OUT OF MANY

VOLUME B
1850–1920

OUT OF MANY

A HISTORY
OF THE
AMERICAN PEOPLE

THIRD EDITION

JOHN MACK FARAGHER
Yale University

MARI JO BUHLE
Brown University

DANIEL CZITROM
Mount Holyoke College

SUSAN H. ARMITAGE
Washington State University

Prentice Hall, Upper Saddle River, New Jersey 07458

Library of Congress Cataloging–in–Publication Data
Out of many: a history of the American people / John Mack Faragher
　. . . [et al.]. — 3rd ed., Combined ed.
　　p.　cm.
　Includes bibliographical references and index.
　ISBN 0-13-949760-9
　1. United States—History.　I. Faragher, John Mack
E178.1.0935　2000　　　　　　　　　　　98–34110
973—dc21　　　　　　　　　　　　　　　　CIP

Editorial Director: Charlyce Jones Owen
Executive Editor: Todd R. Armstrong
Development Editor: David Chodoff
Production Editor: Louise Rothman
Creative Director: Leslie Osher
Art Director: Anne Bonanno Nieglos
Editor-in-Chief of Development: Susanna Lesan
Marketing Manager: Sheryl Adams
Interior and Cover Designer: Thomas Nery
Cover Art: William Hahn, *Market Scene, Sansome Street,*
　　San Francisco (detail), Crocker Art Museum, Sacramento,
　　CA. E.B. Crocker Collection.

AVP, Director of Production and Manufacturing: Barbara Kittle
Manufacturing Manager: Nick Sklitsis
Manufacturing Buyer: Lynn Pearlman
Photo Researcher: Barbara Salz
Photo Editor: Lorinda Morris-Nantz
Copy Editor: Sylvia Moore
Editorial Assistant: Holly Jo Brown
Line Art Coordinator: Guy Ruggiero
Cartographers: Alice and William Thiede/
　　CARTO-GRAPHICS
Electronic Page Layout: Scott Garrison and Rosemary Ross

Credits and acknowledgments for materials borrowed from other sources and reproduced,
with permission, in this textbook appear on pages C–1 – C–3.

This book was set in 11/12 Weiss by the HSS in-house formatting
and production services groups and was printed and bound by RR Donnelley & Sons Company.
The cover was printed by Phoenix Color Corp.

© 2000, 1997, 1994 by Prentice-Hall, Inc.
Upper Saddle River, New Jersey 07458

Printed in the United States of America
10 9 8 7 6 5 4 3 2 1

ISBN 0-13-010032-3

Prentice-Hall International (UK) Limited, *London*
Prentice-Hall of Australia Pty. Limited, *Sydney*
Prentice-Hall Canada Inc., *Toronto*
Prentice-Hall Hispanoamericana, S.A., *Mexico*
Prentice-Hall of India Private Limited, *New Delhi*
Prentice-Hall of Japan, Inc., *Tokyo*
Pearson Education Asia Pte. Ltd., *Singapore*
Editora Prentice-Hall do Brasil, Ltda., *Rio de Janeiro*

TO OUR STUDENTS,
OUR SISTERS,
AND OUR BROTHERS

BRIEF CONTENTS

CONTENTS

16 The Civil War, 1861–1865   447

17 Reconstruction, 1863–1877 481

20 Commonwealth and Empire, 1870–1900   578

21 Urban America and the Progressive Era, 1900–1917 609

22 World War I, 1914–1920   642

■ **AMERICAN COMMUNITIES:**
Vigilante Justice in Bisbee, Arizona   643

MAPS

CHARTS, GRAPHS, AND TABLES

PREFACE

Out of Many, A History of the American People, third edition, offers a distinctive and timely approach to American history, highlighting the experiences of diverse communities of Americans in the unfolding story of our country. These communities offer a way of examining the complex historical forces shaping people's lives at various moments in our past. The debates and conflicts surrounding the most momentous issues in our national life—independence, emerging democracy, slavery, westward settlement, imperial expansion, economic depression, war, technological change—were largely worked out in the context of local communities. Through communities we focus on the persistent tensions between everyday life and those larger decisions and events that continually reshape the circumstances of local life. Each chapter opens with a description of a representative community. Some of these portraits feature American communities struggling with one another: African slaves and English masters on the rice plantations of colonial Georgia, or Tejanos and Americans during the Texas war of independence. Other chapters feature portraits of communities facing social change: the feminists of Seneca Falls, New York, in 1848; the sitdown strikers of Flint, Michigan, in 1934; and the African Americans of Montgomery, Alabama, in 1955. As the story unfolds we find communities growing to include ever larger groups of Americans: The soldiers from every colony who forged the Continental Army into a patriotic national force at Valley Forge during the American Revolution; the movie-goers who dreamed a collective dream of material prosperity and upward mobility during the 1920s; and the Americans linked in ever-growing numbers in the virtual communities of cyberspace as the twenty-first century begins.

Out of Many is also the only American history text with a truly continental perspective. With community vignettes from New England to the South, the Midwest to the far West, we encourage students to appreciate the great expanse of our nation. For example, a vignette of seventeenth-century Santa Fé, New Mexico illustrates the founding of the first European settlements in the New World. We present territorial expansion into the American West from the point of view of the Mandan villagers of the upper Missouri River of North Dakota. We introduce the policies of the Reconstruction era through the experience of African Americans in the Sea Island of South Carolina. This continental perspective drives home to students

that American history has never been the preserve of any particular region.

In these ways *Out of Many* breaks new ground, but without compromising its coverage of the traditional turning points that we believe are critically important to an understanding of the American past. Among these watershed events are the Revolution and the struggle over the Constitution, the Civil War and Reconstruction, and the Great Depression and World War II. In *Out of Many*, however, we seek to *integrate* the narrative of national history with the story of the nation's many diverse communities. The Revolutionary and Constitutional period tried the ability of local communities to forge a new unity, and success depended on their ability to build a nation without compromising local identity. The Civil War and Reconstruction formed a second great test of the balance between the national ideas of the revolution and the power of local and sectional communities. The Depression and the New Deal demonstrated the impotence of local communities and the growing power of national institutions during the greatest economic challenge in our history. *Out of Many* also looks back in a new and comprehensive way—from the vantage point of the beginning of a new century and the end of the Cold War—at the salient events of the last fifty years and their impact on American communities. The community focus of *Out of Many* weaves the stories of the people and of the nation into a single compelling narrative.

SPECIAL FEATURES

With each edition of *Out of Many* we have sought to strengthen its unique integration of the best of traditional American history with its innovative community-based focus and strong continental perspective. A wealth of special features and pedagogical aids reinforces our narrative and helps students grasp key issues.

◆ **Community and Diversity.** *Out of Many*, third edition, opens with an introduction, titled "Community and Diversity," that acquaints students with the major themes of the book, providing them with a framework for understanding American history.

◆ **Immigration and Community: The Changing Face of Ethnicity in America.** This feature, new to this edition, highlights the impact of the immigrant experience on the formation of American communities. There are four Immigration and Community features in the book. The first covers the colonial period through 1800, the second covers from 1800 to 1860, the third covers from 1860 to 1930, and the last covers the period since 1930. Each is six pages long and opens with an overview of the character of immigration during the period in question. This overview is followed by a section called "In Their Own Words" that consists of extracts from primary sources written by immigrants themselves and by native-born Americans in response to the new arrivals. Study questions at the end of each Immigration and Community feature ask students to relate issues raised in the overview and documents to broader issues in American history.

◆ **History and the Land.** These features focus on the geographical dimension of historical change to give students an appreciation of the relationship between geography and history. Each elucidates an important historical trend or process with a map and a brief explanatory essay.

◆ **American Communities.** Each chapter opens with an American Communities vignette that relates the experience of a particular community to the broader issues discussed in the chapter.

◆ **Maps.** *Out of Many,* third edition, has more maps than any other American history textbook. Many maps include topographical detail that helps students appreciate the impact of geography on history.

◆ **Overview tables.** Overview tables, also new to this edition, provide students with a summary of complex issues.

◆ **Graphs, charts and tables.** Every chapter includes one or more graphs, charts, or tables that help students understand important events and trends.

◆ **Photos and illustrations.** The abundant illustrations in *Out of Many,* third edition, include many images that have never before been used in an American history text. None of the images is anachronistic—each one dates from the historical period under discussion. Extensive captions treat the

images as visual primary source documents from the American past, describing their source and explaining their significance.

◆ **Chapter-opening outlines and key topics lists.** These pedagogical aids provide students with a succinct preview of the material covered in each chapter.

◆ **Chronologies.** A chronology at the end of each chapter helps students build a framework of key events.

◆ **Review Questions.** Review questions help students review, reinforce, and retain the material in each chapter and encourage them to relate the material to broader issues in American history.

◆ **Recommended Reading and Additional Bibliography.** The works on the short, annotated Recommended Reading list at the end of each chapter have been selected with the interested introductory student in mind. The extensive Additional Bibliography provides a comprehensive overview of current scholarship on the subject of the chapter.

CLASSROOM ASSISTANCE PACKAGE

In classrooms across the country, many instructors encounter students who perceive history as merely a jumble of names, dates, and events. *Out of Many,* third edition, brings our dynamic past alive for these students with a text and accompanying print and multimedia classroom assistance package that combine sound scholarship, engaging narrative, and a rich array of pedagogical tools.

PRINT SUPPLEMENTS
Instructor's Resource Manual

A true time-saver in developing and preparing lecture presentations, the *Instructor's Resource Manual* contains chapter outlines, detailed chapter overviews, lecture topics, discussion questions, readings, and information on audio-visual resources.

Test Item File

Prepared by Gisela Ables, Mike McCormick, and David Aldstadt, Houston Community College

The *Test Item File* offers a menu of more than 1,500 multiple-choice, identification, matching, true-false, and essay test questions and 10–15 questions per chapter on maps found in each chapter. The guide includes a collection of blank maps that can be photo-copied and used for map testing purposes or for other class exercises.

Prentice Hall Custom Test

This commercial-quality computerized test management program, available for Windows, DOS, and Macintosh environments, allows instructors to select items from the Test Item File and design their own exams.

Transparency Pack

Prepared by Robert Tomes, St. John's University

This collection of more than 160 full-color transparency acetates provides instructors with all the maps, charts, and graphs in the text for use in the classroom. Each transparency is accompanied by a page of descriptive material and discussion questions.

Study Guide, Volumes I and II

Prepared by Elizabeth Neumeyer, Kellogg Community College, and S. Ross Doughty, Ursinus College

Each chapter in the *Study Guide* includes a chapter commentary and outline, identification terms, multiple-choice questions, short essay questions, map questions, and questions based on primary source extracts.

Documents Set, Volumes I and II

Prepared by John Mack Faragher, Yale University, and Daniel Czitrom, Mount Holyoke College

The authors have selected and carefully edited more than 300 documents that relate directly to the themes and content of the text and organized them into five general categories: community, social history, government, culture, and politics. Each document is approximately two pages long and includes a brief introduction and study questions intended to encourage students to analyze the document critically and relate it to the content of the text. The Documents Set is available at a substantial discount when packaged with *Out of Many*.

Retrieving the American Past: A Customized U.S. History Reader

Written and developed by leading historians and educators, this reader is an on-demand history database that offers 52 compelling modules on topics in American History, such as: Women on the Frontier, The Salem Witchcraft Scare, The Age of Industrial Violence, and Native American Societies, 1870–1995. Approximately 35 pages in length, each module includes an introduction, several primary documents and secondary sources, follow-up questions, and recommendations for further reading. By deciding which modules to include and the order in which they will appear, instructors can compile the reader they want to use. Instructor-originated material—other readings, exercises—can be included. Contact your local Prentice Hall Representative for more information about this exciting custom publishing option.

Understanding and Answering Essay Questions

Prepared by Mary L. Kelley, San Antonio College

This brief guide suggests helpful study techniques as well as specific analytical tools for understanding different types of essay questions and provides precise guidelines for preparing well-crafted essay answers. The guide is available free to students when packaged with *Out of Many*.

Reading Critically About History

Prepared by Rose Wassman and Lee Rinsky, both of DeAnza College

This brief guide provides students with helpful strategies for reading a history textbook. It is available free when packaged with *Out of Many*.

Themes of the Times

Themes of the Times is a newspaper supplement prepared jointly by Prentice Hall and the premier news publication, *The New York Times*. Issued twice a year, it contains recent articles pertinent to American history. These articles connect the classroom to the world. For information about a reduced-rate subscription to *The New York Times*, call toll-free: (800) 631–1222.

MULTIMEDIA SUPPLEMENTS

History on the Internet

This brief guide introduces students to the origin and innovations behind the Internet and World Wide Web and provides clear strategies for navigating the web to find historical materials. Exercises within and at the end of the chapters allow students to practice searching the wealth of resources available to the student of history. This 48-page supplementary book is free to students when packaged with *Out of Many*.

Out of Many CD-ROM

This innovative electronic supplement takes advantage of the interactive capabilities of multimedia technology to enrich students' understanding of the geographic dimension of history with animated maps, timelines, and related on-screen activities tied to key issues in each chapter of *Out of Many*.

Out of Many Companion Website
Address: http://www.prenhall.com/faragher

With the *Out of Many* Companion Website, students can now take full advantage of the World Wide Web and use it in tandem with the text to enrich their study of American history. The Companion Website ties the text to related material available on the Internet. Its instructional features include chapter objectives, study questions, news updates, and labeling exercises.

The American History CD-ROM
This vast library of more than 2500 images was compiled by Instructional Resources Corporation for instructors for creating slide shows and supplementing lectures. Among its resources are 68 film sequences, 200 works of art, and more than 100 maps. It also includes an overview of historical periods narrated by Charles Kuralt.

ACKNOWLEDGMENTS

In the years it has taken to bring *Out of Many* from idea to reality and to improve it in successive editions, we have often been reminded that although writing history sometimes feels like isolated work, it actually involves a collective effort. We want to thank the dozens of people whose efforts have made the publication of this book possible.

At Prentice Hall, Todd Armstrong, Executive Editor, gave us his full support and oversaw the entire publication process. David Chodoff, Senior Development Editor, greatly helped to strengthen the book's most distinctive features with his careful attention to detail and clarity. Susanna Lesan, now Editor-in-Chief of Development, worked with us on the first edition of the text; without her efforts this book would never have been published. Louise Rothman, Production Editor, oversaw the entire complicated production process in an exemplary fashion. Barbara Salz, our photo researcher, expertly tracked down the many pertinent new images that appear in this edition.

Among our many other friends at Prentice Hall we also want to thank: Phil Miller, President; Charlyce Jones Owen, Editorial Director; Sheryl Adams, Marketing Manager; Leslie Osher, Creative Design Director; Anne Nieglos, Art Director; Patterson Lamb, Copy Editor; and Holly Jo Brown, Editorial Assistant.

Although we share joint responsibility for the entire book, the chapters were individually authored: John Mack Faragher wrote chapters 1–8; Mari Jo Buhle wrote chapters 18–20, 25–26, 29–30; Daniel Czitrom wrote chapters 17, 21–24, 27–28, 31; and Susan Armitage wrote chapters 9–16.

Historians around the country greatly assisted us by reading and commenting on our chapters for this and previous editions. We want to thank each of them for the commitment of their valuable time.

Donald Abbe, Texas Tech University, TX
Richard H. Abbott, Eastern Michigan University, MI
Guy Alchon, University of Delaware, DE
Don Barlow, Prestonsburg Community College, KY
William Barney, University of North Carolina, NC
Alwyn Barr, Texas Tech University, TX
Debra Barth, San Jose City College, CA
Peter V. Bergstrom, Illinois State University, IL
William C. Billingsley, South Plains College, TX
Peter H. Buckingham, Linfield College, OR
Bill Cecil-Fronsman, Washburn University of Topeka, KS
Victor W. Chen, Chabot College, CA
Jonathan M. Chu, University of Massachusetts, MA
P. Scott Corbett, Oxnard College, CA
Matther Coulter, Collin Country Community College, TX
Virginia Crane, University of Wisconsin, Oshkosh, WI
Jim Cullen, Harvard University, MA
Thomas J. Curran, St. John's University, NY
Richard V. Damms, Ohio State University, OH
Elizabeth Dunn, Baylor University, TX
Emmett G. Essin, Eastern Tennessee State Unversity, TN
Mark F. Fernandez, Loyola University, IL
Leon Fink, University of North Carolina, Chapel Hill, NC
Michael James Foret, University of Wisconsin, Stevens Point, WI
Joshua B. Freeman, Columbia University, NY
Glenda E. Gilmore, Yale University, CT
Don C. Glenn, Diablo Valley College, CA
Lawrence Glickman, University of South Carolina, SC
Kenneth Goings, Florida Atlantic University, FL
Mark Goldman, Tallahassee Community College, FL
Gregory L. Goodwin, Bakersfield College, CA
Gretchen Green, University of Missouri, Kansas City, MO
Emily Greenwald, University of Nebraska at Lincoln, NE
Mark W. T. Harvey, North Dakota State University, ND
James A. Hijiya, University of Massachusetts at Dartmouth, MA
Raymond M. Hyser, James Madison University, VA
John Inscoe, University of Georgia, GA

John C. Kesler, Lakeland Community College, OH
Peter N. Kirstein, Saint Xavier University, IL
Frank Lambert, Purdue University, IN
Susan Rimby Leighow, Millersville University, PA
Janice M. Leone, Middle Tennessee University, TN
Glenn Linden, Southern Methodist University, Dallas, TX
George Lipsitz, University of California, San Diego, CA
Judy Barrett Litoff, Bryant College, RI
Jesus Luna, California State University, CA
Larry Madaras, Howard Community College, MD
Lynn Mapes, Grand Valley State University, MI
John F. Marszalek, Mississippi State University, MS
Scott C. Martin, Bowling Green State University, OH
Robert L. Matheny, Eastern New Mexico University, NM
Thomas Matijasic, Prestonsburg Community College, KY
M. Delores McBroome, Humboldt State University, CA
Gerald McFarland, University of Massachusetts, Amherst, MA
Sam McSeveney, Vanderbilt University, TN
Warren Metcalf, Arizona State University, AZ
M. Catherine Miller, Texas State University, TX
Norman H. Murdoch, University of Cincinnati, OH
Gregory H. Nobles, Georgia Institute of Technology, GA
Dale Odom, University of Texas at Denton, TX
Sean O'Neill, Grand Valley State University, MI
Edward Opper, Greenville Technical College, Greenville, SC
Charles K. Piehl, Mankato State University, MN
Carolyn Garrett Pool, University of Central Oklahoma, OK
Christie Farnham Pope, Iowa State University, IA
Susan Porter-Benson, University of Missouri, MO
Russell Posner, City College of San Francisco, CA
John Powell, Penn State University, Erie, PA
Sarah Purcell, Central Michigan University, MI
Joseph P. Reidy, Howard University, DC
Marilyn D. Rhinehart, North Harris College, TX

Leo P. Ribuffo, George Washington University, DC
Judy Ridner, California State University at Northridge, CA
Neal Salisbury, Smith College, MA
Roberto Salmon, University of Texas-Pan American, TX
Steven Schuster, Brookhaven Community College, TX
Megan Seaholm, University of Texas, Austin, TX
Nigel Sellars, University of Oklahoma, Norman, OK
John David Smith, North Carolina State University, NC
Patrick Smith, Broward Community College, FL
Mark W. Summers, University of Kentucky, KY
John D. Tanner, Jr., Palomar College, CA
Robert R. Tomes, St. John's University, NY
Michael Miller Topp, University of Texas at El Paso, TX
John Trickel, Richland Community College, IL
Steve Tripp, Grand Valley State University, MI
Fred R. Van Hartesveldt, Fort Valley State University, GA
Philip H. Vaughan, Rose State College, OK
Robert C. Vitz, Northern Kentucky University, KY
F. Michael Williams, Brevard Community College, FL
Charles Regan Wilson, University of Mississippi, MS
Harold Wilson, Old Dominion University, VA
William Woodward, Seattle Pacific University, WA
Loretta E. Zimmerman, University of Florida, FL

Each of us depended on a great deal of support and assistance with the research and writing that went into this book. We want to thank: Kathryn Abbott, Nan Boyd, Krista Comer, Crista DeLuzio, Keith Edgerton, Carol Frost, Jesse Hoffnung Garskof, Jane Gerhard, Todd Gernes, Melani McAlister, Cristiane Mitchell, J. C. Mutchler, Tricia Rose, Gina Rourke, and Jessica Shubow.

Our families and close friends have been supportive and ever so patient over the many years we have devoted to this project. But we want especially to thank Paul Buhle, Meryl Fingrutd, Bob Greene, and Michele Hoffnung.

ABOUT THE AUTHORS

Chris Freitag

JOHN MACK FARAGHER

John Mack Faragher is Arthur Unobskey Professor of American History at Yale University. Born in Arizona and raised in southern California, he received his B.A. at the University of California, Riverside, and his Ph.D. at Yale University. He is the author of *Women and Men on the Overland Trail* (1979), which won the Frederick Jackson Turner Award of the Organization of American Historians, *Sugar Creek: Life on the Illinois Prairie* (1986), and *Daniel Boone: The Life and Legend of an American Pioneer* (1992). He is also the editor of *The American Heritage Encyclopedia* (1988).

DANIEL CZITROM

Daniel Czitrom is Professor and Chair of History at Mount Holyoke College. He received his B.A. from the State University of New York at Binghamton and his M.A. and Ph.D. from the University of Wisconsin, Madison. He is the author of *Media and the American Mind: From Morse to McLuhan* (1982), which won the First Books Award of the American Historical Association. His scholarly articles and essays have appeared in the *Journal of American History, American Quarterly, The Massachusetts Review*, and *The Atlantic*. He is currently completing *Mysteries of the City: Culture, Politics, and the Underworld in New York, 1870–1920*.

MARI JO BUHLE

Mari Jo Buhle is Professor of American Civilization and History at Brown University, specializing in American women's history. She is the author of *Women and American Socialism, 1870–1920* (1981) and *Feminism and its Discontents: A Century of Struggle with Psychoanalysis* (1998). She is also coeditor of *Encyclopedia of the American Left*, second edition (1998). She currently serves as an editor of a series of books on women and American history for the University of Illinois Press. Professor Buhle held a fellowship (1991–1996) from the John D. and Catherine T. MacArthur Foundation.

SUSAN H. ARMITAGE

Susan H. Armitage is Professor of History at Washington State University. She earned her Ph.D. from the London School of Economics and Political Science. Among her many publications on western women's history are three coedited books, *The Women's West* (1987), *So Much To Be Done: Women on the Mining and Ranching Frontier* (1991), and *Writing the Range: Race, Class, and Culture in the Women's West* (1997). She is the editor of *Frontiers: A Journal of Women's Studies*.

COMMUNITY & DIVERSITY

One of the most characteristic features of our country has always been its astounding variety. The American people include the descendants of native Indians, colonial Europeans, Africans, and migrants from virtually every country and continent. Indeed, as we enter the new century the nation is absorbing a tide of immigrants from Latin America and Asia that rivals the great tide of immigrants from eastern and southern Europe that arrived at the beginning of the twentieth century. Moreover, the United States is one of the world's largest nations, incorporating more than 3.6 million square miles of territory. The struggle to make a nation out of our many communities is what much of American history is all about. That is the story told in this book.

Every human society is made up of communities. A community is a set of relationships that link men, women, and their families into a coherent social whole, more than the sum of its parts. In a community people develop the capacity for unified action. In a community people learn, often through trial and error, how to transform and adapt to their environment. The sentiment that binds the members of a community together is the origin of group identity and ethnic pride. In the making of history, communities are far more important than even the greatest of leaders, for the community is the institution most capable of passing a distinctive historical tradition to future generations.

Communities bind people together in multiple ways. They can be as small as the local neighborhood, in which people maintain face-to-face relations, or as large as the imagined entity of the nation. This book examines American history from the perspective of community life—an ever widening frame that has included larger and larger groups of Americans.

Networks of kinship and friendship, and connections across generations and among families, establish the bonds essential to community life. Shared feelings about values and history establish the basis for common identity. In communities, people find the power to act collectively in their own interest. But American communities frequently took shape as a result of serious conflicts among groups, and within communities there often has been significant fighting among competing groups or classes. Thus the term community,

John L. Krimmel, Election Day in Philadelphia (1815).

as we employ it here, includes tension and discord as well as harmony and agreement.

For years there have been persistent laments about the "loss of community" in modern America. But community has not disappeared—it is continually being reinvented. Until the late eighteenth century, community was defined primarily by space and local geography. The closer one gets to the present, the more community is reshaped by new and powerful historical forces such as the nation state, the marketplace, industrialization, the corporation, mass immigration, and electronic media.

The American Communities vignettes that open each chapter of *Out of Many* reflect this shift. Most of the vignettes in the pre–Civil War chapters focus on geographically-defined communities, such as the ancient Indian city at Cahokia, or the experiment in industrial urban planning in early nineteenth-century Lowell, Massachusetts. In the post–Civil War chapters different and more modern kinds of communities make their appearance—the community of Holly-

Ralph Fasanella, Sunday Afternoon—Stickball Game, 1953

wood movie audiences in the 1920s, or the "virtual communities" made possible by new computer technologies. Also, the nearer we get to the present, the more we find Americans struggling to balance their membership in several communities simultaneously. These are defined not simply by local spatial arrangements, but by categories as varied as racial and ethnic groups, occupations, political affiliations, and consumer preferences.

The title for our book was suggested by the Latin phrase selected by John Adams, Benjamin Franklin, and Thomas Jefferson for the Great Seal of the United States: *E Pluribus Unum*—"Out of Many Comes Unity." These men understood that unity could not be imposed by a powerful central authority but had

to develop out of mutual respect among Americans of different backgrounds. The revolutionary leadership expressed the hope that such respect could grow on the basis of a remarkable proposition: "We hold these truths to be self-evident, that all men are created equal; that they are endowed by their Creator with certain unalienable rights; that among these are life, liberty, and the pursuit of happiness." The national government of the United States would preserve local and state authority but would guarantee individual rights. The nation would be strengthened by guarantees of difference.

Out of Many—that is the promise of America, and the premise of this book. The underlying dialectic of American history, we believe, is that as a people

William Hahn, Market Scene, Sansome Street, San Francisco.

we need to locate our national *unity* in the celebration of the *differences* that exist among us; these differences can be our strength, as long as we affirm the promise of the Declaration. Protecting the "right to be different," in other words, is absolutely fundamental to the continued existence of democracy, and that right is best protected by the existence of strong and vital communities. We are bound together as a nation by the ideal of local and cultural differences protected by our common commitment to the values of our revolution.

Today—with the many social and cultural conflicts that abound in the United States—some Americans have lost faith in that vision. But our history shows that the promise of American unity has always been problematic. Centrifugal forces have been powerful in the American past, and at times the country has seemed about to fracture into its component parts. Our transformation from a collection of groups and regions into a nation has been marked by painful and often violent struggles. Our past is filled with conflicts between Indians and colonists, masters and slaves,

Patriots and Loyalists, Northerners and Southerners, Easterners and Westerners, capitalists and workers, and sometimes the government and the people. Americans often appear to be little more than a contentious collection of peoples with conflicting interests, divided by region and background, race and class.

Our most influential leaders also sometimes suffered a crisis of faith in the American project of "liberty and justice for all." Thomas Jefferson not only believed in the inferiority of African Americans, but he feared that immigrants from outside the Anglo-American tradition might "warp and bias" the development of the nation "and render it a heterogeneous, incoherent, distracted mass." We have not always lived up to the American promise, and there is a dark side to our history. It took the bloodiest war in American history to secure the human rights of African Americans, and the struggle for full equality continues nearly a century and a half later. During the great influx of immigrants in the early twentieth century, fears much like Jefferson's led to movements to *Americanize* the foreign born by forcing them, in the words of one leader, "to give up the languages, customs, and methods of life which they have brought with them across the ocean, and adopt instead the language, habits, and customs of this country, and the general standards and ways of American living." Similar thinking motivated Congress at various times to bar the immigration of Asians and other ethnic groups into the country, and to force assimilation on American Indians by denying them the freedom to practice their religion or even to speak their own language. Such calls for restrictive unity resound in our own day.

But other Americans have argued for a more idealistic version of *Americanization*. "What is the American, this new man?" asked the French immigrant Michel Crévecoeur in 1782. "A strange mixture of blood which you will find in no other country," he answered; in America, "individuals of all nations are melted into a new race of men." A century later Crévecoeur was echoed by historian Frederick Jackson Turner, who believed that "in the crucible of the frontier, the immigrants were Americanized, liberated, and fused into a mixed race, English in neither nationality nor characteristics. The process has gone on from the early days to our own."

The process by which diverse communities have come to share a set of common American values is one of the most fundamental aspects of our history. It did not occur, however, because of compulsory *Americanization* programs, but because of free public education, popular participation in democratic politics, and the impact of popular culture. Contemporary America does have a common culture: we laugh at the same television sitcoms and share the same aspirations to own a home and send our children to college—all unique American traits.

To a degree that too few Americans appreciate, this common culture resulted from a complicated process of mutual discovery that took place when different ethnic and regional groups encountered one another. Consider just one small and unique aspect of our culture, the barbecue. Americans have been barbecuing since before the beginning of written history. Early settlers adopted this technique of cooking from the Indians—the word itself comes from a native term for a framework of sticks over a fire on which meat was slowly cooked. Colonists typically barbecued pork, fed on Indian corn. African slaves lent their own touch by introducing the use of hot sauces. Thus the ritual that is a part of nearly every American family's Fourth of July silently celebrates the heritage of diversity that went into making our common culture.

The American educator John Dewey recognized this diversity early in this century. "The genuine American, the typical American is himself a hyphenated character," he declared, "international and interracial in his make-up." The point about our "hyphenated character," Dewey believed, "is to see to it that the hyphen connects instead of separates." We, the authors of *Out of Many*, share Dewey's perspective on American history. "Creation comes from the impact of diversity," wrote the American philosopher Horace Kallen. We also endorse Kallen's vision of the American promise: "A democracy of nationalities, cooperating voluntarily and autonomously through common institutions, . . . a multiplicity in a unity, an orchestration of mankind." And now, let the music begin.

CHAPTER FIFTEEN

THE COMING CRISIS
THE 1850s

AMERICAN COMMUNITIES
Illinois Communities Debate Slavery

On seven occasions through the late summer and autumn of 1858, each at one of seven small Illinois towns—Ottawa, Freeport, Jonesboro, Charleston, Galesburg, Quincy, and Alton—thousands of Illinois farmers and townspeople put aside their daily routines and customary chores; climbed into carriages, farm wagons, carts, and conveyances of all sorts; and converged on the town green. Entertained by brass bands, pageantry, and vast quantities of food and local gossip, they waited impatiently for the main event, the chance to take part in the debate on the most urgent question of the day—slavery. Two Illinois politicians—Democratic senator Stephen A. Douglas and his Republican challenger, Springfield lawyer Abraham Lincoln, the principal figures in the debates—presented their views in three hours of closely reasoned argument. But they did not speak alone. Cheers, boos, groans, and shouted questions from active, engaged listeners punctuated all seven of the now famous confrontations between the two men. Although commonly referred to as the Lincoln-Douglas debates, these were really community events in which Illinois citizens—people who, like Americans everywhere, held varying political beliefs—took part. Some individuals were proslavery, some antislavery, and many were undecided, but all were agreed that democratic politics gave them the means to air their opinions and resolve their differences.

"The prairies are on fire," announced the *New York Evening Post* correspondent who covered the debates. "It is astonishing how deep an interest in politics this people take." The reason was clear: by 1858, the American nation was in deep political crisis. The decade-long effort to solve the problem of the future of slavery had failed. For most of this time Washington politicians trying to build broad national parties with policies acceptable to voters in both the North and the South had done their best not to talk about slavery. Thus, that the Lincoln-Douglas debates were devoted to one issue alone—slavery and the future of the Union—showed how serious matters had become.

Democrat Stephen Douglas was the leading Democratic contender for the 1860 presidential nomination, but before he could mount a campaign for national office he had first to win reelection to the Illinois seat he had held in the U.S. Senate for twelve years. His vote against allowing slavery in Kansas had alienated him from the strong southern wing of his own party and had put him in direct conflict with its top leader, President James Buchanan. Because the crisis of the Union was so severe and Douglas's role so pivotal, his reelection campaign clearly previewed the 1860 presidential election. For the sake of its future, the Republican Party had to field a strong opponent: it found its candidate in Abraham Lincoln.

Lincoln had represented Illinois in the House of Representatives in the 1840s but had lost political support in 1848 because he opposed the Mexican-American War. Developing a prosperous Springfield law practice, he had been an influential member of the Illinois Republican Party since its founding in 1856. Although he had entered political life as a Whig, Lincoln was radicalized by the issue of the extension of slavery. Even though his wife's family were Kentucky slave owners, Lincoln's commitment to freedom and his resistance to the spread of slavery had now become absolute: for him, freedom and Union were inseparable.

Much less well known than Douglas, Lincoln was the underdog in the 1858 Senate race and thus it was he who challenged Douglas to debate. As they squared off in the seven Illinois towns, Douglas and Lincoln were an amusing sight. Douglas was short (5 feet, 4 inches) and his build was very square; his nickname was "the Little Giant." Lincoln, on the other hand, was very tall (6 feet, 4 inches) and very thin. Both were eloquent and powerful speakers—and they had to be. The three-hour debates were held without amplification of any kind. Nevertheless, in every town, audiences of 10,000 to 15,000 listened attentively and responded vocally to each speaker's long and thought-packed arguments.

Douglas had many strengths going into the debates. He spoke for the Union, he claimed, pointing out that the Democratic Party was a national party whereas the Republican Party was only sectional. He repeatedly appealed to the racism of much of his audience with declarations such as, "I would not blot out the great inalienable rights of the white men for all the negroes that ever existed!" He repeatedly called his opponent a "Black Republican," implying that Lincoln and his party favored the social equality of whites and blacks, even race mixing.

Lincoln did *not* believe in the social equality of the races, but he did believe wholeheartedly that slavery was a moral wrong. Pledging the Republican Party to the "ultimate extinction" of slavery, Lincoln continually warned that Douglas's position would lead to the opposite result: the spread of slavery everywhere. Although in this argument Lincoln was addressing the northern fear of an expansionist "slave power," he strove at the

same time to present himself as a moderate. He did not favor the breakup of the Union, but he never wavered from his antislavery stance.

The first of the seven debates, held in Ottawa on Saturday, August 21, 1858, showed not only the seriousness but the exuberance of the democratic politics of the time. By early morning the town was jammed with people. The clouds of dust raised by carriages driving to Ottawa, one observer complained, turned the town into "a vast smoke house." By one o'clock the town square was filled to overflowing. At two o'clock, just as the debate was about to begin, the wooden awning over the speakers' platform collapsed under the weight of those sitting on it, delaying the start for half an hour. But then the debate got under way, enthralling an estimated 12,000 people. Ottawa, in northern Illinois, was pro-Republican, and the audience heckled Douglas unmercifully. At the second debate, a week later in Freeport, Douglas's use of the phrase "Black Republicans" drew angry shouts of "White, white" from the crowd. But as the debates moved south in the state, where Democrats predominated, the tables were turned, and Lincoln sometimes had to plead for a chance to be heard.

Although Douglas won the 1858 senatorial election in Illinois, the acclaim that Lincoln gained in the famous debates helped establish the Republicans' claim to be the only party capable of stopping the spread of slavery and made Lincoln himself a strong contender for the Republican presidential nomination in 1860. But the true winners of the Lincoln-Douglas debates were the people of Illinois who gathered peacefully to discuss the most serious issue of their time. The young German immigrant Carl Schurz, who attended the Quincy debate, was deeply impressed by its democratic character. He noted, "There was no end of cheering and shouting and jostling on the streets of Quincy that day. But in spite of the excitement created by the political contest, the crowds remained very good-natured, and the occasional jibes flung from one side to the other were uniformly received with a laugh." The Illinois people who participated in the community debates of 1858 showed the strong faith Americans held in their democratic institutions and the hope—finally shattered in the election of 1860—that a lasting political solution to the problem of slavery could be found.

Illinois

Key Topics

- The failure of efforts by the Whigs and the Democrats to find a lasting political compromise on the issue of slavery

- The end of the Second American Party System and the rise of the Republican Party

- The secession of the southern states following the Republican Party victory in the election of 1860

AMERICA IN 1850

In 1850, after half a century of rapid growth and change, America was a very different nation from the republic of 1800. Geographic expansion, population increase, economic development, and the changes wrought by the market revolution had transformed the struggling new nation. Economically, culturally, and politically Americans had forged a strong sense of national identity.

Expansion and Growth

America was now a much larger nation than it had been in 1800. Through war and diplomacy, the country had grown to continental dimensions, more than tripling in size from 890,000 to 3 million square miles. Its population had increased enormously: from 5.3 million in 1800 to more than 23 million, 4 million of whom were African American slaves and 2 million new immigrants, largely from Germany and Ireland. Comprising just sixteen states in 1800, America in 1850 had thirty-one, and more than half of the population lived west of the Appalachians. America's cities had undergone the most rapid half-century of growth they were ever to experience.

America was also much richer: it is estimated that real per capita income doubled between 1800 and 1850, moving the nation decisively out of the "developing" category. Southern cotton, which had contributed so much to American economic growth, continued to be the nation's principal export, but it was no longer the major influence on the domestic economy. The growth of manufacturing in the Northeast and the rapid opening up of rich farmlands in the Midwest fostered the interdependence of these two regions, which was aided by the rapid growth and consolidation of railway links between them in the 1850s. The future of the United States as a manufacturing nation, second only to Britain, and as a major exporter of agricultural products was assured. Nevertheless, the development of manufacturing in the Northeast and the increased economic importance of the Midwest had serious domestic political implications. As the South's share of responsibility for economic growth waned, so did its political importance—at least in the eyes of many Northerners. Thus the very success of the United States both in geographic expansion and economic development served to undermine the role of the slave South in national politics and to hasten the day of open conflict between it and the free-labor North and Midwest.

Cultural Life and Social Issues

By 1850 the first shock of the far-reaching social changes caused by the market revolution had been absorbed. The conflicting social impulses played out in the politics and reform movements of the Jacksonian period were gradually giving way to new middle-class values, institutions, and ideas. Newspapers, magazines, and communication improvements of all kinds created a national audience for American scholars and writers. Since the turn of the century, American writers had struggled to find distinctive American themes, and these efforts bore fruit in the 1850s in the burst of creative activity termed "the American Renaissance." During this decade, Henry Thoreau, Nathaniel Hawthorne, Walt Whitman, Herman Melville, Emily Dickinson, Frederick Douglass, and others wrote works of fiction and nonfiction that are considered American classics.

During the American Renaissance, American writers pioneered new literary forms. Nathaniel Hawthorne, in stories like "Young Goodman Brown" (1835), raised the short story to a distinctive American literary form. Poets like Walt Whitman and Emily Dickinson experimented with unrhymed and "off-rhyme" verse, Whitman (in *Leaves of Grass,* published in 1855) to celebrate the boisterous pleasures of everyday life in New York City, Dickinson (who lived as a recluse in Amherst, Massachusetts) to catch her every fleeting thought and feeling in scraps of poetry that were not published until after her death. Another recluse, Henry David Thoreau, published *Walden* in 1854. A pastoral celebration of his life at Walden Pond, in Concord, Massachusetts, the essay was also a searching meditation on the cost to the individual of the loss of contact with nature that was a consequence of the market revolution.

Indeed, most of the writers of the American Renaissance were social critics. In *The Scarlet Letter* (1850) and *The House of the Seven Gables* (1851), both set in Puritan New England in the colonial period, Nathaniel Hawthorne brilliantly explored the moral choices faced by individuals as they try to reconcile repressive social expectations with private desires. Hawthorne's friend Herman Melville, in his great work *Moby Dick* (1851), drew on his own personal experience to write about the lives of ordinary sailors on a whaling voyage, but the story had deeper meanings. Melville's novel of Captain Ahab's obsessive search for the white whale is a profound study of the nature of good and evil and a critique of American society in the 1850s. The strongest social critique, however, was Frederick Douglass's starkly simple autobiography, *Narrative of the Life of Frederick Douglass* (1845), which told of his brutal life as a slave.

The most successful American novel of the mid-nineteenth century was about the great issue of the day, slavery. In writing *Uncle Tom's Cabin*, Harriet Beecher Stowe combined the literary style of the then-popular women's domestic novels (discussed in Chapter 12) with vivid details of slavery culled from firsthand accounts by northern abolitionists and escaped slaves. Stowe, the daughter of the reforming clergyman Lyman Beecher,

had married a Congregational minister and was herself a member of the evangelical movement. She had long been active in antislavery work, and a new Fugitive Slave Law passed in 1850 impelled her to write a novel that would persuade everyone of the evils of slavery. She wrote every night at her kitchen table after putting her six children to bed, and, as she said later, the events of the novel came to her "with a vividness that could not be denied," making her feel like "an instrument of God."

Stowe's famous novel told a poignant story of the Christ-like slave Uncle Tom, who patiently endured the cruel treatment of an evil white overseer, Simon Legree. Published in 1851, it was a runaway best seller. More than 300,000 copies were sold in the first year, and within ten years the book had sold more than 2 million copies, becoming the all-time American best-seller in proportion to population. Turned into a play that remained popular throughout the nineteenth century, Uncle Tom's Cabin reached an even wider audience. Scenes from the novel such as that of Eliza carrying her son across the ice-choked Ohio River to freedom, Tom weeping for his children as he was sold south, and the death of little Eva are among the best-known passages in

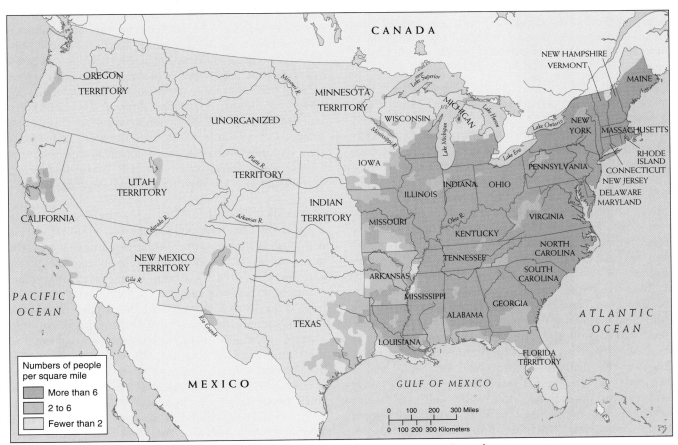

U.S. Population and Settlement, 1850   By 1850, the United States was a continental nation. Its people, whom Thomas Jefferson had once thought would not reach the Mississippi River for forty generations, had not only passed the river but leapfrogged to the west coast. In comparison to the America of 1800 (see the map on p. 233) the growth was astounding.

The Webbs, a free African American family, toured northern cities performing dramatic readings from Uncle Tom's Cabin. *An all-time best-seller, the novel outlasted the Civil War and, adapted into dramatic form, remained popular with theater audiences through the second half of the nineteenth century.*

all of American literature. *Uncle Tom's Cabin* was more than a heart-tugging story: it was a call to action. In 1863, when Harriet Beecher Stowe was introduced to Abraham Lincoln, the president remarked, "So you're the little woman who wrote the book that made this great war!"

Political Parties and Slavery

Stowe's novel clearly spoke to the growing concern of the American people. Slavery had long been a divisive issue in national politics. Until the 1840s, compromises had always been found, most notably in the Constitution itself (see Chapter 8) and in the Missouri Crisis of 1820 (see Chapter 9). But the struggle over the place of slavery in the vast new territories gained in the Mexican-American War gave rise to intractable new sectional arguments. The year 1850 opened to the most serious political crisis the United States had ever known. The struggle over the issue of slavery in the territories had begun in 1846 with the Wilmot Proviso and was still unresolved. Increasingly, both politicians and ordinary people began to consider the almost unthinkable possibility of disunion. As politician James Buchanan wrote to a friend early in the year, "The blessed Union of these states is now in greater danger than it has ever been since the adoption of the federal

Constitution." He feared that the two great national parties, the Whigs and the Democrats, would not be able to find a solution to the increasingly sectional division between North and South over slavery.

The Second American Party System forged in the great controversies of Andrew Jackson's presidency (see Chapter 10) was a national party system. In their need to mobilize great masses of recently enfranchised voters to elect a president every four years, politicians created organized party structures that overrode deeply rooted sectional differences. Politicians from all sections of the country cooperated because they knew their party could not succeed without national appeal. At a time when the ordinary person still had very strong sectional loyalties, the mass political party created a national community of like-minded voters. Yet by the election of 1848 sectional interests were eroding the political "glue" in both parties. Although each party still appeared united, sectional fissures already ran deep.

Political splits were preceded by divisions in other social institutions. Disagreements about slavery had already split the country's great religious organizations into northern and southern groups, the Presbyterians in 1837, the Methodists in 1844, and the Baptists in 1845. (Some of these splits turned out to be permanent. The Southern Baptist Convention, for example, is still a separate body.) Theodore Weld, the abolitionist leader, saw these splits as inevitable: "Events…have for years been silently but without a moment's pause, settling the basis of two great parties, the nucleus of one slavery, of the other, freedom." Indeed, the abolitionists had been posing this simple yet uncompromising choice between slavery or freedom since the 1830s. Moreover, they had been insisting on a compelling distinction: as Liberty Party spokesman Salmon P. Chase said, "Freedom is national; slavery only is local and sectional."

States' Rights and Slavery

But was freedom national and slavery sectional, or was it the other way around? Southern politicians took the latter view, as their foremost spokesman, South Carolina's John C. Calhoun, made ringingly clear throughout his long career.

In 1828 Calhoun had begun the protracted Nullification Crisis by asserting the constitutional right of states to "nullify" national laws that were harmful to their interests (see Chapter 10). Calhoun argued, as others have since, that the states' rights doctrine protected the legitimate rights of a minority in a democratic system governed by majority rule.

In 1847, Calhoun responded to the 1846 Wilmot Proviso with an elaboration of the states' rights argument. In spite of the apparent precedents of the Northwest Ordinance of 1787 and the Missouri Compromise, Calhoun argued that Congress did not have a constitutional right to prohibit slavery in the territories. The territories, he said, were the common property of all the states, north and south, and Congress could not discriminate against slave owners as they moved west. On the contrary, Calhoun argued, slave owners had a constitutional right to the protection of their property wherever they moved. Of course, Calhoun's legally correct description of African American slaves as property enraged abolitionists. But on behalf of the South, Calhoun was expressing the belief—and the fear—that his interpretation of the Constitution was the only protection for slave owners, whose right to own slaves (a fundamental right in southern eyes) was being attacked. Calhoun's position on the territories quickly became southern dogma: anything less than full access to the territories was unconstitutional. Slavery, Calhoun and other Southerners insisted, had to be national.

As Congressman Robert Toombs of Georgia put the case in 1850, there was very little room for compromise:

> I stand upon the great principle that the South has the right to an equal participation in the territories of the United States....She will divide with you if you wish it, but the right to enter all or divide I shall never surrender....Deprive us of this right and appropriate the common property to yourselves, it is then your government, not mine. Then I am its enemy....Give us our just rights, and we are ready...to stand by the Union....Refuse [them], and for one, I will strike for independence.

Northern Fears of "The Slave Power"

The words of Southerners like Calhoun and Toombs confirmed for many Northerners the warnings of antislavery leaders that they were endangered by a menacing "slave power." Liberty Party leader James Birney, in a speech in 1844, was the first to add this phrase to the nation's political vocabulary. "The slave power," Birney explained, was a group of aristocratic slave owners who not only dominated the political and social life of the South but conspired to control the federal government as well, posing a danger to free speech and free institutions throughout the nation.

Birney's "slave power" was a caricature of the influence slave owners wielded over southern politics and of the increasingly defensive and monolithic response of southern representatives in national politics after 1830 (see Chapter 11). The proslavery strategy of maintaining supremacy in the Senate by having at least as many slave as free states admitted to the Union (a plan that required slavery expansion) and of maintaining control, or at least veto power, over presidential nominees seemed, in southern eyes, to be nothing less

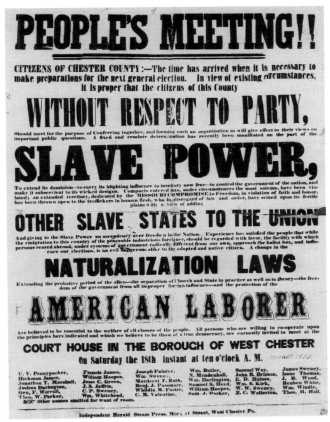

This strident poster warns that "the Slave Power" aims "to control the government of the nation, and make it subservient to its wicked designs." For good measure, the poster also appeals to nativist fears and to workers.

than ordinary self-defense. But to antislavery advocates, these actions looked like a conspiracy by sectional interests to control national politics. Birney's warnings about "the slave power" seemed in 1844 merely the overheated rhetoric of an extremist group of abolitionists. But the defensive southern political strategies of the 1850s were to convince an increasing number of northern voters that "the slave power" did in fact exist. Thus in northern eyes the South became a demonic monolith that threatened the national government.

Two Communities, Two Perspectives

Ironically, it was a common belief in expansion that made the arguments between Northerners and Southerners so irreconcilable. Southerners had been the strongest supporters of the Mexican-American War, and they still hoped to expand into Cuba, believing that the slave system must grow or wither. On the other hand, although many northern Whigs had opposed the Mexican-American War, most did so for antislavery reasons, not because they opposed expansion. The strong showing of the Free-Soil Party (which evolved out of the Liberty Party) in the election of 1848 (10 percent of the popular vote) was proof of that. Basically, both North and South believed in manifest destiny, but each on its own terms.

Similarly, both North and South used the language of basic rights and liberties in the debate over expansion. But Free-Soilers were speaking of personal liberty, whereas Southerners meant their right to own a particular kind of property (slaves) and to maintain a way of life based on the possession of that property. In defending its own rights, each side had taken measures that infringed on the rights of the other. Southerners pointed out that abolitionists had libeled slave owners as a class and that they had bombarded the South with unwanted literature, abused the right of petition to Congress, incited slaves to rebellion, and actively helped slaves to escape. For their part, Northerners accused slave owners of censorship of the mails; imposition of the "gag rule" (repealed in 1844), which prohibited any petition against slavery from being read to or discussed by Congress; suppression of free speech in the South; and, of course, of committing the moral wrong of enslaving others in the first place.

By 1850, North and South had created different communities. To antislavery Northerners, the South was an economic backwater dominated by a small slave-owning aristocracy that lived off the profits of forced labor and deprived poor whites of their democratic rights and the fruits of honest work. The slave system was not only immoral but a drag on the entire nation, for, in the words of Senator William Seward of New York, it subverted the "intelligence, vigor and energy" that were essential for national growth. In contrast, the dynamic and enterprising commercial North boasted a free labor ideology that offered economic opportunity to the common man and ensured his democratic rights (see Chapter 12).

Things looked very different through southern eyes. Far from being economically backward, the South, through its export of cotton, was, according to Southerners, the great engine of national economic growth from which the North benefited. Slavery was not only a blessing to an inferior race but the cornerstone of democracy, for it ensured the freedom and independence of all white men without entailing the bitter class divisions that marked the North. Slave owners accused northern manufacturers of hypocrisy for practicing "wage slavery" without the paternal benevolence they claimed to bestow on their slaves. The North, James Henry Hammond of South Carolina charged, had eliminated the "name [of slavery], but not the thing," for "your whole hireling class of manual laborers and 'operatives'…are essentially slaves."

By the early 1850s, these vastly different visions of the North and the South—the result of many years of political controversy—had become fixed, and the chances of national reconciliation increasingly slim. Over the course of the decade, many Americans came to believe that the place of slavery in the nation's life had to be permanently settled. And they increasingly wondered whether their two sectional communities—one slave, one free—could continue to be part of a unitary national one.

THE COMPROMISE OF 1850

By 1850 the issue raised by the Wilmot Proviso—whether slavery should be extended to the new territories—could no longer be ignored. Overnight, the California Gold Rush had turned a remote frontier into a territory with a booming population. In 1849 both

In 1850, the three men who had long represented America's three major regions attempted to resolve the political crisis brought on by the applications of California and Utah for statehood. Henry Clay is speaking; John C. Calhoun stands third from right; and Daniel Webster is seated at the left with his head in his hand. Both Clay and Webster were ill, and Calhoun died before the compromise of 1850 was arranged by a younger group of politicians led by Stephen A. Douglas.

OVERVIEW

THE GREAT SECTIONAL COMPROMISES

Missouri Compromise	1820	Admits Missouri to the Union as a slave state and Maine as a free state; prohibits slavery in the rest of the Louisiana Purchase Territory north of 36°30′.
		Territory Covered: The entire territory of the Louisiana Purchase, exclusive of the state of Louisiana, which had been admitted to the Union in 1812.
Compromise of 1850	1850	Admits California to the Union as a free state, settles the borders of Texas (a slave state); sets no conditions concerning slavery for the rest of the territory acquired from Mexico.
		Territory Covered: The territory that had been part of Mexico before the end of the Mexican-American War and the Treaty of Guadalupe Hidalgo (1848): part of Texas, California, Utah Territory (now Utah, Nevada, and part of Colorado), and New Mexico Territory (now New Mexico and Arizona).

California and Utah applied for statehood. Should these territories be admitted as slave or free states? A simmering border war between Texas (a slave state) and New Mexico, which seemed likely to be a free state, had to be settled, as did the issue of the debts Texas had incurred as an independent republic. Closer to home, antislavery forces demanded the end of slavery in the District of Columbia, while slave owners complained that Northerners were refusing to return escaped slaves, as federal law mandated.

Debate and Compromise

The Compromise of 1850 was the final act in the political careers of the three aging men who in the public mind best represented America's sections: Westerner Henry Clay; Southerner John C. Calhoun; and Daniel Webster, spokesman for the North. It was sadly appropriate to the bitter sectional argument of 1850 that the three men contributed great words to the debate but that the compromise itself was enacted by younger men. Calhoun brought an aura of death with him to the Senate as he sat, shrouded in flannels, listening to the speech that he was too ill to read for himself. He died less than a month later, still insisting on the right of the South to secede if necessary to preserve its way of life. Daniel Webster claimed to speak "not as a Massachusetts man, nor as a Northern man, but as an American....I speak today for the preservation of the Union." He rejected southern claims that peaceable secession was possible or desirable and pleaded with abolitionists to compromise

enough to keep the South in the Union. Clay, claiming he had "never before risen to address any assemblage so oppressed, so appalled, and so anxious," argued eloquently for compromise, but left the Senate in ill health before his plea was answered.

On July 9, 1850, in the midst of the debate, President Zachary Taylor died of acute gastroenteritis, caused by a hasty snack of fruit and cold milk at a Fourth of July celebration. A bluff military man, Taylor had been prepared to follow Andrew Jackson's precedent during the Nullification Crisis of 1832 and simply demand that southern dissidents compromise. When Vice President Millard Fillmore assumed the presidency, however, he helped adjust the Compromise of 1850 to southern liking. Fillmore was a moderate northern Whig and more prosouthern than the southern-born Taylor had been. Moreover, although Clay had assembled all the necessary parts of the bargain, it was not he but members of a younger political generation, and in particular the rising young Democrat from Illinois, Stephen Douglas, who drove the Compromise of 1850 through Congress. The final product consisted of five separate bills (it had been impossible to obtain a majority for a comprehensive measure), embodying three separate compromises.

First, California was admitted as a free state, but the status of the remaining former Mexican possessions was left to be decided by popular sovereignty (a vote of the territory's inhabitants) when they applied for statehood. (Utah's application for statehood was not accepted until 1896 because of controversy over the Mormon practice of polygamy.) The result was, for the time being,

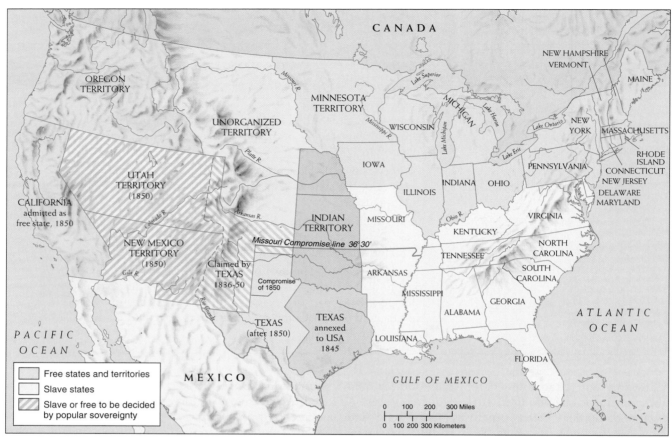

The Compromise of 1850   *The Compromise of 1850 reflected heightened sectional tensions by being even messier and more awkward than the Missouri Compromise of 1820. California was admitted as a free state, the borders of Texas were settled, and the status of the rest of the former Mexican territory was left to be decided later by popular sovereignty. No consistent majority voted for the five separate bills that made up the compromise.*

fifteen slave states and sixteen free states. Second, Texas (a slave state) was required to cede land to New Mexico Territory (free or slave status undecided). In return, the federal government assumed $10 million of debts Texas incurred before it became a state. Finally, the slave trade, but not slavery itself, was ended in the District of Columbia, but a stronger fugitive slave law was enacted.

Jubilation and relief greeted the news that compromise had been achieved. In Washington, where the anxiety and concern had been greatest, drunken crowds serenaded Congress, shouting, "The Union is saved!" That was certainly true for the moment, but analysis of the votes on the five bills that made up the compromise revealed no consistent majority. The sectional splits within each party that had existed before the compromise remained. Antislavery northern Whigs and proslavery southern Democrats, each the larger wing of their party, were the least willing to compromise. Southern Whigs and northern Democrats were the forces for moderation, but each group was dwindling in popular appeal as sectional animosities grew.

In the country as a whole, the feeling was that the problem of slavery in the territories had been solved. The *Philadelphia Pennsylvanian* was confident that "peace and tranquillity" had been ensured, and the *Louisville Journal* said that a weight seemed to have been lifted from the heart of America. But as former Liberty Party spokesman Salmon P. Chase, now a senator from Ohio, soberly noted, "The question of slavery in the territories has been avoided. It has not been settled." The most immediately inflammatory measure of the compromise was the Fugitive Slave Act.

The Fugitive Slave Act

From the early days of their movement, northern abolitionists had urged slaves to escape, promising assistance and support when they reached the North. Some free African Americans had offered far more than verbal support. Among them, Harriet Tubman, an escaped slave from Maryland, was one of the most famous. Tubman made nineteen return trips and brought almost 300 slaves to freedom, among them all the other members of her family. Northerners had long been appalled by professional slave catchers, who zealously seized African Americans in the North and took them south into slavery again. Most abhorrent in northern eyes was that captured black people were at the mercy of slave catchers because they had no legal right to defend themselves. In more than one case, a northern free African American was captured in his own community and helplessly shipped into slavery.

Solomon Northup was one such person. In his widely sold account *Twelve Years a Slave*, published in 1853, he told a harrowing tale of being kidnapped in Washington, the nation's capital, and shipped south. Northup spent twelve years as a slave before he was able to send a message to northern friends to bring the legal proof to free him. As a result of stories like Northup's and the very effective publicity generated by abolitionists, nine northern states passed personal liberty laws between 1842 and 1850, serving notice that they would not cooperate with federal recapture efforts. These northern laws enraged Southerners, who had long been convinced that all Northerners, not just abolitionists, were actively hindering efforts to reclaim their escaped slaves. At issue were two distinct definitions of "rights": Northerners were upset at the denial of legal and personal rights to escaped slaves; Southerners saw illegal infringement of their property rights. Southerners insisted that a strong federal law be part of the Compromise of 1850.

The Fugitive Slave Law, enacted in 1850, dramatically increased the power of slave owners to capture escaped slaves. The full authority of the federal government now supported slave owners, and although fugitives were guaranteed a hearing before a federal commissioner, they were not allowed to testify on their own behalf. Furthermore, the new law imposed federal penalties on citizens who protected or assisted fugitives, or who did not cooperate in their return. In Boston, the center of the abolitionist movement, reaction to the new law was fierce. When an escaped slave named Shadrach Minkins was seized in February 1851, a group of African American men broke into the courtroom, overwhelmed the federal marshals, seized Minkins, and sent him safely to Canada. Although the action had community support—a Massachusetts jury defiantly refused to convict the perpetrators—many people, including Daniel Webster and President Fillmore, condemned it as "mob rule."

The federal government responded with overwhelming force. In April 1851, 300 armed soldiers were mobilized to prevent the rescue of Thomas Sims, who was being shipped back into slavery. In the most famous case in Boston, a biracial group of armed abolitionists led by Unitarian clergyman Thomas Wentworth Higginson stormed the federal courthouse in 1854 in an attempt to save escaped slave Anthony Burns. The

rescue effort failed, and a federal deputy marshal was killed. President Pierce sent marines, cavalry, and artillery to Boston to reinforce the guard over Burns and ordered a federal ship to be ready to deliver the fugitive back into slavery. When the effort by defense lawyers to argue for Burns's freedom failed, Bostonians raised money to buy his freedom. But the U.S. attorney, ordered by the president to enforce the Fugitive Slave Law in all circumstances, blocked the purchase. The case was lost, and Burns was marched to the docks through streets lined with sorrowing abolitionists. Buildings were shrouded in black and draped with American flags hanging upside down, while bells tolled as if for a funeral.

The Burns case radicalized many Northerners. Conservative Whig George Hilliard wrote to a friend, "When it was all over, and I was left alone in my office, I put my face in my hands and wept. I could do nothing less." During the 1850s, 322 black fugitives were sent back into slavery; only 11 were declared free. Northern popular sentiment and the Fugitive Slave Law, rigorously enforced by the federal government, were increasingly at odds. The northern abolitionists who used force to rescue captured slaves were breaking the law, but they were winning the battle for public opinion.

In this volatile atmosphere, escaped African Americans wrote and lectured bravely on behalf of freedom. Frederick Douglass, the most famous and eloquent of the fugitive slaves, spoke out fearlessly in support of armed resistance. "The only way to make the Fugitive Slave Law a dead letter," he said in 1853, "is to make a half dozen or more dead kidnappers." Openly active in the underground network that helped slaves reach safety in Canada, Douglass himself had been constantly in danger of capture until his friends bought his freedom in 1847. Harriet Jacobs, who escaped to the North after seven years in hiding in the South, wrote bitterly in her *Incidents in the Life of a Slave Girl* (1861) that the Fugitive Slave Law made her feel that "I was, in fact, a slave in New York, as subject to slave laws as I had been in a slave state....I had been chased during half my life, and it seemed as if the chase were never to end." Threatened by owners who came north for her, Jacobs went into hiding again, until she was informed that friends had arranged her purchase: "A gentleman near me said, 'It's true; I have seen the bill of sale.' 'The bill of sale!' Those words struck me like a blow. So I was sold at last! A human being sold in the free city of New York!"

The Fugitive Slave Law brought home the reality of slavery to residents of the free states. In effect, this law made slavery national and forced northern communities to confront what that meant. Although most people were still unwilling to grant social equality to the free African Americans who lived in the northern states, more and more had come to believe that the institution of slavery was wrong. The strong northern reaction against the Fugitive Slave Law also had consequences in the South. As Democrat Cave Johnson of Tennessee warned, "If the fugitive slave bill is not enforced in the North, the moderate men of the South…will be overwhelmed by the 'fire-eaters,'" the extremists who favored immediate secession. Northern protests against the Fugitive Slave Law bred suspicion in the South and encouraged secessionist thinking. These new currents of public opinion were reflected in the election of 1852.

The Election of 1852

The first sign of the weakening of the national party system in 1852 was the difficulty both parties experienced at their nominating conventions. With long-time party leaders like Henry Clay now dead, William Seward of New York became the unofficial party head, much to the displeasure of southern Whigs. Seward preferred General Winfield Scott (a military hero like the party's previous two candidates) to the prosouthern Fillmore, and after fifty-two ballots, managed to get him nominated. Many southern Whigs were angered and alienated by the choice and either abstained during the voting, like Georgia's Alexander Stephens, or, like Robert Toombs, cast a protest vote for the Democratic candidate. Although southern Whigs were still elected to Congress, their loyalty to the national party was strained to the breaking point. The Whigs never again fielded a presidential candidate.

The Democrats had a wider variety of candidates: Lewis Cass of popular sovereignty fame; Stephen Douglas, architect of the Compromise of 1850; and James Buchanan, described as a "Northern man with Southern principles." Cass, Douglas, and Buchanan competed for forty-nine ballots, each strong enough to block the others but not strong enough to win. Finally the party turned to a handsome, affable nonentity, Franklin Pierce of New Hampshire, who was thought to have southern sympathies. Uniting on a platform pledging "faithful execution" of all parts of the Compromise of 1850, including the Fugitive Slave Law, Democrats polled well in the South and in the North. Most Democrats who had voted for the Free-Soil Party in 1848 voted for Pierce. So, in record numbers, did immigrant Irish and German voters, who were eligible for citizenship after three years' residence. The strong immigrant vote for Pierce was a sign of the strength of the Democratic machines in northern cities (see Chapter 13), and reformers complained, not for the last time, about widespread corruption and "vote buying" by urban ward bosses. Overall, however, "Genl. Apathy is the strongest candidate out here," as one Ohioan reported. Pierce easily won the 1852 election, 254 electoral votes to 42. Voter turnout was below 70 percent, lower than it had been since 1836.

"Young America": The Politics of Expansion

Pierce entered the White House in 1853 on a wave of good feeling. Massachusetts Whig Amos Lawrence reported, "Never since Washington has an administration commenced with the hearty [good]will of so large a portion of the country." This goodwill was soon strained by Pierce's support for the expansionist adventures of the "Young America" movement.

The "Young America" movement was a group within the Democratic Party whose members used manifest destiny to justify their desire for conquest of Central America and Cuba. Young America expansionists had glanced covetously southward since the end of the Mexican-American War. President Polk himself had wanted to buy Cuba and to intervene in Mexican politics but was rebuffed by Congress (see Chapter 14). During the Pierce administration, several private "filibusters" (from the Spanish *filibustero*, meaning an "adventurer" or "pirate") invaded Caribbean and Central American countries, usually with the declared intention of extending slave territory. The best-known of the filibusters, William Walker, was also the most improbable. Short, slight, and soft-spoken, Walker led not one but three invasions of Nicaragua. After the first invasion in 1855, Walker became ruler of the country and encouraged settlement by southern slave owners, but was unseated by a regional revolt in 1857. His subsequent efforts to regain control of the country failed, and on the last he was captured and executed by firing squad in Honduras.

The Pierce administration, not directly involved in the filibustering, was deeply involved in an effort to obtain Cuba. In 1854, Pierce authorized his minister to Spain, Pierre Soulé, to try to force the unwilling Spanish to sell Cuba for $130 million. Soulé met in Ostend, Belgium, with the American ministers to France and England, John Mason and James Buchanan, to compose the offer, which was a mixture of cajolements and threats. At first appealing to Spain to recognize the deep affinities between the Cubans and American Southerners that made them "one people with one destiny," the document went on to threaten to "wrest" Cuba from Spain if necessary. This amazing document, which became known as the Ostend Manifesto, was supposed to be secret but was soon leaked to the press. Deeply embarrassed, the Pierce administration was forced to repudiate it.

The complicity between the Pierce administration and proslavery expansionists was foolhardy and lost it the northern goodwill with which it had begun. The sectional crisis that preceded the Compromise of 1850 had made obvious the danger of reopening the territorial issue. Ironically, it was not the Young America expansionists but the prime mover of the Compromise of 1850 himself, Stephen A. Douglas, who reignited the sectional struggle over slavery expansion.

THE CRISIS OF THE NATIONAL PARTY SYSTEM

In 1854, Douglas introduced the Kansas-Nebraska Act, proposing to open those lands that had been the northern part of Indian Territory to American settlers under the principle of popular sovereignty. He thereby reopened the question of slavery in the territories. Douglas knew he was taking a political risk, but he believed he could satisfy both his expansionist aims and his presidential ambitions. He was wrong. Instead, he pushed the national party system into crisis, first killing the Whigs and then destroying the Democrats.

The Kansas-Nebraska Act

Until 1854, white Americans thought of Kansas only as a passageway to other places farther west. A part of Indian Territory, Kansas was peopled largely by tribes who had been moved from their original homes in the East. In the great Indian removals of the 1830s, these tribes had been promised the Kansas lands "as

long as grass grows and water flows." The promise was broken in 1854, when prior treaties were ignored and the northern part of Indian Territory was thrown open to white settlement.

Stephen Douglas introduced the Kansas-Nebraska Act to further the construction of a transcontinental railroad, which he ardently supported as a way to foster American democracy and commerce. He wanted the rail line to terminate in Chicago, in his own state of Illinois, rather than in the rival St. Louis, but for that to happen, the land west of Iowa and Missouri had to be organized into territories (the first step toward statehood). To get Congress to agree to the organization of the territories, however, Douglas would need the votes of southern Democrats, who would be unwilling to support him unless the territories were open to slavery. Douglas also coveted his party's nomination for the presidency in 1856, and would need the continuing support of southern Democrats to secure it.

Douglas thought he was solving his problem by proposing that the status of slavery in the new

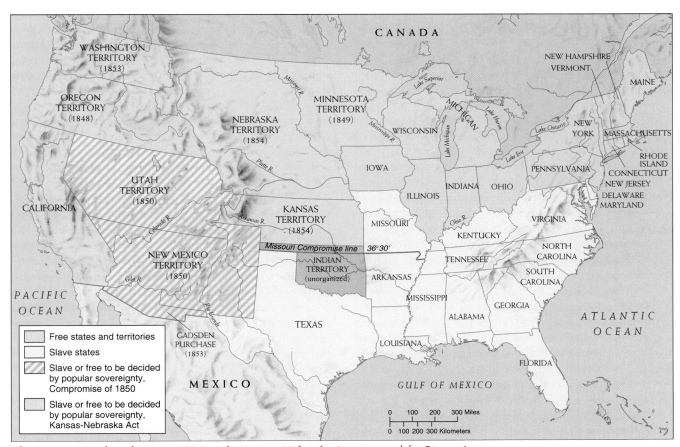

The Kansas-Nebraska Act, 1854   *The Kansas-Nebraska Act, proposed by Steven A. Douglas in 1854, opened the central and northern Great Plains to settlement. The act had two major faults: it robbed Indian peoples of half the territory guaranteed to them by treaty, and, because it repealed the Missouri Compromise Line, it opened up the lands to warring proslavery and antislavery factions.*

territories be governed by the principle of popular sovereignty. Democratic politicians had favored this democratic-sounding slogan, vague enough to appeal to both proslavery and antislavery voters, ever since 1848. Douglas thought Southerners would support his bill because of its popular sovereignty provision, and Northerners because it favored a northern route for the transcontinental railroad. Privately, Douglas believed that the topography of the Kansas-Nebraska region was unsuitable for slave agriculture and that the region's inhabitants would decide to enter the Union as free states. Douglas chose also to downplay the price he had to pay for southern support—by allowing the possibility of slavery in the new territories his bill in effect repealed the Missouri Compromise of 1820, which barred slavery north of latitude 36°30′.

The Kansas-Nebraska bill passed, but it badly strained the major political parties. Southern Whigs voted with southern Democrats in favor of the measure, northern Whigs rejected it absolutely, creating an irreconcilable split that left Whigs unable to field a presidential candidate in 1856. The damage to the Democratic Party was almost as great. In the congressional elections of 1854, northern Democrats lost two-thirds of their seats (a drop from ninety-one to twenty-five), giving the southern Democrats (who were solidly in favor of slavery extension) the dominant voice both in Congress and within the party.

Douglas had committed one of the greatest miscalculations in American political history. A storm of protest arose throughout the North. More than 300 large anti-Nebraska rallies occurred during congressional consideration of the bill, and the anger did not subside. Douglas, who confidently believed that "the people of the North will sustain the measure when they come to understand it," found himself shouted down more than once at public rallies when he tried to explain the bill. "I could travel from Boston to Chicago," he ruefully commented, "by the light of my own [burning] effigy."

The Kansas-Nebraska bill shifted a crucial sector of northern opinion: the wealthy merchants, bankers, and manufacturers (called "Cotton Whigs") who had economic ties with southern slave owners and had always disapproved of abolitionist activity. Convinced that the bill would encourage antislavery feeling in the North, Cotton Whigs urged southern politicians to vote against it, only to be ignored. Passage of the Kansas-Nebraska Act convinced many northern Whigs that compromise with the South was impossible. Even as sober a newspaper as the *New York Times* regarded the act as "part of this great scheme for extending and perpetuating the supremacy of the Slave Power." Joining the antislavery cause were some Cotton Whigs like manufacturer Amos Lawrence of Massachusetts, who had so

warmly welcomed the prospect of sectional peace at the beginning of the Pierce administration. Lawrence provided the financial backing for the first group of antislavery New Englanders who settled Kansas in 1854, and in gratitude they named their town for him.

In Kansas itself in 1854, hasty treaties were concluded with the Indian tribes who owned the land. Some, such as the Kickapoos, Shawnees, Sauks, and Foxes, agreed to relocate to small reservations. Others, like the Delawares, Weas, and Iowas, agreed to sell their lands to whites. Still others, such as the Cheyennes and Sioux, kept the western part of Kansas Territory (now Colorado)—until gold was discovered there in 1859. Once the treaties were signed, both proslavery and antislavery white settlers began to pour in, and the battle was on.

"Bleeding Kansas"

The first to claim land in Kansas were residents of nearby Missouri, itself a slave state. Egged on by Democratic senator David Atchison of Missouri (who took a leave of absence from Congress to lead them), Missourians took up land claims, established proslavery strongholds such as the towns of Leavenworth, Kickapoo, and Atchison, and repeatedly and blatantly swamped Kansas elections with Missouri votes. In 1855, in the second of several notoriously fraudulent elections, 6,307 ballots were cast in a territory that had fewer than 3,000 eligible voters. The rest of the votes—all proslavery—were cast by "border ruffians," as they proudly called themselves, from Missouri. These were frontiersmen, fond of boasting that they could "scream louder, jump higher, shoot closer, get drunker at night and wake up soberer in the morning than any man this side of the Rocky Mountains."

Northerners quickly responded, with the encouragement of sympathetic politicians. Free-Soil (antislavery) New Englanders were recruited to Kansas by the New England Emigrant Aid Society, founded by abolitionist Eli Thayer of Massachusetts. The first party of New Englanders arrived in the summer of 1854 and established the free-soil town of Lawrence. More than a thousand others had joined them by the following summer. Lawrence quickly blossomed from a town of tent homes to one of solid log cabins, a church, a sawmill, stores, and a stone foundation for what became the Free State Hotel, sponsored by the Emigrant Aid Society. These migrants were all free-soilers, and many were religious reformers as well. The contrast of values between them and the border ruffians was almost total. When nondrinking William Phillips stiffly refused a friendly offer of a drink from a Missourian, the border ruffian burst out, "That's just it! This thing of temperance and abolitionism and the Emigrant Aid Society are all the same kind of thing."

Kansas soon became a bloody battleground as the two factions struggled to secure the mandate of "popular sovereignty." Free-Soilers in Lawrence received shipments of heavy crates, innocuously marked "BOOKS" but actually containing Sharps repeating rifles, sent by eastern supporters. For their part, the border ruffians—already heavily armed, with Bowie knives in their boots, revolvers at their waists, rifles slung from their shoulders, and swords at their sides—called for reinforcements. David Atchison exhorted Alabamans: "Let your young men come forth to Missouri and Kansas! Let them come well armed!"

In the summer of 1856 these lethal preparations exploded into open warfare. First, proslavery forces burned and looted the town of Lawrence. The Free State Hotel, among other buildings, was burned to the ground. In retaliation, a grim old man named John Brown led his sons in a raid on the proslavery settlers of Pottawatomie Creek, killing five unarmed people. A wave of violence ensued. Armed bands roamed the countryside, and burnings and killings became commonplace. John Brown and his followers were just one of many bands of marauding murderers who were never arrested, never brought to trial, and never stopped from committing further violence. Peaceful residents of large sections of rural Kansas were repeatedly forced to flee to the safety of military forts when rumors of one or another armed band reached them.

This engraving shows "Border Ruffians" from Missouri lining up to vote for slavery in the Kickapoo, Kansas Territory election of 1855. The widespread practice of illegal voting and of open violence earned Kansas the dreadful nickname of "Bleeding Kansas."

The rest of the nation watched in horror as the residents of Kansas slaughtered each other in the pursuit of sectional goals. Americans' pride in their nation's great achievements was threatened by the endless violence in one small part—but a part that increasingly seemed to represent the divisions of the whole.

The Politics of Nativism

Meanwhile, sectional pressures continued to reshape national politics. The breakup of the Whig Party coincided with one of the strongest bursts of nativism, or anti-immigrant feeling, in American history, a reaction to the Democratic Party's success in capturing the support of the rapidly growing population of mostly Catholic foreign-born voters (see Chapter 13 and "Immigration and Community: The Changing Nature of Ethnicity in America, 1800–1860," p. 380).

Irish immigrants in particular voted Democratic, both in reaction to Whig hostility (as in Boston) and because of their own antiblack prejudices. Frequently in competition with free African Americans for low-paying jobs, Irish immigrants were more likely to share the attitudes of Southerners than those of abolitionists. Violent urban riots in which free African Americans were the scapegoats periodically erupted in northern cities such as Cincinnati (1829), Providence (1831), New York (1834), and Philadelphia (1834 and 1842).

The reformist and individualistic attitudes of many Whigs inclined them toward nativism and toward the new American Party, which formed in 1850 to give political expression to anti-immigrant feeling. Many Whigs disapproved of the new immigrants because they were poor, Catholic, and often disdainful of the temperance movement. The Catholic Church's opposition to the liberal European revolutions of 1848 also fueled anti-Catholic fears. If America's new Catholic immigrants opposed the revolutions in which other Americans took such pride (believing them to be modeled on the American example), how could the future of America's own democracy be ensured? Finally, nativist Whigs held immigration to be solely responsible for the increases in crime and the rising cost of relief for the poor that accompanied the rapid urban growth of the 1830s and 1840s.

Women reformers were as prone to nativism as men. As early as 1838, the influential Lydia Sigourney wrote in alarm in her *Letters to Mothers* about the "influx of untutored foreigners" that had made the United States "a repository for the waste and refuse of other nations." Sigourney urged women to organize an internal missionary movement that would carry the principles of middle-class American domesticity to the unenlightened foreigners.

Nativism drew former Whigs, especially young men in white-collar and skilled blue-collar

Cartoons like this one sought to couple concerns about temperance (suggested by the barrels of Irish whiskey and German lager beer) with nativist claims that immigrant voters were voting illegally (indicated by the struggle in the background).

occupations, to the new American Party. At the core of the party were several secret fraternal societies open only to native-born Protestants who pledged never to vote for a Catholic (on the grounds that all Catholics took their orders straight from the pope in Rome—a fear that was to be voiced again by Southern Baptists in 1960 when John F. Kennedy ran for president). When questioned about their beliefs, party members maintained secrecy by answering, "I know nothing"—Hence the popular name for American Party members, Know-Nothings. Few Know-Nothings were wealthy: most were workers or small farmers whose jobs or ways of life were threatened by the cheap labor and unfamiliar culture of the new immigrants.

Know-Nothings scored startling victories in northern state elections in 1854, winning control of the legislature in Massachusetts and polling 40 percent of the vote in Pennsylvania. No wonder one Pennsylvania Democrat reported, "Nearly everybody seems to have gone altogether deranged on Nativism." Although most of the new immigrants lived in the North, resentment and anger against them was national, and the American Party initially polled well in the South, attracting the votes of many former southern Whigs. But in the 1850s, no party could ignore slavery, and in 1855 the American Party split into northern (antislavery) and southern (proslavery) wings. Soon after this split, many people who had voted for the Know-Nothings shifted their support to another new party, one that combined many characteristics of the Whigs with a westward-looking, expansionist, free-soil policy. This was the Republican Party, founded in 1854.

The Republican Party and the Election of 1856

In 1854 a Massachusetts voter described the elections in his state in terms of "freedom, temperance, and Protestantism against slavery, rum, and Romanism," linking nativism with sectional politics. "Slavery, rum, and Romanism" were supposed to describe the national Democratic Party, whose supporters included southern slave owners and northern immigrant Catholics. "Freedom, temperance, and Protestantism," were meant to characterize the Republican Party. Many constituencies, however, found room in the new party. Its supporters included many former northern Whigs who opposed slavery absolutely, many Free-Soil Party supporters who opposed the expansion of slavery but were willing to tolerate it in the South, and many northern reformers concerned about temperance and Catholicism. The Republicans also attracted the economic core of the old Whig Party—the merchants and industrialists who wanted a strong national government to promote economic growth by supporting a protective tariff, transportation improvements, and cheap land for western farmers. In quieter times it would have taken this party a while to sort out all its differences and become a true political community. But because of the sectional crisis, the fledgling party nearly won its very first presidential election.

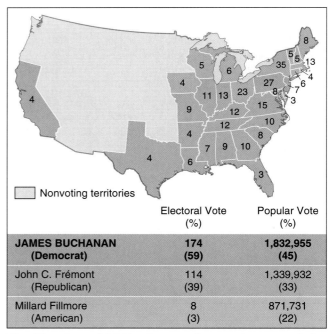

Nonvoting territories

	Electoral Vote (%)	Popular Vote (%)
JAMES BUCHANAN (Democrat)	**174 (59)**	**1,832,955 (45)**
John C. Frémont (Republican)	114 (39)	1,339,932 (33)
Millard Fillmore (American)	8 (3)	871,731 (22)

The Election of 1856 *Because three parties contested the 1856 election, Democrat James Buchanan was a minority president. Although Buchanan alone had national support, Republican John Frémont won most of the free states, and Millard Fillmore of the American Party gained 40 percent of the vote in most of the slave states.*

The immediate question facing the nation in 1856 was which new party, the Know-Nothings or the Republicans, would emerge the stronger. But the more important question was whether the Democratic Party could hold together. The two strongest contenders for the Democratic nomination were President Pierce and Stephen A. Douglas. Douglas had proposed the Kansas-Nebraska Act and Pierce had actively supported it. Both men therefore had the support of the southern wing of the party. But it was precisely their support of this act that made Northerners oppose both of them. The Kansas-Nebraska Act's divisive effect on the Democratic Party now became clear: no one who had voted on the bill, either for or against, could satisfy both wings of the party. A compromise candidate was found in James Buchanan of Pennsylvania, the "Northern man with Southern principles." Luckily for him, he had been ambassador to Great Britain at the time of the Kansas-Nebraska Act and thus had not had to commit himself.

The election of 1856 appeared to be a three-way contest that pitted Buchanan against explorer John C. Frémont of the Republican Party and the American (Know-Nothing) Party's candidate, former president Millard Fillmore. In fact, the election was two separate contests, one in the North and one in the South. The southern race was between Buchanan and Fillmore. Frémont's name appeared on the ballot in only four southern states, all in the Upper South, and even there he polled almost no votes. Fillmore received strong support from many former southern Whigs. Although he carried only the state of Maryland, he attracted more than 40 percent of the vote in ten other slave states. Buchanan, though, won the electoral votes in all those states.

Frémont decisively defeated Buchanan in the North, winning eleven of sixteen free states. Nationwide he garnered 1.3 million votes to Buchanan's 1.8 million. Buchanan won the election with only 45

OVERVIEW

POLITICAL PARTIES SPLIT AND REALIGN

Whig Party	Ran its last presidential candidate in 1852. The candidate, General Winfield Scott, alienated many southern Whigs and the party was so split it could not field a candidate in 1856.
Democratic Party	Remained a national party through 1856, but Buchanan's actions as president made southern domination of the party so clear that many northern Democrats were alienated. Stephen Douglas, running as a northern Democrat in 1860, won 29 percent of the popular vote; John Breckinridge, running as a southern Democrat, won 18 percent.
Liberty Party	Antislavery party ran James G. Birney for president in 1844. He won 62,000 votes, largely from northern antislavery Whigs.
Free-Soil	Ran Martin Van Buren, former Democratic president, in 1848. Gained 10 percent of the popular vote, largely from Whigs but also from some northern Democrats.
American (Know-Nothing) Party	Nativist party made striking gains in 1854 congressional elections, attracting both northern and southern Whigs. In 1856, its presidential candidate Millard Fillmore won 21 percent of the popular vote.
Republican Party	Founded in 1854. Attracted many northern Whigs and northern Democrats. Presidential candidate John C. Frémont won 33 percent of the popular vote in 1856; in 1860 Abraham Lincoln won 40 percent and was elected in a four-way race.

percent of the popular vote because he was the only national candidate. His southern support, plus the electoral votes of Pennsylvania, New Jersey, Illinois, Indiana, and California gave him the victory. But the Republicans, after studying the election returns, claimed "victorious defeat," for they realized that in 1860 the addition of just two more northern states to their total would mean victory. Furthermore, the Republican Party had clearly defeated the American Party in the battle to win designation as a major party. These were grounds for great optimism—and for great concern, for the Republican Party was a sectional rather than a national party; it drew almost all its support from the North. Southerners viewed its very existence as an attack on their vital interests. Thus the rapid rise of the Republicans posed a growing threat to national unity.

The election of 1856 attracted one of the highest voter turnouts in American history—79 percent. Ordinary people had come to share the politicians' concern about the growing sectional rift. The combined popular vote for Buchanan and Fillmore (67 percent) showed that most voters, north and south, favored politicians who at least claimed to speak for national rather than sectional interests. The northern returns also showed something else. Northerners had decided that the threat posed by the expansion of slavery was greater than that posed by the new immigrants; although it never disappeared, nativism subsided. The Buchanan administration, however, proved unequal to the task of resolving the free versus slave issue, and the nation began an inexorable slide into civil war.

THE DIFFERENCES DEEPEN

In one dreadful week in 1856 the people of the United States heard, in quick succession, about the looting and burning of Lawrence, Kansas, about John Brown's retaliatory massacre at Pottawatomie, and about unprecedented violence on the Senate floor. In the last of these incidents, Senator Charles Sumner of Massachusetts suffered permanent injury in a vicious attack by Congressman Preston Brooks of South Carolina. Trapped at his desk, Sumner was helpless as Brooks beat him so hard with his cane that it broke. Blood streaming from his head, Sumner escaped only by wrenching loose his desk from the screws that held it to the floor. A few days earlier, Sumner had given an insulting antislavery speech entitled "The Crime against Kansas." Using the abusive, accusatory style favored by abolitionists, he had singled out for ridicule

Senator Andrew Butler of South Carolina, charging him with choosing "the harlot, slavery" as his mistress. Senator Butler was Preston Brooks's uncle; in Brooks's mind, he was simply avenging an intolerable affront to his uncle's honor. So far had the behavioral codes of North and South diverged that each man found his own action perfectly justifiable and the action of the other outrageous. Their attitudes were mirrored in their respective sections.

The *Dred Scott* Decision

Although James Buchanan firmly believed that he alone could hold together the nation so riven by hatred and violence, his self-confidence outran his abilities. When he entered the White House in March 1857 Buchanan was the oldest president (sixty-five) ever elected and a veteran of forty years of politics. Unfortunately, despite his experience, he was indecisive at moments that called for firm leadership. He was also so deeply indebted to the strong southern wing of the Democratic Party that he could not take the impartial actions necessary to heal "Bleeding Kansas." And his support for a momentous prosouthern decision by the Supreme Court further aggravated sectional differences.

In *Dred Scott v. Sandford*, decided on March 6, 1857, two days after James Buchanan was sworn in, a southern-dominated Supreme Court attempted—and failed—to solve the political controversy over slavery. Dred Scott had been a slave all his life. His owner, army surgeon John Emerson, had taken Scott on his military assignments during the 1830s to Illinois (a free state) and Wisconsin Territory (a free territory by the Missouri Compromise line). During that time Scott married another slave, Harriet, and their daughter Eliza was born in free territory. Emerson and the Scotts then returned to Missouri (a slave state) and there, in 1846, Dred Scott sued for his freedom and that of his wife and the daughter born in Wisconsin Territory (who as women had no legal standing of their own) on the grounds that residence in free lands had made them free. It took eleven years for the case to reach the Supreme Court, and by then its importance was obvious to everyone.

Chief Justice Roger B. Taney, of Maryland, seventy-nine years old, hard of hearing and failing of sight, insisted on reading his majority opinion in its entirety, a process that took four excruciating hours. Declaring the Missouri Compromise

SOUTHERN CHIVALRY — ARGUMENT versus CLUB'S.

The beating of Senator Charles Sumner by Congressman Preston Brooks on the Senate floor horrified Northerners but won the approval of Southerners.

unconstitutional, Taney asserted that the federal government had no right to interfere with the free movement of property throughout the territories. Taney was in effect making John C. Calhoun's states' rights position, always considered an extremist southern position, the law of the land. He then dismissed the Dred Scott case on the grounds that only citizens could bring suits before federal courts and that black people—slave or free—were not citizens. With this bold judicial intervention into the most heated issue of the day, Taney intended to settle the controversy over the expansion of slavery once and for all. Instead, he enflamed the conflict.

The five southern members of the Supreme Court concurred in Taney's decision, as did one Northerner, Robert C. Grier. Historians have found that President-elect Buchanan had pressured Grier, a fellow Pennsylvanian, to support the majority. Two of the three other Northerners vigorously dissented, and the last voiced other objections. This was clearly a sectional decision, and the response to it was sectional. Southerners expressed great satisfaction and strong support for the Court. The *Louisville Democrat* said, "The decision is right...but whether or not [it is right], what this tribunal decides the Constitution to be, that it is; and all patriotic men will acquiesce." More bluntly, the *Georgia Constitutionalist* announced, "Southern opinion upon the subject of southern slavery...is now the supreme law of the land...and opposition to southern opinion upon this subject is now opposition to the Constitution, and morally treason against the Government."

Northerners disagreed. Few were quite so contemptuous as the *New York Tribune*, which declared that the decision was "entitled to just as much moral weight as would be the judgment of a majority of those congregated in any Washington bar-room." Still, many were so troubled by the Dred Scott decision that for the first time they found themselves seriously questioning the power of the Supreme Court to establish the "law of the land." Many northern legislatures denounced the decision. New York passed a resolution declaring that the Supreme Court had lost the confidence and respect of the people of that state and another refusing to allow slavery within its borders "in any form or under any pretense, or for any time, however short." New York Republicans also proposed an equal suffrage amendment for free African Americans, who were largely disenfranchised by a stringent property qualification for voting. But this was too liberal for the state's voters, who defeated it. This racist attitude was a bitter blow to free African Americans in the North. Frederick Douglass was so disheartened that he seriously considered emigrating to Haiti.

For the Republican Party, the Dred Scott decision represented a formidable challenge. By invalidating the Missouri Compromise, the decision

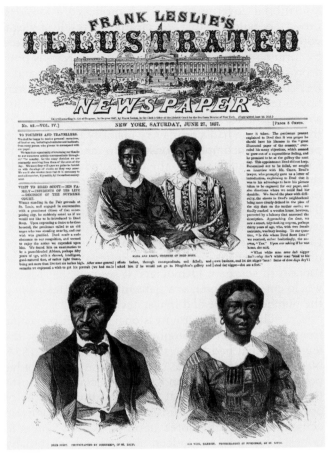

These sympathetic portraits of Harriet and Dred Scott and their daughters in 1857 helped to shape the northern reaction to the Supreme Court decision that denied the Scotts' claim for freedom. The infamous Dred Scott decision, which was intended to resolve the issue of slavery expansion, instead heightened angry feelings in both North and South.

swept away the free soil foundation of the party. But to directly challenge a Supreme Court decision was a weighty matter. The most sensational Republican counterattack—made by both Abraham Lincoln and William Seward—was the accusation that President Buchanan had conspired with the southern Supreme Court justices to subvert the American political system by withholding the decision until after the presidential election. Lincoln also raised the frightening possibility that "the next Dred Scott decision" would legalize slavery even in free states that abhorred it. President Buchanan's response to events in Kansas, including the drafting of a proslavery constitution, also stoked political antagonisms.

The Lecompton Constitution

In Kansas, the doctrine of popular sovereignty led to continuing civil strife and the political travesty of two territorial governments. The first election of officers to a territorial government in 1855 produced a lopsided proslavery outcome that was clearly the result of illegal voting by Missouri border ruffians. Free-soilers protested by forming their own government, giving Kansas both a proslavery territorial legislature in Lecompton and a free-soil government in Topeka. Because free-soil voters boycotted a June 1857 election for a convention to write a constitution for the territory once it reached statehood, the convention had a proslavery majority that wrote the proslavery Lecompton constitution and applied to Congress for admission to the Union under its terms. In the meantime, in October free-soil voters had participated in relatively honest elections for the territorial legislature, elections that returned a clear free-soil majority. Nevertheless, Buchanan, in the single most disastrous mistake of his administration, endorsed the proslavery constitution because he feared to lose the support of southern Democrats. It seemed that Kansas would enter the Union as a sixteenth slave state, making the number of slave and free states equal.

Unexpected congressional opposition came from none other than Stephen Douglas, author of the legislation that had begun the Kansas troubles in 1854. Now, in 1857, in what was surely the bravest step of his political career, Douglas opposed the Lecompton constitution on the grounds that it violated the principle of popular sovereignty. He insisted that the Lecompton constitution must be voted upon by Kansas voters in honest elections (as indeed Buchanan had initially promised). Douglas's decision was one of principle, but it was also motivated by the realization that a proslavery vote would never be accepted by the northern wing of the Democratic Party. Defying James Buchanan, his own president, Douglas voted with the majority in Congress in April 1858 to refuse admission to Kansas under the Lecompton constitution. In a new referendum, the people of Kansas also rejected the Lecompton constitution, 11,300 to 1,788. In 1859 Kansas held another constitutional convention, this one dominated by delegates from the new Republican Party. Kansas was finally admitted as a free state in January 1861.

The defeat of the Lecompton constitution did not come easily. There was more bloodshed in Kansas: sporadic ambushes and killings, including a mass shooting of nine free-soilers. And there was more violence in Congress: a free-for-all involving almost thirty congressmen broke out in the House late one night after an exchange of insults between Republicans and southern Democrats. There was conflict on still another level— the Democratic Party was breaking apart. Douglas had intended to preserve the Democrats as a national party, but instead he lost the support of the southern wing. Southerners reviled him, one claiming that Douglas was "stained with the dishonor of treachery without a parallel." Summing up these events, Congressman Alexander Stephens of Georgia wrote glumly to his brother: "All things here are tending my mind to the conclusion that the Union cannot and will not last long."

The Panic of 1857

Adding to the growing political tensions was the short but sharp depression of 1857 and 1858. Technology played a part. In August 1857, the failure of an Ohio investment house—the kind of event that had formerly taken weeks to be widely known—was the subject of a news story flashed immediately over telegraph wires to Wall Street and other financial markets. A wave of panic selling ensued, leading to business failures and slowdowns that threw thousands out of work. The major cause of the panic was a sharp but temporary downturn in agricultural exports to Britain, and recovery was well under way by early 1859. In the meantime, Republicans and some northern Democrats in Congress proposed to raise tariffs to help industries hurt by the depression but were outvoted by about half of northern Democrats and almost all southern representatives. The South had resisted protective tariffs since the 1820s (see Chapter 10), but now the opposition was regarded, in the bitter

This painting by Charles G. Rosenberg and James H. Cafferty shows a worried crowd exchanging the latest news on Wall Street during the Panic of 1857. This was the first economic depression in which the telegraph played a part by carrying bad financial news in the West to New York much more rapidly than in the past.

words of one Republican, as yet another example of a Congress "shamelessly prostituted, in a base subserviency to the Slave Power."

Because it affected cotton exports less than northern exports, the Panic of 1857 was less harmful to the South than to the North. Southerners took this as proof of the superiority of their economic system to the free-labor system of the North, and some could not resist the chance to gloat. Senator James Henry Hammond of South Carolina drove home the point in his celebrated "King Cotton" speech of March 1858:

> When the abuse of credit had destroyed credit and annihilated confidence; when thousands of the strongest commercial houses in the world were coming down...when you came to a dead lock, and revolutions were threatened, what brought you up?...We have poured in upon you one million six hundred thousand bales of cotton just at the moment to save you from destruction....We have sold it for $65,000,000, and saved you.

It seemed that all matters of political discussion were being drawn into the sectional dispute. The next step toward disunion was an act of violence perpetrated by the grim abolitionist from Kansas, John Brown.

John Brown's Raid

In the heated political mood of the late 1850s, some improbable people became heroes. None was more improbable than John Brown, the self-appointed avenger who slaughtered unarmed proslavery men in Kansas in 1856. In 1859, Brown proposed a wild scheme to raid the South and start a general slave uprising. He believed, as did most northern abolitionists, that discontent among southern slaves was so great that such an uprising needed only a spark to get going. Significantly, free African Americans—among them Frederick Douglass—did not support Brown, thinking his first planned foray, to raid the federal arsenal at Harpers Ferry, Virginia, was doomed to failure. They were right. On October 16, 1859, Brown led a group of twenty-two white and African American men against the arsenal. However, he had made no provision for escape. Even more incredible, he had not notified the Virginia slaves whose uprising it was supposed to be. In less than a day the raid was over. Eight of Brown's men (including two of his sons) were dead, no slaves had joined the fight, and Brown himself was captured. Moving quickly to prevent a lynching by local mobs, the state of Virginia tried and convicted Brown, while he was still weak from the wounds of battle, of treason, murder, and fomenting insurrection.

Ludicrous in life, possibly insane, Brown was nevertheless a noble martyr. In his closing speech prior

JOHN BROWN AT HARPER'S FERRY.

In a contemporary engraving, John Brown and his followers are shown trapped inside the armory at Harper's Ferry in October 1859. Captured, tried, and executed, Brown was regarded as a martyr in the North and a terrorist in the South.

to sentencing, Brown was magnificently eloquent: "Now, if it is deemed necessary that I should forfeit my life for the furtherance of the end of justice, and mingle my blood further with the blood of my children and with the blood of millions in this slave country whose rights are disregarded by wicked, cruel, and unjust enactments, I say, let it be done."

Brown's death by hanging on December 2, 1859, was marked throughout northern communities with public rites of mourning not seen since the death of George Washington. Church bells tolled, buildings were draped in black, ministers preached sermons, prayer meetings were held, abolitionists issued eulogies. Ralph Waldo Emerson said that Brown would "make the gallows as glorious as the cross," and Henry David Thoreau called him "an angel of light." In a more militant frame of mind, abolitionist Wendell Phillips announced, "The lesson of the hour is insurrection." Naturally, not all Northerners supported Brown's action. Northern Democrats and conservative opinion generally repudiated him. In New York, for example, 20,000 merchants signed a petition for a public meeting designed to reassure the South of northern good intentions. But many people, while rejecting Brown's raid, did support the antislavery cause that he represented.

Brown's raid shocked the South because it aroused the greatest fear, that of slave rebellion. Southerners believed that northern abolitionists were provoking slave revolts, a suspicion apparently confirmed when documents captured at Harpers Ferry revealed that Brown had the financial support of half a dozen members of the northern elite. These "Secret Six"—Gerrit Smith, George Stearns, Franklin Sanborn, Thomas Wentworth Higginson, Theodore Parker, and Samuel Gridley Howe—had been willing to finance armed attacks on the slave system.

Even more shocking to Southerners than the raid itself was the extent of northern mourning for Brown's death. Although the Republican Party disavowed Brown's actions, Southerners simply did not believe the party's statements. Southerners wondered how they could stay in the Union in the face of "Northern insolence." The *Richmond Enquirer* reported, "The Harpers Ferry invasion has advanced the cause of disunion more than any other event that has happened since the formation of [the] government." The alarm in up-country South Carolina was so great that vigilance committees were formed in every district. Throughout the next year, these committees remained armed and ready to deal with strangers (they might be abolitionists) and any hint of slave revolt. This extreme defensiveness was not a good portent for the election year of 1860. Looking to the presidential race, Senator Robert Toombs of Georgia warned that the South would "never permit this Federal government to pass into the traitorous hands of the Black Republican party."

Talk of secession as the only possible response to the northern "insults" of the 1850s—the armed protests against the Fugitive Slave Law, the rejection of the Lecompton constitution, and now the support for John Brown's raid—was common throughout the South. Although the majority of Southerners probably rejected secession, the political passions of the election year fostered secessionist thinking.

THE SOUTH SECEDES

By 1860, sectional differences had caused one national party, the Whigs, to collapse. The second national party, the Democrats, stood on the brink of dissolution. Not only the politicians but ordinary people in both the North and the South were coming to believe there was no way to avoid what in 1858 William Seward (once a Whig, now a Republican) had called an "irrepressible conflict."

The Election of 1860

The split of the Democratic Party into northern and southern wings that had occurred during President Buchanan's tenure became official at the Democratic nominating conventions in 1860. The party convened first in Charleston, South Carolina, the center of seces-

sionist agitation. It was the worst possible location in which to attempt to reach unity. Although Stephen Douglas had the support of the plurality of delegates, he did not have the two-thirds majority necessary for nomination. As the price of their support, Southerners insisted that Douglas support a federal slave code—a guarantee that slavery would be protected in the territories. Douglas could not agree without violating his own belief in popular sovereignty and losing his northern support. After ten days, fifty-nine ballots, and two southern walkouts, the convention ended where it had begun: deadlocked. Northern supporters of Douglas were angry and bitter: "I never heard Abolitionists talk more uncharitably and rancorously of the people of the South than the Douglas men," one reporter wrote. "They say they do not care...where the South goes."

In June, the Democrats met again in Baltimore. The Douglasites, recognizing the need for a united party, were eager to compromise wherever they could, but most southern Democrats were not. More than a third of the delegates bolted. Later, holding a convention of their own, they nominated Buchanan's vice president John C. Breckinridge of Kentucky. The remaining two-thirds of the Democrats nominated Douglas, but everyone knew that a Republican victory was inevitable. To make matters worse, some southern Whigs joined with some border-state nativists to form the Constitutional Union Party, which nominated John Bell of Tennessee.

Republican strategy was built on the lessons of the 1856 "victorious defeat." The Republicans planned to carry all the states Frémont had won, plus Pennsylvania, Illinois, and Indiana. The two leading Republican contenders were Senator William H. Seward of New York and Abraham Lincoln of Illinois. Seward, the party's best-known figure, had enemies among party moderates, who thought he was too radical, and among nativists with whom he had clashed in the New York Whig Party. Lincoln, on the other hand, appeared new, impressive, more moderate than Seward, and certain to carry Illinois. Lincoln won the nomination on the third ballot.

The election of 1860 presented voters with one of the clearest choices in American history. On the key issue of slavery, Breckinridge supported its extension to the territories; Lincoln stood firmly for its exclusion. Douglas attempted to hold the middle ground with his principle of popular sovereignty; Bell vaguely favored compromise as well. The Republicans offered other platform planks designed to appeal to northern voters: a homestead act (free western lands), support for a transcontinental railroad, other internal improvements, and a higher tariff. Although they spoke clearly against the extension of slavery, Republicans sought to dispel their radical abolitionist image. The Republican platform condemned John Brown's raid as "the gravest of crimes," repeatedly denied that Republicans favored the social

OVERVIEW

THE IRREPRESSIBLE CONFLICT

Declaration of Independence	1776	Thomas Jefferson's denunciation of slavery deleted from the final version.
Northwest Ordinance	1787	Slavery prohibited in the Northwest Territory (north of the Ohio River).
Constitution	1787	Slavery unmentioned but acknowledged in Article I, section 2, counting three-fifths of all African Americans, slave and free, in a state's population, and in Article I, section 9, which barred Congress from prohibiting the international slave trade for twenty years.
Louisiana Purchase	1803	Louisiana admitted as a slave state in 1812; no decision about the rest of Louisiana Purchase.
Missouri Compromise	1820	Missouri admitted as a slave state, but slavery prohibited in Louisiana Purchase north of 36°30'.
Wilmot Proviso	1846	Proposal to prohibit slavery in territory that might be gained in Mexican-American War causes splits in national parties.
Compromise of 1850	1850	California admitted as free state; Texas (already admitted, 1845) is a slave state, the rest of Mexican Cession to be decided by popular sovereignty. Ends the slave trade in the District of Columbia but a stronger Fugitive Slave Law, leading to a number of violent recaptures, arouses northern antislavery opinion.
Kansas-Nebraska Act	1854	At the urging of Stephen A. Douglas, Congress opens Kansas and Nebraska Territories for settlement under popular sovereignty. Open warfare between proslavery and antislavery factions breaks out in Kansas.
Lecompton Constitution	1857	President James Buchanan's decision to admit Kansas to the Union with a proslavery constitution is defeated in Congress.
Dred Scott Decision	1857	The Supreme Court's denial of Dred Scott's case for freedom is welcomed in the South, condemned in the North.
John Brown's Raid and Execution	1859	Northern support for John Brown shocks the South.
Democratic Party Nominating Conventions	1860	The Democrats are unable to agree on a candidate; two candidates, one northern (Stephen A. Douglas) and one southern (John C. Breckinridge) split the party and the vote, thus allowing Republican Abraham Lincoln to win.

equality of black people, and strenuously affirmed that they sought to preserve the Union. In reality, Republicans simply did not believe the South would secede if Lincoln won. In this the Republicans were not alone; few Northerners believed southern threats—Southerners had threatened too many times before.

Breckinridge insisted that he and his supporters were loyal to the Union—as long as their needs concerning slavery were met. The only candidate who spoke urgently and openly about the impending threat of secession was Douglas. Breaking with convention, Douglas campaigned personally, in both the North and, bravely, in the hostile South, warning of the danger of dissolution and presenting himself as the only truly national candidate. Realizing his own chances for election were slight, he told his private

This Republican Party poster for the election of 1860 combines the party's major themes: free land, free soil, opposition to "the Slave Power" (the slogan "Free Speech"), and higher tariffs. But above all was the message, "THE UNION MUST AND SHALL BE PRESERVED."

secretary, "Mr. Lincoln is the next President. We must try to save the Union. I will go South."

In accordance with tradition, Lincoln did not campaign for himself, but many other Republicans spoke for him. In an estimated 50,000 campaign speeches they built the image of "Honest Abe," the candidate who really had been born in a log cabin. The Republicans made a special effort, headed by Carl Schurz, to attract the German immigrant vote. They were successful with German Protestants but less so with Catholics, who were put off by the Republicans' lingering reputation for nativism. The general mood among the northern electorate was one of excitement and optimism. The Republicans were almost certain to win and to bring, because of their uncompromising opposition to the expansion of slavery, an end to the long sectional crisis. "I will vote the Republican ticket next Tuesday," wrote New York businessman and former Whig George Templeton Strong. "The only alternative is everlasting submission to the South." The Republicans did not campaign in the South; Breckinridge did not campaign in the North. Each side was therefore free to believe the worst about the other. All parties, North and South, campaigned with oratory, parades and rallies, free food and drink. Even in the face of looming crisis, this presidential campaign was the best entertainment of the day.

In spite of Breckinridge's protestations of loyalty to the Union, the mood in the Deep South was close to mass hysteria. Rumors of slave revolts—in Texas,

Alabama, and South Carolina—swept the region, and vigilance committees sprang up to counter the supposed threat. Responding to the rumors, Alabaman Sarah R. Espy wrote in her diary, "The country is getting in a deplorable state owing to the depredations committed by the Abolitionist[s] especially in Texas; and the safety of the country depend[s] on who is elected to the presidency." Apparently, southern voters talked of little else, as another Alabaman, Benjamin F. Riley, recalled: "Little else was done this year, than discuss politics. Vast crowds would daily assemble at the places of popular resort, to canvass the questions at issue. Stump speaking was a daily occurrence. Men were swayed more by passion than by calm judgment."

In the South Carolina up-country, the question of secession dominated races for the state legislature. Candidates such as A. S. Wallace of York, who advocated "patriotic forbearance" if Lincoln won, were soundly defeated. The very passion and excitement of the election campaign moved Southerners toward extremism. Even the weather—the worst drought and heat wave the South had known for years—contributed to the tension.

The election of 1860 produced the second highest voter turnout in U.S. history (81.2 percent, topped only by 81.8 percent in 1876). The election turned out to be two regional contests: Breckinridge versus Bell in the South, Lincoln versus Douglas in the North. Breckinridge carried eleven slave states with 18 percent of the popular vote; Bell carried Virginia, Tennessee, and Kentucky with 13 percent of the popular vote. Lincoln won all eighteen of the free states (he split New Jersey with Douglas) and almost 40 percent of the popular vote. Douglas carried only Missouri, but gained nearly 30 percent of the popular vote. Lincoln's electoral vote total was overwhelming: 180 to a combined 123 for the other three candidates. But although Lincoln had won 54 percent of the vote in the northern states, his name had not even appeared on the ballot in ten southern states. The true winner of the 1860 election was sectionalism.

The South Leaves the Union

Charles Francis Adams, son and grandson of presidents, wrote in his diary on the day Lincoln was elected, "The great revolution has actually taken

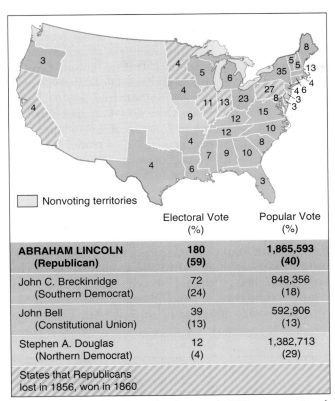

	Electoral Vote (%)	Popular Vote (%)
ABRAHAM LINCOLN (Republican)	**180 (59)**	**1,865,593 (40)**
John C. Breckinridge (Southern Democrat)	72 (24)	848,356 (18)
John Bell (Constitutional Union)	39 (13)	592,906 (13)
Stephen A. Douglas (Northern Democrat)	12 (4)	1,382,713 (29)

☐ Nonvoting territories

▨ States that Republicans lost in 1856, won in 1860

The Election of 1860   *The election of 1860 was a sectional election. Lincoln won no votes in the South, Breckinridge none in the North. The contest in the North was between Lincoln and Douglas, and although Lincoln swept the electoral vote, Douglas's popular vote was uncomfortably close. The large number of northern Democratic voters opposed to Lincoln was a source of political trouble for him during the Civil War.*

place.... The country has once and for all thrown off the domination of the Slaveholders." That was precisely what the South feared.

The results of the election shocked Southerners. They were humiliated and frightened by the prospect of becoming a permanent minority in a political system dominated by a party pledged to the elimination of slavery. In southern eyes the Republican triumph meant they would become unequal partners in the federal enterprise, their way of life (the slave system) existing on borrowed time. As a Georgia newspaper said ten days after Lincoln's election, "African slavery, though panoplied by the Federal Constitution, is doomed to a war of extermination. All the powers of a Government which has so long sheltered it will be turned to its destruction. The only hope for its preservation, therefore, is out of the Union." And Mary Boykin Chesnut, member of a well-connected South Carolina family, confided to her diary, "The die is cast—no more vain regrets—sad forebodings are useless. The stake is life or death."

The governors of South Carolina, Alabama, and Mississippi, each of whom had committed his state to

secession if Lincoln were elected, immediately issued calls for special state conventions. At the same time, calls went out to southern communities to form vigilance committees and volunteer militia companies. A visiting Northerner, Sereno Watson, wrote to his brother in amazement: "This people is apparently gone crazy. I do not know how to account for it & have no idea what might be the end of it. Union men, Douglas men, Breckinridge men are alike in their loud denunciation of submission to Lincoln's administration. There are of course those who think differently but they scarcely dare or are suffered to open their mouths." In the face of this frenzy, cooperationists (the term used for those opposed to immediate secession) were either intimidated into silence or simply left behind by the speed of events.

On December 20, 1860, a state convention in South Carolina, accompanied by all the hoopla and excitement of bands, fireworks displays, and huge rallies, voted unanimously to secede from the Union. James Buchanan, the lame-duck president (Lincoln would not be inaugurated until March), did nothing. In the weeks that followed, conventions in six other southern states (Mississippi, Florida, Alabama, Georgia, Louisiana, and Texas) followed suit, with the support, on average, of 80 percent of their delegates. Although there was genuine division of opinion in the South (especially in Georgia and Alabama, along customary up-country—low-country lines) none of the Deep South states held anywhere near the number of Unionists that Republicans had hoped. Throughout the South, secession occurred because Southerners no longer believed they had a choice. "Secession is a desperate remedy," acknowledged South Carolina's David Harris, "but of the two evils I do think it is the lesser."

In every state that seceded, the joyous scenes of South Carolina were repeated as the decisiveness of action replaced the long years of anxiety and tension. People danced in the streets, most believing the North had no choice but to accept secession peacefully. They ignored the fact that eight other slave states (Delaware, Maryland, Kentucky, Missouri, Virginia, North Carolina, Tennessee, and Arkansas) had not acted—though the latter four states would secede after war broke out. Just as Republicans had miscalculated in thinking southern threats a mere bluff, so secessionists now miscalculated in believing they would be able to leave the Union in peace.

The North's Political Options

What should the North do? Buchanan continued to do nothing. The decision thus rested with Abraham Lincoln, even before he officially became president. One possibility was compromise, and many proposals were suggested, ranging from full adoption of the Breckinridge campaign platform to reinstatement of the Missouri Compromise line. Lincoln cautiously refused them all, making it clear that he would not compromise on the extension of slavery, which was the South's key demand. He hoped, by appearing firm but moderate, to discourage additional southern states from seceding while giving pro-Union Southerners time to organize. He succeeded in his first aim, but not in the second. Lincoln and most of the Republican Party had seriously overestimated the strength of pro-Union sentiment in the South.

A second possibility, suggested by Horace Greeley of the *New York Tribune*, was to let the seven seceding states "go in peace." This is what many secessionists expected, but too many Northerners—including Lincoln himself—believed in the Union for this to happen. As Lincoln said, what was at stake was "the necessity of proving that popular government is not an absurdity. We must settle this question now, whether in a free government the minority have the right to break up the government whenever they choose." At stake was all the accumulated American pride in the federal government as a model for democracies the world over.

The third possibility was force, and this was the crux of the dilemma. Although he believed their action was wrong, Lincoln was loath to go to war to force the seceding states back into the Union. On the other hand, he refused to give up federal powers over military forts and customs posts in the South. These were precisely the powers the seceding states had to command if they were to function as an independent nation. A confrontation was bound to come. Abraham Lincoln, not for the last time, was prepared to wait for the other side to strike the first blow.

Establishment of the Confederacy

In February, delegates from the seven seceding states met in Montgomery, Alabama, and created the Confederate States of America. They wrote a constitution that was identical to the Constitution of the United States, with a few crucial exceptions: it strongly supported states' rights and made the abolition of slavery practically impossible. These two

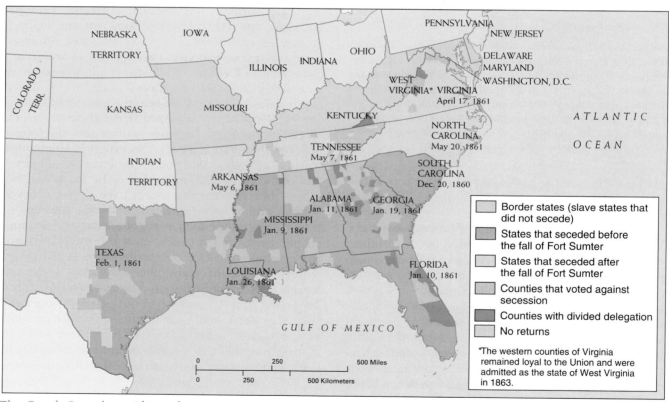

The South Secedes   *The southern states that would constitute the Confederacy seceded in two stages. The states of the Lower South seceded before Lincoln took office. Arkansas and three states of the Upper South—Virginia, North Carolina, and Tennessee—waited until after the South fired on Fort Sumter. And four border slave states—Delaware, Maryland, Kentucky and Missouri—chose not to secede. Every southern state (except South Carolina) was divided on the issue of secession, generally along up-country—low-country lines. In Virginia, this division was so extreme that West Virginia split off to become a separate nonslave state and was admitted to the Union in 1863.*

clauses did much to define the Confederate enterprise. It was difficult to avoid the conclusion that the structure of the new Confederacy had been decided by the southern dependence on slave labor. L. W. Spratt of South Carolina confessed as much in 1859: "We stand committed to the South, but we stand more vitally committed to the cause of slavery. It is, indeed, to be doubted whether the South [has] any cause apart from the institution which affects her." The South's entire defense of slavery was built on a commitment to individualism and decentralization: the rights of the slave owner over his slaves; the right of freedom claimed by all white men; and the rights of individual states versus the federal government. The military defense of the South, however, would require a strong central government. This was to be the South's basic dilemma throughout the Civil War.

The Montgomery convention passed over the fire-eaters—the men who had been the first to urge secession—and chose Jefferson Davis of Mississippi as president and Alexander Stephens of Georgia as vice president of the new nation. Both men were known as moderates. Davis, a slave owner who had been a general in the Mexican-American War and secretary of war in the Pierce administration, who was currently a senator from Mississippi, had expressed his own uncertainties by retaining his Senate seat for two weeks after Mississippi seceded. Stephens, a former leader in the Whig party, had been a cooperationist delegate to Georgia's convention, where he urged that secession not be undertaken hastily.

The choice of moderates was deliberate, for the strategy of the new Confederate state was to argue that secession was a normal, responsible, and expectable course of action, and nothing for the North to get upset about. This was the theme that President Jefferson Davis of the Confederate States of America struck in his Inaugural Address, delivered to a crowd of 10,000 from the steps of the State Capitol at Montgomery, Alabama on February 18, 1861. "We have changed the constituent parts," Davis said, "but not the system of our Government." Secession was a legal and peaceful step that, Davis said, quoting from the Declaration of Independence, "illustrates the American idea that governments rest on the consent of the governed...and that it is the right of the people to alter or abolish them at will whenever they become destructive of the ends for which they were established." After insisting that "a just perception of mutual interest [should] permit us peaceably to pursue our separate political [course]," Davis concluded, "Obstacles may retard, but they cannot long prevent, the progress of a movement sanctified by its justice and sustained by a virtuous

Abraham Lincoln's inauguration on March 4, 1861, *shown here in* Leslie's Illustrated Newspaper, *symbolized the state of the nation. As he took the oath to become president of a divided country, Lincoln stood before a Capitol building with a half-finished dome and was guarded by soldiers who feared a Confederate attack. Politicians had long been concerned about the dangers of sectionalism in American life. But most ordinary people had taken for granted the federal Union of states—and the ability of slave and nonslave states to coexist.*

people." This impressive inaugural prompted a deeply moved correspondent for the *New York Herald* to report, "God does not permit evil to be done with such earnest solemnity, such all-pervading trust in His Providence, as was exhibited by the whole people on that day."

Lincoln's Inauguration

The country as a whole waited to see what Abraham Lincoln would do, which at first appeared to be very little. In Springfield, Lincoln refused to issue public statements before his inaugural (although he sent many private messages to Congress and to key military officers), for fear of making a delicate situation worse. Similarly, during a twelve-day whistle-stopping rail-

CHRONOLOGY

1820	Missouri Compromise
1828–32	Nullification Crisis
1846	Wilmot Proviso
1848	Treaty of Guadalupe Hidalgo ends Mexican-American War
	Zachary Taylor elected president
	Free-Soil Party formed
1849	California and Utah seek admission to the Union as free states
1850	Compromise of 1850
	California admitted as a free state
	American (Know-Nothing) Party formed
	Zachary Taylor dies, Millard Fillmore becomes president
1851	North reacts to Fugitive Slave Law
	Harriet Beecher Stowe's *Uncle Tom's Cabin* published
1852	Franklin Pierce elected president
1854	Ostend Manifesto
	Kansas-Nebraska Act
	Treaties with Indians in northern part of Indian Territory renegotiated
	Republican Party formed as Whig Party dissolves
1855	William Walker leads first filibustering expedition to Nicaragua
1856	Burning and looting of Lawrence, Kansas
	John Brown leads Pottawatomie massacre
	Attack on Senator Charles Sumner
	James Buchanan elected president
1857	Dred Scott decision
	President Buchanan accepts proslavery Lecompton constitution in Kansas
	Panic of 1857
1858	Congress rejects Lecompton constitution
	Lincoln-Douglas debates
1859	John Brown's raid on Harpers Ferry
1860	Four parties run presidential candidates
	Abraham Lincoln elected president
	South Carolina secedes from Union
1861	Six other Deep South states secede
	Confederate States of America formed
	Lincoln takes office

road trip east from Springfield, he was careful to say nothing controversial. Eastern intellectuals, already suspicious of a mere "prairie lawyer," were not impressed. Finally, hard evidence of an assassination plot forced Lincoln to abandon his whistle-stops at Harrisburg and, protected by Pinkerton detectives, to travel incognito into Washington "like a thief in the night," as he complained. These signs of moderation and caution did not appeal to an American public with a penchant for electing military heroes. Americans wanted leadership and action.

Lincoln continued, however, to offer nonbelligerent firmness and moderation. And at the end of his Inaugural Address on March 4, 1861, as he stood ringed by federal troops called out in case of a Confederate attack, the new president offered unexpected eloquence:

I am loath to close. We are not enemies, but friends. We must not be enemies. Though passion may have strained, it must not break our bonds of affection. The mystic chords of memory, stretching from every battlefield, and patriot grave, to every living heart and hearthstone, all over this broad land, will yet swell the chorus of the Union, when again touched, as surely they will be, by the better angels of our nature.

CONCLUSION

Americans had much to boast about in 1850. Their nation was vastly larger, richer, and more powerful than it had been in 1800. But the issue of slavery was slowly dividing the North and the South, two communities with similar origins and many common bonds. The following decade was marked by frantic efforts at political compromise, beginning with the Compromise of 1850, continuing with the Kansas-Nebraska Act of 1854, and culminating in the Supreme Court's 1859 decision in the Dred Scott case. Increasingly, the ordinary people of the two regions demanded resolution of the crisis. The two great parties of the Second American Party System, the Democrats and the Whigs, unable to find a solution, were destroyed. Two new sectional parties—the Republican Party and a southern party devoted to the defense of slavery—fought the 1860 election, but Southerners refused to accept the national verdict. Politics had failed: the issue of slavery was irreconcilable. The only remaining recourse was war. But although Americans were divided, they were still one people. That made the war, when it came, all the more terrible.

REVIEW QUESTIONS

1. What aspects of the remarkable economic development of the United States in the first half of the nineteenth century contributed to the sectional crisis of the 1850s?

2. How might the violent efforts by abolitionists to free escaped slaves who had been recaptured and the federal armed enforcement of the Fugitive Slave Act have been viewed differently by merchants (the so-called Cotton Whigs), Irish immigrants, and abolitionists?

3. Consider the course of events in "Bloody Kansas" from Douglas's Kansas-Nebraska Act to the Congressional rejection of the Lecompton constitution. Were these events the inevitable result of the political impasse in Washington, or could other decisions have been taken that would have changed the outcome?

4. The nativism of the 1850s that surfaced so strongly in the Know-Nothing Party was eclipsed by the crisis over slavery. But nativist sentiment has been a recurring theme in American politics. Discuss why it was strong in the 1850s and why it might have emerged periodically since then.

5. Evaluate the character and actions of John Brown. Was he the hero proclaimed by northern supporters or the terrorist condemned by the South?

6. Imagine that you lived in Illinois, home state to both Douglas and Lincoln, in 1860. How would you have voted in the presidential election, and why?

RECOMMENDED READING

William L. Barney, *The Secessionist Impulse: Alabama and Mississippi in 1860* (1974). Covers the election of 1860 and the subsequent conventions that led to secession.

Don E. Fehrenbacher, *The Dred Scott Case: Its Significance in American Law and Politics* (1978). A major study by the leading historian on this controversial decision.

Eric Foner, *Free Soil, Free Labor, Free Men: The Ideology of the Republican Party before the Civil War* (1970). A landmark effort that was among the first studies to focus on free labor ideology of the North and its importance in the political disputes of the 1850s.

Lacey K. Ford Jr., *Origins of Southern Radicalism: The South Carolina Upcountry, 1800–1860* (1988). One of a number of recent studies of the attitudes of up-country farmers, who in South Carolina supported secession wholeheartedly.

Homan Hamilton, *Prologue to Conflict: The Crisis and Compromise of 1850* (1964). The standard source on the Compromise of 1850.

Bruce Levine, *Half Slave and Half Free: The Roots of the Civil War* (1992). Good survey of the contrasting attitudes of North and South.

Alice Nichols, *Bleeding Kansas* (1954). The standard source on the battles over Kansas.

David M. Potter, *The Impending Crisis, 1848-1861* (1976). A comprehensive account of the politics leading up to the Civil War.

Anne C. Rose, *Voices of the Marketplace: American Thought and Culture, 1830–1860* (1995). A new study that considers the effects of the concepts of Christianity, democracy, and capitalism on American cultural life.

Kenneth M. Stampp, *America in 1857: A Nation on the Brink* (1990). A study of the "crucial" year by a leading southern historian.

Albert J. Von Frank, *The Trials of Anthony Burns: Freedom and Slavery in Emerson's Boston* (1998). An eloquent study of the trial and the links between transcendentalist and abolitionist opinion.

ADDITIONAL BIBLIOGRAPHY

The Controversy over Slavery

Richard H. Abbott, *Cotton and Capital: Boston Businessmen and Antislavery Reform, 1854–1868* (1991)

Eugene Berwanger, *The Frontier against Slavery: Western Anti-Negro Prejudice and the Slavery Extension Controversy* (1967)

Stanley W. Campbell, *The Slave Catchers* (1970)

David B. Davis, *The Slave Power Conspiracy and the Paranoid Style* (1969)

W. Ehrlich, *They Have No Rights: Dred Scott's Struggle for Freedom* (1979)

P. Finkelman, *An Imperfect Union: Slavery, Freedom, and Comity* (1981)

C. C. Goen, *Broken Churches, Broken Nation* (1985)

Thomas F. Grossett, *Uncle Tom's Cabin and American Culture* (1985)

Joseph Herring, *The Enduring Indians of Kansas: A Century and a Half of Acculturation* (1990)

J. R. McKivigan, *The War against Proslavery Religion* (1984)

William Lee Miller, *Arguing About Slavery: The Great Battle in the United States Congress* (1996)

H. Craig Miner and William E. Unrau, *The End of Indian Kansas* (1978)

Thomas D. Morris, *Free Men All: The Personal Liberty Laws of the North, 1780–1861* (1974)

Allan Nevins, *The Ordeal of the Union*, vols. 1–2 (1947)

Roy Nichols, *The Disruption of American Democracy* (1948)

Joseph G. Rayback, *Free Soil: The Election of 1848* (1970)

J. Rossbach, *Ambivalent Conspirators: John Brown, the Secret Six and a Theory of Black Political Violence* (1982)

Thomas P. Slaughter, *Bloody Dawn: The Christiana Riots and Racial Violence in the Antebellum North* (1991)

Kenneth M. Stampp, *The Causes of the Civil War*, rev. ed. (1974)

Joanna L. Stratton, *Pioneer Women: Voices from the Kansas Frontier* (1981)

Gerald W. Wolff, *The Kansas-Nebraska Bill: Party, Section, and the Coming of the Civil War* (1977)

Bertram Wyatt-Brown, *Yankee Saints and Southern Sinners* (1985)

The Crisis of the National Party System

Thomas B. Alexander, *Sectional Stress and Party Strength* (1967)

Tyler Anbinder, *Nativism and Slavery: The Northern Know-Nothings and the Politics of the 1850s* (1992)

J. H. Baker, *Affairs of Party: The Political Culture of Northern Democrats in the Mid-Nineteenth Century* (1983)

F. J. Blue, *The Free Soilers: Third Party Politics* (1973)

G. B. Forgie, *Patricide in the House Divided* (1981)

Ronald Formisano, *The Birth of Mass Political Parties: Michigan, 1827–1861* (1971)

William E. Gienapp, *The Origins of the Republican Party, 1852–1856* (1987)

Michael Holt, *Forging a Majority: The Formation of the Republican Party in Pittsburgh, 1848–1860* (1969)

———, *The Political Crisis of the 1850's* (1978)

Thelma Jennings, *The Nashville Convention* (1980)

Robert W. Johannsen, *The Lincoln-Douglas Debates* (1965)

Paul Kleppner, *The Third Electoral System, 1853–1892: Parties, Voters, and Political Cultures* (1979)

John Mayfield, *Rehearsal for Republicanism: Free Soil and the Politics of Antislavery* (1980)

Richard Sewell, *Ballots for Freedom: Antislavery Politics in the United States, 1837–1865* (1976)

The South Secedes

William. L. Barney, *The Road to Secession* (1972)

Charles H. Brown, *Agents of Manifest Destiny: The Lives and Times of the Filibusters* (1980)

Steven A. Channing, *Crisis of Fear: Secession in South Carolina* (1970)

William J. Cooper, *The South and the Politics of Slavery* (1978)

Avery O. Craven, *The Growth of Southern Nationalism 1848–1861* (1953)

John Hope Franklin, *A Southern Odyssey: Travelers in the Antebellum North* (1976)

———, *The Militant South 1800–1861* (1956)

William W. Freehling, *The Road to Disunion*, vol. I: *Secessionists at Bay, 1776–1854* (1991)

William H. Goetzmann, *When the Eagle Screamed: The Romantic Horizon in American Diplomacy, 1800–1860* (1966)

Michael P. Johnson, *Toward a Patriarchal Republic: The Secession of Georgia* (1977)

———, *Secession and Conservatism in the Lower South: The Social and Ideological Bases of Secession in Georgia, 1860–1861* (1983)

Michael P. Johnson and James L. Roark, eds., *No Chariot Let Down: Charleston's Free People of Color on the Eve of the Civil War* (1984)

Robert E. May, *The Southern Dream of a Caribbean Empire, 1854–1861* (1973)

John McCardell, *The Idea of a Southern Nation: Southern Nationalists and Southern Nationalism, 1830–1861* (1979)

Rollin G. Osterweis, *Romanticism and Nationalism in the Old South* (1949)

David M. Potter, *The South and the Sectional Conflict* (1968)

Basil Rauch, *American Interest in Cuba* (1948)

William O. Scroggs, *Filibusters and Financiers: The Story of William Walker and His Associates* (1960)

K. M. Stampp, *And the War Came: The North and the Secession Crisis 1860–1861* (1950)

Joe A. Stout, *The Liberators: Filibustering Expeditions into Mexico, 1848–1862, and the Last Thrust of Manifest Destiny* (1973)

Ronald L. Takaki, *A Proslavery Crusade: The Agitation to Reopen the African Slave Trade* (1971)

J. Mills Thornton, *Politics and Power in a Slavery Society* (1978)

Eric H. Walter, *The Fire-Eaters* (1992)

C. Vann Woodward, *American Counterpoint: Slavery and Racism in the North–South Dialogue* (1971)

R. A. Wooster, *The Secession Conventions of the South* (1962)

Biography

K. J. Bauer, *Zachary Taylor: Soldier, Planter, Statesman of the Old Southwest* (1985)

D. H. Donald, *Charles Sumner and the Coming of the Civil War* (1960)

Donald E. Fehrenbacher, *Prelude to Greatness: Lincoln in the 1850's* (1962)

Joan Hedrick, *Harriet Beecher Stowe: A Life* (1994)

Robert W. Johannsen, *Stephen A. Douglas* (1973)

Stephen Oates, *To Purge This Land with Blood: A Biography of John Brown* (1970)

———, *With Malice toward None: A Life of Abraham Lincoln* (1977)

CHAPTER SIXTEEN

THE CIVIL WAR

1861–1865

Winslow Homer, *Near Andersonville*, 1865. Oil on canvas. Photograph by Armen Shamalian Photographers. The Newark Museum. Gift of the Corbin family in memory of their parents Hannah Stockton Corbin and Horace Kellogg Corbin.

AMERICAN COMMUNITIES
Mother Bickerdyke Connects Northern Communities to Their Boys at War

In May 1861 the Reverend Edward Beecher interrupted his customary Sunday service at Brick Congregational Church in Galesburg, Illinois, to read a disturbing letter to the congregation. Two months earlier, Galesburg had proudly sent 500 of its young men off to join the Union army. They had not yet been in battle. Yet, the letter reported, an alarming number were dying of diseases caused by inadequate food, medical care, and sanitation at the crowded military camp in Cairo, Illinois. Most army doctors were surgeons, trained to operate and amputate on the battlefield. They were not prepared to treat soldiers sick with dysentery, pneumonia, typhoid, measles—all serious, frequently fatal diseases that could often be cured with careful nursing. The letter writer, appalled by the squalor and misery he saw around him, complained of abuses by the army. The Union army, however, was overwhelmed with the task of readying recruits for battle and had made few provisions for their health when not in combat.

The shocked and grieving members of Beecher's congregation quickly decided to send not only supplies but one of their number to inspect the conditions at the Cairo camp and to take action. In spite of warnings from a veteran of the War of 1812 that army regulations excluded women from encampments, the congregation voted to send their most qualified member, Mary Ann Bickerdyke, a middle-aged widow who made her living as a "botanic physician." This simple gesture of community concern launched the remarkable Civil War career of "the Cyclone in Calico," who defied medical officers and generals alike in her unceasing efforts on behalf of ill, wounded, and convalescent Union soldiers.

"Mother" Bickerdyke, as she was called, let nothing stand in the way of helping her "boys." When she arrived in Cairo, she immediately set to work cleaning the hospital tents and the soldiers themselves and finding and cooking nourishing food for them. Ordered to leave by the hospital director, who resented her interference, she blandly continued her work. When he reported her to the commanding officer, General Benjamin Prentiss, she quickly convinced the general to let her stay. "I talked sense to him," she later said.

From a peacetime point of view, what Mother Bickerdyke was doing was not unusual. Every civilian hospital had a matron who made sure patients were supplied with clean bed linen and bandages and were fed the proper convalescent diet. But in the context of the war—the sheer number of soldiers, the constant need to set up new field hospitals and commandeer scarce food for an army on the move—it was unusual indeed and required an unusual person. A plain spoken, hardworking woman, totally unfazed by rank or tender masculine egos, Mother Bickerdyke single-mindedly devoted herself to what she called "the Lord's work." The ordinary soldiers loved her; wise generals supported her. Once, when an indignant officer's wife complained about Bickerdyke's rudeness, General William Tecumseh Sherman joked, "You've picked the one person around here who outranks me. If you want to lodge a complaint against her, you'll have to take it to President Lincoln."

By their actions, Mother Bickerdyke and others like her exposed the War Department's inability to meet the needs of the nation's first mass army. And like the Galesburg congregation, other communities all over the North rallied to make up for the department's shortcomings with supplies and assistance. The efforts of women on the local level—for example, to make clothing for men from their communities who had gone off to the war—quickly took on national dimensions. The Women's Central Association of Relief (WCAR), whose organizers were mostly reformers experienced in the abolitionist, temperance, and education movements, eventually had 7,000 chapters throughout the North. Its volunteers raised funds, made and collected a variety of items—food, clothes, medicine, bandages, and more than 250,000 quilts and comforters—and sent them to army camps and hospitals. Volunteers also provided meals, housing, and transportation to soldiers on furlough. All told, association chapters supplied an estimated $15 million worth of goods to the Union troops.

In June 1861, responding to requests by officials of the WCAR for formal recognition of the organization, President Abraham Lincoln created the United States Sanitary Commission and gave it the power to investigate and advise the Medical Bureau. Henry Bellows, a Unitarian clergyman, became president of the organization, and Frederick Law Olmsted, the author of influential books about the slaveholding South and later the designer of New York's Central Park, was named its executive secretary. The commission's more than 500 "sanitary inspectors" (usually men) instructed soldiers in such matters as water supply, placement of latrines, and safe cooking.

Although at first she worked independently and remained suspicious of all organizations (and even of many other relief workers), in 1862 Mother Bickerdyke was persuaded to become an official agent of "the Sanitary," as it was known. The advantage to her was access to the commission's warehouses and the ability to order from them precisely what she needed. The advantage to the Sanitary was that Mother Bickerdyke was an unequaled fundraiser. In speaking tours throughout Illinois, she touched her female listeners with moving stories of wounded boys whom she had cared for as if they were her own sons. Her words to men were more forceful. It was a man's business to fight, she said. If he was too old or ill to fight with a gun, he should fight with his dollars. With the help of Bickerdyke's blunt appeals, the Sanitary raised $50 million for the Union war effort.

As the Civil War continued, Mother Bickerdyke became a key figure in the medical support for General Ulysses S. Grant's campaigns along the Mississippi River. She was with the army at Shiloh, and as Grant slowly fought his way to Vicksburg she set up convalescent hospitals in Memphis. Grant authorized her to commandeer any army wagons she needed to transport supplies. Between fifty and seventy "contrabands" (escaped former slaves) worked on her laundry crew. On the civilian side, the Sanitary Commission authorized her to draw on its supply depots in Memphis, Cairo, Chicago, and elsewhere. She was thus in a practical sense a vital "middlewoman" between the home front and the battlefield—and in a symbolic and emotional sense too, as a stand-in for all mothers who had sent their sons to war.

The Civil War was a community tragedy, ripping apart the nation's political fabric and producing more casualties than any other war in the nation's history. Yet in another sense, it was a community triumph. Local communities directly supported and sustained their soldiers on a massive scale in unprecedented ways. As national unity failed, the strength of local communities, symbolized by Mother Bickerdyke, endured.

Memphis

KEY TOPICS

- The social and political changes created by the unprecedented nature and scale of the Civil War

- The major military campaigns of the war
- The central importance of the end of slavery to the war efforts of North and South

COMMUNITIES MOBILIZE FOR WAR

A neutral observer in March 1861 might have seen ominous similarities. Two nations—the United States of America (shorn of seven states in the Deep South) and the Confederate States of America—each blamed the other for the breakup of the Union. Two new presidents—Abraham Lincoln and Jefferson Davis—each faced the challenging task of building and maintaining national unity. Two regions—North and South—scorned each other and boasted of their own superiority. But the most basic similarity was not yet apparent: both sides were unprepared for the ordeal that lay ahead.

Fort Sumter: The War Begins

In their Inaugural Addresses, both Abraham Lincoln and Jefferson Davis prayed for peace but positioned themselves for war. Careful listeners to both addresses realized that the two men were on a collision course. Jefferson Davis claimed that the Confederacy would be forced to "appeal to arms...if...the integrity of our territory and jurisdiction [is] assailed." Lincoln said, "The power confided to me will be used to hold, occupy, and possess the property and places belonging to the government." One of those places, Fort Sumter, in South Carolina, was claimed by both sides.

Fort Sumter, a major federal military installation, sat on a granite island at the entrance to Charleston harbor. So long as it remained in Union hands, Charleston, the center of secessionist sentiment, would be immobilized. Realizing its military and symbolic importance, South Carolinians had begun demanding that the fort be turned over to them even before they seceded. Thus it was hardly surprising that Fort Sumter would provide President Lincoln with his first crisis.

With the fort dangerously low on supplies, Lincoln had to decide whether to abandon it or risk the fight that might ensue if he ordered it resupplied. In a process he would follow on many other occasions, Lincoln first hesitated, canvassed opinions of all kinds, and then took cautious and careful action (even as some of his cabinet urged more decisive steps). On April 6, Lincoln notified the governor of South Carolina that he was sending a relief force to the fort carrying only food and no military supplies. Now the decision rested with Jefferson Davis. Like Lincoln, Davis faced a divided cabinet; unlike Lincoln, however, he opted for decisive action. On April 10 he ordered General P. G. T. Beauregard to demand the surrender of Fort Sumter and to attack it if the garrison did not comply. On April 12, as Lincoln's relief force neared Charleston harbor, Beauregard opened fire. Two days later, the defenders surrendered and the Confederate Stars and Bars rose over Fort Sumter. The people of Charleston celebrated wildly. "I did not know," wrote Mary Boykin Chesnut in her diary, "that one could live such days of excitement."

The Call to Arms

Even before the attack on Fort Sumter, the Confederate Congress had authorized a volunteer army of 100,000 men to serve for twelve months. There was no difficulty finding volunteers. Men flocked to enlist, and their communities sent them off in ceremonies featuring bands, bonfires, and belligerent oratory. Most of that oratory, like Jefferson Davis's Inaugural Address (see Chapter 15), evoked the Revolutionary War and the right of free people to resist tyranny. In many places, the response to the hostilities at Fort Sumter was even more visceral. The first war circular, printed in Hickman County, Tennessee, trumpeted, "To Arms! Our Southern soil must be defended. We must not stop to ask who brought about war, who is at fault, but let us go and do battle...and then settle the question of who is to blame." Exhilarated by their own rapid mobilization, most Southerners believed that Unionists were cowards who would not be able to face up to southern bravery. "Just throw three or four shells among those blue-bellied Yankees," one North Carolinian boasted, "and they'll scatter like sheep." The cry of "On to Washington!" was raised throughout the South, and orators confidently predicted that the city would be captured and the war concluded within sixty days. For the early recruits, war was a patriotic adventure.

The "thunderclap of Sumter" startled the North into an angry response. The apathy and uncertainty that had prevailed since Lincoln's election disappeared, to be replaced by strong feelings of patriotism. On April 15, Lincoln issued a proclamation calling for 75,000 state militiamen to serve in the federal army for ninety days. Enlistment offices were swamped with so many enthusiastic volunteers that many men were sent home. Free African Americans, among the most eager to serve, were turned away: this was not yet a war for or by black people.

Public outpourings of patriotism were common. New Yorker George Templeton Strong recorded one example on April 18: "Went to the [City] Hall. The [Sixth] Massachusetts Regiment, which arrived here last night, was marching down on its way to Washington. Immense crowd; immense cheering. My eyes filled with tears, and I was half choked in sympathy with the contagious excitement. God be praised for the unity of feeling here! It is beyond, very far beyond, anything I hoped for."

The mobilization in Chester, Pennsylvania, was typical of the northern response to the outbreak of war. A patriotic rally was held at which a company of volunteers (the first of many from the region) calling themselves the "Union Blues" were mustered into the Ninth Regiment of Pennsylvania Volunteers amid cheers and band music. As they marched off to Washington (the gathering place for the Union army), companies of home guards were organized by the men who remained behind. Within a month, the women of Chester had organized a countywide system of war relief that sent a stream of clothing, blankets, bandages, and other supplies to the local troops and provided assistance to their families at home. Such relief organizations, some formally organized, some informal, emerged in every community, North and South, that sent soldiers off to the Civil War. These organizations not only played a vital role in supplying the troops but maintained the human, local link on which so many soldiers depended. In this sense, every American community accompanied its young men to war. And every American community stood to suffer terrible losses when its young men went into battle.

This patriotic painting shows the departure of New York's Seventh Regiment for Washington in mid-April of 1861. Stirring scenes like this occurred across the nation following "the thunderclap of Sumter" as communities mobilized for war.

The Border States

The first secession, between December 20, 1860, and February 1, 1861, had taken seven Deep South states out of the Union. Now, in April, the firing on Fort Sumter and Lincoln's call for state militias forced the other southern states to take sides. Courted—and pressured—by both North and South, four states of the Upper South (Virginia, Arkansas, Tennessee, and North Carolina) joined the original seven in April and May 1861. Virginia's secession tipped the other three toward the Confederacy. The capital of the Confederacy was now moved to Richmond. This meant that the two capitals—Richmond and Washington—were less than 100 miles apart.

Still undecided was the loyalty of the northernmost tier of slave-owning states: Missouri, Kentucky, Maryland, and Delaware. Each controlled vital strategic assets. Missouri not only bordered the Mississippi River but controlled the routes to the west. Kentucky controlled the Ohio River. The main railroad link with the West ran through Maryland and the hill region of western Virginia (which split from Virginia to become the free state of West Virginia in 1863). Delaware controlled access to Philadelphia. Finally, were Maryland to secede, the nation's capital would be completely surrounded by Confederate territory.

Delaware was loyal to the Union (less than 2 percent of its population were slaves), but Maryland's loyalty was divided, as an ugly incident on April 19 showed. When the Sixth Massachusetts Regiment (the one Strong had cheered in New York) marched through Baltimore, a hostile crowd of 10,000 Southern sympathizers, carrying Confederate flags, pelted the troops with bricks, paving stones, and bullets. Finally, in desperation the troops fired on the crowd, killing twelve people and wounding others. In retaliation, Southern sympathizers burned the railroad bridges to the North and destroyed the telegraph line to Washington, cutting off communication between the capital and the rest of the Union for six days.

Lincoln's response was swift and stern. He stationed Union troops along Maryland's crucial railroads, declared martial law in Baltimore, and arrested the suspected ringleaders of the pro-Confederate mob and held them without trial. In July, he ordered the detention of thirty-two secessionist legislators and many sympathizers. Thus was Maryland's loyalty to the Union ensured.

In detaining the Baltimore agitators, Lincoln suspended the writ of habeas corpus, the constitutional requirement that authorities explain to a court their reasons for arresting someone. Chief Justice Roger B. Taney of the Supreme court ruled that the president had no right to do this, but Lincoln at first ignored him. Later Lincoln argued that the suspension of certain civil rights might be necessary to suppress rebellion. The arrests in Maryland were the first of a number of violations of basic civil rights during the war, all of which the president justified on the basis of national security.

Like Maryland, the loyalties of the other border states were also divided. Missouri was plagued by guerrilla battles (reminiscent of the prewar "Bleeding Kansas") throughout the war. In Kentucky, division took the form of a huge illegal trade with the Confederacy through neighboring Tennessee, to which Lincoln, determined to keep Kentucky in the Union, turned a blind eye. The conflicting loyalties of the border states were often mirrored within families. Kentucky senator John J. Crittenden had two sons who were major generals, one in the Union army and the other in the Confederate army. Such family divisions reached all the way to the White House: three brothers of Kentucky-born Mary Todd Lincoln, the president's wife, died fighting for the Confederacy.

That Delaware, Maryland, Missouri, and Kentucky chose to stay in the Union was a severe blow to the Confederacy. Among them, the four states could have added 45 percent to the white population and military manpower of the Confederacy and 80 percent to its manufacturing capacity. Almost as damaging, the decision of four slave states to stay in the Union punched a huge hole in the Confederate argument that the southern states were forced to secede to protect the right to own slaves.

The Battle of Bull Run

Once sides had been chosen and the initial flush of enthusiasm had passed, the nature of the war, and the mistaken notions about it, soon became clear. The event that shattered the illusions was the first battle of Bull Run, at Manassas Creek in Virginia in July 1861. Confident of a quick victory, a Union army of 35,000 men marched south, crying "On to Richmond!" So lighthearted and unprepared was the Washington community that the troops were accompanied not only by journalists but by a crowd of politicians and sightseers. At first the Union troops held their ground against the 25,000 Confederate troops commanded by General P. G. T. Beauregard (of Fort Sumter fame). But when 2,300 fresh Confederate troops arrived as reinforcements, the untrained northern troops broke ranks in an uncontrolled retreat that swept up the frightened sightseers as well. Soldiers and civilians alike retreated in disarray to Washington. Confederate Mary Boykin Chesnut recorded in her diary, "We might have walked into Washington any day for a week after Manassas, such was the consternation and confusion there." But the Confederates lacked the organization and the strength to follow the retreating Union troops and capture the capital.

Bull Run was sobering—and prophetic. The Civil War was the most lethal military conflict in American history, leaving a legacy of devastation on the battlefield and desolation at home. It claimed the lives of nearly 620,000 soldiers, more than the the First and Second World Wars combined. One out of every four soldiers who fought in the war never returned home.

The Relative Strengths of North and South

Overall, in terms of both population and productive capacity, the Union seemed to have a commanding edge over the Confederacy. The North had two and a half times the South's population (22 million to 9 million, of whom 3.5 million were slaves) and enjoyed an even greater advantage in industrial capacity (nine times that of the South). The North produced almost all of the nation's firearms (97 percent), had 71 percent of its railroad mileage, and produced 94 percent of its cloth and 90 percent of its footwear. The North seemed able to feed, clothe, arm, and transport all the soldiers it chose. These assets were ultimately to prove decisive: by the end of the war the Union had managed to field more than 2 million soldiers to the Confederacy's 800,000.

But in the short term the South had important assets to counter them.

The first was the nature of the struggle. For the South, this was a defensive war in which, as the early volunteers showed, the most basic principle of the defense of home and community united almost all white citizens, regardless of their views about slavery. The North would have to invade the South and then control it against guerrilla opposition to win. The parallels with the Revolutionary War were unmistakable. Most white Southerners were confident that the North, like Great Britain in its attempt to subdue the rebellious colonies, would turn out to be a lumbering giant against whom they could secure their independence.

Second, the military disparity was less extreme than it appeared. Although the North had manpower, its troops were mostly untrained. The professional federal army numbered only 16,000, and most of its experience had been gained in small Indian wars. Moreover, the South, because of its tradition of honor and belligerence (see Chapter 11), appeared to have an advantage in military leadership. More than a quarter of

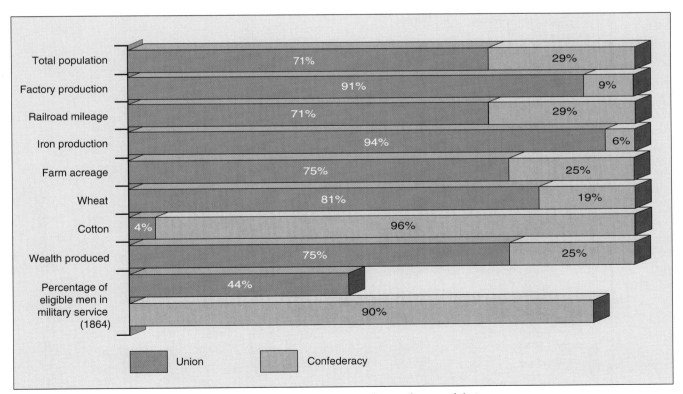

Comparative Resources, North and South, 1861 *By 1865, the North's overwhelming advantage in population, industrial strength, railroad mileage, agricultural productivity, and wealth had proved decisive in assuring victory. But initially these strengths made little difference in a struggle that began as a traditional war of maneuver in which the South held the defensive advantage. Only slowly did the Civil War become a modern war in which all of the resources of society, including the property and lives of civilians, were mobilized for battle.*

Source: *The Times Atlas of World History* (Maplewood, New Jersey: Hammond, 1978).

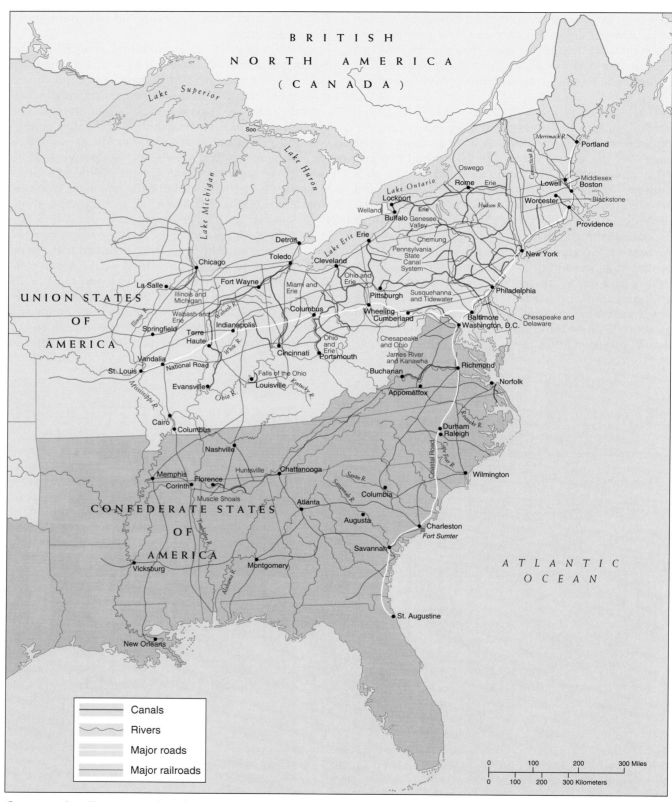

Comparative Transportation Systems, 1860 *Transportation systems were an important index of comparative strength: the North had almost three times the railroad mileage of the South. The relative lack of transportation hurt the Confederacy by hindering its ability to move troops and to distribute military and medical supplies.*

all the regular army officers chose to side with the South. The most notable was Robert E. Lee. Offered command of the Union army by President Lincoln, Lee hesitated but finally decided to follow his native state, Virginia, into the Confederacy, saying, "I have been unable to make up my mind to raise my hand against my native state, my relatives, my children, and my home."

Finally, the North's economic advantages, which were eventually decisive, initially seemed unimportant. The South could feed itself, and many soldiers brought their own weapons, uniforms, horses, and sometimes slaves when they enlisted. It was widely believed that slavery would work to the South's advantage, for slaves could continue to do the vital plantation work while their

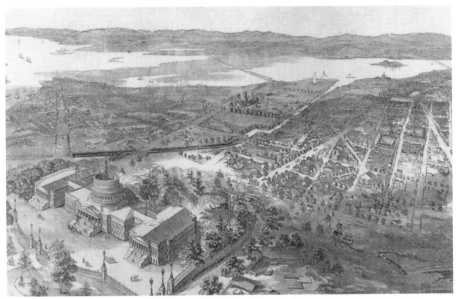

This aerial view of Washington shows the nation's capital during the Civil War as it underwent an abrupt transition from a small slave-owning community to the busy hub of the Union's war effort. Throughout the Civil War, the unfinished dome of the Capitol Building loomed over the city, its incompleteness symbolizing the divided state of the nation.

masters went off to war. But above all, the South had the weapon of cotton. "Cotton is King," James Henry Hammond had announced in 1858, at the height of the cotton boom that made the 1850s the most profitable decade in southern history. Because of the crucial role of southern cotton in industrialization, Hammond had declared, "The slaveholding South is now the controlling power of the world." Southerners were confident that the British and French need for southern cotton would soon bring those countries to recognize the Confederacy as a separate nation.

THE LINCOLN PRESIDENCY

The Civil War forced the federal government to assume powers unimaginable just a few years before. Abraham Lincoln took as his primary task to lead and unify the nation in his responsibility as commander in chief. He found the challenge almost insurmountable. Fortunately, the nation had found in Lincoln a man with the moral courage and the political skill to chart a course through the many conflicting currents of northern public opinion.

Lincoln as Party Leader and War President

Lincoln's first task as president was to assert control over his own cabinet. Because he had few national contacts outside the Republican Party, Lincoln chose to staff his cabinet with other Republicans, including, most unusually, several who had been his rivals for the presidential nomination. Secretary of State William

Seward, widely regarded as the leader of the Republican Party, at first expected to "manage" Lincoln as he had Zachary Taylor in 1848, but he soon became the president's willing partner. On the other hand, Treasury Secretary Salmon P. Chase, a staunch abolitionist, adamantly opposed concessions to the South and considered Lincoln too conciliatory. Chase, a key member of a group known as the Radical Republicans, remained a vocal and dangerous critic. That the Republican Party was a not-quite-jelled mix of former Whigs, abolitionists, moderate Free-Soilers, and even some prowar Democrats made Lincoln's task as party leader much more difficult than it might otherwise have been.

After the fall of Fort Sumter, military necessity prompted Lincoln to call up the state militias, order a naval blockade of the South, and vastly expand the military budget. Breaking with precedent, he took these actions without congressional sanction because Congress was not in session. Military necessity—the need to hold the border states—likewise prompted other early actions, such as the suspension of habeas corpus and the acceptance of Kentucky's ambiguous neutrality. Over howls of protest from abolitionists, the president also repudiated an unauthorized declaration issued by General John C. Frémont, military commander in Missouri, in August 1861 that would have freed Missouri's slaves, because he feared it would lead to the secession of Kentucky and Maryland.

Although James K. Polk had assumed responsibility for overall American military strategy during the

President Abraham Lincoln visits General George McClellan in 1862 after Antietam. Although as a young congressman Lincoln had objected to President James K. Polk's active participation in Mexican-American War strategy, he found himself taking a major role as commander in chief during the Civil War. His relationship with McClellan was especially difficult, for he could never convince the general to overcome his habitual caution.

Mexican-American War (see Chapter 14), Lincoln was the first president to act as commander in chief in both a practical and a symbolic way. He actively directed military policy, although he sometimes wondered whether he would ever find generals capable of carrying out his orders. Lincoln's involvement in military strategy sprang from his realization that a civil war presented problems different from those of a foreign war of conquest. Lincoln wanted above all to persuade the South to rejoin the Union, and his every military move was dictated by the hope of eventual reconciliation—hence his cautiousness, and his acute sense of the role of public opinion. Today we recognize Lincoln's exceptional abilities and eloquent language, but in his own time some of his most moving statements fell on deaf ears.

The War Department

The greatest expansion in government power during the war was in the War Department, which by early 1862 was faced with the unprecedented challenge of feeding, clothing, and arming 700,000 Union soldiers. Initially the government relied on the individual states to equip and supply their vastly expanded militias. States often contracted directly with textile mills and shoe factories to clothe their troops. In many northern cities volunteer groups sprang up to recruit regiments, buy them weapons, and send them to Washington. Other such community groups, like the one in Chester, Pennsylvania, focused on clothing and providing medical care to soldiers. By January 1862 the War Department, under the able direction of Edwin M.

Stanton, a former Democrat from Ohio, was able to perform many basic functions of procurement and supply without too much delay or corruption. But the size of the Union army and the complexity of fully supplying it demanded constant efforts at all levels—government, state, and community—throughout the war. Thus, in the matter of procurement and supply, as in mobilization, the battlefront was related to the home front on a scale that Americans had not previously experienced.

Taxes and the Greenback Dollar

Although Lincoln was an active commander in chief, he did not believe it was the job of the president to direct economic policy. This, he believed, was the task of Congress. In this important respect, the Civil War was fundamentally different from American wars of the twentieth century, during which executive control over economic policy was deemed essential. Yet the need for money for the vast war effort was pressing. Treasury Secretary Chase worked closely with Congress to develop ways to finance the war. They naturally turned to the nation's economic experts—private bankers, merchants, and managers of large businesses. With the help of Philadelphia financier Jay Cooke, the Treasury used patriotic appeals to sell war bonds to ordinary people in amounts as small as $50. Cooke sold $400 million in bonds, taking for himself what he considered a "fair commission." By the war's end, the United States had borrowed $2.6 billion for the war effort, the first example in American history of the mass financing of war. Additional sources of revenue were sales taxes and the first federal income tax (of 3 percent). Imposed in August 1861, the income tax affected only the affluent: anyone with an annual income under $800 was exempt.

Most radical of all was Chase's decision—which was authorized only after a bitter congressional fight—to print and distribute Treasury notes (paper money). Until then, the money in circulation had been a mixture of coins and state bank notes issued by 1,500 different state banks. The Legal Tender Act of February 1862 created a national currency, which, because of its color, was popularly known as the greenback. In 1863 Congress passed the National Bank Act, which prohibited state banks from issuing their own notes and forced them to apply for federal charters. Thus was the first uniform national currency created, at the expense of the independence that many state banks had prized. "These are extraordinary times, and extraordinary measures must be resorted to in order to save our Government and preserve our nationality," pleaded Congressman Elbridge G. Spaulding, sponsor of the legislation. Only through this appeal to wartime necessity were Spaulding and his allies able to overcome the opposition, for the switch to a national currency was widely recognized as a major step toward centralization of economic power in the hands of the federal government. Such a measure would have been unthinkable if southern Democrats had still been part of the national government. The absence of southern Democrats also made possible passage of a number of Republican economic measures not directly related to the war.

Politics and Economics: The Republican Platform

Although the debate over slavery had overshadowed everything else, in 1860 the Republican Party had campaigned on a comprehensive program of economic development. Once in office, Republicans quickly passed the Morrill Tariff Act (1861); by 1864, this and subsequent measures had raised tariffs to more than double their prewar rate. In 1862 and 1864, Congress created two federally chartered corporations to build a transcontinental railroad—the Union Pacific Railroad Company, to lay track westward from Omaha, and the Central Pacific, to lay track eastward from California— thus fulfilling the dreams of the many expansionists who believed America's economic future lay in trade with Asia across the Pacific Ocean. Two other measures, both passed in 1862, had long been sought by Westerners. The Homestead Act gave 160 acres of public land to any citizen who agreed to live on it for five years, improve it by building a house and cultivating some of the land, and pay a small fee. The Morrill Land Grant Act gave states public land that would allow them to finance land-grant colleges offering education to ordinary citizens in practical skills such as agriculture, engineering, and military science. Coupled with this act, the establishment of a federal Department of Agriculture in 1862 gave American farmers a big push toward modern commercial agriculture.

This package revealed the Whig origins of many Republicans, for in essence the measures amounted to an updated version of Henry Clay's American System of national economic development (see Chapter 9). They were to have a powerful nationalizing effect, connecting ordinary people to the federal government in new ways. As much as the extraordinary war measures, the enactment of the Republican program increased the role of the federal government in national life. Although many of the executive war powers lapsed when the battles ended, the accumulation of strength by the federal government, which southern Democrats would have opposed had they been in Congress, was never reversed.

Diplomatic Objectives

To Secretary of State William Seward fell the job of making sure that Britain and France did not extend diplomatic recognition to the Confederacy. Although Southerners had been certain that King Cotton would gain them European support, they were wrong. British public opinion, which had strongly supported the abolition of slavery within the British Empire in the 1830s, would not now countenance the recognition of a new nation based on slavery. British cotton manufacturers found economic alternatives, first using up their backlog of southern cotton and then turning to Egypt and India for new supplies. In spite of Union protests, however, both Britain and France did allow Confederate vessels to use their ports, and British shipyards sold six ships to the Confederacy. But in 1863, when the Confederacy commissioned Britain's Laird shipyard to build two ironclad ships with pointed prows for ramming, the Union threatened war and the British government made sure that the Laird rams were never delivered. Seward had wanted to threaten Britain with war earlier, in 1861, when the prospect of diplomatic recognition for the Confederacy seemed most likely, but Lincoln had overruled him, cautioning, "One war at a time."

Nonbelligerence was also the Union response in 1863, when France took advantage of the Civil War to invade Mexico and install the Austrian archduke Maximilian as emperor. This was a serious violation of the Monroe Doctrine that could have led to war, but fearing that France might recognize the Confederacy or invade Texas, Seward had to content himself with refusing to recognize the new Mexican government. In the meantime he directed Union troops to gain a stronghold in Texas as soon as possible. In November, five months after the French marched into Mexico City, Union troops seized Brownsville, a town on the Texas-Mexico border, sending a clear signal to the French to go no further. In 1866, after the Civil War, strong diplomatic pressure from Seward convinced the French to withdraw from Mexico. The following year, the hapless Maximilian was captured and shot during a revolt led by a future Mexican president, Benito Juárez.

Although the goal of Seward's diplomacy— preventing recognition of the Confederacy by the European powers—was always clear, its achievement was uncertain for more than two years. Northern fears and southern hopes seesawed with the fortunes of battle. Not until the victories at Vicksburg and Gettysburg in July 1863 could Seward be reasonably confident of success.

Confederate President Jefferson Davis (in the largest chair) and his cabinet are shown meeting with Confederate general Robert E. Lee in this 1866 lithograph. Davis carefully selected his cabinet to represent the South's major states. Shown here, left to right, are Stephen R. Mallory, Judah P. Benjamin, Leroy P. Walker, Davis, Lee, John Reagan, Christopher Memminger, Alexander Stephens, and Robert Toombs.

THE CONFEDERACY

Lincoln faced a major challenge in keeping the North unified enough to win the war, but Jefferson Davis's challenge was even greater. He had to create a Confederate nation. The Confederate States of America was a loose grouping of eleven states, each believing strongly in states' rights. Yet in the Confederacy, as in the Union, the conduct of the war required central direction.

Jefferson Davis as President

Although Jefferson Davis had held national cabinet rank (as secretary of war under president Franklin Pierce), had experience as an administrator, and was a former military man (none of which was true of Abraham Lincoln), he was unable to hold the Confederacy together. Perhaps no one could have. Born, like Lincoln, in Kentucky, Davis ultimately settled in Mississippi, where he became a rich planter. Davis was thus a "cotton nabob" (one of the newly rich class of slave owners), and as such was as scorned by some members of the old southern aristocracy as was Abraham Lincoln by some members of the northern elite. Davis's problems, however, were as much structural as they were personal.

Davis's first cabinet of six men, appointed in February 1861, included a representative from each of the states of the first secession except Mississippi, which was represented by Davis himself. This careful attention to the equality of the states pointed to the fundamental problem that Davis was unable to overcome. For all of

its drama, secession was a conservative strategy for preserving the slavery-based social and political structure that existed in every southern state. A shared belief in states' rights—that is, in their own autonomy—was a poor basis on which to build a unified nation. Davis, who would have preferred to be a general rather than a president, lacked Lincoln's persuasive skills and political astuteness. Although he saw the need for unity, he was unable to impose it. Soon his autonomous style of leadership—he wanted to decide every detail himself—angered his generals, alienated cabinet members, and gave southern governors reason to resist his orders. By the second year of the war, when rich slave owners were refusing to give up their privileges for the war effort, Davis no longer had the public confidence and support he needed to coerce them. After the first flush of patriotism had passed, the Confederacy never lived up to its hope of becoming a unified nation.

Diplomatic Hopes

The failure of "cotton diplomacy" was a crushing blow. White Southerners were stunned that Britain and France would not recognize their claim to independence. Well into 1863, the South hoped that a decisive battlefield victory would change the minds of cautious Europeans. In the meantime, plantations continued to grow cotton, but the Confederacy withheld it from market, hoping that lack of raw material for their textile mills would lead the British and French to recognize the Confederacy. The British reacted indignantly, claiming that the withholding of cotton was economic blackmail and that to yield "would be ignominious beyond measure," as Lord Russell put it. Because British textile manufacturers found new sources of cotton, when the Confederacy ended the embargo in 1862 and began to ship its great surplus, the world price of cotton plunged. Then too, the Union naval blockade, weak at first, began to take effect. Cotton turned out to be not so powerful a diplomatic weapon after all.

The Sinews of War

Perhaps the greatest southern failure was in the area of finances. At first the Confederate government tried to raise money from the states, but governors refused to impose new taxes. By the time uniform taxes were levied in 1863, it was too late. Heavy borrowing and the printing of great sums of paper money produced runaway inflation (a ruinous rate of 9,000 percent by 1865, compared with 80 percent in the North). Inflation, in turn, caused incalculable damage to morale and prospects for unity.

After the initial surge of volunteers, enlistment in the military fell off, as it did in the North also. In April 1862, the Confederate Congress passed the first draft law in American history, and the Union Congress followed suit in March 1863. The southern law declared that all able-bodied men between eighteen and thirty-five were eligible for three years of military service. Purchase of substitutes was allowed, as in the North, but in the South the price was uncontrolled, rising eventually to $10,000 in Confederate money. The most disliked part of the draft law was a provision exempting one white man on each plantation with twenty or more slaves. This provision not only seemed to disprove the earlier claim that slavery freed white men to fight, but it aroused class resentments. A bitter phrase of the time complained, "It's a rich man's war but a poor man's fight."

Contradictions of Southern Nationalism

In the early days of the war, Jefferson Davis successfully mobilized feelings of regional identity and patriotism.

Many Southerners felt part of a beleaguered region that had been forced to resist northern tyranny. But most Southerners felt loyalty to their own state and local communities, not to a Confederate nation. The strong belief in states' rights and aristocratic privilege undermined the Confederate cause. Some Southern governors resisted potentially unifying actions such as moving militias outside their home states. Broader measures, such as general taxation, were widely evaded by rich and poor alike. The inequitable draft was only one of many things that convinced the ordinary people of the South that this was a war for privileged slave owners, not for them. With its leaders and citizens fearing (perhaps correctly) that centralization would destroy what was distinctively southern, the Confederacy was unable to mobilize the resources—financial, human, and otherwise—that might have prevented its destruction by northern armies.

THE FIGHTING THROUGH 1862

Just as political decisions were often driven by military necessity, the basic northern and southern military strategies were affected by political considerations as much as by military ones. The initial policy of limited war, thought to be the best route to ultimate reconcil-

The contrast between the hope and valor of these young southern volunteer soldiers, photographed shortly before the first battle of Bull Run, and the later advertisements for substitutes is marked. Southern exemptions for slave owners and lavish payment for substitutes increasingly bred resentment among the ordinary people of the South.

Cook Collection. Valentine Museum, Richmond, Virginia.

SUBSTITUTE NOTICES.

WANTED—A SUBSTITUTE for a conscript, to serve during the war. Any good man over the age of 35 years, not a resident of Virginia, or a foreigner, may hear of a good situation by calling at Mr. GEORGE BAGBY'S office, Shockoe Slip, to-day, between the hours of 9 and 11 A. M. [jy 9—1t*] A COUNTRYMAN.

WANTED—Two SUBSTITUTES—one for artillery, the other for infantry or cavalry service. Also, to sell, a trained, thoroughbred cavalry HORSE. Apply to DR. BROOCKS, Corner Main and 12th streets, or to T. T. BROOCKS, jy 9—3t* Petersburg, Va.

WANTED—Immediately, a SUBSTITUTE. A man over 35 years old, or under 18, can get a good price by making immediate application to Room No. 50, Monument Hotel, or by addressing "J. W.," through Richmond P. O. jy 9—1t*

WANTED—A SUBSTITUTE, to go into the 24th North Carolina State troops, for which a liberal price will be paid. Apply to me at Dispatch office this evening at 4 o'clock P. M. jy 9—1t* R. R. MOORE.

WANTED—A SUBSTITUTE, to go in a first-rate Georgia company of infantry, under the heroic Jackson. A gentleman whose health is impaired, will give a fair price for a substitute. Apply immediately at ROOM, No. 13, Post-Office Department, third story, between the hours of 10 and 3 o'clock. jy 9—6t*

WANTED—Two SUBSTITUTES for the war. A good bonus will be given. None need apply except those exempt from Conscript. Apply to-day at GEORGE I. HERRING'S, jy 9—1t* Grocery store, No. 56 Main st.

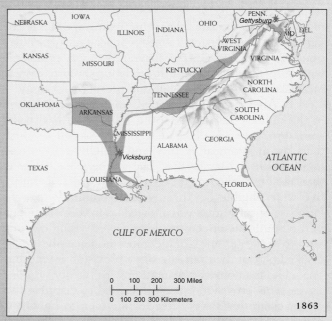

Overall Strategy of the Civil War

In 1861 General Winfield Scott, then the Union's general in chief, proposed the so-called Anaconda plan for subduing the South, which involved strangling it by a blockade at sea and control of the Mississippi rather than directly assaulting its territory. Important aspects of this plan—the blockade of the Confederate coast and the attempt to divide the Confederacy by controlling the Mississippi—became part of the Union's overall war strategy. Union leaders realized, however, that they could not win the war without conquering Confederate territory. The South's strategy was defensive. If its armies could hold out long enough for the North to tire of fighting, its independence would be secured.

By the end of 1862, the Union had captured the sea islands of South Carolina and Georgia and areas of North Carolina, Ulysses S. Grant had won important victories in Tennessee, and Admiral David Farragut had taken New Orleans and advanced up the Mississippi. But in the East, Union armies were consistently stymied by Robert E. Lee's Army of Northern Virginia.

The turning point of the war came in 1863 with General George Gordon Meade's defeat of Lee at Gettysburg (July 1–3) and Grant's capture of Vicksburg (July 4). These two great victories turned the tide in favor of the Union. The Confederates never again mounted a major offensive, and total Union control of the Mississippi exposed the Lower South to Union advance.

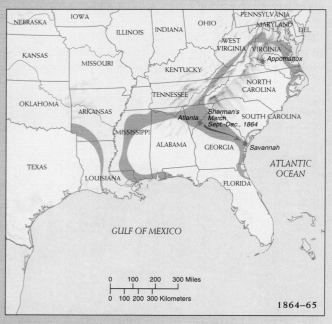

In 1864–65, Grant (now in command of all the Union armies) and General William Tecumseh Sherman brought the war home to the South. Sherman's destructive "March to the Sea" divided the South's heartland, and Grant's hammering tactics kept Lee under constant pressure in northern Virginia. Finally, on April 9, 1865, Lee surrendered to Grant at Appomattox, thus ending the bloodiest war in the nation's history.

iation, ran into difficulties because of the public's impatience for victories. But victories, as the mounting slaughter made clear, were not easy to achieve.

The War in Northern Virginia

The initial northern strategy, dubbed by critics the Anaconda Plan (after the constricting snake), envisaged slowly squeezing the South with a blockade at sea and on the Mississippi River. Proposed by the general in chief, Winfield Scott, a native of Virginia, it avoided invasion and conquest in the hope that a strained South would recognize the inevitability of defeat and thus surrender. Lincoln accepted the basics of the plan, but public clamor for a fight pushed him to agree to the disastrous battle of Bull Run and then to a major buildup of Union troops in northern Virginia under General George B. McClellan.

Dashing in appearance, McClellan was extremely cautious in battle. In March 1862, after almost a year spent drilling the raw Union recruits and after repeated exhortations by an impatient Lincoln, McClellan committed 120,000 troops to what became known as the Peninsular campaign. The objective was to capture Richmond, the Confederate capital. McClellan had his troops and their supplies ferried from Washington to Fortress Monroe, near the mouth of the James River, in 400 ships, an effort that took three weeks. Inching up the James Peninsula toward Richmond, he tried to avoid battle, hoping his overwhelming numbers would convince the South to surrender. By June, McClellan's troops were close enough to Richmond to hear the church bells ringing—but not close enough for victory. In a series of battles known as the Seven Days, Robert E. Lee (who had just assumed command of the Confederacy's Army of Northern Virginia) boldly counterattacked, repeatedly catching McClellan off guard. Taking heavy losses as well as inflicting them, Lee drove McClellan back. In August, Lee routed another Union army, commanded by General John Pope, at the second battle of Bull Rull (Second Manassas). Lincoln, alarmed at the threat to Washington and disappointed by McClellan's inaction, ordered him to abandon the Peninsular campaign and return to the capital.

Jefferson Davis, like Abraham Lincoln, was an active commander in chief. And like Lincoln, he responded to a public that clamored for more action than a strictly defensive war entailed. After the Seven Days victories, Davis supported a Confederate attack on Maryland. At the same time, he issued a proclamation urging the people of Maryland to make a separate peace. But in the brutal battle of Antietam on September 17, 1862, which claimed more than 5,000 dead and 19,000 wounded, McClellan's army checked Lee's advance. Lee retreated to Virginia, inflicting terrible losses on northern troops at Fredricksburg when they

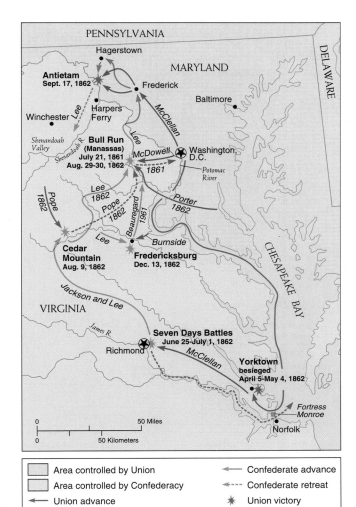

Major Battles in the East, 1861–1862   *Northern Virginia was the most crucial and the most constant theater of battle. The prizes were the two opposing capitals, Washington and Richmond, only 70 miles apart. By the summer of 1862, George B. McClellan, famously cautious, had achieved only stalemate in the Peninsular campaign. He did, however, turn back Robert E. Lee at Antietam in September.*

again made a thrust toward Richmond in December, 1862. The war in northern Virginia was stalemated: neither side was strong enough to win, but each was too strong to be defeated.

Shiloh and the War for the Mississippi

Although most public attention was focused on the fighting in Virginia, battles in Tennessee and along the Mississippi River proved to be the key to eventual Union victory. The rising military figure in the West was Ulysses S. Grant, who had once resigned from the service because of a drinking problem. Reenlisting as a colonel after the capture of Fort Sumter, Grant was promoted to brigadier general within two months. In February 1862

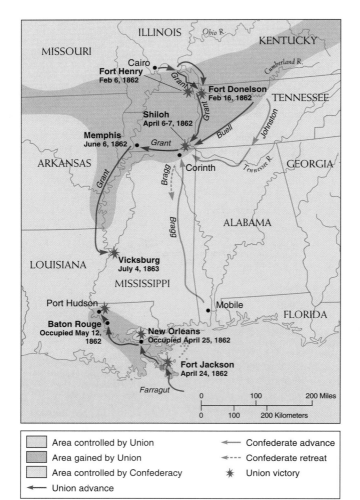

Major Battles in the West, 1862–1863   *Ulysses S. Grant waged a mobile war, winning at Fort Henry and Fort Donelson in Tennessee in February 1862 and at Shiloh in April, and capturing Memphis in June. He then laid siege to Vicksburg, as Admiral David Farragut captured New Orleans and began to advance up the Mississippi River.*

Grant captured Fort Henry and Fort Donelson, on the Tennessee and Cumberland Rivers, establishing Union control of much of Tennessee and forcing Confederate troops to retreat into northern Mississippi.

Moving south with 28,000 men, Grant met a 40,000-man Confederate force commanded by General Albert Sidney Johnston at Shiloh Church in April. Seriously outnumbered on the first day, Grant's forces were reinforced by the arrival of 35,000 troops under the command of General Don Carlos Buell. After two days of bitter and bloody fighting in the rain, the Confederates withdrew. The losses on both sides were enormous: the North lost 13,000 men, the South 11,000, including General Johnston, who bled to death. McClellan's Peninsular campaign was already under way when Grant won at Shiloh, and Jefferson Davis,

concerned about the defense of Richmond, refused to reinforce the generals who were trying to stop Grant. Consequently, Union forces kept moving, capturing Memphis in June and beginning a campaign to eventually capture Vicksburg, "the Gibraltar of the Mississippi." Grant and other Union generals faced strong Confederate resistance, and progress was slow. Earlier that year, naval forces under Admiral David Farragut had captured New Orleans and then continued up the Mississippi River. By the end of 1862 it was clearly only a matter of time before the entire river would be in Union hands. Arkansas, Louisiana, and Texas would then be cut off from the rest of the Confederacy.

The War in the Trans-Mississippi West

Although only one western state, Texas, seceded from the Union, the Civil War was fought in small ways in many parts of the West. Southern hopes for the extension of slavery into the Southwest were reignited by the war. Texans mounted an attack on New Mexico, which they had long coveted, and kept their eyes on the larger prizes of Arizona and California. A Confederate force led by General Henry H. Sibley occupied Santa Fe and Albuquerque early in 1862 without resistance, thus posing a serious Confederate threat to the entire Southwest. Confederate hopes were dashed, however, by a ragtag group of 950 miners and adventurers organized into the first Colorado Volunteer Infantry Regiment. After an epic march of 400 miles from Denver, which was completed in thirteen days despite snow and high winds, the Colorado militia stopped the unsuspecting Confederate troops in the battle of Glorieta Pass on March 26–28, 1862. This dashing action, coupled with the efforts of California militias to safeguard Arizona and Utah from seizure by Confederate sympathizers, secured the Far West for the Union.

Other military action in the West was less decisive. The chronic fighting along the Kansas-Missouri border set a record for brutality when Confederate William Quantrill's Raiders made a predawn attack on Lawrence, Kansas, in August 1863, massacring 150 inhabitants and burning the town. Another civil war took place in Indian Territory, south of Kansas. The southern Indian tribes who had been removed there from the Old Southwest in the 1830s included many who were still bitter over the horrors of removal by federal troops and sympathized with the Confederacy. Furthermore, the Confederacy actively sought Indian support by offering Indian people representation in the Confederate Congress. Consequently, many Indians fought for the South, among them Stand Watie, who became a Confederate military officer. Union victories at Pea Ridge (in northwestern Arkansas) in 1862 and near Fort Gibson (in Indian Territory) in 1863 secured the area for the Union but did little to stop dissension among the Indian groups themselves. After the Civil War the victorious federal government used the tribes' wartime support for the Confederacy as a justification for demanding further land cessions.

Elsewhere in the West, other groups of Indians found themselves caught up in the wider war. An uprising by the Santee Sioux in Minnesota occurred in August 1862, just as McClellan conceded defeat in the Peninsular campaign in Virginia. Alarmed whites, certain that the uprising was a Confederate plot, ignored legitimate Sioux grievances and responded in kind to Sioux ferocity. In little more than a month, 500–800 white settlers and an even greater number of Sioux were killed. Thirty-eight Indians were hanged in a mass execution in Mankato on December 26, 1862, and subsequently all Sioux were expelled from Minnesota. In 1863, U.S. Army Colonel Kit Carson invaded Navajo country in Arizona in retaliation for Indian raids on U.S. troops. Eight thousand Navajos were forced on the brutal "Long Walk" to Bosque Redondo on the Pecos River in New Mexico, where they were held prisoner until a treaty between the United States and the Navajos was signed in 1868.

The hostilities in the West showed that no part of the country, and none of its inhabitants, could remain untouched by the Civil War.

The Naval War

The Union's naval blockade of the South, intended to cut off commerce between the Confederacy and the rest of the world, was initially unsuccessful. The U.S. Navy had only thirty-three ships with which to blockade 189 ports along 3,500 miles of coastline. Southern blockade runners evaded Union ships with ease: only an estimated one-eighth of all Confederate shipping was stopped in 1862. Moreover, the Confederacy licensed British-made privateers to strike at northern shipping. In a two-year period one such Confederate raider, the *Alabama*, destroyed sixty-nine Union

ships with cargoes valued at $6 million. Beginning in 1863, however, as the Union navy became larger, the blockade began to take effect. In 1864 a third of the blockade runners were captured, and in 1865 half of them. As a result, fewer and fewer supplies reached the South.

North and South also engaged in a brief duel featuring the revolutionary new technology of ironclading. The Confederacy refitted a scuttled Union vessel, the *Merrimac*, with iron plating and renamed it the *Virginia*. On March 8, 1862, as McClellan began his Peninsular campaign, the *Virginia* steamed out of Norfolk harbor to challenge the Union blockade. The iron plating protected the *Virginia* from the fire of the Union ships, which found themselves defenseless against its ram and

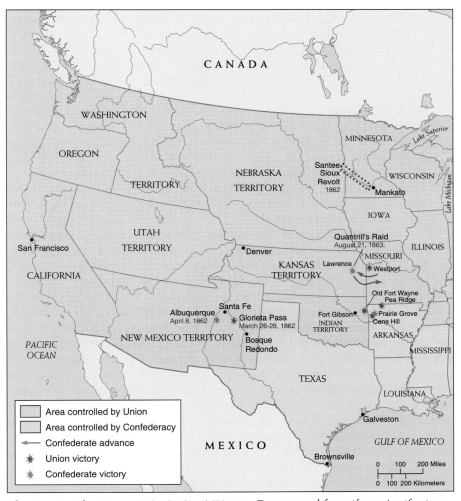

The War in the Trans-Mississippi West   *Far removed from the major theaters of battle, the Far West was nevertheless a rich prize in the Civil War. Battles in remote places like Glorieta Pass, New Mexico, were decisive in holding the Far West for the Union. The battles in Kansas and Indian Territory, however, arose primarily from prewar antagonisms and settled little.*

Source: Warren Beck and Ynez Haase, *Historical Atlas of the American West* (Norman: University of Oklahoma Press, 1989).

its powerful guns. Two Union ships went down, and the blockade seemed about to be broken. But the North had an experimental ironclad of its own, the *Monitor*, which was waiting for the *Merrimac* when it emerged from port on March 9. The *Monitor*, which looked like "an immense shingle floating on the water, with a gigantic cheese box rising from its center," was the ship of the future, for the "cheese box" was a revolving turret, a basic component of battleships to come. The historic duel between these first two ironclads was inconclusive, and primitive technology together with limited resources made them of little consequence for the rest of the war. But this brief duel prefigured the naval and land battles of the world wars of the twentieth century as much as did the massing of huge armies on the battlefield.

For the Union, the most successful naval operation in the first two years of the war was not the blockade but the seizing of exposed coastal areas. The Sea Islands of South Carolina were taken, as were some of the North Carolina islands and Fort Pulaski, which commanded the harbor of Savannah, Georgia. Most damaging to the South was the capture of New Orleans.

The Black Response

The capture of Port Royal in the South Carolina Sea Islands in 1861 was important for another reason. Whites fled at the Union advance, but 10,000 slaves greeted the troops with jubilation and shouts of gratitude. Union troops had unwittingly freed these slaves in advance of any official Union policy on the status of slaves in captured territory.

Early in the war, an irate Southerner who saw three of his slaves disappear behind Union lines at Fortress Monroe, Virginia, demanded the return of his property, citing the Fugitive Slave Law. The Union commander, Benjamin Butler, replied that the Fugitive Slave Law no longer applied and that the escaped slaves were "contraband of war." News of Butler's decision spread rapidly among the slaves in the region of Fortress Monroe. Two days later, eight runaway slaves appeared; the next day, fifty-nine black men and women arrived at the fort. Union commanders had found an effective way to rob the South of its basic workforce. The "contrabands," as they were known, were put to work building fortifications and doing other useful work in northern camps. Washington, D.C., became a refuge for contrabands, who crowded into the capital to join the free black people who lived there (at 9,000, they were one of the largest urban black populations outside the Confederacy). Many destitute contrabands received help from the Contraband Relief Association. Modeled on the Sanitary Commission, the association was founded by former slave Elizabeth Keckley, seamstress to Mary Todd Lincoln, the president's wife.

As Union troops drove deeper into the South, the black response grew. When Union General William Tecumseh Sherman marched his army through Georgia in 1864, 18,000 slaves—entire families, people of all ages—flocked to the Union lines. By the war's end, nearly a million black people, fully a quarter of all the slaves in the South, had "voted with their feet" for the Union.

THE DEATH OF SLAVERY

The overwhelming response of black slaves to the Union advance changed the nature of the war. As increasing numbers of slaves flocked to Union lines, the conclusion was unmistakable: the southern war to defend the slave system did not have the support of slaves themselves. Any northern policy that ignored the issue of slavery and the wishes of the slaves was unrealistic.

The Politics of Emancipation

Abraham Lincoln had always said that this was a war for the Union, not a war about slavery. In his Inaugural Address, he had promised to leave slavery untouched in the South. Although Lincoln personally abhorred slavery, his official policy was based on a realistic assessment of several factors. At first, he hoped to give pro-Union forces in the South a chance to consolidate and to prevent the outbreak of war. After the war began, he was impelled by the military necessity of holding the border states (Delaware, Maryland, Kentucky, and Missouri), where slavery was legal.

Finally, Lincoln was worried about unity in the North. Even within the Republican Party, before the war only a small group of abolitionists had favored freeing the slaves. Most Republicans were more concerned about the expansion of slavery than they were about the lives of slaves themselves. They did not favor the social equality of black people, whom they considered inferior. The free-soil movement, for example, was as often antiblack as it was antislave. For their part, most northern Democrats were openly antiblack. Irish workers in northern cities had rioted against free African Americans, with whom they often competed for jobs. There was also the question of what would become of slaves who were freed. Even the most fervent abolitionists had refused to face up to this issue. Finally, northern Democrats effectively played on racial fears in the 1862 congressional elections, warning that freed slaves would pour into northern cities and take jobs from white laborers.

Nevertheless, the necessities of war edged Lincoln toward a new position. In March 1862 he proposed that every state undertake gradual, compensated emancipation, after which former slaves would be resettled in Haiti and Panama (neither of which was under U.S. control). This unrealistic colonization scheme, as well as the reluctance of politicians in the border states to consider emancipation, doomed the proposal.

Radical Republicans chafed at Lincoln's conservative stance. In August 1862 Horace Greeley, editor of the *New York Tribune*, pressed the point in an open letter to the president: "On the face of this wide earth, Mr. President, there is not one disinterested, determined, intelligent champion of the Union cause who does not feel that all attempts to put down the Rebellion and at the same time uphold its inciting cause are preposterous and futile." Greeley's statement was incorrect, for many Northerners did not care what happened to the slaves but did care what happened to the Union. Lincoln's famous answer implicitly acknowledged the many shades of public opinion and cast his decision in terms of military necessity: "If I could save the Union without freeing any slave, I would do it; and if I could save it by freeing all the slaves, I would do it; and if I could do it by freeing some and leaving others alone, I would also do that. What I do about Slavery and the colored race, I do because I believe it helps to save this Union."

In fact, Lincoln had already made up his mind to issue an Emancipation Proclamation, and was simply waiting for the right moment. Following the Union victory at Antietam in September 1862, Lincoln issued a preliminary decree: unless the rebellious states returned to the Union by January 1, 1863, he would declare their slaves "forever free." Although Lincoln did not expect the Confederate states to surrender because of his proclamation, the decree increased the pressure on the South by directly linking the slave system to the war effort. Thus the freedom of black people became part of the struggle. Frederick Douglass, the voice of black America, wrote, "We shout for joy that we live to record this righteous decree."

On January 1, 1863, Lincoln duly issued the final Emancipation Proclamation, which turned out to be just as tortuous as his response to Greeley in August. The proclamation freed the slaves in the areas of rebellion—the areas the Union did not control—but specifically exempted slaves in the border states and in former Confederate areas conquered by the Union. Lincoln's purpose was to meet the abolitionist demand for a war against slavery while not losing the support of conservatives, especially in the border states. But the proclamation was so equivocal that Lincoln's own secretary of state, William Seward, remarked sarcastically, "We show our sympathy with slavery by emancipating slaves where we cannot reach them and holding them in bondage where we can set them free." And in Britain, where Lincoln had hoped to make a favorable impression on the public, government officials were more puzzled than impressed by the proclamation.

One group greeted the Emancipation Proclamation with open celebration. On New Year's Day, hundreds of African Americans gathered outside the White House and cheered the president. They called to him, as pastor Henry M. Turner recalled, that "if he would come out of that palace, they would hug him to death." Realizing the symbolic importance of the proclamation, free African Americans predicted that the news would encourage southern slaves either to flee to Union lines or refuse to work for their masters. Both of these things were already happening as African Americans seized on wartime changes to reshape white-black relations in the South. In one sense, then, the Emancipation Proclamation simply gave a name to a process already in motion.

Abolitionists set about moving Lincoln beyond his careful stance in the Emancipation Proclamation. Reformers such as Elizabeth Cady Stanton and Susan B. Anthony lobbied and petitioned for a constitutional amendment outlawing slavery. Lincoln agreed with them, and encouraged the Republican Party to support such an amendment in its 1864 election platform. Congress, at Lincoln's urging, approved and sent to the states a statement banning slavery throughout the United States. Quickly ratified by the Union states in 1865, the statement became the Thirteenth Amendment to the Constitution. (The southern states, being in a state of rebellion, could not vote.) Lincoln's firm support for this amendment is a good indicator of his true feelings about slavery when he was free of the kinds of military and political considerations taken into account in the Emancipation Proclamation.

Black Fighting Men

As part of the Emancipation Proclamation, Lincoln gave his support for the first time to the recruitment of black soldiers. Early in the war, eager black volunteers had been bitterly disappointed at being turned away. Many, like Robert Fitzgerald, a free African American from Pennsylvania, found other ways to serve the Union cause. Fitzgerald first drove a wagon and mule for the Quartermaster Corps, and later, in spite of persistent seasickness, he served in the Union navy. After the Emancipation Proclamation, however, Fitzgerald was able to do what he had wanted to do all along: be a soldier. He enlisted in the Fifth Massachusetts Cavalry, a regiment that, like all the units in which black soldiers served, was 100 percent African American but commanded by white officers. The most famous black regiment, the Fifty-fourth Massachusetts Colored Infantry, was commanded by abolitionist Robert Gould Shaw of Boston, who was killed in action along with half of his troops in a fruitless attack on Fort Wagner, South Carolina, in 1863. Thomas Wentworth Higginson, the Unitarian minister who had supported John Brown, led another of the first black regiments, the First South Carolina Volunteers.

In Fitzgerald's company of eighty-three men, half came from slave states and had run away to enlist; the other half came mostly from the North but also from Canada, the West Indies, and France. Other regiments had volunteers from Africa. The proportion of volunteers from the loyal border states (where slavery was still legal) was upwards of 25 percent—a lethal blow to the slave system in those states.

After a scant two months of training, Fitzgerald's company was sent on to Washington and thence to battle in northern Virginia. Uncertain of the reception they would receive in northern cities with their history of antiblack riots, Fitzgerald and his comrades were pleasantly surprised. "We are cheered in every town we pass through," he wrote in his diary. "I was surprised to see a great many white people weeping as the train moved South." White people had reason to cheer: black volunteers, eager and willing to fight, made up 10 percent of the Union army. Nearly 200,000 African Americans (one out of every five black males in the nation) served in the Union army or navy.

A fifth of them—37,000—died defending their own freedom and the Union.

Military service was something no black man could take lightly. He faced prejudice of several kinds. In the North, most white people believed that black people were inferior both in intelligence and in courage. Most army officers shared these opinions— but usually not those who had volunteered to lead black troops. Thus African American soldiers had to prove themselves in battle. The performance of black soldiers at Fort Wagner and in battles near Vicksburg, Mississippi, in 1863 helped to change the minds of the Union army command. In the battle of Milliken's Bend, untrained and poorly armed former slaves fought desperately—and successfully. "The bravery of the blacks...completely revolutionized the sentiment of the army with regard to the employment of negro troops," wrote Charles Dana, assistant secretary of war. "I heard prominent officers who formerly in private had sneered at the idea of negroes fighting express themselves after that as heartily in favor of it."

Among the Confederates, however, the feeling was very different. They hated and feared African American troops and threatened to treat any captured black soldier as an escaped slave subject to execution. On at least one occasion, the threats were carried out. In 1864 Confederate soldiers massacred 262 black soldiers at Fort Pillow, Tennessee, after they had surrendered. Although large-scale episodes such as this were rare (especially after President Lincoln threatened retaliation), smaller ones were not. On duty near Petersburg, Virginia, Robert Fitzgerald's company lost a picket to Confederate hatred: wounded in the leg, he was unable to escape from Confederate soldiers, who smashed his skull with their musket butts. Fitzgerald wrote in his diary, "Can such men eventually triumph? God forbid!"

Another extraordinary part of the story of the African American soldiers was their reception by black people in the South, who were overjoyed at the sight of armed black men, many of them former slaves themselves, wearing the uniform of the Union army. As his regiment entered Wilming-

When the family of Robert and Cornelia Fitzgerald posed for a group picture in the 1890s, Robert Fitzgerald proudly dressed in the Union Army uniform he had worn during the Civil War. Fitzgerald's pride in his war service, doubtless shared by many African American veterans, was an important family memory of the fight against slavery.

ton, North Carolina, one soldier wrote, "Men and women, old and young, were running throughout the streets, shouting and praising God. We could then truly see what we have been fighting for."

Robert Fitzgerald's own army career was brief. Just five months after he enlisted, he caught typhoid fever. Hearing of his illness, Fitzgerald's mother traveled from Pennsylvania and nursed him, probably saving his life. Eventually, 117 members of his regiment died of disease—and only 7 in battle. Eight months after he had enlisted, Fitzgerald was discharged for poor eyesight. His short military career nevertheless gave him, in the words of a granddaughter, the distinguished lawyer Pauli Murray, "a pride which would be felt throughout his family for the next century."

African American soldiers were not treated equally by the Union army. They were segregated in camp, given the worst jobs, and paid less than white soldiers ($10 a month rather than $13). Although they might not be able to do much about the other kinds of discrimination, the men of the Fifty-fourth Massachusetts found an unusual way to protest their unequal pay: they refused to accept it, preferring to serve the army for free until it decided to treat them as free men. The protest was effective; in June 1864 the War Department equalized the wages of black and white soldiers.

In other ways the army service of black men made a dent in northern white racism. Massachusetts, the state where abolitionist feeling was the strongest, went the furthest by enacting the first law forbidding discrimination against African Americans in public facilities. Some major cities, among them San Francisco, Cincinnati, Cleveland, and New York, desegregated their streetcars. Several states—Ohio, California, Illinois—repealed statutes that had barred black people from testifying in court or serving on juries. But above all, as Frederick Douglass acutely saw, military service permanently changed the status of African Americans. "Once let the black man get upon his person the brass letters, U.S., let him get an eagle on his button and a musket on his shoulder and bullets in his pocket," Douglass said, and "there is no power on earth that can deny that he has earned the right to citizenship."

THE FRONT LINES AND THE HOME FRONT

Civil War soldiers wrote millions of letters home, more proportionately than in any American war. Their letters and the ones they received in return were links between the front lines and the home front, between the soldiers and their home communities. They are a testament to the patriotism of both Union and Confederate troops, for the story they tell is frequently one of slaughter and horror.

The Toll of War

In spite of early hopes for what one might call a "brotherly" war, one that avoided excessive brutality, Civil War battles were appallingly deadly. One reason was technology: improved weapons, particularly modern rifles, had much greater range and accuracy than the muskets they replaced. The Mexican-American War had been fought with smooth-bore muskets, which were slow to reload and accurate only at short distances. As Ulysses Grant said, "At a distance of a few hundred yards, a man could fire at you all day [with a musket] without your finding out." The new Springfield and Enfield rifles were accurate for a quarter of a mile or more.

Civil War generals, however, were slow to adjust to this new reality. Almost all Union and Confederate generals remained committed to the conventional military doctrine of massed infantry offensives—the Jomini doctrine—that they had learned in their military classes at West Point. Part of this strategy had been to "soften up" a defensive line before an infantry assault, but now the range of the new rifles made artillery itself vulnerable to attack. As a result, generals relied less on "softening up" than on immense numbers of infantrymen, hoping that enough of them would survive the withering rifle fire to overwhelm the enemy line. Enormous casualties were a consequence of this basic strategy.

Medical ignorance was another factor in the casualty rate. Because the use of antiseptic procedures was in its infancy, men often died because minor wounds became infected. Gangrene was a common cause of death. Disease was an even more frequent killer, taking twice as many men as were lost in battle. The overcrowded and unsanitary conditions of many camps were breeding grounds for smallpox, dysentery, typhoid, pneumonia, and, in the summer, malaria. The devastating effect of disease was apparent, for example, in McClellan's Peninsular campaign. Among his 130,000 men, nearly a quarter of the unwounded were ill in July 1862. The knowledge that this situation could only deteriorate during August and September—the most disease-ridden months—was one of the reasons Lincoln decided to recall McClellan and his army.

Both North and South were completely unprepared to handle the supply and health needs of their large armies. Twenty-four hours after the battle of Shiloh, most of the wounded still lay on the field in the rain. Many died of exposure; some, unable to help themselves, drowned. Nor were the combatants prepared to deal with masses of war prisoners, as the shocking example of the Confederate prison camp of Andersonville in northern Georgia demonstrated. Andersonville was an open stockade with no shade or shelter erected early in 1864 to hold 10,000 northern prisoners, but by midsummer it held 33,000. During the worst weeks of that summer, 100 prisoners died of disease, exposure, or malnutrition each day.

Army Nurses

Many medical supplies that the armies were unable to provide were donated by the United States Sanitary Commission in the North, as described in the opening of this chapter, and by women's volunteer groups in the South. But in addition to supplies, there was also an urgent need for skilled nurses to care for wounded and convalescent soldiers. Nursing within a family context was widely considered to be women's work. Caring for sick family members was a key domestic responsibility for women, and most had considerable experience with it. But taking care of strange men in hospitals was another thing. There were strong objections that such work was "unseemly" for respectable women.

Under the pressure of wartime necessity, and over the objections of most army doctors—who resented the challenge to their authority from people no different than their daughters or wives—women became army nurses. Hospital nursing, previously considered a job only disreputable women would undertake, now became a suitable vocation for middle-class women. Under the leadership of veteran reformer Dorothea Dix of the asylum movement (see Chapter 13), and in cooperation with the Sanitary Commission (and with the vocal support of Mother Bickerdyke), by the war's end more than 3,000 northern women had worked as paid army nurses and many more as volunteers.

One of the volunteers was Ellen Ruggles Strong of New York, who, over her husband's objections, insisted on nursing in the Peninsular campaign of 1862. "The little woman has come out amazingly strong during these two months," George Templeton Strong wrote in his diary with a mixture of pride and condescension. "Have never given her credit for a tithe of the enterprise, pluck, discretion, and force of character that she has shown. God bless her." Other women organized other volunteer efforts outside the Sanitary Commission umbrella. Perhaps the best known was Clara Barton, who had been a government clerk before the war and consequently knew a number of influential members of Congress. Barton organized nursing and the distribution of medical supplies; she also used her congressional contacts to force reforms in army medical practice, of which she was very critical.

Southern women were also active in nursing and otherwise aiding soldiers, though the South never boasted a single large-scale organization like the Sanitary Commission. The women of Richmond volunteered when they found the war on their doorstep in the summer of 1862. During the Seven Days Battles, thousands of wounded poured into Richmond; many died in the streets because there was no room for them in hospitals. Richmond women first established informal "roadside hospitals" to meet the need, and their activities expanded from there. As in the North, middle-class women at first faced strong resistance from army doctors and even their own families, who believed that a field hospital was "no place for a refined lady." Kate Cumming of Mobile, who nursed in Corinth, Mississippi, after the Battle of Shiloh, faced down such reproofs, though she confided to her diary that nursing wounded men was very difficult: "Nothing that I had ever heard or read had given me the faintest idea of the horrors witnessed here." She and her companion nurses persisted and became an important part of the Confederate medical services. For southern women, who had been much less active in the public life of their communities than their northern reforming sisters, this Civil War activity marked an important break with prewar tradition.

Although women had made important advances, most army nurses and medical support staff were men. One volunteer nurse was the poet Walt Whitman, who visited wounded soldiers in the hospital in Washington, D.C. Horrified at the suffering he saw, Whitman also formed a deep admiration for the "incredible

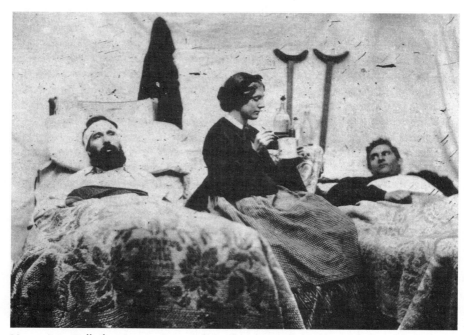

Nurse Ann Bell shown preparing medicine for a wounded soldier. Prompted by the medical crisis of the war, women such as Bell and "Mother" Bickerdyke actively participated in the war effort as nurses.

dauntlessness" of the common soldier in the face of slaughter and privation. While never denying the senselessness of the slaughter, Whitman nevertheless found hope in the determined spirit of the common man and woman.

The Life of the Common Soldier

The conditions experienced by the eager young volunteers of the Union and Confederate armies included massive, terrifying, and bloody battles, apparently unending, with no sign of victory in sight. Soldiers suffered from the uncertainty of supply, which left troops, especially in the South, without uniforms, tents, and sometimes even food. They endured long marches over muddy, rutted roads while carrying packs weighing fifty or sixty pounds. Disease was rampant in

The Metropolitan Museum of Art, Gift of Mrs. Frank B. Porter

This painting helped to establish the reputation of the young artist Winslow Homer, for in it he broke with the tradition of heroic battle scenes and focused instead on the psychology of defeat. In a landscape devastated by battle, three disarmed Confederate prisoners of war await the decision of a Union general on their future. The prisoners, although bedraggled, appear psychologically undefeated, evoking an expression of sympathy from their captor.

their dirty, verminous, and unsanitary camps, and hospitals were so dreadful that more men left them dead than alive. Many soldiers had entered military service with unrealistic, even romantic ideas about warfare. The Mexican-American War had been short and glorious (or at least far enough away to seem so), and the Revolutionary War was even more shrouded in myth. Reality was thus a rude shock, and not all soldiers reacted as nobly as those glorified by Walt Whitman. Desertion was common: an estimated one of every nine Confederate soldiers and one of every seven Union soldiers deserted. Unauthorized absence was another problem. At Antietam, Robert E. Lee estimated that unauthorized absence reduced his strength by a third to a half.

Another widespread phenomenon was fraternization between the two sides. A southern private, for example, wrote about how he celebrated the Fourth of July after the Seven Days Battles in 1862: "There are blackberries in the fields so our boys and the Yanks made a bargain not to fire at each other, and went out in the field, leaving one man on each post with the arms, and gathered berries together and talked over the fight, and traded tobacco and coffee and newspapers as peacefully and kindly as if they had not been engaged for...seven days in butchering one another." In October 1861 a Louisiana man wrote to his brother-in-law: "You spoke as if you had some notion of volunteering. I advise you to stay at home." Once the initial patriotic fervor had waned, attitudes such as his were increasingly common, both on the battlefield and at home.

Wartime Politics

In the earliest days of the war, Northerners had joined together in support of the war effort. Democrat Stephen A. Douglas, Lincoln's defeated rival, paid a visit to the White House to offer Lincoln his support, then traveled home to Illinois, where he addressed a huge rally of Democrats in Chicago: "There can be no neutrals in this war, only patriots— or traitors!" Within a month, Douglas was dead at age forty-eight. The Democrats had lost the leadership of a broad-minded man who might have done much on behalf of northern unity. By 1862 Democrats had split into two factions: the War Democrats and the Peace Democrats, or Copperheads (from the poisonous snake).

Despite the split in the party in 1860 and the secession of the South, the Democratic Party remained a powerful force in northern politics. It had received 44 percent of the popular vote in the North in the 1860 election and its united opposition to the emancipation of slaves explains much of Lincoln's equivocal action on this issue. But the Peace Democrats went far beyond opposition to emancipation, denouncing the draft, martial law, and the high-handed actions of "King Abraham." Echoing old complaints against the Whigs, Peace Democrats appealed to the sympathies of western farmers by warning that agriculture was being hurt by the Republican Party's tariff and industrial policies. At the same time, they appealed to urban workers and immigrants with racist warnings that Republican policies would bring a flood of black workers into northern cities.

The leader of the Copperheads, Clement Vallandigham, a former Ohio congressman, advocated an armistice and a negotiated peace that would "look only to the welfare, peace and safety of the white race, without reference to the effect that settlement may have on the African." Western Democrats, he threatened, might form their own union with the South, excluding New England with its radical abolitionists and high-tariff industrialists.

At the time, long before Grant captured Vicksburg and gained control of the Mississippi River, Lincoln could not afford to take Vallandigham's threats lightly. Besides, he was convinced that some Peace Democrats were members of secret societies—the Knights of the Golden Circle and the Sons of Liberty—that had been conspiring with the Confederacy. In 1862, Lincoln proclaimed that all people who discouraged enlistments in the army or otherwise engaged in disloyal practices would be subject to martial law. In all, 13,000 people were arrested and imprisoned, including Vallandigham, who was exiled to the Confederacy. Lincoln rejected all protests, claiming that his arbitrary actions were necessary for national security.

Lincoln also faced challenges from the radical faction of his own party. As the war continued, the Radicals gained strength: it was they who pushed for emancipation in the early days of the war and for harsh treatment of the defeated South after it ended. The most troublesome Radical was Salmon P. Chase, who in December 1862 caused a cabinet crisis when he encouraged Senate Republicans to complain that Secretary of State William Seward was "lukewarm" in his support for emancipation. This Radical challenge was a portent of the party's difficulties after the war, which Lincoln did not live to see—or prevent.

Economic and Social Strains on the North

Wartime needs caused a surge in northern economic growth, but the gains were unequally distributed. Early in the war, some industries suffered: textile manufacturers could not get cotton, and shoe factories that had made cheap shoes for slaves were without a market. But other industries boomed—bootmaking, shipbuilding, and the manufacture of woolen goods such as blankets and uniforms, to give just three examples. Coal mining expanded, as did ironmaking, especially the manufacture of iron rails for railroads. Agricultural goods were in great demand, promoting further mechanization of farming. The McCormick brothers grew rich from sales of their reapers. Once scorned as a "metal grasshopper," the ungainly-looking McCormick reaper made hand harvesting of grain a thing of the past and led to great savings in manpower. Women, left to tend the family farm while the men went to war, found that with mechanized equipment they could manage the demanding task of harvesting.

Meeting wartime needs enriched some people honestly, but speculators and profiteers also flourished, as they have in every war. By the end of the war, government contracts had exceeded $1 billion. Not all of this business was free from corruption. New wealth was evident in every northern city. *Harper's Monthly* reported that "the suddenly enriched contractors, speculators, and stock-jobbers...are spending money with a profusion never before witnessed in our country." Some people were appalled at the spectacle of wealth in the midst of wartime suffering. Still, some of the new wealth went to good causes. Of the more than $3 million raised by the female volunteers of the United States Sanitary Commission, some came from gala Sanitary Fairs designed to attract those with money to spend.

For most people, however, the war brought the day-to-day hardship of inflation. During the four years of the war, the North suffered an inflation rate of 80 percent, or nearly 15 percent a year. This annual rate, three times what is generally considered tolerable, did much to inflame social tensions. Wages rose only half as much as prices, and workers responded by joining unions and striking. Thirteen occupational groups, among them tailors, coal miners, and railroad engineers, formed unions during the Civil War. Manufacturers, bitterly opposed to unions, freely hired strikebreakers (many of whom were African Americans, women, or immigrants) and formed organizations of their own to prevent further unionization and to blacklist union organizers. Thus both capital and labor moved far beyond the small, localized confrontations of the early industrial period. The formation of large-scale organizations, fostered by wartime demand, laid the groundwork for the national battle between workers and manufacturers that would dominate the last part of the nineteenth century.

Another major source of social tension was conscription. The Union draft, introduced in March 1863, was based on the theory that the very threat of coercion would stimulate reenlistments and encourage volunteering. It soon became clear, however, that coercion, backed by federal marshals, was necessary to fill the ranks. Especially unpopular was a provision in the draft law that allowed the hiring of substitutes or the payment of a commutation fee of $300. The most likely source of substitutes was recent immigrants who had not yet filed for citizenship and were thus not yet eligible to be drafted. It is estimated that immigrants (some of whom were citizens) made up 20 percent of the Union army. Substitution had been accepted in all previous European and American wars. It was so common that President Lincoln, though overage, tried to set an example by paying for a substitute himself. The Democratic Party, however, made substitution an inflammatory issue.

Pointing out that $300 was almost a year's wages for an unskilled laborer, they denounced the draft law (88 percent of Democratic congressmen had voted against it). They appealed to popular resentment by calling it "aristocratic legislation" and to fear by running headlines such as "Three Hundred Dollars or Your Life."

As practiced in the local communities, conscription was indeed often marred by favoritism and prejudice. Local officials called up many more poor than rich men and selected a higher proportion of immigrants than nonimmigrants. In reality, however, only 7 percent of all men called to serve actually did so. About 25 percent hired a substitute, another 45 percent were exempted for "cause" (usually health reasons), and another 20–25 percent simply failed to report to the community draft office. Nevertheless, by 1863 many northern urban workers believed that the slogan "a rich man's war but a poor man's fight," though coined in the South, applied to them as well.

A black man is lynched during the New York City Draft Riots in July 1863. Free black people and their institutions were major victims of the worst rioting in American history until then. The riots were less a protest against the draft than an outburst of frustration over urban problems that had been festering for decades.

The New York City Draft Riots

In the spring of 1863 there were protests against the draft throughout the North. Riots and disturbances broke out in many cities, and several federal enrollment officers were killed. The greatest trouble occurred in New York City between July 13 and July 16, 1863, where a wave of working-class looting, fighting, and lynching claimed the lives of 105 people, many of them African American. The rioting, the worst up to that time in American history, was quelled only when five units of the U.S. Army were rushed from the battlefield at Gettysburg, where they had been fighting Confederates the week before.

The riots had several causes. Anger at the draft and racial prejudice were what most contemporaries saw. George Templeton Strong, a staunch Republican, believed that the "brutal, cowardly ruffianism and plunder" was instigated by Confederate agents stirring up "the rabble" of "the lowest Irish day laborers." From a historical perspective, however, the riots had less to do with the war than with the urban growth and tensions described in Chapter 13. The Civil War made urban problems worse and heightened the visible contrast between the lives of the rich and those of the poor.

These tensions exploded, but were not solved, during those hot days in the summer of 1863.

Ironically, African American men, a favorite target of the rioters' anger, were a major force in easing the national crisis over the draft. Though they had been barred from service until 1863, African American volunteers ultimately composed one-tenth of the Union army. Nearly 200,000 black soldiers filled the manpower gap that the controversial draft was meant to address.

The Failure of Southern Nationalism

The war brought even greater changes to the South. As in the North, war needs led to expansion and centralization of government control over the economy. In many cases, Jefferson Davis himself initiated government control (over railroads, shipping, and war production, for example), often in the face of protest or inaction by governors who favored states' rights. The expansion of government brought sudden urbanization, a new experience for the predominantly rural South. The population of Richmond, the Confederate capital, almost tripled, in large part because the Confederate bureaucracy grew to 70,000 people. Because of the need for military manpower, a good part of the Confederate bureaucracy consisted of women, who were referred to as "government girls." All of this—government control, urban growth, women in the paid workforce—was new to Southerners, and not all of it was welcomed.

Even more than in the North, the voracious need for soldiers fostered class antagonisms. When small yeoman farmers went off to war, their wives and families struggled to farm on their own, without the help of mechanization, which they could not afford, and without the help of slaves, which they had never owned. But wealthy men could be exempted from the draft if they had more than twenty slaves. Furthermore, many upper-class Southerners—at least 50,000—avoided military service by paying liberally ($5,000 and more) for substitutes. In the face of these inequities, desertions from the Confederate army soared. One Mississippi soldier spoke for many when he said that "he did not propose to fight for the rich men while they were at home having a good time." But the rich men, the South's traditional ruling class, paid little attention to such complaints.

Worst of all was the starvation. The North's blockade and the breakdown of the South's transportation system restricted the availability of food in the South, and these problems were vastly magnified by runaway inflation. Prices in the South rose by an unbelievable 9,000 percent. Speculation and hoarding by the rich made matters even worse. Women and children were left destitute, and a government-sponsored civilian relief program was soon diverted to meet the pressing needs of the military. Ordinary people suffered. "It is folly for a poor mother to call on the rich people about here," one woman wrote bitterly. "Their hearts are of steel; they would sooner throw what they have to spare to the dogs than give it to a starving child."

In the spring of 1863 food riots broke out in four Georgia cities (Atlanta among them) and in North Carolina. In Richmond, more than a thousand people, mostly women, broke into bakeries and snatched loaves of bread, crying "Bread! Bread! Our children are starving while the rich roll in wealth!" When the bread riot threatened to turn into general looting, Jefferson Davis himself appealed to the crowd to disperse—but found he had to threaten the rioters with gunfire before they would leave. A year later, Richmond stores sold eggs for $6 a dozen and butter for $25 a pound. One woman wept, "My God! How can I pay such prices? I have seven children; what shall I do?"

Increasingly, the ordinary people of the South, preoccupied with staying alive, refused to pay taxes, to provide food, or to serve in the army. Soldiers were drawn home by the desperation of their families as well as the discouraging course of the war. By January 1865 the desertion rate had climbed to 8 percent a month.

At the same time, the life of the southern ruling class was irrevocably altered by the changing nature of slavery. By the end of the war, one-quarter of all slaves had fled to the Union lines, and those who remained often stood in a different relationship to their owners. As white masters and overseers left to join the army, white women were left behind on the plantation to cope with shortages, grow crops, and manage the labor of slaves. Lacking the patriarchal authority of their husbands, white women found that white-black relationships shifted, sometimes drastically (as when slaves fled) and sometimes more subtly. Slaves increasingly made their own decisions about when and how they would work, and they refused to accept the punishments that would have accompanied this insubordination in prewar years. One black woman, implored by her mistress not to reveal the location of a trunk of money and silver plate when the invading Yankees arrived, looked her in the eye and said, "Mistress, I can't lie over that; you bought that silver plate when you sold my three children."

Peace movements in the South were motivated by a confused mixture of realism, war weariness, and the animosity of those who supported states' rights and opposed Jefferson Davis. The anti-Davis faction was led by his own vice president, Alexander Stephens, who early in 1864 suggested a negotiated peace. Peace sentiment was especially strong in North Carolina, where more than a hundred public meetings in support of negotiations were held in the summer of 1863. Davis would have none of it, and he commanded enough votes in the Confederate Congress to enforce his will and to suggest that peace sentiment was traitorous. The Confederacy, which lacked a two-party system, had no official way to consider alternatives. Thus the peace sentiment, which grew throughout 1864, flourished outside the political system in secret societies such as the Heroes of America and the Red Strings. As hopes of Confederate victory slipped away, conflict expanded beyond the battlefield to include the political struggles that southern civilians were fighting among themselves.

THE TIDE TURNS

As Lincoln's timing of the Emancipation Proclamation showed, by 1863 the nature of the war was changing. The proclamation freeing the slaves struck directly at the southern home front and the civilian workforce. That same year, the nature of the battlefield war changed as well. McClellan's notion of a limited war with modest battlefield casualties was gone forever. The Civil War became the first total war.

The Turning Point of 1863

In the summer of 1863 the moment finally arrived when the North could begin to hope for victory. But for the Union army the year opened with stalemate in the East and slow and costly progress in the West. For the South, 1863 represented its highest hopes for military success and for diplomatic recognition by Britain or France.

Attempting to break the stalemate in northern Virginia, General Joseph "Fighting Joe" Hooker and a

Union army of 130,000 men attacked a Confederate army half that size at Chancellorsville in May. In response, Robert E. Lee daringly divided his forces, sending General Thomas "Stonewall" Jackson and 30,000 men on a day-long flanking movement that caught the Union troops by surprise. Although Jackson was killed (shot by his own men by mistake), Chancellorsville was a great Confederate victory. However, Confederate losses were also great: 13,000 men, representing more than 20 percent of Lee's army (versus 17,000 Union men).

Though weakened, Lee moved to the attack. In June, in his second and most dangerous single thrust into Union territory, he moved north into Maryland and Pennsylvania. His purpose was as much political as military: he hoped that a great Confederate victory would lead Britain and France to intervene in the war and demand a negotiated peace. The ensuing battle of Gettysburg, July 1–3, 1863, was another horrible slaughter. On the last day, Lee sent 15,000 men, commanded by George Pickett, to attack the heavily defended Union center. The charge was suicidal. When the Union forces opened fire at 700 yards, one southern officer reported, "Pickett's division just seemed to melt away....Nothing but stragglers came back." The next day a Union officer reported, "I tried to ride over the field but could not, for dead and wounded lay too thick to guide a horse through them."

Pickett's Charge, one historian has written, was the perfect symbol of the entire Confederate war effort: "matchless valor, apparent initial success, and ultimate disaster." Lee retreated from the field, leaving more than one-third of his army behind—28,000 men killed, wounded, or missing. Union general George Meade elected not to pursue with his battered Union army (23,000 casualties). "We had them in our grasp," Lincoln said in bitter frustration. "We had only to stretch forth our arms and they were ours. And nothing I could say or do could make the Army move." Nevertheless, Lee's great gamble had failed; he never again mounted a major offensive.

The next day, July 4, 1863, Ulysses S. Grant took Vicksburg, Mississippi, after a costly siege. The combined news of Gettysburg and Vicksburg dissuaded Britain and France from recognizing the Confederacy and checked the northern peace movement. It also tightened the North's grip on the South, for the Union now controlled the entire Mississippi River. In November, Generals Grant and Sherman broke the Confederate hold on Chattanooga, Tennessee, thereby opening the way to Atlanta.

Grant and Sherman

In March 1864, President Lincoln called Grant east and appointed him general in chief of all the Union

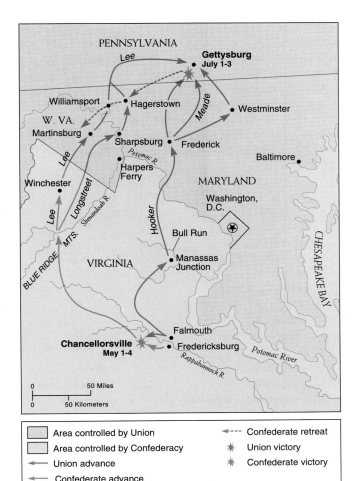

The Turning Point: 1863 *In June, Lee boldly struck north into Maryland and Pennsylvania, hoping for a victory that would cause Britain and France to demand a negotiated peace on Confederate terms. Instead, he lost the hard-fought battle of Gettysburg, July 1–3. The very next day, Grant's long siege of Vicksburg succeeded. These two great Fourth of July victories turned the tide in favor of the Union. The Confederates never again mounted a major offensive. Total Union control of the Mississippi now exposed the Lower South to attack.*

forces. Lincoln's critics were appalled. Grant was an uncouth Westerner (like the president) and (unlike the president) was rumored to have a drinking problem. Lincoln replied that if he knew the general's brand of whiskey he would send a barrel of it to every commander in the Union army.

Grant devised a plan of strangulation and annihilation. While he took on Lee in northern Virginia, he sent General William Tecumseh Sherman to defeat Confederate general Joe Johnston's Army of Tennessee, which was defending the approach to Atlanta. Both Grant and Sherman exemplified the new kind of warfare. They aimed to inflict maximum damage on the fabric of southern life,

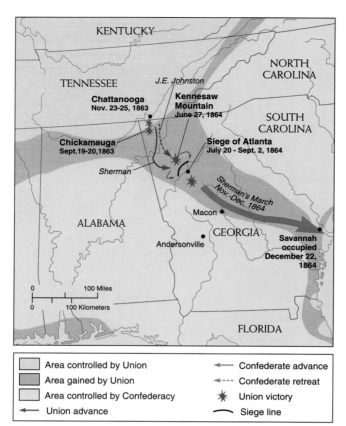

Sherman's Campaign in Georgia, 1864   *Ulysses S. Grant and William Tecumseh Sherman, two like-minded generals, commanded the Union's armies in the final push to victory. While Grant hammered away at Lee in northern Virginia, Sherman captured Atlanta in September (a victory that may have been vital to Lincoln's reelection) and began his March to the Sea in November 1864.*

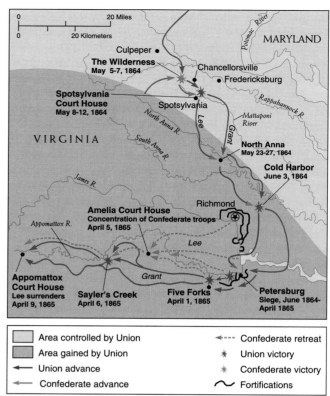

The Final Battles in Virginia, 1864–1865   *In the war's final phase early in 1865, Sherman closed one arm of a pincers by marching north from Savannah while Grant attacked Lee's last defensive positions in Petersburg and Richmond. Lee retreated from them on April 2 and surrendered at Appomattox Court House on April 9, 1865.*

hoping that the South would choose to surrender rather than face total destruction. This decision to broaden the war so that it directly affected civilians was new in American military history and prefigured the total wars of the twentieth century.

In northern Virginia, Grant pursued a policy of destroying civilian supplies. He said he "regarded it as humane to both sides to protect the persons of those found at their homes, but to consume everything that could be used to support or supply armies." One of those supports was slaves. Grant welcomed fleeing slaves to Union lines and encouraged army efforts to put them to work or enlist them as soldiers. He also cooperated with the efforts of groups like the New England Freedmen's Aid Society, which sent northern volunteers (many of them women) into Union-occupied parts of the South to educate former slaves. (The Freedmen's Bureau, authorized by Congress in March 1865, continued this work into Reconstruction. One of the northern teachers who

went south in 1866 to work for the bureau was Robert Fitzgerald, the former soldier.) But the most famous example of the new strategy of total war was General Sherman's 1864 march through Georgia.

Sherman captured Atlanta on September 2, 1864, after outmaneuvering and outfighting Johnson and his successor, John Bell Hood. Atlanta lay in ruins as Sherman and his troops entered the city. With the rest of Georgia now vulnerable, gloom enveloped the South. "Since Atlanta I have felt as if all were dead within me, forever," Mary Boykin Chesnut wrote in her diary. "We are going to be wiped off the earth."

In November, Sherman set out to march the 285 miles to the coastal city of Savannah, living off the land and destroying everything in his path. His military purpose was to tighten the noose around Robert E. Lee's army in northern Virginia by cutting off Mississippi, Alabama, and Georgia from the rest of the Confederacy. But his second purpose, openly stated, was to "make war so terrible" to the people of the South, to "make them so sick of war that generations would pass away before they would again appeal to it." Accordingly, he told his men to seize, burn, or destroy everything in their path (but, significantly, not to harm civilians).

One Union soldier wrote to his father, "You can form no idea of the amount of property destroyed by us on this raid....A tornado 60 miles in width from Chattanooga to this place 290 miles away could not have done half the damage we did." A southern woman supplied the details: "The fields were trampled down and the road was lined with carcasses of horses, hogs and cattle that the invaders, unable either to consume or to carry with them, had wantonly shot down to starve our people and prevent them from making their crops. The stench in some places was unbearable." It was estimated that Sherman's army did $100 million worth of damage. "They say no living thing is found in Sherman's track," Mary Boykin Chesnut wrote, "only chimneys, like telegraph poles, to carry the news of [his] attack backwards."

Terrifying to white southern civilians, Sherman was initially hostile to black Southerners as well. In the interests of speed and efficiency, his army turned away many of the 18,000 slaves who flocked to it in Georgia, causing a number to be recaptured and reenslaved. This callous action caused such a scandal in Washington that Secretary of War Edwin Stanton arranged a special meeting in Georgia with Sherman and twenty African American ministers who spoke for the freed slaves. This meeting in itself was extraordinary: no one had ever asked slaves what they wanted. Equally extraordinary was Sherman's response in Special Field Order 15, issued in January 1865: he set aside more than 400,000 acres of Confederate land to be given to the freed slaves in forty-acre parcels. This was war of a kind that white Southerners had never imagined.

The 1864 Election

The war complicated the 1864 presidential election, aggravating the usual political factionalism. Public opinion about Lincoln and the conduct of the war had been on a roller coaster, soaring to great heights with news of Union victories and plunging during long periods of stalemate. Just as in the Mexican-American War, the "instant news" provided by the telegraph and special correspondents pulled people out of their daily lives and fixed their attention on the war. But the Civil War was much larger and much nearer. Almost everyone had a son or a father or a brother at the front, or knew someone in their community who did. The war news was personal.

Lincoln was renominated during a low period. Opposed by the Radicals, who thought he was too conciliatory toward the South, and by Republican conservatives, who disapproved of the Emancipation Proclamation, Lincoln had little support within his own party. Secretary of the Treasury Salmon P. Chase, a man of immense ego, went so far as to encourage his supporters to propose him, rather than Lincoln, as the party's nominee.

The Democrats had an appealing candidate: General George McClellan, a war hero (always a favorite with American voters) who was known to be sympathetic to the South, although he was unwilling to endorse the plank of the Democratic Party platform that proclaimed the war a failure and proposed an armistice to end it. Other Democrats played shamelessly on the racist fears of the urban

This striking photograph by Thomas C. Roche shows a dead Confederate soldier, killed at Petersburg on April 3, 1865, only six days before the surrender at Appomattox. The new medium of photography conveyed the horror of the war with a gruesome reality to the American public.

working class, accusing Republicans of being "negro-lovers" and warning that racial mixing lay ahead.

A deeply depressed Lincoln fully expected to lose the election. "I am going to be beaten," he told an army officer in August 1864, "and unless some great change takes place badly beaten." A great change did take place: Sherman captured Atlanta on September 2. Jubilation swept the North: some cities celebrated with 100-gun salutes. Lincoln won the election with 55 percent of the popular vote. Seventy-eight percent of the soldiers voted for him rather than for their former commander. The vote probably saved the Republican Party from extinction. Furthermore, the election was important evidence of northern support for Lincoln's policy of unconditional surrender for the South. There would be no negotiated peace; the war would continue.

In many ways, Lincoln's reelection was extraordinary. Ordinary people and war-weary soldiers had voted to continue a difficult and divisive conflict. This was the first time in American history that the people had been able to vote on whether they were willing to continue wartime hardships, and that 45 percent of the electorate voted against Lincoln suggests how severe those hardships were.

Nearing the End

As Sherman devastated the lower South, Grant was locked in struggle with Lee in northern Virginia.

Grant did not favor subtle strategies. He bluntly said, "The art of war is simple enough. Find out where your enemy is. Get at him as soon as you can. Strike at him as hard as you can, and keep moving on." Following this plan, Grant eventually hammered Lee into submission, but at enormous cost. Lee had learned the art of defensive warfare (his troops called him "the King of Spades" because he made them dig trenches so often), and he inflicted heavy losses on the Union army in a succession of bloody encounters in the spring and summer of 1864: almost 18,000 at the battle of the Wilderness, more than 8,000 at Spotsylvania, and 12,000 at Cold Harbor. At Cold Harbor, Union troops wrote their names and addresses on scraps of paper and pinned them to their backs, so certain were they of being killed or wounded in battle. Grim and terrible as Grant's strategy was, it proved effective. Rather than pulling back after his failed assaults, he kept moving South, finally settling in for a prolonged siege of Lee's forces at Petersburg. The North's great advantage in population finally began to tell. There were more Union soldiers to replace those lost in battle, but there were no more white Confederates.

In desperation, the South turned to what had hitherto been unthinkable: arming slaves to serve as soldiers in the Confederate army. As Jefferson Davis said in February 1865, "We are reduced to choosing whether the negroes shall fight for or against us."

But—and this was the bitter irony—the African American soldiers and their families would have to be promised freedom or they would desert to the Union at the first chance they had. Even though Davis's proposal had the support of General Robert E. Lee, the Confederate Congress balked at first. As one member said, the idea was "revolting to Southern sentiment, Southern pride, and Southern honor." Another candidly admitted, "If slaves make good soldiers our whole theory of slavery is wrong." Finally, on March 13, the Confederate Congress authorized a draft of black soldiers—without mentioning freedom. Although two regiments of African American soldiers were immediately organized in Richmond, it was too late. The South never had to

Abraham Lincoln toured Richmond, the Confederate capital, just hours after Jefferson Davis had fled. This photograph, taken April 4, 1865, shows Yankee cavalry horses in the foreground and the smoldering city in the background. It gives a sense of the devastation suffered by the South and the immense task of rebuilding and reconciliation that Lincoln would not live to accomplish.

publicly acknowledge the paradox of having to offer slaves freedom so that they would fight to defend slavery.

By the spring of 1865, public support for the war simply disintegrated in the South. Starvation, inflation, dissension, and the prospect of military defeat were too much. In February, Jefferson Davis sent his vice president, Alexander Stephens, to negotiate terms at a peace conference at Hampton Roads. Lincoln would not countenance anything less than full surrender, although he did offer gradual emancipation with compensation for slave owners. Davis, however, insisted on southern independence at all costs. Consequently, the Hampton Roads conference failed and southern resistance faded away. In March 1865, Mary Boykin Chesnut recorded in her diary: "I am sure our army is silently dispersing. Men are going the wrong way all the time. They slip by now with no songs nor shouts. They have given the thing up."

Lincoln's assassination, just days after Lee's surrender at Appomattox, was a stunning blow. This lithograph shows the elaborate funeral cortege in New York City on April 25, 1865, just one of the many ceremonies that marked Lincoln's final trip to Springfield, Illinois, his burying place.

Appomattox

Grant's hammering tactics worked—slowly. In the spring of 1865 Lee and his remaining troops, outnumbered two to one, still held Petersburg and Richmond. Starving, short of ammunition, and losing men in battle or to desertion every day, Lee retreated from Petersburg on April 2. The Confederate government fled Richmond, stripping and burning the city. Seven days later, Lee and his 25,000 troops surrendered to Grant at Appomattox Court House. Grant treated Lee with great respect and set a historic precedent by giving the Confederate troops parole. This meant they could not subsequently be prosecuted for treason. Grant then sent the starving army on its way with three days' rations for every man. Jefferson Davis, who had hoped to set up a new government in Texas, was captured in Georgia on May 10. The war was finally over.

Death of a President

Sensing that the war was near its end, Abraham Lincoln visited Grant's troops when Lee withdrew from Petersburg on April 2. Thus it was that Lincoln came to visit Richmond, and to sit briefly in Jefferson Davis's presidential office, soon after Davis had left it. As Lincoln walked the streets of the burned and pillaged city, black people poured out to see him

and surround him, shouting "Glory to God! Glory! Glory! Glory!" Lincoln in turn said to Admiral David Porter: "Thank God I have lived to see this. It seems to me that I have been dreaming a horrid dream for four years, and now the nightmare is gone." Lincoln had only the briefest time to savor the victory. On the night of April 14, President and Mrs. Lincoln went to Ford's Theater in Washington. There Lincoln was shot at point-blank range by John Wilkes Booth, a Confederate sympathizer. He died the next day. For the people of the Union, the joy of victory was muted by mourning for their great leader. After a week of observances in Washington, Lincoln's coffin was loaded on a funeral train that slowly carried him back to Springfield. All along the railroad route, day and night, in small towns and large, people gathered to see the train pass and to pay their last respects. At that moment, the Washington community and the larger Union community were one and the same.

The nation as a whole was left with Lincoln's vision for the coming peace, expressed in the unforgettable words of his Second Inaugural Address:

> With malice toward none, with charity for all, with firmness in the right as God gives us to see the right, let us strive on to finish the work we are in, to bind up the nation's wounds, to care for him who shall have borne the battle and for his widow and his orphan, to do all which may achieve and cherish a just and lasting peace among ourselves and with all nations.

CHRONOLOGY

1861 March: Morrill Tariff Act

April: Fort Sumter falls; war begins

April: Mobilization begins

April–May: Virginia, Arkansas, Tennessee, and North Carolina secede

June: United States Sanitary Commission established

July: First Battle of Bull Run

1862 February: Legal Tender Act

February: Battles of Fort Henry and Fort Donelson

March: Battle of Pea Ridge

March: Battle of the *Monitor* and the *Merrimack*

March–August: George B. McClellan's Peninsular campaign

March: Battle of Glorieta Pass

April: Battle of Shiloh

April: Confederate Conscription Act

April: David Farragut captures New Orleans

May: Homestead Act

June–July: Seven Days Battles

July: Pacific Railway Act

July: Morrill Land Grant Act

August: Santee Sioux Uprising, Minnesota

September: Battle of Antietam

December: Battle of Fredericksburg

1863 January: Emancipation Proclamation

February: National Bank Act

March: Draft introduced in the North

March: Colonel Kit Carson sends 8,000 Navajos on the "Long Walk" to Bosque Redondo, New Mexico Territory

April: Richmond bread riot

May: Battle of Chancellorsville

June: French occupy Mexico City

July: Battle of Gettysburg

July: Surrender of Vicksburg

July: New York City Draft Riots

November: Battle of Chattanooga

November: Union troops capture Brownsville, Texas

1864 March: Ulysses S. Grant becomes general in chief of Union forces

April: Fort Pillow massacre

May: Battle of the Wilderness

May: Battle of Spotsylvania

June: Battle of Cold Harbor

September: Atlanta falls

November: Abraham Lincoln reelected president

November–December: William Tecumseh Sherman's March to the Sea

1865 April: Richmond falls

April: Robert E. Lee surrenders at Appomattox

April: Lincoln assassinated

December: Thirteenth Amendment to the Constitution becomes law

CONCLUSION

In 1865, a divided people had been forcibly reunited by battle. Their nation, the United States of America, had been permanently changed by civil war. Devastating losses among the young men of the country—the greatest such losses the nation was ever to suffer— would affect not only their families but all of postwar society. Politically, the deepest irony of the Civil War was that only by fighting it had America become completely a nation. For it was the war that broke down local isolation. Ordinary citizens in local communities, North and South, developed a national perspective as they sent their sons and brothers to be soldiers, their daughters to be nurses and teachers. Then, too, the federal government, vastly strengthened by wartime necessity, reached the lives of ordinary citizens more than ever before. The question now was whether this strengthened but divided national community, forged in battle, could create a just peace.

REVIEW QUESTIONS

1. At the outset of the Civil War, what were the relative advantages of the North and the South, and how did they affect the final outcome?
2. In the absence of the southern Democrats, in the early 1860s the new Republican Congress was able to pass a number of party measures with little opposition. What do these measures tell you about the historical roots of the Republican Party? More generally, how do you think we should view legislation passed in the absence of the customary opposition, debate, and compromise?
3. The greatest problem facing Jefferson Davis and the Confederacy was the need to develop a true feeling of nationalism. Can the failure of this effort be blamed on Davis's weakness as a leader alone, or are there other causes?
4. In what ways can it be said that the actions of African Americans, both slave and free, came to determine the course of the Civil War?
5. Wars always have unexpected consequences. List some of these consequences both for soldiers and for civilians in the North and in the South.
6. Today, Abraham Lincoln is considered one of our greatest presidents, but he did not enjoy such approval at the time. List some of the contemporary criticisms of Lincoln, and evaluate them.

RECOMMENDED READING

Nina Brown Baker, *Cyclone in Calico: The Story of Mary Ann Bickerdyke* (1952). Mother Bickerdyke's wartime career is told in homely detail.

Iver Bernstein, *The New York City Draft Riots* (1990). A social history that places the famous riots in the context of the nineteenth century's extraordinary urbanization.

Paul Escott, *After Secession: Jefferson Davis and the Failure of Confederate Nationalism* (1978). A thoughtful study of Davis's record as president of the Confederacy.

Drew Gilpin Faust, *Mothers of Invention: Women of the Slaveholding South in the American Civil War* (1996). A major study that considers the importance of gender at the white South's "moment of truth."

Alvin Josephy, *The Civil War in the West* (1992). A long-needed study, by a noted western historian, of the course of the war in the Trans-Mississippi West.

William Quentin Maxwell, *Lincoln's Fifth Wheel: The Political History of the United States Sanitary Commission* (1956). A useful study of the major northern volunteer organization.

James M. McPherson, *The Negro's Civil War: How American Negroes Felt and Acted during the War for the Union* (1965). One of the earliest documentary collections on African American activity in wartime.

———, *Battle Cry of Freedom: The Civil War Era* (1988). An acclaimed, highly readable synthesis of much scholarship on the war.

———, *The Atlas of the Civil War* (1994). Detailed battle diagrams with clear descriptions.

Pauli Murray, *Proud Shoes: The Story of an American Family* (1956). Murray tells the proud story of her African American family and her grandfather, Robert Fitzgerald.

Phillip Shaw Paludan, *"A People's Contest": The Union at War, 1861–1865* (1988). A largely successful social history of the North during the war.

ADDITIONAL BIBLIOGRAPHY

The Lincoln Presidency and the Northern Home Front

Richard Franklin Bensel, *Yankee Leviathan: The Origins of Central State Authority in America, 1859–1877* (1991)

David Donald, *Liberty and Union* (1978)

Eric Foner, *Politics and Ideology in the Age of the Civil War* (1980)

George M. Frederickson, *The Inner Civil War: Northern Intellectuals and the Crisis of the Union* (1965)

J. Matthew Gallman, *The North Fights the Civil War: The Home Front* (1994)

Ernest A. McKay, *The Civil War and New York City* (1990)

James M. McPhersen, *Abraham Lincoln and the Second American Revolution* (1990)

Mark E. Neely, *The Fate of Liberty: Abraham Lincoln and Civil Liberties* (1991)

Phillip Shaw Paludan, *The Presidency of Abraham Lincoln* (1994)

William E. Parrish, *Turbulent Partnership: Missouri and the Union, 1861–1865* (1963)

James Rawley, *The Politics of Union: Northern Politics during the Civil War* (1974)

Heather Cox Richardson, *The Greatest Nation of the Earth: Republican Economic Policies during the Civil War* (1997)

Anne C. Rose, *Victorian America and the Civil War* (1992)

Joel Sibley, *A Respectable Minority: The Democratic Party in the Civil War Era, 1860–1868* (1977)

Lewis P. Simpson, *Mind and the American Civil War* (1989)

John L.Thomas, ed., *Abraham Lincoln and the American Political Tradition* (1986)

Hans L. Trefousse, *The Radical Republicans* (1968)

Thomas H. O'Connor, *Civil War Boston: Homefront and Battlefield* (1997)

Bell I. Wiley, *The Life of Johnny Reb* (1943)

———, *The Life of Billy Yank* (1952)

Maris A. Vinovskis, ed., *Toward a Social History of the American Civil War: Exploratory Essays* (1990)

T. Harry Williams, *Lincoln and His Generals* (1952)

Gary Wills, *Lincoln at Gettysburg: Words that Remade America* (1992)

The Death of Slavery

Herman Belz, *A New Birth of Freedom: The Republican Party and Freedmen's Rights, 1861–1866* (1976)

Ira Berlin, et al., *Slaves No More: Three Essays on Emancipation and the Civil War* (1992)

Ira Berlin, et al., eds., *Freedom, A Documentary History of Emancipation, 1861–1867*, Series 1, Volume I: *The Destruction of Slavery* (1985)

———, et al., eds. *Freedom, A Documentary History of Emancipation, 1861–1867*, Series 1, Volume II: *The Wartime Genesis of Free Labor: The Upper South* (1993)

———, et al., eds. *Freedom, A Documentary History of Emancipation, 1861–1867*, Series 1, Volume III: *The Wartime Genesis of Free Labor: The Lower South* (1990)

———, et al., eds. *Freedom, A Documentary History of Emancipation, 1861–1867*, Series 2: *The Black Military Experience* (1988)

John Hope Franklin, *The Emancipation Proclamation* (1963)

Benjamin Quarles, *The Negro in the Civil War* (1953)

Willie Lee Rose, *Rehearsal for Reconstruction: The Port Royal Experiment* (1964)

The Confederacy and the Southern Home Front

Steven V. Ash, *When the Yankees Came: Conflict and Chaos in the Occupied South 1861–1865* (1995)

Daniel W. Crofts, *Reluctant Confederates: Upper South Unionists in the Secession Crisis* (1989)

William C. Davis, *"A Government of Our Own": The Making of the Confederacy* (1994)

Wayne K. Durrill, *War of Another Kind: A Southern Community in the Great Rebellion* (1990)

Clement Eaton, *A History of the Southern Confederacy* (1954)

Drew Gilpin Faust, *The Creation of Confederate Nationalism* (1988)

Robert M. Myers, ed., *The Children of Pride: A True Story of Georgia and the Civil War* (1972)

Phillip S. Paludan, *Victims: A True History of the Civil War* (1981)

George C. Rable, *Civil Wars: Women and the Crisis of Southern Nationalism* (1989)

———, *The Confederate Republic: A Revolution against Politics* (1994)

Charles W. Ramsdell, *Behind the Lines in the Southern Confederacy* (1944)

James L. Roark, *Masters without Slaves: Southern Planters in the Civil War and Reconstruction* (1978)

Daniel E. Sutherland, *Seasons of War: The Ordeal of a Confederate Community 1861–1865* (1995)

Emory M. Thomas, *The Confederate Nation, 1861–1865* (1979)

LeeAnn Whites, *The Civil War as a Crisis in Gender: Augusta, Georgia, 1860–1890* (1995)

Bell I. Wiley, *The Plain People of the Confederacy* (1943)

The Fighting

Michael Barton, *Good Men: The Character of Civil War Soldiers* (1981)

Ken Burns, *The Civil War* (1990)

Bruce Catton, *A Stillness at Appomattox* (1953)

Shelby Foote, *The Civil War: A Narrative*, 3 vols. (1958–1974)

Joseph T. Glatthaar, *Forged in Battle: The Civil War Alliance of Black Soldiers and White Officers* (1990)

———, *The March to the Sea and Beyond: Sherman's Troops in the Savannah and Carolinas Campaign* (1985)

Mark Grimsley, *The Hard Hand of War: Union Policy toward Southern Civilians, 1861–1865* (1995)

Edward Hagerman, *The American Civil War and the Origins of Modern Warfare* (1988)

Gerald F. Linderman, *Embattled Courage: The Experience of Combat in the American Civil War* (1987)

Reid Mitchell, *The Vacant Chair: The Northern Soldier Leaves Home* (1993)

Allan Nevins, *The War for the Union*, 4 vols. (1959–71)

Edwin S. Redkey, ed., *A Grand Army of Black Men: Letters from African-American Soldiers in the Union Army, 1861–1865* (1992)

Charles Royster, *The Destructive War: William Tecumseh Sherman, Stonewall Jackson, and the Americans* (1991)

Biography

William C. Davis, *Jefferson Davis: The Man and His Hour* (1991)

William S. Feeley, *Grant: A Biography* (1980)

Thomas E. Schott, *Alexander H. Stephens of Georgia: A Biography* (1988)

Stephen W. Sears, *George B. McClellan: The Young Napoleon* (1988)

Emory M. Thomas, *Robert E. Lee: A Biography* (1995)

CHAPTER SEVENTEEN

RECONSTRUCTION

1863–1877

AMERICAN COMMUNITIES
Hale County, Alabama: From Slavery to Freedom in a Black Belt Community

On a bright Saturday morning in May 1867, 4,000 former slaves eagerly streamed into the town of Greensboro, bustling seat of Hale County in west-central Alabama. They came to hear speeches from two delegates to a recent freedmen's convention in Mobile and to find out about the political status of black people under the Reconstruction Act just passed by Congress. Tensions mounted in the days following this unprecedented gathering as military authorities began supervising voter registration for elections to the upcoming constitutional convention that would rewrite the laws of Alabama. On June 13, John Orrick, a local white, confronted Alex Webb, a politically active freedman, on the streets of Greensboro. Webb had recently been appointed a voter registrar for the district. Orrick swore he would never be registered by a black man, and shot Webb dead. Hundreds of armed and angry freedmen formed a posse to search for Orrick, but failed to find him. Galvanized by Webb's murder, 500 local freedmen formed a chapter of the Union League, the Republican Party's organizational arm in the South. The chapter functioned as both a militia company and a forum to agitate for political rights.

Violent political encounters between black people and white people were common in southern communities in the wake of the Civil War. The war had destroyed slavery and the Confederacy, but left the political and economic status of newly emancipated African Americans unresolved. Communities throughout the south struggled over the meaning of freedom in ways that reflected their particular circumstances. The 4 million freed people constituted roughly one-third of the total southern population, but the black–white ratio in individual communities varied enormously. In some places the Union army had been a strong presence during the war, hastening the collapse of the slave system and encouraging experiments in free labor. Other areas remained relatively untouched by the fighting. In some areas small farms prevailed; in others, including Hale County, large plantations dominated economic and political life.

West-central Alabama had emerged as a fertile center of cotton production just two decades before the Civil War. There African Americans, as throughout the South's black belt, constituted more than three-quarters of the population. The region was virtually untouched by fighting until the very end of the Civil War. But with the arrival of federal troops in the spring of 1865, African Americans in Hale County, like their counterparts elsewhere, began to challenge the traditional organization of plantation labor.

One owner, Henry Watson, found that his entire workforce had deserted him at the end of 1865. "I am in the midst of a large and fertile cotton growing country," Watson wrote to a partner.

"Many plantations are entirely without labor, many plantations have insufficient labor, and upon none are the laborers doing their former accustomed work." Black women refused to work in the fields, preferring to stay home with their children and tend garden plots. Nor would male field hands do any work, such as caring for hogs, that did not directly increase their share of the cotton crop.

Above all, freed people wanted more autonomy. Overseers and owners thus grudgingly allowed them to work the land "in families," letting them choose their own supervisors and find their own provisions. The result was a shift from the gang labor characteristic of the antebellum period, in which large groups of slaves worked under the harsh and constant supervision of white overseers, to the sharecropping system, in which African American families worked small plots of land in exchange for a small share of the crop. This shift represented less of a victory for newly freed African Americans than a defeat for plantation owners, who resented even the limited economic independence it forced them to concede to their black workforce.

Only a small fraction—perhaps 15 percent—of African American families were fortunate enough to be able to buy land. The majority settled for some version of sharecropping, while others managed to rent land from owners, becoming tenant farmers. Still, planters throughout Hale County had to change the old routines of plantation labor. Local African Americans also organized politically. In 1866 Congress had passed the Civil Rights Act and sent the Fourteenth Amendment to the Constitution to the states for ratification; both promised full citizenship rights to former slaves. Hale County freedmen joined the Republican Party and local Union League chapters. They used their new political power to press for better labor contracts, demand greater autonomy for the black workforce, and agitate for the more radical goal of land confiscation and redistribution. "The colored people are very anxious to get land of their own to live upon independently; and they want money to buy stock to make crops," reported one black Union League organizer. "The only way to get these necessaries is to give our votes to the [Republican] party . . . making every effort possible to bring these blessings about by reconstructing the State." Two Hale County former slaves, Brister Reese and James K. Green, won election to the Alabama state legislature in 1869.

It was not long before these economic and political gains prompted a white counterattack. In the spring of 1868, the Ku Klux Klan—a secret organization devoted to terrorizing and intimidating African Americans and their white Republican allies—came to Hale County. Disguised in white sheets, armed with guns and whips, and making nighttime raids on horseback, Klansmen flogged, beat, and murdered freed people. They intimidated voters and silenced political activists. Planters used Klan terror to dissuade former slaves from leaving plantations or organizing for higher wages.

With the passage of the Ku Klux Klan Act in 1871, the federal government cracked down on the Klan, breaking its power temporarily in parts of the former Confederacy. But no serious effort was made to stop Klan terror in the west Alabama black belt, and planters there succeeded in reestablishing much of their social and political control.

The events in Hale County illustrate the struggles that beset communities throughout the South during the Reconstruction era after the Civil War. The destruction of slavery and the Confederacy forced African Americans and white people to renegotiate their old economic and political roles. These community battles both shaped and were shaped by the victorious and newly expansive federal government in Washington. In the end, Reconstruction was only partially successful. Not until the "Second Reconstruction" of the twentieth-century civil rights movement would the descendants of Hale County's African Americans begin to enjoy the full fruits of freedom—and even then not without challenge.

Greensboro

KEY TOPICS

- Competing political plans for reconstructing the defeated Confederacy

- Difficult transition from slavery to freedom for African Americans

- The political and social legacy of Reconstruction in the southern states

- Post–Civil War transformations in the economic and political life of the North

THE POLITICS OF RECONSTRUCTION

When General Robert E. Lee's men stacked their guns at Appomattox, the bloodiest war in American history ended. More than 600,000 soldiers had died during the four years of fighting, 360,000 Union and 260,000 Confederate. Another 275,000 Union and 190,000 Confederate troops had been wounded. Although President Abraham Lincoln insisted early on that the purpose of the war was to preserve the Union, by 1863 it had evolved as well into a struggle for African American liberation. Indeed the political, economic, and moral issues posed by slavery were the root cause of the Civil War, and the war ultimately destroyed slavery, although not racism, once and for all.

The Civil War also settled the Constitutional crisis provoked by the secession of the Confederacy and its justification in appeals to states' rights . The name "United States" would from now on be understood as a singular rather than a plural noun, signaling an important change in the meaning of American nationality. The old notion of the United States as a voluntary union of sovereign states gave way to the new reality of a single nation in which the federal government took precedence over the individual states. The key historical developments of the Reconstruction era revolved around precisely how the newly strengthened national government would define its relationship with the defeated Confederate states and the 4 million newly freed slaves.

The Defeated South

The white South paid an extremely high price for secession, war, and defeat. In addition to the battlefield casualties, the Confederate states sustained deep material and psychological wounds. Much of the best agricultural land lay waste, including the rich fields of northern Virginia, the Shenandoah Valley, and large sections of Tennessee, Mississippi, Georgia, and South Carolina. Many towns and cities—including Richmond, Atlanta, and Columbia, South Carolina—were in ruins. By 1865, the South's most precious commodities, cotton and African American slaves, no longer were measures of wealth and prestige. Retreating

Confederates destroyed most of the South's cotton to prevent its capture by federal troops. What remained was confiscated by Union agents as contraband of war. The former slaves, many of whom had fled to Union lines during the latter stages of the war, were determined to chart their own course in the reconstructed South as free men and women.

It would take the South's economy a generation to overcome the severe blows dealt by the war. In 1860 the South held roughly 25 percent of the nation's wealth; a decade later it controlled only 12 percent. Many white Southerners resented their conquered status, and white notions of race, class, and "honor" died hard. A white North Carolinian, for example, who had lost almost everything dear to him in the war—his sons, home, and slaves—recalled in 1865 that in spite of all his tragedy he still retained one thing. "They've left me one inestimable privilege—to hate 'em. I git up at half-past four in the morning, and sit up till twelve at night, to hate 'em." As late as 1870 the Reverend Robert Lewis Dabney of Virginia wrote: "I do not forgive. I try not to forgive. What! forgive those people, who have invaded our country, burned our cities, destroyed our homes, slain our young men, and spread desolation and ruin over our land! No, I do not forgive them."

Emancipation proved the bitterest pill for white Southerners to swallow, especially the planter elite. Conquered and degraded, and in their view robbed of their slave property, white people responded by regarding African Americans more than ever as inferior to themselves. In the antebellum South white skin had defined a social bond that transcended economic class. It gave even the lowliest poor white a badge of superiority over even the most skilled slave or prosperous free African American. Emancipation, however, forced white people to redefine their world. Many believed that without white direction, the freed people would languish, become wards of the state, or die off. Most white people believed that African Americans were too lazy to take care of themselves and survive. At the very least, whites reasoned, the South's agricultural economy would suffer at the hands of allegedly undisciplined and inefficient African Americans. The specter of political power and social equality for African Americans made

Charleston, South Carolina, in 1865, after Union troops had burned the city. In the aftermath of the Civil War, scenes like this were common throughout the South. The destruction of large portions of so many southern cities and towns contributed to the postwar economic hardships faced by the region.

racial order the consuming passion of most white Southerners during the Reconstruction years. In fact, racism can be seen as one of the major forces driving Reconstruction and, ultimately, undermining it.

Abraham Lincoln's Plan

By late 1863, Union military victories had convinced President Lincoln of the need to fashion a plan for the reconstruction of the South (see Chapter 16). Lincoln based his reconstruction program on bringing the seceded states back into the Union as quickly as possible. He was determined to respect private property (except in the case of slave property), and he opposed imposing harsh punishments for rebellion. His Proclamation of Amnesty and Reconstruction of December 1863 offered "full pardon" and the restoration of property, not including slaves, to white Southerners willing to swear an oath of allegiance to the United States and its laws, including the Emancipation Proclamation. Prominent Confederate military and civil leaders were excluded from Lincoln's offer, though he indicated that he would freely pardon them.

The president also proposed that when the number of any Confederate state's voters who took the oath of allegiance reached 10 percent of the number who had voted in the election of 1860, this group could establish a state government that Lincoln would recognize as legitimate. Fundamental to this Ten Percent Plan was acceptance by the reconstructed governments of the abolition of slavery. Lincoln's plan was designed less as a blueprint for Reconstruction than as a way to shorten

the war and gain white people's support for emancipation. It angered those Republicans—known as Radical Republicans—who advocated not only equal rights for the freedmen but a tougher stance toward the white South. As a result, when Arkansas and Louisiana met the president's requirements for reentry into the Union, Congress refused to seat their representatives.

In July 1864, Senator Benjamin F. Wade of Ohio and Congressman Henry W. Davis of Maryland, both Radicals, proposed a harsher alternative to the Ten Percent Plan. The Wade-Davis bill required 50 percent of a seceding state's white male citizens to take a loyalty oath before elections could be held for a convention to rewrite the state's constitution. The bill also guaranteed equality before the law (although not suffrage) for former slaves. Unlike the president, the Radicals saw Reconstruction as a chance to effect a fundamental transformation of southern society. They thus wanted to delay the process until war's end and to limit participation to a small number of southern Unionists. Lincoln viewed Reconstruction as part of the larger effort to win the war and abolish slavery. He wanted to weaken the Confederacy by creating new state governments that could win broad support from southern white people. The Wade-Davis bill threatened his efforts to build political consensus within the southern states, and Lincoln therefore pocket-vetoed it, by refusing to sign it within ten days of the adjournment of Congress.

Redistribution of southern land among former slaves posed another thorny issue for Lincoln, Congress, and federal military officers. As Union armies occupied parts of the South, commanders had improvised a variety of arrangements involving confiscated plantations and the African American labor force. For example, in 1862 General Benjamin F. Butler began a policy of transforming slaves on Louisiana sugar plantations into wage laborers under the close supervision of occupying federal troops. Butler's policy required slaves to remain on the estates of loyal planters, where they would receive wages according to a fixed schedule, as well as food and medical care for the aged and sick. Abandoned plantations would be leased to northern investors. Butler's successor, General Nathaniel P. Banks, extended this system throughout occupied Louisiana. By 1864 some 50,000 African American laborers on nearly 1,500 Louisiana estates worked either directly for the government or for individual planters under contracts supervised by the army.

In January 1865, General William T. Sherman issued Special Field Order 15, setting aside the Sea Islands off the Georgia coast and a portion of the South Carolina low-country rice fields for the exclusive settlement of freed people. Each family would receive forty acres of land and the loan of mules from the army—the origin, perhaps, of the famous call for "forty acres and a

"Freedom to Slaves!", a Union commander's notice of the Emancipation Proclamation. Civil War, 1863.

A Union commander notifies the citizens of Winchester, Virginia, of President Abraham Lincoln's Emancipation Proclamation. Union officers throughout the South had to improvise arrangements for dealing with African Americans who streamed into Union army camps. For many newly freed slaves, the call for taking up "useful occupations" meant serving the Union forces in their neighborhoods as laborers, cooks, spies, and soldiers.

mule" that would soon capture the imagination of African Americans throughout the South. Sherman's intent was not to revolutionize southern society but to relieve the demands placed on his army by the thousands of impoverished African Americans who followed his march to the sea. By the summer of 1865 some 40,000 freed people, eager to take advantage of the general's order, had been settled on 400,000 acres of "Sherman land."

Conflicts within the Republican Party prevented the development of a systematic land distribution program. Still, Lincoln and the Republican Congress supported other measures to aid the emancipated slaves. In March 1865 Congress established the Freedmen's Bureau. Along with providing food, clothing, and fuel to destitute former slaves, the bureau was charged with supervising and managing "all the abandoned lands in the South and the control of all subjects relating to refugees and freedmen." The act that established the bureau also stated that forty acres of abandoned or confiscated land could be leased to freed slaves or white Unionists, who would have an option to purchase after three years and "such title thereto as the United States can convey." To guarantee the end of slavery once the war ended, Republicans drafted the Thirteenth Amendment, declaring that "neither slavery nor involuntary servitude, except as a punishment for crime . . . , shall

exist within the United States." This amendment passed both houses of Congress by January 1865 and was ratified by the necessary three-fourths of the states on December 18, 1865—eight months after Lee's surrender.

At the time of Lincoln's assassination, his Reconstruction policy remained unsettled and incomplete. In its broad outlines the president's plans had seemed to favor a speedy restoration of the southern states to the Union and a minimum of federal intervention in their affairs. But with his death the specifics of postwar Reconstruction had to be hammered out by a new president, Andrew Johnson of Tennessee, a man whose personality, political background, and racist leanings put him at odds with the Republican-controlled Congress.

Andrew Johnson and Presidential Reconstruction

Andrew Johnson, a Democrat and former slaveholder, was a most unlikely successor to the martyred Lincoln. By trade a tailor, educated by his wife, Johnson overcame his impoverished background and served as state legislator, governor, and U.S. senator. Throughout his career Johnson had championed yeoman farmers and viewed the South's plantation aristocrats with contempt. He was the only southern member of the U.S. Senate to remain loyal to the Union, and he held the planter elite responsible for secession and defeat. In 1862 Lincoln appointed Johnson to the difficult post of military governor of Tennessee. There he successfully began wartime Reconstruction and cultivated Unionist support in the mountainous eastern districts of that state.

In 1864 the Republicans, in an appeal to northern and border state "War Democrats," nominated Johnson for vice president. But despite Johnson's success in Tennessee and in the 1864 campaign, many Radical Republicans distrusted him, and the hardscrabble Tennessean remained a political outsider in Republican circles. In the immediate aftermath of Lincoln's murder, however, Johnson appeared to side with those Radical Republicans who sought to treat the South as a conquered province. "Treason is a crime and must be made odious," Johnson declared. "Traitors must be impoverished. . . . They must not only be punished, but their social power must be destroyed." The new president also hinted at indicting prominent Confederate officials for treason, disfranchising them, and confiscating their property.

Such tough talk appealed to Republicans. But support for Johnson quickly faded as the new president's policies unfolded. Johnson defined Reconstruction as the province of the executive, not the legislative branch, and he planned to restore the Union as quickly as possible. He blamed individual Southerners—the planter elite—rather than entire states for leading the South down the disastrous road to secession. In line with this philosophy, Johnson outlined mild terms for reentry to the Union.

In the spring of 1865 Johnson granted amnesty and pardon, including restoration of property rights except slaves, to all Confederates who pledged loyalty to the Union and support for emancipation. Fourteen classes of Southerners, mostly major Confederate officials and wealthy landowners, were excluded. But these men could apply individually for presidential pardons. The power to pardon his former enemies—the Old South's planter elite—gratified Johnson and reinforced his class bias. It also helped win southern support for his lenient policies, for Johnson pardoned former Confederates liberally. In September 1865 Johnson granted an average of a hundred pardons a day, and during his tenure he pardoned roughly 90 percent of those who applied. Significantly, Johnson instituted this plan while Congress was not in session.

Johnson also appointed provisional governors for seven of the former Confederate states, requiring them to hold elections for state constitutional conventions. Participation in this political process was limited to white people who had been pardoned or who had taken a loyalty oath. Johnson also called on state conventions to repudiate secession, acknowledge the abolition of slavery, and void state debts incurred during the war. By the fall of 1865 ten of the eleven Confederate states claimed to have met Johnson's requirements to reenter the Union. On December 6, 1865, in his first annual message to Congress, the president declared the "restoration" of the Union virtually complete. But a serious division within the federal government was taking shape, for the Congress was not about to allow the president free rein in determining the conditions of southern readmission.

Andrew Johnson used the term "restoration" rather than "reconstruction." A lifelong Democrat with ambitions to be elected president on his own in 1868, Johnson hoped to build a new political coalition composed of northern Democrats, conservative Republicans, and southern Unionists. Firmly committed to white supremacy, he opposed political rights for the freedmen. In 1866, after Frederick Douglass and other black leaders had met with him to discuss black suffrage, Johnson told an aide: "Those damned sons of bitches thought they had me in a trap! I know that damned Douglass; he's just like any nigger, and he would sooner cut a white man's throat than not." Johnson's open sympathy for his fellow white Southerners, his antiblack bias, and his determination to control the course of Reconstruction placed him on a collision course with the powerful Radical wing of the Republican Party.

The Radical Republican Vision

Most Radicals were men whose careers had been shaped by the slavery controversy. At the core of their thinking lay a deep belief in equal political rights and equal economic opportunity, both guaranteed by a powerful national government. They argued that once free labor, universal education, and equal rights were implanted in the South, that region would be able to share in the North's material wealth, progress, and fluid social mobility. Representative George W. Julian of Indiana typified the Radical vision for the South. He called for elimination of the region's "large estates, widely scattered settlements, wasteful agriculture, popular ignorance, social degradation, the decline of manufactures, contempt for honest labor, and a pampered oligarchy." This process would allow Republicans to develop "small farms, thrifty tillage, free schools, social independence, flourishing manufactures and the arts, respect for honest labor, and equality of political rights."

In the Radicals' view, the power of the federal government would be central to the remaking of southern society, especially in guaranteeing civil rights and suffrage for freedmen. In the most far-reaching proposal, Representative Thaddeus Stevens of Pennsylvania called for the confiscation of 400 million acres belonging to the wealthiest 10 percent of Southerners, to be redistributed to black and white yeomen and northern land buyers. "The whole fabric of southern society must be changed," Stevens told Pennsylvania Republicans in September 1865, "and never can it be done if this opportunity is lost. How can republican institutions, free schools, free churches, free social intercourse exist in a mingled community of nabobs and serfs? If the South is ever to be made a safe republic let her lands be cultivated by the toil of the owners."

Northern Republicans were especially outraged by the stringent "black codes" passed by South Carolina, Mississippi, Louisiana, and other states. These were designed to restrict the freedom of the black labor force and keep freed people as close to slave status as possible. Laborers who left their jobs before contracts expired would forfeit wages already earned and be subject to arrest by any white citizen. Vagrancy, very broadly defined, was punishable by fines and involuntary plantation labor. Apprenticeship clauses obliged black children to work without pay for employers. Some states attempted to bar African Americans from land ownership. Other laws specifically denied African Americans equality with white people in civil rights, excluding them from juries and prohibiting interracial marriages.

The black codes underscored the unwillingness of white Southerners to accept the full meaning of freedom for African Americans. Mississippi's version contained a catchall section levying fines and possible imprisonment for any former slaves "committing riots, routs, affrays, trespasses, malicious mischief, cruel treatment to animals, seditious speeches, insulting gestures, language, or acts, or assaults on any person, disturbance of the peace, exercising the function of a minister of

This wood engraving appeared in Frank Leslie's Illustrated Newspaper, May 5, 1864. It depicted "vagrant" African Americans in New Orleans being rounded up by the Provost Guard, in compliance with Louisiana's restrictive "Black Code." These types of images helped raise concerns in the North about the treatment of recently freed slaves.

the Gospel without a license . . . vending spiritous or intoxicating liquors, or committing any other misdemeanor, the punishment of which is not specifically provided for by law."

The Radicals, although not a majority of their party, were joined by moderate Republicans as growing numbers of Northerners grew suspicious of white southern intransigence and the denial of political rights to freedmen. When the Thirty-ninth Congress convened in December 1865, the large Republican majority prevented the seating of the white Southerners elected to Congress under President Johnson's provisional state governments. Republicans also established the Joint Committee on Reconstruction. After hearing extensive testimony from a broad range of witnesses, it concluded that not only were old Confederates back in power in the South but that black codes and racial violence required increased protection for African Americans.

As a result, in the spring of 1866 Congress passed two important bills designed to aid African Americans. The landmark Civil Rights bill, which bestowed full citizenship on African Americans, overturned the 1857 Dred Scott decision and the black codes. It defined all persons born in the United States (except Indian peoples) as national citizens, and it enumerated various rights, including the rights to make and enforce contracts, to sue, to give evidence, and to buy and sell property. Under this bill, African Americans acquired "full and equal benefit of all laws and proceedings for the security of person and property as is enjoyed by white citizens."

Congress also voted to enlarge the scope of the Freedmen's Bureau, empowering it to build schools and pay teachers, and also to establish courts to prosecute those charged with depriving African Americans of their civil rights. The bureau achieved important, if limited, success in aiding African Americans. Bureau-run schools helped lay the foundation for southern public education. The bureau's network of courts allowed freed people to bring suits against white people in disputes involving violence, nonpayment of wages, or unfair division of crops. The very existence of courts hearing public testimony by African Americans provided an important psychological challenge to traditional notions of white racial domination.

An angry President Johnson vetoed both of these bills. In opposing the Civil Rights bill, Johnson denounced the assertion of national power to protect African American civil rights, claiming it was a "stride toward centralization, and the concentration of all legislative powers in the national Government." In the case of the Freedmen's Bureau, Johnson argued that Congress lacked jurisdiction over the eleven unrepresented southern states. But Johnson's intemperate attacks on the Radicals—he damned them as traitors unwilling to restore the Union—united moderate and Radical Republicans and they succeeded in overriding the vetoes. Congressional Republicans, led by the Radical faction, were now unified in challenging the president's power to direct Reconstruction and in using national authority to define and protect the rights of citizens.

In June 1866, fearful that the Civil Rights Act might be declared unconstitutional and eager to settle the basis for the seating of southern representatives, Congress passed the Fourteenth Amendment. The amendment defined national citizenship to include former slaves ("all persons born or naturalized in the United States") and prohibited the states from violating the privileges of citizens without due process of law. It also empowered Congress to reduce the representation of any state that denied the suffrage to males over twenty-one. Republicans adopted the Fourteenth Amendment as their platform for the 1866 congressional elections and suggested that southern states would have to ratify it as a condition of readmission. President Johnson, meanwhile, took to the stump in August to support conservative Democratic and Republican candidates. His unrestrained speeches often degenerated into harangues, alienating many voters and aiding the Republican cause.

For their part, the Republicans skillfully portrayed Johnson and northern Democrats as disloyal and white Southerners as unregenerate. Republicans began an effective campaign tradition known as "waving the bloody shirt"—reminding northern voters of the hundreds of thousands of Yankee soldiers left dead or maimed by the war. In the November 1866 elections, the Republicans increased their majority in both the House and the Senate and gained control of all the northern states. The stage was now set for a battle between the president and Congress. Was it to be Johnson's "restoration" or Congressional Reconstruction?

Congressional Reconstruction and the Impeachment Crisis

United against Johnson, Radical and moderate Republicans took control of Reconstruction early in 1867. In March Congress passed the First Reconstruction Act over Johnson's veto. This act divided the South into five military districts subject to martial law. To achieve restoration, southern states were first required to call new constitutional conventions, elected by universal manhood suffrage. Once these states had drafted new constitutions, guaranteed African American voting rights, and ratified the Fourteenth Amendment, they were eligible for readmission to the Union. Supplementary legislation, also passed over the president's veto, invalidated the provisional governments established by Johnson, empowered the military to administer voter registration, and required an oath of loyalty to the United States.

Congress also passed several laws aimed at limiting Johnson's power. One of these, the Tenure of Office Act, stipulated that any officeholder appointed by the president with the Senate's advice and consent could not be removed until the Senate had approved a successor. In this way, congressional leaders could protect Republi-

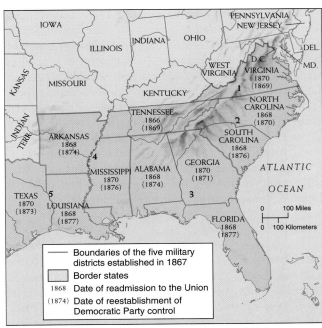

Reconstruction of the South, 1866–1877   *Dates for the readmission of former Confederate states to the Union and the return of Democrats to power varied according to the specific political situations in those states.*

cans, such as Secretary of War Edwin M. Stanton, entrusted with implementing Congressional Reconstruction. In August 1867, with Congress adjourned, Johnson suspended Stanton and appointed General Ulysses S. Grant interim secretary of war. This move enabled the president to remove generals in the field that he judged to be too radical and replace them with men who were sympathetic to his own views. It also served as a challenge to the Tenure of Office Act. In January 1868, when the Senate overruled Stanton's suspension, Grant broke openly with Johnson and vacated the office. Stanton resumed his position and barricaded himself in his office when Johnson attempted to remove him once again.

Outraged by Johnson's relentless obstructionism, and seizing upon his violation of the Tenure of Office Act as a pretext, Radical and moderate Republicans in the House of Representatives again joined forces and voted to impeach the president by a vote of 126 to 47 on February 24, 1868, charging him with eleven counts of high crimes and misdemeanors. To ensure the support of moderate Republicans, the articles of impeachment focused on violations of the Tenure of Office Act. The case against Johnson would have to be made on the basis of willful violation of the law. Left unstated were the Republicans' real reasons for wanting the president removed: Johnson's political views and his opposition to the Reconstruction Acts.

An influential group of moderate Senate Republicans feared the damage a conviction might do to the constitutional separation of powers. They also worried about the political and economic policies that might be pursued by Benjamin Wade, the president pro tem of the Senate and a leader of the Radical Republicans, who, because there was no vice president, would succeed to the presidency if Johnson were removed from office. Behind the scenes during his Senate trial, Johnson agreed to abide by the Reconstruction Acts. In May, the Senate voted 35 for conviction, 19 for acquittal—one vote shy of the two-thirds necessary for removal from office. Johnson's narrow acquittal established the precedent that only criminal actions by a president—not political disagreements—warranted removal from office.

The Election of 1868

By the summer of 1868, seven former Confederate states (Alabama, Arkansas, Florida, Louisiana, North Carolina, South Carolina, and Tennessee) had ratified the revised constitutions, elected Republican governments, and ratified the Fourteenth Amendment. They had thereby earned readmission to the Union. Though Georgia, Mississippi, Texas, and Virginia still awaited readmission, the presidential election of 1868 offered some hope that the Civil War's legacy of sectional hate and racial tension might finally ease.

Republicans nominated Ulysses S. Grant, the North's foremost military hero. An Ohio native, Grant had graduated from West Point in 1843, served in the Mexican War, and resigned from the army in 1854. Unhappy in civilian life, Grant received a second chance during the Civil War. He rose quickly to become commander in the western theater, and he later destroyed Lee's army in Virginia. Although his armies suffered terrible losses, Grant enjoyed tremendous popularity after the war, especially when he broke with Johnson. Totally lacking in political experience, Grant admitted after receiving the nomination that he had been forced into it in spite of himself: "I could not back down without leaving the contest for power for the next four years between mere trading politicians, the elevation of whom, no matter which party won, would lose to us, largely, the results of the costly war which we have gone through."

Significantly, at the very moment that the South was being forced to enfranchise former slaves as a prerequisite for readmission to the Union, the Republicans rejected a campaign plank endorsing black suffrage in the North. Their platform left "the question of suffrage in all the loyal States . . . to the people of those States." State referendums calling for black suffrage failed in eight northern states between 1865 and 1868, succeeding only in Iowa and Minnesota. The Democrats, determined to reverse Congressional Reconstruction, nominated Horatio Seymour, former governor of New York and a long-

time foe of emancipation and supporter of states' rights. Democrats North and South exploited the race question to garner votes. Their platform blasted the Republicans for subjecting the nation "in time of profound peace, to military despotism and negro supremacy." The party sought "the abolition of the Freedmen's Bureau; and all political instrumentalities designed to secure negro supremacy."

Throughout the South, violence marked the electoral process. The Ku Klux Klan, founded as a Tennessee social club in 1866, emerged as a potent instrument of terror (see the opening of this chapter). In Louisiana, Arkansas, Georgia, and South Carolina the Klan threatened, whipped, and murdered black and white Republicans to prevent them from voting. This terrorism enabled the Democrats to carry Georgia and Louisiana, but it ultimately cost the Democrats votes in the North. In the final tally, Grant carried twenty-six of the thirty-four states for an electoral college victory of 214 to 80. But he received a popular majority of less than 53 percent, beating Seymour by only 306,000 votes. Significantly, more than 500,000 African American voters cast their ballots for Grant, demonstrating their overwhelming support for the Republican Party. The Republicans also retained large majorities in both houses of Congress.

In February 1869, Congress passed the Fifteenth Amendment, providing that "the right of citizens of the United States to vote shall not be denied or abridged . . . on account of race, color, or previous condition of servitude." Noticeably absent was language prohibiting the states from imposing educational, residential, or other qualifications for voting. Moderate Republicans feared that filling these discriminatory loopholes might make it difficult to obtain ratification for the amendment by the required three-quarters of the states. To enhance the chances of ratification, Congress required the three remaining unreconstructed states—Mississippi, Texas, and Virginia—to ratify both the Fourteenth and Fifteenth Amendments before readmission. They did so and rejoined the Union in early 1870. The Fifteenth Amendment was ratified in February 1870. In the narrow sense of simply readmitting the former Confederate states to the Union, Reconstruction was complete.

Woman Suffrage and Reconstruction

The battles over the political status of African Americans proved an important turning point for women as well. The Fourteenth and Fifteenth Amendments, which granted citizenship and the vote to freedmen, both inspired and frustrated women's rights activists. Many of these women had long been active in the abolitionist movement. During the war, they had actively supported the union cause through their work

RECONSTRUCTION AMENDMENTS TO THE CONSTITUTION, 1865–1870

Amendment and Date Passed by Congress	Main Provisions	Ratification Process (¾ of all states including ex-Confederate states required)
13 (January 1865)	Prohibited slavery in the United States	December 1865 (27 states, including 8 southern states)
14 (June 1866)	• Conferred national citizenship on all persons born or naturalized in the United States • Reduced state representation in Congress proportionally for any state disfranchising male citizens • Denied former Confederates the right to hold state or national office • Repudiated Confederate debt.	July 1868 (after Congress makes ratification a prerequisite for readmission of ex-Confederate states to the Union)
15 (February 1869)	Prohibited denial of suffrage because of race, color, or previous condition of servitude	March 1870 (ratification required for readmission of Virginia, Texas, Mississippi, and Georgia)

in the National Woman's Loyal League and the United States Sanitary Commission. Elizabeth Cady Stanton and Susan B. Anthony, two leaders with long involvement in both the antislavery and feminist movements, objected to the inclusion of the word "male" in the Fourteenth Amendment. "If that word 'male' be inserted," Stanton predicted in 1866, "it will take us a century at least to get it out."

Insisting that the causes of the African American vote and the women's vote were linked, Stanton, Anthony, and Lucy Stone founded the American Equal Rights Association in 1866. The group launched a series of lobbying and petition campaigns to remove racial and sexual restrictions on voting from state constitutions. In Kansas, for example, an old antislavery battlefield, the association vigorously supported two 1867 referendums that would have removed the words "male" and "white" from the state's constitution. But Kansas voters rejected both woman suffrage and black suffrage. Throughout the nation, the old abolitionist organizations and the Republican Party emphasized passage of the Fourteenth and Fifteenth Amendments and withdrew funds and support from the cause of woman suffrage. Disagreements over these amendments divided suffragists for decades.

The radical wing, led by Stanton and Anthony, opposed the Fifteenth Amendment, arguing that ratification would establish an "aristocracy of sex," enfranchising all men while leaving women without political privileges. In arguing for a Sixteenth Amendment that would secure the vote for women, they used racist and elitist appeals. They urged "American women of wealth, education, virtue, and refinement" to support the vote for women and oppose the Fifteenth Amendment "if you do not wish the lower orders of Chinese, Africans, Germans, and Irish, with their low ideas of womanhood to make laws for you and your daughters." Other women's rights activists, including Lucy Stone and Frederick Douglass, asserted that "this hour belongs to the Negro." They feared a debate over woman suffrage at the national level would jeopardize passage of the two amendments.

By 1869 woman suffragists had split into two competing organizations. The moderate American Woman Suffrage Association (AWSA), led by Lucy Stone, Julia Ward Howe, and Henry Blackwell, focused on achieving woman suffrage at the state level. It maintained close ties with the Republican Party and the old abolitionist networks, worked for the Fifteenth Amendment, and actively sought the support of men. The more radical wing founded the all-female National Woman

Susan B. Anthony (1820–1906) and Elizabeth Cady Stanton (1815–1902), the two most influential leaders of the woman suffrage movement, ca. 1892. Anthony and Stanton broke with their longtime abolitionist allies after the Civil War when they opposed the Fifteenth Amendment. They argued that the doctrine of universal manhood suffrage it embodied would give constitutional authority to the claim that men were the social and political superiors of women. As founders of the militant National Woman Suffrage Association, Stanton and Anthony established an independent woman suffrage movement with a broader spectrum of goals for women's rights and drew millions of women into public life during the late nineteenth century.

Suffrage Association (NWSA). For the NWSA, the vote represented only one part of a broad spectrum of goals inherited from the Declaration of Sentiments manifesto adopted at the first women's rights convention held in 1848 at Seneca Falls, New York (see Chapter 13).

Although women did not win the vote in this period, they did establish an independent suffrage movement that eventually drew millions of women into political life. The NWSA in particular demonstrated that self-government and democratic participation in the public sphere were crucial for women's emancipation. Stanton and Anthony toured the country, speaking to women's audiences and inspiring the formation of suffrage societies. The NWSA's weekly magazine, *Revolution*, became a forum for feminist ideas on divorce laws, unequal pay, women's property rights, and marriage. The failure of woman suffrage after the Civil War was less a result of factional fighting than of the larger defeat of Radical Reconstruction and the ideal of expanded citizenship.

THE MEANING OF FREEDOM

For 4 million slaves, freedom arrived in various ways in different parts of the South. In many areas, slavery had collapsed long before Lee's surrender at Appomattox. In regions far removed from the presence of federal troops, African Americans did not learn of slavery's end until the spring of 1865. There were thousands of sharply contrasting stories, many of which revealed the need for freed slaves to confront their owners. One Virginia slave, hired out to another family during the war, had been working in the fields when a friend told her she was now free. "Is dat so?" she exclaimed. Dropping her hoe, she ran the seven miles to her old place, confronted her former mistress, and shouted, "I'se free! Yes, I'se free! Ain't got to work fo' you no mo'. You can't put me in yo' pocket now!" Her mistress burst into tears and ran into the house. That was all the former slave needed to see. But regardless of specific regional circumstances, the meaning of "freedom" would be contested for years to come.

The deep desire for independence from white control formed the underlying aspiration of newly freed slaves. For their part, most southern white people sought to restrict the boundaries of that independence. As individuals and as members of communities transformed by emancipation, former slaves struggled to establish economic, political, and cultural autonomy. They built on the twin pillars of slave culture—the family and the church—to consolidate and expand African American institutions and thereby laid the foundation for the modern African American community.

Emancipation greatly expanded the choices available to African Americans. It helped build confidence in their ability to effect change without deferring to white people. Freedom also meant greater uncertainty and risk. But the vast majority of African Americans were more than willing to take their chances. Many years later, one former Texas slave pondered the question "What I likes bes, to be slave or free?" She answered: "Well, it's dis way. In slavery I owns nothin' and never owns nothin'. In freedom I's own de home and raise de family. All dat cause me worryment and in slavery I has no worryment, but I takes de freedom."

Moving About

The first impulse of many emancipated slaves was to test their freedom. The simplest, most obvious way to do this involved leaving home. By walking off a plantation, coming and going without restraint or fear of punishment, African Americans could savor freedom. Throughout the summer and fall of 1865, observers in the South noted enormous numbers of freed people on the move. One former slave squatting in an abandoned tent outside Selma, Alabama, explained his feeling to a northern journalist: "I's want to be free man, cum when I please, and nobody say nuffin to me, nor order me roun'." When urged to stay on with the South Carolina family she had served for years as a cook, a slave woman replied firmly: "No, Miss, I must go. If I stay here I'll never know I am free."

Yet many who left their old neighborhoods returned soon afterward to seek work in the general vicinity, or even on the plantation they had left. Many wanted to separate themselves from former owners, but not from familial ties and friendships. Others moved away altogether, seeking jobs in nearby towns and cities. Many former slaves left predominantly white counties, where they felt more vulnerable and isolated, for new lives in the relative comfort of predominantly black communities. In most southern states, there was a significant population shift toward black belt plantation counties and towns after the war. Many African Americans, attracted by schools, churches, and fraternal societies as well as the army, preferred the city. Between 1865 and 1870, the African American population of the South's ten largest cities doubled, while the white population increased by only 10 percent.

Disgruntled planters had difficulty accepting African American independence. During slavery, they had expected obedience, submission, and loyalty from African Americans. Now many could not understand why so many former slaves wanted to leave despite urgent pleas to continue working at the old place. The deference and humility white people expected from African Americans could no longer be taken for granted. Indeed, many freed people went out of their way to reject the old subservience. Moving about freely was one way of doing this, as was refusing to tip one's hat to white people, ignoring former masters or mistresses in the streets, and refusing to step aside on sidewalks. After encountering an African American who would not step aside, Eliza Andrews, a Georgia plantation mistress, complained, "It is the first time in my life that I have ever had to give up the sidewalk to a man, much less to negroes!" When freed people staged parades, dances, and picnics to celebrate their new freedom, as they did, for example, when commemorating the Emancipation Proclamation, white people invariably condemned them angrily for "insolence," "outrageous spectacles," or "putting on airs."

The African American Family

Emancipation allowed freed people to strengthen family ties. For many former slaves, freedom meant the opportunity to reunite with long-lost family members. To track down relatives, freed people trekked to faraway places, put ads in newspapers, sought the help of Freedmen's Bureau agents, and questioned anyone who might have information about loved ones. Many thousands of family reunions, each with its own story, took place after the war. To William Curtis of Georgia, whose father had been sold to a Virginia planter, "that was the best thing about the war setting us free, he could come back to us." One North Carolina slave, who had seen his parents separated by sale, recalled many years later what for him had been the most significant aspect of freedom. "I has got thirteen great-gran' chilluns an' I know whar dey ever'one am. In slavery times dey'd have been on de block long time ago."

Thousands of African American couples who had lived together under slavery streamed to military and civilian authorities and demanded to be legally married. By 1870, the two-parent household was the norm for a large majority of African Americans. "In their eyes," a Freedmen's Bureau agent reported, "the work of emancipation was incomplete until the families which had been dispersed by slavery were reunited." For many freed people the attempt to find lost relatives dragged on for years. Searches often proved frustrating, exhausting, and ultimately disappointing. Some "reunions" ended painfully with the discovery that spouses had found new partners and started new families.

Emancipation brought changes to gender roles within the African American family as well. By serving in the Union army, African American men played a more direct role than women in the fight for freedom. In the political sphere, black men could now serve on juries, vote, and hold office; black women, like their white counterparts, could not. Freedmen's Bureau agents designated the husband as household head and established lower wage scales for women laborers. African American editors, preachers, and politicians regularly quoted the biblical injunction that wives submit to their husbands. African American men asserted their male authority, denied under slavery, by insisting their wives work at home instead of in the fields.

For years after 1865, southern planters complained about the scarcity of women and children available for field work. African American women generally wanted to devote more time than they had under slavery to caring for their children and to performing such domestic chores as cooking, sewing, gardening, and laundering. Yet African American women continued to work outside the home, engaging in seasonal field labor for wages or working a family's rented plot. Most rural black families barely eked out a living, and thus the labor of every family member was essential to survival. The key difference from slave times was that African American families themselves, not white masters and overseers, decided when and where women and children worked.

African American Churches and Schools

The creation of separate African American churches proved the most lasting and important element of the energetic institution building that went on in post-emancipation years. Before the Civil War, southern Protestant churches had relegated slaves and free African Americans to second-class membership. Black worshipers were required to sit in the back during services, they were denied any role in church governance, and they were excluded from Sunday schools. Even in larger cities, where all-black congregations sometimes built their own churches, the law required white pastors. In rural areas, slaves preferred their own preachers to the sermons of local white ministers who quoted Scripture to justify slavery and white supremacy. "That old white preachin' wasn't nothin'," former slave Nancy Williams recalled. "Old white preachers used to talk with their tongues without sayin' nothin', but Jesus told us slaves to talk with our hearts."

In communities around the South, African Americans now pooled their resources to buy land and build their own churches. Before these structures were completed, they might hold services in a railroad boxcar, where Atlanta's First Baptist Church began, or in an outdoor arbor, the original site of the First Baptist Church of Memphis. By late 1866 Charleston's African American community could boast of eleven churches in the city—five Methodist, two Presbyterian, two Episcopalian, one Baptist, and one Congregational. In rural areas, different denominations frequently shared the same church building. Churches became the center not only for religious life but for many other activities that defined the African American community: schools, picnics, festivals, and political meetings. They also helped spawn a host of organizations devoted to benevolence and mutual aid, such as burial societies, Masonic lodges, temperance clubs, and trade associations.

The church became the first social institution fully controlled by African Americans. In nearly every community ministers, respected for their speaking and organizational skills, were among the most influential leaders. By 1877 the great majority of black Southerners had withdrawn from white-dominated churches. In South Carolina, for example, only a few hundred black Methodists attended biracial churches, down from over 40,000 in 1865. The various Protestant denominations competed for the allegiance of African American worshipers. Among Methodists, the African Methodist

Episcopal Church, originally founded in 1816, gained ascendancy over white-dominated rivals. Black Baptist churches, with their decentralized and democratic structure and more emotional services, attracted the greatest number of freed people. By the end of Reconstruction the vast majority of African American Christians belonged to black Baptist or Methodist churches.

The rapid spread of schools reflected African Americans' thirst for self-improvement. Southern states had prohibited education for slaves. But many free black people managed to attend school, and a few slaves had been able to educate themselves. Still, over 90 percent of the South's adult African American population was illiterate in 1860. Access to education thus became a central part of the meaning of freedom. Freedmen's Bureau agents repeatedly expressed amazement at the number of makeshift classrooms organized by African Americans in rural areas. A bureau officer described these "wayside schools": "A negro riding on a loaded wagon, or sitting on a hack waiting for a train, or by the cabin door, is often seen, book in hand delving after the rudiments of knowledge. A group on the platform of a depot, after carefully conning an old spelling book, resolves itself into a class."

African American communities received important educational aid from outside organizations. By 1869 the Freedmen's Bureau was supervising nearly 3,000 schools serving over 150,000 students throughout the South. Over half the roughly 3,300 teachers in these schools were African Americans, many of whom had been free before the Civil War. Other teachers included dedicated northern white women, volunteers sponsored by the American Missionary Association (AMA). The bureau and the AMA also assisted in the founding of several black colleges, including Tougaloo, Hampton, and Fisk, designed to train black teachers. Black self-help proved crucial to the education effort. Throughout the South in 1865 and 1866, African Americans raised money to build schoolhouses, buy supplies, and pay teachers. Black artisans donated labor for construction, and black families offered room and board to teachers.

Land and Labor after Slavery

Most newly emancipated African Americans aspired to quit the plantations and to make new lives for themselves. Leaving the plantation was not as simple as walking off. Some freed people did find jobs in railroad building, mining, ranching, or construction work. Others raised subsistence crops and tended vegetable gardens as squatters. However, white planters tried to retain African Americans as permanent agricultural laborers. Restricting the employment of former slaves was an important goal of the black codes. For example, South Carolina legislation in 1865 provided that "no person of color shall pursue or practice the art, trade, or business of an artisan, mechanic, or shopkeeper, or any other trade employment, or business, besides that of husbandry, or that of a servant under contract for service or labor" without a special and costly permit.

The majority of African Americans hoped to become self-sufficient farmers. As *DeBow's Review* observed in 1869, the freedman showed "great anxiety to have his little home, with his horse, cow, and hogs, separate and apart from others." Many former slaves believed they were entitled to the land they had worked throughout their lives. General Oliver O. Howard, chief commissioner of the Freedmen's Bureau, observed that many "supposed that the Government [would] divide among them the lands of the conquered owners, and furnish them with all that might be necessary to begin life as an independent farmer." This perception was not merely a wishful fantasy. The Freedmen's Bureau Act of 1865 specifically required that abandoned land be leased for three years in forty-acre lots, with an option to buy. Frequent reference in the Congress and the press to the question of land distribution made the idea of "forty acres and a mule" not just a pipe dream but a matter of serious public debate.

Above all, African Americans sought economic autonomy, and ownership of land promised the most independence. "Give us our own land and we take care of ourselves," was how one former slave saw it. "But widout land, de ole massas can hire us or starve us, as dey please." At a Colored Convention in Montgomery, Alabama, in May 1867, delegates argued that the property now owned by planters had been "nearly all earned by the sweat of our brows, not theirs. It has been forfeited to the government by the treason of its owners, and is liable to be confiscated whenever the Republican Party demands it."

But by 1866 the federal government had already pulled back from the various wartime experiments involving the breaking up of large plantations and the leasing of small plots to individual families. President Johnson directed General Howard of the Freedmen's Bureau to evict tens of thousands of freed people settled on confiscated and abandoned land in southeastern Virginia, southern Louisiana, and the Georgia and South Carolina low country. These evictions created a deep sense of betrayal among African Americans. A former Mississippi slave, Merrimon Howard, bitterly noted that African Americans had been left with "no land, no house, not so much as a place to lay our head. . . . We were friends on the march, brothers on the battlefield, but in the peaceful pursuits of life it seems that we are strangers."

A variety of labor arrangements could be found in southern agriculture in the immediate postwar years. Each featured both advantages and disadvantages for planters and freed people. Writing in 1866, white planter Percy Roberts identified three distinct "systems of hire" for working the land: money wages, share wages, and sharecropping. Under both the money wage and share wage systems, planters contracted former slaves to work in large gangs, paying them either in

Leaving for Kansas, Harper's Weekly, May 17, 1879. *This drawing depicts a group of southern freedpeople on their way to Kansas. Black disillusionment following the end of Reconstruction led thousands of African Americans to migrate to Kansas, where they hoped to find the political rights, economic opportunities, and freedom from violence denied them in the South. Most of these "Exodusters" (after the biblical story of the Israelite Exodus from Egypt) lacked the capital or experience to establish themselves as independent farmers on the Great Plains. Yet few chose to go back to the South, where their former masters had returned to political and economic power.*

cash (money wage) or with a share of the crop that the workers divided among themselves (share wage). Freedmen's Bureau agents, who generally advocated the money wage arrangement, would often help freedmen negotiate labor contracts with planters. Planters tended to prefer the money wage system because it clearly defined laborers as hirelings and gave planters more direct control over the labor force—for example, by enabling them to discharge the hands they thought inefficient. Yet most planters were forced to adopt share wages at the insistence of black laborers who were adamantly opposed to serving as mere hirelings.

But both the money wage and share wage systems were unsatisfactory from the perspective of freed people. Both systems relied on the gang labor approach so reminiscent of slavery. And both systems often left African Americans at the mercy of unscrupulous planters who cheated them of their wages or fair

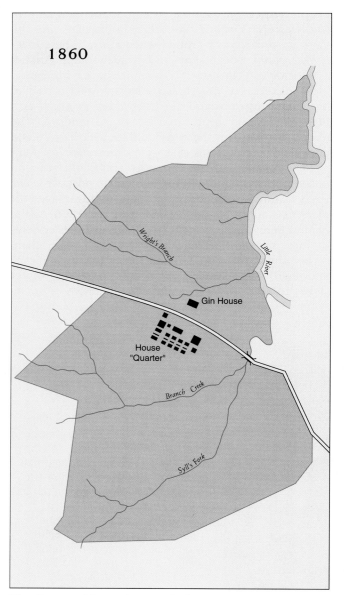

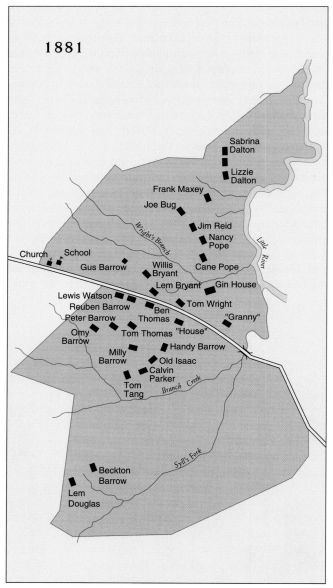

The Barrow Plantation, Oglethorpe County, Georgia, 1860 and 1881 (approx. 2,000 acres)   *These two maps, based on drawings from* Scribner's Monthly, *April 1881, show some of the changes brought by emancipation. In 1860 the plantation's entire black population lived in the communal slave quarters, right next to the white master's house. In 1881 black sharecropper and tenant families lived on individual plots, spread out across the land. The former slaves had also built their own school and church.*

shares. Above all, the deep desire for economic improvement and greater autonomy led many African Americans to press for an alternative. By the late 1860s, black people's resistance to working in gangs and their desire to establish independent homesteads forced planters into a compromise system, sharecropping, that emerged as the dominant form of working the land.

Under sharecropping arrangements, individual families contracted with landowners to be responsible for a specific plot. Large plantations were thus broken into family-sized farms. Generally, sharecropper families received one-third of the year's crop if the owner furnished implements, seed, and draft animals, or one-half if they provided their own supplies. African Americans preferred sharecropping to gang labor, as it allowed families to set their own hours and tasks and offered freedom from white supervision and control. For planters, the system stabilized the work force by requiring sharecroppers to remain until the harvest and to employ all family members. It also offered a way around the chronic shortage of cash and credit that plagued the postwar South. But as the *Southern Argus* of Selma, Alabama, editorialized, sharecropping was "an unwilling concession to the freedmen's desire to become a proprietor. . . . It is not a voluntary association from similarity of aims and interests." Freed people did not aspire to sharecropping. Owning land outright or tenant farming (renting land) were both more desirable. But though black sharecroppers clearly enjoyed more autonomy than in the past, the vast majority never achieved economic independence or land ownership. They remained a largely subordinate agricultural labor force.

Sharecropping came to dominate the southern agricultural economy and African American life in particular. By 1880 about 80 percent of the land in the black belt states—Mississippi, Alabama, and Georgia—had been divided into family-sized farms. Nearly three-quarters of black Southerners were sharecroppers. Through much of the black belt, family and community were one. Often several families worked adjoining parcels of land in common, pooling their labor in order to get by. Men usually oversaw crop production. Women went to the fields seasonally during planting or harvesting, but they mainly tended to household chores and child care. In addition, women frequently held jobs that might bring in cash, such as raising chickens or taking in laundry. The cotton harvest engaged all members of the community, from the oldest to the youngest. Cotton picking remained a difficult, labor-intensive task that took priority over all other work.

The Origins of African American Politics

Although the desire for autonomy had led African Americans to pursue their economic and religious goals largely apart from white people, inclusion rather than separation was the objective of early African American political activity. The greatest political activity by African Americans occurred in areas occupied by Union forces during the war. In 1865 and 1866, African Americans throughout the South organized scores of mass meetings, parades, and petitions that demanded civil equality and the right to vote. In the cities, the growing web of churches and fraternal societies helped bolster early efforts at political organization.

Hundreds of African American delegates, selected by local meetings or churches, attended statewide political conventions held throughout the South in 1865 and 1866. Previously free African Americans, as well as black ministers, artisans, and veterans of the Union army, tended to dominate these proceedings, setting a pattern that would hold throughout Reconstruction. Convention debates sometimes reflected the tensions within African American communities, such as friction between poorer former slaves and better-off free black people, or between lighter- and darker-skinned African Americans. But most of these state gatherings concentrated on passing resolutions on issues that united all African Americans. The central concerns were suffrage and equality before the law. Black Southerners firmly proclaimed their identification with the nation's history and republican traditions. The 1865 North Carolina freedmen's convention was typical in describing universal manhood suffrage as "an essential and inseparable element of self-government." It also praised the Declaration of Independence as "the broadest, the deepest, the most comprehensive and truthful definition of human freedom that was ever given to the world."

The passage of the First Reconstruction Act in 1867 encouraged even more political activity among African Americans. The military started registering the South's electorate, ultimately enrolling approximately 735,000 black and 635,000 white voters in the ten unreconstructed states. Five states—Alabama, Florida, Louisiana, Mississippi, and South Carolina—had black electoral majorities. Fewer than half the registered white voters participated in the elections for state constitutional conventions in 1867 and 1868. In contrast, four-fifths of the registered black voters cast ballots in these elections. Much of this new African American political activism was channeled through local Union League chapters throughout the South. However, as the fate of Alex Webb in Hale County, Alabama, again makes clear, few whites welcomed this activism.

Begun during the war as a northern, largely white middle-class patriotic club, the Union League now became the political voice of the former slaves. Union League chapters brought together local African Americans, soldiers, and Freedmen's Bureau agents to demand the vote and an end to legal discrimination

Electioneering at the South, Harper's Weekly, July 25, 1868. *Throughout the Reconstruction-era South, newly freed slaves took a keen interest in both local and national political affairs. The presence of women and children at these campaign gatherings illustrates the importance of contemporary political issues to the entire African American community.*

against African Americans. It brought out African American voters, instructed freedmen in the rights and duties of citizenship, and promoted Republican candidates. Not surprisingly, newly enfranchised freedmen voted Republican and formed the core of the Republican Party in the South.

In 1867 and 1868, the promise of Radical Reconstruction enlarged the scope of African American political participation and brought new leaders to the fore. Many were teachers, preachers, or others with useful skills, such as literacy. For most ordinary African Americans, politics was inseparable from economic issues, especially the land question. Grassroots political organizations frequently intervened in local disputes with planters over the terms of labor contracts. African American political groups closely followed the congressional debates over Reconstruction policy and agitated for land confiscation and distribution. Perhaps most important, politics was the only arena where black and white Southerners might engage each other on an equal basis. As the delegates to an Alabama convention asserted in 1867: "We claim exactly the same rights, privileges and immunities as are enjoyed by white men—we ask nothing more and will be content with nothing less. . . . The law no longer knows white nor black, but simply the men, and consequently we are entitled to ride in public conveyances, hold office, sit on juries and do everything else which we have in the past been prevented from doing solely on the ground of color."

SOUTHERN POLITICS AND SOCIETY

By the summer of 1868, when the South had returned to the Union, the majority of Republicans believed the task of Reconstruction to be finished. Ultimately, they put their faith in a political solution to the problems facing the vanquished South. That meant nurturing a viable two-party system in the southern states, where no Republican Party had ever existed. If that could be accomplished, Republicans and Democrats would compete for votes, offices, and influence, just as they did in northern states. Most Republican congressmen were moderates, conceiving Reconstruction in limited terms. They rejected radical calls for confiscation and redistribution of land, as well as permanent military rule of the South. The Reconstruction Acts of 1867 and 1868 laid out the requirements for the readmission of southern states, along with the procedures for forming and electing new governments.

Yet over the next decade the political structure created in the southern states proved too restricted and fragile to sustain itself. Republicans had to employ radical means to protect their essentially conservative goals. To most southern whites the active participation of African Americans in politics seemed extremely dangerous. Federal troops were needed to protect Republican governments and their supporters from violent opposition. Congressional action to monitor southern elections and protect black voting rights became routine. Despite initial successes, southern Republicanism proved an unstable coalition of often conflicting elements, unable to sustain effective power for very long. By 1877, Democrats had regained political control of all the former Confederate states.

Southern Republicans

Three major groups composed the fledgling Republican coalition in the postwar South. African American voters made up a large majority of southern Republicans throughout the Reconstruction era. Yet African Americans outnumbered whites in only three southern states—South Carolina, Mississippi, and Louisiana. They made up roughly one-quarter of the population in Texas, Tennessee, and Arkansas, and between 40 and 50 percent in Virginia, North Carolina, Alabama, Florida, and Georgia. Thus, Republicans would have to attract white support to win elections and sustain power.

A second group consisted of white Northerners, derisively called "carpetbaggers" by native white Southerners. One Democratic congressman in 1871 said the term "applied to the office seeker from the North who came here seeking office by the negroes, by arraying their political passions and prejudices against the white people of the community." In fact, most carpet-baggers combined a desire for personal gain with a commitment to reform the "unprogressive" South by developing its material resources and introducing Yankee institutions such as free labor and free public schools. Most were veterans of the Union army who stayed in the South after the war. Others included Freedmen's Bureau agents and businessmen who had invested capital in cotton plantations and other enterprises.

Carpetbaggers tended to be well educated and from the middle class. Albert Morgan, for example, was an army veteran from Ohio who settled in Mississippi after the war. When he and his brother failed at running a cotton plantation and sawmill, Morgan became active in Republican politics as a way to earn a living. He won election to the state constitutional convention, became a power in the state legislature, and risked his life to keep the Republican organization alive in the Mississippi delta region. Although they made up a tiny percentage of the population, carpetbaggers played a disproportionately large role in southern politics. They won a large share of Reconstruction offices, particularly in Florida, South Carolina, and Louisiana and in areas with large African American constituencies.

The third major group of southern Republicans were the native whites pejoratively termed "scalawags." They had even more diverse backgrounds and motives than the northern-born Republicans. Some were prominent prewar Whigs who saw the Republican Party as their best chance to regain political influence. Others viewed the party as an agent of modernization and economic expansion. "Yankees and Yankee notions are just what we want in this country," argued Thomas Settle of North Carolina. "We want their capital to build factories and workshops. We want their intelligence, their energy and enterprise." Their greatest influence lay in the up-country strongholds of southern Unionism, such as eastern Tennessee, western North Carolina, and northern Alabama. Loyalists during the war, traditional enemies of the planter elite (most were small farmers), these white Southerners looked to the Republican Party for help in settling old scores and relief from debt and wartime devastation.

Deep contradictions strained the alliance of these three groups. Southern Republicans touted themselves as the "party of progress and civilization" and promised a new era of material progress for the region. Republican state conventions in 1867 and 1868 voiced support for internal improvements, public schools, debt relief, and railroad building. Yet few white Southerners identified with the political and economic aspirations of African Americans. Nearly every party convention split between "confiscation radicals" (generally African Americans) and moderate elements committed to white

control of the party and to economic development that offered more to outside investors than to impoverished African Americans and poor whites.

Reconstructing the States: A Mixed Record

With the old Confederate leaders barred from political participation, and with carpetbaggers and newly enfranchised African Americans representing many of the plantation districts, Republicans managed to dominate the ten southern constitutional conventions of 1867–69. Well-educated carpetbaggers usually chaired the important committees and drafted key provisions of the new constitutions. Most of the delegates were southern white Republicans. African Americans formed a majority of the conventions in Louisiana and South Carolina, but they were generally under-represented. In all, there were 258 African Americans among the 1,027 convention delegates at the ten conventions.

This poster, ca. 1880, honored seven prominent ex-slaves, including U.S. Senators Hiram R. Revels and Blanche K. Bruce, both representing Mississippi. In the center is Frederick Douglass. This poster was typical of many other Reconstruction-era prints celebrating the entry of African Americans into state and national legislatures.

Most of the conventions produced constitutions that expanded democracy and the public role of the state. The new documents guaranteed the political and civil rights of African Americans, and they abolished property qualifications for officeholding and jury service, as well as imprisonment for debt. They created the first state-funded systems of education in the South, to be administered by state commissioners. The new constitutions also mandated establishment of orphanages, penitentiaries, and homes for the insane. The changes wrought in the South's political landscape seemed quite radical to many. In 1868, only three years after the end of the war, Republicans came to power in most of the southern states. By 1869 new constitutions had been ratified in all the old Confederate states. "These constitutions and governments," one South Carolina Democratic newspaper vowed bitterly, "will last just as long as the bayonets which ushered them into being, shall keep them in existence, and not one day longer."

Republican governments in the South faced a continual crisis of legitimacy that limited their ability to legislate change. They had to balance reform against the need to gain acceptance, especially by white Southerners. Their achievements were thus mixed. In the realm of race relations there was a clear thrust toward equal rights and against discrimination. Republican legislatures followed up the federal Civil Rights Act of 1866 with various antidiscrimination clauses in new constitutions and laws prescribing harsh penalties for civil rights violations. While most African Americans supported autonomous African American churches, fraternal societies, and schools, they insisted that the state be color-blind. African Americans could now be employed in police forces and fire departments, serve on juries, school boards, and city councils, and hold public office at all levels of government.

Segregation, though, became the norm in public school systems. African American leaders often accepted segregation because they feared that insistence on integrated education would jeopardize funding for the new school systems. They generally agreed with Frederick Douglass that separate schools were "infinitely superior" to no schools at all. So while they opposed constitutional language requiring racial segregation in schools, most African Americans were less interested in the abstract ideal of integrated education than in ensuring educational opportunities for their children and employment for African American teachers. Many, in fact, believed all-black schools offered a better chance of securing these goals.

Patterns of discrimination persisted. Demands by African Americans to prohibit segregation in railroad cars, steamboats, theaters, and other public spaces revealed and heightened the divisions within the Republican Party. Moderate white Republicans feared such laws would only further alienate potential white supporters. But by the early 1870s, as black influence and assertiveness grew, laws guaranteeing equal access to transportation and public accommodation were passed in many states. By and large, though, such civil rights laws were difficult to enforce in local communities.

In economic matters, Republican governments failed to fulfill African Americans' hopes of obtaining land. Few former slaves possessed the cash to buy land in the open market, and they looked to the state for help. Republicans tried to weaken the plantation system and promote black ownership by raising taxes on land. Yet even when state governments seized land for nonpayment of taxes, the property was never used to help create black homesteads. In Mississippi, for example, 6 million acres, or about 20 percent of the land, had been forfeited by 1875. Yet virtually all of it found its way back to the original owners after they paid minimal penalties.

Republican leaders emphasized the "gospel of prosperity" as the key to improving the economic fortunes of all Southerners, black and white. Essentially, they envisioned promoting northern-style capitalist development—factories, large towns, and diversified agriculture—through state aid. Much Republican state lawmaking was devoted to encouraging railroad construction. Between 1868 and 1873 state legislatures passed hundreds of bills promoting railroads. Most of the government aid consisted not of direct cash subsidies but of official endorsements of a company's bonds. This government backing gave railroad companies credibility and helped them raise capital. In exchange, states received liens on railroads as security against defaults on payments to bondholders.

Between 1868 and 1872 the southern railroad system was rebuilt and over 3,000 new miles of track added, an increase of almost 40 percent. But in spite of all the new laws, it proved impossible to attract significant amounts of northern and European investment capital. The obsession with railroads drew resources from education and other programs. As in the North, it also opened the doors to widespread corruption and bribery of public officials. Finally, the frenzy of railroad promotion soon led to an overextension of credit and to many bankruptcies, saddling Republican governments with enormous debts. Railroad failures eroded public confidence in the Republicans' ability to govern. The "gospel of prosperity" ultimately failed to modernize the economy or solidify the Republican Party in the South.

White Resistance and "Redemption"

The emergence of a Republican Party in the reconstructed South brought two parties but not a two-party system to the region. The opponents of Reconstruction, the Democrats, refused to acknowledge Republi-

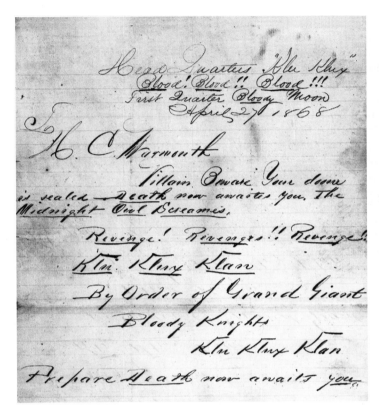

The Ku Klux Klan emerged as a potent political and social force during Reconstruction, terrorizing freedpeople and their white allies. An 1868 Klan warning threatens Louisiana governor Henry C. Warmoth with death. Warmoth, an Illinois-born "carpetbagger," was the state's first Republican governor. Two Alabama Klansmen, photographed in 1868, wear white hoods to protect their identities.

cans' right to participate in southern political life. In their view, the Republican Party, supported primarily by the votes of former slaves, was the partisan instrument of the northern Congress. Since Republicans controlled state governments, this denial of legitimacy meant, in effect, a rejection of state authority itself. In each state, Republicans were split between those who urged conciliation in an effort to gain white acceptance and those who emphasized consolidating the party under the protection of the military.

From 1870 to 1872 the Ku Klux Klan fought an ongoing terrorist campaign against Reconstruction governments and local leaders. Although not centrally organized, the Klan was a powerful presence in nearly every southern state. It acted as a kind of guerrilla military force in the service of the Democratic Party, the planter class, and all those who sought the restoration of white supremacy. Klansmen employed violence to intimidate African Americans and white Republicans, murdering innocent people, driving them from their homes, and destroying their property. Planters sometimes employed Klansmen to enforce labor discipline

by driving African Americans off plantations to deprive them of their harvest share.

In October 1870, after Republicans carried Laurens County in South Carolina, bands of white people drove 150 African Americans from their homes and murdered 13 black and white Republican activists. In March 1871, three African Americans were arrested in Meridian, Mississippi, for giving "incendiary" speeches. At their court hearing, Klansmen killed two of the defendants and the Republican judge, and thirty more African Americans were murdered in a day of rioting. The single bloodiest episode of Reconstruction era violence took place in Colfax, Louisiana, on Easter Sunday 1873. Nearly 100 African Americans were murdered after they failed to hold a besieged courthouse during a contested election. One former Confederate officer observed that the Klan's goal was "to defy the reconstructed State Governments, to treat them with contempt, and show that they have no real existence."

Southern Republicans looked to Washington for help. In 1870 and 1871 Congress passed three Enforcement Acts designed to counter racial terrorism.

These declared interference with voting a federal offense, provided for federal supervision of voting, and authorized the president to send the army and suspend the writ of habeas corpus in districts declared to be in a state of insurrection. The most sweeping measure was the Ku Klux Klan Act of April 1871, which made the violent infringement of civil and political rights a federal crime punishable by the national government. Attorney General Amos T. Akerman prosecuted hundreds of Klansmen in North Carolina and Mississippi. In October 1871 President Grant sent federal troops to occupy nine South Carolina counties and round up thousands of Klan members. By the election of 1872 the federal government's intervention had helped break the Klan and restore a semblance of law and order .

The Civil Rights Act of 1875 outlawed racial discrimination in theaters, hotels, railroads, and other public places. But the law proved more an assertion of principle than a direct federal intervention in southern affairs. Enforcement required African Americans to take their cases to the federal courts, a costly and time-consuming procedure.

As wartime idealism faded, northern Republicans became less inclined toward direct intervention in southern affairs. They had enough trouble retaining political control in the North. In 1874 the Democrats gained a majority in the House of Representatives for the first time since 1856. Key northern states also began to fall to the Democrats. Northern Republicans slowly abandoned the freedmen and their white allies in the South. Southern Democrats were also able to exploit a deepening fiscal crisis by blaming Republicans for excessive extension of public credit and the sharp increase in tax rates. Republican governments had indeed spent public money for new state school systems, orphanages, roads, and other internal improvements.

Gradually, conservative Democrats "redeemed" one state after another. Virginia and Tennessee led the way in 1869, North Carolina in 1870, Georgia in 1871, Texas in 1873, and Alabama and Arkansas in 1874. In Mississippi, white conservatives employed violence and intimidation to wrest control in 1875 and "redeemed" the state the following year. Republican infighting in Louisiana in 1873 and 1874 led to a series of contested election results, including bloody clashes between black militia and armed whites, and finally to "redemption" by the Democrats in 1877. Once these states returned to Democratic rule, African Americans faced obstacles to voting, more stringent controls on plantation labor, and deep cuts in social services.

Several Supreme Court rulings involving the Fourteenth and Fifteenth Amendments effectively constrained federal protection of African American civil rights. In the so-called Slaughterhouse cases of 1873, the Court issued its first ruling on the Fourteenth Amendment. The cases involved a Louisiana charter that gave a New Orleans meat-packing company a monopoly over the city's butchering business on the grounds of protecting public health. A rival group of butchers had sued, claiming the law violated the Fourteenth Amendment, which prohibited states from depriving any person of life, liberty, or property without due process of law. The Court held that the Fourteenth Amendment protected only the former slaves, not butchers, and that it protected only national citizenship rights, not the regulatory powers of states. The ruling in effect denied the original intent of the Fourteenth Amendment—to protect against state infringement of national citizenship rights as spelled out in the Bill of Rights.

Three other decisions curtailed federal protection of black civil rights. In *U.S. v. Reese* (1876) and *U.S. v. Cruikshank* (1876) the Court restricted congressional power to enforce the Ku Klux Klan Act. Future prosecution would depend on the states rather than on federal authorities. In these rulings the Court held that the Fourteenth Amendment extended the federal power to protect civil rights only in cases involving discrimination by states; discrimination by individuals or groups was not covered. The Court also ruled that the Fifteenth Amendment did not guarantee a citizen's right to vote; it only barred certain specific grounds for denying suffrage—"race, color, or previous condition of servitude." This interpretation opened the door for southern states to disfranchise African Americans for allegedly nonracial reasons. States back under Democratic control began to limit African American voting by passing laws restricting voter eligibility through poll taxes and property requirements.

Finally, in the 1883 Civil Rights Cases decision, the Court declared the Civil Rights Act of 1875 unconstitutional, holding that the Fourteenth Amendment gave Congress the power to outlaw discrimination by states, but not by private individuals. The majority opinion held that black people must no longer "be the special favorite of the laws." Together, these Supreme Court decisions marked the end of federal attempts to protect African American rights until well into the next century.

"King Cotton" and the Crop Lien System

The Republicans' vision of a "New South" remade along the lines of the northern economy failed to materialize. Instead, the South declined into the country's poorest agricultural region. Unlike midwestern and western farm towns burgeoning from trade in wheat, corn, and livestock, southern communities found themselves

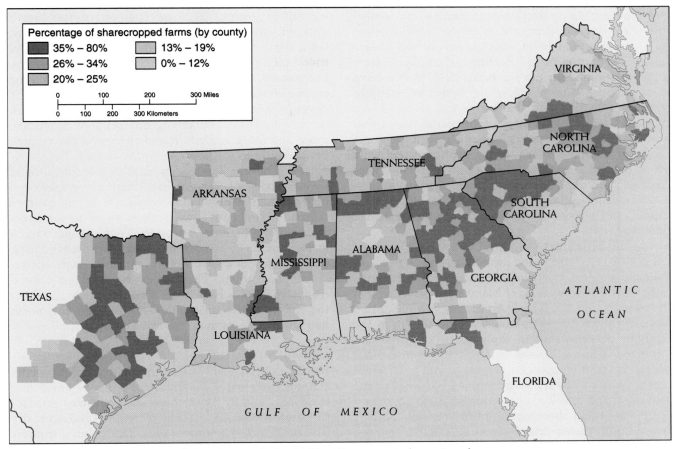

Southern Sharecropping and the Cotton Belt, 1880 *The economic depression of the 1870s forced increasing numbers of southern farmers, both white and black, into sharecropping arrangements. Sharecropping was most pervasive in the cotton belt regions of South Carolina, Georgia, Alabama, Mississippi, and east Texas.*

almost entirely dependent on the price of one commodity. Cotton growing had defined the economic life of large plantations in the coastal regions and black belt communities of the antebellum South. In the post–Civil War years "King Cotton" expanded its realm, as greater numbers of small white farmers found themselves forced to switch from subsistence crops to growing cotton for the market. The transition to cotton dependency developed unevenly, at different speeds in different parts of the South. Penetration by railroads, the availability of commercial fertilizers, and the opening up of new lands to cultivation were key factors in transforming communities from diversified, locally oriented farming to the market-oriented production of cotton.

The spread of the crop lien system as the South's main form of agricultural credit forced more and more farmers, both white and black, into cotton growing. This system developed because a chronic

shortage of capital and banking institutions made local merchants and planters the sole source of credit. They advanced loans to small owners, sharecroppers, and tenant farmers only in exchange for a lien, or claim, on the year's cotton crop. Merchants and planters frequently charged exorbitant interest rates on advances, as well as marking up the prices of the goods they sold in their stores. Taking advantage of the high illiteracy rates among poor Southerners, landlords and merchants easily altered their books to inflate the figures. At the end of the year, sharecroppers and tenants found themselves deep in debt to stores (many owned by Northerners) for seed, supplies, and clothing. Despite hard work and even bountiful harvests, few small farmers could escape from heavy debt.

As more and more white and black farmers turned to cotton growing as the only way to obtain credit, expanding production depressed prices. Competition from new cotton centers in the world market, such as Egypt and India, accelerated the downward spiral. As cotton prices declined alarmingly, from roughly eleven cents per pound in 1875 to five cents in 1894, per capita wealth in the South fell steadily, equaling only one-third that of the East, Midwest, or West by the 1890s. Cotton dependency had other repercussions. The planters lacked capital to purchase the farm equipment needed to profitably cultivate wheat or corn, and their reliance on cheap labor kept them wedded to cotton. Planters persisted in employing hand labor and mule power. As soil depletion took its toll, crop outputs, or yields per acre, either remained steady or fell.

Small farmers caught up in a vicious cycle of low cotton prices, debt, and dwindling food crops found their old ideal of independence sacrificed to the cruel logic of the cotton market. Many must have sympathized with men like John F. Armstrong, a white cotton farmer in the Georgia up-country, who fled from the crushing burdens of debt, only to be captured and returned. "I just got tired of working for the other fellow," he grimly explained. "I worked and toiled from year to year and all the fruits of my labor went to the man who never struck a lick. . . . I never made anything."

By 1880, about one-third of the white farmers and nearly three-quarters of the African American farmers in the cotton states were sharecroppers or tenants. Of the roughly 1.1 million farms in the nine large cotton-planting states that year, sharecroppers worked 301,000 of them. Many former slaves and poor white people had tried subsistence farming in the undeveloped backcountry. Yet to obtain precious credit, most found themselves forced to produce cotton for market and thus became enmeshed in the debt-ridden crop lien system. In traditional cotton producing areas, especially the black belt, landless farmers growing cotton had replaced slaves growing cotton. In the up-country and newer areas of cultivation, cotton-dominated commercial agriculture, with landless tenants and sharecroppers as the main workforce, had replaced the more diversified subsistence economy of the antebellum era.

RECONSTRUCTING THE NORTH

Abraham Lincoln liked to cite his own rise as proof of the superiority of the northern system of "free labor" over slavery. "There is no permanent class of hired laborers amongst us," Lincoln asserted. "Twenty-five years ago, I was a hired laborer. The hired laborer of yesterday, labors on his own account today; and will hire others to labor for him tomorrow. Advancement—improvement in condition—is the order of things in a society of equals." But the triumph of the North brought with it fundamental changes in the economy, labor relations, and politics that brought Lincoln's ideal vision into question. The spread of the factory system, the growth of large and powerful corporations, and the rapid expansion of capitalist enterprise all hastened the development of a large unskilled and routinized work force. Rather than becoming independent producers, more and more workers found themselves consigned permanently to wage labor.

The old Republican ideal of a society bound by a harmony of interests had become overshadowed by a grimmer reality of class conflict. A violent national railroad strike in 1877 was broken only with the direct intervention of federal troops. That conflict struck many Americans as a turning point. Northern society, like the society of the South, appeared more hierarchical than equal. That same year, the last federal troops withdrew from their southern posts, marking the end of the Reconstruction era. By then, the North had undergone its own "reconstruction" as well.

The Age of Capital

In the decade following Appomattox, the North's economy continued the industrial boom begun during the Civil War. By 1873, America's industrial production had grown 75 percent over the 1865 level. By that time, too, the number of nonagricultural workers in the North had surpassed the number of farmers. Between 1860 and 1880 the number of wage earners in manufacturing and construction more than doubled, from 2 million to over 4 million. Only Great Britain boasted a larger manufacturing economy than the United States. During the same period, nearly 3 million immigrants arrived in America, almost all of whom settled in the North and West.

The railroad business both symbolized and advanced the new industrial order. Shortly before the Civil War, enthusiasm mounted for a transcontinental line. Private companies took on the huge and expensive job of construction, but the federal government funded the project, providing the largest subsidy in American history. The Pacific Railway Act of 1862 granted the Union Pacific and the Central Pacific rights to a broad swath of land extending from Omaha, Nebraska, to Sacramento, California. An 1864 act bestowed a subsidy of $15,000 per mile of track laid over smooth plains country and varying larger amounts up to $48,000 per mile in the foothills and mountains of the Far West. The Union Pacific employed gangs of Irish American and African American workers to lay track heading west from Omaha, while the Central Pacific brought in more than 10,000 men from China to handle the difficult work in the Sierra Nevada mountain region.

Completion of the transcontinental railroad, May 10, 1869, as building crews for the Union Pacific and Central Pacific meet at Promontory Point, Utah. The two locomotive engineers salute each other, while the chief engineers for the two railroads shake hands. Construction had begun simultaneously from Omaha and Sacramento in 1863, with the help of generous subsidies from Congress. Work crews, consisting of thousands of ex-soldiers, Irish immigrants, and imported Chinese laborers, laid nearly 1,800 miles of new track.

On May 10, 1869, Leland Stanford, the former governor of California and president of the Central Pacific Railroad, traveled to Promontory Point in Utah Territory to hammer a ceremonial golden spike, marking the finish of the first transcontinental line. Other railroads went up with less fanfare. The Southern Pacific, chartered by the state of California, stretched from San Francisco to Los Angeles, and on through Arizona and New Mexico to connections with New Orleans. The Atchison, Topeka, and Santa Fe reached the Pacific in 1887 by way of a southerly route across the Rocky Mountains. The Great Northern, one of the few lines financed by private capital, extended west from St. Paul, Minnesota, to Washington's Puget Sound.

Railroads paved the way for the rapid settlement of the West, and both rural and urban areas grew dramatically over the next several decades. The combined population of Minnesota, the Dakotas, Nebraska, and Kansas, for example, jumped from 300,000 in 1860 to over 2 million in 1880. In the fifty years after 1870, the nation's railroad system expanded to more than a quarter million miles—more than all the rest of the world's railroad track combined.

Railroad corporations became America's first big businesses. Railroads required huge outlays of investment capital, and their growth increased the economic power of banks and investment houses centered in Wall Street. Bankers often gained seats on boards of directors, and their access to capital some-

times gave them the real control of lines. By the early 1870s the Pennsylvania Railroad stood as the nation's largest single company, with more than 20,000 employees. A new breed of aggressive entrepreneur sought to ease cutthroat competition by absorbing smaller companies and forming "pools" that set rates and divided the market. A small group of railroad executives, including Cornelius Vanderbilt, Jay Gould, Collis P. Huntington, and James J. Hill, amassed unheard-of fortunes. When he died in 1877, Vanderbilt left his son $100 million. By comparison, a decent annual wage for working a six-day week was around $350.

A growing number of Republican politicians maintained close connections with railroad interests. Railroad promoters, lawyers, and lobbyists became ubiquitous figures in Washington and state capitals, wielding enormous influence among lawmakers. "The galleries and lobbies of every legislature," one Republican leader noted, "are thronged with men seeking . . . an advantage." Railroads benefited enormously from government subsidies. Between 1862 and 1872 Congress alone awarded more than 100 million acres of public lands to railroad companies and provided them over $64 million in loans and tax incentives.

Some of the nation's most prominent politicians routinely accepted railroad largesse. Republican senator William M. Stewart of Nevada, a member of the Committee on Pacific Railroads, received a gift of 50,000 acres of land from the Central Pacific for his services. Senator Lyman Trumbull of Illinois took an annual retainer from the Illinois Central. The worst scandal of the Grant administration grew out of corruption involving railroad promotion. As a way of diverting funds for the building of the Union Pacific Railroad, an inner circle of Union Pacific stockholders created the dummy Crédit Mobilier construction company. In return for political favors, a group of prominent Republicans received stock in the company. When the scandal broke in 1872, it ruined Vice President Schuyler Colfax politically and led to the censure of two congressmen.

Other industries also boomed in this period, especially those engaged in extracting minerals and processing natural resources. Railroad growth stimulated expansion in the production of coal, iron, stone, and lumber, and these also received significant government aid. For example, under the National Mineral Act of 1866, mining companies received millions of acres of free public land. Oil refining enjoyed a huge expansion in the 1860s and 1870s. As with railroads, an early period of fierce competition soon gave way to concentration. By the late 1870s John D. Rockefeller's Standard Oil Company controlled almost 90 percent of the nation's oil-refining capacity. The production of pig iron tripled from 1 million tons in 1865 to 3 million tons in 1873. Between 1869 and 1879 both the capital investment and the number of workers in iron nearly doubled. Coal production shot up from 17 million tons in 1861 to 72 million tons in 1880. The size of individual ironworks and coal mines—measured by the number of employees and capital invested—also grew in these years, reflecting the expanding scale of industrial enterprise as a whole.

Liberal Republicans and the Election of 1872

With the rapid growth of large-scale, capital-intensive enterprises, Republicans increasingly identified with the interests of business rather than the rights of freedmen or the antebellum ideology of "free labor." The old Civil War–era Radicals had declined in influence. State Republican parties now organized themselves around the spoils of federal patronage rather than grand causes such as preserving the Union or ending slavery. Despite the Crédit Mobilier affair, Republicans had no monopoly on political scandal. In 1871 New York City newspapers reported the shocking story of how Democratic Party boss William M. Tweed and his friends had systematically stolen tens of millions from the city treasury. The "Tweed Ring" had received enormous bribes and kickbacks from city contractors and businessmen. Grotesquely caricatured by Thomas Nast's cartoons in *Harper's Weekly*, Tweed emerged as the preeminent national symbol of an increasingly degraded and dishonest urban politics. But to many, the scandal represented only the most extreme case of the routine corruption that now plagued American political life.

By the end of President Grant's first term, a large number of disaffected Republicans sought an alternative. They were led by a small but influential number of intellectuals, professionals, businessmen, and reformers who articulated an ideology that helped reshape late-nineteenth-century politics. The Liberal Republicans, as they called themselves, shared several core values. First, they emphasized the doctrines of classical economics, stressing the law of supply and demand, free trade, defense of property rights, and individualism. They called for a return to limited government, arguing that bribery, scandal, and high taxes all flowed from excessive state interference in the economy.

Liberal Republicans were also suspicious of expanding democracy. "Universal suffrage," Charles Francis Adams Jr. wrote in 1869, "can only mean in plain English the government of ignorance and vice— it means a European, and especially Celtic, proletariat on the Atlantic coast, an African proletariat on the shores of the Gulf, and a Chinese proletariat on the Pacific." Liberal Republicans believed that politics ought to be the province of "the best men"—educated and well-to-do men like themselves, devoted to the "science of government." They proposed civil service reform as the best way to break the hold of party machines on patronage. Competitive examinations, they argued, were the best way to choose employees for government posts. At a time when only a very small fraction of Americans attended college, this requirement would severely restrict the pool of government workers.

Although most Liberal Republicans had enthusiastically supported abolition, the Union cause, and equal rights for freedmen, they now opposed continued federal intervention in the South. The national government had done all it could for the former slaves; they must now take care of themselves. "Root, Hog, or Die" was the harsh advice offered by Horace Greeley, editor of the *New York Tribune*. In the spring of 1872 a diverse collection of Liberal Republicans nominated Greeley to run for president. A longtime foe of the Democratic Party, Greeley nonetheless won that party's presidential nomination as well. He made a new policy for the South the center of his campaign against Grant. The "best men" of both sections, he argued, should support a more generous Reconstruction policy based on "universal amnesty and impartial suffrage." All Americans, Greeley urged, must put the Civil War behind them and "clasp hands across the bloody chasm."

Grant easily defeated Greeley, carrying every state in the North and winning 56 percent of the popular vote. Most Republicans were not willing to abandon the regular party organization, and "waving the bloody shirt" was still a potent vote-getter. But the 1872 election accelerated the trend toward federal abandonment of African American citizenship rights. The Liberal Republicans quickly faded as an organized political force. But their ideas helped define a growing conservative consciousness among the northern public. For the rest of the century, their political and economic views attracted a growing number of middle-class professionals and businessmen. This agenda included retreat from the ideal of racial justice, hostility toward trade unions, suspicion of working-class and immigrant political power, celebration of competitive individualism, and opposition to government intervention in economic affairs.

The Depression of 1873

In the fall of 1873 the postwar boom came to an abrupt halt as a severe financial panic triggered a deep economic depression. The collapse resulted from commercial overexpansion, especially speculative investing in the nation's railroad system. The investment banking house of Jay Cooke and Company failed in September 1873 when it found itself unable to market millions of dollars in Northern Pacific Railroad bonds. Soon other banks and brokerage houses, especially those dealing in railroad securities, caved in as well, and the New York Stock Exchange suspended operations. By 1876 half the nation's railroads had defaulted on their bonds. Over the next two years more than 100 banks folded and 18,000 businesses shut their doors. The depression that began in 1873 lasted sixty-five months—the longest economic contraction in the nation's history until then.

The human toll of the depression was enormous. As factories began to close across the nation, the unemployment rate soared to about 15 percent. In many cities the jobless rate was much higher; roughly one-quarter of New York City workers were unemployed in 1874. Many thousands of men took to the road in search of work, and the "tramp" emerged as a new and menacing figure on the social landscape. The

The Tramp, Harper's Weekly, *September 2, 1876. The depression that began in 1873 forced many thousands of unemployed workers to go "on the tramp" in search of jobs. Men wandered from town to town, walking or riding railroad cars, desperate for a chance to work for wages or simply for room and board. The "tramp" became a powerful symbol of the misery caused by industrial depression and, as in this drawing, an image that evoked fear and nervousness among the nation's middle class.*

Pennsylvania Bureau of Labor Statistics noted that never before had "so many of the working classes, skilled and unskilled . . . been moving from place to place seeking employment that was not to be had." Farmers were also hard hit by the depression. Agricultural output continued to grow, but prices and land values fell sharply. As prices for their crops fell, farmers had a more difficult time repaying their fixed loan obligations; many sank deeper into debt.

During the winter of 1873, New York labor leaders demanded to know what measures would be taken "to relieve the necessities of the 10,000 homeless and hungry men and women of our city whose urgent appeals have apparently been disregarded by our public servants." Mass meetings of workers in New York and other cities issued calls to government officials to create jobs through public works. But these appeals were rejected. Indeed, many business leaders and political figures denounced even meager efforts at charity. E. L. Godkin wrote in the Christmas 1875 issue of the *Nation* that "free soup must be prohibited, and all classes must learn that soup of any kind, beef or turtle, can be had only by being paid for." Men such as Godkin saw the depression as a natural, if painful, part of the business cycle, one that would allow only the strongest enterprises (and workers) to survive. They dismissed any attempts at government interference, in the form of either job creation or poor relief.

Increased tensions, sometimes violent, between labor and capital reinforced the feeling of many Americans that the nation was no longer immune from European-style class conflict. The depression of the 1870s prompted workers and farmers to question the old free-labor ideology that celebrated a harmony of interests in northern society. More people voiced anger at and distrust of large corporations that exercised great economic power from outside their communities. Businessmen and merchants, meanwhile, especially in large cities, became more conscious of their own class interests. New political organizations such as Chicago's Citizens' Association united businessmen in campaigns for fiscal conservatism and defense of property rights. In national politics, the persistent depression made the Republican Party, North and South, more vulnerable than ever.

The Electoral Crisis of 1876

With the economy mired in depression, Democrats looked forward to capturing the White House in 1876. New scandals plaguing the Grant administration also weakened the Republican Party. In 1875, a conspiracy surfaced between distillers and U.S. revenue agents to cheat the government out of millions in tax revenues. The government secured indictments against more than 200 members of this "Whiskey Ring," including Orville E. Babcock, Grant's private secretary. Though acquitted, thanks to Grant's intervention, Babcock resigned in disgrace. In 1876, Secretary of War William W. Belknap was impeached for receiving bribes for the sale of trading posts in Indian Territory, and he resigned to avoid conviction.

Though Grant himself was never implicated in any wrongdoing, Democrats hammered away at his administration's low standard of honesty in government. For president they nominated Governor Samuel J. Tilden of New York, who brought impeccable reform credentials to his candidacy. In 1871 he had helped expose and prosecute the "Tweed Ring" in New York City. As governor he had toppled the "Canal Ring," a graft-ridden scheme involving inflated contracts for repairs on the Erie Canal. In their platform, the Democrats linked the issue of corruption to an attack on Reconstruction policies. They blamed the Republicans for instituting "a corrupt centralism" that subjected southern states to "the rapacity of carpetbag tyrannies," riddled the national government "with incapacity, waste, and fraud," and "locked fast the prosperity of an industrious people in the paralysis of hard times."

Republican nominee Rutherford B. Hayes, governor of Ohio, also sought the high ground. As a lawyer in Cincinnati he had defended runaway slaves. Later he had distinguished himself as a general in the Union army. Republicans charged Tilden with disloyalty during the war, income tax evasion, and close relations with powerful railroad interests. Hayes promised, if elected, to support an efficient civil service system, to vigorously prosecute officials who betrayed the public trust, and to introduce a system of free universal education.

On an election day marred by widespread vote fraud and violent intimidation, Tilden received 250,000 more popular votes than Hayes. But Republicans refused to concede victory, challenging the vote totals in the electoral college. Tilden garnered 184 uncontested electoral votes, one shy of the majority required to win, while Hayes received 165. The problem centered in 20 disputed votes from Florida, Louisiana, South Carolina, and Oregon. In each of the three southern states two sets of electoral votes were returned. In Oregon, which Hayes had unquestionably carried, the Democratic governor replaced a disputed Republican elector with a Democrat.

The crisis was unprecedented. In January 1877 Congress moved to settle the deadlock, estab-

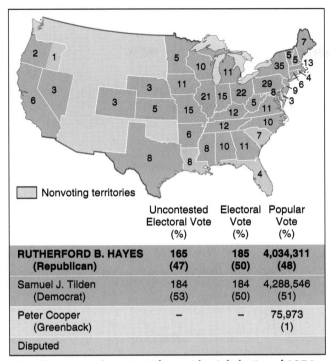

	Uncontested Electoral Vote (%)	Electoral Vote (%)	Popular Vote (%)
RUTHERFORD B. HAYES (Republican)	**165 (47)**	**185 (50)**	**4,034,311 (48)**
Samuel J. Tilden (Democrat)	184 (53)	184 (50)	4,288,546 (51)
Peter Cooper (Greenback)	–	–	75,973 (1)
Disputed			

The Election of 1876   *The presidential election of 1876 left the nation without a clear-cut winner.*

lishing an Electoral Commission composed of five senators, five representatives, and five Supreme Court justices; eight were Republicans and seven were Democrats. The commission voted along strict partisan lines to award all the contested electoral votes to Hayes. Outraged by this decision, Democratic congressmen threatened a filibuster to block Hayes's inauguration. Violence and stalemate were avoided when Democrats and Republicans struck a compromise in February. In return for Hayes's ascendance to the presidency, the Republicans promised to appropriate more money for Southern internal improvements, to appoint a Southerner to Hayes's cabinet, and to pursue a policy of noninterference ("home rule") in southern affairs.

Shortly after assuming office, Hayes ordered removal of the remaining federal troops in Louisiana and South Carolina. Without this military presence to sustain them, the Republican governors of those two states quickly lost power to Democrats. "Home rule" meant Republican abandonment of freed people, Radicals, carpetbaggers, and scalawags. It also effectively nullified the Fourteenth and Fifteenth Amendments and the Civil Rights Act of 1866. The "Compromise of 1877" completed repudiation of the idea, born during the Civil War and pursued during Congressional

Reconstruction, of a powerful federal government protecting the rights of all American citizens. As one black Louisianan lamented, "The whole South—every state in the South—had got into the hands of the very men that held us slaves." Other voices hailed this turning point in policy. "The negro," declared the *Nation,* "will disappear from the field of national politics. Henceforth, the nation, as a nation, will have nothing more to do with him."

CONCLUSION

Reconstruction succeeded in the limited political sense of reuniting a nation torn apart by civil war. The Radical Republican vision, emphasizing racial justice, equal civil and political rights guaranteed by the Fourteenth and Fifteenth Amendments, and a new southern economy organized around independent small farmers, never enjoyed the support of the majority of its party or the northern public. By 1877 the political force of these ideals was spent and the national retreat from them nearly complete.

The end of Reconstruction left the way open for the return of white domination in the South. The freed people's political and civil equality proved only temporary. It would take a "Second Reconstruction," the civil rights movement of the next century, to establish full black citizenship rights once and for all. The federal government's failure to pursue land reform left former slaves without the economic independence needed for full emancipation. Yet the newly autonomous black family, along with black-controlled churches, schools, and other social institutions, provided the foundations for the modern African American community. If the federal government was not yet fully committed to protecting equal rights in local communities, the Reconstruction era at least pointed to how that goal might be achieved.

Even as the federal government retreated from the defense of equal rights for black people, it took a more aggressive stance as the protector of business interests. The Hayes administration responded decisively to one of the worst outbreaks of class violence in American history by dispatching federal troops to several northern cities to break the Great Railroad Strike of 1877. In the aftermath of Reconstruction, the struggle between capital and labor had clearly replaced "the southern question" as the number one political issue of the day. "The overwhelming labor question has dwarfed all other questions into nothing," wrote an Ohio Republican. "We have home questions enough to occupy attention now."

CHRONOLOGY

1865	Freedmen's Bureau established
	Abraham Lincoln assassinated
	Andrew Johnson begins Presidential Reconstruction
	Black codes begin to be enacted in southern states
	Thirteenth Amendment ratified
1866	Civil Rights Act passed
	Congress approves Fourteenth Amendment
	Ku Klux Klan founded
1867	Reconstruction Acts, passed over President Johnson's veto, begin Congressional Reconstruction
	Tenure of Office Act
	Southern states call constitutional conventions
1868	President Johnson impeached by the House, but acquitted in Senate trial
	Fourteenth Amendment ratified
	Most southern states readmitted to Union
	Ulysses S. Grant elected president
1869	Congress approves Fifteenth Amendment
	Union Pacific and Central Pacific tracks meet at Promontory Point in Utah Territory

	Suffragists split into National Woman Suffrage Association and American Woman Suffrage Association
1870	Fifteenth Amendment ratified
1871	Ku Klux Klan Act passed
	"Tweed Ring" in New York City exposed
1872	Liberal Republicans break with Grant and Radicals, nominate Horace Greeley for president
	Crédit Mobilier scandal
	Grant reelected president
1873	Financial panic and beginning of economic depression
	Slaughterhouse cases
1874	Democrats gain control of House for first time since 1856
1875	Civil Rights Act
1876	Disputed election between Samuel Tilden and Rutherford B. Hayes
1877	Electoral Commission elects Hayes president
	President Hayes dispatches federal troops to break Great Railroad Strike and withdraws last remaining federal troops from the South

REVIEW QUESTIONS

1. How did various visions of a "reconstructed" South differ? How did these visions reflect the old political and social divisions that had led to the civil war?
2. What key changes did emancipation make in the political and economic status of African Americans? Discuss the expansion of citizenship rights in the post–Civil War years. To what extent did women share in the gains made by African Americans?
3. What role did such institutions as the family, the church, schools, and political parties play in the African American transition to freedom?
4. How did white Southerners attempt to limit the freedom of former slaves? How did these efforts succeed, and how did they fail?
5. Evaluate the achievements and failures of Reconstruction governments in the southern states.
6. What were the crucial economic changes occurring in the North and South during the Reconstruction era?

RECOMMENDED READING

Michael Les Benedict, *The Impeachment and Trial of Andrew Johnson* (1973). The best history of the impeachment crisis.

Laura F. Edwards, *Gendered Strife & Confusion: The Political Culture of Reconstruction* (1997). An ambitious analysis of how gender ideologies played a key role in shaping the party politics and social relations of the Reconstruction-era South.

Michael W. Fitzgerald, *The Union League Movement in the Deep South* (1989). Uses the Union League as a lens through which to examine race relations and the close connections between politics and economic change in the post–Civil War South.

Eric Foner, *Reconstruction: America's Unfinished Revolution, 1863–1877* (1988). The most comprehensive and thoroughly researched overview of the Reconstruction era.

William Gillette, *Retreat from Reconstruction: A Political History, 1867–1878* (1979). Covers the national political scene, with special attention to the abandonment of the ideal of racial equality.

Jacqueline Jones, *Labor of Love, Labor of Sorrow* (1985). Includes excellent material on the work and family lives of African American women in slavery and freedom.

Leon Litwack, *Been in the Storm So Long: The Aftermath of Slavery* (1979). A richly detailed analysis of the transition from slavery to freedom; excellent use of African American sources.

Michael Perman, *Emancipation and Reconstruction, 1862–1879* (1987). A short but very useful overview of Reconstruction, emphasizing racial issues and the end of slavery.

Edward Royce, *The Origins of Southern Sharecropping* (1993). A sophisticated, tightly argued work of historical sociology that explains how sharecropping emerged as the dominant form of agricultural labor in the post–Civil War South.

Mark W. Summers, *Railroads, Reconstruction, and the Gospel of Prosperity* (1984). The best study of the economic and political importance of railroad building in this era.

Allen W. Trelease, *White Terror: The Ku Klux Klan Conspiracy and Southern Reconstruction* (1971). The most complete account of Klan activity and the efforts to suppress it.

ADDITIONAL BIBLIOGRAPHY

The Politics of Reconstruction

Richard H. Abbott, *The Republican Party and the South, 1855–1877* (1986)

Herman Belz, *Emancipation and Equal Rights* (1978)

Michael Les Benedict, *A Compromise of Principle: Congressional Republicans and Reconstruction* (1974)

Michael Kent Curtis, *No State Shall Abridge: The Fourteenth Amendment and the Bill of Rights* (1990)

Ellen Carol DuBois, *Feminism and Suffrage* (1978)

Eric Foner, *Politics and Ideology in the Age of the Civil War* (1980)

William C. Harris, *With Charity for All: Lincoln and the Restoration of the Union* (1997)

Robert Kaczorowski, *The Politics of Judicial Interpretation: The Federal Courts, Department of Justice, and Civil Rights, 1866–1876* (1985)

James McPherson, *Ordeal by Fire: The Civil War and Reconstruction* (1982)

Kenneth M. Stampp, *The Era of Reconstruction, 1865–1877* (1965)

The Meaning of Freedom

Ira Berlin et al., eds., *Freedom: A Documentary History*, 3 vols. (1985–91)

W. E. B. Du Bois, *Black Reconstruction* (1935)

Barbara J. Fields, *Slavery and Freedom on the Middle Ground* (1985)

Eric Foner, *Freedom's Lawmakers: A Directory of Black Officeholders during Reconstruction* (1996)

Herbert G. Gutman, *The Black Family in Slavery and Freedom* (1976)

Thomas Holt, *Black over White: Negro Political Leadership in South Carolina during Reconstruction* (1977)

Lynda J. Morgan, *Emancipation in Virginia's Tobacco Belt* (1992)

Nell Irvin Painter, *Exodusters* (1977)

Howard N. Rabinowitz, *Race Relations in the Urban South, 1865–1890* (1978)

Roger L. Ransom and Richard Sutch, *One Kind of Freedom: The Economic Consequences of Emancipation* (1977)

Southern Politics and Society

Dan T. Carter, *When the War Was Over: The Failure of Self Reconstruction in the South, 1865–1877* (1985)

Richard N. Current, *Those Terrible Carpetbaggers* (1988)

Stephen Hahn, *The Roots of Southern Populism* (1983)

William C. Harris, *The Day of the Carpetbagger: Republican Reconstruction in Mississippi* (1979)

Michael S. Perman, *Reunion without Compromise: The South and Reconstruction, 1865–1868* (1973)

———, *The Road to Redemption: Southern Politics, 1868–1979* (1984)

Howard N. Rabinowitz, *The First New South, 1865–1920* (1991)

James Roark, *Masters without Slaves* (1977)

Jonathan M. Wiener, *Social Origins of the New South* (1978)

Reconstructing the North

Stephen Buechler, *The Transformation of the Woman Suffrage Movement* (1986)

Morton Keller, *Affairs of State* (1977)

James C. Mohr, ed., *Radical Republicans in the North* (1976)

David Montgomery, *Beyond Equality: Labor and the Radical Republicans, 1862–1872* (1967)

Keith I. Polakoff, *The Politics of Inertia: The Election of 1876 and the End of Reconstruction* (1973)

Mark W. Summers, *The Era of Good Stealings* (1993)

Margaret S. Thompson, *The "Spider Web": Congress and Lobbying in the Age of Grant* (1985)

C. Vann Woodward, *Reunion and Reaction: The Compromise of 1877 and the End of Reconstruction* (1956)

Biography

Fawn M. Brodie, *Thaddeus Stevens* (1959)

David Donald, *Charles Sumner and the Rights of Man* (1970)

Russell Duncan, *Freedom's Shore: Tunis Campbell and the Georgia Freedmen* (1986)

William S. McFeely, *Frederick Douglass* (1989)

———, *Grant: A Biography* (1981)

———, *Yankee Stepfather: General O. O. Howard and the Freedmen* (1968)

Hans L. Trefousse, *Andrew Johnson* (1989)

CHAPTER EIGHTEEN

CONQUEST AND SURVIVAL
THE TRANS-MISSISSIPPI WEST, 1860–1900

AMERICAN COMMUNITIES
The Oklahoma Land Rush

D ecades after the event, cowboy Evan G. Barnard vividly recalled the preparations made by settlers when Oklahoma territorial officials announced the opening of No Man's Land to the biggest "land rush" in American history. "Thousands of people gathered along the border. . . . As the day for the race drew near the settlers practiced running their horses and driving carts." Finally the morning of April 22, 1889, arrived. "At ten o'clock people lined up . . . ready for the great race of their lives." Like many others, Barnard displayed his guns prominently on his hips, determined to discourage competitors from claiming the 160 acres of prime land that he intended to grab for himself.

Evan Barnard's story was one strand in the larger tale of the destruction and creation of communities in the trans-Mississippi West. In the 1830s, the federal government designated what was to become the state of Oklahoma as Indian Territory, reserved for the Five Civilized Tribes (Cherokees, Chickasaws, Choctaws, Creeks, and Seminoles) that had been forcibly removed from their eastern lands. All five tribes had reestablished themselves as sovereign republics in Indian Territory. The Cherokees and Chocktaws became prosperous cotton growers. The Creeks managed large herds of hogs and cattle, and the Chickasaws grazed not only cattle but sheep and goats on their open fields. The Five Tribes also ran sawmills, gristmills, and cotton gins. Indian merchants were soon dealing with other tribespeople as well as licensed white traders and even contracting with the federal government.

The Civil War, however, took a heavy toll on their success. Some tribes, slaveholders themselves, sided with the Confederacy; others with the Union. When the war ended, more than 10,000 people—nearly one-fifth of the population of Indian Territory—had died. To make matters worse, new treaties required the Five Tribes to cede the entire western half of the territory for the resettlement of tribes from other regions, including the former northern Indian territory of Nebraska and Kansas.

Western Oklahoma thereby became home to thousands of newly displaced peoples, including the Pawnees, Peorias, Ottawas, Wyandots, and Miamis. Many small tribes readily took to farming and rebuilt their communities. But the nomadic, buffalo-hunting Kiowas, Cheyennes, Comanches, and Arapahoes did not settle so peacefully. They continued to traverse the plains until the U.S. Army finally forced them onto reservations. Eventually, more than 80,000 tribespeople were living on twenty-one separate reservations in western Oklahoma, all governed by agents appointed by the federal government.

The opening of the unassigned far western district of Oklahoma known as No Man's Land to non-Indian homesteading, however, signaled the impending end of Indian sovereignty. Many non-Indians saw this almost 2 million acre strip as a Promised

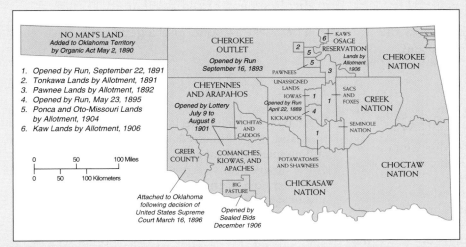

Oklahoma Territory *Land openings to settlers came at different times, making new land available through various means.*

Inside map legend:

NO MAN'S LAND
*Added to Oklahoma Territory
by Organic Act May 2, 1890*

1. *Opened by Run, September 22, 1891*
2. *Tonkawa Lands by Allotment, 1891*
3. *Pawnee Lands by Allotment, 1892*
4. *Opened by Run, May 23, 1895*
5. *Ponca and Oto-Missouri Lands
   by Allotment, 1904*
6. *Kaw Lands by Allotment, 1906*

0   50   100 Miles
0   50   100 Kilometers

CHEROKEE OUTLET
Opened by Run September 16, 1893

KAWS
OSAGE RESERVATION
Lands by Allotment 1906
CHEROKEE NATION

PAWNEES

CHEYENNES AND ARAPAHOS
Opened by Lottery July 9 to August 6 1901

UNASSIGNED LANDS
IOWAS
Opened by Run April 22, 1889
KICKAPOOS

SACS AND FOXES
CREEK NATION
SEMINOLE NATION

WICHITAS AND CADDOS

GREER COUNTY
Attached to Oklahoma following decision of United States Supreme Court March 16, 1896

COMANCHES, KIOWAS, AND APACHES

BIG PASTURE
Opened by Sealed Bids December 1906

POTAWATOMIS AND SHAWNEES

CHICKASAW NATION

CHOCTAW NATION

Land, perfect for dividing into thousands of small farms. African Americans, many of whom were former slaves of Indian planters, appealed to the federal government for the right to stake claims there. Another group of would-be homesteaders, known as "Boomers," quickly tired of petitioning and invaded the district in 1880, only to be booted out by the Tenth Cavalry. Meanwhile, the railroads, seeing the potential for lucrative commerce, put constant pressure on the federal government to open No Man's Land for settlement. In 1889 the U.S. Congress finally gave in.

Cowboy Barnard was just one of thousands to pour into No Man's Land on April 22, 1889. Many homesteaders simply crossed the border from Kansas. Southerners, dispossessed by warfare and economic ruin in their own region, were also well represented. Market-minded settlers claimed the land nearest the railroads, and by nightfall of April 22 had set up tent cities along the tracks. In a little over two months, after 6,000 homestead claims had been filed, the first sod houses appeared, sheltering growing communities of non-Indian farmers, ranchers, and other entrepreneurs.

Dramatic as it was, the land rush of 1889 was only one in a series of events that soon dispossessed Oklahoma's Indians of their remaining lands. First the federal government broke up the estates held collectively by various tribes in western Oklahoma, assigning to individuals the standard 160-acre allotment and allowing non-Indian homesteaders to claim the rest. In 1898, Congress passed the Curtis Act, formally dissolving Indian Territory and dispossessing the Five Tribes. Members of the former Indian nations were directed to dismantle their governments, abandon their estates, and join the ranks of other homesteaders. They nevertheless retained many of their tribal customs and managed to regain sovereign status in 1977.

Later generations of Oklahomans often celebrated their historic ties to the Indian nations. At formal ceremonies marking statehood, just before the newly elected governor took the oath of office, a mock wedding ceremony united a tough and virile cowboy with a demure and submissive Indian maiden. By this time, in 1907, tribespeople were outnumbered in Oklahoma by ten to one.

By this time also, nearly one-quarter of the entire population of the United States lived west of the Mississippi River. Hundreds of new communities, supported primarily by cattle ranching, agriculture, mining, or other industries, had not only grown with the emerging national economy but helped to shape it in the process. The newcomers displaced communities that had formed centuries earlier. They also drastically transformed the physical landscape. Through their activities and the support of Easterners, the United States realized an ambition that John L. O'Sullivan had described in 1845 as the nation's "manifest destiny to overspread the continent" and remake it in a new image.

Indian Territory (Oklahoma)

KEY TOPICS

- The impact of western expansion on Indian societies

- The West as an "internal empire" and the development of new technologies and new industries

- The creation of new communities and the displacement of old communities

- The West as myth and legend

INDIAN PEOPLES UNDER SIEGE

The tribespeople living west of the Mississippi River keenly felt the pressure of the gradual incorporation of the West into the nation. The Oregon Trail opened the Northwest to large numbers of non-Indian settlers, and by 1845 nearly 5,000 people had braved the six- to eight-month journey by wagon to reach present-day Oregon and Washington. The following year, the United States reached an agreement with Great Britain for the division of the Oregon Country. Then came the addition of the vast territories taken from Mexico following the Mexican-American War. California quickly became a state in 1850, Oregon in 1859. Congress consolidated the national domain in the next decades by granting territorial status to Utah, New Mexico, Washington, Dakota, Colorado, Nevada, Arizona, Idaho, Montana, and Wyoming. The purchase of Alaska in 1867 added an area twice the size of Texas and extended the nation beyond its contiguous borders so that it reached almost to Russia and the North Pole. The federal government made itself the custodian of all these thinly settled regions, permitting limited self-rule, with appointed governors supervising the transition from territorial status to statehood.

Tribespeople struggled to preserve their ways of life under these changing conditions, but their prospects dimmed considerably following the discovery of gold in California in 1848 and the completion of the transcontinental railroad in 1869. White settlers, hoping to build a new life for themselves, rushed into these new territories and repeatedly invaded Indian lands west of the Mississippi. Violent outbreaks between white emigrants and Indian peoples became increasingly commonplace. Since the Jefferson administration, federal officials had promoted the assimilation of Indian peoples; they now became even more determined to break up their tribal councils and to bring them into the American mainstream.

On the Eve of Conquest

Before the European colonists reached the New World, tribespeople of the Great Plains, Southwest, and Far West had occupied the lands for more than twenty thousand years. Hundreds of tribes totaling perhaps a million members had adapted to such extreme climates as the desert aridity of present-day Utah and Nevada, the bitter cold of the northern plains, and the seasonally heavy rain of the Pacific Northwest. Many cultivated maize (corn), foraged for wild plants, fished, or hunted game. Several tribes built cities with several thousand inhabitants and traded across thousands of miles of western territory.

Invasion by the English, Spanish, and other Europeans brought disease, religious conversion, and new patterns of commerce. But geographic isolation still gave many tribes a margin of survival unknown in the East. At the close of the Civil War, approximately 360,000 Indian people still lived in the trans-Mississippi West, the majority of them in the Great Plains.

The surviving tribes adapted to changing conditions. The Plains Indians learned to ride the horses and shoot the guns introduced by Spanish and British traders. The Pawnees migrated farther westward to evade encroaching non-Indian settlers, while the Sioux and the Comanches fought neighboring tribes to gain control of large stretches of the Great Plains. The southwestern Hopis and Zunis, conquered earlier by the Spanish, continued to trade extensively with the Mexicans who lived near them. Some tribes took dramatic steps toward accommodation with white ways. Even before they were uprooted and moved across the Mississippi River, the Cherokees had become literate in English, converted to Christianity, established a constitutional republic, and become a nation of farmers.

Legally, the federal government had long regarded Indian tribes as autonomous nations residing within American boundaries and had negotiated numerous treaties with them over land rights and commerce. But pressured by land-hungry whites, several states had violated these federal treaties so often that the U.S. Congress passed the Indian Removal Act of 1830 (Chapter 10), which provided funds to relocate all eastern tribes by force if necessary. The Cherokees challenged this legislation, and

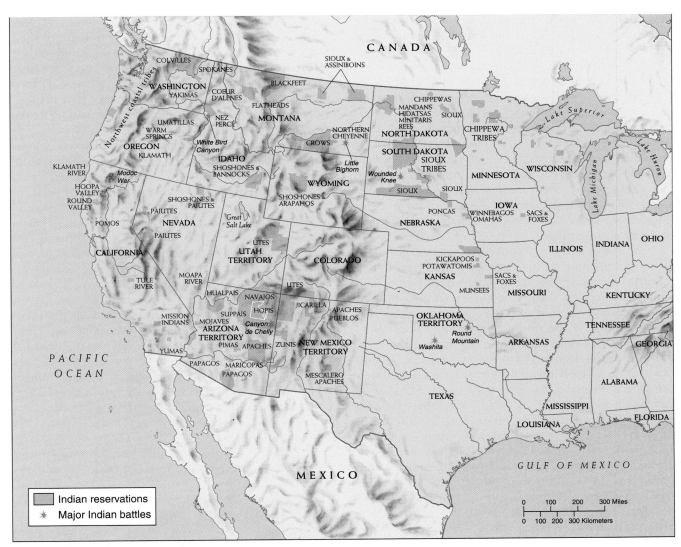

Major Indian Battles and Indian Reservations, 1860–1900   *As commercial routes and white populations passed through and occupied Indian lands, warfare inevitably erupted. The displacement of Indians to reservations opened access by farmers, ranchers, and investors to natural resources and to markets.*

the Supreme Court ruled in their favor in *Cherokee Nation v. Georgia* (1831). Ignoring the court's decision, President Andrew Jackson, known as a hardened Indian fighter, forced many tribes to cede their land and remove to Indian Territory. There, it was believed, they might live undisturbed by whites and gradually adjust to "civilized" ways. But soon, the onslaught of white settlers, railroad entrepreneurs, and prospectors rushing for gold pressured tribes to cede millions of their acres to the United States. In 1854, to open the Kansas and Nebraska Territories for white settlement, the federal government simply abolished the northern half of Indian Territory. As demand for resources and land accelerated, the entire plan for a permanent Indian Territory fell apart.

Reservations and the Slaughter of the Buffalo

As early as the 1840s, highly placed officials had outlined a plan to subdue the intensifying rivalry over natural resources and land. Under the terms of their proposal, individual tribes would agree to live within clearly defined zones—reservations—and, in exchange, the Bureau of Indian Affairs would provide guidance while U.S. military forces ensured protection. This reservation policy also reflected the vision of many "Friends of the Indian," educators and Protestant missionaries who aspired to "civilize the savages." By the end of the 1850s eight western reservations had been established where Indian peoples were induced to speak English, take up farming, and convert to Christianity. The U.S. commissioner of Indian affairs

Luke Lea predicted that reservations would speed the "ultimate incorporation" of the Indians "into the great body of our citizen population."

Several tribes did sign treaties, although often under duress. High-handed officials, such as governor Isaac Stevens of Washington Territory, made no attempt at legitimate negotiations, choosing instead to intimidate or deceive Indian peoples into signing away their lands. Most of the tribes in Washington responded by remaining in their old villages. But Stevens finally had his way. State officials moved the Indians onto three reservations after their leaders signed away 45,000 square miles of tribal land. The Suquamish leader Seattle admitted defeat but warned the governor: "Your time of decay may be distant, but it will surely come."

Those tribes that moved to reservations often found federal policies inadequate to their needs. The federal government repeatedly reduced the size of land allotments, forcing tribes to compete with each other for increasingly scarce resources and making subsistence farming on the reservation virtually impossible. The Medicine Lodge Treaty of 1867 assigned reservations in existing Indian Territory to Comanches, Plains (Kiowa) Apaches, Kiowas, Cheyennes, and Arapahoes, bringing these tribes together with Sioux, Shoshones, Bannocks, and Navajos. All told, more than 100,000 people found themselves competing intensely for survival. Over the next decade, a group of Quakers appointed by President Ulysses S. Grant attempted to mediate differences among the tribes and to supply the starving peoples with food and seed. At the same time, white prospectors and miners continued to flood the Dakota Territory. "They crowded in," Iron Teeth recalled bitterly, "so we had to move out." Moreover, corrupt officials of the Bureau of Indian Affairs routinely diverted funds for their own use and reduced food supplies, a policy promoting malnutrition, demoralization, and desperation.

The nomadic tribes that traditionally hunted and gathered over large territories saw their freedom sharply curtailed. The Lakotas, or Western Sioux, a loose confederation of bands scattered across the northern Great Plains, were one of the largest and most adaptive of all Indian nations. Seizing buffalo-hunting territory from their rivals, the Pawnees and the Crows, the Sioux had learned

to follow the herds on horseback. Buffalo meat and hides fed and clothed the Sioux and satisfied many of their other needs as well. Images of buffalo appeared in their religious symbols and ceremonial dress. The Sioux were also vision seekers. Young men and women pursued dreams that would provide them guidance for a lifetime; elders themselves followed dreams that might guide the destiny of the entire tribe or nation.

The mass slaughter of the buffalo by whites brought the crisis provoked by the increasing restriction of the Plains peoples to a peak. In earlier eras, vast herds of buffalo had literally darkened the western horizon. Buffalo grazed over distances of several hundred miles, searching for water and wallowing in mud to fend off insects. As gunpowder and the railroad came to the range, the number of buffalo fell rapidly. Non-Indian traders avidly sought buffalo fur for coats, hide for leather, and heads for trophies. New rifles, like the .50 caliber Sharps, could kill at 600 feet; one sharpshooter bragged of killing 3,000 buffalo. Army commanders encouraged the slaughter, accurately predicting that starvation would break tribal resistance to the reservation system. Their food sources practically destroyed and their way of life undermined, many Great Plains tribes, including many Sioux, concluded that they could only fight or die.

The Indian Wars

Under these pressures, a handful of tribes organized themselves and their allies to resist both federal poli-

Chief Red Cloud in an 1868 photograph. The Oglala Sioux spiritual leader is seen with Red Dog, Little Wound, interpreter John Bridgeman (on his right), American Horse, and Red Shirt (on his left). He ventured to Washington with his delegation to discuss with President Ulysses S. Grant the various provisions of the peace treaty, just signed, to end the violent conflict over the Bozeman Trail.

cies and the growing wave of white settlers. The over-whelming majority of tribespeople did not take up arms. But settlers, thousands of them Civil War veterans with weapons close at hand, responded to real or imaginary threats with their own brands of violence.

Large-scale war erupted in 1864. Having decided to terminate all treaties with tribes in eastern Colorado, territorial governor John Evans encouraged a group of white civilians, the Colorado Volunteers, to stage repeated raids through Cheyenne campgrounds. Seeking protection, chief Black Kettle brought a band of 800 Cheyennes to a U.S. fort and received orders to set up camp at Sand Creek. Feeling secure in this arrangement, Black Kettle sent out most of his men to hunt. The next morning, on November 29, 1864, the Colorado Volunteers attacked. While Black Kettle held up a U.S. flag and a white truce banner, the disorderly group of 700 men, many of them drunk, slaughtered 105 Cheyenne women and children and 28 men. They mutilated the corpses and took scalps back to Denver to exhibit as trophies. Iron Teeth, a Cheyenne woman who survived, remembered seeing a woman "crawling along on the ground, shot, scalped, crazy, but not yet dead." Months after the Sand Creek Massacre, bands of Cheyennes, Sioux, and Arapahoes were still retaliating, burning civilian outposts and sometimes killing whole families.

The Sioux played the most dramatic roles in the Indian Wars. In 1851, believing the U.S. government would recognize their own rights of conquest over other Indian tribes, the Sioux relinquished large tracts of land as a demonstration of good faith. But within a decade, a mass invasion of miners and the construction of military forts along the Bozeman Trail in Wyoming, the Sioux's principal buffalo range, threw the tribe's future into doubt. During the Great Sioux War of 1865–67, the Oglala Sioux warrior Red Cloud fought the U.S. Army to a stalemate and forced the government to abandon its forts, which the Sioux then burned to the ground. The Treaty of Fort Laramie, signed in 1868, created the Great Sioux Reservation, which included the present state of South Dakota west of the Missouri River, but restored only a temporary peace to the region.

The Treaty of Fort Laramie granted the Sioux the right to occupy the Black Hills, or Paha Sapa, their sacred land, "as long as the grass shall grow," but the discovery of gold soon undermined this guarantee. White prospectors hurriedly invaded the territory. Directed to quash rumors of fabulous deposits of the precious metal, Lieutenant Colonel George Armstrong Custer led a surveying expedition to the Black Hills during the summer of 1874, but, contrary to plan, the Civil War hero described rich veins of ore that could be cheaply extracted. The U.S. Congress then pushed

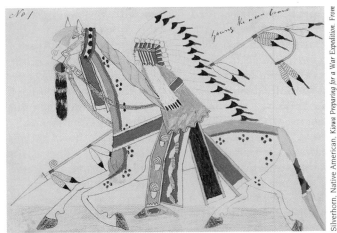

Silverhorn, Native American, Kiowa Preparing for a War Expedition. From Sketchbook, 1887. Gift of Mrs. Terrell Bartlett. McNay Art Museum, San Antonio, Texas.

Preparing for a War Expedition, *ca. 1887. This sketch on paper was made by an Indian artist, Silverhorn, who had himself taken part in the final revolt of the Kiowas in 1874. He later became a medicine man, and then served as a private in the U.S. Cavalry at Fort Sill, Oklahoma Territory.*

to acquire the territory for Americans. To protect their land, Sioux, Cheyenne, and Arapaho warriors, ranging between two thousand and nine thousand in number, moved into war camps during the summer of 1876 and prepared for battle.

The most flamboyant of army commanders (and in the eyes of many of his own troops, the most irresponsible), Custer developed an ambitious plan to subdue the rebellious tribes. He even invited newspaper reporters to come along as he set off to establish a fort in the Black Hills. After several skirmishes, he decided to rush ahead of other army regiments to a site that was known to white soldiers as Little Bighorn and to Lakotas as Greasy Grass. This foolhardy move offered the allied Cheyenne and Sioux warriors a perfect opportunity to cut off Custer's logistical and military support. On June 25, 1876, Custer and his troops were wiped out by one of the largest Indian contingents ever assembled, an estimated 2,000 to 4,000 warriors.

"Custer's Last Stand" gave Indian-haters the emotional ammunition to whip up public excitement. After Custer's defeat, spiritual leader Sitting Bull reportedly said, "Now they will never let us rest." The U.S. Army tracked down the disbanded Indian contingents one by one and forced them to surrender. In February, 1877, the U.S. government formally took possession of the Black Hills. After the defiant warrior Crazy Horse was fatally stabbed while under arrest at a U.S. army camp, Sioux leadership in the Indian Wars came to an end.

Among the last to hold out against the reservation system were the Apaches in the Southwest. Most Apache bands had abided the Medicine Lodge Treaty of 1867, and in 1872 Cochise, one of the ablest

Apache chiefs, agreed to live with his people on a reservation on a portion of the tribe's ancestral land. Cochise died two years later, and some of the Apache bands, unable to tolerate the harsh conditions on the reservation, returned to their old ways of seizing territory and stealing cattle. For the next ten years, Cochise's successor Geronimo led intermittent raids against white outposts in the rough Arizona terrain.

Pursued by the U.S. Army, the Apaches earned a reputation as intrepid warriors. Their brilliant strategists and horse-riding braves became legendary for lightning-swift raids followed by quick disappearances. The Kiowas and the Comanches, both powerful tribes, joined the Apaches in one of the bloodiest conflicts, the Red River War of 1874–75. The U.S. Army ultimately prevailed less by military might than by denying Indians access to food. Even after the Red River War, small-scale warfare sputtered on. Not until September 1886, his band reduced to only thirty people, did Geronimo finally surrender, ending the Indian Wars.

The Nez Percé

In crushing the Plains tribes, the U.S. government had conquered those peoples who had most actively resisted the advance of non-Indians into the West. But even tribes that had long tried to cooperate found themselves embattled. The Nez Percé (pierced nose), given their name by French Canadian trappers who thought they had seen members of the tribe wearing shells in their septums, for generations regarded themselves as good friends to white traders and settlers. Living in the plateau where Idaho, Washington, and Oregon now meet, they saved the Lewis and Clark expedition from starvation. The Nez Percé occasionally assisted U.S. armies against hostile tribes, and many of them were converts to Christianity.

The discovery of gold on Nez Percé territory in 1860 changed their relations with whites for the worse. Pressed by prospectors and mining companies, government commissioners, in the treaty of 1863, demanded the Nez Percé cede 6 million acres, nine-tenths of their land, at less than ten cents per acre. Some the Nez Percé leaders agreed to the terms of the treaty, which had been fraudulently signed on behalf of the entire tribe, but others refused. Old Chief Tukekas, one of the first to convert to Christianity, threw away his Bible and returned to his old religion. His son and successor, Chief Joseph, swore to protect the peoples of the Wallowa Valley in present-day Oregon. At first federal officials listened to Nez Percé complaints against the treaty and decided to allow them to remain on their land. Responding to pressure from settlers and politicians, however, they almost immediately reversed their decision, ordering the Nez Percé, including Chief

Joseph and his followers, to sell their land and to move onto the reservation.

Intending to comply, Chief Joseph's band set out from the Wallowa Valley with their livestock and all the possessions they could carry. When U.S. troops fired on a Nez Percé truce team, however, the Nez Percé fought back, repulsing the attackers and killing one-third of them. Chief Joseph and his people then undertook a monumental journey in search of sanctuary in Canada. Brilliantly outmaneuvering vengeful U.S. troops sent to intercept them, the 750 Nez Percé—including women, children, and the elderly—retreated for some 1,400 miles into Montana and Wyoming through mountains and prairies, and across the Bitterroot range. Along the way they unintentionally terrified tourists at the newly created Yellowstone National Park. Over the three and a half months of their journey, Nez Percé braves fought 2,000 regular U.S. troops and eighteen Indian auxiliary detachments in eighteen separate engagements and two major battles. U.S. troops finally trapped the Nez Percé in the Bear Paw Mountains of northern Montana, just 30 miles from the Canadian border. Suffering from hunger and cold, they surrendered.

General Sherman remarked admiringly at the Nez Percé's ingenious tactics, courage, and avoidance of cruelty. Newspapers described Chief Joseph as a "Red Napoleon" defying overwhelming odds. (Actually, Joseph did not plan military strategy but mainly attended to the needs of dependent tribal members.)

Promised they would be returned to Oregon, the Nez Percé were sent instead to disease-ridden bottomland near Fort Leavenworth in Kansas, and then to Oklahoma. Arguing for the right of his people to return to their Oregon reservation, Joseph spoke eloquently, through an interpreter, to Congress in 1879. "Treat all men alike. Give them all the same law. Give them all an even chance to live and grow. All men were made by the same Great Spirit Chief," Joseph pleaded. Government officials appeared willing to allow him and his people to return to their homeland until white settlers in Idaho objected. The last remnant of Joseph's band were deported under guard to a non-Nez Percé reservation in Washington, where Chief Joseph died in 1904 "of a broken heart" and where his descendants continue to live in exile to this day.

THE INTERNAL EMPIRE

Since the time of Christopher Columbus, the Americas had inspired in Europeans visions of a land of incredible wealth, free for the taking. In the nineteenth century, the North American continent, stretching across scarcely populated territories toward the Pacific Ocean, revived this fantasy, espe-

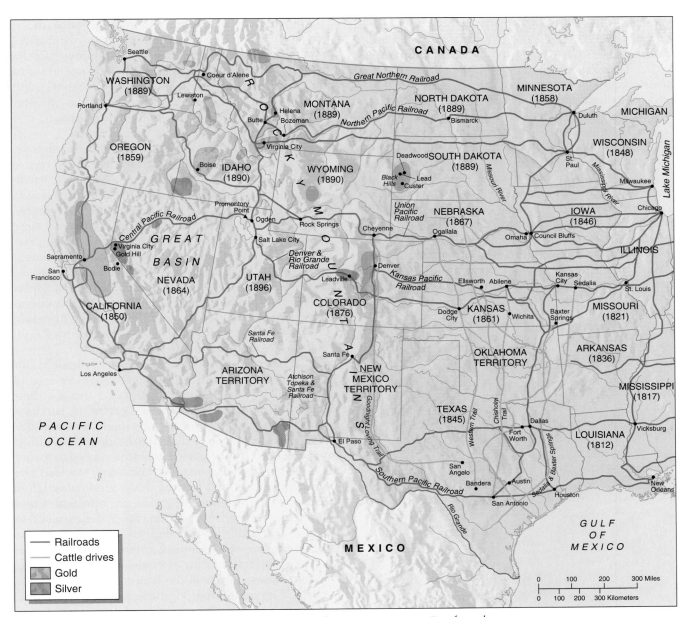

Railroad Routes, Cattle Trails, Gold and Silver Rushes, 1860–1900 *By the end of the nineteenth century, the vast region of the West was crosscut by hundreds of lines of transportation and communication. The trade in precious metals and in cattle helped build a population almost constantly on the move, following the rushes for gold or the herds of cattle.*

Source: Encyclopedia of American Social History.

cially as early reports conjured dreams of mountains of gold and silver. Determined to make their fortunes, be it from copper in Arizona, wheat in Montana, or oranges in California, numerous adventurers traveled west. As a group they carried out the largest migration and greatest commercial expansion in American history.

But the settlers themselves also became the subjects of a huge "internal empire" whose financial, political, and industrial centers of power remained in the East. A vast system of international markets also shaped the development of mines, farms, and new communities even as Americans romantically imagined the West to be the last frontier of individual freedom and wide-open spaces. Only a small number of settlers actually struck it rich. Meanwhile, older populations—Indian peoples, Hispanic peoples, and more recently settled communities like the Mormons—struggled to create places for themselves in this new order.

Mining Communities

The discovery of gold in California in 1848 roused fortune seekers from across the United States, Europe, and as far away as China and Chile. Within a year, prospecting parties overran the western territories, setting a pattern for intermittent rushes for gold, silver, and copper that extended from the Colorado mountains to the Arizona deserts to California, Oregon, Washington, and Alaska to the Black Hills of South Dakota. Mining camps and boomtowns soon dotted what had once been thinly settled regions. The population of California alone jumped from 14,000 in 1848 to 223,856 just four years later. More than any other industry or commercial enterprise, mining fostered western expansion.

The first miners required little preparation to stake their claims. The miner needs nothing, the military governor of California announced, "but his pick

A "hard rock" miner demonstrates the tiring and often dangerous task of hammering a drill into a rock to prepare a blasting hole. New technologies, such as diamond-headed drills, quickly revolutionized the extractive process, but potentially lethal hazards, including cave-ins and poisonous gases, remained great.

and shovel and tin pan with which to dig and wash the gravel." A handful of individual prospectors did strike it rich. Many more found themselves employees of the so-called bonanza kings, the owners or operators of the most lucrative enterprises. Only in 1896–97, with news of "gold on the Klondike" in Alaska, did prospectors again hit on a vein worth millions of dollars.

The mining industry quickly grew from its treasure-hunt origins into a grand corporate enterprise. The Comstock Lode of silver, discovered by Henry Comstock along the Carson River in Nevada in 1858, sent about 10,000 miners across the Sierra Nevada from California, but few individuals came out wealthy. Comstock himself eventually sold his claims for a mere $11,000 and two mules. Those reaping the huge profits were the entrepreneurs who could afford to invest in the heavy—and expensive—equipment necessary to drill more than 3,000 feet deep and to hire engineers with the technical knowledge to manage the operations. Having secured a capital investment of nearly $900,000, the owners of the Gould and Curry mill, built on the Comstock Lode, did very well.

The most successful mineowners bought out the smaller claims and built an entire industry around their stakes. They found investors to finance their expansion and used the borrowed capital to purchase the latest in extractive technology, such as new explosives, compressed-air or diamond-headed rotary drills, and wire cable. They gained access to timber to fortify their underground structures and water to feed the hydraulic pumps that washed down mountains. They built smelters to refine the crude ore into ingots and often financed railroads to transport the product to distant markets. By the end of the century, the Anaconda Copper Mining Company had expanded into hydroelectricity to become one of the most powerful corporations in the nation.

The mining corporations laid the basis for a new economy as well as an interim government and established many of the region's first white settlements. Before the advent of railroads, ore had to be brought out of and supplies brought into mining areas by boats, wagons, and mules traveling hundreds of miles over rough territory. The railroad made transportation of supplies and products easier and faster. The shipping trade meanwhile grew into an important industry of its own, employing thousands of merchants, peddlers, and sailors. Dance halls, saloons, theaters, hospitals, and newspapers followed. Gold Hill and nearby Virginia City, Nevada, began as a cluster of small mining camps and by the early 1860s became a thriving urban community of nearly 6,000 people. A decade later, the population had quadrupled, but it subsequently fell sharply as the mines gave out. Occasionally, ore veins lasted long enough—as in Butte, Montana, center of the copper-mining district—to create permanent cities.

Many short-lived boomtowns were known as "Helldorados." Men outnumbered women by as much as ten to one, and very few lived with families or stayed very long. They often bunked with male kin and worked alongside friends or acquaintances from their hometown. Some lived unusually well, feasting on oysters trucked in at great expense. Amateur sporting events, public lectures, and large numbers of magazines and books filled many of their leisure hours. But the town center was usually the saloon, where, as one observer complained, men "without the restraint of law, indifferent to public opinion, and unburdened by families, drink whenever they feel like it, whenever they have the money to pay for it, and whenever there is nothing else to do."

The western labor movement began in these camps, partly as a response to dangerous working conditions. In the hardrock mines of the 1870s, one of every thirty workers was disabled, one of eighty killed. Balladeers back in Ireland sang of Butte as the town "where the streets were paved with Irish bones," and departing emigrants promised their mothers that they would never go underground in Montana. Miners began to organize in the 1860s, demanding good pay for dangerous and life-shortening work. By the end of the century they had established the strongest unions in the West.

Violence on both sides characterized western labor relations. When mineowners' private armies "arrested" strikers or fought their unions with rifle fire, miners burned down the campsites, seized trains loaded with ore, and sabotaged company property. The miners' unions also helped to secure legislation mandating a maximum eight-hour day for certain jobs and workmen's compensation for injuries. Such laws were enacted in Idaho, Arizona, and New Mexico by the 1910s, long before similar laws in most eastern states.

The unions fought hard, but they did so exclusively for the benefit of white workers. The native-born and the Irish and Cornish immigrants (from Cornwall, England) far outnumbered other groups before the turn of the century, when Italians, Slavs, and Greeks began to replace them. Labor unions eventually admitted these new immigrants, but refused Chinese, Mexican, and Indian workers. In 1869 white miners at the Comstock Lode rioted to protest the employment of Chinese miners. In Arizona, Mexican Americans had secured jobs in the copper and silver mines, but they usually received less pay and worked under worse conditions than white workers.

When prices and ore production fell sharply, not even unions could stop the owners from shutting down the mines and leaving ghost towns in their wake.

Often they also left behind an environmental disaster. Hydraulic mining, which used water cannons to blast hillsides and expose gold deposits, drove tons of rock and earth into the rivers and canyons. By the late 1860s southern California's rivers were clogged, producing floods that wiped out towns and farms. In 1893 Congress finally passed the Caminetti Act, giving the state the power to regulate the mines. (The act also created the Sacramento River Commission, which began to replace free-flowing rivers with canals and dams). Underground mining continued unregulated, using up whole forests for timbers and filling the air with dangerous, sulfurous smoke.

Mormon Settlements

While western expansion fostered the growth of new commercial cities such as the numerous if unstable mining towns, it simultaneously placed new restrictions on established communities. The Mormons (members of the Church of Jesus Christ of Latter-Day Saints) had fled western New York in the 1830s for Illinois and Missouri, only to face greater persecution in the Midwest. When their founder, Joseph Smith, was lynched after proclaiming the doctrine of polygamy (plural wives), the community sought refuge in the West. Led by their new prophet, Brigham Young, the Mormons migrated in 1846–47 to the Great Basin in present-day Utah and formed an independent theocratic state, called Deseret. However, their dream was cut short in 1850 when Congress set up Utah Territory. In 1857 President James Buchanan declared the Mormons to be in "a state of substantial rebellion" (for being an independent state in U.S. territory) and sent the U.S. Army to occupy the territory.

Although federal troops remained until the outbreak of the Civil War in 1861, the Mormon population continued to grow. By 1860 more than 40,000 Mormons lived in Utah Territory. Contrary to federal law, church officials forbade the selling of land. Mormons instead held property in common. They created sizable settlements complemented by satellite villages joined to communal farmlands and a common pasture. Relying on agricultural techniques learned from local Indian tribes, the Mormons built dams for irrigation and harvested a variety of crops from desert soil. Eventually nearly 500 Mormon communities spread from Oregon to Idaho to Arizona.

But as territorial rule tightened, the Mormons saw their unique way of life once again threatened. The newspapers and the courts repeatedly assailed the Mormons for the supposed sexual excesses of their system of "plural marriage," condemning them as heathens and savages. "There is an irrepressible conflict," one journalist wrote, "between the Mormon power and the principles upon which our free institu-

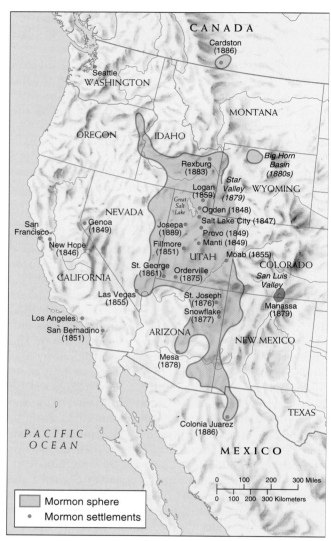

Mormon Cultural Diffusion, ca. 1883 *Mormon settlements permeated many sparsely populated sections of Idaho, Nevada, Arizona, Wyoming, Colorado, and New Mexico. Built with Church backing and the strong commitment of community members, they survived and even prospered in adverse climates.*

tions are established, and one or the other must succumb." Preceded by prohibitory federal laws enacted in 1862 and 1874, the Supreme Court finally ruled against polygamy in the 1879 case of *United States v. Reynolds,* which granted the freedom of belief but not the freedom of practice. In 1882 Congress passed the Edmunds Act, which effectively disfranchised those who believed in or practiced polygamy and threatened them with fines and imprisonment. Equally devastating was the Edmunds-Tucker Act, passed five years later, which destroyed the temporal power of the Mormon Church by confiscating all assets over $50,000 and establishing a federal commission to over-

see all elections in the territory. By the early 1890s Mormon leaders officially renounced plural marriage.

Polygamy had actually been practiced by no more than 15 percent to 20 percent of Mormon families, but it had been important to their sense of messianic mission. Forced to abandon the practice, they gave up most other aspects of their distinctive communal life, including the common ownership of land. By the time Utah became a state in 1896, Mormon communities resembled in some ways the society that the original settlers had sought to escape. They nevertheless combined their religious cohesion with leadership in the expanding regional economy to become a major political force in the West.

The Southwest

American expansionism transformed deserts and grasslands that had been contested for centuries among world powers. In 1845, Texas was annexed as a state, and the following year President James K. Polk whipped up a border dispute with Mexico into a war. The one-sided conflict ended in 1848 with the United States taking fully half of all Mexican territory—the future states of Arizona, California, Nevada, and Utah and parts of New Mexico, Wyoming, and Colorado. The Gadsden Purchase of 1853 rounded off this prize, giving the United States possession of all the land north of the Rio Grande.

The Treaty of Guadalupe Hidalgo, which ended the Mexican-American War, allowed the Hispanic people north of the Rio Grande to choose between immigrating to Mexico or staying in what was now the United States. But the new Mexican-American border, one of the longest unguarded boundaries in the world, could not successfully sever communities that had been connected for centuries. Despite the change in sovereignty, elites and common folk alike continued to travel back and forth between the two nations, and the majority of people who became U.S. citizens retained their identity as Mexicans. Even those who migrated farther north, a process that accelerated after the discovery of gold in California and the silver strikes in Nevada, kept their ties with friends and family in Mexico. What gradually emerged was an economically and socially interdependent zone, the Anglo-Hispanic borderlands linking the United States and Mexico.

Equality, however, did not provide the basis for relationships between the two nations and their peoples. Although under the treaty all Hispanics were formally guaranteed citizenship and the "free enjoyment of their liberty and property," local Anglos (as the Mexicans called white Americans) often violated these provisions and, through fraud or coercion, took control of the land. The Sante Fe Ring, a group of lawyers, politicians, and land speculators, stole millions of acres from the public

Thomas Allen, *Market Plaza*, 1878–1879. Oil on canvas, 26 x 39½ in. Witte Museum, San Antonio, Texas.

Mexican Americans in San Antonio continued to conduct their traditional market bazaar well after the incorporation of this region into the United States. Forced off the land and excluded from the better-paying jobs in the emerging regional economy, many Mexicanos and especially women sought to sell the products of their own handiwork for cash or for bartered food and clothing.

domain and grabbed over 80 percent of the Mexicano landholdings in New Mexico alone. More often, Anglos used new federal laws to their own benefit.

For a time, Arizona and New Mexico seemed to hold out hope for a mutually beneficial interaction between Mexicanos and Anglos. A prosperous class of Hispanic landowners, with long-standing ties to Anglos through marriage, had established itself in cities like Albuquerque and Tucson, old Spanish towns that had been founded in the seventeenth and eighteenth centuries. Estevan Ochoa, merchant, philanthropist, and the only Mexican to serve as mayor of Tucson following the Gadsden Purchase, managed to build one of the largest business empires in the West. In Las Cruces, New Mexico, an exceptional family such as the wealthy Amadors could shop by mail from Bloomingdales, travel to the World's Fair in Chicago, and send their children to English-language Catholic schools. Even the small and struggling Mexicano middle class could afford such modern conveniences as kitchen stoves and sewing machines. These Mexican elites, well integrated into the emerging national economy, continued to wield political power as ranchers, landlords, and real estate developers until the end of the century. They secured passage of bills for education in their regions and often served as superintendents of local schools. Several

prominent merchants became territorial delegates to Congress.

The majority of Mexicans who had lived in the mountains and deserts of the Southwest for well over two centuries were less prepared for these changes. Most had worked outside the commercial economy, farming and herding sheep for their own subsistence. Before 1848 they had few contacts with the outside world. With the Anglos came land closures as well as commercial expansion prompted by railroad, mining, and timber industries. Many poor families found themselves crowded onto plots too small for subsistence farming. Many turned to seasonal labor on the new Anglo-owned commercial farms, where they became the first of many generations of poorly paid migratory workers. Other Mexicanos adapted by taking jobs on the railroad or in the mines. Meanwhile their wives and daughters moved to the new towns and cities in such numbers that by the end of the century Mexicanos had become a predominantly urban population, dependent on wages for survival.

Women were quickly drawn into the expanding network of market and wage relations. They tried to make ends meet by selling produce from their backyard gardens; more often they worked as seamstresses or laundresses. Formerly at the center of a communal society, Mexicanas found themselves with fewer options in the cash economy. What wages they could now earn fell below even the low sums paid to their husbands, and women lost status within both the family and community.

Occasionally, Mexicanos organized to reverse these trends or at least to limit the damage done to their communities. In South Texas in 1859, Juan Cortina and sixty of his followers pillaged white-owned stores and killed four Anglos who had gone unpunished for murdering several Mexicans. "Cortina's War" marked the first of several sporadic rebellions. As late as the 1880s, Las Corras Blancas, a band of agrarian rebels in New Mexico, were destroying railroad ties and posting demands for justice on fences of the new Anglo farms and ranches. Other Mexicanos organized more peacefully. *El Alianzo Hispano-Americano* (the Hispanic-American Alliance) was formed "to protect and fight for the rights of Spanish Americans" through political action. *Mutualistes* (mutual aid societies) provided sickness and death benefits to Mexican families.

Despite many pressures, Mexicanos preserved much of their cultural heritage. Many persisted in older ways because they had few choices and because their family and religion reinforced tradition. The Roman Catholic Church retained its influence in the community, and most Mexicans continued to turn to the church to baptize infants, to celebrate the feast day of their patron saints, to marry, and to bury the dead. Special saints like the Virgin of Guadalupe and distinctive holy days like the Day of the Dead survived along with fiestas celebrating the change of seasons. Many communities continued to commemorate Mexican national holidays, such as *Cinco de Mayo* (the fifth of May), marking the Mexican victory over French invaders in the battle of Puebla in 1862. Spanish language and Spanish place names continued to distinguish the Southwest.

But for the encroaching Anglo majority, large regions in the West had been "won" from the populations who had previously settled the region. Americans had brought in commercial capitalism, their political and legal systems, as well as many of their social and cultural institutions. Ironically, though, even after statehood, white settlers would still be only distant representatives of an empire whose financial, political, and industrial centers remained in the Northeast. In return for raw produce or ore drawn out of soil or rock, they received washtubs, clothes, and whiskey; model legal statutes; and doctors, lawyers, and teachers. But they were often frustrated by their continued isolation and enraged at the federal regulations that governed them and at the eastern investors and lawyers who seemed poised on all sides to rob them of the fruits of their labor. Embittered Westerners, along with Southerners, would form the core of a nationwide discontent that would soon threaten to uproot the American political system.

THE CATTLE INDUSTRY

The slaughter of the buffalo made way for the cattle industry, one of the most profitable businesses in the West. Texas longhorns, introduced by the Spanish, numbered over 5 million at the close of the Civil War and represented a potentially plentiful supply of beef for eastern consumers. In the spring of 1866, entrepreneurs such as Joseph G. McCoy began to build a spectacular cattle market in the western part of Kansas, where the Kansas Pacific Railroad provided crucial transportation links to slaughtering and packing houses and commercial distributors in Kansas City, St. Louis, and Chicago.

In 1867 only 35,000 head of cattle reached McCoy's new stockyards in Abilene, but 1868 proved

the first of many banner years. Drovers pushed herd after herd north from Texas through Oklahoma on the trail marked out by part-Cherokee trader Jesse Chisholm. Great profits were made on Texas steers bought for $7–$9 a head and sold in Kansas for upward of $30. In 1880 nearly 2 million cattle were slaughtered in Chicago alone. For two decades, cattle represented the West's bonanza industry.

Cowboys

The great cattle drives depended on the cowboy, a seasonal or migrant worker. After the Civil War, cowboys—one for every 300–500 head on the trail—rounded up herds of Texas cattle and drove them as much as 1,500 miles north to grazing ranches or to the stockyards where they were readied for shipping by rail to eastern markets. The boss supplied the horses, the cowboy his own bedroll, saddle, and spurs. The workday lasted from sunup to sundown, with short night shifts for guarding the cattle. Scurvy, a widespread ailment, could be traced to the basic chuckwagon menu of sowbelly, beans, and coffee, a diet bereft of fruits and vegetables. The cowboy worked without protection from rain or hail, and severe dust storms could cause temporary blindness. As late as 1920, veterans of the range complained that no company would sell life insurance to a cowboy.

In return for his labor, the cowboy received at the best of times about $30 per month. Wages were usually paid in one lump sum at the end of a drive, a policy that encouraged cowboys to spend their money quickly and recklessly in the booming cattle towns of Dodge City, Kansas, or Cheyenne, Wyoming. In the 1880s, when wages began to fall along with the price of beef, cowboys fought back by stealing cattle or by forming unions. In 1883 many Texas cowboys struck for higher wages; nearly all Wyoming cowboys struck in 1886. Aided by the legendary camaraderie fostered in the otherwise desolate conditions of the long drive, cowboys, along with miners, were among the first western workers to organize against employers.

Like other parts of the West, the cattle range was ethnically diverse. Between one-fifth and one-third of all workers were Indian, Mexican, or African American. Indian cowboys worked mainly on the northern plains and in Indian Territory; the vaqueros, who had previously worked on the Mexican cattle haciendas, or huge estates, predominated in South Texas and California. After the Civil War, hundreds of African Americans took the trail north from Texas.

Like the vaqueros, African American cowboys were highly skilled managers of cattle. Some were sons of former slaves who had been captured from the African territory of Gambia, where cattle-raising was an age-old art. Unlike Mexicans, they earned wages comparable to those paid to Anglos and especially during the early years worked in integrated drover parties. By the 1880s, as the center of the cattle industry shifted to the more settled regions around the northern ranches, African Americans were forced out and turned to other kinds of work. Although the majority of Anglo cowboys also came from the South and shared with former slaves the hope of escaping the postwar economic devastation of their region, they usually remained loyal to the racial hierarchy of the Confederacy.

Cowgirls and Prostitutes

Sally Redus, wife of an early Texas cattleman, once accompanied her husband on the long drive from Texas to Kansas. Carrying her baby on her lap, she most likely rode the enormous distance "sidesaddle," with both legs on one side of the horse. Although few women worked as trail hands, they did find jobs on the ranches, usually in the kitchen or laundry. Occasionally a husband and wife worked as partners, sharing even the labor of wrangling cattle, and following her husband's death, a woman might take over altogether. The majority of women attended to domestic chores, caring for children and maintaining the household. Their daughters, however, enjoyed better prospects. By the end of the century, women reared on ranches were riding astride, "clothespin style," roping calves, branding cattle or cutting their ears to mark

them, and castrating bulls. But not until 1901 did a woman dare to enter an official rodeo contest.

In cattle towns, many women worked as prostitutes. During the first cattle drive to Abilene in 1867, a few women were so engaged; but by the following spring, McCoy's assistant recalled, "they came in swarms, & as the weather was warm 4 or 5 girls could huddle together in a tent very comfortably." Although some women worked in trailside "hoghouses," the best-paid prostitutes congregated in "brothel districts" or "tenderloins." Most cattle towns boasted at least one dance hall where prostitutes plied their trade. Dodge city had two: one with white prostitutes for white patrons; another with black prostitutes for both white and black men. Although prostitution was illegal in most towns, the laws were rarely enforced until the end of the century, when reformers led campaigns to shut down the red-light districts.

Perhaps 50,000 women engaged in prostitution west of the Mississippi during the second half of the nineteenth century. Like most cowboys, most prostitutes were unmarried and in their teens or twenties. Often fed up with underpaid jobs in dressmaking or domestic service, they found few alternatives to prostitution in the cattle towns, where the cost of food and lodging was notoriously high. Still, earnings in prostitution were slim, except during the cattle-shipping season when young men outnumbered women by as much as three to one.

In the best of times, a fully employed Wichita prostitute might earn $30 per week, nearly two-thirds of which would go for room and board. Injury or even death from violent clients, addiction to narcotics such as cocaine or morphine, and venereal disease were workaday dangers.

Community and Conflict on the Range

The combination of prostitution, gambling, and drinking discouraged the formation of stable communities. According to a Kansas proverb, "There's no Sunday west of Junction City and no god west of Salina." Personal violence was notoriously commonplace on the streets and in the barrooms of cattle towns and mining camps populated mainly by young, single men. Many western towns such as Wichita outlawed the carrying of handguns, but

Curly Wolves Howled on Saturday Night, *a commercial woodcut from the 1870s. The artist, recording this scene at a tavern near Billings, Montana, captured what he called a "Dude and a Waitress" dancing the "Bull Calves' Medley on the Grand Piano." Illustrations depicting a wild and lively West appeared prominently in magazines like* Harper's Weekly, *which circulated mainly among readers east of the Mississippi.*

enforcement usually lagged. Local specialty shops and mail-order catalogues continued to sell weapons with little regulation. But contrary to popular belief, gunfights were relatively rare. Local police officers, such as Wyatt Earp and "Wild Bill" Hickok, worked mainly to keep order among drunken cowboys.

After the Civil War, violent crime, assault, and robbery rose sharply throughout the United States. In the West, the most prevalent crimes were horse theft and cattle rustling, which peaked during the height of the open range period and then fell back by the 1890s. Death by legal hanging or illegal lynching—at "necktie parties" in which the victims were "jerked to Jesus"—was the usual sentence. In the last half of the century, vigilantes acting outside the law mobilized more than 200 times, claiming altogether more than 500 victims.

The "range wars" of the 1870s produced violent conflicts. By this time, both farmers and sheep herders were encroaching on the fields where cattle had once grazed freely. Sheep chew grass down to its roots, making it practically impossible to raise cattle on land they have grazed. Farmers meanwhile set about building fences to protect their domestic livestock and property. Great cattle barons fought back against farmers by ordering cowboys to cut the new

barbed-wire fences. Rivalry among the owners of livestock was even more vicious, particularly in the Southwest and Pacific Northwest. In these areas, Mexicano shepherds and Anglo cattlemen often fought each other for land. In Lincoln County, New Mexico, the feuds grew so intense in 1878 that one faction hired gunman Billy the Kid to protect its interests. President Rutherford B. Hayes finally sent troops to halt the bloodshed.

The cattle barons helped to bring about their own demise, but they did not go down quietly. Ranchers eager for greater profits, and often backed by foreign capital, overstocked their herds, and eventually the cattle began to deplete the limited supply of grass. Finally, in 1885–87, a combination of summer drought and winter blizzards killed 90 percent of the cattle in the West. Prices also declined sharply. Many big ranchers fell into bankruptcy. Along the way, they often took out their grievances against the former cowboys who had gathered small herds for themselves. They charged these small ranchers with cattle rustling, taking them to court or, in some cases, rounding up lynching parties. As one historian has written, violence was "not a mere sideshow" but "an intrinsic part of western society."

Statehood and Ethnic Settlement

The process for admitting new states to the Union was established by Congress in the Northwest Ordinance of 1787, before the ratification of the Constitution. Although the pace at which this process operated and the way it was controlled varied from region to region and over time, its formal rules changed little. Each new state was admitted when its free population reached 60,000 and its constitution was approved by Congress, entitling those citizens eligible to vote to become full participants in the political system.

Each of the western states that entered the Union in the late nineteenth and early twentieth centuries had its own distinctive ethnic and racial composition. North Dakota, which became a state in 1889, had long had a large Native American population. An influx of newcomers, many of them European immigrants, boosted its population quickly by 1900. As the map at the right indicates, ethnic groups of European background tended to settle in clusters, mainly where they had purchased large blocs of fertile land from promoters. Nonwhites sought (or were confined to) remote locations. Much of the state remained practically uninhabited.

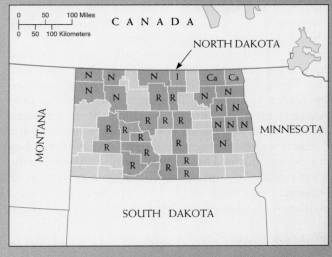

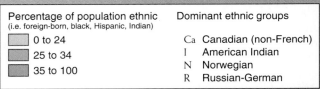

Percentage of population ethnic
(i.e. foreign-born, black, Hispanic, Indian)

- 0 to 24
- 25 to 34
- 35 to 100

Dominant ethnic groups

Ca Canadian (non-French)
I American Indian
N Norwegian
R Russian-German

Source: James R. Shortridge, *The Great Plains.* Cayton, Gorn, Williams, *Encyclopedia of American History*, II.

FARMING COMMUNITIES ON THE PLAINS

The vision of a huge fertile garden extending from the Appalachians to the Pacific Ocean had inspired Americans since the early days of the republic. But the first explorers who actually traveled through the Great Plains quashed this dream. "The Great Desert" was the name they gave to the region stretching west from Kansas and Nebraska, north to Montana and the Dakotas, and south again to Oklahoma and Texas. Few trees fended off the blazing sun of summer or promised a supply of lumber for homes and fences. The occasional river or stream flowed with "muddy gruel" rather than pure, sweet water. Economically, the entire region appeared as hopelessly barren as it was vast. It took massive improvements in both transportation and farm technology—as well as unrelenting advertising and promotional campaigns—to open the Great Plains to widescale agriculture.

The Homestead Act

The Homestead Act of 1862 offered the first incentive to prospective white farmers. This act granted a quarter section (160 acres) of the public domain free to any settler who lived on the land and improved it for at least five years; or a settler could buy the land for $1.25 per acre after only six months' residence. Approximately 605 million acres of public domain became available for settlement.

Homesteaders achieved their greatest success in the central and upper Midwest where the soil was rich and weather relatively moderate. But those settlers lured to the Great Plains by descriptions of land "carpeted with soft grass—a sylvan paradise" found themselves locked in a fierce struggle with the harsh climate and arid soil. The average holding could rarely furnish a livelihood, even with hard work.

Rather than filing a homestead claim with the federal government, most settlers acquired their land outright. State governments and land companies usually held the most valuable land near transportation and markets, and the majority of farmers were willing to pay a hefty price for these benefits. A few women speculators did very well, particularly in the Dakotas, where they acquired acreage under the generous terms of the Homestead Act, not to farm but to sell when prices for land increased. Before the turn of the century, farm acreage west of the Mississippi had tripled, but perhaps only 10 percent of all farmers got their start under homestead provisions. The big-time land speculators gained the most, plucking choice locations at bargain prices.

The dream of a homestead nevertheless died hard. Five years after the passage of the Homestead Act, *New York Tribune* editor Horace Greeley still advised his readers to strike off "into the broad, free West" and "make yourself a farm from Uncle Sam's generous domain, you will crowd nobody, starve nobody, and . . . neither you nor your children need evermore beg for Something to Do." He was wrong. Although the Homestead Act did spark the largest migration in American history, it did not lay the foundation for a nation of prosperous family farms.

Populating the Plains

The rapid settlement of the West could not have taken place without the railroad. Although the Homestead Act offered prospective farmers free land, it was the railroad that promoted settlement, brought people to their new homes, and carried crops and cattle to eastern markets. The railroads therefore wielded tremendous economic and political power throughout the West. Their agents—reputed to know every cow in the district—made major decisions regarding territorial welfare. In designing routes and locating depots, railroad companies put whole communities "on the map," or left them behind.

Along with providing transportation links between the East and West and potential markets as distant as China, the western railroads directly encouraged settlement. Unlike the railroads built before the Civil War, which followed the path of villages and towns, the western lines preceded settlement. Bringing people west became their top priority, and the railroad companies conducted aggressive promotional and marketing campaigns. Agents enticed Easterners and Europeans alike with long-term loans and free transportation by rail to distant points in the West. The railroads also sponsored land companies to sell parcels of their own huge allotments from the federal government. The National Land Company, founded in Chicago in 1869, alone organized sixteen colonies of mainly European immigrants in parts of Kansas and Colorado. The Santa Fe Railroad sent agent C. B. Schmidt to Germany, where he managed to entice nearly 60,000 Germans to settle along the rail line.

More than 2 million Europeans, many recruited by professional promoters, settled the Great Plains between 1870 and 1900. Some districts in Minnesota seemed to be virtual colonies of Sweden; others housed the largest number of Finns in the New World. In sparsely settled North Dakota, Scandinavians constituted 30 percent of the population, with Norwegians the largest group. Nebraska, whose population as early as 1870 was 25 percent foreign-born, concentrated Germans, Swedes, Danes, and Czechs. A smaller portion of European immigrants reached Kansas, still fewer the territories to the south where Indian and Hispanic peoples and African Americans remained the major ethnic populations. But Germans outnumbered all other immigrants by far.

Many immigrants found life on the Great Plains difficult but endurable. "Living in Nebraska," the locals joked, "is a lot like being hanged; the initial shock is a bit abrupt, but once you hang there for awhile you sort of get used to it." The German Russians who settled the Dakotas discovered soil similar to that of their homeland but weather that was even more severe. Having earlier fled religious persecution in Germany for Russia, they brought with them heavy coats and the technique of using sun-dried bricks to build houses in areas where lumber was scarce. These immigrants often provided examples for other settlers less familiar with such harsh terrain.

Having traveled the huge distance with kin or members of their Old World villages, immigrants tended to form tight-knit communities on the Great Plains. Often they advised others still at home to join them and gradually enlarged their distinctive settlements. Many married only within their own group. For example, only 3 percent of Norwegian men married women of a different ethnic background. Like many Mexicanos in the Southwest, several immigrant groups retained their languages well into the twentieth century, usually by sponsoring parochial school systems and publishing their own newspapers. A few groups closed their communities to outsiders. The Poles who migrated to central Nebraska in the 1880s, for example, formed an exclusive settlement; and the German Hutterites, who disavowed private property, lived as much as possible in seclusion in the Bon Homme colony of South Dakota, established in 1874.

Among the native-born settlers of the Great Plains, the largest number had migrated from states bordering the Mississippi River, all of which lost population in the decade after the enactment of the Homestead Act. Settling as individual families rather than as whole communities, they faced an exceptionally solitary life on the Great Plains. The usual rectangular homestead of 160 acres placed farm families at least a half-mile and often much farther from each other. To stave off isolation, homesteaders sometimes built their homes on the adjoining corners of their plots. Still, the prospect of doing better, which brought most homesteaders to the Great Plains in the first place, caused many families to keep seeking greener pastures. Mobility was so high that between one-third and one-half of all households pulled up stakes within a decade.

Communities eventually flourished in prosperous towns like Grand Island, Nebraska; Coffeyville, Kansas; and Fargo, North Dakota, that served the larger agricultural region. Built alongside the railroad, they grew into commercial centers, home to banking, medical, legal, and retail services. Town life fostered a special intimacy; even in the county graveyard, it was said, a town resident remained among neighbors. But closeness did not necessarily promote social equality or even friendship. A social hierarchy based on education (for the handful of doctors and lawyers) and, more important, investment property (held mainly by railroad agents and bankers) governed relationships between individuals and families. Religion also played a large part in defining these differences. Upwards of 70 percent of town residents were church-affiliated, the largest group comprising Roman Catholics, followed by Methodists, Lutherans, Baptists, and Presbyterians. Reinforced by family ties and ethnic affiliation, religious allegiances just as often provided a basis for conflict as for community.

Work, Dawn to Dusk

By the 1870s the Great Plains, once the home of buffalo and Indian hunters, was becoming a vast farming region populated mainly by immigrants from Europe and white Americans from east of the Mississippi. In place of the first one-room shanties, sod houses, and log cabins stood substantial frame farmhouses, along with a variety of other buildings like barns, smokehouses, and stables. But the built environment took nothing away from the predominating vista—the expansive fields of grain. "You have no idea, Beulah," wrote a Dakota farmer to his wife, "of what [the wheat farms] are like until you see them. For mile after mile there is not a sign of a tree or stone and just as level as the floor of your house. . . . Wheat never looked better and it is nothing but wheat, wheat, wheat."

Most farm families survived, and prospered if they could, through hard work, often from dawn to dusk. Men's activities in the fields tended to be seasonal, with heavy work during planting and harvest; at other times, their labor centered on construction or repair of buildings and on taking care of livestock. Women's activities were usually far more routine, week in and week out: cooking and canning of seasonal fruit and vegetables, washing, ironing, churning cream for butter, and keeping chickens for their eggs. Women might occasionally take in boarders, usually young men working temporarily in railroad construction, and they tended to the young children. Many women complained about the ceaseless drudgery, especially when they watched their husbands invest in farm equipment rather than domestic appliances. Others, however, relished the challenge. An Iowa woman, for example, liked "to have whole control of my house; can say I am monarch of all I survey and none to dispute my right."

Children also joined in the family's labors. Milking the cows, hauling water, and running errands to neighboring farms could be done by the children, once they had reached the age of nine or so. The "one-room school," where all grades learned together, taught the basics of literacy and arithmetic that a future farmer or commercial employee would require. Sons might be expected to work for ten to twenty years on the family farm, generally for their subsistence alone. Older sons and daughters alike might move to the nearest town to find wagework and contribute their earnings to the family coffer.

The harsh climate and unyielding soil nevertheless

These homesteaders in Nebraska, 1886, confronted the typically harsh conditions of treeless plains by erecting sod huts. They often brought with them an assortment of seeds and seedlings for spring plantings and a small number of livestock. A good fall harvest would provide the cash for building more substantial frame houses and outbuildings and encourage other homesteaders to settle near them. Communities eventually grew from these crude beginnings.

forced all but the most reclusive families to seek out friends and neighbors. Many hands were needed to clear the land for cultivation or for road beds, to raise houses and barns, or to bring in a harvest before a threatening storm. Neighbors might agree to work together haying, harvesting, and threshing grain. They also traded their labor, calculated by the hour, for use of equipment or for special assistance. A well-to-do farmer might "rent" his threshing machine in exchange for a small cash fee and, for instance, three days' labor. His wife might barter her garden produce for her neighbor's bread and milk or for help during childbirth or disability. Women often combined work and leisure in quilting bees and sewing circles, where they made friends while sharing scraps of material and technical information. Whole communities turned out for special events, such as the seasonal husking bees and apple bees, which were organized mainly by women.

Much of this informal barter, however, resulted from lack of cash rather than a lasting desire to cooperate. When annual harvests were bountiful, even the farm woman's practice of bartering goods with neighbors and local merchants—butter and eggs in return for yard goods or seed—diminished sharply, replaced by cash transactions. Still, wheat production proved unsteady in the last half of the nineteenth century, and few farm families could remain reliant wholly on themselves.

For many farmers, the soil simply would not yield a livelihood, and they often owed more money than they took in. Start-up costs, including the purchase of land and equipment, put many farmers deep in debt to local creditors. Some lost their land altogether. By 1880, when the Bureau of the Census began to compile statistics on tenant-operated farms, nearly 18 percent of the farms in Nebraska were worked by tenants; a decade later the portion had risen to nearly one-quarter. By the turn of the century, more than one-third of all farmers in the United States were tenants on someone else's land.

The Garden of Eden was not to be found on the prairies or on the plains, no matter how hard the average farm family worked. Again and again foreclosures wiped out the small landowner through dips in commodity prices, bad decisions, natural disasters, or illness. In one especially bad year, 1881, a group of farmers in western Iowa chose to burn off rather than harvest their wheat because the yield promised to be so small. Many farmers stood only a step away from financial disaster, wondering if they had chosen the best life for themselves and their families. The swift growth of rural population soon ended. Although writers and orators alike continued to celebrate the family farm as the source of virtue and economic well-being, the hard reality of big money and political power told a far different story.

THE WORLD'S BREADBASKET

During the second half of the nineteenth century western farms employed the most intensive and extensive methods of agricultural production in the world. Hard-working farmers brought huge numbers of acres under cultivation, while new technologies allowed them to achieve unprecedented levels of efficiency in the planting and harvesting of crops. As a result, western agriculture became increasingly tied to international trade, and modern capitalism soon ruled western agriculture, as it did the mining and cattle industries.

New Production Technologies

Only after the trees had been cleared and grasslands cut free of roots could the soil be prepared for planting. But as farmers on the Great Plains knew so well, the sod west of the Mississippi did not yield readily to cultivation and often broke the cast-iron plows typically used by eastern farmers. Farther west, some farmers resorted to drills to plant seeds for crops such as wheat and oats. Even in the best locations, where loamy, fertile ground had built up over centuries into eight or more inches of decayed vegetation, the preliminary breaking, or "busting," of the sod required hard labor. One man would guide a team of five or six oxen pulling a plow through the soil, while another regulated the depth of the cut, or furrow. But, as a North Dakota settler wrote to his wife back in Michigan, after the first crop the soil became as "soft as can be, any team [of men and animals] can work it."

Agricultural productivity depended as much on new technology as on the farmers' hard labor. In 1837 John Deere had designed his famous "singing plow" that easily turned prairie grasses under and turned up even highly compacted soils. Around the same time, Cyrus McCormick's reaper began to be used for cutting

This "thirty-three horse team harvester" was photographed at the turn of the century in Walla Walla, Washington. Binding the grain into sheaves before it could hit the ground, the "harvester" cut, threshed, and sacked wheat in one single motion.

HAND VS. MACHINE LABOR ON THE FARM, CA. 1880

Crop	Time Worked		Labor Cost	
	Hand	Machine	Hand	Machine
Wheat	61 hours	3 hours	$3.55	$0.66
Corn	39 hours	15 hours	3.62	1.51
Oats	66 hours	7 hours	3.73	1.07
Loose Hay	21 hours	4 hours	1.75	0.42
Baled Hay	35 hours	12 hours	3.06	1.29

grain; by the 1850s his factories were turning out reapers in mass quantities. McCormick's design featured ridges of triangular knives, like sharks' teeth, that mechanically sliced through the stalks as the reaper moved forward under horse-power or, later, machine-power. The harvester, invented in the 1870s, drew the cut stalks upward to a platform where two men could bind them into sheaves; by the 1880s an automatic knotter tied them together. Drastically reducing the number of people traditionally required for this work, the harvester increased the pace many times over.

Improvements were not limited to the reaper and harvester, although these machines underwent continuous redesign and were enhanced first by steam and eventually gas power. From the 1840s on, the U.S. Patent Office recorded an astonishing number of agricultural inventions. The introduction of mechanized corn planters and mowing or raking machines for hay all but completed the technological arsenal.

In the 1890s, the U.S. commissioner of labor measured the impact of technology on farm productivity. Before the introduction of the wire binder in 1875, he reported, a farmer could not plant more than 8 acres of wheat if he were to harvest it successfully without help; by 1890 the same farmer could rely on his new machine to handle 135 acres with relative ease and without risk of spoilage. The improvements in the last half of the century allowed an average farmer to produce up to ten times more than was possible with the old implements.

Scientific study of soil, grain, and climatic conditions was another factor in the record output. Heretofore, farmers had to rely on tradition or to experiment with whatever the grain merchants had to offer. Beginning in the mid-nineteenth century, federal and state governments added inducements to the growing body of expertise, scientific information, and hands-on advice. Through the Morrill Act of 1862, "land-grant" colleges acquired space for campuses in return for promising to institute agricultural programs. The Department of Agriculture, which attained cabinet status in

1889, and the Weather Bureau (transferred from the War Department in 1891) also made considerable contributions to farmers' knowledge. The federal Hatch Act of 1887, which created a series of experimental agricultural stations, passed along new information, especially in the areas of soil minerals and plant growth. Many states added their own agricultural stations, usually connected with state colleges and universities.

Nature nevertheless often reigned over technological innovation and seemed in places to take revenge against these early successes. West of the 98th meridian—a north–south line extending through western Oklahoma, central Kansas and Nebraska, and eastern Dakota—perennial dryness due to an annual rainfall of less than 28 inches constantly threatened to turn soil into dust and to break plows on the hardened ground. Summer heat burned out crops and ignited grass fires. Mountains of winter snows turned rivers into spring torrents that flooded fields; heavy fall rains washed crops away. Even good weather invited worms and flying insects to infest the crops. During the 1870s grasshoppers in clouds a mile long ate everything organic, including tree bark and clothes. Mormons erected a statue to the gulls who made a surprise appearance in Utah to eat the "hoppers"; however, most farmers were not as lucky as the Mormons.

Producing for the Market

From the Midwest to the far reaches of the Great Plains, farming changed in important ways during the last third of the nineteenth century. Although the family remained the primary source of labor, farmers tended to put more emphasis on production for exchange rather than for home use. They continued to plant vegetable gardens and often kept fowl or livestock for the family's consumption, but farmers raised crops mainly for the market and measured their own success or failure in terms of cash products.

Most large-scale farmers specialized in one or two crops, such as corn, rye, or barley, and sent their goods by railroad to eastern distributors and thence to national and international markets. Wheat farmers in particular prospered. With the world population increasing at a rapid rate, the international demand for wheat was enormous, and American farmers made huge profits from the sale of this crop. Wheat production ultimately served as a barometer of the agricultural economy in the West. Farmers in all corners of the region, from Nebraska to California, expanded or contracted their holdings and planned their crops according to the price of wheat.

The new machines and expanding market did not necessarily guarantee success. Land, draft animals, and equipment remained very expensive, and start-up costs could keep a family in debt for decades. A year of good returns often preceded a year of financial disaster. Weather conditions, international markets, and railroad and steamship shipping prices all proved equally unpredictable and heartless.

Farmers who settled on good lands in the 1860s and 1870s were more fortunate than those to follow. These pioneers, who began with only a little capital and worked twenty or thirty years to build up livestock and crops, frequently reached old age knowing that they could leave productive farmland to their sons or daughters. Latecomers found most of the good land already locked up in production or too expensive to acquire.

The new technology and scientific expertise favored the large, well-capitalized farmer over the small one. Such is the story of the large-scale wheat operations in the great Red River Valley of North Dakota. Here a shrewd worker such as Oliver Dalrymple could take advantage of a spectacular bonanza. When Dalrymple started out in 1875, he managed a farm owned by two officials of the Northern Pacific Railroad. He cleared their land, planted wheat, and yielded a sizable harvest the first year. He did much better the second year and began to invest in his own farm. A decade later his operations included 32,000 acres in wheat and 2,000 in oats. Dalrymple now had the financial resources to use the latest technology to harvest these crops and to employ up to one thousand seasonal laborers at a time. The majority of farmers with fewer resources expanded at more modest rates. Between 1880 and 1900 average farm size in the seven leading grain-growing states increased from 64.4 acres to more than 100 acres.

California

The trend toward big farms reached an apex in California, where farming as a business quickly superseded farming as a way of life. The conclusion of the Mexican-American War in 1848 coincided with the beginning of the Gold Rush, and the Anglos flooding the new territory wanted the land that had been occupied for centuries by the Spanish-speaking peoples, the Californios. The U.S. Congress created the Lands Claims Commission in 1851 to examine the great land-grant system that had been introduced by the Spaniards. Although many Californios ultimately saw their holdings validated by the Supreme Court, the cost of litigation had forced many into debt. Then, after a period of frenzied land speculation, capitalists mainly from San Francisco and Sacramento took ownership of many farms in northern California. Many of these haciendas held some of the best farming land in the state and were replete with dams, canals, and other expensive earthworks demanded by the arid soil. The new owners introduced new technologies and invested huge amounts of capital, setting the pattern for the state's prosperous agribusiness. Farms of nearly 500 acres dominated the California landscape in 1870; by the turn of the century, two-thirds of the state's arable land was in 1,000-acre farms. As land reformer and social commentator Henry George noted, California was "not a country of farms but a country of plantations and estates."

This scale of production made California the national leader in wheat production by the mid-1880s. But it also succeeded dramatically with fruit and vegetables. Large- and medium-sized growers, shrewdly combined in cooperative marketing associations during the 1870s–80s, used the new refrigerator cars to ship their produce in large quantities to the East and even to Europe. By 1890, cherries, apricots, and oranges, packed with mountains of ice, made their way into homes across the United States.

California growers learned quickly that they could satisfy consumer appetites and even create new ones. Orange producers packed their products individually in tissue paper, a technique designed to convince eastern consumers that they were about to eat a luxury fruit. By the turn of the century, advertisers for the California Citrus Growers' Association described oranges as a necessity for good health, inventing the trademark "Sunkist" to be stamped on each orange. Meanwhile California's grape growing grew into a big business, led by promoter and winemaker Paul Masson. Long considered inferior to French wines, California wines found a ready market at lower prices. Other grape growers made their fortunes in raisins. By the early twentieth century, one association trademarked its raisins as "Sun Maid" and packaged them for schoolchildren in the famous nickel box.

By 1900, California had become the model for American agribusiness, not the home of self-sufficient homesteaders but the showcase of heavily capitalized farm factories. Machines soon displaced animals and even many people. Many Californios tried to hold onto their traditional forms of labor if not their land, only to become the backbone of the state's migrant work force. Intense battles in the state legislature over land and irrigation rights underscored the message that powerful forces had gathered in California to promote large-scale agricultural production.

The Toll on the Land

The delicate ecologies of the West perished more quickly under human pressure than those prevailing anywhere else on the continent. Viewing the land as a resource to command, the new inhabitants often looked past the existing flora and fauna toward a landscape remade strictly for commercial purposes. The changes they produced in some areas were nearly as cataclysmic as those that occurred during the Ice Age.

Banishing many existing species, farmers "improved" the land by introducing exotic plants and animals—that is, biological colonies indigenous to other regions and continents. Some of the new plants and animals flourished in alien surroundings; many did not. Farmers also unintentionally introduced new varieties of weeds, insect pests, and rats. Surviving portions of older grasslands and meadows eventually could be found only alongside railroad tracks, in graveyards, or inside national parks.

Numerous species disappeared altogether or suffered drastic reduction. The grizzly bear, for example, an animal exclusive to the West, could once be found in large numbers from the Great Plains to California and throughout much of Alaska; by the early decades of the twentieth century, one nature writer estimated that only 800 survived, mostly in Yellowstone National Park. At the same time the number of wolves declined from perhaps as many as 2 million to just 200,000. "If you count the buffalo for hides and the antelope for backstraps and the passenger pigeons for target practice and the Indian ponies (killed by whites, to keep the Indian poor)," one scholar estimates, "it is conceivable that 500 million creatures died" on the Plains alone. By the mid-1880s, no more than 5,000 buffalo survived in the entire United States, and little remained of the once vast herds but great heaps of bones sold for $7.50 per ton.

The slaughter of the buffalo had a dramatic impact, not only on the fate of the species but also on the grasslands of the Great Plains. Overall, the biological diversity of the region had been drastically reduced. Unlike the grizzly and wolf, buffalo had not been exclusively Western animals. Before European colonization they had grazed over an area of 3 million square miles, nearly to the east coast; as the herds moved on, the grasslands were replenished. Having killed off the giant herds, ranchers and farmers quickly shifted to cattle and sheep production. Unlike the roaming buffalo, these livestock did not range widely

and soon devoured the native grasses down to their roots. With the ground cover destroyed, the soil eroded and became barren. By the end of the century, huge dust storms formed across the windswept plains.

New forests, many settlers hoped, would improve the weather, restore the soil, and also provide a source for fencing and fuel. In 1873 the U.S. Congress passed the Timber Culture Act, which allotted homesteaders an additional 160 acres of land in return for planting and cultivating forty acres of trees. Because residence was not required, and because tree planting could not be assessed for at least thirteen years, speculators filed for several claims at once, then turned around and sold the land without having planted a single tree. Although some forests were restored, neither the weather nor the soil improved.

Large-scale commercial agriculture also took a heavy toll on inland waters. Before white settlement, rainfall had drained naturally into lakes and underground aquifers, and watering spots were abundant throughout the Plains. Farmers mechanically rerouted and dammed water to irrigate their crops, causing many bodies of water to disappear and the water table to drop significantly. Successful farmers pressed for ever greater supplies of water. In 1887 the state of California formed irrigation districts, securing bond issues for construction of canals, and other western states followed. But by the 1890s, irrigation had seemed to reach its limit without federal support. The Newlands or National Reclamation Act of 1902 added 1 million acres of irrigated land, and state irrigation districts added more than 10 million acres. Expensive to taxpayers, and ultimately benefiting corporate farmers rather than small landowners, these projects further diverted water and totally transformed the landscape.

Although western state politicians and federal officials debated water rights for decades, they rarely considered the impact of water policies on the environment. Lake Tulare in California's Central Valley, for example, had occupied up to 760 square miles. After farmers began to irrigate their land by tapping the rivers that fed Tulare, the lake shrank dramatically, covering a mere 36 square miles by the early twentieth century. Finally the lake, which had supported rich aquatic and avian life for thousands of years, disappeared entirely. The land left behind, now wholly dependent on irrigation, grew so alkaline in spots that it could no longer be used for agricultural purposes.

The need to maintain the water supply indirectly led to the creation of national forests and the Forest Service. Western farmers supported the General Land Revision Act of 1891, which gave the president the power to establish forest reserves to protect watersheds against the threats posed by lumbering, overgrazing, and forest fires. In the years that followed,

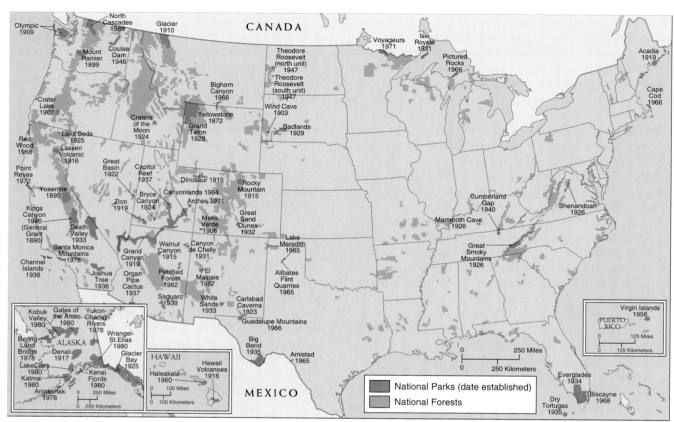

The Establishment of National Parks and Forests *The setting aside of land for national parks saved large districts of the West from early commercial development and industrial degradation, setting a precedent for the later establishment of additional parks in economically marginal but scenic territory. The West, home to the vast majority of park space, became a principal site of tourism by the end of the nineteenth century.*

President Benjamin Harrison established 15 forest reserves exceeding 16 million acres, and President Grover Cleveland added more than 21 million acres. But only in 1897 did the secretary of the interior finally gain the authority to regulate the use of these reserves.

The Forest Management Act of 1897 and the National Reclamation Act of 1902 set the federal government on the path of large-scale regulatory activities. The Forest Service was established in 1905, and in 1907 forest reserves were transferred from the Department of the Interior to the Department of Agriculture. The federal government would now play an even larger role in economic development of the West, dealing mainly with corporate farmers and ranchers eager for improvements.

THE WESTERN LANDSCAPE

Throughout the nineteenth century, many Americans viewed western expansion as the nation's "manifest destiny," and just as many marveled at the region's natural and cultural wonders. Their fascination grew with the proliferation of printed literature, "Wild West" entertainments, sideshows, and traveling exhibits featuring western themes. The public east of the Mississippi craved stories about the West and visual images of its sweeping vistas. Artists and photographers built their reputations in what they saw and imagined. Scholars, from geologists and botanists to historians and anthropologists, toured the trans-Mississippi West in pursuit of new data. The region and its peoples came to represent what was both unique and magnificent about the American landscape.

Nature's Majesty

Alexis de Tocqueville, the famed commentator on American society, found little beauty in the land west of the Mississippi. Writing in the 1830s, he described the landscape as "more and more uneven and sterile," the soil "punctured in a thousand places by primitive rocks sticking out here and there like the bones of a skeleton when sinews of flesh have perished." By the end of the century, scores of writers had provided an entirely different image of the American West. They described spectacular, breathtaking natural sites like the

Grand Tetons and High Sierras, vast meadows of waving grasses and beautiful flowers, expansive canyons and rushing white rivers, and exquisite deserts covered with sagebrush or dotted with flowering cactus and enticing precisely for their stark qualities. A traveler through Yellowstone country recalled "the varied scenery" of the West and its "stupendous & remarkable manifestations of nature's forces," an impression destined to stay with him "as long as memory lasts."

Moved by such reveries, the federal government began to set aside huge tracts of land as nature reserves. In 1864 Congress passed the Yosemite Act, which placed the spectacular cliffs and giant sequoias under the management of the state of California. Meanwhile, explorers returned to the East awestruck by the varied terrain of the Rocky Mountains, the largest mountain chain in North America. These early visitors described huge sky-high lakes, boiling mud, and spectacular waterfalls. Finally, in 1871, the federal government funded a major undertaking by a team of researchers from the Geological and Geographical Survey of the Territories, which included the early landscape photographer William H. Jackson and the painter Thomas Moran. These researchers brought back to Congress visual proof of the monumental scenery of the West, including the Grand Canyon. In 1872 Congress named Yellowstone the first national park. Yosemite and Sequoia in California, Crater Lake in Oregon, Mount Ranier in Washington, and Glacier in Montana all became national parks between 1890 and 1910.

Landscape painters, particularly the group that became known as the Rocky Mountain School, also piqued the public's interest in western scenery. Exhibited in galleries and museums and reproduced in popular magazines, their sketches and paintings circulated western imagery throughout the country and through much of Europe. In the 1860s German-born Albert Bierstadt, equipped with a camera, traveled the Oregon Trail. Using his photographs as inspiration, Bierstadt painted mountains so wondrous that they seemed nearly surreal, projecting a divine aura behind the majesty of nature. His "earthscapes"— huge canvases with exacting details of animals and plants— thrilled viewers and sold for tens of thousands of dollars.

The Legendary Wild West

Legends of the Wild West grew into a staple of popular culture just as the actual work of cowboys became more routine. By the end of the century, many Americans, rich and poor alike, imagined the West as a land of promise and opportunity and, above all, of excitement and adventure. Future president Theodore Roosevelt helped to promote this view. Soon after his election to the New York state assembly in 1882, Roosevelt was horrified to see himself lampooned in the newspapers as a dandy and weakling. A year later, after buying a ranch in South Dakota, he began to reconstruct his public image. He wrote three books recounting his adventures in the West, claiming that they had not only instilled in him personal bravery and "hardihood" but self-reliance. In 1886 he was back in New York, running for mayor as the "Cowboy of the Dakotas." In April 1899, he addressed the members of Chicago's elite Hamilton Club, inviting them to join him in "the strenuous life" as exemplified by their Indian-fighter ancestors. Indeed, by this time many Americans had joined Roosevelt in imagining the West as a source of rejuvenation and virility. Young men at Harvard and Yale universities, for example, had named their hunting clubs after Daniel Boone and Davy Crockett. The West, as Roosevelt insisted, meant "vigorous manhood."

The first "westerns," the "dime novels" that sold in the 1860s in editions of 50,000 or more, reflected

Albert Bierstadt: Merced River, Yosemite Valley, 1866. Oil on canvas, 36 x 50 in. The Metropolitan Museum of Art. Gift of the sons of William Paton, 1909.

Albert Bierstadt became one of the first artists to capture on enormous canvases the vastness and rugged terrain of mountains and western wilderness. Many other artists joined Bierstadt to form the Rocky Mountain School. In time, the camera largely replaced the paintbrush, and most Americans formed an image of these majestic peaks from postcards and magazine illustrations.

these myths. Competing against stories about pirates, wars, crime, and sea adventures, westerns outsold the others. Edward Zane Carroll Judson's *Buffalo Bill, the King of the Border Men*, first published in 1869, spawned hundreds of other novels, thousands of stories, and an entire magazine devoted to Buffalo Bill. Even before farmers had successfully halted the free-grazing of cattle, writers made tough cowboys and high-spirited women into legends of the Wild West. Real-life African American cowboy Nat Love lived on in the imaginations of many generations as Edward L. Wheeler's dime novel hero "Deadwood Dick," who rode the range as a white cowboy in black clothes in over thirty stories. His girlfriend "Calamity Jane"—"the most reckless buchario in ther Hills"—also took on mythic qualities.

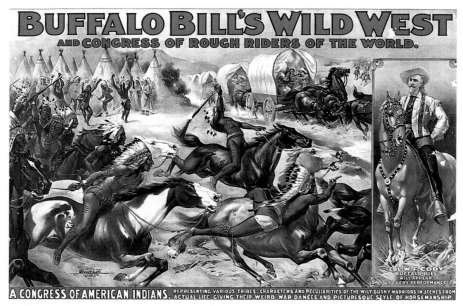

Buffalo Bill's "Wild West Show" poster from 1899. William Cody's theatrical company toured the United States and Europe for decades, reenacting various battles and occasionally switching to football (cowboys versus Indians). Cody's style set the pace for both rodeos and Western silent films.

Railroad promoters and herd owners actively promoted these romantic and heroic images. Cowman Joseph McCoy staged Wild West shows in St. Louis and Chicago, where Texas cowboys entertained prospective buyers by roping calves and breaking horses. Many cowboys played up this imaginary role, dressing and talking to match the stories told about them. "The drovers of the seventies were a wild and reckless bunch," recalled cowboy Teddy Blue. Typically, they had worn a "wide brimmed beaver hat, black or brown with a low crown, fancy shirts, high heeled boots, and sometimes a vest." In the 1880s cowboys adopted the high-crowned Stetson hat, ornately detailed shirts with pockets, and striped or checked pants. The first professional photographers often made their living touring the West, setting up studios where cowboys and prostitutes posed in elaborate costumes.

For thirty years, Wild West shows toured the United States and Europe. The former Pony Express rider, army scout, and famed buffalo hunter William F. Cody hit upon the idea of an extravaganza that would bring the legendary West to those who could never experience it in person. "Buffalo Bill" Cody made sharpshooter Annie Oakley a star performer. Entrancing crowds with her stunning accuracy with pistol or rifle, Oakley shot dimes in midair and cigarettes from her husband's mouth. Cody also hired Sioux Indians and hundreds of cowboys to perform in mock stagecoach robberies and battles. Shows like Custer's Last Stand

thrilled crowds, including Britain's Queen Victoria. Revamped as the rodeo, the Wild West show long outlasted Buffalo Bill, who died in 1917.

With far less fanfare, many veteran cowboys enlisted themselves on "dude ranches" for tourists or performed as rope twirlers or yodeling singers in theaters across the United States. In 1902 Owen Wister's novel *The Virginian* fixed in the popular imagination the scene of the cowboy facing down the villain and saying, "When you call me that, smile."

The "American Primitive"

New technologies of graphic reproduction encouraged painters and photographers to provide new images of the West, authentic as well as fabricated. A young German American artist, Charles Schreyvogel, saw Buffalo Bill's tent show in Buffalo and decided to make the West his life's work. His canvases depicted Indian warriors and U.S. cavalry fighting furiously but without blood and gore. Charles Russell, a genuine cowboy, painted the life he knew, but also indulged in imaginary scenarios, producing paintings of buffalo hunts and first encounters between Indian peoples and white explorers.

Frederic Remington, the most famous of all the western artists, left Yale Art School to visit Montana in 1881, became a Kansas sheep herder and tavern owner, and then returned to painting. Inspired by newspaper stories of the army's campaign against the Apaches, he made himself into a war correspondent and captured vivid scenes of battle in his sketches. Painstakingly accurate in physical details, especially of horses, his paintings celebrated the "winning of the West" from the Indian peoples. By the turn of the century, Remington was the chief magazine illustrator of western history.

Remington joined hundreds of other painters and engravers in reproducing the most popular historic event: Custer's Last Stand. Totally fictionalized by white artists to show a heroic General Custer personally holding off advancing Indian warriors, these renditions dramatized the romance and tragedy of conquest. Indian artists recorded Custer's defeat in far less noble fashion.

Photographers often produced highly nuanced portraits of Indian peoples. Dozens of early photographers from the Bureau of American Ethnology captured the gaze of noble tribespeople or showed them hard at work digging clams or grinding corn. President Theodore Roosevelt praised Edward Sheriff Curtis for vividly conveying tribal virtue. Generations later, in the 1960s and 1970s, Curtis's photographs again captured the imagination of western enthusiasts, who were unaware or unconcerned that this sympathetic artist had often posed his subjects or retouched his photos to blur out any artifacts of white society.

Painters and photographers led the way for scholarly research on the various Indian societies. The early ethnographer and pioneer of fieldwork in anthropology, Lewis Henry Morgan, devoted his life to the study of Indian family or kinship patterns, mostly of eastern tribes such as the Iroquois, who adopted him into their Hawk Clan. In 1851 he published *League of the Ho-de-no-sau-nee, or Iroquois*, considered the first scientific account of an Indian tribe. A decade later Morgan ventured into Cheyenne country to examine the naming patterns of this tribe. In his major work, *Ancient Society*, published in 1877, he posited a universal process of social evolution leading from savagery to barbarism to civilization.

One of the most influential interpreters of the cultures of living tribespeople was the pioneering ethnographer Alice Cunningham Fletcher. In 1879, Fletcher met Suzette (Bright Eyes) La Flesche of the Omaha tribe, who was on a speaking tour to gain support for her people, primarily to prevent their removal from tribal lands. Fletcher, then forty-two years old, accompanied La Flesche to Nebraska, telling the Omahas that she had come "to learn, if you will let me, something about your tribal organization, social customs, tribal rites, traditions and songs. Also to see if I can help you in any way." After transcribing hundreds of songs, Fletcher became well known as an expert on Omaha music. She also supported the Omahas' campaign to gain individual title to tribal lands, eventually drafting legislation that was enacted

by Congress as the Omaha Act of 1882. In 1885 Fletcher produced for the U.S. Senate a report titled *Indian Education and Civilization*, one of the first general statements on the status of Indian peoples. As a founder of the American Anthropological Society and president of the American Folk-Lore Society, she encouraged further study of Indian societies.

While white settlers and the federal government continued to threaten the survival of tribal life, Indian lore became a major pursuit of scholars and amateurs alike. Adults and children delighted in turning up arrowheads. Fraternal organizations such as the Elks and Eagles borrowed tribal terminology. The Boy Scouts and Girl Scouts, the nation's premier youth organizations, used tribal lore to instill strength of character. And the U.S. Treasury stamped images of tribal chiefs and of buffalo on the nation's most frequently used coins.

THE TRANSFORMATION OF INDIAN SOCIETIES

In 1871, the U.S. government formally ended the treaty system, eclipsing without completely abolishing the sovereignty of Indian nations. Still, the tribes persisted. Using a mixture of survival strategies from farming and trade to the leasing of reservation lands, they both adapted to changing conditions and maintained old traditions.

Reform Policy and Politics

By 1880, many Indian tribes had been forcibly resettled on reservations, but very few had adapted to white ways. For decades, reformers, mainly from the Protestant churches, had lobbied Congress for a program of salvation through assimilation, and they looked to the Board of Indian Commissioners, created in 1869, to carry out this mission. The board often succeeded in mediating conflicts among the various tribes crowded onto reservations but made far less headway in converting them to Christianity or transforming them into prosperous farming communities. The majority of Indian peoples lived in poverty and misery, deprived of their traditional means of survival and more often than not subjected to fraud by corrupt government officials and private suppliers. Reformers who observed these conditions firsthand nevertheless remained unshaken in their belief that tribespeople must be raised out of the darkness of ignorance into the light of civilization. Many conceded, however, that the reservation system might not be the best means to this end.

Unlike most Americans, who saw the conquest of the West as a means to national glory, some reformers were genuinely outraged by the government's continuous violation of treaty obligations and the military enforcement of the reservation policy. One of the most influential was Helen Hunt Jackson, a noted poet and author of children's stories. In 1879 Jackson had attended a lecture in Hartford, Connecticut, by a chief of the Ponca tribe whose destitute people had been forced from their Dakota homeland. Heartstruck, Jackson lobbied former abolitionists such as Wendell Phillips to work for Indians' rights and herself began to write against government policy. Her book-length exposé, *A Century of Dishonor*, published in 1881, detailed the mistreatment of Indian peoples.

Jackson threw herself into the Indian Rights Association, an offshoot of the Women's National Indian Association (WNIA), which had been formed in 1874 to rally public support for a program of assimilation. The two organizations helped to place Protestant missionaries in the West to work to eradicate tribal customs as well as to convert Indian peoples to Christianity. According to the reformers' plans, men would now farm as well as hunt, while women would leave the fields to take care of home and children. Likewise, all communal practices would be abandoned in favor of individually owned homesteads, where families could develop in the "American" manner and even celebrate proper holidays such as the Fourth of July. Children, hair trimmed short, would be placed in boarding schools where, removed

from their parents' influence, they would shed traditional values and cultural practices. By 1882 the WNIA had gathered 100,000 signatures on petitions urging Congress to phase out the reservation system, establish universal education for Indian children, and award title to 160 acres to any individual willing to work the land.

The Dawes Severalty Act, passed by Congress in 1887, incorporated many of these measures and established federal Indian policy for decades to come. The act allowed the president to distribute land not to tribes but to individuals legally "severed" from their tribes. The commissioner of Indian affairs rendered the popular interpretation that "tribal relations should be broken up, socialism destroyed and the family and autonomy of the individual substituted. The allotment of land in severalty, the establishment of local courts and police, the development of a personal sense of independence and the universal adoption of the English language are means to this end."

Those individuals who accepted the land allotment of 160 acres and agreed to allow the government to sell unallotted tribal lands (with some funds set aside for education) could petition to become citizens of the United States. A little over a decade after its enactment, many reformers believed that the Dawes Act had resolved the basis of the "Indian problem." Hollow Horn Bear, a Sioux chief, offered a

OVERVIEW

MAJOR INDIAN TREATIES AND LEGISLATION OF THE LATE NINETEENTH CENTURY

1863	Nez Percé Treaty	Signed illegally on behalf of the entire tribe in which the Nez Percé abandoned 6 million acres of land in return for a small reservation in northeastern Oregon. Led to Nez Percé wars, which ended in 1877 with surrender of Chief Joseph.
1867	Medicine Lodge Treaty	Assigned reservations in existing Indian Territory to Comanches, Plains (Kiowa), Appaches, Kiowas, Cheyennes, and Arapahoes, bringing these tribes together with Sioux, Shoshones, Bannocks, and Navajos.
1868	Treaty of Fort Laramie	Successfully ended Red Cloud's war by evacuating federal troops from Sioux Territory along the Bozeman Trail; additionally granted Sioux ownership of the western half of South Dakota and rights to use Powder River county in Wyoming and Montana.
1871		Congress declares end to treaty system.
1887	Dawes Severalty Act	Divided communal tribal land, granting the right to petition for citizenship to those Indians who accepted the individual land allotment of 160 acres. Successfully undermined sovereignty.

Students at Toledo Indian School, Iowa, August 1899. Young women of various tribes boarded at this school, which offered them lessons in several subjects and training for adult life among white Americans. Their teachers hoped to prepare them for a future Christian marriage and motherhood.

different opinion, judging the Dawes Act to be "only another trick of the whites."

The Dawes Act successfully undermined tribal sovereignty but offered little compensation. Indian religions and sacred ceremonies were banned, the telling of legends and myths forbidden, and shaman and medicine men imprisoned or exiled for continuing their traditional practices. "Indian schools" forbade Indian languages, clothing styles, and even hair fashions in order to "kill the Indian . . . and save the man," as one schoolmaster put it.

These and other measures did little to integrate Indians into white society. Treated as savages, Indian children fled most white schools. Nor did adults receive much encouragement to become property holders. Government agencies allotted them inferior farmland, inadequate tools, and little training for agricultural self-sufficiency. Seeing scant advantage in assimilating, only a minority of adults dropped their tribal religion for Christianity or their communal ways for the accumulation of private property. Within the next forty years, the Indian peoples lost 60 percent of the reservation land remaining in 1887 and 66 percent of the land allotted to them as homesteaders. The tenets of the Dawes Act were not reversed until 1934. In that year, Congress passed the Indian Reorganization Act, which affirmed the integrity of Indian cultural institutions and returned some land to tribal ownership (see Chapter 24).

The Ghost Dance

After the passage of the Dawes Severalty Act, one more cycle of rebellion remained for the Sioux. In 1888, the Paiute prophet Wovoka, ill with scarlet fever, had a vision during a total eclipse of the sun. In his vision, the Creator told him that if the Indian peoples learned to love each other, they would be granted a special place in the afterlife. The Creator also gave him the Ghost Dance, which the prophet performed for others and soon spread throughout the tribe. The Sioux came to believe that when the day of judgment came, all Indian peoples who had ever lived would return to their lost world and white peoples would vanish from the earth. The chant sounded:

The whole world is coming.
A nation is coming, a nation is coming.
The Eagle has brought the message to the tribe.
The father says so, the father says so.
Over the whole earth they are coming.
The buffalo are coming, the buffalo are coming.
The Crow has brought the message to the tribe,
The Father says so, the Father says so.

Many white settlers and federal officials feared the Ghost Dancers, even though belief in a sudden divine judgment was common among Christians and Jews. Before the Civil War, Protestant groups such as the Millerites had renounced personal property and prepared themselves for the millennium. But after decades of Indian warfare, white Americans took the Ghost Dance as a warning of tribal retribution rather than a religious ceremony. As thousands of Sioux danced to exhaustion, local whites demanded the practice be stopped. A group of the Sioux led by Big Foot, now fearing mass murder, moved into hiding in the Bad Lands of South Dakota.

The U.S. Seventh Cavalry, led in part by survivors of the battle of Little Bighorn, pursued them. The three hundred undernourished Sioux, freezing and without horses, agreed to accompany the troops to Wounded Knee Creek on the Pine Ridge Reservation. There, on December 29, 1890, while the peace-seeking Big Foot, who had personally raised a white flag of surrender, lay dying of pneumonia, they were surrounded by soldiers armed with automatic guns. The U.S. troops expected the Sioux to surrender their few remaining weapons, but an accidental gunshot from one deaf brave who misunderstood the command caused panic on both sides.

Within minutes, 200 Sioux had been cut down and dozens of soldiers wounded, mostly by their own cross fire. For two hours soldiers continued to shoot at anything that moved—mostly women and children straggling away. Many of the injured froze to

This 1916 photograph of Chief American Horse shows the Oglala Sioux leader accepting his tribe's allotment from government agents at Pine Ridge, South Dakota. A veteran of the "Fetterman Massacre" during Red Cloud's war for the Bozeman Trail during the 1860s, American Horse had seen his people's territory reduced in size from more than 2.5 million acres to less than 150,000.

death in the snow; others were transported in open wagons and finally laid out on beds of hay under Christmas decorations at the Pine Ridge Episcopal church. The massacre, which took place almost exactly four hundred years after Columbus "discovered" the New World for Christian civilization, seemed to mark the final conquest of the continent's indigenous peoples.

Black Elk later recalled, "I can see that something else died there in the bloody mud, and was buried in the blizzard. A people's dream died there. It was a beautiful dream. . . . The nation's hoop is broken and scattered. There is no center any longer, and the sacred tree is dead."

Endurance and Rejuvenation

The most tenacious tribes were those occupying land rejected by white settlers or distant from their new communities. Still, not even an insular, peaceful agricultural existence on semi-arid, treeless terrain necessarily provided protection. Nor did a total willingness to accept white offers peacefully prevent attack.

The Pimas of Arizona, for instance, had a well-developed agricultural system adapted to a scarce supply of water, and they rarely warred with other tribes. After the arrival of white settlers, they integrated Christian

symbolism into their religion, learned to speak English, and even fought with the U.S. cavalry against the Apaches. Still, the Pimas saw their lands stolen, their precious waterways diverted, and their families impoverished.

The similarly peaceful Yana tribes of California, hunters and gatherers rather than farmers, were even less fortunate. Suffering enslavement, prostitution, and multiple new diseases from white settlers, they faced near extinction within a generation. One Yana tribe, the Yahi, chose simply to disappear. For more than a decade, they lived in caves and avoided all contact with white settlers.

Many tribes found it difficult to survive in the proximity of white settlers. The Flatheads, for example, seemed to Indian commissioners in the Bitterroot region of Montana to be destined for quick assimilation. They had refused to join the Ghost Dance and had agreed to sell their rich tribal land and move to a new reservation. But while waiting to be moved, the dispossessed Flatheads nearly starved. When they finally reached the new reservation in October 1891, the remaining 250 Flatheads put on their finest war paint and whooped and galloped their horses, firing guns in the air in celebration. But disappointment and tragedy lay ahead. The federal government drastically reduced the size of the reservation, using a large part of it to provide a national reserve for buffalo. Only handfuls of Flatheads, mostly elderly, continued to live together in pockets of rural poverty.

A majority of tribes, especially smaller ones, sooner or later reached numbers too low to maintain their collective existence. Intermarriage, although widely condemned by the white community, drew many young people outside their Indian communities. Some tribal leaders also deliberately chose a path toward assimilation. The Quapaws, for example, formally disbanded in the aftermath of the Dawes Severalty Act. The minority that managed to prosper in white society as tradespeople or farmers abandoned their language, religious customs, and traditional ways of life. Later generations petitioned the federal government and regained tribal status, established ceremonial grounds and cultural centers (or bingo halls), and built up one of the most durable powwows in the state. Even so, much of the tribal lore that had underpinned distinct identity had simply vanished.

A small minority of tribes, grown skillful in adapting to dramatically changing circumstances, managed to persist and even grow. Never numbering more than a few thousand people, during the late eighteenth century the Cheyennes had found themselves caught geographically between aggressive tribes in the Great Lakes region and had migrated into the Missouri area, where they split into small village-sized communities. By the mid-nineteenth century they had become expert horse traders on the Great Plains, well prepared to meet the massive influx of white settlers by shifting their location frequently. They avoided the worst of the pestilence that spread from the diseases white people carried, and likewise survived widespread intermarriage with the Sioux in the 1860s and 1870s. Instructed to settle, many Cheyenne took up elements of the Christian religion and became farmers, also without losing their tribal identity. Punished by revenge-hungry soldiers after the battle of Little Bighorn, their lands repeatedly taken away, they still held on. The Cheyennes were survivors.

The Navajos experienced an extraordinary renewal, largely because they built a life in territory considered worthless by whites. Having migrated to the Southwest from the northwestern part of the continent perhaps 700 years earlier, the *Diné* ("the People") as they called themselves had already survived earlier invasions by the Spanish. In 1863 they had been conquered again through the cooperation of hostile tribes led by the famous Colonel Kit Carson. Their crops burned, their fruit trees destroyed, 8,000 Navajo were forced in the 300-mile "Long Walk" to the desolate Bosque Redondo reservation, where they nearly starved. Four years later, the Indian Bureau allowed the severely reduced tribe to return to a fraction of its former lands.

CHRONOLOGY

1848	Treaty of Guadalupe Hidalgo
1849–1860s	California Gold Rush
1853	Gadsden Purchase
1858	Comstock Lode discovered
1859	Cortina's War in South Texas
1862	Homestead Act makes free land available
	Morrill Act authorizes "land-grant" colleges
1865–1867	Great Sioux War
1866	Texas cattle drives begin
	Medicine Lodge Treaty established reservation system
	Alaska purchased
1869	Board of Indian Commissioners created
	Buffalo Bill, the King of the Border Men, sets off "Wild West" publishing craze
1870s	Grasshopper attacks on the Great Plains
1872	Yellowstone National Park created
1873	Timber Culture Act
	Red River War
1874–1875	Sioux battles in Black Hills of Dakotas
1876	Custer's Last Stand
1877	Defeat of the Nez Percé
1881	Helen Hunt Jackson, *A Century of Dishonor*
1882	Edmunds Act outlaws polygamy
1885–87	Droughts and severe winters cause the collapse of the cattle boom
1887	Dawes Severalty Act
1890	Sioux Ghost Dance movement
	Massacre of Lakota Sioux at Wounded Knee
	Census Bureau announces the end of the frontier line
1887	Forest Management Act gives the federal government authority over forest reserves

By 1880 the Navajos' population had returned to nearly what it had been before their conquest by white Americans. Quickly depleting the deer and antelope on their hemmed-in reservation, they had to rely on sheep alone as a food reserve for years of bad crops. With their wool rugs and blankets much in demand in the East, the Navajos increasingly turned to crafts, including eventually silver jewelry as well as weaving, to survive. Although living on the economic margin, they persevered to become the largest Indian nation in the United States.

The nearby Hopis, like the Navajos, survived by stubbornly clinging to lands unwanted by white settlers and by adapting to drastically changing conditions. A famous tribe of "desert people," the Hopis had lived for centuries in their cliff cities. Their highly developed theological beliefs, peaceful social system, sand paintings, and kachina dolls interested many educated and influential whites. The resulting publicity helped them gather the public supporters and financial resources to fend off further threats to their reservations.

Fortunate northwestern tribes remained relatively isolated from white settlers until the early twentieth century, although they had begun trading with white visitors centuries earlier. Northwestern peoples relied largely on salmon and other resources of the region's rivers and bays. In potlatch ceremonies, leaders redistributed tribal wealth and maintained their personal status and the status of their tribe by giving lavish gifts to invited guests. Northwest peoples also made intricate wood carvings, including commemorative "totem" poles, that recorded their history and identified their regional status. Northwestern peoples maintained their cultural integrity in part through connections with kin in Canada, as did southern tribes with kin in Mexico.

In Canada and Mexico, native populations suffered less pressure from new populations and retained more tribal authority than in the United States.

Indian nations approached their nadir as the nineteenth century came to a close. The descendants of the great pre-Columbian civilizations had been conquered by foreigners, their population reduced to fewer than 250,000. Under the pressure of assimilation, the remaining tribespeople became known to non-Indians as "the vanishing Americans." It would take several generations before Indian sovereignty experienced a resurgence.

CONCLUSION

The transformation of the trans-Mississippi West pointed up the larger meaning of expansion. Almost overnight, mines opened, cities grew, and farms and cattle ranches spread out across the vast countryside. New communities formed rapidly and often displaced old ones. In 1890 the director of the U.S. Census announced that the nation's "unsettled area has been so broken into by isolated bodies of settlement that there can hardly be said to be a frontier line."

The development of the West met the nation's demand for mineral resources for its expanding industries and agricultural products for the people of the growing cities. Envisioning the West as a cornucopia whose boundless treasures would offer themselves to the willing pioneer, most of the new residents failed to calculate the odds against their making a prosperous livelihood as miners, farmers, or petty merchants. Nor could they appreciate the long-term consequences of the violence they brought with them from the battlefields of the Civil War to the far reaches of the West.

REVIEW QUESTIONS

1. Discuss the role of federal legislation in accelerating and shaping the course of westward expansion.
2. How did the incorporation of western territories into the United States affect Indian nations such as the Sioux or the Nez Percé? Discuss the causes and consequences of the Indian Wars. Discuss the significance of reservation policy and the Dawes Severalty Act for tribal life.
3. What were some of the major technological advances in mining and in agriculture that promoted the development of the western economy?
4. Describe the unique features of Mexicano communities in the Southwest before and after the mass immigration of Anglos. How did changes in the economy affect the patterns of labor and the status of women in these communities?
5. What role did the Homestead Act play in western expansion? How did farm families on the Great Plains divide chores among their members? What factors determined the likelihood of economic success or failure?
6. Describe the responses of artists, naturalists, and conservationists to the western landscape. How did their photographs, paintings, and stories shape perceptions of the West in the East?

RECOMMENDED READING

Alfred L. Bush and Lee Clark Mitchell, *The Photograph and the American Indian* (1994). A comprehensive study of photos of Indians by various American photographers from 1840 to the present.

William Cronon, George Miles, and Jay Gitlin, eds., *Under an Open Sky: Rethinking America's Western Past* (1992). A useful collection of essays. Reinterpreting older evidence and adding new data, these essays stress the bitter conflicts over territory, the racial and gender barriers against democratic community models, and the tragic elements of western history.

Jon Gjerde, *The Minds of the West: Ethnocultural Evolution in the Rural Middle West, 1830–1914* (1997). A combination cultural and economic history that weighs the importance of ethnicity in the shaping of American identities in the farming regions of the Middle West. Gjerde pays close attention to the religious institutions and systems of belief of European immigrants as the basis of community formation.

Lisbeth Haas, *Conquests and Historical Identities in California, 1769–1936* (1995). A multiethnic history, centered in San Juan Capistrano, that examines the political intersection of geography and community formation. The author studies the processes of Americanization among the Spanish and Indian populations who settled this land.

John C. Hudson, *Making the Corn Belt: A Geographical History of Middle-Western Agriculture* (1994). An ecologically oriented study of corn growing that traces its development from Indians to Southerners moving westward.

Elizabeth Jameson and Susan Armitage, eds., *Writing the Range* (1997). A collection of essays on women in the U.S. West that presents an inclusive historical narrative based on the experiences of women of differing backgrounds, races, and ethnic groups.

Patricia Nelson Limerick, *The Legacy of Conquest: The Unbroken Past of the American West* (1987). A controversial and popular revisionist history of the West. Focused on conflict, Limerick's study shows the frontier most of all as a site of racial antagonism.

John G. Neihardt, *Black Elk Speaks: Being the Life Story of a Holy Man of the Oglala Sioux* (1961). A classic "as-told-to" autobiographical account published originally in 1932. Black Elk recalls the tragedy of his tribe's destruction with the events around George Armstrong Custer and the battle of Little Bighorn.

Glenda Riley, *Building and Breaking Families in the American West* (1996). Essays covering the variety of cultures in the American West and organized topically to highlight courtship, marriage and intermarriage, and separation and divorce.

Thomas E. Sheridan, *Los Tucsonenses: The Mexican Community in Tucson, 1854–1941* (1986). A highly readable account of Mexican-American communities in the Southwest. Sheridan shows how a mid-century accommodation of Anglos and Mexicanos faded with the absorption of the region into the national economy and with the steady displacement of Mexicano community from its agricultural landholdings.

Robert M. Utley, *The Lance and the Shield: The Life and Times of Sitting Bull* (1993). A careful reinterpretation of a spiritual leader's attempt to secure religious freedom for Indian peoples.

Richard White, *"It's Your Misfortune and None of My Own": A History of the American West* (1991). A wide-ranging history of the West with emphasis on cultural contact and the environment. White shows that conflicting cultures with little understanding of each other clashed tragically, with great losses to the environment and the hopes of a democratic American community.

ADDITIONAL BIBLIOGRAPHY

Indian Peoples and Indian-White Relations

Patricia Albers and Beatrice Medicine Albers, *The Hidden Half: Studies of Plains Indian Women* (1983)

Morris W. Foster, *Being Comanche: A Social History of an American Indian Community* (1991)

E. Richard Hart, ed., *Zuni and the Courts: A Struggle for Sovereign Land Rights* (1995)

Frederick E. Hoxie, *A Final Promise: The Campaign to Assimilate the Indians, 1880–1920* (1984)

Douglas R. Hurt, *Indian Agriculture in America* (1987)

Albert L. Hurtado, *Indian Survival on the California Frontier* (1988)

Douglas C. McChristian, *The U.S. Army in the West, 1870–1880: Uniforms, Weapons and Equipment* (1995)

Catherine Price, *The Oglala People, 1841–1879* (1996)

Glenda Riley, *Women and Indians on the Frontier, 1825–1915* (1984)

Richard White, *The Roots of Dependency: Subsistence, Environment, and Social Change among the Choctaws, Pawnees, and Navajos* (1983)

Robert Wooster, *The Military and United States Indian Policy, 1865–1902* (1988)

Internal Empire

Susan Armitage and Elizabeth Jameson, eds., *The Women's West* (1987)

Susan Armitage, Ruth B. Moynihan, and Christiane Fischer Dichamp, eds., *So Much to Be Done: Women Settlers on the Mining and Ranching Frontier* (1990)

Sarah Deutsch, *No Separate Refuge: Culture, Class and Gender on an Anglo-Hispanic Frontier in the American Southwest, 1880–1940* (1987)

David M. Emmons, *The Butte Irish: Class and Ethnicity in an American Mining Town, 1875–1925* (1989)

Mario R. Garcia, *Desert Immigrants: The Mexicans of El Paso, 1880–1920* (1981)

Marion S. Goldman, *Gold Diggers and Silver Miners: Prostitution and Social Life on the Comstock* (1981)

Richard Griswold del Castillo, *The Los Angeles Barrio, 1850–1890* (1979)

B. Carmon Hardy, *Solemn Covenant: The Mormon Polygamous Passage* (1992)

Douglas Monroy, *Thrown among Strangers: The Making of Mexican Culture in Frontier California* (1993)

David Montejano, *Anglos and Mexicans in the Making of Texas, 1836–1986* (1987)

Robert J. Rosenbaum, *Mexicano Resistance in the Southwest* (1981)

Jonathan D. Rosenblum, *Copper Crucible: How the Arizona Miners' Strike of 1893 Recast Labor-Management Relations in America* (1996)

Lucy E. Salyer, *Laws Harsh as Tigers: Chinese Immigrants and the Shaping of Modern Immigration Law* (1996)

Ranching and Farming

Leonard J. Arrington and Davis Bitton, *The Mormon Experience*, 2d ed. (1992)

Allan G. Bogue, *From Prairie to Corn Belt: Farming on the Illinois and Iowa Prairies in the Nineteenth Century* (1963)

Anne M. Butler, *Daughters of Joy, Sisters of Misery: Prostitutes in the American West, 1865–1890* (1985).

Harry Sinclair Drago, *The Great Range Wars* (1985)

Philip Durham and Everett L. Jones, *The Negro Cowboys* (1965)

C. Mark Hamilton, *Nineteenth-Century Mormon Architecture and City Planning* (1995)

Robert C. Haywood, *Victorian West: Class and Culture in Kansas Cattle Towns* (1991)

Stan Hoig, *The Oklahoma Land Rush of 1889* (1984)

Lawrence Jelinek, *Harvest Empire: A History of California Agriculture*, 2d ed. (1982)

Frederick C. Luebke, ed., *Ethnicity on the Great Plains* (1980).

D. Aidan McQuillan, *Prevailing over Time: Ethnic Adjustment on the Kansas Prairies, 1875–1925* (1990)

Donald J. Pisani, *From Family Farm to Agribusiness* (1984)

Sonya Salamon, *Prairie Patrimony: Family, Farming, and Community in the Midwest* (1992)

Paul I. Wellman, *The Trampling Herd: The Story of the Cattle Range in America* (1988)

Jack Weston, *The Real American Cowboy* (1985)

Ellen Jane Marris Wheeler, ed., *Cherokee Outlet Cowboy: Recollections of Laban S. Records* (1996)

The West, the Land, and the Imagination

Robert F. Berkhoffer Jr., *The White Man's Indian: Images of the American Indian from Columbus to the Present* (1978)

Christine Bold, *Selling the West: Popular Western Fiction, 1860–1960* (1987)

William H. Goetzmann and William N. Goetzmann, *The West of the Imagination* (1986)

L.G. Moses, *Wild West Shows and the Images of American Indians, 1883–1933* (1996)

Alexander Nemertov, *Frederic Remington & Turn-of-the-Century America* (1995)

Richard Orsi, Alfred Runte, and Marlene Smith-Barazini, eds., *Yosemite and Sequoia: A Century of California National Parks* (1993)

Donald J. Pisani, *To Reclaim a Divided West: Water, Law, and Public Policy, 1848–1901* (1993)

Joseph G. Rosa, *Wild Bill Hickok: The Man and His Myth* (1996)

Richard Slotkin, *Gunfighter Nation: The Myth of the Frontier in 20th-Century America* (1992)

Raymond William Steadman, *Shadows of the Indian: Stereotypes in American Culture* (1982)

Richard White and Patricia Nelson Limerick, *The Frontier in American Culture* (1994)

Donald Worcester, *Rivers of Empire: Water, Aridity, and the Growth of the American West* (1985)

Biography

Matthew Baigell, *Albert Bierstadt* (1981)

Louise Barnett, *Touched by Fire: The Life, Death, and Mythic Afterlife of George Armstrong Custer* (1996)

Angie Debo, *Geronimo* (1976)

Joan T. Mark, *A Stranger in Her Native Land: Alice Fletcher and the American Indians* (1988)

Valerie Mathes, *Helen Hunt Jackson and Her Indian Reform Legacy* (1990)

Glenda Riley, *Life and Legacy of Annie Oakley* (1994)

Mari Sandoz, *Crazy Horse, the Strange Man of the Oglalas* (1961)

Elinore Pruitt Stewart, *Letters of a Woman Homesteader* (1914; 1989)

Edwin R. Sweeny, *Cochise, Chiricahua Apache Chief* (1991)

John Tusha, *Billy the Kid, His Life and Legend* (1994)

CHAPTER NINETEEN

THE INCORPORATION OF AMERICA

1865–1900

Looking north on State Street, Chicago, in 1899; oil over a photograph. The Granger Collection.

AMERICAN COMMUNITIES
Packingtown, Chicago, Illinois

Approaching Packingtown, the neighborhood adjoining the Union Stockyards, the center of Chicago's great meat-packing industry, one noticed first the pungent odor, a mixture of smoke, fertilizer, and putrid flesh, blood, and hair from the slaughtered animals. A little closer, the stench of the uncovered garbage dump blended in. Finally one crossed "Bubbly Creek," a lifeless offshoot of the Chicago River aptly named for the effect of the carbolic acid gas that formed from the decaying refuse poured in by the meat-packing plants. Railroads crisscrossed the entire area, bringing in thousands of animals each day and carrying out meat for sale in markets across the country.

Packingtown occupied about one square mile of land bounded by stockyards, packing plants, and freight yards. With a population of 30,000–40,000 at the end of the nineteenth century, it was a rapidly growing community of old and new immigrants who depended on the meat-packing industry for their livelihood. An average household included six or seven people—parents, two or three children, and two or three boarders. They lived typically in wooden houses divided into four or more flats. Although Irish, Germans, Bohemians, Poles, Lithuanians, and Slovaks were squeezed together in this solidly working-class neighborhood, strong ethnic identities persisted. Few households included residents of more than one nationality, and interethnic marriages were rare. Nearly everyone professed the Roman Catholic faith, yet each ethnic group maintained its own church and often its own parochial school, where children were taught in their parents' language. Political organizations, fraternal societies, and even gymnastic clubs and drama groups reflected these ethnic divisions.

The one local institution that bridged the different groups was the saloon. Located on virtually every street corner, saloons offered important services to the community, hosting weddings and dances, providing meeting places for trade unions and fraternal societies, and cashing paychecks. During the frequent seasons of unemployment, Packingtown workers spent a lot of time in saloons. Here they often made friends across ethnic divisions, an extension of their common work experience in the nearby stockyard and packinghouses.

Most of the meat-packing industry's first "knife men"—the skilled workers in the "killing gangs" that managed the actual slaughtering and cutting operations—were German and Irish. Many had learned their butcher's craft in the Old Country. Below them were the common laborers, mainly recent immigrants from eastern Europe. Having no previous experience in meat packing, these workers found themselves in the lowest paid jobs, such as the by-product manufacturing of glue and oleo. A sizable portion had never before earned wages. They soon discovered, as one Lithuanian laborer put it, that "money was everything and a man without money must die." But the money available—a daily wage of $2 (or less)—was often not enough. The death rate from tuberculosis in Packingtown was thought to be the highest in Chicago and among the highest in the nation.

The Packingtown community was bound into an elaborate economic network that reached distant parts of the United States, transforming the way farmers raised livestock and grains, railroads operated, and consumers ate their meals. These workers helped make Chicago a gateway city, a destination point for raw materials coming in from the West as well as a point of export for products of all kinds.

Chicago meat packers, led by the "big five" of Armour, Cudahy, Morris, Schwarzschild and Sulzberger, and Swift, expanded more than 900 percent between 1870 and 1890, dominating the national market for meat and establishing a standard for monopoly capitalism in the late nineteenth century. In the process, they also became the city's largest manufacturing employer. They built huge, specialized factories during the 1860s and 1870s that speeded the killing process and—thanks to mountains of ice brought by rail from ponds and lakes—operated year round. The introduction of an efficiently refrigerated railroad car in the 1880s made it possible to ship meat nationwide. Consumers had long believed that only meat butchered locally was safe to eat, but now cheap Chicago-packed beef and pork began to appear on every meat-eater's table. Local packinghouses throughout the Midwest succumbed to the ruthless competition from Chicago.

Chicago's control of the mass market for meat affected all aspects of the industry. Midwestern farmers practically abandoned raising calves on open pastures. Instead, they bought two-year-old steers from the West and fattened them on homegrown corn in feedlots, making sure that bulk went into edible parts rather than muscle and bone. The feedlot—a kind of rural factory—replaced pasture just as pasture had earlier supplanted prairie grasslands.

Few of the workers in Chicago's stockyards had seen a farm since they left their homelands. But as the working hands of what poet Carl Sandburg would later call the "City of the Big Shoulders," "Hog Butcher for the World," they played their part, along with the farmer, the grain dealer, the ironworker, the teamster, and many others in bringing together the neighboring countryside, distant regions, and the city in a common endeavor.

Chicago

KEY TOPICS

- The rise of big business and the formation of the national labor movement

- The growth of cities

- The transformation of southern society

- The Gilded Age

- Changes in education

- Commercial amusements and organized sports

THE RISE OF INDUSTRY, THE TRIUMPH OF BUSINESS

At the time of the Civil War, the typical American business firm was a small enterprise, owned and managed by a single family, and producing goods for a local or regional market. By the turn of the century, businesses depending on large-scale investments had organized as corporations and grown to unforeseen size. These mammoth firms could afford to mass-produce goods for national and even international markets. At the helm stood unimaginably wealthy men such as Andrew Carnegie, Philip Danforth Armour, Jay Gould, and John D. Rockefeller, all powerful leaders of a new national business community.

A Revolution in Technology

In the decades after the Civil War, American industry transformed itself into a new wonder of the world. The Centennial Exposition of 1876, held in Philadelphia, celebrated not so much the American Revolution 100 years earlier as the industrial and technological promise of the century to come. Its central theme was power. In the main building—at the time the largest on earth—the visiting emperor of Brazil marked the opening day by throwing a switch on a giant steam engine. Examining the telephone, which he had never before seen in operation, he gasped, "My God, it talks!" Patented that year by Alexander Graham Bell, the telephone signaled the rise of the United States to world leadership in industrial technology.

The year 1876 also marked the opening of Thomas Alva Edison's laboratory in Menlo Park, New Jersey, one of the first devoted to industrial research. Not yet thirty years old, Edison could already claim credit for the mimeograph, the multiplex telegraph, and the stock ticker. In October 1879 his research team hit upon its most marketable invention, an incandescent lamp that burned for more than thirteen hours. On December 31 Edison brought 3,000 people by a special train to witness the sight of hundreds of electric lights illuminating his shop and neighborhood streets. By 1882 the Edison Electric Light Company had launched its service in New York City's financial district. A wondrous source of light and power, electricity revolutionized both industry and urban life.

By this time American inventors, who had filed nearly half a million patents since the close of the Civil War, were previewing the marvels of the next century. Henry Ford, working as an electrical engineer for the Detroit Edison Company, was already experimenting with the gasoline-burning internal combustion engine and designing his own automobile. By 1900 American companies had produced more than 4,000 automobiles. The prospect of commercial aviation emerged in 1903 when Wilbur and Orville Wright staged the first airplane flight near Kitty Hawk, North Carolina.

A major force behind economic growth in the decades after the Civil War was the completion of the transcontinental railroad in 1869. The addition of three more major lines (Southern Pacific, Northern Pacific, and the Atchison, Topeka, and Santa Fe) in the early 1880s and the Great Northern a decade later completed the most extensive transportation network in the world. The nation's first big business, railroads linked cities in every state and serviced a nationwide market for goods. Freight trains carried the bountiful natural resources, such as iron, coal, and minerals that supplied the raw materials for industry, as well as food for the growing urban populations.

Advances in transportation and communication promoted the progressively westward relocation of industry. The geographic center of manufacturing (as computed by the gross value of products) was near the middle of Pennsylvania in 1850, in western Pennsylvania by 1880, and near Mansfield, Ohio, in 1900. Flour milling moved from the east coast to Rochester, New York, then to Ohio, and finally to Minneapolis and Kansas City. The manufacture of agricultural equipment relocated from central New York to Illinois and Wisconsin, while the production of wire moved from Massachusetts to Illinois.

Industry grew at an unprecedented and previously unimaginable pace. The output of capital goods rose at more than 7 percent per year (compared to less than 5 percent annually before the Civil War). In 1865

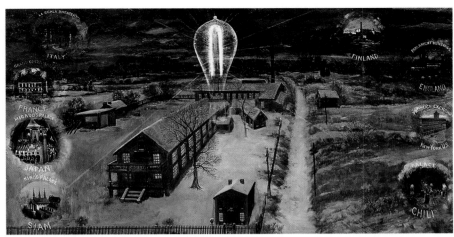

A *whimsical rendition of Thomas Edison's laboratories in Menlo Park, New Jersey, ca.*
1880. The commercial artist imagined a giant electric light illuminating the entire region.
Six weeks after Edison announced the invention of the electric light in 1879, the stock
market turned jittery and gas company shares fell sharply: investors feared his "magic."

the annual production of goods was estimated at $2 billion; by 1900 it stood at $13 billion, transforming the United States from fourth to first in the world in terms of productivity. By the early twentieth century, American industry manufactured one-third of the world's goods.

Mechanization Takes Command

This second industrial revolution depended on many factors, but none was more important than the application of new technologies to increase the productivity of labor and the volume of goods. Machines, factory managers, and workers together created a system of continuous production by which more could be made, and faster, than anywhere else on earth. Higher productivity depended not only on machinery and technology but on economies of scale and speed, reorganization of factory labor and business management, and the unparalleled growth of a market for goods of all kinds.

All these changes depended in turn on a new source of fuel, anthracite coal, which was widely used after 1850. By the late 1880s many factories had begun to replace waterpower with steam, generated by huge boilers fired by coal or coke. These reliable and relatively inexpensive sources of energy made possible dramatic changes in the industrial uses of light, heat, and motion. Equally important, coal fueled the great open-hearth furnaces and mills of the iron and steel industry. By the end of the century, the United States steel industry was the world's largest, churning out rails to carry trains and frames and parts to speed production by machines. Not only machines for manufacturing goods but machines for making more machines were at the heart of mass production.

In addition to new machinery, new systems of mass production replaced wasteful and often chaotic practices and speeded up the delivery of finished goods. In the 1860s meat packers set up one of the earliest production lines. The process of converting livestock into meat began with a live animal. A chain around the hind leg whirled the body to an overhead rail, which carried it to slaughter—all in barely half a minute's time. Then hair and bristles were removed by a scraping machine, the carcass shifted to a conveyer belt where the chest was split and the organs removed, and the body placed in a cooler. This "disassembly line" displaced patterns of hand labor that were centuries old. Although opponents of meat eating looked with horror upon the mechanization of animal slaughter, comparing the process to modern warfare, the production line became standard in most areas of manufacturing.

Sometimes the invention of a single machine could instantly transform production, mechanizing every stage from processing the raw material to packaging the product. The cigarette-making machine, patented in 1881, shaped the tobacco, encased it in an endless paper tube, and snipped off the tube at cigarette-length intervals. This machine could produce more than 7,000 cigarettes per hour, replacing the worker who at best made 3,000 per day. After a few more improvements, fifteen machines could meet the total demand for American cigarettes. Diamond brand matches were soon produced in the same fashion and came to dominate the world market. Within a generation, continuous production also revolutionized the making of furniture, cloth, grain products, soap, and canned goods; the refining, distilling, and processing of animal and vegetable fats; and eventually the manufacture of automobiles.

The Expanding Market for Goods

To distribute the growing volume of goods, businesses demanded new techniques of marketing and merchandising. For generations, legions of sellers, or "drummers," had worked their routes, pushing goods, especially hardware and patent medicines, to individual buyers and retail stores. The appearance of mail-order houses after the Civil War accompanied the consolidation of the railroad lines and the expansion of the postal system. Rates were lowered for freight and

Patterns of Industry, 1900 *Industrial manufacturing concentrated in the Northeast and Midwest, while the raw materials for production came mostly from other parts of the nation.*

postage alike, and railroad stations opened post offices and sold money orders. By 1896 rural free delivery had reached distant communities.

Growing directly out of these services, the successful Chicago-based mail-order houses drew rural and urban consumers into a common marketplace. Sears, Roebuck and Company (which began by selling watches by mail) and Montgomery Ward (which started out with a mail-order catalogue of merchandise) offered an enormous variety of goods, from shoes to buggies to gasoline stoves and cream separators. The Montgomery Ward catalogue provided "a real link between us and civilization," a Nebraska farmwoman wrote. The mail-order catalogue also returned to rural folks the fruits of their own labor, now processed and packaged for easy use. The Sears catalogue offered Armour's summer sausage as well as Aunt Jemima's Pancake Flour and Queen Mary Scotch Oatmeal, both made of grains that came from the agricultural heartland. In turn, the purchases made by farm families through the Sears catalogue sent cash flowing into Chicago.

The chain store achieved similar economies of scale. By 1900, a half-dozen grocery chains had sprung up. The largest was A&P, originally named the Great Atlantic and Pacific Tea Company to celebrate the completion of the transcontinental railroad. Frank and Charles Woolworth offered inexpensive variety goods in five-and-ten-cent stores, of which more than 1,000 were established in the United States and Great Britain by 1919. Other chains selling drugs, costume jewelry, shoes, cigars, and furniture soon appeared, offering a greater selection of goods and lower prices than the small, independent stores. Hurt financially by this competition, community-based retailers headed the lobby for antichain legislation.

The department stores reigned over the urban market. These palaces of merchandise, with their attractive displays and convenient arrangements of goods, enticed buyers and browsers alike. Opening shortly after the Civil War, department stores began to take up much of the business formerly enjoyed by specialty shops, offering a spectrum of services that included restaurants, rest rooms, ticket agencies, nurseries, reading rooms, and post offices. Elegantly appointed with imported carpets, sweeping marble staircases, and crystal chandeliers, the department store

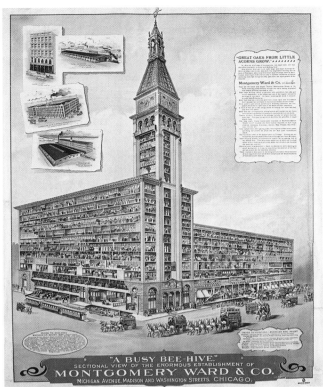

Lithograph, ICHi-01622. "A Busy Bee-Hive." Montgomery Ward & Co., Michigan Avenue, Madison, and Washington Streets, Chicago. Boston, MA, ca. 1899, printed by Forbes Company.

Montgomery Ward & Company, Chicago, ca. 1870s.
This "sectional view" imaginatively strips away exterior walls
to show the activity of each department of the great mail-order
firm. The artist suggests that all who work at the Ward
Company must be overwhelmingly busy simply to meet
customer demand.

raised retailing to new heights. By the close of the century, the names of Marshall Field of Chicago, Filene's of Boston, The Emporium of San Francisco, Wanamaker's of Philadelphia, and Macy's of New York had come to represent the splendors of those great cities as well as the apex of mass retailing.

Advertising lured customers to the department stores, the chains, and the independent neighborhood shops. The advertising revolution began in 1869, when Francis Wayland Ayer founded the earliest advertising agency, but the firm did not hire its first full-time copy writers until 1891. Ayer's handled the accounts of such companies as Montgomery Ward, Procter & Gamble, and the National Biscuit Company. With the help of this new sales tool, gross revenues of retailers raced upward from $8 million in 1860 to $102 million in 1900.

Integration, Combination, and Merger

Business leaders moved purposefully to exercise greater control of the American economy and to enlarge their own commercial empires. In every aspect of their business, from procurement of raw materials to the organization of production, from the conditions of labor to

the climate of public opinion, they acted shrewdly. The contracts and high protective tariffs of the Civil War era had given American businesses an enormous boost. The business cycle, alternating between rapid growth and sharp decline, also promoted the rise of big business. Major economic setbacks in 1873 and 1893 wiped out weaker competitors, allowing the strongest firms to rebound swiftly and to expand their sales and scale of operation during the recovery period. Purchasing more efficient machines and speeding up production, American corporations commanded the heights of the national and even world markets in the last half of the century.

Businesses grew in two distinct if overlapping ways. Through vertical integration a firm aspired to control production at every step of the way—from raw materials through processing to transport and merchandising of the finished items. Agricultural processing firms such as Gustavus Swift in meat and James Buchanan Duke's American Tobacco Company often integrated "forward" in this fashion. In 1899 the United Fruit Company began to build a network of wholesale houses, and within two years it had opened distribution centers in twenty-one major cities. Eventually United Fruit directed an elaborate system of Central American plantations and temperature-controlled shipping and storage facilities for its highly perishable bananas. The firm became one of the nation's largest corporations, its "empire in bananas" dominating the economic and political life of whole nations in Central America.

The second means of growth, horizontal combination, entailed gaining control of the market for a single product. The most famous case was the Standard Oil Company, founded by John D. Rockefeller in 1870. Operating out of Cleveland in a highly competitive but lucrative field, Rockefeller recognized the urgency of bringing "some order out of what has rapidly become a state of chaos." He first secured preferential rates from railroads to transport Standard's oil. He then convinced or coerced other local oil operators to sell their stock to him; by 1880 he controlled over 90 percent of the nation's oil-refining industry.

The Standard Oil Trust, established in 1882, "was the first in the field," wrote journalist Ida Tarbell, "and it has furnished the methods, the charter, and the traditions for its followers." Rockefeller himself recognized the larger implications. "This movement," he wrote proudly, "was the origin of the whole system of modern economic administration. It has revolutionized the way of doing business all over the world. . . . The day of combination is here to stay."

Horizontal combinations, which secured unprecedented control over output and prices, produced a highly concentrated business economy over which a few very large firms prevailed. To protect trade and commerce and restore competition by encouraging small business, Congress in 1890 passed the Sherman Antitrust Act, which outlawed "every . . . combination . . . in restraint of trade." Ironically, the courts interpreted the law in ways that inhibited the organization of trade unions (on the ground that they restricted the free flow of labor) while supporting the consolidation of business. Between 1898 and 1902, more than 2,600 firms vanished, 1,200 in 1899 alone. By 1910 the industrial giants that would dominate the American economy until the last half of the twentieth century—U.S. Rubber, Goodyear, American Smelting and Refining, Anaconda Copper, General Electric, Westinghouse, Nabisco, Swift and Company, Armour, International Harvester, Eastman-Kodak, and American Can—had already been created.

The Gospel of Wealth

The preeminent financiers and corporation magnates not only took pride in the collective triumph of the business community but felt spiritually fulfilled by the accumulation of wealth. Ninety percent of the nation's business leaders were Protestant, and the majority attended church services regularly. They attributed their personal achievement to hard work and perseverance and made these the principal tenets of a new faith that imbued the pursuit of wealth with old-time religious zeal. "God gave me my money," declared John D. Rockefeller, and Baptist minister Russell Conwell's pamphlet *Acres of Diamonds*, which sold more than 1 million copies, argued that to build a fortune was a profound Christian duty. "To make money honestly," he preached, "is to preach the gospel."

One version of this "gospel of wealth" justified the ruthless behavior of entrepreneurs who accumulated unprecedented wealth and power through shady deals and conspiracies. Speculator Jay Gould, known in the popular press as "the Worst Man in the World," wrung his fortune, it was widely believed, from the labor of others. Through a series of financial maneuvers (one of which allegedly drove a partner to suicide) and such high-handed measures as sending armed employees to seize a factory, he rose quickly from his modest origins in western New York state. After abandoning his tanning business for stock trading, Gould gained notoriety on Wall Street for bribing, threatening, and conspiring against his competitors.

Speculation in railroads proved to be Gould's forte. He took over the Erie Railroad, paying off New York legislators to get the state to finance its expansion. Now a major player, Gould acquired the U.S. Express Company by pressuring and tricking its stockholders. Threatened with arrest, he sold off his shares for $9 million and moved on to the Union Pacific, where he cut wages, precipitated strikes, and manipulated elections in the western and Plains states. When caricatured in the press as a great swindler, Gould bought

the leading newspapers and kept reporters in line by giving them valuable tips on stocks. At his death, the New York World called Jay Gould "an incarnation of cupidity and sordidness" whose life symbolized "idolatrous homage [to] the golden calf."

Andrew Carnegie—"the Richest Man in the World"—offered a strikingly different model of success. He represented the "captain of industry" who had risen from the ranks through diligence and who refused to worship wealth for its own sake. A poor immigrant boy from Scotland, Carnegie had studied bookkeeping at night while working days in a textile mill. At age thirteen he had become a messenger for Western Union, and by age seventeen he was the fastest telegraph key operator in Pittsburgh. In 1852 the superintendent of the Penn-

The Two Philanthropists *by Joseph Keppler, from* Puck Magazine, *February 23, 1888. This famous artist of the late nineteenth century drew caricatures of magnates Jay Gould and Cornelius Vanderbilt, stressing not their "good works" but their less than beneficent control of the nation's railroads and telegraph systems. Illustrated magazines, such as* Puck, *reproduced such drawings in quantity, due in part to technological advances in the lithographic process.*

sylvania Railroad's western division hired the young man as his secretary and personal telegrapher. Well placed to learn the principles of the business, Carnegie stepped into the superintendent's job seven years later. He improved passenger train service while investing brilliantly to build up funds for his next venture, steel. By exploiting his talents for management and self-promotion, Carnegie was soon able to place the new industry on the same powerful financial footing as the railroads.

A genius at vertical integration, Carnegie built an empire in steel. He consistently undercut his strongest competitors by using the latest technology, following his own system of cost analysis, and selling steel as cheaply as possible. By 1900 Carnegie managed the most efficient steel mills in the world and accounted for one-third of American output. When he sold out to J. P. Morgan's new United States Steel Corporation for $480 million in 1901, his personal share came to $225 million.

By 1890 Carnegie, only five feet three inches tall, was an industrial giant with a personality to match. From one point of view, he was still a factory despot who underpaid his employees and ruthlessly managed their work lives. But to the patrons of the public libraries, art museums, concert halls, colleges, and universities he funded, he was the greatest philanthropist of the age. At the time of his death, he had given away his massive personal fortune. In his book *The Gospel of Wealth* (1900) Carnegie insisted that "there is no genuine, praiseworthy success in life if you are not honest, truthful, and fair-dealing."

Whether following the rough road of Gould or the smooth path of Carnegie, the business community effected sweeping changes in the larger society. One such change took place in the way most Americans perceived greatness. Even as they schemed to control market forces, the captains of industry praised the system of free enterprise. They endorsed the principles of social Darwinism, or survival of the fittest— the timely doctrine devised from the famed naturalist Charles Darwin's scientific theories of evolution that purportedly explained, and justified, why some Americans grew rich while others remained poor. Meanwhile, Horatio Alger published more than 100 rags-to-riches novels celebrating the outrageous good fortune of self-made men. Some Americans nevertheless feared that the cost of progress achieved by such principles might be more than the nation could afford.

LABOR IN THE AGE OF BIG BUSINESS

It was a common item of faith among most working people that, as labor reformer George E. McNeill put it in 1877, "labor produces all the wealth of the

world. . . . [The laborer] makes civilization possible." Like the gospel of wealth, the "gospel of work" affirmed the dignity of hard work, the virtue of thrift, and the importance of individual initiative. Both doctrines elaborated the simple phrase adorning many needlework samplers, "Work Is Prayer." But unlike business leaders, the philosophers of American working people did not believe in riches as the proof of work well done, or in the lust for power as the driving force of progress. On the contrary, they contended that honesty and competence should become the cornerstones of a society "so improved that labor shall become a blessing instead of a curse," recognized by all as the badge of the morally responsible citizen.

This faith inspired a slender minority, less than 3 percent of the work force, to form unions in various trades and industries. Despite its small size, the labor movement represented the most significant and lasting response of workers to the rise of big business and the consolidation of corporate power.

The Changing Status of Labor

The momentous growth of manufacturing in the last half of the nineteenth century required a parallel expansion of the workforce. Self-employment became less common, and the United States became a nation of wage workers or employees. The 1870 census revealed that wage workers already totaled almost 5 million (3.5 million in industry) of the nearly 13 million gainfully employed persons. Farmers still accounted for 3 million or so, agricultural laborers for nearly 4 million. By the end of the century, two-thirds of all Americans worked for wages.

The new system required a vast number of people. Many young men and women fled the family farm for the promise of a paying job in industry. A smaller number escaped the peonage system of agricultural labor in the South. By far the largest proportion came from Europe or Asia. Between 1860 and 1890, 10 million people immigrated to the United States. Although the lure of jobs brought many to American shores, political or economic crisis in their homelands also proved a major incentive. The Irish were forced off the land in their native country, while in Germany and Great Britain many factory workers fled industrial depressions. A 1910 report on twenty-one industries estimated that nearly 53 percent of all wage workers were foreign-born, with two-thirds coming from southern and eastern Europe. In many occupations—meat processing, clothing and textile manufacturing, cigar making, and mining, for example—immigrants predominated.

The accelerating growth of industry, especially the steady mechanization of production, shaped this expanding pool of wage workers in two major ways: it

Between 1852 and the Chinese Exclusion Act of 1882, approximately 322,000 Chinese immigrated to the United States. Many helped to built the Central Pacific Railroad and, after fulfilling their labor contracts, moved on to work as cooks or laundry workers in mining and timber camps. Nearly 90 percent of all American Chinese settled in the West. This family, celebrating a wedding, posed for a photographer in Idaho City, Idaho, their new hometown.

dramatically changed employer-employee relations; and it created wholly new categories of workers. Both, in turn, fostered competition among workers and created often hazardous work conditions.

For most craft workers, the new system destroyed long-standing practices and chipped away at their customary autonomy. As the pioneer of scientific management, Frederick Winslow Taylor, explained, the company must "take all the important decisions . . . out of the hands of workmen." Although only a few companies adopted Taylor's specific policies before the turn of the century, workers in major industries lost control over production processes. Teams of iron-workers, for example, had previously set the rules of production as well as their wages while the company supplied equipment and raw materials. Once steel replaced iron, most companies gradually introduced a new managerial structure. Workers now faced constant supervision, higher production quotas, and new, faster machinery. Highly skilled cabinetmakers, who for generations had brought their own tools to the factory, were largely replaced with "green hands"— immigrants, including many women, who could operate new woodworking machines with minimal training and close supervision.

Not all trades conformed to this pattern. The garment industry, for example, grew at a very fast pace in New York, Boston, Chicago, Philadelphia, Cleveland, and St. Louis but retained older systems of labor along with the new. On the one hand were highly mechanized factories that employed hundreds of thou-

sands of young immigrant women. On the other was the outwork system, established well before the Civil War, which employed ever-larger numbers of families working at home on sewing machines or by hand. Companies fostered extreme competition between these two groups of workers, continually speeding up the pace by increasing daily production quotas. Paid by the piece—a seam stitched, a collar turned, a button attached—workers labored faster and longer at home or in the factory to forestall a dip in wages. Meanwhile, in older trades such as machine tooling and textiles, the surviving craft jobs continued to pass from fathers to sons, nephews, or family friends.

Wholly new trades or expanding occupational fields brought an unprecedented number of women into the wage system. In the trades least affected by technological advances, such as domestic service, African American and immigrant women in particular found employment in cities such as Atlanta, Boston, New York, and Chicago. Meanwhile, English-speaking white women moved into clerical positions in the rapidly expanding business sector. After the typewriter and telephone came into widespread use in the 1890s, the number of women employed in office work rose even faster. In retailing there was a legion of nearly 60,000 saleswomen ruled over by male superintendents, floorwalkers, and buyers. Overall, at the turn of the century, 8.6 million women worked outside their homes—nearly triple the number in 1870.

By contrast, African American men found themselves excluded from many fields. In Cleveland, for example, the number of black carpenters declined after 1870, just as the volume of construction increased rapidly. African American men were also driven from restaurant service and barred from newer trades like boilermaking, plumbing, electrical work, and paper-hanging, which European immigrants secured for themselves.

The impact of discriminatory or exclusionary practices fell hardest on workers who had been recruited from China in earlier decades. Driven by severe famine and political turmoil in their homeland and drawn by news of jobs in the California Gold Rush, 322,000 Chinese—mostly young men between the ages of sixteen and twenty-four—came to the United States between 1850 and 1882. Many signed up as contract laborers, agreeing to work for four or five years in railroad construction without wages in return for ocean transport. Once their contracts expired and they sought other jobs, they were viewed as potential competitors by white workers and proprietors of small businesses. In 1877 rioters calling for deportation measures destroyed Chinese neighborhoods. In 1882 Congress passed the Chinese Exclusion Act, which suspended Chinese immigra-

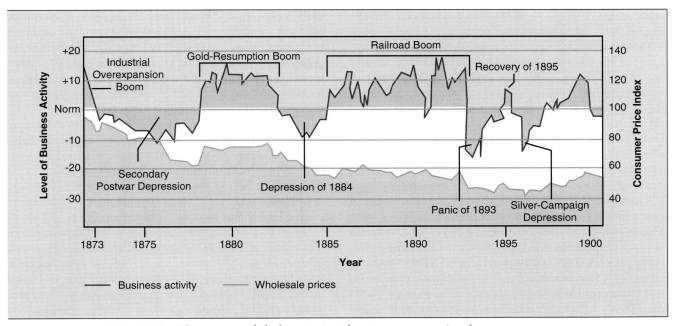

U.S. Economy, 1873–1900   *The economy of the late nineteenth century was a series of sharp ups and downs. Each "boom" was swiftly followed by a "bust," often of greater duration. Although wholesale prices fell, most consumers lacked sufficient income to enjoy fully the bounty of cheaper goods.*

Source: Bernard Bailyn et al., *The Great Republic*, 3d ed. (Lexington, Mass.: D. C. Heath, 1985), p. 552.

tion, limited the civil rights of resident Chinese, and forbade their naturalization.

For even the best-placed wage earners, the new workplace could be unhealthy, even dangerous. Meat packing produced its own hazards—the dampness of the pickling room, the sharp blade of the slaughtering knife, and the noxious odors of the fertilizer department. Factory owners often locked fire doors from the outside, failed to mark high-voltage wires, and took little or no action to limit the emission of toxic fumes. Extractive workers, such as coal and copper miners, endured the worst conditions of all. Mineshaft air could suddenly turn poisonous; sudden cave-ins could make escape all but impossible. Moreover, machines ran faster in American factories than anywhere else in the world, and workers who could not keep up or suffered serious injury found themselves without a job.

Even under less hazardous conditions, workers complained about the tedium of performing repetitive tasks for many hours each day. Although federal employees had been granted the eight-hour day in 1868, most workers still toiled upward of ten or twelve hours. "Life in a factory," one textile operative grumbled, "is perhaps, with the exception of prison life, the most monotonous life a human being can live." Nor could glamour be found in the work of saleswomen in the elegant department stores. Clerks could not sit down, despite workdays as long as sixteen hours in the busy season, or hold "unnec-

essary conversations" with customers or other clerks. Despite these disadvantages, most women preferred sales and manufacturing jobs to domestic service. Household workers, especially live-in servants, were on call seven days a week, enjoying at best an occasional afternoon off. Most workers tolerated unsafe conditions or tedious jobs as the price of steady employment.

The boom-and-bust business cycle made periods of unemployment routine in the lives of most workers. Between 1866 and 1897, fourteen years of prosperity stood against seventeen of hard times. The major depressions of 1873–79 and 1893–97 were the worst in the nation's history up to that time. Three "minor" recessions (1866–67, 1883–85, and 1890–91) did not seem insignificant to the millions who lost their jobs during those periods. "At one time they drive us like slaves," a labor official complained in 1883, "and at other times we have to beg for work." During that year, 40 percent of all industrial workers lived below the poverty line ($500 per year). Whereas a highly skilled worker might earn between $800 and $1,000 per year, a common laborer received only $1.50 for a day's work.

Mobilization against the Wage System

Many workers who abhorred the wage system experimented with worker-owned factories. Others dismissed such an alternative as far-fetched and concentrated instead on improving conditions in their trades by stabilizing wages and above all by shortening hours. In the second half of the nineteenth century, a national labor movement embracing both views took shape.

The National Labor Union (NLU) was formed in 1866. William Sylvis, its founder and president, wished to halt the spread of the wage system. He insisted that through "cooperation we will become a nation of employers—the employers of our own labor. The wealth of the land will pass into the hands of those who produce it." Annual NLU conventions passed resolutions advocating banking reforms to permit workers to borrow enough money to launch their own factories. The NLU achieved a maximum enrollment of approximately 300,000 members but disintegrated soon after Sylvis's death, its goal unrealized.

The Noble and Holy Order of the Knights of Labor, founded by a group of Philadelphia garment cutters in 1869, became the largest labor organization in the nineteenth century. Led by Grand Master Workman Terence V. Powderly, the order sought to bring together all wage earners regardless of skill in a "great brotherhood." Only by organizing widely, one member insisted, would workers be able to achieve their "emancipation" from "the thraldom and loss of wage slavery." Growing slowly at first, the Knights enrolled 110,000 members by 1885.

The Knights endorsed a variety of reform measures—more land set aside for homesteading, the abolition of contract and child labor, monetary reform, and a graduated income tax—to offset the power of the manufacturers. Above all they advocated a system of producers' cooperatives. Local assemblies launched thousands of small co-ops, such as the Our Girls Cooperative Manufacturing Company established by Chicago seamstresses. These worker-run factories generated great enthusiasm among the participants, who shared all profits and made collective decisions on prices and wages. The Knights also sponsored consumer cooperatives for members, often operating small grocery stores from their own assembly buildings. Other co-ops, such as cigar shops, sold items to the broader working-class community. Local banks and other businesses, however, viewed co-ops as competitors, and many refused to extend them credit or sell them goods at wholesale prices. Ultimately, the co-ops could not compete against heavily capitalized enterprises such as chain or department stores.

The Knights reached their peak during the great campaign for a shorter workday. At the close of the Civil War, eight-hour leagues had formed to advocate a "natural" rhythm of eight hours for work, eight hours for sleep, and eight hours for leisure. After staging petition campaigns, marches, and a massive strike in New York City, the movement collapsed during the economic recession of the 1870s. But it was revived early in the next decade, and this time the campaign aroused widespread public support. Consumers boycotted those brands of beer, bread, and other products made in longer-hour shops. Newspaper advertisements announced "eight-hour" shoes, "eight-hour" romance novels, and "eight-hour" picnics and concerts sponsored by groups eager for the reform.

During the first weeks of May 1886, more than a third of a million workers walked off their jobs. Approximately 200,000 of them won shorter hours, including Packingtown's workers, who joined the Knights of Labor en masse. To celebrate, Chicago cattle butchers led a huge parade, accompanied by twelve bands and twenty-eight decorated wagons.

The eight-hour campaign swelled the ranks of the Knights of Labor. Workers ordinarily excluded from craft unions joined the Knights. Nearly 3,000 women formed their own "ladies assemblies" or joined mixed locals. Leonora Barry, appointed to organize women, helped to increase their share of membership to 10 percent, or nearly 50,000 workers from the textile, garment, shoe, and carpet industries. African Americans—20,000 to 30,000 of them nationally—also joined the Knights, forming separate assemblies within the organization. Like the NLU, however, the Knights supported the Chinese Exclusion Act and advocated further restrictions on immigration.

A tragedy in Chicago's Haymarket Square on May 4, 1886, however, undercut the Knights' gains. A protest rally on that day against police violence following a series of confrontations between strikers and police was unfolding quietly when an unidentified person threw a bomb. One police officer was killed outright and seven others were fatally wounded. The police then fired wildly into the dispersing crowd, killing several people. During the next weeks, newspaper editorials warned of imminent, bloody revolution in the nation's streets. In several cities, club-wielding police broke up rallies, raided the offices of labor assemblies and ethnic fraternal clubs, and threatened immigrant unionists with deportation. Chicago authorities arrested anarchist leaders and in a sensational trial sentenced them to death, although no evidence linked them to the actual bombing. Four of the anarchists were hanged, another committed suicide, and three others remained jailed until Illinois governor John Peter Altgeld pardoned them in 1893.

The Knights of Labor suffered irreparable setbacks during the rest of 1886 and 1887. Employers' associations successfully pooled funds to rid their factories of troublesome organizers and announced that companies would no longer bargain with unions. In Packingtown, the Big Five firms drew up a blacklist to get rid of labor organizers and quickly reinstituted the ten-hour day. The Knights' leadership, shaken by these events, desperately sought to regain respectability by denouncing the "Haymarket martyrs." Most remaining members simply dropped out. The wage system had triumphed.

The American Federation of Labor

The events of 1886 also signaled the rise of a very different kind of organization, the American Federation of Labor (AFL). Unlike the NLU or the Knights, the AFL accepted the wage system. Following a strategy of "pure and simple unionism," the AFL sought to gain recognition of its union status to bargain with employers for better working conditions, higher wages, and shorter hours. In return it offered compliant firms the benefit of amenable day-to-day relations with the most highly skilled wage earners. Only if companies refused to bargain in good faith would union members strike.

The AFL originated in the craft unions revived from earlier times or founded in the decade after the Civil War. National organizations for individual crafts, such as machinists and typographers, set their own agendas. At the same time, combined assemblies of skilled workers appeared in most major cities outside the South. During the business upswing of the early 1880s, delegates from eight national unions formed the Federation of Organized Trades and Labor Unions of the United States and Canada. In 1886 this organization became the American Federation of Labor.

The new federation, with twelve national unions and 140,000 affiliated members, declared war on the Knights of Labor. In the wake of the Haymarket tragedy and collapse of the eight-hour movement, the AFL pushed ahead of its rival by organizing craft workers. AFL president Samuel Gompers refused to include unskilled workers, including African Americans, women, and most new immigrants. As Gompers put it, such a "heterogeneous stew of divergent and discordant customs, languages and institutions" was "impossible to organize" and even unworthy of equal status. By successfully limiting the job market and policing unskilled workers for employers, the AFL unionist became the "aristocrat of labor," the best-paid worker in the world.

By the end of the century, the AFL had enrolled only 10 percent of the nation's workers. It could not slow the steady advance of mechanization, which diminished the craft worker's autonomy and eliminated some of the most desirable jobs. But the AFL had achieved a degree of respectability that the Knights of Labor had commanded only briefly. Local politicians courted AFL members' votes, and Labor Day, first celebrated in the 1880s, became a national holiday in 1894.

THE INDUSTRIAL CITY

Before the Civil War, manufacturing had centered in the countryside, in burgeoning factory towns such as Lowell, Massachusetts, and Troy, New York. The expanding rail system promoted new growth in the older commercial cities of Boston, Philadelphia, and New York and created urban outposts like Minneapolis, Kansas City, and Denver. By the end of the nineteenth century, 90 percent of all manufacturing took place in cities. The metropolis stood at the center of the growing industrial economy, a magnet drawing raw material, capital, and labor and the key distribution point for manufactured goods.

The industrial city inspired both great hope and great trepidation. Civic leaders often bragged about its size and rate of growth; immigrants wrote to their countryfolk of its pace, both exciting and exhausting. Philosopher Josiah Strong described the city as the nation's "storm center." "Here luxuries are gathered—everything that dazzles the eye, or tempts the appetite" as well as, he pointedly added, "the desperation of starvation." Whatever the assessment, the city dominated the nation's economic, social, and cultural life.

Populating the City

The United States was on its way to becoming an urban nation. The population of cities grew at double the rate of the nation's population as a whole. In 1860 only sixteen cities had more than 50,000 residents. By 1890 one-third of all Americans were city dwellers. Eleven cities claimed more than 250,000 people. Both Chicago and Philadelphia had 1 million inhabitants. By 1900 New York City was home to almost 3.5 million people.

The major cities—New York, Chicago, Philadelphia, St. Louis, Boston, and Baltimore—achieved international fame for the size and diversity of their populations. Many of their new residents had migrated from rural communities within the United States. Between 1870 and 1910, an average of nearly 7,000 African Americans moved north each year, hoping to escape the poverty and oppression prevailing in the South and to find better-paying jobs. By the end of the century, nearly 80 percent of African Americans in the North lived in urban areas. Among those aged sixteen to thirty-five in all native-born groups, urban women outnumbered men. Whereas young white men in particular aspired to inherit the family farm or seek a fortune in the West, their sisters sought jobs in urban manufacturing, commercial trades, and housekeeping.

Immigrants and their children were the major source of urban population growth in the late nineteenth century. Most of those in the first wave of immi-

Population

- ∘ 0 – 9,999
- ○ 10,000 – 49,999
- ◯ 50,000 – 499,999
- ◯ 500,000 – 999,999
- ◯ 1,000,000 – 2,000,000
- ◯ Over 2,000,000

- Established city before 1880
- Newly emerging city, 1880–1900
- Urban-industrial core
- 1880 population
- 1900 population

Patterns in Urban Growth in Turn-of-the-Century America

By the turn of the century, the ten largest cities in the United States were located in the Northeast and the Midwest. The rapid growth of these cities reflected the rise of industry and commerce in the nation's urban-industrial core and the demand for labor that accompanied it. New York City, Chicago, Philadelphia, St. Louis, and Boston, for example, attracted new immigrants who found jobs in the these cities' huge ready-to-wear clothing industries and other light manufacturing shops. Chicago, Pittsburgh, Detroit, and Buffalo became the home of working-class families who looked for their livelihood to these cities' giant steel mills and packinghouse plants.

The growth of cities in the western and southern states reflected the expansion of the nation's railroads in those regions and the efficient transportation of goods and people that expansion made possible. The growth of Atlanta, for example, was tied to the expansion of the southern rail system. Like Chicago in the Midwest and Los Angeles in the West, Atlanta became a hub and distribution center for regionally produced goods.

gration, before the Civil War, had settled in the countryside. In contrast, after the war it was the industrial city that drew the so-called "new" immigrants, who came primarily from eastern and southern Europe. At the turn of the century Chicago had more Germans than all but a few German cities and more Poles than most Polish cities; New York had more Italians than a handful of the largest Italian cities, and Boston had nearly as many Irish as Dublin. In almost every group except the Irish, men outnumbered women.

Like rural migrants, immigrants came to the American city to take advantage of the expanding opportunities for employment. While many hoped to build a new home in the land of plenty, many others intended to work hard, save money, and return to their families in the Old Country. In the 1880s, for example, nearly half of all Italian, Greek, and Serbian men returned to their native lands. Others could not return to their homelands or did not wish to. Jews, for instance, had emigrated to escape persecution in Russia

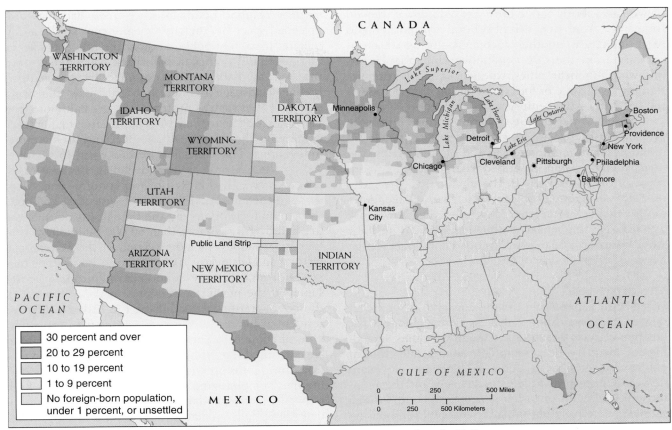

Population of Foreign Birth by Region, 1880   *European immigrants after the Civil War settled primarily in the industrial districts of the northern Midwest and parts of the Northeast. French Canadians continued to settle in Maine, Cubans in Florida, and Mexicans in the Southwest, where earlier immigrants had established thriving communities.*

Source: Clifford L. Lord and Elizabeth H. Lord, *Lord & Lord Historical Atlas of the United States* (New York: Holt, 1953).

and Russian-dominated Polish and Romanian lands. A Yiddish writer later called this generation the "Jews without Jewish memories. . . . They shook them off in the boat when they came across the seas. They emptied out their memories."

Of all groups, Jews had the most experience with urban life. Forbidden to own land in most parts of Europe and boxed into shtetls (villages), Jews had also formed thriving urban communities in Vilna, Berlin, London, and Vienna. Many had worked in garment manufacturing in, for example, London's East End, and followed a path to American cities like New York, Rochester, Philadelphia, or Chicago where the needle trades flourished.

Other groups, the majority coming from rural parts of Europe, sought out their kinfolk in American cities, where they could most easily find housing and employment. Bohemians settled largely in Chicago, Pittsburgh, and Cleveland. They often lived and worked near German immigrants, although in poorer

housing and in less skilled jobs as lumberyard workers, cigar rollers, and garment workers. French Canadians, a relatively small group of a few hundred thousand, emigrated from Quebec and settled almost exclusively in New England and upper New York State. Finding work mainly in textile mills, they transformed smaller industrial cities like Woonsocket, Rhode Island, into French-speaking communities. Cubans, themselves often first- or second-generation immigrants from Spain, moved to Ybor City, a section of Tampa, Florida, to work in cigar factories. Still other groups tended toward cities dominated by fishing, shoemaking, or even glassblowing, a craft carried directly from the Old Country. Italians, the most numerous among the new immigrants, settled mainly in northeastern cities. With few skills and little education, they often became laborers, laying railroad track, excavating subways, and erecting buildings.

Resettlement in an American city did not necessarily mark the end of the immigrants' travels.

Newcomers, both native-born and immigrant, moved frequently from one neighborhood to another and from one city to another. As manufacturing advanced outward from the city center, working populations followed. American cities experienced a total population turnover three or four times during each decade of the last half of the century.

The American city was transformed under the pressure of these various groups. In 1882, when 1.2 million people immigrated to the United States, the novelist Henry James described what he called a "sharp sense of dispossession." To the immigrants, the scene was also disquieting. Before he left his village, Alessandro DeLuca remembered hearing that New York was not only bigger but better than any city in Italy. After he arrived, he felt disillusioned and doubted that he would ever "find here my idea."

The Urban Landscape

Faced with a population explosion and an unprecedented building boom, the cities encouraged the creation of many beautiful and useful structures, including commercial offices, sumptuous homes, and efficient public services—but at a cost. Builders and city planners often disregarded the natural beauty and the architectural landmarks of earlier generations. Laid out in a simple geometric gridiron pattern, streets and housing ran over the sites of hills that had been leveled, ponds that had been filled, farmlands and farm houses that had been eradicated. Factories often occupied the best sites, near waterways where goods could be easily transported and wastes dumped.

The majority of the population, who worked in dingy factories, lived in crowded tenements designed to maximize the use of space by impoverished families. Built by the thousands after the Civil War, the typical "dumbbell" model in New York City sat on a lot 25 feet by 100 feet and rose to five stories. Each floor was subdivided into four family units of no more than three rooms each. One room served as a combined cooking and living room, the remaining two as bedrooms. By 1890 New York's Lower East Side packed more than 700 people per acre into back-to-back buildings, producing one of the highest population densities in the world.

At the other end of the urban social scale, New York's Fifth Avenue, St. Paul's Summit Avenue, Chicago's Michigan Avenue, and San Francisco's Nob Hill fairly gleamed with new mansions and town houses. Commonwealth Avenue marked Boston's fashionable Back Bay district, built on a filled-in 450-acre tidal flat. State engineers planned this community, with its magnificent boulevard, uniform five-story brownstones, and back alleys designed for deliveries. Like

wealthy neighborhoods in other cities, Back Bay also provided space for the city's magnificent public architecture, its stately public library, fine arts and science museums, and orchestra hall. Back Bay opened onto the Fenway Park system designed by the nation's premier landscape architect, Frederick Law Olmsted.

Cities such as Boston, Chicago, Baltimore, and San Francisco managed to rebuild after major fires, employing the latest technological and architectural innovations. The Chicago Fire broke out in October 1871—though not, as legend had it, because "Mrs. O'Leary's cow" had kicked over a lantern—and swept through the ramshackle wooden houses that had been thrown up for workers. By the time it was doused, the fire had destroyed more than 60,000 buildings within four square miles, including much of the commercial district, and left nearly 100,000 people homeless. Louis H. Sullivan, recently schooled in Europe, eagerly surveyed the newly cleared sites in the aftermath of the conflagration. Although he did little to improve residential living, he came up with a plan for a new type of commercial building, the skyscraper, a "proud and soaring thing, rising in [such] sheer exultation that from bottom to top it is a unit without a single dissenting line." Emphasizing vertical grandeur rising as high as twenty stories, and using iron, steel, and masonry to deter fires, Sullivan made the skyscraper the symbol of the modern city.

Architects played a key role in what is sometimes called the American Renaissance or City Beautiful movement. Grand concrete boulevards were constructed at enormous public cost. New sports amphitheaters dazzled the public and evoked pride in the city's accomplishments. New schools, courthouses, capitols, hospitals, museums, and department stores arose. Influenced by the Parisian Beaux-Arts style, architects regularly replaced the simple Greek Revival buildings constructed earlier in the century with domed palaces. These massive, often highly ornate structures expressed the city's pride in its commercial success. The city center also became more congested and noisy, making it a more desirable place to visit than to live.

The city inspired other architectural marvels. Opened in 1883, the Brooklyn Bridge won wide acclaim from engineers, journalists, and poets as the most original American construction. Designed by John Roebling, who died from an accident early in its construction, and by his son Washington Roebling, who became an invalid during its construction, the bridge was considered an aesthetic and practical wonder. Its soaring piers, elegant arches, and intricate steel cables convey an image of strength and elasticity, inspiring a belief among artists and writers in the potential of technology to unite function and beauty. The Brooklyn

Bridge also helped to speed the transformation of rural townships into suburban communities.

The emergence of inexpensive, rapid mass transportation systems also altered the spatial design of cities. Like the railroad but on a smaller scale, streetcars and elevated railroads changed business dramatically because they moved traffic of many different kinds—information, people, and goods—faster and farther than before. Although San Francisco introduced the first mechanically driven cable car in 1873, within a decade Chicago would claim the most extensive cable car system in the world. By 1895 more than 800 communities operated systems of electrically powered cars or trolleys on track reaching 10,000 miles. Two years later Boston rerouted a mile and a half of track underground, establishing the nation's first subway trolley. In 1902 New York opened its subway system, which would grow to become the largest in the nation.

By making it possible for a great number of workers to live in communities distant from their place of employment, mass transportation also allowed cities to grow dramatically. In 1880 New York City's surface transit system alone accommodated more than 150 million riders annually, a large proportion traveling into Manhattan from Queens and Brooklyn. Suburbs like Dorchester and Brookline sprang up outside Boston, offering many professional workers quiet residential retreats from the city's busy downtown. New retail and service businesses followed as the dynamism of the great city radiated outward while the bulk of industry and pollution remained behind.

The City and the Environment

Electric trolleys eliminated the tons of waste from horsecars that had for decades fouled city streets. But the new rail systems also increased congestion and created new safety hazards for pedestrians. During the 1890s, 600 people were killed each year by Chicago's trains. To relieve congestion, Chicago as well as New York and Boston elevated portions of their rapid transit systems and in the process placed entire communities under the shadow of noisy and rickety wooden platforms. Despite many technologi-

In *his watercolor* The Bowery at Night, *painted in 1895, W. Louis Sonntag Jr. shows a New York City scene transformed by electric light. Electricity transformed the city in other ways as well, as seen in the electric streetcars and elevated railroad.*

cal advances, the quality of life in the nation's cities did not necessarily improve.

In the half-century after the Civil War, efforts to improve sanitary conditions absorbed many urban tax dollars. Modern water and sewer systems constituted a hidden city of pipes and wires mirroring the growth of the visible city above ground. Although cast iron pipes and steam pumps had delivered water into cities since the early part of the century, the filtration systems introduced in the 1890s greatly improved water quality and, by providing cleaner water, played an important role in reducing the incidence of typhoid. By the 1880s, bathrooms with showers and flush toilets had become standard features in hospitals and in many middle-class homes.

These advances did not in themselves eradicate serious environmental problems. Most cities continued to dump sewage in nearby bodies of water. Moreover, rather than outlawing upriver dumping by factories, municipal governments usually moved to establish separate clean-water systems through the use of reservoirs. Meanwhile the filthy rivers, such as the Providence and Woonasquatucket Rivers in Providence, Rhode Island, were paved over as they passed through downtown. The Chicago River was reversed through an engineering feat so as to transport sewage away from Lake Michigan, the city's source of drinking water. Chicago's residents enjoyed cleaner tap water, but downriver communities began to complain about the unendurable stench from the diverted flow.

The unrestricted burning of coal to fuel the railroads and to heat factories and homes after 1880 greatly intensified urban air pollution. Noise levels continued to rise in the most compacted living and industrial areas. Overcrowded conditions and inadequate sanitary facilities bred tuberculosis, smallpox, and scarlet fever, among other contagious diseases. Children's diseases like whooping cough and measles spread rapidly through poor neighborhoods such as Packingtown. A major yellow fever epidemic in 1878 prompted the creation of the National Board of Health, which in turn began to advise state and city officials and provide emergency assistance. But only after the turn of the century, amid an intensive campaign against municipal corruption, did laws and administrative practices address the serious problems of public health (see Chapter 21).

Meanwhile the distance between the city and the countryside narrowed. Naturalists had hoped for large open spaces—a buffer zone—to preserve farmland and wild areas, protect future water supplies, and diminish regional air pollution. But soon the industrial landscape invaded the countryside. Nearby rural lands not destined for private housing or commercial development became sites for water treatment and sewage plants, garbage dumps, and graveyards—services essential to the city's growing population.

THE NEW SOUTH

"Fifteen years have gone over" since the Civil War, journalist Whitelaw Reid complained, yet the South "still sits crushed, wretched, busy displaying and bemoaning her wounds." Physically and financially devastated by the war, the South had little investment capital and relatively few banks to manage it. The area was economically stagnant, its per capita wealth only 27 percent of that of the northeastern states. The South's remote countryside receded into greater isolation, while its few urban regions moved very slowly into the era of modern industry and technology. As late as 1880 mining and manufacturing employed only 5 percent of Alabama's workforce. At the turn of the century southern industries lagged far behind enterprises in other regions of the country. Their progress was held back by dependence on northern finance capital, continued reliance on cotton production, and the legacy of slavery.

Industrialization

In the 1870s a vocal and powerful new group of Southerners headed by Henry Woodfin Grady, editor of the *Atlanta Constitution*, insisted that the region enjoyed a great potential in its abundant natural resources of coal, iron, turpentine, tobacco, and lumber. Grady and his peers envisioned a "New South" where modern textile mills operated efficiently and profitably close to the sources of raw goods, the expansive fields of cotton, and a plentiful and cheap supply of labor, unrestricted by unions or by legal limitations on the employment of children. Arguing against those planters who aspired to rejuvenate the agricultural economy based on the cultivation of a few staple crops, this group forcefully promoted industrial development and welcomed northern investors.

Northern investors secured huge concessions from state legislatures, including land, forest, and mineral rights and large tax exemptions. Exploiting the incentives, railroad companies laid over 22,000 miles of new track, connecting the region to national markets and creating new cities. By 1890 a score of large railroad companies, mainly centered in New York, held more than half of all the track in the South. Northern-owned lumber companies meanwhile stripped southern forests.

Northerners also employed various means to protect their investments from southern competition. By the late 1870s southern merchants, with help from foreign investors, had begun to run iron factories around Birmingham, Alabama. Southern iron production was soon encroaching on the northeastern market. Andrew Carnegie toured the city's iron mills and then declared, "The South is Pennsylvania's most formidable industrial enemy." Carnegie first attempted to stave off competition by ordering the railroads to charge higher freight fees to Birmingham's iron producers. By the turn of the century, his successor corporation, U.S. Steel, implemented a simpler solution: buying several Birmingham plants and taking over production.

The production of cotton textiles followed a similar course. Powerful merchants and large landowners, realizing that they could make high profits by controlling the cotton crop from field to factory, promoted the vertical integration of the cotton industry. The Mississippi Valley Cotton Planters' Association, for example, advised planters to "set up spindles in the cotton fields"—that is, to build mills on their land. Meanwhile, New South promoters in Atlanta hosted the International Cotton Exposition of 1881 in a bold public relations campaign to attract investors.

The number of mills in the South grew from 161 in 1880 to 400 in 1900. The latest machines ran the new mills, and the South boasted the first factory fully equipped with electricity. Production in the four leading cotton-manufacturing states—North Carolina, South Carolina, Georgia, and Alabama—skyrocketed, far outpacing the New England mills.

Yet this achievement did not necessarily represent an absolute gain for the South. Northern manufacturers, including many New England mill owners, responded creatively to the report of the 1900 census on manufacturing that "the return upon investment in southern cotton mills has greatly exceeded that upon factories in the North." Recognizing the potential for great profit in new factories and cheap labor, they shifted their investments to the South. By the 1920s, northern investors held much of the South's wealth, including the major textile mills, but returned through employment or social services only a small share of the profits to the region's people.

Beyond iron or steel and textiles, southern industry remained largely extractive and, like the South itself, rural. Turpentine and lumbering businesses pushed ever farther into diminishing pine forests, the sawmills and distilleries moving with them. Toward the end of the century, fruit canning and sugar refining flourished. For the most part, southern enterprises mainly produced raw materials for consumption or use in the North, thereby perpetuating the economic imbalance between the sections.

The governing role of capital investments from outside the region reinforced long-standing relationships. Even rapid industrialization—in iron, railroad, and textiles—did not match the level achieved in the North. The rise of the New South reinforced, rather than refuted, the region's status as a dependent economy: the South relied on the North for capital and administration while deriving few long-term benefits from the relationship.

Southern Labor

Reconstruction and its demise (see Chapter 17) profoundly affected working conditions in the region. For instance, Captain Ellison Alger Smyth, who organized a group of white Southerners, the Red Shirts, to curtail the political influence of African Americans, established a whites-only policy for the workforce of his Pelzer Mill, which he founded in 1881 in Greenville, South Carolina. Textile barons such as Smyth, who became known as the "dean of southern Cotton manufacturers," helped to pass legislation and to devise informal rules that spread racial segregation throughout southern society.

The advance of southern industry did little to improve the working lives of most African Americans, although large numbers moved to the new manufacturing centers and growing cities in search of better-paying jobs. African American men did find work with the railroads; in booming cities like Atlanta they even gained skilled positions in the construction trades and worked as bricklayers, carpenters, and painters. For the most part, however, African Americans were limited to unskilled, low-paying jobs. In the textile mills and cigarette factories, which employed both black and white workers, the work force was rigidly

African American women working as sweepers, Belton, South Carolina, in 1899. Despite the rise of industry in the New South, African Americans found few new avenues for employment. The majority continued to work in agricultural labor or domestic service.

segregated. African Americans were assigned mainly to janitorial jobs and rarely worked alongside the white workers who tended the machines. Nearly all African American women who earned wages did so as household workers. Girls as young as ten years worked as domestics or as child-nurses, while the vast majority of older women did laundry. By 1880 Atlanta's washerwomen outnumbered the African American men who worked as common laborers.

In general, white workers fiercely protected their relatively privileged positions. Locals of the all-white carpenters' union maintained a segregation policy so absolute that if too few members were available for a job, the union would send for out-of-town white workers rather than employ local members of the black carpenters' union. In Atlanta in 1897, 1,400 white women mill operatives went on strike when the company proposed to hire two black spinners.

Only at rare moments did southern workers unite across racial lines. In the 1880s, the Knights of Labor briefly organized both black and white workers. At its high point, the Knights' local union, District Assembly 92, enrolled two-thirds of Richmond's 5,000 tobacco operatives and made significant inroads among quarry workers, coopers, typographers, iron molders, and builders. But when white politicians and local newspapers began to raise the specter of black domination, the Knights were forced to retreat. Across the region their organization collapsed. The few successful unions remained for generations the exclusive claim of white skilled workers.

Wages throughout the South were low for both black and white workers. In Richmond, white skilled workers in the iron trades, including plumbers, carpenters, and gas fitters, made 10 percent to 30 percent less in 1890 than comparable workers elsewhere in the United States. Southern textile workers' wages were barely half those of New Englanders. In the 1880s, when investors enjoyed profits ranging from 30 percent to 75 percent, southern mill workers earned as little as twelve cents per hour. Black men earned at or below the poverty line of $300 per year, while black women rarely earned more than $120 and white women about $220 annually. The poorest paid workers were children.

As industry expanded throughout the nation, so too did the number of children earning wages, especially in the South. In 1896 only one in twenty Massachusetts mill operatives was younger than sixteen, but one in four North Carolina cotton mill workers was. Traditions rooted in the agricultural economy reinforced the practice of using the labor of all family members, even the very young. The same principle operated among Polish immigrant families in the South: even five-year-olds joined their parents to work in oyster-canning factories. Seasonal labor, such as picking crops or grinding sugarcane, put families on the move, making community life and formal education all but impossible. Not until well into the twentieth century did compulsory school attendance laws effectively restrict child labor in the South.

A system of convict labor also thrived in the South. Public work projects of all kinds, especially in remote areas, employed disciplinary methods and created living and working conditions reminiscent of slavery. With African Americans constituting up to 90 percent of the convict work force, public officials felt little need to justify the occasional practice of capturing unsuspecting black strangers and placing them alongside criminals in labor gangs. Transported and housed like animals—chained together by day and confined in portable cages at night—these workers suffered high mortality rates. Southern leaders took pride in what they called the "good roads movement"—the chief use of convict labor—as proof of regional progress.

The Transformation of Piedmont Communities

The impact of the New South was nowhere greater than in the Piedmont. The region, where the tidewater ends and water power can be used for mills, extends from southern Virginia and the central Carolinas into northern Alabama and Georgia. After 1870, long-established farms and plantations gave way to railroad tracks, textile factories, numerous mill villages, and a few sizable cities. By the turn of the century, five Piedmont towns had populations over 10,000. Even more dramatic was the swelling number of small towns with populations between 1,000 and 5,000—from fourteen in 1870 to fifty-two in 1900. Once the South's backcountry, the Piedmont now surpassed New England to stand first in the world in the production of yarn and cloth.

Rural poverty, even more than persuasive arguments by labor recruiters, encouraged many farm families to strike out for a new life in the mill town. As prices of cotton or tobacco fell and farmers' debts to the merchants rose, many families turned to tenant farming and its life of hopeless indebtedness. Those with the least access to land and credit—mainly widows and their children and single women—were the first to go into the mills. Then families sent their children. Some families worked in the mills on a seasonal basis, between planting and harvesting. But as the agricultural crisis deepened, more and more people abandoned the countryside entirely for what they called "public work." In the mill, workers hoped, they could do better.

The majority of these families found themselves residents of a company town, owned "lock, stock and barrel" by the manufacturers who employed them. A mill community typically comprised rows of single-family houses, a small school, several churches, a company-owned store, and the home of the superintendent who governed everyone's affairs. The manager of the King Cotton Mill in Burlington, North Carolina, not only kept the company's accounts in order, purchased raw material, and sold the finished yarn, but even bought Christmas presents for the workers' children. It was not unknown for a superintendent to prowl the neighborhood to see which families burned their lanterns past nine o'clock at night and, finding a violator, to knock on the door and tell the offenders to go to bed. Millworkers frequently complained that they had no private life at all. A federal report published shortly after the turn of the century concluded that "all the affairs of the village and the conditions of living of all the people are regulated entirely by the mill company. Practically speaking, the company owns everything and controls everything, and to a large extent controls everybody in the mill village."

Mill superintendents also relied on schoolteachers and clergy to set the tone of community life. They hired and paid the salaries of Baptist and Methodist ministers to preach a faith encouraging workers to be thrifty, orderly, temperate, and hardworking. Ministers conducted evening prayer services, brought men and women into the choir, and sponsored Bible classes and missionary societies. The schools, similarly subsidized by the company, reinforced the lesson of moral and social discipline required of industrial life and encouraged students to follow their parents into the mill. But it was mainly young children between six and eight years old who attended school. When more hands were needed in the mill, superintendents plucked out these youngsters and sent them to join their older brothers and sisters who were already at work.

Piedmont mill villages like Greenville, South Carolina, and Burlington, Charlotte, and Franklinville, North Carolina, nevertheless developed a cohesive character typical of isolated rural communities. The new residents maintained many aspects of their agricultural pasts, tilling small gardens and keeping chickens, pigs, and cows in their yards. Factory owners rarely paved roads or sidewalks or provided adequate sanitation. Mud, flies, and diseases such as typhoid fever flourished. Millworkers endured poverty and health hazards by strengthening community ties through intermarriage. Within a few generations, most of the village residents had, according to one study, "some connection to each other, however distant, by marriage," blood, or both. Even the men and women without families boarded in households where privacy was scarce and collective meals created a familylike atmosphere. Historians have called this complex of intimate economic, family, and community ties the customs of incorporation.

CULTURE AND SOCIETY IN THE GILDED AGE

The growth of industry and spread of cities had a profound impact on all regions of the United States. During the final third of the century the standard of living climbed, although unevenly and erratically. Real wages (pay in relation to the cost of living) rose, fostering improvements in nutrition, clothing, and housing. More and cheaper products were within the reach of all but the very poor. Food from the farms became more abundant and varied—grains for bread or beer; poultry, pork, and beef; fresh fruits and vegetables from California. Although many Americans continued to acknowledge the moral value of hard work, thrift, and self-sacrifice, the explosion of consumer goods and services promoted sweeping changes in behavior and beliefs. Nearly everyone felt the impact of the nation's wealth, although in vastly different ways.

"Conspicuous Consumption"

Labeled the "Gilded Age" by humorist and social critic Mark Twain, the era following the Civil War favored the growth of a new class united in its pursuit of money and leisure. The well-to-do enjoyed great status throughout the nineteenth century, but only after the war did upper-class Americans form national networks to consolidate their power. Business leaders

built diverse stock portfolios and often served simultaneously on the boards of several corporations. Similarly, they intertwined their interests by joining the same religious, charitable, athletic, and professional societies. They sent their sons to private boarding schools such as St. Paul's, then on to Harvard, Yale, or Princeton. Their wives and children vacationed together in the sumptuous new seashore and mountain resorts, while they themselves made deals at their leisure in new downtown social clubs and on the golf links of suburban country clubs. Just as Dun and Bradstreet ranked the leading corporations, the Social Register identified the 500 families that controlled most of the nation's wealth.

According to economist and social critic Thorstein Veblen, the rich had created a new style of "conspicuous consumption." The Chicago mansion of real estate tycoon Potter Palmer, for example, was constructed in 1885 without exterior doorknobs. Not only could no one enter uninvited, but a visitor's calling card supposedly passed through the hands of twenty-seven servants before admittance was allowed. At the nearby McCormick mansion, dinner guests chose from a menu printed in French. A vice president of the Chicago & Northwestern Railroad, Perry H. Smith, built his marble palace in the style of the Greek Renaissance. Its ebony staircase was trimmed in gold, its butler's pantry equipped with faucets not only for hot and cold water but for iced champagne. The women who oversaw these elaborate households themselves served as measures of their husbands' status, according to Veblen, by adorning themselves in jewels, furs, and dresses of the latest Paris design.

"Conspicuous consumption" reached toward new heights of extravagance. In New York, wealthy families hosted dinner parties for their dogs or pet monkeys, dressing the animals in fancy outfits for the occasion. Railroad magnate "Diamond Jim" Brady commonly enjoyed after-theater snacks at the city's "lobster palaces," where he consumed vast quantities of food—oysters for an appetizer, two soups, fish, a main dinner of beef and vegetables, punches and sherbet on the side, dessert, and coffee and quarts of orange juice.

Perhaps no display of wealth matched the ostentation of the "cottages" of Newport, Rhode Island, where the rich created a summer community centering on consumption. Architect H. H. Richardson and his protégés built manor houses more magnificent than the English homes they mimicked. Here wealthy young men and women engaged in new amateur sports such as polo, rowing, and lawn tennis. Young and old alike joined in yachting and golf tournaments.

Toward the end of the century, the wealthy added a dramatic public dimension to the "high life."

New York's Waldorf-Astoria hotel, which opened in 1897, incorporated the grandeur of European royalty but with an important difference. Because rich Americans wanted to be watched, the elegantly appointed corridors and restaurants were visible to the public through huge windows, and floor-to-ceiling mirrors allowed diners to observe one another. The New York rich also established a unique custom to welcome the New Year: they opened wide the curtains of their Fifth Avenue mansions so that passersby could marvel at the elegant decor.

The wealthy also became the leading patrons of the arts as well as the chief importers of art treasures from Europe and Asia. They provided the bulk of funds for the new symphonies, operas, and ballet companies, which soon rivaled those of Continental Europe. Nearly all major museums and art galleries, including the Boston Museum of Fine Arts, the Philadelphia Museum of Art, the Art Institute of Chicago, and the Metropolitan Museum of Art in New York, were founded during the last decades of the nineteenth century. Many were the gifts of individual donors, such as the libraries, museums, and galleries in Pittsburgh that all bore the name "Carnegie."

Gentility and the Middle Class

A new middle class, very different from its predecessor, formed during the last half of the century. The older middle class comprised the owners or superintendents of small businesses, doctors, lawyers, teachers, and ministers and their families. The new middle class included these professionals but also the growing number of salaried employees—the managers, technicians, clerks, and engineers who worked in the complex web of corporations and government. Long hours of labor earned their families a modest status and sufficient income to live securely in style and comfort.

Most middle-class American families valued their home not simply as a sign of their social station but as a haven from the tumultuous society outside. For as little as $10 a month, a family could finance the construction of a suburban retreat from the noise, filth, and dangers of the city. This peaceful domestic setting, with its manicured lawns and well-placed shrubs, afforded family members both privacy and rejuvenation. But to accomplish this goal, middle-class families had to separate business activities from leisure, and the breadwinner from his family for most of the day. Assisted by modern transportation systems, men often traveled one to two hours each day, five or six days a week, to their city offices and back again. Women and children stayed behind.

The interior design of middle-class homes reflected a desire for refinement. A rush of new magazines and volumes on homemaking, like Harriet Spof-

ford's *Art Decoration* (1879), set the standards, including elaborate front entryways, wallpapers stenciled by housewives themselves, stained-glass windows, and solid furniture. Reserved for visitors, the parlor featured upholstered furniture, inexpensive prints of famous paintings, and framed photographs of family members. Outside, the fenced-in yard served as a safe playground for small children and their pets.

Middle-class women found themselves devoting a large part of their day to housework. They frequently employed one or two servants but relied increasingly on the many new household appliances to get their work done. Improvements in the kitchen stove, such as the conversion from wood fuel to gas, saved a lot of time. Yet, simultaneously, with the widespread circulation of cookbooks and recipes in newspapers and magazines, as well as the availability of new foods, the preparation of meals became more complex and time-consuming. New devices such as the eggbeater speeded some familiar tasks, but the era's

Franklin Park, Boston by Maurice Prendergast, ca. 1897, reflects the "impressionist" influence on changing artistic sensibility. Influenced by current European techniques, many contemporary American painters abandoned realist or photographic-like representational styles for a subjective artistic view of nature or society. One of their favorite subjects was the emerging middle class at play.

Maurice Brazil Prendergast (American, 1858–1924), *Franklin Park, Boston*, 1895–97, watercolor and graphite on paper, 17½ x 13⅝ inches, Daniel J. Terra Collection, Terra Museum of American Art. Photograph © 1996, Terra Museum of American Art, Chicago.

fancy culinary practices offset any gains. Similarly, the new carpet sweepers surpassed the broom in efficiency, but the fashionable high-napped carpeting demanded more care. The foot-powered treadle sewing machine, a staple of the middle-class home, encouraged the fashion-conscious housewife to produce fancier clothing for herself and her family. Thus, rather than diminishing with technological innovation, household work expanded to fill the time available.

Almost exclusively white, Anglo-Saxon, and Protestant, the new middle class embraced "culture" not for purposes of "conspicuous consumption" but as a means of self-improvement and moral uplift. Whole families visited the new museums and art galleries. One of the most cherished institutions, the annual week of lectures at the Chautauqua campgrounds in upstate New York, brought thousands of families together in pursuit of knowledge of literature and the fine arts. The middle class also provided the bulk of patrons for the new public libraries.

Middle-class families applied the same standards to their leisure activities. What one sporting-goods entrepreneur rightly called the "gospel of EXERCISE" involved men and women in calisthenics and outdoor activities, not so much for pleasure as for physical and mental discipline. Hiking was a favorite among both men and women and required entirely new outfits: for women, loose upper garments and skirts short enough to prevent dragging; for men, rugged outer wear and jaunty hats. Soon men and women began camping out, with almost enough amenities to re-create a middle-class home in the woods. Roller skating and ice skating, which became crazes shortly after the Civil War, took place in specially designed rinks in almost every major town. By the 1890s, the "safety" bicycle had also been marketed. It replaced the large-wheel variety, which was difficult to keep upright. A good-quality "bike" cost $100 and, like the piano, was a symbol of middle-class status.

Leisure became the special province of middle-class childhood. Removed from factories and shops and freed from many domestic chores, children enjoyed creative play and physical activity. Summer camps, offering several weeks of sports and handicrafts, attracted many children to New England during this period. The toy market boomed, and lower printing prices helped children's literature flourish. *The Brownie Book* (1898), about imaginary elflike beings, was tremendously popular. Children's magazines such as *St. Nicholas* and *Youth's Companion* were filled with stories, poems, and pictures. Slightly older children read Westerns, sports novels of many kinds, and such perennial and uplifting classics as *Little Women* and *Black Beauty*.

Life in the Streets

Immigrants often weighed the material abundance they found in the United States against their memories of the Old Country. One could "live better" here, but only by working much harder. In letters home, immigrants described the riches of the new country but warned friends and relatives not to send weaklings, who would surely die of stress and strain. Even if their bodies thrived, their spirits might sink amid the alien and intense commercialism of American society. In many immigrant communities, alcoholism and suicide rates did soar above contemporary European standards. Germans in Chicago, it was said half jokingly, drank more beer and whiskey than all the Germans in Germany. Each group had its own phrase to express its feelings of disenchantment. Embittered German immigrants called their new land Malhuerica, "misfortune"; Jews called it Ama Reka, Hebrew for "without soul"; and Slavs referred to it as Dollerica.

To alleviate the stress of adjustment to life in an unfamiliar city, newcomers often established close-knit ethnic communities. European immigrants usually preferred to live together with people from their own country of origin, if possible from their home district. The poorest of new immigrants, like the Italians of Providence, Rhode Island, or the Slavs of Homestead, Pennsylvania, made special sacrifices to resettle with people who would be familiar to them. Aunts and uncles became almost as dear as parents, cousins as close as brothers and sisters. Young adults married within their communities, often setting up households within a few blocks of their parents and not infrequently within the same "triple-decker" or tenement.

Many newcomers, having little choice about their place of residence, concentrated in districts marked off by racial or ethnic lines. In San Francisco, city ordinances prevented Chinese from operating laundries in most of the city's neighborhoods, effectively confining the population to Chinatown. In Los Angeles and San Antonio, Mexicans lived in distinctive barrios. In most cities, African American families were similarly compelled to remain in the dingiest, most crime-ridden, and dangerous sections of town.

Young people who had left their families behind, whether in Europe or in the American countryside, usually took rooms in small residential hotels or boardinghouses. The Young Men's Christian Association, established in the 1850s, and the Young Women's Christian Association, organized a decade later, provided temporary residences mainly to native-born, white, self-supporting men and women. The most successful "women adrift," such as clerical workers and retail clerks, lived in the new furnished-room districts bordering the city's business center. The least prosperous landed on skid row, where homeless people spent time in the rough taverns, eating free lunches in return for purchased beer, waiting for casual labor, and sometimes trading sexual favors for money.

The working-class home did not necessarily ensure privacy or offer protection from the dangers of the outside world. In the tenements, families often shared their rooms with other families or paying boarders. During the summer heat, adults, children, and boarders alike competed for a sleeping place on the fire escape or roof, and all year round noise resounded through paper-thin walls. But so complex and varied were income levels and social customs that no single pattern emerged. Packingtown's Slovaks, Lithuanians, and Poles, for example, frequently took in boarders, yet Bohemians rarely did. Neither did the skilled iron rollers who worked at the Carnegie Steel Company in Homestead, Pennsylvania. These well-paid craft workers often owned their own homes, boasting parlors and even imported Belgian carpets. At the other extreme, Italian immigrants, who considered themselves fortunate to get work with a shovel, usually lived in overcrowded rented apartments, just a paycheck away from eviction.

Whether it was a small cottage or a tenement flat, the working-class home involved women and children in routines of household labor without the aid of the new mechanical devices. In addition to cooking and cleaning, women used their cramped domestic space for work that provided a small income. They gathered their children—and their husbands after a hard day's labor—to sew garments, wrap cigars, string beads, or paint vases for a contractor who paid them by the piece. And they cooked and cleaned for the boarders whose rent supplemented the family income. In short, the home was a second workplace, usually involving the entire family.

Despite working people's slim resources, their combined buying power created new and important markets for consumer goods. Often they bought shoddy replicas of products sold to the middle class: cheaper canned goods, inferior cuts of meat, and partially spoiled fruit. Several leading clothing manufacturers specialized in inexpensive ready-to-wear items, usually copied from patterns designed for wealthier consumers but constructed hastily from flimsy materials. Patent medicines for ailments caused by working long periods in cramped conditions sold well in working-class communities, where money for doctors was scarce. These nostrums failed to restore health, except perhaps through the power of suggestion. On the other hand, their high alcohol content might lift people's spirits, if only temporarily. The close quarters of the urban neighborhood allowed immigrants to preserve many Old World

The intersection of Orchard and Hester Streets on New York's Lower East Side, photographed ca. 1905. Unlike the middle classes, who worked and played hidden away in offices and private homes, the Jewish lower-class immigrants who lived and worked in this neighborhood spent the greater parts of their lives on the streets. Here children and adults mingle, partaking in both business and conversation.

customs. In immigrant communities such as Chicago's Packingtown, Pittsburgh's Poletown, New York's Lower East Side, or San Francisco's Chinatown, people usually spoke their native language while visiting their friends and relatives. The men might play cards while women and children gathered in the stairwell or on the front stoop to trade stories. In good weather they walked and talked, an inexpensive pastime common in European cities. No organization was as important as the fraternal society, which sponsored social clubs and provided insurance benefits. Immigrants also re-created Old World religious institutions such as the church or synagogue, or secular institutions such as German family-style taverns or Russian Jewish tearooms. They replicated their native cuisine (as much as available foods allowed), sang their own songs accompanied by polka, mazurka, or tamburitza music according to tradition, and married, baptized children, and buried the dead according to Old World customs.

In the cosmopolitan cities, immigrants, by being innovative entrepreneurs as well as best customers, helped to shape the emerging popular culture. German immigrants, for example, created Tin Pan Alley, the center of the popular music industry, and wrote such well-liked ballads as "Down by the Old Mill Stream." They also became the first promoters of ragtime, which found its way north from Storyville, the red-light district of New Orleans. Created by African American and creole bands, ragtime captivated those teenage offspring of immigrants who rushed to the new dance halls. Disdaining their parents' sentimental favorites, such as "Beautiful Dreamer," the youngsters seemed to associate the new syncopated sounds with the pulse of urban life. They also gave ragtime musicians paying work and budding musical entrepreneurs the idea that music with African American roots could become the biggest commercial entertainment of all.

In the same years, the first great amusement parks began to enthrall masses of immigrants and other city dwellers. The most spectacular was Coney Island, at the southern edge of Brooklyn, New York, which grew out of a series of fancy hotels and gambling (and prostitution) parlors. When developers realized that "wholesome fun" for the masses could pay better than upper-class leisure or lower-class vice, they decided to transform Coney Island into a magnificent seaside park filled with ingenious amusements such as water slides, mechanized horse races, roller coasters, and fun houses. It opened in 1895. On the rides or at the nearby beach, young men and women could easily meet apart from their parents, cast off their inhibitions, and enjoy a hug or kiss. Or they could simply stroll through the grounds, looking at exotic performers, enjoying make-believe trips to the Far East or even the moon, entranced by fantastic towers, columns, minarets, and lagoons lit up at night to resemble dreams rather than reality. Here millions of working-class people enjoyed cheap thrills that offset the hardships of their working lives.

CULTURES IN CONFLICT, CULTURE IN COMMON

The new commercial entertainments gave Americans from various backgrounds more in common than they would otherwise have had. On New York's Lower East Side, for instance, theater blossomed with dramas that Broadway would adopt years later, while children dreamed of going "uptown" where the popular songs they heard on the streets were transcribed onto sheet music and sold in stores throughout the city. Even so, nothing could smooth the tensions caused by conflicting claims to the same resources, such as public schools and urban parks.

Education

As industries grew and cities expanded, so did the nation's public school system. Business and civic leaders realized that the welfare of society now depended on an educated population, one possessing the skills and knowledge required to keep both industry and government running. In the last three decades of the nineteenth century, the idea of universal free schooling, at least for white children, took hold. Kindergartens in particular flourished. St. Louis, Missouri, opened the first public school kindergarten in 1873, and by the turn of the century more than 4,000 similar programs throughout the country enrolled children between the ages of three and seven.

The number of public high schools also increased, from 160 in 1870 to 6,000 by the end of the century. In Chicago alone, average daily attendance increased sixfold. Despite this spectacular growth, which was concentrated in urban industrial areas, as late as 1890 only 4 percent of children between the ages of fourteen and seventeen were enrolled in school, the majority of them girls planning to become teachers or office workers. Most high schools continued to serve mainly the middle class. In 1893 the National Education Association reaffirmed the major purpose of the nation's high schools as preparation for college, rather than for work in trades or industry, and endorsed a curriculum of rigorous training in the classics, such as Latin, Greek, and ancient history. The expected benefits of this kind of education rarely outweighed the immediate needs of families who depended on their children's wages.

Higher education also expanded along several lines. Agricultural colleges formed earlier in the century developed into institutes of technology and took their places alongside the prestigious liberal arts colleges. To extend learning to the "industrial classes," Representative Justin Morrill of Vermont sponsored the Morrill Federal Land Grant Act of 1862, which funded a system of state colleges and universities for teaching agriculture and mechanics "without excluding other scientific and classic studies." Meanwhile, established private institutions like Harvard, Yale, Princeton, and Columbia grew, with the help of huge endowments from business leaders such as Rockefeller and Carnegie. By 1900, sixty-three Catholic colleges were serving mainly the children of immigrants from Ireland and eastern and southern Europe. Still, as the overall number of colleges and universities grew from 563 in 1870 to nearly 1,000 by 1910, only 3 percent of the college-age population took advantage of these new opportunities.

One of the most important developments occurred in the area of professional training. Although medical and law schools dated from the mid-eighteenth century, their numbers grew rapidly after the Civil War. Younger professions, such as engineering, pharmacy, and journalism, also established specialized training institutions. In 1876 the Johns Hopkins University pioneered a program of research and graduate studies, and by the end of the century several American universities, including Stanford University and the University of Chicago, offered advanced degrees in the arts and sciences.

This expansion benefited women, who previously had had little access to higher education. After the Civil War, a number of women's colleges were founded, beginning in 1865 with Vassar, which set the academic standard for the remainder of the century. Smith and Wellesley followed in 1875, Bryn Mawr in 1885. By the end of the century 125 women's colleges offered a first-rate education comparable to that given to men at Harvard, Yale, or Princeton. Meanwhile, coeducation grew at an even faster rate; by 1890, 47 percent of the nation's colleges and universities admitted women. The proportion of women college students changed dramatically. Women constituted 21 percent of undergraduate enrollments in 1870, 32 percent in 1880, and 40 percent in 1910. Despite these gains, many professions remained closed to women.

An even greater number of women enrolled in vocational courses. Normal schools, which offered one- or two-year programs for women who planned to become elementary school teachers, developed a collegiate character after the Civil War and had become accredited state teachers' colleges by the end of the century. Normal schools enrolled many women from rural areas, particularly from poor families. Upon graduation, these women filled the personnel ranks of the rapidly expanding system of public education. Other institutions, many founded by middle-class philanthropists, also prepared women for vocations. For example, the first training school for nurses opened in Boston in 1873, followed in 1879 by a diet kitchen that taught women to become cooks in the city's hospitals. Founded in 1877, the Women's Educational and Industrial Union offered a multitude of classes to Boston's wage-earning women, ranging from elementary French and German to drawing, watercolors, oil and china painting, to dressmaking, millinery, stenography, typing, as well as crafts less familiar to women, such as upholstering, cabinetmaking, and carpentry. In the early 1890s, when the entering class at a large women's college like Vassar still averaged under 100, the Boston Women's Educational and Industrial Union reported that its staff of 83 served an estimated 1,500 clients per day. By that time, one of its most well-funded programs was a training school for domestic servants.

The leaders of the business community had also begun to promote manual training for working-class and immigrant boys. One leading San Francisco merchant described the philosophy behind this movement as a desire to train boys "to earn a living with little study and plenty of work." Craft unionists in several cities actively opposed this development, preferring their own methods of apprenticeship to training programs they could not control. But local associations of merchants and manufacturers lobbied hard for "industrial education" and raised funds to supplement the public school budget. In 1884 the Chicago Manual Training School opened teaching "shop work" along with a few academic subjects, and by 1895 all elementary and high schools in the city offered courses that trained working-class boys for future jobs in industry and business.

The expansion of education did not benefit all Americans or benefit them all in the same way. Because African Americans were prohibited from enrolling in colleges attended by white students, special colleges were founded in the southern states shortly after the Civil War. All-black Atlanta and Fisk both soon offered a rigorous curriculum in the liberal arts. Other institutions, such as Hampton, founded in 1868, specialized in vocational training, mainly in manual trades. Educator Booker T. Washington encouraged African Americans to resist "the craze for Greek and Latin learning" and to strive for practical instruction. In 1881 he founded the Tuskegee Institute in Alabama to provide industrial education and moral uplift. By the turn of the century, Tuskegee enrolled 1,400 men and women in more than thirty different vocational courses, including special cooking classes for homemakers and domestic servants. Black colleges, including Tuskegee, trained so many teachers that by the century's end the majority of black schools were staffed by African Americans.

The nation's educational system was becoming more inclusive and yet more differentiated. The majority of children attended school for several years or more. At the same time, students were tracked—by race, gender, and class—to fill particular roles in an industrial society.

Leisure and Public Space

Most large cities set aside open land for leisure-time use by residents. New York's Central Park opened for ice skating in 1858, providing a model for urban park systems across the United States. These parks were rolling expanses, cut across by streams and pathways and footbridges and set off by groves of trees, ornamental shrubs, and neat flower gardens. According to the designers' vision, the urban middle class might find here a respite from the stresses of modern life. To ensure this possibility, posted regulations forbade many activities, ranging from walking on the grass to gambling, picnicking or ball playing without permission, and speeding in carriages.

The working classes had their own ideas about the use of parks and open land. Trapped in overcrowded tenements, they wanted space for sports, picnics, and lovers' trysts. Young people openly defied ordinances that prohibited play on the grassy knolls, while their elders routinely voted against municipal bonds that did not include funds for more recreational space in their communities. Immigrant ward representatives on the Pittsburgh city council, for instance, argued that band shells for classical music meant little to their constituents, while spaces suitable for sports meant much.

Eventually, most park administrators set aside some sections for playgrounds and athletic fields and others for public gardens and band shells. Yet intermittent conflicts erupted. The Worcester, Massachusetts, park system, for example, allowed sports leagues to schedule events but prohibited pickup games. This policy gave city officials more control over the use of the park for outdoor recreation but at the same time forced many ball-playing boys into the streets. When working-class parents protested, city officials responded by instituting programs of supervised play, to the further dismay of the children.

Public drinking of alcoholic beverages, especially on Sunday, provoked similar disputes. Pittsburgh's "blue laws," forbidding businesses to open on Sunday, were rigidly enforced when it came to neighborhood taverns, while large firms like the railroads enjoyed exemptions. Although the Carnegie Institute hoped to discourage Sunday drinking by sponsoring alternative events, such as free organ recitals and other concerts, many working people, especially beer-loving German immigrants, continued to treat Sunday as their one day of relaxation and gathered for picnics in the city's parks.

Toward the end of the century, many park administrators relaxed the rules and expanded the range of permitted activities. By this time, large numbers of the middle class had become sports enthusiasts and pressured municipal governments to turn meadowlands into tennis courts and golfing greens. In the 1890s bicycling brought many women into the parks. Still, not all city residents enjoyed these facilities. Officials in St. Louis, for example, barred African Americans from the city's grand Forest Park and set aside the smaller Tandy Park for their use. After challenging this policy in court, African Americans won a few concessions, such as the right to picnic at any time in Forest Park and to use the golf course on Monday mornings.

One of the finest American painters of the period, known for realistic depictions of physical exertion in amateur athletics, Thomas Eakins here turned his attention to the commercial baseball park. The batter and catcher appear as well-poised athletes, dignified in their dress and manner—everything that the baseball player of the late nineteenth century was not very likely to be.

Thomas Eakins, *Baseball Players*, 1875. Watercolor. The Rhode Island School of Design Museum of Art

National Pastimes

Toward the end of the century, the younger members of the urban middle class had begun to find common ground in lower-class pastimes, especially ragtime music. Introduced to many Northerners by the African American composer Scott Joplin at the Chicago World's Fair of 1893, "rag" quickly became the staple of entertainment in the new cabarets and nightclubs. Middle-class urban dwellers began to seek out ragtime bands and congregated in nightclubs and even on rooftops of posh hotels to listen and dance and even to drink.

Vaudeville, the most popular form of commercial entertainment since the 1880s, also bridged middle- and working-class tastes. Drawing on a variety-show tradition of singers, dancers, comedians, jugglers, and acrobats who had entertained Americans since colonial days, "vaude" became a big business that made ethnic and racial stereotypes and the daily frustrations of city life into major topics of amusement. Vaudeville palaces—ten in New York, six in Philadelphia, five in Chicago, and at least one in every other large city—attracted huge, "respectable" crowds that sampled between twenty and thirty dramatic, musical, and comedy acts averaging fifteen minutes each. One study estimated that before vaudeville gave way to movie theaters in the 1920s, between 14 and 16 percent of all city dwellers attended shows at least once a week. Sunday matinees were especially popular with women and children.

Sports, however, outdistanced all other commercial entertainments in appealing to all kinds of fans and managing to create a sense of national identity. No doubt the most popular parks in the United States were the expanses of green surrounded by grandstands and marked by their unique diamond shape—the baseball field. During the last quarter of the nineteenth century the amateur sport of gentlemen and Union soldiers suddenly became the "national pastime." Both American and English children had for years been playing a form of baseball, known mainly as "rounders," when a group of young men in Manhattan formed the Knickerbocker Base Ball Club in 1845 and proceeded to set down the game's rules in writing. Baseball clubs soon formed in many cities, and shortly after the Civil War traveling teams with regular schedules made baseball a professional sport. The formation of the National League in 1876 encouraged other spectator sports, but for generations baseball remained the most popular.

Rowdy behavior gave the game a working-class ambience. Well-loved players known for their saloon brawls occasionally disappeared for a few days on "benders." Team owners, themselves often proprietors of local breweries, counted heavily on beer sales in the parks. Having to contend with hundreds of drunken fans, officials maintained order only with great difficulty. Outfielders occasionally leaped into the grandstand to punch spectators who had heckled them. To attract more subdued middle-class fans, the National League raised admission prices, banned the sale of alcohol, and observed Sunday blue laws. Catering to a working-class audience, the American Association kept the price of admission low, sold liquor, and played ball on Sunday.

Baseball, like many other sports, soon became tied to the larger business economy. Entrepreneur Albert Spalding, manager and then president of the Chicago White Stockings, quickly came to see baseball as a source of multiple profits. He procured the exclusive rights to manufacture the official ball and the rule book, while producing large varieties of other sporting equipment. Meanwhile, he built impressive baseball parks in Chicago with seating for 10,000 and special private boxes above the grandstands for the wealthy. He easily became the foremost figure in the National League.

Spalding also succeeded in tightening the rules of participation in the sport. In 1879 he dictated

CHRONOLOGY

1862	Morrill Act authorizes "land-grant" colleges		Chinese Exclusion Act passed
			Standard Oil Trust founded
1866	National Labor Union founded	1886	Campaigns for eight-hour workday peak
1869	Knights of Labor founded		Haymarket riot and massacre discredit the Knights of Labor
1870	Standard Oil founded		American Federation of Labor founded
1871	Chicago Fire		
1873	Financial panic brings severe depression	1890	Sherman Antitrust Act passed
		1893	Stock market panic precipitates severe depression
1876	Baseball's National League founded		
	Alexander Graham Bell patents the telephone	1895	Coney Island opens
		1896	Rural free delivery begins
1879	Thomas Edison invents the incandescent bulb	1900	Andrew Carnegie's *Gospel of Wealth* recommends honesty and fair dealing
	Depression ends		
1881	Tuskegee Institute founded	1901	U.S. Steel Corporation formed
1882	Peak of immigration to the United States (1.2 million) in the nineteenth century		

the "reserve clause" that prevented players from negotiating a better deal and leaving the team that originally signed them. He encouraged his player-manager "Cap" Anson to forbid the White Stockings to play against any team with an African American member, thereby setting the standard for professional baseball. The firing of Moses "Fleet" Walker from the Cincinnati team in 1884 marked the first time the color line had been drawn in a major professional sport. Effectively excluded, African Americans organized their own traveling teams. In the 1920s they formed the Negro Leagues, which produced some of the nation's finest ballplayers.

Players occasionally organized to regain control over their sport. They frequently complained about low wages and arbitrary rules, and like factory workers in the 1880s they formed their own league, the Brotherhood of Professional Base Ball Players, with profits divided between participants and investors. This effort failed, partly because fans would not desert the established leagues, but mostly because successful baseball franchises demanded large quantities of capital. American sports had become big business.

As attendance continued to grow, the enthusiasm for baseball straddled major social divisions, bringing together Americans of many backgrounds, if only on a limited basis. By the end of the century, no section of the daily newspaper drew more readers than the sports pages. Although it interested relatively few women, sports news riveted the attention of men from all social classes. Loyalty to the "home team" helped to create an urban identity, while individual players became national heroes.

CONCLUSION

By the end of the nineteenth century, industry and the growing cities had opened a new world for Americans. Fresh from Europe or from the native countryside, ordinary urban dwellers struggled to form communities of fellow newcomers through work and leisure, in the factory, the neighborhood, the ballpark, and the public school. Their "betters," the wealthy and the new middle class, meanwhile made and executed the decisions of industry and marketing, established the era's grand civic institutions, and set the tone for high fashion and art.

Rich and poor alike shared many aspects of the new order. Yet inequality persisted and increased, as much a part of the new order as the Brooklyn Bridge or advertising. During the mostly prosperous 1880s, optimists believed that unfair treatment based on region, on class, and perhaps even on race and gender might ease in time. By the depressed 1890s, however, these hopes had worn thin, and the lure of overseas empire appeared as one of the few goals that held together a suffering and divided nation.

REVIEW QUESTIONS

1. Discuss the sources of economic growth in the decades after the Civil War. Historians often refer to this period as the era of the "second industrial revolution." Do you agree with this description?

2. Describe the impact of new technologies and new forms of production on the routines of industrial workers. How did these changes affect African American and women workers in particular? What role did trade unions play in this process?

3. Choose one major city, such as Boston, New York, Chicago, Birmingham, or San Francisco, and discuss changes in its economy, population, and urban space in the decades after the Civil War.

4. Discuss the role of northern capital in the development of the New South. How did the rise of industry affect the lives of rural Southerners? Analyze these changes from the point of view of African Americans.

5. How did urban life change during the Gilded Age? How did economic development affect residential patterns? How did the middle class aspire to live during the Gilded Age? How did their lifestyles compare with those of working-class urbanites?

6. How did the American educational system change to prepare children for their adult roles in the new industrial economy?

7. How did the rise of organized sports and commercial amusements reflect and shape social divisions at the end of the century? Which groups were affected most (or least) by new leisure activities?

RECOMMENDED READING

James R. Barrett, *Work and Community in the Jungle* (1987). A very close study of the Packingtown district of Chicago, Illinois, at the turn of the century. Barrett describes the transformation of animals to meat in great stockyards and processing plants. He also provides rich documentation of neighborhood life.

Alfred D. Chandler Jr., *The Visible Hand: The Managerial Revolution in American Business* (1977). A highly acclaimed study of corporate management. Chandler shows how the rapid growth in the scale of business, as well as its influence in public life, brought about a new type of executive with skills for national decision making and close links with others of his kind.

William Cronon, *Nature's Metropolis* (1991). Analyzes the changing economic and political relationship between the city of Chicago and the surrounding countryside. Cronon demonstrates through a variety of evidence the tight interdependence of urban and rural regions.

Herbert G. Gutman, *Work, Culture and Society in Industrializing America: Essays in American Working-Class and Social History* (1977). Influential essays on the formation of working-class communities in the nineteenth century. Gutman focuses on the role of immigrants in transforming the values and belief systems of working-class Americans in the throes of industrialization.

John F. Kasson, *Amusing the Millions: Coney Island at the Turn of the Century* (1978). A heavily illustrated account of America's favorite amusement park. Kasson sees Coney Island as the meeting point for shrewd entrepreneurs and pleasure-seeking immigrants, its amusements and architectural styles emblematic of a special era in American history.

Alice Kessler-Harris, *Out to Work: A History of Wage-Earning Women in the United States* (1982). A comprehensive survey of women's increasing participation in the labor force. Kessler-Harris documents women's role in trade unions but also the impact on family patterns and ideas about women's role in American society.

Kenneth L. Kusmer, *A Ghetto Takes Shape, Black Cleveland, 1870–1930* (1976). A keen analysis of a long-standing African American community. Kusmer shows how blacks suffered downward mobility and increased segregation as their skilled jobs and small-business opportunities were given to European immigrants.

Lawrence H. Larsen, *The Rise of the Urban South* (1985). Studies of the changing South. In Larson's view, the true New South was the city, for relatively few had lived there before the late nineteenth century, but rural values remained vital, especially in religious life and voting patterns.

David F. Noble, *America by Design: Science, Technology and the Rise of Corporate Capitalism* (1977). A view of scientific advancement and its connections with the expanding economy. Noble shows how scientific breakthroughs were often created for, but especially adapted to, corporate purposes.

Dave Roediger and Franklin Rosemont, eds., *Haymarket Scrapbook* (1986). A large, beautifully illustrated book about the events and consequences of the Haymarket tragedy.

Roy Rosenzweig, *Eight Hours for What We Will: Workers and Leisure in an Industrial City, 1870–1920* (1983). Analyzes class and cultural conflicts over recreational space. This valuable book treats the city park as the arena for conflict over whether public community life should be uplifting (devoted to nature walks and concerts) or entertaining (for drinking, courting, and amusement).

Alan Trachtenberg, *The Incorporation of America: Culture and Society in the Gilded Age* (1982). One of the best and most readable overviews of the post–Civil War era. Trachtenberg devotes great care to describing the rise of the corporation to the defining institution of national life, and the reorientation of culture to reflect the new middle classes employed by the corporation.

ADDITIONAL BIBLIOGRAPHY

Science, Technology, and Industry

David A. Hounshell, *From the American System to Mass Production, 1800–1932* (1984)

David Landes, *The Unbound Prometheus: Technological Change and Industrial Development* (1969)

Walter Licht, *Industrializing America: The Nineteenth Century* (1995)

A. J. Millard, *Edison and the Business of Innovation* (1990)

Leonard S. Reich, *The Making of American Industrial Research: Science and Business at G.E. and Bell, 1876–1926* (1985)

Howard Segal, *Technological Utopianism in American Culture* (1985)

Business and the Economy

Wendy Gambler, *The Female Economy: The Millinery and Dressmaking Trades, 1860–1930* (1997)

Robert Higgs, *Competition and the Economy: Blacks in the American Economy, 1865–1914* (1977)

Howard Horwitz, *By the Law of Nature: Form and Value in Nineteenth Century America* (1990)

John Ingham, *Iron Barons: A Social Analysis of an Urban Elite* (1978)

Naomi R. Lamoreaux, *The Great Merger Movement in American Business, 1895–1904* (1985)

Daniel Nelson, *Managers and Workers: Origins of the Factory System in the United States, 1880–1920* (1975)

Sarah Lyons Watts, *Order against Chaos: Business Culture and Labor Ideology in America, 1800–1915* (1991)

Olivier Zunz, *Making America Corporate, 1870–1920* (1990)

Working Class and Labor

Eric Arnesen, *Waterfront Workers of New Orleans: Race, Class, and Politics, 1863–1923* (1991)

John Bodnar, *Immigration and Industrialization: Ethnicity in an American Mill Town* (1977)

Lisa M. Fine, *The Souls of the Skyscraper: Female Clerical Workers in Chicago, 1870–1930* (1990)

Leon Fink, *Workingmen's Democracy: The Knights of Labor and American Politics* (1983)

Victoria C. Hattam, *Labor Visions and State Power* (1993)

David M. Katzman, *Seven Days a Week: Women and Domestic Service in Industrializing America* (1978)

David Montgomery, *The Fall of the House of Labor: The Workplace, the State, and American Labor Activism, 1865–1925* (1987)

Dominic A. Pacyga, *Polish Immigrants and Industrial Chicago* (1991)

Daniel T. Rodgers, *The Work Ethic in Industrial America, 1850–1920* (1978)

The Industrial City

Lewis F. Fried, *Makers of the City* (1990)

John S. Garner, ed., *The Midwest in American Architecture* (1991)

James Gilbert, *Perfect Cities: Chicago's Utopias of 1893* (1991)

Dolores Hayden, *The Grand Domestic Revolution: A History of Feminist Designs for American Homes, Neighborhoods, and Cities* (1981)

Scott Molloy, *Trolley Wars: Streetcar Workers on the Line* (1996)

Roy Rosenzweig and Elizabeth Blackmar, *The Park and the People: A History of Central Park* (1993)

John R. Stilgoe, *Borderland: Origins of the American Suburb, 1820–1939* (1988)

The New South

Edward L. Ayers, *The Promise of the New South* (1992)

Don Doyle, *New Men, New Cities, New South* (1990)

Jacquelyn D. Hall, et al., *Like a Family: The Making of a Southern Cotton Mill World* (1987)

Gerald D. Jaynes, *Branches without Roots: Genesis of the Black Working Class in the American South, 1862–1882* (1986)

Cathy McHugh, *Mill Family: The Labor System in the Southern Textile Industry, 1880–1915* (1988)

Allen Tullos, *Habits of Industry: White Culture and the Transformation of the Carolina Piedmont* (1989)

Society and Culture

Elaine S. Abelson, *When Ladies Go A-Thieving* (1989)

Stuart Blumin, *The Emergence of the Middle Class* (1989)

Perry Duis, *The Saloon: Public Drinking in Chicago and Boston, 1880–1920* (1983)

John F. Kasson, *Rudeness and Civility: Manners in Nineteenth-Century Urban America* (1992)

Lawrence W. Levine, *Black Culture and Black Consciousness* (1977)

Patricia Marks, *Bicycles, Bangs, and Bloomers: The New Woman in the Popular Press* (1990)

Steven A. Riess, *City Games: The Evolution of American Urban Society and the Rise of Sports* (1989)

Barbara M. Solomon, *In the Company of Educated Women: A History of Women and Higher Education in America* (1985)

Louise L. Stevenson, *The Victorian Homefront: American Thought and Culture, 1860–1880* (1991)

Biography

Robert V. Bruce, *Alexander Graham Bell and the Conquest of Solitude* (1973)

Helen Lefkowitz Horowitz, *The Power and Passion of M. Carey Thomas* (1994)

Stuart B. Kaufman, *Samuel Gompers and the Rise of the American Federation of Labor, 1884–1896* (1973)

Murray Klein, *The Life and Legend of Jay Gould* (1986)

Emily Toth, *Kate Chopin: The Life of the Author of* The Awakening (1990)

Robert C. Twombly, *Louis Sullivan* (1986)

CHAPTER TWENTY

COMMONWEALTH AND EMPIRE

1870–1900

R. F. Zogbaum, *Dewey at Manila*, 1899. Oil on canvas, 60 x 48 inches, Vermont State House, Montpelier, Vermont.

AMERICAN COMMUNITIES
The Cooperative Commonwealth

Edward Bellamy's *Looking Backward* (1888), the century's best-selling novel after Harriet Beecher Stowe's *Uncle Tom's Cabin*, tells the story of a young man who awakens in the year 2000 after a sleep lasting more than 100 years. He is surprised to learn that Americans had solved their major problems. Poverty, crime, war, taxes, air pollution—even housework—no longer exist. Nor are there politicians, capitalists, bankers, or lawyers. Most amazing, gone is the great social division between the powerful rich and the suffering poor. In the year 2000 everyone lives in material comfort, happily and harmoniously. No wonder Bellamy's hero shudders at the thought of returning to the late nineteenth century, a time of "worldwide bloodshed, greed and tyranny."

Community and cooperation are the key concepts in Bellamy's utopian tale. The nation's businesses, including farms and factories, have been given over to the collective ownership of the people. Elected officials now plan the production and distribution of goods for the common well-being. With great efficiency, they even manage huge department stores and warehouses full of marvelous manufactured goods and oversee majestic apartment complexes with modern facilities for cooking, dining, and laundering. To get the necessary work done, an industrial army enlists all adult men and women, but automated machinery has eliminated most menial tasks. The workday is only four hours; vacations extend to six months of each year. At forty-five everyone retires to pursue hobbies, sports, and culture.

Bellamy envisioned his technological utopia promoting the "highest possible physical, as well as mental, development for everyone." There was nothing fantastic in this plan, the author insisted. It simply required Americans to share equally the abundant resources of their land. If the nation's citizens actually lived up to their democratic ideals, Bellamy declared, the United States would become a "cooperative commonwealth," that is, a nation governed by the people for their common welfare.

Bellamy, a journalist and writer of historical fiction from Chicopee Falls, Massachusetts, moved thousands of his readers to action. His most ardent fans endorsed his program for a "new nation" and formed the Nationalist movement, which by the early 1890s reached an apex of 165 clubs. Terence V. Powderly of the Knights of Labor declared himself a Nationalist. Many leaders of the woman suffrage movement also threw in their support. They endorsed *Looking Backward*'s depiction of marriage as a union of "perfect equals" and admired Bellamy's sequel, *Equality* (1897), which showed how women might become "absolutely free agents" by ending their financial dependence on men.

During the 1890s Bellamy's disciples actually attempted to create new communities along the lines set forth in *Looking Backward*. The best known and longest lasting of these settlements was

579

established in Point Loma, California, in 1897. Situated on 330 acres, with avenues winding through gardens and orchards newly planted with groves of eucalyptus trees, Point Loma was known for its physical beauty. Many young married couples chose to live in small bungalows, which were scattered throughout the colony's grounds; others opted for private rooms in a large communal building. Either way, they all met twice daily to share meals and usually spent their leisure hours together. On the ocean's edge the residents constructed an outdoor amphitheater and staged plays and concerts.

The colony's founder, Katherine Tingley, described Point Loma as "a practical illustration of the possibility of developing a higher type of humanity." No one earned wages, but all 500 residents lived comfortably. They dressed simply in clothes manufactured by the community's women. The majority of the men worked in agriculture. They conducted horticultural experiments that yielded new types of avocados and tropical fruits and eventually produced over half of the community's food supply. Children, who slept in a special dormitory from the time they reached school age, enjoyed an outstanding education. They excelled in the fine arts, including music and drama, and often demonstrated their talents to audiences in nearby San Diego.

The Point Loma community never met all its expenses, but with the help of donations from admirers across the country it remained solvent for decades. Baseball entrepreneur Albert Spalding, who lived there during his retirement, helped make up the financial deficit. As late as the 1950s the community still had some seventy-five members living on about 100 acres of land.

Even relatively successful cooperative communities such as Point Loma, however, could not bring about the changes that Bellamy hoped to see, and he knew it. Only a mobilization of citizens nationwide could overturn the existing hierarchies and usher in the egalitarian order depicted in *Looking Backward*. Without such a rigorous challenge, the economic and political leadership that had been emerging since the Civil War would continue to consolidate its power and become even further removed from popular control.

The last quarter of the nineteenth century saw just such a challenge, producing what one historian calls "a moment of democratic promise." Ordinary citizens sought to renew the older values of community through farm and labor organizations as well as philanthropic and charitable societies. They could not clearly see, however, that the fate of the nation depended increasingly on events beyond its territorial boundaries. Business leaders and politicians had proposed their own vision of the future: an American empire extending to far distant lands.

Point Loma

KEY TOPICS

- The growth of federal and state governments and the consolidation of the modern two-party system

- The development of mass protest movements

- Economic and political crisis in the 1890s

- The United States as a world power

- The Spanish-American War

TOWARD A NATIONAL GOVERNING CLASS

The basic structure of government changed dramatically in the last quarter of the nineteenth century. Mirroring the fast-growing economy, public administration expanded at all levels—municipal, county, state, and federal—and took on greater responsibility for regulating society, especially market and property relations. Whereas most political theorists continued to advise that the best government is the one that governs least, governments began to do much more than simply maintain order.

This expansion offered ample opportunities for politicians who were eager to compete against one another for control of the new mechanisms of power. Political campaigns, especially those staged for the presidential elections, became mass spectacles, and votes became precious commodities. The most farsighted politicians attempted to rein in the growing corruption and to promote both efficiency and professionalism in the expanding structures of government.

The Growth of Government

Before the Civil War, local governments attended mainly to the promotion and regulation of trade and relied on private enterprise to supply vital services such as fire protection and water supply. As cities became more responsible for their residents' well-being, they introduced professional police and fire-fighting forces and began to finance school systems, public libraries, and parks. Municipal ownership and administration of basic services became so common that by the end of the century only nine of the nation's fifty largest cities still depended on private corporations for their water supplies.

This expansion demanded huge increases in local taxation. Boston, for example, spent five times more per resident in 1875 than it did just thirty years earlier, and its municipal debt rose from $784,000 to more than $27 million. The city now paid the salaries of many civil servants, including a growing class of sanitary engineers. By 1880 one of every eight New York voters appeared on a government payroll.

At the national level, mobilization for the Civil War and Reconstruction had demanded an unprecedented degree of coordination, and the federal government continued to expand under the weight of new tasks and responsibilities. Federal revenues also skyrocketed, from $257 million in 1878 to $567 million in 1900. The administrative bureaucracy also grew dramatically, from 50,000 employees in 1871 to 100,000 only a decade later.

The modern apparatus of departments, bureaus, and cabinets took shape amid this upswing. The Department of Agriculture was established in 1862 to provide information to farmers and to consumers of farm products. The Department of the Interior, which had been created in 1849, grew into the largest and most important federal department after the Post Office. It came to comprise more than twenty agencies, including the Bureau of Indian Affairs, the U.S. Geological Survey, and the Bureau of Territorial and International Affairs. The Department of the Treasury, responsible for collecting federal taxes and customs as well as printing money and stamps, grew from 4,000 employees in 1873 to nearly 25,000 in 1900. The Pension Act of 1890 made virtually

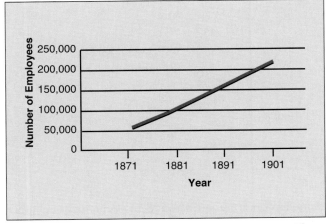

Federal Employment by Decade, 1871–1901   *The expansion of government created a bureaucracy of employees and great opportunities for political patronage.*

Source: David Nachmias and David H. Rosenbloom, *Bureaucratic Government USA* (New York: St. Martin's Press, 1980), p. 39.

OVERVIEW

PRESIDENTIAL POLITICS, 1868–1900

Presidential election year	Winning candidate (party)	Popular vote margin	Major issues
1868	Ulysses S. Grant (Republican)	5.4 percent	• Reconstruction • Suffrage for African American men • Monetary reform
1872	Ulysses S. Grant (Republican)	11.9 percent	• Civil Service reform • Government regulation • Reconstruction
1876	Rutherford B. Hayes (Republican)	-3 percent (election decided in House)	• Reconstruction • Corruption
1880	James A. Garfield (Republican)	.4 percent	• Monetary reform • Civil Service reform • Pensions for veterans • Chinese exclusion • Tariff
1884	Grover Cleveland (Democratic)	.3 percent	• Corruption • Civil Service reform • Tariff • Monetary reform
1888	Benjamin Harrison (Republican)	-.7 percent (Harrison won with a majority of electoral votes)	• Tariff • Veteran pension
1892	Grover Cleveland (Democratic)	3.1 percent	• Tariff • Government ownership of railroads • Monetary reform
1896	William McKinley (Republican)	3.4 percent	• Tariff • Monetary reform • Regulation of railroads
1900	William McKinley (Republican)	6.2 percent	• Imperialism • Monetary reform • Tariff

every Union army veteran and his dependents eligible for benefits; within a decade the Veterans Bureau became known as "the largest executive bureau in the world," employing nearly 60,000 men and women.

The nation's first independent regulatory agency, the Interstate Commerce Commission (ICC), was created in 1887 to bring order to the growing patchwork of state laws concerning railroads. The five-member commission appointed by the president approved freight and passenger rates set by the railroads. The ICC could take public testimony on possible violations, examine company records, and generally oversee enforcement of the law. This set a precedent for future regulation of trade as well as for positive government—that is, for the intervention of the government into the affairs of private enterprise. The establishment of the ICC also marked a shift in the balance of power from the states to the federal government.

The Machinery of Politics

Only gradually did Republicans and Democrats adapt to the demands of governmental expansion. The Republican Party continued to run on its Civil War record, pointing to its achievements in reuniting the nation and in passing new reform legislation. Democrats, by contrast, sought to reduce the influence of the federal government, slash expenditures, repeal legislation, and protect states' rights. While Republicans held on to their long-time constituencies, Democrats gathered support from southern white voters and immigrants newly naturalized in the North. But neither party commanded a clear majority of votes until the century drew to a close.

Presidents in the last quarter of the century—Rutherford B. Hayes (1877–81), James A. Garfield (1881), Chester A. Arthur (1881–85), Grover Cleveland (1885–89), Benjamin Harrison (1889–93), and Cleveland again (1893–97)—did not espouse a clear philosophy of government. They willingly yielded power to Congress and the state legislatures. Only 1 percent of the popular vote separated the presidential candidates in three of five elections between 1876 and 1892. Congressional races were equally tight, less than 2 percentage points separating total votes for Democratic and Republican candidates in all but one election in the decade before 1888. Democrats usually held a majority in the House and Republicans a majority in the Senate, but neither party had sufficient strength to govern effectively. One result was that Congress passed little legislation before 1890.

One major political issue of the late nineteenth century was the tariff. First instituted in 1789 to raise revenue for the young republic, the tariff imposed a fee on imported goods, especially manufactured commodities. Soon its major purpose became the protection of the nation's "infant industries" from foreign competition. Manufacturing regions, especially the Northeast, favored a protective policy, while agricultural regions like the South opposed high tariffs as unfair to farmers who had to pay the steep fees on imported necessities. Democrats, with a stronghold among southern voters, argued for sharp reductions in the tariff as a way to save the rural economy and to give a boost to workers. Republicans, who represented mainly business interests, raised tariffs to new levels on a wide array of goods during the Civil War and retained high tariffs as long as they held power.

Although their platforms encompassed broad national issues, none more important than the tariff, both political parties operated essentially as state or

Cleveland campaign noisemaker, 1892. Museum of American Political Life, University of Hartford. Photo by Sally Andersen-Bruce.

This wooden noisemaker was designed for Grover Cleveland's presidential campaign in 1892. Pursuing the voters, political campaigners devised ingenious signs, buttons, and other miscellaneous novelties for supporters to display, especially at public demonstrations. When shaken vigorously, noisemakers literally demanded the attention of bystanders.

local organizations. Successful politicians responded primarily to the particular concerns of their constituents. To please local voters, Democrats and Republicans repeatedly crosscut each other by taking identical positions on controversial issues.

Candidates of both parties urged their "regulars" to turn out and pursued swing voters furiously. "We work through one campaign," quipped one candidate, "take a bath and start in on the next." Election paraphernalia—leaflets or pamphlets, banners, hats, flags, buttons, inscribed playing cards, or clay pipes featuring a likeness of a candidate's face or the party symbol—became a major expense for both parties. Partisans embraced the Democratic donkey or the Republican elephant as symbols of party fidelity. And voters did turn out. During the last quarter of the century, participation in presidential elections peaked at nearly 80 percent of those eligible to vote. Thousands, in fact, voted several times on any given election day; voters who had died, or had never lived, also miraculously cast ballots.

The rising costs of maintaining local organizations and orchestrating mammoth campaigns drove party leaders to seek ever-larger sources of revenue. Winners often seized and added to the "spoils" of office through an elaborate system of payoffs. Legislators who supported government subsidies for railroad corporations, for instance, commonly received stock in return and sometimes cash bribes. At the time, few politicians or business leaders regarded these practices as unethical.

At the local level, powerful bosses and political machines dominated both parties. Democrats William Marcy Tweed of New York's powerful political organization, Tammany Hall, and Michael "Hinky Dink" Kenna of Chicago specialized in giving municipal jobs to loyal voters and holiday food baskets to their families. Tweed's machine wooed working-class voters by expanding city services in their neighborhoods and even by staging major sporting events or entertainments for the Irish Americans and German Americans who made up over half of New York City's population. Hundreds of smaller political machines ruled cities and rural courthouses through a combination of "boodle" (bribe money) and personal favors.

Many federal jobs, meanwhile, changed hands each time the presidency passed from one party to another. More than 50 percent of all federal jobs were patronage positions—nearly 56,000 in 1881—jobs that could be awarded to loyal supporters as part of the "spoils" of the winner. Observers estimated that decisions about congressional patronage filled one-third of all legislators' time.

Noted critic John Jay Chapman, looking back at the history of candidates and elections, suggested that "the change of motive power behind the party organizations—from principles to money—was silently effected during the thirty years which followed the [Civil] war." No wonder Bellamy's utopian community operated without politicians and political parties.

One Politician's Story

A typical politician of the age was James Garfield, the nation's twentieth president. Born in a frontier Ohio log cabin in 1831, Garfield briefly worked as a canal boat driver, an experience he later exploited as proof of his humble origins. A Civil War hero—he fought at Shiloh, was honored for gallantry at Chickamauga, and was a major general when he took a seat in Congress in 1863—the Ohio legislator carefully prepared his move into the national political arena.

While serving in Congress, Garfield seemed at first committed to social reform. He introduced a bill to create a Department of Education, arguing that public education would prove the best stepping-stone to equality. He denounced his own Republican Party for allowing corruption to flourish during Ulysses S. Grant's administration. The nation's "next great fight," he insisted, would pit the people against the corporations.

With the failure of Reconstruction, Garfield shifted his stance and began to espouse more conservative views. Nearly defeated in a Democratic congressional landslide in 1874, he concluded that "the intelligence of the average American citizen" fell short of the demands of the democratic system. As a result, he came out against universal suffrage. Garfield now looked to the probusiness faction of the Republican Party as a vehicle for realizing his personal ambition. After six years of shrewd maneuvering, trading votes and favors to build his reputation, Garfield became the party's candidate for the 1880 presidential election. In a mediocre race with no outstanding issues, Garfield won by less than 40,000 popular votes out of 9 million cast.

Garfield the idealist had grown into Garfield the machine politician and lackluster president. He had already shown himself indecisive and even indifferent to governing when a frustrated patronage seeker shot him just 200 days after his inauguration. Like other presidents of his era, Garfield assumed that the nation's chief executive served as his party's titular leader and played mainly a ceremonial role in office.

The Spoils System and Civil Service Reform

For decades, critics in both parties had been calling without success for legislation to improve the quality of government. As early as 1865, Republican representative Thomas A. Jenckes of Rhode Island proposed a bill for civil service reform. Congress, however, feared that such a measure would hamper candidates in their relentless pursuit of votes. President Hayes took up the cause, introducing a few reforms in the New York Customhouse and federal post offices, but Congress again refused to join in a major reform effort. Finally, a group consisting of mainly professors, newspaper editors, lawyers, and ministers organized the Civil Service Reform Association and enlisted Democratic senator George H. Pendleton to sponsor reform legislation in Congress.

In January 1883, a bipartisan congressional majority passed the Pendleton Civil Service Reform Act. This measure allowed the president to create, with Senate approval, a three-person commission to draw up a set of guidelines for executive and legislative appointments. The commission established a system of standards for various federal jobs and instituted "open, competitive examinations for testing the fitness of applicants for public service." The Pendleton Act also barred political candidates from soliciting campaign contributions from government workers. Patronage did not disappear, but public service did improve.

Many departments of the federal government took on a professional character similar to that which doctors, lawyers, and scholars were imposing on their fields through regulatory societies such as the American Medical Association and the American Historical Association. At the same time, the federal judiciary began to act more aggressively to establish the parameters of government. With the Circuit Courts of Appeals Act of 1891, Congress granted the U.S. Supreme Court the right to review any case—state or federal—at will.

The move to transform government into a professional enterprise involved people from many walks of life, but no group more than lawyers. Lawyers began to organize citywide and statewide societies and in 1878 formed the American Bar Association (ABA). In 1894 New York introduced an examining board to control admission to legal practice, and many states followed its example. By the turn of the century, more than 40 percent of the members of Congress were lawyers, and lawyers dominated in the Senate.

Despite reforms like the Pendleton Act and the increasing dominance of legal professionals in government, many observers, Edward Bellamy among them, remained convinced that "insiders" controlled government, pulling the levers of party machinery or spending money to influence important decisions. Bellamy, concluding that the growing legion of politicians and civil servants failed to address the needs of ordinary citizens, advised Americans to organize their communities for the specific purpose of wresting control of government from the hands of politicians.

FARMERS AND WORKERS ORGANIZE THEIR COMMUNITIES

In the late 1860s farmers and workers began to organize. Within two decades, they built powerful national organizations to oppose, as a Nebraska newspaper put it, "the wealthy and powerful classes who want the control of government to plunder the people." Though short on financial resources, farmers and workers raised the most significant challenge to the two-party system since the Civil War—the populist movement.

The Grange

In 1867 farmers on the Great Plains formed the Patrons of Husbandry for their own "social, intellectual, and moral improvement." Led by Oliver H. Kelley, an employee of the Department of Agriculture, this fraternal society resembled the secretive Masonic order. Whole families staffed a complex array of offices engaged in mysterious rituals involving passwords, flags, songs, and costumes. In many farming communities, the headquarters of the local chapter, known as the Grange (a word for "farm"), became the center of social activity, the site of summer dinners and winter dances.

As a result of economic hardship among farmers, the Grange movement spread rapidly. The price of

Kingfisher Reformer, May 3, 1894

The symbols chosen by Grange artists represented their faith that all social value could be traced to honest labor and most of all to the work of the entire farm family. The hardworking American required only the enlightenment offered by the Grange to build a better community.

wheat and corn had boomed in the immediate aftermath of the Civil War, but following the Panic of 1873, farm families saw their hopes for prosperity wither. Blizzards, drought, and grasshopper infestations in the early 1870s left farmers on the Great Plains barely surviving. Competition from producers in Canada, Australia, Argentina, Russia, and India, meanwhile, contributed to steadily falling prices for grains and cotton, hurting farmers throughout the trans-Mississippi West and the South. Most farmers found themselves operating at a loss; many slid to the verge of bankruptcy. In the hope of improving their condition through collective action, many farmers joined their local Grange. The Patrons of Husbandry soon swelled to more than 1.5 million members.

Grangers blamed hard times on the exorbitant fees of big businesses, especially railroads and banks, which they reviled as a band of "thieves in the night." They fumed at American farm equipment manufacturers, such as Cyrus McCormick, for selling their wares more cheaply in Europe than in the United States. To purchase equipment and raw materials, farmers borrowed money, accruing debts averaging twice that of Americans not engaged in business. Eastern land companies, Grangers charged, not only imposed usurious interest rates but granted mortgages on terms too short to allow farmers to turn their fortunes around.

Grangers mounted their most concerted assault on the railroad corporations. With bribes, the railroads had secured the support of state legislators for a highly discriminatory rate policy. Farmers commonly paid more to ship their crops short distances than over long hauls. In 1874 several midwestern states responded to Granger pressure and passed a series of so-called Granger laws establishing maximum shipping rates.

Grangers also complained to their lawmakers about the price-fixing policies of grain wholesalers, warehousers, and operators of grain elevators. In 1873 the Illinois legislature passed a Warehouse Act establishing maximum rates for storing grains. Chicago firms challenged the legality of this measure, but in *Munn v. Illinois* (1877) the Supreme Court upheld the law, ruling that states had the power to regulate private property in the public interest.

Determined to "buy less and produce more," Grangers created a vast array of cooperative enterprises for both the purchase of supplies and the marketing of crops. They established local grain elevators, set up retail stores, and even manufactured some of their own farm machinery. As early as 1872 the Iowa Grange claimed to control one-third of the grain elevators and warehouses in the state. In other states Grangers ran banks as well as fraternal life and fire insurance companies.

The deepening depression of the late 1870s came at the worst possible moment for the Patrons of Husbandry, wiping out most of their cooperative programs. By 1880 Grange membership had fallen to 100,000. Meanwhile, the Supreme Court overturned most of the key legislation regulating railroads. The Patrons of Husbandry had nonetheless promoted a model of cooperation that would remain at the heart of agrarian protest movements until the end of the century.

The Farmers' Alliance

Agrarian unrest did not end with the decline of the Grange but instead moved south. In the 1880s farmers organized in communities where both poverty and the crop-lien system prevailed (see Chapter 17). Conservative newspaper writers and politicians advised farmers to trim expenditures and to diversify out of cotton into other crops. But with household budgets that had already fallen from $50 to as low as $10 a year, southern farmers had no leeway to cut expenses. And the cost of shipping perishable crops made diversification untenable despite the low price of cotton. In response to these conditions, Texas farmers—proclaiming "Equal Rights to All, Special Privileges to None"—began to organize.

In 1889, under the leadership of Charles W. Macune and William Lamb, several regional organizations joined forces to create the National Farmers' Alliance and Industrial Union. The next year the combined movement claimed 3 million white members. African American farmers joined the separate Colored Farmers' Alliance and Cooperative Union, which emerged in Texas and Arkansas and quickly spread across the South, ultimately claiming more than a million members of its own. The development of these parallel organizations reflected both practical necessity in a region of increasing racial segregation and the racism of white farmers.

The Farmers' Alliance claimed that power concentrated in the hand of a new governing class had resulted in "the impoverishment and bondage of so many." Members pledged themselves to restore democracy through "agitation, education, and cooperation."

Southern farmers readily translated their anger over falling cotton prices into intense loyalty to the one organization pledged to the improvement of their lot. With more than 500 chapters in Texas alone, and cooperative stores complemented by cooperative merchandising of crops, the Southern Farmers' Alliance became a viable alternative to the capitalist marketplace—if only temporarily. The alliance-run Texas Cotton Exchange failed in 1889, mainly because banks refused to accept as legal tender the vouchers its members used among themselves.

Large farmers' organizations in Minnesota, Nebraska, Iowa, Kansas, and the Dakota territory joined forces in the Northern Farmers' Alliance on the Plains states. During 1886 and 1887, summer drought followed winter blizzards and ice storms, reducing wheat harvests by one-third on the Plains. Locusts and cinch bugs ate much of the rest. As if this were not enough, prices on the world market fell sharply for what little remained. Many farmers left the land; western Kansas lost nearly half its population by the early 1890s. Skilled agitators played upon these hardships—especially the overpowering influence of railroads over the farmers' lives—boosting the alliance movement. By 1890 the Kansas Alliance alone claimed 130,000 members.

Grangers had pushed legislation that would limit the salaries of public officials, provide public school students with books at little or no cost, establish a program of teacher certification, and widen the admissions policies of the new state colleges. But only rarely did they put up candidates for office. In comparison, the Farmers' Alliance had few reservations about taking political stands or entering electoral races. At the end of the 1880s regional alliances drafted campaign platforms demanding state ownership of the railroads, a graduated income tax, lower tariffs, restriction of land ownership to citizens, and easier access to money through "the free and unlimited coinage of silver." In several states, alliance candidates for local and state office won local elections. By 1890 the alliances had gained control of the Nebraska legislature and held the balance of power in Minnesota and South Dakota.

Workers Search for Power

Like farmers, urban workers organized protest movements during the 1870s. The depression following the Panic of 1873, which produced 25 percent unemployment in many cities, served as a catalyst for organization. In New York City, a group marched to City Hall to present a petition on behalf of 10,000 workers who were without jobs or homes. Turned back repeatedly by the police, the organizers decided to stage a rally to advertise their demand for a steady job at a living wage. City officials refused to grant a permit. When 7,000 working-class men and women showed up on January 13, 1874, a battalion of 1,600 police—nearly two-thirds of the city's force—rushed into the crowd and began striking out indiscriminately with their clubs. This incident, known as the Tompkins Square Riot, inaugurated an era of unprecedented labor conflict and violence.

The railroad industry became the focus of protests by workers and farmers alike. Within the few months after the Panic of 1873, workers struck so many times that the New York Railroad Gazette complained, "Strikes are . . . as much a disease of the body politic as the measles or indigestion are of our physical organization." Although most of these strikes ended in failure, they revealed the readiness of workers to spell out their grievances in a direct and dramatic manner. They also suggested how strongly many townspeople, including merchants who depended on workers' wages, would support local strikes.

Despite these warnings, the railroad corporations were unprepared for the Great Uprising of 1877, the first nationwide strike. The strike began in Martinsburg, West Virginia, where workers protesting a 10 percent wage cut uncoupled all engines. No trains would run, they promised, until wages were restored. Within a few days, the strike had spread along the railroad routes to New York, Buffalo, Pittsburgh, Chicago, Kansas City, and San Francisco. In all these cities, workers in various industries and masses of the unemployed formed angry crowds, defying armed militia ordered to disperse them by any means. Meanwhile, strikers halted train traffic. They seized carloads of food for hungry families, and in St. Louis workers even took over the city's administration.

The rioting persisted for nearly a week, spurring business leaders to call for the deportation, arrest, or execution of strike leaders. Law and Order Leagues swept through working-class neighborhoods and broke up union meetings. Fearing a "national insurrection," President Hayes set a precedent by calling in the U.S. Army to suppress the strike. In Pittsburgh, federal troops equipped with semi-automatic machine guns fired into a

Strikes by State, 1880   *Most strikes after the Uprising of 1877 could be traced to organized trades, concentrated in the manufacturing districts of the Northeast and Midwest.*

Source: Carville Earle, *Geographical Inquiry and American Historical Problems* (Stanford, Calif.: Stanford University Press, 1992).

crowd and killed more than 20 people. By the time the strike finally ended, more than 100 people were dead.

Memories of the Uprising of 1877 haunted business and government officials for decades, prompting the creation of the National Guard and the construction of armories in working-class neighborhoods. Workers also drew lessons from the events. Before the end of the century, more than 6 million workers would strike in industries ranging from New England textiles to southern tobacco factories to western mines. The labor movement also expanded its sphere of influence to the halls of city government. While the Farmers' Alliance put up candidates in the South and Plains states, workers launched labor parties in dozens of industrial towns and cities.

In New York City, popular economist and land reformer Henry George, with the ardent support of the city's Central Labor Council and the Knights of Labor, put himself forward in 1886 as candidate for mayor on the United Labor Party ticket. His best-selling book, *Progress and Poverty* (1879), advocated a sweeping tax on all property to generate enough revenue to allow all Americans to live in comfort. Especially popular among Irish Americans, who had seen their homeland swallowed up by British landlords, George's ideas also appealed to German Americans, who, with the Irish, made up the heart of the city's labor movement. George called upon "all honest citizens" to join in independent political action as "the only hope of exposing and breaking up the extortion and speculation by which a standing army of professional politicians corrupt the people whom they plunder."

Tammany Hall delivered many thousands of the ballots cast for George straight into the Hudson River. Nevertheless, George managed to finish a respectable second with 31 percent of the vote, running ahead of young patrician Theodore Roosevelt.

Although his campaign ended in defeat, George had issued a stern warning to the entrenched politicians. Equally important, his impressive showing encouraged labor groups in other cities to form parties calling for the defeat of the "power of aggregated wealth." The results, in local elections around the country, stunned Republicans and Democrats alike.

In the late 1880s labor parties won seats on many city councils and state legislatures. Candidates of the Milwaukee People's Party won the race for mayor, a seat in the state senate, six seats in the state assembly, and one seat in Congress. In smaller industrial towns where workers outnumbered the middle classes, labor parties did especially well. In Rochester, New Hampshire, with a population of only 7,000, the Knights of Labor encouraged workers in shoe factories to put up their own candidates for office. From 1889 through 1891 Rochester workers elected a majority slate, from city council to mayor.

Women Build Alliances

Women helped build both the labor and agrarian protest movements while campaigning for their own rights as citizens. Like woman suffrage leader Elizabeth Cady Stanton, they believed that "government based on caste and class privilege cannot stand." In its place, as Bellamy predicted in *Equality*, would arise a new cooperative order in which women would be "absolutely free agents in the disposition of themselves."

Women in the Knights of Labor endorsed the order's political planks while putting forth their own set of demands. In 1886 sixteen women attending the

Sixteen women were among the 660 delegates attending the 1886 convention of the Knights of Labor in Richmond, Virginia. Elizabeth Rodgers, who holds her two-week-old daughter, joined the organization as a housewife. The mother of twelve children, she was also the first woman elected to head a district assembly. The majority of women delegates worked in shoe factories or textile mills.

national convention lobbied for the creation of a special department "to investigate the abuses of which our sex is subjected by unscrupulous employers, to agitate the principles which our Order teaches of equal pay for equal work and the abolition of child labor." The delegates accepted the plan with little dissent and appointed knit-goods worker Leonora M. Barry general investigator. With perhaps 65,000 women members at its peak, the Knights ran day-care centers for the children of wage-earning mothers and occasionally even set up bakery cooperatives to reduce the drudgery of cooking.

Women made a similar mark on farmers' organizations. The Patrons of Husbandry issued a charter to a local chapter only when women were well represented on its rolls, and in the 1870s delegates to its conventions routinely gave speeches endorsing woman suffrage and even dress reform. The Farmers' Alliance continued this policy, enjoining women to assist their fathers, husbands, or sons in agitation efforts. Whole families shared in social programs, such as songfests on Sunday afternoons, lecture series, and contests featuring antimonopoly games. In both the Northern and Southern Alliances, women made up perhaps one-quarter of the membership, and several advanced through the ranks to become leading speakers and organizers. Mary E. Lease, who achieved lasting fame for advising farmers to raise less corn and more hell, vividly expressed their sense of purpose. "Ours is a grand, a holy mission," she proclaimed, "to drive from our land and forever abolish the triune monopoly of land, money, and transportation."

Women in both the Knights of Labor and the Farmers' Alliance found their greatest leader in Frances E. Willard, the most famous woman of the nineteenth century. Willard assumed that the women who guarded their families' physical and spiritual welfare would, if granted the right to vote, extend their influence throughout the whole society. From 1878 until her death in 1897, Willard presided over the Woman's Christian Temperance Union (WCTU), at the time the largest organization of women in the world, and encouraged her numerous followers to "do everything." She mobilized nearly 1 million women to, in her words, "make the whole world HOMELIKE." WCTU members preached total abstinence from the consumption of alcohol, but they also worked to reform the prison system, eradicate prostitution, and eliminate the wage system. Willard went so far as to draw up plans for a new system of government whereby all offices, right up to the presidency, would be shared jointly by men and women. She also became a member of the Knights of Labor and endorsed the platform of the Farmers' Alliance.

Under Willard's leadership, the WCTU grew into the major force behind the campaign for woman suffrage, far surpassing the American Woman Suffrage Association and the National Woman Suffrage Association. By 1890, when the two rival suffrage associations merged to form the National American Woman Suffrage Association, the WCTU had already pushed the heart of the suffrage campaign into the Plains states and the West. In Iowa, Nebraska, Colorado, and especially Kansas, agitation for the right to vote provided a political bridge among women organized in the WCTU, Farmers' Alliance, Knights of Labor, and various local suffrage societies.

In 1891 representatives from various women's organizations formed the National Women's Alliance. The founding convention called for "full equality of the sexes," "harmony and unity of action among the Sisterhood" of the nation, "prevention of war," and the rejection of alcohol, tobacco, and narcotics as injurious to health. The organization's newspaper, the *Farmer's Wife*, spelled out basic principles in epigrams like "Give our women encouragement and victory is yours" and "Put 1000 women lecturers in the field and the revolution is here."

Although women lecturers such as Kansas's Annie Diggs were outstanding crowd pleasers, women in the Knights of Labor and the Farmers' Alliance failed to gain equality within the protest movements. Most political parties endorsed by these organizations included planks calling for equal wages for equal work but refused to endorse woman suffrage. Only in Colorado did local third-party candidates support the 1893 campaign that secured women's right to vote in that state. In the Southern Alliance, women themselves opposed women's enfranchisement. It was, however, an increasing emphasis on electoral politics that effectively placed voteless women on the sidelines.

Farmer-Labor Unity

In December 1890 the Farmers' Alliance called a meeting at Ocala, Florida, to press for a national third-party movement. This was a risky proposition because local chapters, like the Grangers before them, often allied themselves with Democrats or Republicans. The Southern Alliance hoped to capture control of the Democratic Party, while many farmers in the Plains states voted Republican. In some areas, though, the Farmers' Alliance established its own parties, put up full slates of candidates for local elections, won majorities in state legislatures, and even sent a representative to Congress. Reviewing these successes, delegates at Ocala decided to push ahead and form a national party, and they appealed to other farm, labor, and reform organizations to join them. Edward Bellamy advised his followers to take advantage of "the largest opportunity yet presented in the history of our movement" and support the third-party effort.

The time had come, the Alliance announced, "to establish the moral solidarity of the farmer and

toiler societies." In February 1892, representatives from the Farmers' Alliance, the Knights of Labor, and the National Colored Farmers' Alliance, among others, met in St. Louis under a broad banner that read: "We do not ask for sympathy or pity. We ask for justice." After much deliberation, the 1,300 delegates adopted a platform for the new People's Party. It called for government ownership of railroads, banks, and telegraph lines, prohibition of large landholding companies, a graduated income tax, an eight-hour workday, and restriction of immigration. Its preamble, written by Minnesota's Ignatius Donnelly, declared: "We seek to restore the government of the Republic to the hands of 'the plain people' with which class it originated." The People's Party convened again in Omaha in July 1892 and nominated James Baird Weaver of Iowa for president and, to please the South, the Confederate veteran James Field from Virginia for vice president.

The Populists, as supporters of the People's Party styled themselves, quickly became a major factor in American politics. In some southern states, Populists cooperated with local Republicans in sponsoring "pepper and salt" state and local tickets that put black and white candidates on a single slate. To hold their voters, some Democrats adopted the Populist platform wholesale; others resorted to massive voter fraud and intimidation. In the West, Democrats threw their weight behind the Populist ticket mainly to defeat the ruling Republicans.

Democrat Grover Cleveland regained the presidency in 1892 (he had previously served from 1885 to 1889), but Populists scored a string of local victories. They ran strongest in Idaho, Nevada, Colorado, Kansas, and North Dakota, winning 50 percent or more of the vote. Nationwide, they elected three governors, ten representatives to Congress, and five senators. The national ticket received more than 1 million votes (8.5 percent of the total) and 22 electoral college votes—the only time since the Civil War that a third party had received any electoral votes. Despite poor showings among urban workers east of the Mississippi, Populists looked forward to the next round of state elections in 1894. But the great test would come with the presidential election in 1896.

THE CRISIS OF THE 1890s

Populist Ignatius Donnelly wrote in the preface to his pessimistic novel *Caesar's Column* (1891) that industrial society appears to be a "wretched failure" to "the great mass of mankind." On the road to disaster rather than to the egalitarian community that Bellamy had envisioned, "the rich, as a rule, hate the poor; and the poor are coming to hate the rich . . . society divides itself into two hostile camps. . . . They wait only for the drum beat and the trumpet to summon them to armed conflict."

A series of events in the 1890s shook the confidence of many citizens in the reigning political system. But nothing was more unsettling than the severe economic depression that consumed the nation. Many feared—while others hoped—that the entire political system would topple.

Financial Collapse and Depression

Railroads were at the center of the economic growth of the late nineteenth century. By the early 1890s they represented capital totaling $2.5 billion. As a result, when the nation's major rail lines went bankrupt in 1893, the business boom of nearly two decades ended and the entire economy ground to a halt. The depression that followed made the hard times of the 1870s appear a mere rehearsal for worse misery to come.

Jacob Coxey's "Commonwealth of Christ Army," 1894. Attracting the sympathetic attention of working people and the hostility of most of the wealthier classes, "Industrial Armies" marched through U.S. cities en route to the nation's capital.

The collapse of the Philadelphia and Reading Railroad in March 1893, followed by the downfall of the National Cordage Company, precipitated a crisis in the stock market and sent waves of panic splashing over banks across the country. In a few months, more than 150 banks went into receivership and hundreds more closed; nearly 200 railroads and more than 15,000 businesses also slipped into bankruptcy. In the steel industry alone thirty companies collapsed within six months of the panic. Agricultural prices meanwhile plummeted to new lows. Subsequent bank failures and stock market declines held back recovery until 1897, when the economy slowly began to pick up again. The new century arrived before prosperity returned.

The depression brought untold hardships. In many cities, unemployment rates reached 25 percent; Samuel Gompers, head of the American Federation of Labor (AFL), estimated nationwide unemployment at 3 million. "I have seen more misery in this last week than I ever saw in my life before," wrote a young reporter from Chicago. Few people starved, but millions suffered. Inadequate diets prompted a rise in communicable diseases, such as tuberculosis and pellagra.

Men and women begged for food or turned to charities for free bread and clothing. Tens of thousands "rode the rails" or went "on the tramp" to look for work, hoping that their luck might change in a new city or town. Some panhandled for the nickel that could buy a mug of beer and a free lunch at a saloon. By night they slept in parks or, in the colder months, flocked to the "bum tanks" of the city jail or to fleabag hotels. In New York City alone, with more than 20,000 homeless people, thousands ended up in jail. Newspapers warned against this "menace" and blamed the growing crime rates on the "dangerous classes."

Another Populist, Jacob Sechler Coxey, decided to gather the masses of unemployed into a huge army and then to march to Washington, D.C., to demand from Congress a public works program. On Easter Sunday, 1894, Coxey left Massillon, Ohio, with several hundred followers. Meanwhile, brigades from Boston, Los Angeles, San Francisco, Tacoma, Denver, Salt Lake City, Reno, Butte, and Omaha joined his "petition in boots." Communities across the country welcomed the marchers, but U.S. attorney general Richard C. Olney, a former lawyer for the railroad companies, conspired with state and local officials to halt them. Only 600 men and women reached the nation's capital, where the police first clubbed and then arrested the leaders for trespassing on the grass. Coxey's Army quickly disbanded, but not before voicing the public's growing impatience with government apathy toward the unemployed.

Strikes and Labor Solidarity

Meanwhile, in several locations the conflict between labor and capital had escalated to the brink of civil war.

In 1892, general strikes shut down industries in New Orleans and Buffalo and spread throughout the mining territories of east Tennessee.

Wage cuts in the silver and lead mines of northern Idaho led to one of the bitterest conflicts of the decade. To put a brake on organized labor, mineowners had formed a "protective association," and in March 1892 they announced a lower wage scale throughout the Coeur d'Alene district. After the miners' union refused to accept the cut, the owners locked out all union members and brought in strikebreakers. After three months of stalemate, union members loaded a railcar with explosives and blew up a mine. Strikebreakers fled while mineowners appealed to the Idaho governor for assistance. A force of 1,500 state and federal troops occupied the district. Strikebreakers were brought back in, and more than 300 union members were herded into bullpens, where they were kept under unsanitary conditions for several weeks before their trial. Ore production meanwhile resumed, and by November, when troops were withdrawn, the mineowners declared a victory. But the miners' union survived, and most members eventually regained their jobs. "We have made a fight that we are proud of and propose to continue it to the end," one striker declared. The following spring, Coeur d'Alene miners sent delegates to Butte, Montana, where they helped form the Western Federation of Miners, which soon became one of the strongest labor organizations in the nation.

Coeur d'Alene strikers had been buoyed by the news that steelworkers at Homestead, Pennsylvania, had likewise taken guns in hand to defend their union. Members of the Amalgamated Iron, Steel and Tin Workers, the most powerful union of the AFL, had carved out an admirable position for themselves in the Carnegie Steel Company. Well paid, proud of their skills, the unionists customarily directed their unskilled helpers without undue influence of company supervisors. Determined to gain control over every stage of production, Carnegie and his chairman, Henry C. Frick, decided not only to lower wages but to break the union.

In 1892, when the Amalgamated's contract expired, Frick announced a drastic wage cut. He also ordered a wooden stockade built around the factory, with grooves for rifles and barbed wire on top. The workers went on strike in late June. When Homestead's city government refused to assign police to disperse them, Frick sent in a heavily armed private army to do the job. After a day-long gun battle between strikers and the hired army, the governor sent the Pennsylvania National Guard to restore order. Carnegie's factory reopened, with strikebreakers doing the work.

After four months, the union was forced to concede a crushing defeat, not only for itself but in effect for all steelworkers. The Carnegie company reduced its work force by 25 percent, lengthened the workday, and cut wages 25 percent for those who remained on the job. If the Amalgamated Iron, Steel and Tin Workers, known throughout the industry as the "aristocrats of labor," could be brought down, less-skilled workers could expect little from the corporate giants. Within a decade, every major steel company operated without union interference.

But the spirit of labor solidarity did not die. Just two years after the strikes at Coeur d'Alene and Homestead, the greatest railway strike since 1877 again dramatized the extent of collusion between the government and corporations to crush the labor movement.

Like Lowell, Massachusetts, sixty years earlier, the town of Pullman, Illinois, just south of Chicago, had been regarded as a model industrial community. Its creator and proprietor, George Pullman, had manufactured luxurious "sleeping cars" for railroads since 1881. He built his company as a self-contained community, with the factory at the center, surrounded by modern cottages, a library, churches, an independent water supply, and even its own cemetery. The Pullman Palace Car Company deducted rent, library fees, and grocery bills from each worker's weekly wages. In good times workers enjoyed a decent livelihood, although many resented Pullman's autocratic control of their daily affairs.

When times grew hard, the company cut wages by as much as one-half, in some cases down to less than $1 a day. Charges for food and rent remained unchanged. Furthermore, factory supervisors sought to make up for declining profits by driving workers to produce more. In May 1894, after Pullman fired members of a committee that had drawn up a list of grievances, workers voted to strike.

Pullman workers found their champion in Eugene V. Debs, who had recently formed the American Railway Union (ARU) to bring all railroad workers into one organization. Just one month before the Pullman workers voted to strike, Debs and the ARU had scored a victory over the Great Northern rail line. Debs now advised caution, but delegates to an ARU convention voted to support a nationwide boycott of all Pullman cars. This action soon turned into a sympathy strike by railroad workers across the country. Support for the strike was especially strong in the western states.

Compared to the Uprising of 1877, the orderly Pullman strike at first produced little violence. ARU officials urged strikers to ignore all police provocations and hold their ground peacefully. But Attorney General Olney, claiming that the ARU was disrupting mail shipments (actually Debs had banned such interference), issued a blanket injunction against the strike. On July 4, President Cleveland sent federal troops to Chicago, over Illinois governor John Peter Altgeld's objections. After a bitter confrontation that left thirteen people dead and more than fifty wounded, the army dispersed the strikers. For the next week, railroad workers in twenty-six other states resisted federal troops, and a dozen more people were killed. On July 17, the strike finally ended when federal marshals arrested Debs and other leaders. Debs was sentenced to six months in jail.

"The Debs of fable," wrote the editor of a Unitarian weekly, "lighted a fire in the car yards of Chicago. The Debs of fact lighted an idea in the dangerous shadows of the Republic." Assailing the arrogance of class privilege that encouraged the government to use brute force against its citizens, Debs concluded that the labor movement could not regain its dignity under the present system. An avid fan of Bellamy's *Looking Backward*, he came out of jail a committed socialist. A few years later he tried to create a utopian colony that would prove the viability of cooperation in both working and living arrangements. This attempt failed to get off the ground, and in 1898 Debs moved on to help form a socialist political party.

Across the industrial belt and in the West and Southwest, in railroad towns, factory villages, and farms, tens of thousands of people supported Debs. Debs ran for president as a Socialist in 1900 and in four subsequent elections. But as prosperity returned after the depression of the 1890s, the odds against him grew. Debs, however, made his point on moral grounds. His friend James Whitcomb Riley, the nation's most admired sentimental poet, wrote in rural dialect that Debs had "the kindest heart that ever beat/betwixt here and the jedgment [judgment] seat."

The Social Gospel

Like Edward Bellamy, a growing number of Protestant and Catholic clergy and lay theologians noted a discrepancy between the ideals of Christianity and prevailing attitudes toward the poor. Like Bellamy, they could no longer sanction an economic system that allowed so many to toil long hours under unhealthy conditions and for subsistence wages. Moved by the human suffering accompanying the major depressions of the 1870s and 1890s, leading clergy envisioned a new cooperative order based on the principles of Christ's gospels and demanded that the church lead the way. In 1889 Episcopalian clergyman W. D. P. Bliss, a charter member of Boston's Bellamy Nationalist club, began to publish a monthly magazine, the *Dawn*, whose motto was "He works for God who works for man."

Coinciding with an upswing in religious revivals in the nation's cities, some liberal congregations broke away from established churches to side with the working class and the immigrant poor. Ministers called for civil service reform and the end of child labor. Supporting labor's right to organize and, if necessary, to strike, they petitioned government officials to regulate corporations and place a limit on profits. Washington Gladden, a Congregationalist minister, warned that if

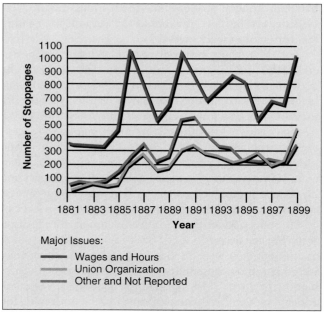

Work Stoppages, 1881–1899 *The number of strikes over wages and hours peaked in the years of 1886, 1890, and 1899, as workers in various trades and industries acted to protect or better their situations. By contrast, strikes for union recognition by employees—waged mostly by skilled workers—rose slowly but steadily until the economic depression of the 1890s. As the depression eased, strikes again increased.*

Source: United States Bureau of the Census, *Historical Statistics of the United States, Colonial Times to 1957* (Washington, D.C.: Bureau of the Census, 1960), p. 99.

churches continued to ignore pressing social problems they would devolve into institutions whose sole purpose was to preserve obscure rituals and superstitions. In the wake of the great railroad strikes of 1877, he had called upon his congregation in Columbus, Ohio, to take an active part in the fight against social injustice. Gladden's *Applied Christianity* (1886) appealed to the nation's business leaders to return to Christ's teachings.

Less famous but more numerous, local Protestant ministers and community leaders likewise sought to restore what they considered the true spirit of Christianity. As labor reformer George McNeill wrote in 1890, some ministers might be the servants of wealth, but in the long run "the influence of the teachings of the Carpenter's Son" will "counteract the influence of Mammon," the biblical embodiment of greed. McNeill looked forward to the day when "every man shall have according to his needs." Although the social gospel spread most rapidly through the northern industrial cities, southern African Americans espoused their own version. They reinterpreted the Gospel as Jesus' promise to emancipate their race from satanic white power brokers. The biblical republic of "Beulahland" became their model of redemption.

The depression of the 1890s produced an outpouring of social gospel treatises. The very popular *If Christ Came to Chicago* (1894), by British journalist W. T. Stead, forced readers to confront the "ugly sight" of a city with 200 millionaires and 200,000 unemployed men. It inspired Edward Everett Hale's *If Jesus Came to Boston* (1894), which similarly questioned social inequalities. The most famous tract, *In His Steps* (1896), by Methodist minister Charles M. Sheldon of Topeka, Kansas, urged readers to rethink their actions in the light of the simple question "What would Jesus do?" By 1933 Sheldon's book had sold more than 23 million copies.

Catholics, doctrinally more inclined than Protestants to accept poverty as a natural condition, joined the social gospel movement in smaller numbers. In the early 1880s Polish Americans broke away from the Roman Catholic Church to form the Polish National Church, which was committed to the concerns of working people. Irish Americans, especially prominent in the Knights of Labor, encouraged priests to ally themselves with the labor movement. Pope Leo XIII's encyclical *Rerum Novarum* (1891) endorsed the right of workers to form trade unions.

Women guided the social gospel movement in their communities. In nearly every city, groups of women affiliated with various evangelical Protestant sects raised money to establish small, inexpensive residential hotels for working women, whose low wages rarely covered the price of safe, comfortable shelter. Many of these groups joined to form the Young Women's Christian Association (YWCA), which by 1900 had more than 600 local chapters. The "Y" sponsored a range of services for needy Christian women, ranging from homes for the elderly and for unmarried mothers to elaborate programs of vocational instruction and physical fitness. The Girls Friendly Societies, an organization of young women affiliated with Episcopal churches, sponsored similar programs. Meanwhile Catholic lay women and nuns served the poor women of their faith, operating numerous schools, hospitals, and orphanages.

Although centered in the cities, the social gospel rallied many small-town and rural women, especially ardent admirers of Frances Willard. "The time will come," Willard insisted, "when the human heart will be so much alive that no one could sleep in any given community; if any of that group of human beings were cold, hungry, or miserable."

POLITICS OF REFORM, POLITICS OF ORDER

The severe hardships of the 1890s, following decades of popular unrest and economic uncertainty, led to a crisis in the two-party system, making the presidential election of 1896 a turning point in American politics. Republicans and Democrats continued to enjoy long-standing voter loyalties among specific groups or regions. Particularly in the South, the Democrats could generally depend on the masses of white voters to unite against any movement threatening to compromise the "color line." But Populists showed surprising ingenuity and courage in breaking down barriers against political insurgents.

The Free Silver Issue

Grover Cleveland owed his victory in 1892 over Republican incumbent Benjamin Harrison to the predictable votes of the Democratic "solid South" and to the unanticipated support of such northern states as Illinois and Wisconsin, whose German-born voters turned against the increasingly nativist Republicans. But when the economy collapsed the following year, Cleveland and the Democrats who controlled Congress faced a public eager for action. Convinced that the economic crisis was "largely the result of financial policy . . . embodied in unwise laws," the president called a special session of Congress to reform the nation's currency.

For generations, reformers had advocated "soft" currency—that is, an increase in the money supply that would loosen credit, accelerate economic development, and allow farmers to repay bank loans with "cheaper" money than they had borrowed. "Hard money" conservatives insisted that such a measure would throw the economy into chaos. Nevertheless, during the Civil War the federal government took decisive action, replacing state bank notes with a national paper currency popularly called "greenbacks" (from the color of the bills). In 1873 President Grant signed a Coinage Act that added silver to gold as the precious metal base of currency, presumably lowering the value of specie by adding to its supply. This measure had little real impact on the economy but opened the door to yet more tinkering.

In hard times especially, the currency question simmered. In 1876 philanthropist Peter Cooper ran an independent presidential campaign on a soft money platform and won 50,000 votes. Four years later, Civil War General James Baird Weaver ran on a similar platform for the Greenback-Labor Party and gathered an impressive 300,000 votes. Meanwhile, the gold-standard advocates, concentrated mostly in the business community, argued that the economy had already been damaged by the Coinage Act of 1873, which they called the "Crime of '73." The compromise Sherman Silver Purchase Act of 1890 directed the Treasury to increase the amount of currency coined from silver mined in the West and also permitted the U.S. government to print paper currency backed by the silver. Eastern members of Congress supported this measure when Westerners agreed, in turn, to support the McKinley tariff of 1890, which established the highest import duties yet on foreign goods.

With the economy in ruins, a desperate President Cleveland now demanded the repeal of the Sherman Act, insisting that only the gold standard could pull the nation out of depression. By exerting intense pressure on congressional Democrats, Cleveland got his way in October 1893, but not without ruining his chances for renomination. The midterm elections in 1894 brought the largest shift in congressional power in American history: the Republicans gained 117 seats, while the Democrats lost 113. The "Silver Democrats" of Cleveland's own party vowed revenge and began to look to the Populists, mainly Westerners and farmers who favored "free silver"—that is, the unlimited coinage of silver. Republicans confidently began to prepare for the presidential election of 1896, known as the "battle of the standards."

Populism's Last Campaigns

Populists had been buoyed by the 1894 election, which delivered to their candidates nearly 1.5 million votes, a gain of 42 percent over their 1892 totals. They made impressive inroads into several southern states. West of the Mississippi, political excitement steadily increased. David Waite, the Populist governor of Colorado, talked of a coming revolution and declared, "It is better, infinitely better, that blood should flow [up] to the horses' bridles rather than our national liberties should be destroyed." Still, even in the Midwest where Populists doubled their vote, they managed to win less than 7 percent of the total.

As Populists prepared for the 1896 election, they found themselves at a crossroad: What were they to do with the growing popularity of Democrat William Jennings Bryan? Son of an Illinois judge who had run for Congress unsuccessfully on the Greenback ticket, Bryan had relocated to Nebraska, where he practiced law. A spellbinding orator, he won a congressional seat in 1890. After seizing the Populist slogan "Equal Rights to All, Special Privilege to None," Bryan became a major contender for president of the United States.

Noting the surging interest in free silver, Bryan became its champion. "I don't know anything about free silver," he once admitted, but "the people of Nebraska are for free silver and I am for free silver. I will look up the arguments later." For two years before the 1896 election, Bryan wooed potential voters in a speaking tour that took him to every state in the nation. Pouring new life into his divided party, Bryan pushed Silver Democrats to the forefront.

At the 1896 party convention, the thirty-six-year-old orator thrilled delegates with his evocation of agrarian ideals. "Burn down your cities and leave our farms," Bryan preached, "and your cities will spring up again as if by magic; but destroy our farms and the grass will grow in the streets of every city in the country." What became one of the most famous speeches in Amer-

This Republican campaign poster of 1896 depicts William McKinley standing on sound money and promising a revival of prosperity. The depression of the 1890s shifted the electorate into the Republican column.

ican political history closed on a yet more dramatic note. Spreading his arms to suggest the crucified Christ figure, Bryan pledged to answer all demands for a gold standard by saying, "You shall not press down upon the brow of labor this crown of thorns, you shall not crucify mankind upon a cross of gold." The next day, Bryan won the Democratic presidential nomination.

The Populists knew that the Democrats, in nominating Bryan, had stolen their thunder. Although many feared that the growing emphasis on currency would overshadow their more important planks calling for government ownership of the nation's railroads and communications systems, few Populists had expected either major party to come out for free silver. As the date of their own convention approached, delegates divided over strategy: they could endorse Bryan and give up their independent status; or they could run an independent campaign and risk splitting the silver vote. Neither choice was good. "If we fuse," one Populist explained, "we are sunk; if we don't fuse, all the silver men we have will leave us for the more powerful Democrats."

In the end, the Populists nominated Bryan for president and chose one of their own ranks, the popular Georgian Tom Watson, for the vice-presidential candidate. Most of the state Democratic Party organizations, however, refused to put the "fusion" ticket on the ballot, and Bryan and his Democratic running mate, Arthur Sewall, simply ignored the Populist campaign.

The Republican Triumph

After Cleveland's blunders, Republicans anticipated an easy victory in 1896, but Bryan's nomination, as party stalwart Mark Hanna warned, "changed everything." Luckily, they had their own handsome, knowledgeable, courteous, and ruthless candidate, Civil War veteran William McKinley. Equally important, the Republicans enjoyed an efficient and well-financed machine. Hanna guided a campaign strategy that raised up to $7 million and outspent Bryan more than ten to one. The sheer expense and skill of coordination outdid all previous campaigns and established a precedent for future presidential elections. Using innumerable pamphlets, placards, hats, and parades, Republicans advertised their promise to "re-build out of the ruins of the last four years the stately mansions of national happiness, prosperity and self-respect." In the campaign's final two weeks, organizers dispatched 1,400 speakers to spread the word. Fearful of divisions in their own ranks, Republicans played down the silver issue while emphasizing the tariff and consistently cast adversary Bryan as a dangerous naysayer willing to risk the nation's well-being and cost voters their jobs or worse.

McKinley triumphed in the most important presidential election since Reconstruction. Bryan won 46 percent of the popular vote but failed to carry the Midwest, West Coast, or Upper South. The free silver campaign alienated traditionally Democratic urban voters, who feared soft money would bring higher prices. Many Catholics, uncomfortable with Bryan's Protestant moral piety, also deserted the Democrats, while German American Lutherans voted in especially large numbers for McKinley and for a Republican Congress. Finally, neither the reform-minded middle classes nor impoverished blue-collar workers were convinced that Bryan's grand reform vision really included them. The Populist following, disappointed and disillusioned, dwindled away.

For sixteen years after the 1896 election, Democrats dominated no region but the South. With Republican victories seemingly inevitable, apathy set in, and voter participation began to spiral downward.

Once in office, McKinley promoted a mixture of probusiness and expansionist measures. He supported the Dingley tariff of 1897, which raised

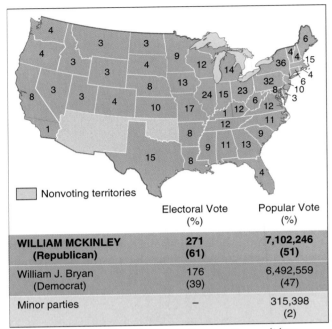

	Electoral Vote (%)	Popular Vote (%)
WILLIAM MCKINLEY (Republican)	**271 (61)**	**7,102,246 (51)**
William J. Bryan (Democrat)	176 (39)	6,492,559 (47)
Minor parties	–	315,398 (2)

Election of 1896, by States *Democratic candidate William Jennings Bryan carried most of rural America but could not overcome Republican William McKinley's stronghold in the populous industrial states.*

import duties to an all-time high and favored the passage of the Gold Standard Act of 1900. In 1897 McKinley also encouraged Congress to create the United States Industrial Commission, which would plan business regulation; in 1898 he promoted a bankruptcy act that eased the financial situation of small businesses; and in the same year he proposed the Erdman Act, which established a system of arbitration to avoid rail strikes. The Supreme Court ruled in concert with the president, finding eighteen railways in violation of antitrust laws and granting states the right to regulate hours of labor under certain circumstances.

McKinley's triumph ended the popular challenge to the nation's governing system. With prosperity returning by 1898 and nationalism rising swiftly, McKinley encouraged Americans to go for "a full dinner pail," the winning Republican slogan of the 1900 presidential election.

The Limits of Democracy

Campaign rhetoric aside, McKinley and Bryan differed only slightly on the major problems facing the nation in 1896. Neither Bryan the reformer nor McKinley the prophet of prosperity addressed the escalation of racism and nativism (anti-immigrant feeling) throughout the nation. After the election, McKinley made white supremacy a major tenet of his foreign policy; Bryan, twice more a presidential contender, championed white rule in the South.

Toward the end of the century, many political observers noted, the nation's patriotic fervor took on a strongly nationalistic and antiforeign tone. Striking workers and their employers alike tended to blame "foreigners" for the hard times. AFL leader Samuel Gompers, himself a Jewish immigrant from Europe, lobbied Congress to restrict immigration from eastern and southern Europe, and even the sons and daughters of earlier immigrants attacked the newcomers as unfit for democracy. Imagining a Catholic conspiracy directed by the pope, semisecret organizations such as the American Protective Association sprang up to defend American institutions. Fourth of July orators continued to celebrate freedom and liberty but more often boasted about the might and power of their nation.

White violence against African Americans reached levels unknown since Reconstruction. Meanwhile, southern local and state governments codified racist ideology by passing discriminatory and segregationist legislation, which became known as Jim Crow laws. Wealthy planters, merchants, and farmers organized to disfranchise black voters and to extend the practice of segregation to cover facilities such as restaurants, public transportation, and even drinking fountains. The United States Supreme Court upheld the new discriminatory legislation. Its decisions in the *Civil Rights Cases* (1883) overturned the Civil Rights Act of 1875, and in *Plessy v. Ferguson* (1896) the Court upheld a Louisiana state law formally segregating railroad cars on the basis of the "separate but equal" doctrine. In *Cumming v. Richmond County Board of Education* (1899), the Court allowed separate schools for blacks and whites, even where facilities for African American children did not exist.

The new restrictions struck especially hard at the voting rights of African Americans. Southern states enacted new literacy tests and property qualifications for voting, demanding proof of $300 to $500 in property and the ability to read and write. Loopholes permitted poor whites to vote even under these conditions, except where they threatened the Democratic Party's rule. "Grandfather clauses," invented in Louisiana, exempted from all restrictions those who had been entitled to vote on January 1, 1867, together with their sons and grandsons, a measure that effectively enfranchised whites while barring African Americans. In 1898 the Supreme Court ruled that poll taxes and literacy requirements enacted in order to prevent blacks (and some poor whites) from voting were a proper means of restricting the ballot to "qualified" voters. By this time, only 5 percent of the southern black electorate voted, and African Americans were barred from public office and jury service. Supreme Court Justice John Marshall Harlan, the lone dissenter in *Plessy v. Ferguson*, lamented that the Court's majority rulings gave power to the states "to place in a condition of legal inferiority a large body of American citizens." Depriving African Americans of equal rights and protection under the law, Jim Crow legislation encouraged states outside the South to pass similar measures.

Racial violence in turn escalated. Not only race riots but thousands of lynchings took place. Between 1882 and the turn of the century, the number of lynchings usually exceeded 100 each year; 1892 produced a record 230 deaths (161 black, 69 white). Mobs often burned or dismembered victims in order to drag out their agony and entertain the crowd of onlookers. Announced in local newspapers, lynchings became public spectacles for entire white families, and railroads sometimes offered special excursion rates for travel to these events.

Antilynching became the one-woman crusade of Ida B. Wells, young editor of a black newspaper in Memphis. After three local black businessmen were lynched in 1892, Wells vigorously denounced the outrage, blaming white business competitors of the victims. Her stand fanned the tempers of local whites, who destroyed her press and forced the outspoken editor to leave the city.

WHITE SUPREMACY!

Attention, White Men!

Grand Torch-Light Procession

At JACKSON,

On the Night of the

Fourth of January, 1890.

The Final Settlement of Democratic Rule and White Supremacy in Mississippi.

GRAND PYROTECHNIC DISPLAY!
Transparencies and Torches Free for all.

All in Sympathy with the Grand Cause are Cordially and Earnestly Invited to be on hand, to aid in the Final Overthrow of Radical Rule in our State.

Come on foot or on horse-back; come any way, but be sure to get there.
Brass Bands, Cannon, Flambeau Torches, Transparencies, Sky-rockets, Etc.

A GRAND DISPLAY FOR A GRAND CAUSE.

Billboard produced for the Mississippi constitutional convention of 1890. Rallying under the banner of "white supremacy," the delegates successfully disfranchised African Americans.

Wells set out to investigate lynching in a systematic fashion. She paid special attention to the common defense of lynching—that it was a necessary response to attempts by black men to rape white women. Her 1895 pamphlet *A Red Record* showed that the vast majority of black lynching victims had not even been accused of rape. In fact, Wells showed, lynching was primarily a brutal device to eliminate African Americans who had become too prosperous or competed with white businesses.

Wells launched an international movement against lynching, lecturing across the country and in Europe, demanding an end to the silence about this barbaric crime. Her work also inspired the growth of a black women's club movement. The National Association of Colored Women, founded in 1896, provided a home for black women activists who had been excluded from white women's clubs. United by a growing sense of racial pride, black women's clubs took up the antilynching cause and also fought to protect black women from exploitation by white men and from charges of sexual depravity.

Tom Watson

Few white reformers rallied to defend African Americans. At its 1899 convention, the National American Woman Suffrage Association appeased new southern white members by voting down a resolution condemning racial segregation in public facilities. A far greater tragedy was a racist turn in the Populist movement, whose leaders even in the South had at times challenged white supremacy. The story of Thomas E. Watson, briefly a champion of interracial unity, illustrates the rise and fall of hopes for an egalitarian South.

Son of a prosperous cotton farmer who had been driven into bankruptcy during the depression of the 1870s, Tom Watson had once campaigned to restore the civil rights of southern African Americans. "Why is not the colored tenant [farmer] open to the conviction that he is in the same boat as the white tenant; the colored laborer with the white laborer?" he asked. Watson planned to overturn Democratic rule by capturing and building up the black vote for the People's Party.

Watson's followers in Georgia were jailed, shot at, denied the protection of the courts, and driven from their churches. Yet tens of thousands regarded him as a savior. Flowers decorated the bridges along his speaking routes, crowds standing in pouring rain begged him to continue speaking, and wagons of loyalists carried Winchester rifles to defend him from armed attack. Preaching government ownership of railroads and banks and political equality for both races, Watson stirred the only truly grass-roots interracial movement the South had yet seen.

By early 1896, however, Watson perceived that the increasing ardor for free silver and the move toward cooperation with Democrats would doom the Populist movement. He nevertheless accepted the nomination for vice president on the "fusion" ticket and campaigned in several states. After McKinley's triumph, Watson withdrew from politics, returning to his Georgia farm to write popular histories of the United States and to plot his future.

Watson returned to public life after the turn of the century but with a totally different approach to race relations. He still bitterly attacked the wealthy classes but now blamed black citizens for conspiring against poor whites. Political salvation now hinged, he concluded, on accommodation to white supremacy. Watson expressed a southern variation of the new national creed that prepared Americans to view the luckless inhabitants of distant lands as ripe for colonization by the United States.

"IMPERIALISM OF RIGHTEOUSNESS"

Many Americans attributed the crisis of 1893–97 not simply to the collapse of the railroads and the stock market but to basic structural problems: an overbuilt economy and an insufficient market for goods. Profits from total sales of manufactured and agricultural products had grown substantially over the level achieved in the 1880s, but output increased even more rapidly. While the number of millionaires shot up from 500 in 1860 to more than 4,000 in 1892, the majority of working people lacked enough income to buy back a significant portion of what they produced. As Republican Senator Albert J. Beveridge of Indiana put it, "We are raising more than we can consume . . . making more than we can use. Therefore, we must find new markets for our produce, new occupation for our capital, new work for our labor."

In 1893 Frederick Jackson Turner reminded Americans that the continent had now been settled. Having passed "from the task of filling up the vacant spaces of the continent," the nation is now "thrown back upon itself," the young historian concluded. Obviously, Americans required a new "frontier" if democracy were to survive.

The White Man's Burden

Turner read his famous essay, "The Significance of the Frontier in American History," at the meeting of the American Historical Association, which was held in Chicago at the time of the World's Fair, less than two months after the nation's economy collapsed. On May Day 1893 crowds flocked to the fair—"a little ideal world, a realization of Utopia . . . [foreshadowing] some far away time when the earth should be as pure, as beautiful, and as joyous as the White City itself." A complex of more than 400 buildings, newly constructed in beaux arts design, commemorated the four hundredth anniversary of Columbus's landing. Such expositions, President McKinley explained, served as "timekeepers of progress."

The captains of Chicago's industry—Armour, Swift, McCormick, Field, and Pullman—had campaigned hard to bring the fair to Chicago and delighted in its triumphant display of American business ingenuity. Agriculture Hall showcased the production of corn, wheat, and other crops and featured a gigantic globe encircled by samples of American-manufactured farm machinery. The symbolism was evident: all eyes were on worldwide markets for American products. Another building housed a model of a canal cut across Nicaragua, suggesting the ease with which American traders might reach Asian markets if transport ships could travel directly from the Caribbean to the Pacific. One of the most popular exhibits, attracting 20,000 people a day, featured a mock ocean liner built to scale by the International Navigation Company, where fair-goers could imagine themselves as "tourists," sailing in luxury to distant parts of the world.

The World's Fair also "displayed" representatives of the people who populated foreign lands. The Midway Plaisance, a strip nearly a mile long and more than 600 feet wide, was an enormous sideshow of re-created Turkish bazaars and South Sea island huts. There were Javanese carpenters, Dahomean drummers, Egyptian swordsmen, and Hungarian Gypsies as well as Eskimos, Syrians, Samoans, and Chinese. Very popular was the World Congress of Beauty, parading "40 Ladies from 40 Nations" dressed in native costume. Another favorite attraction was "Little Egypt," who performed at the Persian Palace of Eros; her *danse du ventre* became better known as the hootchy-kootchy. According to the guidebook, these peoples had come "from the nightsome North and the splendid South, from the wasty West and the effete East, bringing their manners, customs, dress, religions, legends, amusements, that we might know them better." One of the exposition's directors, Frederick Ward Putnam, head of Harvard's Peabody Museum of American Archeology and Ethnology, explained more fully that the gathering gave fair-goers "a grand opportunity to see . . . the material advantages which civilization brings to mankind."

By celebrating the brilliance of American industry and simultaneously presenting the rest of the world's people as a source of exotic entertainment, the planners of the fair delivered a powerful message. Former abolitionist Frederick Douglass, who attended the fair on "Colored People's Day," recognized it immediately. He noted that the physical layout of the fair, by carefully grouping exhibits, sharply divided the United States and Europe from the rest of the world, namely from the nations of Africa, Asia, and the Middle East. Douglass objected to the stark contrast setting off Anglo-Saxons from people of color, an opposition between "civilization" and "savagery." Douglass and Ida

B. Wells jointly wrote a pamphlet that referred to the famed exposition as "a whited sepulcher." Wells advised African Americans to boycott the fair, but Douglass chose to attend. He used the occasion to deliver a speech upbraiding those white Americans who labeled the African American "a moral monster."

The Chicago World's Fair gave material shape to prevalent ideas about the superiority of American civilization and its racial order. At the same time, by showcasing American industries, it made a strong case for commercial expansion abroad. Social gospeler Josiah Strong, a Congregational minister who had begun his career trying to convert Indians to Christianity, provided a timely synthesis. He argued that the United States, as the most economically advanced and most Christian nation in the world, commanded a providential role. Thus linking economic and spiritual expansion, Strong advocated an "imperialism of righteousness." The rest of the world "is to be Christianized and civilized," Strong insisted, by the white Americans, who were best suited to this greatest task of all time. "Pure spiritual Christianity" and a "genius for colonizing" compelled Americans to move beyond their own national interests to consider the needs of the people of Africa and the Pacific and beyond. It was the white American, Strong argued, who had been "divinely commissioned to be, in a peculiar sense, his brother's keeper."

Senator Beveridge faithfully carried this message to Congress, insisting that God "has made us [white, English-speaking people] adept in government that we may administer governments among savages and senile peoples. . . . He has marked the American people as His chosen nation to finally lead in the regeneration of the world." According to many newspaper reporters and editorialists, it would be morally wrong for Americans to shirk what the British poet Rudyard Kipling called the "White Man's Burden."

Foreign Missions

The push for overseas expansion coincided with a major wave of religious evangelism and foreign missions. Early in the nineteenth century, Protestant missionaries, hoping to fulfill what they believed to be a divine command to carry God's message to all peoples and to win converts for their church, had focused on North America. Many disciples, like Strong himself, headed west and stationed themselves on Indian reservations. Others worked among the immigrant populations of the nation's growing cities. As early as the 1820s, however, a few missionaries had traveled to the Sandwich Islands (Hawai'i) in an effort to supplant the indigenous religion with Christianity. After the Civil War, following the formation of the Women's Union Missionary Society of Americans for Heathen Lands, the major evangelical Protestant denominations all sponsored missions directed at foreign lands.

Funded by wealthy men and the vigorous campaigns of female church members, these societies soon attracted a large membership. By the 1890s college campuses blazed with missionary excitement, and the intercollegiate Student Volunteers for Foreign Missions spread rapidly under the slogan "The Evangelicization of the World in This Generation." Magazines bristled with essays such as "The Anglo-Saxon and the World's Redemption." Young Protestant women rushed to join foreign missionary societies. In 1863 there had been only 94 Methodist women missionaries in China; by 1902 the number had jumped to 783. In all, some twenty-three American Protestant churches had established missions in China by the turn of the century, the majority staffed by women. By 1915, more than 3 million women had enrolled in forty denominational missionary societies, surpassing in size all other women's organizations in the United States. Their foreign missions ranged from India and Africa to Syria, the Pacific Islands, and nearby Latin America.

With so many agents in the field, missionaries scored numerous successes. They recruited many "natives," including the "rice-Christians" who feigned conversion in order to be fed by the missions. By 1898 Protestants claimed to have made Christians of more than 80,000 Chinese, a tiny portion of the population but a significant stronghold for American interests in their nation. The missionaries did more than spread the gospel. They taught school, provided rudimentary medical care, offered vocational training programs, and sometimes encouraged young men and women to pursue a college education in preparation for careers in their homelands. Such work depended on, and in turn inspired, enthusiastic church members in the United States.

Outside the churches proper, the YMCA and YWCA, which had set up nondenominational missions for the working poor in many American cities, also embarked on a worldwide crusade to reach non-Christians. By the turn of the century, the YWCA had foreign branches in Ceylon (present-day Sri Lanka) and China. After foreign branches multiplied in the next decade, a close observer ironically suggested that the United States had three great occupying forces: the army, the navy, and the "Y." He was not far wrong.

Missionaries played an important role both in generating public interest in foreign lands and in preparing the way for American economic expansion. As Josiah Strong aptly put it, "Commerce follows the missionary."

An Overseas Empire

Not only missionaries but business and political leaders had set their sights on distant lands. In the 1860s secretary of state William Henry Seward, under Abraham Lincoln and then under Andrew Johnson, encouraged Americans to defer to "a political law—and when I say political law, I mean higher law, a law of Providence—that empire has [had], for the last three thousand years." Seward correctly predicted that foreign trade would play an increasingly important part in the American economy. Between 1870 and 1900 exports more than tripled, from about $400 million to over $1.5 billion. But as European markets for American goods began to contract, business and political leaders of necessity looked more eagerly to Asia as well as to lands closer by.

Since the American Revolution, many Americans had regarded all nearby nations as falling naturally within their own territorial realm, destined to be acquired when opportunity allowed. Seward advanced these imperialist principles in 1867 by negotiating the purchase of Alaska (known at the time as Seward's Icebox) from Russia for 7.2 million dollars, and hoped someday to see the American flag flying over Canada and Mexico. Meanwhile, with European nations launched on their own imperialist missions in Asia and Africa, the United States increasingly viewed the Caribbean as an "American lake" and all of Latin America as a vast potential market for U.S. goods. The crisis of the 1890s transformed this long-standing desire into a perceived economic necessity. Large-scale conquest, however, appeared to American leaders more expensive and less appealing than economic domination and selective colonization. Unlike European imperialists, powerful Americans dreamed of empire without large-scale permanent military occupation and costly colonial administration.

Americans focused their expansionist plans on the Western Hemisphere, determined to dislodge the dominant power, Great Britain. In 1867, when Canada became a self-governing dominion, American diplomats hoped to annex their northern neighbor, believing that Great Britain would gladly accede in order to concentrate its imperial interests in Asia. But Great Britain refused to give up Canada, and the United States backed away. Central and South America proved more accommodating to American designs.

Republican stalwart James G. Blaine, secretary of state under presidents Garfield and Harrison, determined to work out a Good Neighbor policy (a phrase coined by Henry Clay in 1820). "What we want," he explained, "are the markets of these neighbors of ours that lie to the south of us. We want the $400,000,000 annually which to-day go to England, France, Germany and other countries. With these markets secured new life would be given to our manufactures, the product of the Western farmer would be in demand, the reasons for and inducements to strikers, with all their attendant evils, would cease." Bilateral treaties with Mexico, Colombia, the British West Indies, El Salvador, and the Dominican Republic allowed American business to dominate local economies, importing their raw materials at low prices

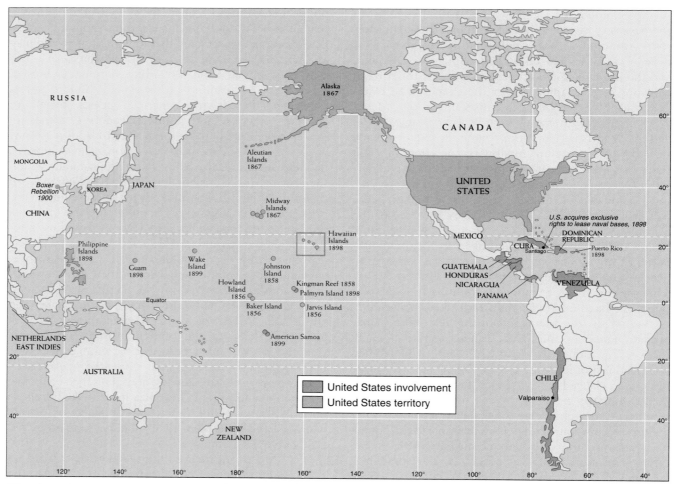

The American Domain, ca. 1900 *The United States claimed numerous islands in the South Pacific and intervened repeatedly in Latin America to secure its economic interests.*

and flooding their local markets with goods manufactured in the United States. Often American investors simply took over the principal industries of these small nations, undercutting national business classes. The first Pan-American Conference, held in 1889–90, marked a turning point in hemispheric relations.

The Good Neighbor policy depended, Blaine knew, on peace and order in the Latin American states. As early as 1875, when revolt shook Venezuela, the Department of State warned European powers not to meddle. If popular uprisings proved too much for local officials, the U.S. Navy would intervene and return American allies to power.

In 1883, wishing to enforce treaties and protect overseas investments, Congress appropriated funds to build up American seapower. Beginning with ninety small ships, over one-third of them wooden, the navy grew quickly to become known as the Great White Fleet. One of the most popular exhibits at the Chicago World's Fair featured full-sized models of the new armor-plated steel battleships. Congress also established

the Naval War College in Newport, Rhode Island, in 1884 to train the officer corps. One of its first presidents, Captain Alfred Thayer Mahan, prescribed an imperialist strategy based on command of the seas. His book, *The Influence of Sea Power upon American History, 1660–1873* (1890), helped to define American foreign policy at the time. Mahan insisted that international strength rested not only on open markets but on the control of colonies. He advocated the annexation of bases in the Caribbean and the Pacific to enhance the navy's ability to threaten or wage warfare.

The annexation of Hawai'i on July 7, 1898, followed nearly a century of economic penetration and diplomatic maneuver. American missionaries, who had arrived in the 1820s to convert Hawai'ians to Christianity, began to buy up huge parcels of land and to subvert the existing feudal system of landholding. They also encouraged American businesses to buy into sugar plantations, and by 1875 U.S. corporations dominated the sugar trade. They tripled the number of plantations by 1880 and sent Hawai'ian sugar duty-free to the

Brought to power with the assistance of American businessmen, Queen Liliuokalani nevertheless sought to limit the outsiders' influence. American marines, Christian missionaries, and sugar planters joined in 1893 to drive her from her throne. A century later, the U.S. government apologized to Hawai'ians for this illegal act.

United States. By this time Hawai'i appeared, in Blaine's opinion, to be "an outlying district of the state of California," and he began to push for annexation. In 1887 a new treaty allowed the United States to build a naval base at Pearl Harbor on the island of Oahu.

The next year, American planters took a step further, arranging the overthrow of a weak king, Kalakaua, and securing a new government allied to their economic interests. In 1891, the new ruler, Queen Liliuokalani, struck back by issuing a constitution granting her more discretionary power. The U.S. minister, prompted by the pineapple magnate Sanford B. Dole, responded by calling for military assistance. On January 16, 1893, U.S. sailors landed on Hawai'i to protect American property. Liliuokalani was deposed, a new provisional government was installed, and Hawai'i was proclaimed an American protectorate (a territory protected and partly controlled by the United States). The American diplomat John L. Stevens, stationed in Hawai'i, eagerly wired Washington that the "Hawai'ian

pear is now fully ripe, and this is the golden hour for the United States to pluck it." President Cleveland refused to consider annexation, but five years later McKinley affirmed a joint congressional resolution under which Hawai'i would become an American territory in 1900. The residents of Hawai'i were not consulted about this momentous change in their national identity.

Hawai'i was often viewed as a stepping-stone to the vast Asian markets. A U.S. admiral envisioned the happy future: "The Pacific is the ocean bride of America—China, Japan and Korea—and their innumerable islands, hanging like necklaces about them, are the bridesmaids. . . . Let us as Americans . . . determine while yet in our power, that no commercial rival or hostile flag can float with impunity over the long swell of the Pacific sea."

To accelerate railroad investment and trade, a consortium of New York bankers created the American China Development Company in 1896. They feared, however, that the tottering Manchu dynasty would fall to European, Russian, and Japanese colonial powers, which would then prohibit trade with the United States. Secretary of State John Hay responded in 1899 by proclaiming the Open Door policy. According to this doctrine, outlined in notes to six major powers, the United States enjoyed the right to advance its commercial interests anywhere in the world, at least on terms equal to those of the other imperialist nations. The Chinese marketplace was too important to lose.

Nationalist rebellion, however, threatened to overwhelm all the outsiders' plans for China. An antiforeign secret society known as the Harmonious Righteous Fists (dubbed "Boxers" by the Western press) rioted repeatedly in 1898 and 1899, actually occupying the capital city of Beijing and surrounding the foreign embassies. Shocked by the deaths of thousands, including many Chinese converts to Christianity, and determined to maintain American economic interests, President McKinley, not bothering to request congressional approval, contributed five thousand U.S. troops to an international army that put down the uprising. The Boxer Rebellion dramatized the Manchu regime's inability to control its own subjects and strengthened John Hay's determination to preserve the economic status quo. A second series of Open Door notes by the secretary of state restated the intention of the United States to trade in China and laid the basis for twentieth-century foreign policy.

THE SPANISH-AMERICAN WAR

During his 1896 campaign, William McKinley firmly committed himself to the principle of economic expansion. It was for him the proper alternative to Edward Bellamy's program for a cooperative commonwealth. Indeed, he once described his "greatest ambition" as achieving American supremacy in world markets. As president, McKinley not only reached out for markets but took his nation into war.

A "Splendid Little War" in Cuba

Cuba had long tempted American investors. As early as the 1840s, advocates of expansion described the nearby Caribbean island, still owned by Spain, as a fruit ripe for picking. Before the Civil War, Southerners hoped to acquire Cuba as a new region for cotton production and the expansion of slavery. After the Civil War Americans invested heavily in sugar mills, tobacco plantations, and mines, and by the early 1890s they held nearly $50 million worth of property on Cuba. In 1894, however, the Wilson-Gorman tariff placed stiff restrictions on Cuban imports to the United States, cutting the volume of trade by as much as 50 percent. The Cuban economy, along with American investments, went into a deep recession, setting the stage for revolution.

As unemployment and unrest spread, nationalist leader José Martí declared that "Cuba must be free from Spain and the United States." Cubans rallied under his leadership until Spanish troops ambushed

and killed Martí in May 1895. Martí's martyrdom fueled the flames of rebellion.

Many Americans, invoking the legacy of their own war for independence, supported the movement for *Cuba Libre*. Grisly stories of Spain's treatment of captured insurrectionists circulated in American newspapers and aroused popular sympathy for the Cuban cause. President Cleveland refused to back the Cuban revolutionaries but urged Spain to grant the island a limited autonomy. Even when Congress passed a resolution in 1896 welcoming the future independence of Cuba, Cleveland and his advisers demurred, determined to avoid war with Spain.

When McKinley took over the presidency, he immediately perceived that the insurrection harmed U.S. investments and might destroy the entire Cuban economy. He nevertheless drew back. In his Inaugural Address he declared, "We want no wars of conquest; we must avoid the temptation of territorial aggression." The tide turned, however, when Spain appeared unable to maintain order. In early 1898 American newspapers published a private letter written by a Spanish diplomat in Washington characterizing the president as weak and opportunistic. Public indignation, whipped up by tabloid press head-

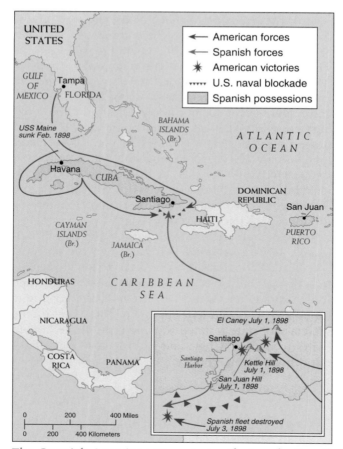

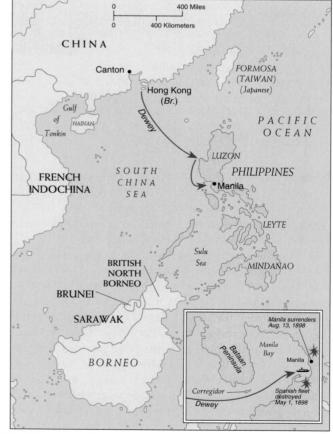

The Spanish-American War *In two theaters of action, the United States used its naval power adeptly against a weak foe.*

lines and sensational stories, turned into frenzy five days later, on February 15, when an explosion ripped through the battleship USS Maine, stationed in Havana harbor ostensibly to rescue American citizens living in Cuba.

McKinley, suspecting war was close, had already begun to prepare for intervention. While newspapers ran banner headlines charging a Spanish conspiracy, the president established a commission to investigate the explosion, which proved to be an accident rather than an act of Spanish aggression. The impatient public meanwhile demanded revenge for the death of 266 American sailors. Soon a new slogan appeared: "Remember the Maine and to Hell with Spain!"

Finally, on April 11, McKinley asked Congress for a declaration of war against Spain. Yet the Senate barely passed the war resolution by a vote of 42 to 35, and only with the inclusion of an amendment by Republican senator Henry Teller of Colorado that disclaimed "any disposition or intention to exercise sovereignty, jurisdiction or control over said island, except for the pacification thereof." McKinley, who opposed any plan to annex Cuba, signed the declaration of war on April 29, 1898.

An outpouring of patriotic joy inspired massive parades, topical songs, and an overpowering enthusiasm. "Populists, Democrats, and Republicans are we," went one jingle, "But we are all Americans to make Cuba free."

Ten weeks later the war was all but over. On land, Lieutenant Colonel Theodore Roosevelt—who boasted of killing Spaniards "like jackrabbits"—led his Rough Riders to victory. On July 3, the main Spanish fleet near Santiago Bay was destroyed; two weeks later Santiago itself surrendered, and the war drew to a close. Although fewer than 400 Americans died in battle, disease and the inept treatment of the wounded claimed more than 5,000 lives. Roosevelt nevertheless felt invigorated by the conflict, agreeing with John Hay that it had been a "splendid little war."

On August 12, at a small ceremony in McKinley's office marking Spain's surrender, the United States secured Cuba's independence but nevertheless denied the island an official role in the proceedings. American businesses tightened their hold on Cuban sugar plantations, while U.S. military forces oversaw the formation of a constitutional convention that made Cuba a protectorate of the United States. Under the Platt Amendment, sponsored by Republican senator Orville H. Platt of Connecticut in 1901, Cuba promised to provide land for American bases; to devote national revenues to paying back debts to the United States; to sign no treaty that would be detrimental to American interests; and to acknowledge the right of the United States to intervene at any time to protect its interests in Cuba. After American troops withdrew from Cuba, the amendment was incorporated into the Cuban-

American Treaty of 1903. This treaty, which remained in place until 1934, paved the way for American domination of the island's sugar industry and contributed to anti-American sentiment among Cuban nationalists.

The United States further advanced its interests in the Caribbean to include Puerto Rico, ceded by Spain, and eventually the Virgin Islands of St. Thomas and St. John, purchased from Denmark in 1917. The acquisition of Pacific territories, including Guam, marked the emergence of the United States as a global colonial power.

War in the Philippines

The Philippines, another of Spain's colonies, seemed an especially attractive prospect, its 7,000 islands a natural way station to the markets of mainland Asia. In 1897 Assistant Secretary of the Navy Theodore Roosevelt and President McKinley had discussed the merits of taking the Pacific colony in the event of war with Spain. At the first opportunity, McKinley acted to bring these islands into the U.S. strategic orbit. Shortly after Congress declared war on Spain, on May 4, the president dispatched 5,000 troops to occupy the Philippines. George Dewey, a Civil War veteran who commanded the American Asiatic Squadron, was ordered to "start offensive action." During the first week

Rebel Cubans, 1898, painted by Herbert Orth. Badly supplied Cuban insurrectos had practiced guerrilla warfare against the Spanish colonizers since the mid-1890s, but after the explosion on the USS Maine, American forces took over the war and abandoned the cause of Cuban self-determination. This picture, by the young U.S. volunteer, was one of a series of sketches later transformed into watercolor and oil paintings.

Courtesy of Mrs. Charles Johnson Post and Miss Phyllis B. Post.

of the conflict, he demolished the Spanish fleet in Manila Bay through seven hours of unimpeded target practice. Once the war ended, McKinley refused to sign the armistice unless Spain relinquished all claims to its Pacific islands. When Spain conceded, McKinley quickly drew up plans for colonial administration. He pledged "to educate the Filipinos, and to uplift and civilize and Christianize them." But after centuries of Spanish rule, the majority of islanders—already Christians—were eager to create their own nation.

The Filipino rebels, like the Cubans, at first welcomed American troops and fought with them against Spain. But when the war ended and they perceived that American troops were not preparing to leave, the rebels, led by Emilio Aguinaldo, turned against their former allies and attacked the American base of operations in Manila in February 1899. Predicting a brief skirmish, American commanders seriously underestimated the population's capacity to endure great suffering for the sake of independence.

U.S. troops had provoked this conflict in various ways. Military leaders, the majority veterans of the Indian wars, commonly described the natives as "gu-gus," and reported themselves, as one said, as "just itching to get at the niggers." While awaiting action, American soldiers repeatedly insulted or physically abused civilians, raped Filipino women, and otherwise whipped up resentment.

The resulting conflict took the form of modern guerrilla warfare, with brutalities on both sides. Instructed to regard every male Filipino over ten years of age as a potential enemy who could be shot without provocation, U.S. troops attacked civilians and destroyed their food, housing, and water supplies. Many American soldiers appeared indifferent to the sight of bloodshed. A. A. Barnes of the Third Regiment, describing the slaughter of 1,000 men, women, and children, wrote home, "I am probably growing hard-hearted, for I am in my glory when I can sight my gun on some dark-skin and pull the trigger." Ordered to take no prisoners, American soldiers forced Filipino civilians to dig their own graves and bragged about killing the wounded. By the time the fighting slowed down in 1902, 4,300 American lives had been lost, and one of every five Filipinos had died in battle or from starvation or disease. On some of the Philippine islands, intermittent fighting lasted until 1935.

The United States nevertheless refused to pull out. In 1901 William Howard Taft headed a commission that established a government controlled by Americans; after 1905, the president appointed a Filipino governor general to maintain the provincial government. Meanwhile, Americans bought up the best land and invested heavily in the island's sugar economy.

The conquest of the Philippines, which remained a U.S. territory until 1946, evoked for its defenders the vision of empire.

"Uncle Sam Teaches the Art of Self-Government," editorial cartoon, 1898. Expressing a popular sentiment of the time, a newspaper cartoonist shows the rebels as raucous children who constantly fight among themselves and need to be brought into line by Uncle Sam. The Filipino leader, Emilio Aguinaldo, appears as a dunce for failing to learn properly from the teacher. The two major islands where no uprising took place, Puerto Rico and Hawai'i, appear as passive but exotically dressed women, ready to learn their lessons.

Once again, Josiah Strong proclaimed judgment over an era. His famous treatise *Expansion* (1900) roundly defended American overseas involvements by carefully distinguishing between freedom and independence. People could achieve freedom, he argued, only under the rule of law. And because white Americans had proven themselves superior in the realm of government, they could best bring "freedom" to nonwhite peoples by setting aside the ideal of national independence for a period of enforced guidance. Many began to wonder, however, whether the United States could become an empire without sacrificing its democratic spirit, and to ask whether the subjugated people were so fortunate under the rule of the United States.

Critics of Empire

No mass movement formed to forestall U.S. expansion, but distinguished figures like Mark Twain, Andrew Carnegie, William Jennings Bryan, and Harvard philosopher William James voiced their opposition strongly. Dissent followed two broad lines of argument. In 1870, when President Grant urged the annexation of Santo Domingo, the nation-state occupying half of the island of Hispaniola (Haiti occupy-

CHRONOLOGY

1867	Grange founded Secretary of State Seward negotiates the purchase of Alaska
1874	Tompkins Square Riot Granger laws begin to regulate railroad shipping rates
1877	Rutherford B. Hayes elected president Great Uprising of 1877
1879	Henry George publishes *Progress and Poverty*
1881	President James A. Garfield assassinated; Chester A. Arthur becomes president
1883	Pendleton Act passed
1884	Grover Cleveland elected president
1887	Interstate Commerce Act creates the Interstate Commerce Commission
1888	Edward Bellamy publishes *Looking Backward* National Colored Farmers' Alliance and Cooperative Union formed Benjamin Harrison elected president
1889	National Farmers' Alliance and Industrial Union formed
1890	Sherman Silver Purchase Act McKinley tariff enacted National American Woman Suffrage Association formed
1891	National Women's Alliance formed Populist (People's) Party formed

1892	Coeur d'Alene miners' strike Homestead strike Ida B. Wells begins crusade against lynching
1893	Western Federation of Miners formed Financial panic and depression World's Columbian Exhibition opens in Chicago
1894	"Coxey's Army" marches on Washington, D. C. Pullman strike
1896	*Plessy v. Ferguson* upholds segregation William McKinley defeats William Jennings Bryan for president
1897	Dingley tariff again raises import duties to an all-time high
1898	Eugene V. Debs helps found Social Democratic Party Hawai'i is annexed Spanish-American War begins Anti-Imperialist League formed
1899	*Cumming v. Richmond County Board of Education* sanctions segregated education Secretary of State John Hay announces Open Door policy Guerrilla war begins in the Philippines
1900	Gold Standard Act Josiah Strong publishes *Expansion*

ing the other half), opponents countered by insisting that the United States stood unequivocally for the right of national self-determination and the consent of the governed. Others opposed annexation on the ground that dark-skinned and "ignorant" Santo Domingans were unworthy of American citizenship. These two contrary arguments, democratic and racist, were sounded repeatedly as the United States joined other nations in the armed struggle for empire.

Organized protest to military action, especially against the widely reported atrocities in the Philippines, owed much to the Anti-Imperialist League, which was founded by a small group of prominent Bostonians. In historic Faneuil Hall, which had witnessed the birth of both the American Revolution and the antislavery movement, a mass meeting was convened in June 1898 to protest the "insane and wicked ambition which is driving the nation to ruin." Within a few months, the league reported 25,000 members. Most supported American economic expansion but advocated free trade rather than political domination as the means to reach this goal. All strongly opposed the annexation of new territories. The league drew followers from every walk of life, including such famous writers as Charles Francis Adams and Mark Twain, *Nation* editor E. L. Godkin, African American scholar W.E.B. Du Bois, and Civil War veteran Thomas Wentworth Higginson.

The Anti-Imperialist League brought together like-minded societies from across the country, encouraged mass meetings, and published pamphlets, poems, and broadsides. *The National Labor Standard* expressed the common hope that all those "who believe in the Republic against Empire should join." By 1899, the league claimed a half-million members. A few outspoken anti-imperialists, such as former Illinois governor John Peter Altgeld, openly toasted Filipino rebels as heroes. Morrison Swift, leader of the Coxey's Army contingent from Massachusetts, formed a Filipino Liberation Society and sent antiwar materials to American troops. Others, such as Samuel Gompers, a league vice president, felt no sympathy for conquered peoples, describing Filipinos as "perhaps nearer the condition of savages and barbarians than any island possessed by any other civilized nation on earth." Gompers simply wanted to prevent colonized nonwhites from immigrating to the United States and "inundating" American labor.

Military leaders and staunch imperialists did not distinguish between racist and nonracist anti-imperialists. They called all dissenters "unhung traitors" and demanded their arrest. Newspaper editors accused universities of harboring antiwar professors, although college students as a group were enthusiastic supporters of the war.

Within the press, which overwhelmingly supported the Spanish-American War, the voices of opposition appeared primarily in African American and labor papers. The *Indianapolis Recorder* asked rhetorically in 1899, "Are the tender-hearted expansionists in the United States Congress really actuated by the desire to save the Filipinos from self-destruction or is it the worldly greed for gain?" The *Railroad Telegrapher* similarly commented, "The wonder of it all is that the working people are willing to lose blood and treasure in fighting another man's battle."

Most Americans put aside their doubts and welcomed the new era of aggressive nationalism. Untouched by the private tragedies of dead or wounded American soldiers and the mass destruction of civilian society in the Philippines, the vast majority could approve Theodore Roosevelt's defense of armed conflict: "No triumph of peace is quite so great as the supreme triumphs of war."

CONCLUSION

The conflicts marking the last quarter of the nineteenth century that pitted farmers, workers, and the proprietors of small businesses against powerful outside interests had offered Americans an important moment of democratic promise. By the end of the century, however, the rural and working-class campaigns to retain a large degree of self-government in their communities had been defeated, their organizations destroyed, their autonomy eroded. The rise of a national governing class and its counterpart, the large bureaucratic state, established new rules of behavior, new sources of prestige, and new rewards for the most successful citizens.

But the nation would pay a steep price, in the next era, for the failure of democratic reform. Regional antagonisms, nativist movements against the foreign-born, and above all deepening racial tensions blighted American society. As the new century opened, progressive reformers moved to correct flaws in government while accepting the framework of a corporate society and its overseas empire. But they found the widening divisions in American society difficult—if not impossible—to overcome.

REVIEW QUESTIONS

1. Discuss some of the problems accompanying the expansion of government during the late nineteenth century. What role did political parties play in this process? Explain how a prominent reformer such as James Garfield might become a leading "machine" politician?

2. What were the major causes and consequences of the populist movement of the 1880s and 1890s? Why did the election of 1896 prove so important to the future of American politics?

3. Discuss the role of women in both the Grange and the People's Party. What were their specific goals?

4. Discuss the causes and consequences of the financial crisis of the 1890s. How did various reformers and politicians respond to the event? What kinds of programs did they offer to restore the economy or reduce poverty?

5. How did the exclusion of African Americans affect the outcome of populism? Explain the rise of Jim Crow legislation in the South, and discuss its impact on the status of African Americans.

6. Describe American foreign policy during the 1890s. Why did the United States intervene in Cuba and the Philippines? What were some of the leading arguments for and against overseas expansion?

RECOMMENDED READING

Ruth Bordin, *Woman and Temperance: The Quest for Power and Liberty, 1873–1900* (1981). Relates the history of the WCTU to other campaigns for women's emancipation in the late nineteenth century and highlights the leadership of Frances E. Willard. Bordin demonstrates the central position temperance occupied in the political struggles of the era.

John G. Cawelti, *Apostles of the Self-Made Man* (1965). Examines the popular cultural obsession with the idea of success. Cawelti analyzes both the myths behind the notion of equal opportunity for all and the methods of popularizing success in the various media of the time.

Lawrence Goodwyn, *Democratic Promise: The Populist Moment in America* (1976). The most detailed study of populism, this book focuses on the economic cooperation and visionary schemes that preceded the populist electoral actions of the 1890s. Goodwin shows that populism was above all a movement aimed to turn back the monopolistic trend in the market economy and return power to the nation's citizens.

Lewis L. Gould, *The Presidency of William McKinley* (1980). A biography and political study of the president who represented a new kind of national leader in several key ways. Gould presents McKinley as product of "machine" politics but also an enlightened and modern administrator.

Michael Kazin, *The Populist Persuasion: An American History* (1995). A fresh interpretation of populist-style movements through the nineteenth and twentieth century that suggests such movements can be either "right" or "left" depending upon circumstances.

Walter LaFeber, *The New Empire: An Interpretation of American Expansion, 1860–1898* (1963). The best overview of U.S. imperial involvement in the late nineteenth century. LaFeber shows how overseas commitments grew out of the economic expansionist assumptions

of American leaders and expanded continuously, if often chaotically, with the opportunities presented by the crises experienced by the older imperial powers.

Nell Irvin Painter, *Standing at Armageddon: The United States, 1877–1919* (1987). Presents a broad overview of racial and industrial conflicts and the political movements that formed in their wake. Painter attempts to show how this period proved decisive to the future history of the United States.

Thomas C. Reeves, *Gentleman Boss: The Life of Chester Alan Arthur* (1975). A detailed treatment of President Arthur as a product of a particular stage in the American political system. Reeves analyzes the conflicts within the Republican Party and the chaos of the Democratic Party, which made Arthur's rise possible.

Emily S. Rosenberg, *Spreading the American Dream: American Economic and Cultural Expansion, 1890–1945* (1982). Insightfully examines the significance of expansionist ideology. Rosenberg studies the cultural and social roots of American foreign policy.

William Appleman Williams, *Empire as a Way of Life: An Essay on the Causes and Character of America's Present Predicament* (1982). A lucid general exploration of American views of empire. Williams shows that Americans allowed the idea of empire and, more generally, economic expansion, to dominate their concept of democracy, especially in the last half of the nineteenth century.

C. Vann Woodward, *The Strange Career of Jim Crow*, 3d rev. ed. (1974). The classic study of southern segregation. Woodward shows how racist laws and customs tightened in the South and in many parts of the North in the last decades of the nineteenth century and how the ideologies of southern society encouraged the rise of Jim Crow legislation.

ADDITIONAL BIBLIOGRAPHY

The Nation and Politics

Cindy Sondik Aron, *Ladies and Gentlemen of the Civil Service* (1987)

Paula C. Baker, *The Moral Frameworks of Public Life: Gender, Politics and the State in Rural New York, 1870–1930* (1991)

Michael Lewis Goldberg, *An Army of Women: Gender and Politics in Gilded Age Kansas* (1997)

Charles Hoffman, *The Depression of the Nineties* (1970)

Morton Keller, *Affairs of the State: Public Life in Late Nineteenth*

Century America (1977)

J. Morgan Kousser, *The Shaping of Southern Politics: Suffrage Restriction and the Establishment of a One Party South* (1974)

Gwendolyn Mink, *Old Labor and New Immigrants in American Political Development* (1986)

Homer E. Socolofsky and Allan B. Spetter, *The Presidency of Benjamin Harrison* (1987)

Tom E. Terrell, *The Tariff, Politics and American Foreign Policy, 1874–1901* (1973)

Richard E. Welch Jr., *The Presidencies of Grover Cleveland* (1988)

Populism

Steven Hahn, *The Roots of Southern Populism* (1983)

Robert C. McMath, *American Populism: A Social History* (1993)

Scott G. McNall, *The Road to Rebellion: Class Formation and Kansas Populism 1865–1900* (1988)

Theodore R. Mitchell, *Political Education in the Southern Farmers' Alliance, 1887–1900* (1987)

Norman Pollack, *The Human Economy: Populism, Capitalism and Democracy* (1990)

Protest and Reform Movements

Beverly Beeton, *Women Vote in the West: The Suffrage Movement, 1869–1896* (1986)

Paul Buhle, *From the Knights of Labor to the New World Order: Labor and Culture in America* (1996)

Susan Curtis, *A Consuming Faith: The Social Gospel and Modern American Culture* (1991)

Barbara Leslie Epstein, *The Politics of Domesticity: Women, Evangelism, and Temperance in Nineteenth-Century America* (1981)

Philip S. Foner, *The Great Labor Uprisings of 1877* (1977)

Paul Krause, *The Battle for Homestead, 1880–1892* (1992)

Ralph E. Luker, *The Social Gospel in Black and White* (1991)

Nina Mjagkij and Margaret Spratt, eds., *Men and Women Adrift: The YMCA and the YWCA in the City* (1997)

Carlos A. Schwantes, *Coxey's Army* (1985)

Sheldon Stromquist, *A Generation of Boomers: The Patterns of Railroad Labor Conflict in Nineteenth Century America* (1987)

Mary Martha Thomas, *The New Woman in Alabama: Social Reform and Suffrage, 1890–1920* (1992)

Imperialism and Empire

Robert L. Beisner, *Twelve against Empire: The Anti-Imperialists, 1898–1900* (1968)

Nupur Chauduri and Margaret Strobel, eds., *Western Women and Imperialism* (1992)

Willard B. Gatewood Jr., *Black Americans and the White Man's Burden* (1975)

David Healy, *Drive to Hegemony: The United States in the Caribbean, 1888–1917* (1988)

Patricia Hill, *The World Their Household: The American Women's Foreign Mission Movement and Cultural Transformation, 1870–1920* (1985)

Amy Kaplan and Donald E. Pease, eds., *Cultures of United States Imperialism* (1993)

Martin Ridge, ed., *History, Frontier and Section: Three Essays by Frederick Jackson Turner* (1993)

Robert W. Rydell, *All the World's a Fair: Vision of Empire at the American International Expositions, 1876–1916* (1984)

Anders Stephanson, *Manifest Destiny: American Expansion and the Empire of Right* (1995)

Rubin F. Weston, *Racism in American Imperialism* (1972)

Spanish-American War and the Philippines

H. W. Brands, *Bound to Empire: The United States and the Philippines* (1992)

Kenton Clymer, *Protestant Missionaries in the Philippines, 1898–1916* (1986)

Graham A. Cosmos, *An Army for Empire* (1971)

Glenn Anthony May, *Battle for Batangas: A Philippine Province at War* (1991)

———, *Social Engineering in the Philippines: The Aims, Execution, and Impact of American Colonial Policy, 1900–1913* (1980)

Stuart Creighton Miller, *"Benevolent Assimilation": The American Conquest of the Philippines, 1899–1903* (1982)

William J. Pomeroy, *Philippines: Colonialism, Collaboration, Resistance* (1992)

Winfred Lee Thompson, *The Introduction of American Law in the Philippines and Puerto Rico, 1889–1905* (1989)

David F. Trask, *The War with Spain in 1898* (1981)

Richard E. Welch, *Response to Imperialism: The United States and the Philippine-American War* (1979)

Biography

Ruth Bordin, *Frances Willard: A Biography* (1986)

Mari Jo Buhle, Paul Buhle, and Harvey J. Kaye, eds., *The American Radical* (1995)

Jane Taylor Nelson, *A Prairie Populist: The Memoirs of Luna Kellie* (1992)

Allan Peskin, *Garfield: A Biography* (1978)

Martin Ridge, *Ignatius Donnelly* (1962)

Nick Salvatore, *Eugene V. Debs* (1982)

Mildred Thompson, *Ida B. Wells-Barnett: An Exploratory Study of an American Black Woman* (1990)

C. Van Woodward, *Tom Watson* (1963)

CHAPTER TWENTY-ONE

URBAN AMERICA AND THE PROGRESSIVE ERA

1900–1917

AMERICAN COMMUNITIES
The Henry Street Settlement House: Women Settlement House Workers Create a Community of Reform

A shy and frightened young girl appeared in the doorway of a weekly home-nursing class for women on Manhattan's Lower East Side. The teacher beckoned her to come forward. Tugging on the teacher's skirt, the girl pleaded in broken English for the teacher to come home with her. "Mother," "baby," "blood," she kept repeating. The teacher gathered up the sheets that were part of the interrupted lesson in bed making. The two hurried through narrow, garbage-strewn, foul-smelling streets, then groped their way up a pitch-dark, rickety staircase. They reached a cramped, two-room apartment, home to an immigrant family of seven and several boarders. There, in a vermin-infested bed, encrusted with dried blood, lay a mother and her newborn baby. The mother had been abandoned by a doctor because she could not afford his fee.

The teacher, Lillian Wald, was a twenty-five-year-old nurse at New York Hospital. Years later she recalled this scene as her baptism by fire and the turning point in her life. Born in 1867, Wald enjoyed a comfortable upbringing in a middle-class German Jewish family in Rochester. Despite her parents' objections, she moved to New York City to become a professional nurse. Resentful of the disdainful treatment nurses received from doctors and horrified by the inhumane conditions at a juvenile asylum she worked in, Wald determined to find a way of caring for the sick in their neighborhoods and homes. With nursing school classmate Mary Brewster, Wald rented a fifth-floor walk-up apartment on the Lower East Side and established a visiting nurse service. The two provided professional care in the home to hundreds of families for a nominal fee of ten to twenty-five cents. They also offered each family they visited information on basic health care, sanitation, and disease prevention. In 1895, philanthropist Jacob Schiff generously donated a red brick Georgian house on Henry Street as a new base of operation.

The Henry Street Settlement stood in the center of perhaps the most overcrowded neighborhood in the world, New York's Lower East Side. Roughly 500,000 people were packed into an area only as large as a midsized Kansas farm. Population density was about 500 per acre, roughly four times the figure for the rest of New York City and far more concentrated than even the worst slums of London or Calcutta. A single city block might have as many as 3,000 residents. Home for most Lower East Siders was a small tenement apartment that might include paying boarders squeezed in alongside the immediate family. Residents were mostly recent immigrants from southern and eastern Europe: Jews, Italians, Germans, Greeks, Hungarians, Slavs. Men, women, and children toiled in the garment shops, small factories, retail stores, breweries, and warehouses to be found on nearly every street. An Irish-dominated machine controlled local political affairs.

The Henry Street Settlement became a model for a new kind of reform community composed essentially of college-educated women who encouraged and supported one another in a wide variety of humanitarian, civic, political, and cultural activities. Settlement house living arrangements closely resembled those in the dormitories of such new women's colleges as Smith, Wellesley, and Vassar. Like these colleges, the settlement house was an "experiment," but one designed, in settlement house pioneer Jane Addams's words, "to aid in the solution of the social and industrial problems which are engendered by the modern conditions of urban life." Unlike earlier moral reformers who tried to impose their ideas from outside, settlement house residents lived in poor communities and worked for immediate improvements in the health and welfare of those communities. Yet as Addams and others repeatedly stressed, the college-educated women were beneficiaries as well. The settlement house allowed them to preserve a collegial spirit, satisfy the desire for service, and apply their academic training.

With its combined moral and social appeal, the settlement house movement attracted many educated young women and grew rapidly. There were six settlement houses in the United States in 1891, 74 in 1897, more than 200 by 1900, and more than 400 by 1910. Few women made settlement work a career. The average stay was less than five years. Roughly half of those who worked in the movement eventually married. Those who did make a career of settlement house work, however, typically chose not to marry, and most lived together with female companions. As the movement flourished, settlement house residents called attention to the plight of the poor and fostered respect for different cultural heritages in countless articles and lectures. Leaders of the movement, including Jane Addams, Lillian Wald, and Florence Kelley, emerged as influential political figures during the progressive era.

Wald attracted a dedicated group of nurses, educators, and reformers to live at the Henry Street Settlement. By 1909 Henry Street had more than forty residents, supported by the donations of well-to-do New Yorkers. Wald and her allies convinced the New York Board of Health to assign a nurse to every public school in the city. They lobbied the Board of Education to create the first school lunch programs. They persuaded the city to set up municipal milk stations to ensure the purity of milk. Henry Street also pioneered tuberculosis treatment and prevention. Its leaders became powerful advocates for playground construction, improved street cleaning, and tougher housing inspection. The settlement's Neighborhood Playhouse became an internationally acclaimed center for innovative theater, music, and dance.

As settlement house workers expanded their influence from local neighborhoods to larger political and social circles, they became, in the phrase of one historian, spearheads for reform. Lillian Wald became a national figure—an outspoken advocate of child labor legislation and woman suffrage and a vigorous opponent of American involvement in World War I. She offered Henry Street as a meeting place to the National Negro Conference in 1909, out of which emerged the National Association for the Advancement of Colored People. It was no cliché for Wald to say, as she did on many occasions, "The whole world is my neighborhood."

New York City

KEY TOPICS

- The political, social, and intellectual roots of progressive reform

- Tensions between social justice and social control

- The urban scene and the impact of new immigration

- Political activism by the working class, women, and African Americans

- Progressivism in national politics

THE CURRENTS OF PROGRESSIVISM

Between the 1890s and World War I, a large and diverse number of Americans claimed the political label "progressive." Progressives could be found in all classes, regions, and races. They shared a fundamental ethos, or belief, that America needed a new social consciousness to cope with the problems brought on by the enormous rush of economic and social change in the post–Civil War decades. Yet progressivism was no unified movement with a single set of principles. It is best understood as a varied collection of reform communities, often fleeting, uniting citizens in a host of political, professional, and religious organizations, some of which were national in scope.

Progressivism drew from deep roots in hundreds of local American communities. At the state level it flowered in the soil of several key issues: ending political corruption, bringing more businesslike methods to governing, and offering a more compassionate legislative response to the excesses of industrialism. As a national movement, progressivism reached its peak in 1912, when the four major presidential candidates all ran on some version of a progressive platform. This last development was an important measure of the extent to which local reform movements like the Henry Street Settlement and new intellectual currents had captured the political imagination of the nation.

The many contradictions and disagreements surrounding the meaning of progressivism have led some historians to dismiss the term as hopelessly vague. Some progressives focused on expanding state and federal regulation of private interests for the public welfare. Others viewed the rapid influx of new immigrants and the explosive growth of large cities as requiring more stringent social controls. Another variant emphasized eliminating corruption in the political system as the key to righting society's wrongs. In the South, progressivism was for white people only. Progressives could be forward looking in their vision or nostalgic for a nineteenth-century world rapidly disappearing. Self-styled progressives often found themselves facing each other from opposite sides of an issue.

Yet at the local, state, and finally national levels, reform rhetoric and energy shaped most of the political and cultural debates of the era. Understanding progressivism in all its complexity thus requires examining what key reform groups, thinkers, and political figures actually did and said under its ambiguous banner.

Unifying Themes

Three basic attitudes underlay the various crusades and movements that emerged in response to the fears gnawing at large segments of the population. The first was anger over the excesses of industrial capitalism and urban growth. At the same time, progressives shared an essential optimism about the ability of citizens to improve social and economic conditions. They were reformers, not revolutionaries. Second, progressives emphasized social cohesion and common bonds as a way of understanding how modern society and economics actually worked. They largely rejected the ideal of individualism that had informed nineteenth-century economic and political theory. For progressives, poverty and success hinged on more than simply individual character; the economy was more than merely a sum of individual calculations. Progressives thus opposed social Darwinism, with its claim that any effort to improve social conditions would prove fruitless because society is like a jungle in which only the "fittest" survive. Third, progressives believed in the need for citizens to intervene actively, both politically and morally, to improve social conditions. They pushed for a stronger government role in regulating the economy and solving the nation's social problems.

Progressive rhetoric and methods drew on two distinct sources of inspiration. One was evangelical Protestantism, particularly the late-nineteenth-century social gospel movement. Social gospelers rejected the idea of original sin as the cause of human suffering. They emphasized both the capacity and the duty of Christians to purge the world of poverty, inequality, and economic greed. A second strain of progressive

OVERVIEW

CURRENTS OF PROGRESSIVISM

	Key Figures	Issues	Institutions/Achievements
Local Communities	Jane Addams, Lillian Wald, Florence Kelley, Frederic C. Howe, Samuel Jones	• Improving health, education, welfare in urban immigrant neighborhoods • Child labor, eight-hour day • Celebrating immigrant cultures • Reforming urban politics • Municipal ownership/regulation of utilities	• Hull House Settlement • Henry Street Settlement • National Consumers League • New York Child Labor Committee • Bureau of Municipal Research
State	Robert M. LaFollette, Hiram Johnson, Al Smith	• Limiting power of railroads, other corporations • Improving civil service • Direct democracy • Applying academic scholarship to human needs	• "Wisconsin Idea" • State Workmen's Compensation • Unemployment Insurance • Public utility regulation
	James K. Vardaman, Hoke Smith	• Disfranchisement of African Americans	• Legalized segregation
National	Theodore Roosevelt	• Trustbusting • Conservation and Western development • National regulation of corporate and financial excesses	• Reclamation Bureau (1902) • U.S. Forest Service (1905) • Food and Drug Administration (1906) • Meat Inspection Act (1906) • Hepburn Act–ICC (1906)
	Woodrow Wilson	• National regulation of corporate and financial excesses • Reform of national banking	• Graduated Income Tax (1913) • Federal Reserve Act (1913) • Clayton Antitrust Act (1914) • Federal Trade Commission (1914)
Intellectual/ Cultural	Jacob Riis	• Muckraking	• *How the Other Half Lives* (1890)
	Lincoln Steffens, Ida Tarbell, Upton Sinclair, S.S. McClure		• *Shame of the Cities* (1902) • *History of Standard Oil* (1904) • *The Jungle* (1906) • *McClure's Magazine*
	John Dewey	• Education reform	• *Democracy and Education* (1916)
	Louis Brandeis	• Sociological jurisprudence	• *Muller v. Oregon* (1908)
	Edwin A. Ross	• Empowering "ethical elite"	• *Social Control* (1901)

Courtesy George Eastman House

Lewis Hine took this photo of a young girl working on a thread spinning frame in a North Carolina cotton mill. Between 1908 and 1918 Hine worked for the National Child Labor Committee, documenting the widespread abuse of child labor in the nation's mills, factories, mines, and canneries. "These pictures," Hine wrote, "speak for themselves and prove that the law is being violated."

thought looked to natural and social scientists to develop rational measures for improving the human condition, believing that experts trained in statistical analysis and engineering could make government and industry more efficient. Progressivism thus offered an uneasy combination of social justice and social control, a tension that would characterize American reform for the rest of the twentieth century.

Women Spearhead Reform

In the 1890s the settlement house movement had begun to provide an alternative to traditional concepts of private charity and humanitarian reform. Settlement workers found they could not transform their neighborhoods without confronting a host of broad social questions: chronic poverty, overcrowded tenement houses, child labor, industrial accidents, public health. As on Henry Street, college-educated, middle-class women constituted a key vanguard in the crusade for social justice. As reform communities, settlement houses soon

discovered the need to engage the political and cultural life of the larger communities that surrounded them.

Jane Addams founded one of the first settlement houses, Hull House, in Chicago in 1889 after years of struggling to find work and a social identity equal to her talents. A member of one of the first generation of American women to attend college, Addams was a graduate of Rockford College. Many educated women were dissatisfied with the life choices conventionally available to them: early marriage or the traditional female professions of teaching, nursing, and library work. Settlement work provided these women with an attractive alternative. Hull House was located in a run-down slum area of Chicago. It had a day nursery, a dispensary for medicines and medical advice, a boardinghouse, an art gallery, and a music school. Addams often spoke of the "subjective necessity" of settlement houses. By this she meant that they gave young, educated women a way to satisfy their powerful desire to connect with the real world. "There is nothing after disease, indigence and guilt," she wrote, "so fatal to life itself as the want of a proper outlet for active faculties."

Social reformer Florence Kelley helped direct the support of the settlement house movement behind groundbreaking state and federal labor legislation. Arriving at Hull House in 1891, Kelley found what she described as a "colony of efficient and intelligent women." In 1893, she wrote a report detailing the dismal conditions in sweatshops and the effects of long hours on the women and children who worked in them. This report became the basis for landmark legislation in Illinois that limited women to an eight-hour workday, barred children under fourteen from working, and abolished tenement labor. Illinois governor John Peter Altgeld appointed Kelley as chief inspector for the new law. In 1895 Kelley published *Hull House Maps and Papers*, the first scientific study of urban poverty in America. Moving to Henry Street Settlement in 1898, Kelley served as general secretary of the new National Consumers' League. With Lillian Wald she established the New York Child Labor Committee and pushed for the creation of the U.S. Children's Bureau, established in 1912.

Kelley, Addams, Wald, and their circle consciously used their power as women to reshape politics in the progressive era. Electoral politics and the state were historically male preserves, but female social progressives turned their gender into an advantage. They built upon the tradition of female moral reform, where women had long operated outside male-dominated political institutions to agitate and organize. Activists like Kelley used their influence in civil society to create new state powers in the service of social justice. They left a legacy that simultaneously expanded the social welfare function of the state and increased women's public authority and influence.

The Urban Machine

Women had to work outside existing political institutions not just because they could not vote, but also because city politics had become a closed and often corrupt system. By the turn of the century Democratic Party machines, usually dominated by first- and second-generation Irish, controlled the political life of most large American cities. The keys to machine strength were disciplined organization and the delivery of essential services to both immigrant communities and business elites. The successful machine politician viewed his work as a business, and he accumulated his capital by serving people who needed assistance. For most urban dwellers, the city was a place of economic and social insecurity. Recent immigrants in particular faced frequent unemployment, sickness, and discrimination. In exchange for votes, machine politicians offered their constituents a variety of services. These included munic-

ipal jobs in the police and fire departments, work at city construction sites, intervention with legal problems, and food and coal during hard times.

For those who did business with the city—construction companies, road builders, realtors—staying on the machine's good side was simply another business expense. In exchange for valuable franchises and city contracts, businessmen routinely bribed machine politicians and contributed liberally to their campaign funds. George Washington Plunkitt, a stalwart of New York's Tammany Hall machine, good-naturedly defended what he called "honest graft": making money from inside information on public improvements. "It's just like lookin' ahead in Wall Street or in the coffee or cotton market. . . . I seen my opportunities and I took 'em."

The machines usually had close ties to a city's vice economy and commercial entertainments. Organized prostitution and gambling, patronized largely by visitors to the city, could flourish only when "protected" by politicians who shared in the profits. Many machine figures began as saloonkeepers, and liquor dealers and beer brewers provided important financial support for "the organization." Vaudeville and burlesque theaters, boxing, horse racing, and professional baseball were other urban enterprises with economic and political links to machines. Entertainment and spectacle made up a central element in the machine political style as well. Constituents looked forward to the colorful torchlight parades, free summer picnics, and riverboat excursions regularly sponsored by the machines.

On New York City's Lower East Side, where the Henry Street Settlement was located, Timothy D. "Big Tim" Sullivan embodied the popular machine style. Big Tim, who had risen from desperate poverty, remained enormously popular with his constituents until his death in 1913. "I believe in liberality," he declared. "I am a thorough New Yorker and have no narrow prejudices. I never ask a hungry man about his past; I feed him, not because he is good, but because he needs food. Help your neighbor but

This *publicity photograph of neighborhood children taking an art class at the Henry Street Settlement, New York City, around 1910, suggested that cultural pursuits and learning could flourish in slum neighborhoods with the help of a settlement house.*

keep your nose out of his affairs." Critics charged that Sullivan controlled the city's gambling and made money from prostitution. But his real fortune came through his investments in vaudeville and the early movie business. Sullivan, whose district included the largest number of immigrants and transients in the city, provided shoe giveaways and free Christmas dinners to thousands every winter. To help pay for these and other charitable activities, he informally taxed the saloons, theaters, and restaurants in the district.

Progressive critics of machine politics routinely exaggerated the machine's power and influence. State legislatures, controlled by Republican rural and small-town elements, proved a formidable check on what city-based machines could accomplish. Reform campaigns that publicized excessive graft and corruption sometimes led voters to throw machine-backed mayors and aldermen out of office. And there were never enough patronage jobs for all the people clamoring for appointments. In the early twentieth century, to expand their base of support, political machines in the Northeast began concentrating more on passing welfare legislation beneficial to working-class and immigrant constituencies. In this way machine politicians often allied themselves with progressive reformers in state legislatures. In New York, for example, Tammany Hall figures such as Robert Wagner, Al Smith, and Big Tim Sullivan worked with middle-class progressive groups to pass child labor laws, factory safety regulations, worker compensation plans, and other efforts to make government more responsive to social needs. As Jewish and Catholic immigrants expanded in number and proportion in the city population, urban machines also began to champion cultural pluralism, opposing prohibition and immigration restrictions and defending the contributions made by new ethnic groups in the cities.

Political Progressives and Urban Reform

Political progressivism originated in the cities. It was both a challenge to the power of machine politics and a response to deteriorating urban conditions. City governments, especially in the Northeast and industrial Midwest, seemed hardly capable of providing the basic services needed to sustain large populations. For example, an impure water supply left Pittsburgh with one of the world's highest rates of death from typhoid, dysentery, and cholera. Most New York City neighborhoods rarely enjoyed street cleaning, and playgrounds were nonexistent. "The challenge of the city," Cleveland progressive Frederic C. Howe said in 1906, "has become one of decent human existence."

Reformers placed much of the blame for urban ills on the machines and looked for ways to restructure city government. The "good government" movement, led by the National Municipal League, fought to make city management a nonpartisan, even nonpolitical, process by bringing the administrative techniques of large corporations to cities. Reformers revised city charters in favor of stronger mayoral power and expanded use of appointed administrators and career civil servants. The New York Bureau of Municipal Research, founded in 1906, became a prototype for similar bureaus around the country. It drew up blueprints for model charters, ordinances, and zoning plans designed by experts trained in public administration.

Business and professional elites became the biggest boosters of structural reforms in urban government. In the summer of 1900 a hurricane in the Gulf of Mexico unleashed a tidal wave on Galveston, Texas. To cope with this disaster, leading businessmen convinced the state legislature to replace the mayor-council government with a small board of commissioners. Each commissioner was elected at large, and each was responsible for a different city department. Under this plan voters could more easily identify and hold accountable those responsible for city services. The city commission, enjoying both policy-making and administrative powers, proved very effective in rebuilding Galveston. By 1917 nearly 500 cities, including Houston, Oakland, Kansas City, Denver, and Buffalo, had adopted the commission form of government. Another approach, the city manager plan, gained popularity in small and midsized cities. In this system, a city council appointed a professional, nonpartisan city manager to handle the day-to-day operations of the community.

Progressive politicians who focused on the human problems of the industrial city championed a different kind of reform, one based on changing policies rather than the political structure. In Toledo, Samuel "Golden Rule" Jones served as mayor from 1897 to 1904. A capitalist who had made a fortune manufacturing oil well machinery, Jones created a strong base of working-class and ethnic voters around his reform program. He advocated municipal ownership of utilities, built new parks and schools, and established an eight-hour day and a minimum wage for city employees. In Cleveland, wealthy businessman Thomas L. Johnson served as mayor from 1901 to 1909. He emphasized both efficiency and social welfare. His popular program included lower streetcar fares, public baths, milk and meat inspection, and an expanded park and playground system.

Progressivism in the Statehouse

Their motives and achievements were mixed, but progressive politicians became a powerful force in many state capitals. In Wisconsin, Republican dissident Robert M. La Follette forged a coalition of angry farmers, small businessmen, and workers with his fiery attacks on railroads and other large corporations. Leader of the progressive faction of the state Republicans, "Fighting Bob" won three terms as governor (1900–1906), then served as a U.S. senator until his death in 1925. As governor he pushed through tougher corporate tax rates, a direct primary, an improved civil service code, and a railroad commission designed to regulate freight charges. La Follette used faculty experts at the University of Wisconsin to help research and write his bills. Other states began copying the "Wisconsin Idea"—the application of academic scholarship and theory to the needs of the people.

La Follette railed against "the interests" and invoked the power of the ordinary citizen. In practice, however, his railroad commission accomplished far less than progressive rhetoric claimed. It essentially represented special interests—commercial farmers and businessmen seeking reduced shipping rates. Ordinary consumers did not see lower passenger fares or reduced food prices. And as commissioners began to realize, the national reach of the railroads limited the effectiveness of state regulation. Although La Follette championed a more open political system, he also enrolled state employees in a tight political machine of his own. The La Follette family would dominate Wisconsin politics for forty years.

Western progressives displayed the greatest enthusiasm for institutional political reform. In the early 1900s, Oregon voters approved a series of constitutional amendments designed to strengthen direct democracy. The two most important were the initiative, which allowed a direct vote on specific measures put on the state ballot by petition, and the referendum, which allowed voters to decide on bills referred to them by the legislature. Other reforms included the direct primary, which allowed voters to cross party lines, and the recall, which gave voters the right to remove elected officials by popular vote. Widely copied throughout the West, all these measures intentionally weakened political parties.

Western progressives also targeted railroads, mining and timber companies, and public utilities for reform. Large corporations such as Pacific Gas and Electric and the Southern Pacific Railroad had amassed enormous wealth and political influence. They were able to corrupt state legislatures and charge consumers exorbitant rates. An alliance between middle-class progressives and working-class voters reflected growing disillusionment with the ideology of individualism that had helped pave the way for the rise of the big corporation. In California, attorney Hiram Johnson won a 1910 progressive campaign for governor on the slogan "Kick the Southern Pacific Railroad Out of Politics." In addition to

winning political reforms, Johnson also put through laws regulating utilities and child labor, mandating an eight-hour day for working women, and providing a state worker compensation plan.

In the South, reform governors, such as James Vardaman of Mississippi and Hoke Smith of Georgia, often drew on the agrarian program and flamboyant oratory of populism. But southern progressives were typically city professionals or businessmen rather than farmers. Like their northern and western counterparts, they focused their attention on strengthening state regulation of railroads and public utilities, improving educational facilities, reforming city governments, and reining in the power of large corporations.

While southern populism had been based in part on a biracial politics of protest, southern progressivism was for white people only. A strident racism accompanied most reform campaigns against entrenched conservative Democratic machines, reinforcing racial discrimination and segregation. Southern progressives supported black disfranchisement as an electoral reform. With African Americans removed from political life, they argued, the direct primary system of nominating candidates would give white voters more influence. Between 1890 and 1910 southern states passed a welter of statutes specifying poll taxes, literacy tests, and property qualifications with the explicit goal of preventing voting by blacks. This systematic disfranchisement of African American voters stripped black communities of any political power. To prevent the disfranchisement of poor white voters under these laws, states established so-called understanding and grandfather clauses. Election officials had discretionary power to decide whether an illiterate person could understand and reasonably interpret the Constitution when read to him. Unqualified white men were also registered if they could show that their grandfathers had voted.

Southern progressives also supported the push toward a fully segregated public sphere. Between 1900 and 1910 southern states strengthened laws requiring separation of races in restaurants, streetcars, beaches, and theaters. Schools were separate but hardly equal. A 1916 Bureau of Education study found that per capita expenditures for education in southern states averaged $10.32 a year for white children and $2.89 for black children. And African American teachers received far lower salaries than their white counterparts. The legacy of southern progressivism was thus closely linked to the strengthening of the legal and institutional guarantees of white supremacy.

New Journalism: Muckraking

Changes in journalism helped fuel a new reform consciousness by drawing the attention of millions to urban poverty, political corruption, the plight of industrial workers, and immoral business practices. As early as 1890, journalist Jacob Riis had shocked the nation with his landmark book *How the Other Half Lives*, a portrait of New York City's poor. A Danish immigrant who arrived in New York City in 1871, Riis became a newspaper reporter, covering the police beat and learning about the city's desperate underside. Riis's book included a remarkable series of photographs he had taken in tenements, lodging houses, sweatshops, and saloons. These striking pictures, combined with Riis's analysis of slum housing patterns, had a powerful impact on a whole generation of urban reformers.

Within a few years, magazine journalists had turned to uncovering the seamier side of American life. The key innovator was S. S. McClure, a young Midwestern editor who in 1893 started America's first large-circulation magazine, *McClure's*. Charging only a dime for his monthly, McClure effectively combined popular fiction with articles on science, technology, travel, and recent history. He attracted a new readership among the urban middle class through aggressive subscription and promotional campaigns, as well as newsstand sales. By the turn of the century *McClure's* and several imitators—*Munsey's, Cosmopolitan, Collier's, Everybody's,* and the *Saturday Evening Post*—had circulations in the hundreds of thousands. Making extensive use of photographs and illustrations, these cheap upstarts soon far surpassed older, more staid and expensive magazines such as the *Atlantic Monthly* and *Harper's* in circulation.

In 1902 McClure began hiring talented reporters to write detailed accounts of the nation's social problems. Lincoln Steffens's series *The Shame of the Cities* (1902) revealed the widespread graft at the center of American urban politics. He showed how big-city bosses routinely worked hand in glove with businessmen seeking lucrative municipal contracts for gas, water, electricity, and mass transit. Ida Tarbell, in her *History of the Standard Oil Company* (1904), thoroughly documented how John D. Rockefeller ruthlessly squeezed out competitors with unfair business practices. Ray Stannard Baker wrote detailed portraits of life and labor in Pennsylvania coal towns.

McClure's and other magazines discovered that "exposure journalism" paid off handsomely in terms of increased circulation. The middle-class public responded to this new combination of factual reporting and moral exhortation. A series such as Steffens's fueled reform campaigns that swept individual communities. Between 1902 and 1908, magazines were full of articles exposing insurance scandals, patent medicine frauds, and stock market swindles. Upton Sinclair's 1906 novel *The Jungle*, a socialist tract set among Chicago packinghouse workers, exposed the filthy sanitation and abysmal working conditions in the stockyards and the meatpacking industry. In an effort to boost sales, Sinclair's publisher devoted an entire issue of a monthly magazine it owned, *World's Work*, to articles and photographs that substantiated Sinclair's devastating portrait.

In 1906, David Graham Phillips, in a series for *Cosmopolitan* called "The Treason of the Senate," argued that many conservative U.S. senators were no more than mouthpieces for big business. President Theodore Roosevelt, upset by Phillips's attack on several of his friends and supporters, coined a new term when he angrily denounced Phillips and his colleagues as "muckrakers" who "raked the mud of society and never looked up." Partly due to Roosevelt's outburst, the muckraking vogue began to wane. By 1907, S. S. McClure's original team of reporters had broken up.

In his landmark book, How the Other Half Lives *(1890), Jacob Riis made innovative use of photographs and statistics to argue for housing reform. This photograph depicts an Italian immigrant family of seven living in a one-room apartment. Overcrowded and dilapidated tenements threatened the entire city "because they are the hot-beds of the epidemics that carry death to the rich and poor alike; the nurseries of pauperism and crime that fill our jails and police courts."*

But muckraking had demonstrated the powerful potential for mobilizing public opinion on a national scale. Reform campaigns need not be limited to the local community. Ultimately, they could engage a national community of informed citizens.

Intellectual Trends Promoting Reform

On a deeper level than muckraking, a host of early-twentieth-century thinkers challenged several of the core ideas in American intellectual life. Their new theories of education, law, economics, and society provided effective tools for reformers. The emergent fields of the social sciences—sociology, psychology, anthropology, and economics—emphasized empirical observation of how people actually lived and behaved in their communities. Progressive reformers linked the systematic analysis of society and the individual characteristic of these new fields of inquiry to the project of improving the material conditions of American society. In doing so they called on the academy for something it had never before been asked to provide—practical help in facing the unprecedented challenges of rapid industrialization and urbanization.

Sociologist Lester Frank Ward, in his pioneering work *Dynamic Sociology* (1883), offered an important critique of social Darwinism, the then orthodox theory that attributed social inequality to natural selection and the "survival of the fittest." Ward argued that the conservative social theorists responsible for social Darwinism, such as Herbert Spencer and William Graham Sumner, had wrongly applied evolutionary theory to human affairs. They had confused organic evolution with social evolution. Nature's method was genetic: unplanned, involuntary, automatic, and mechanical. An octopus had to lay 50,000 eggs to maintain itself; a codfish hatched a million young fish a year in order that two might survive. By contrast, civilization had been built on successful human intervention in the natural processes of organic evolution. The human method was telic: planned, voluntary, rational, dynamic. "Every implement or utensil," Ward argued, "every mechanical device, every object of design, skill, and labor, every artificial thing that serves a human purpose, is a triumph of mind over the physical forces of nature in ceaseless and aimless competition."

Philosopher John Dewey criticized the excessively rigid and formal approach to education found in most American schools. In books such as *The School and Society* (1899) and *Democracy and Education* (1916), Dewey advocated developing what he called "creative intelligence" in students, which could then be put to use in improving society. Schools ought to be "embryonic communities," miniatures of society, where children were encouraged to participate actively in different types of experiences. By cultivating imagination and openness to new experiences, schools could develop creativity and the habits required for systematic inquiry. Dewey placed excessive faith in the power of schools to promote community spirit and democratic values. But his belief that education was the "fundamental method of social progress and reform" inspired generations of progressive educators.

At the University of Wisconsin, John R. Commons founded the new field of industrial relations and organized a state industrial commission that became a model for other states. Working closely with Governor Robert M. La Follette, Commons and his students helped draft pioneering laws in worker compensation and public utility regulation. Another Wisconsin faculty member, economist Richard Ely, argued that the state was "an educational and ethical agency whose positive aim is an indispensable condition of human progress." Ely believed the state must directly intervene to help solve public problems. He rejected the doctrine of laissez faire as merely "a tool in the hands of the greedy." Like Commons, Ely worked with Wisconsin lawmakers, applying his expertise in economics to reforming the state's labor laws.

Progressive legal theorists began challenging the conservative view of constitutional law that had dominated American courts. Since the 1870s the Supreme Court had interpreted the Fourteenth Amendment (1868) as a guarantee of broad rights for corporations. That amendment, which prevented states from depriving "any person of life, liberty, or property, without due process of law," had been designed to protect the civil rights of African Americans against violations by the states. But the Court, led by Justice Stephen J. Field, used the due process clause to strike down state laws regulating business and labor conditions. The Supreme Court and state courts had thus made the Fourteenth Amendment a bulwark for big business and a foe of social welfare measures.

The most important dissenter from this view was Oliver Wendell Holmes Jr. A scholar and Massachusetts judge, Holmes believed the law had to take into account changing social conditions. And courts should take care not to invalidate social legislation enacted democratically. After his appointment to the Supreme Court in 1902, Holmes authored a number of notable dissents to conservative court decisions overturning progressive legislation. Criticizing the majority opinion in *Lochner v. New York* (1905), in which the Court struck down a state law setting a ten-hour day for bakers, Holmes insisted that the Constitution "is not intended to embody a particular theory."

Holmes's pragmatic views of the law seldom convinced a majority of the Supreme Court before the late 1930s. But his views influenced a generation of lawyers who began practicing what came to be called sociological jurisprudence. In *Muller v. Oregon* (1908), the Court upheld an Oregon law limiting the maximum hours for working women. Noting that "woman's physical structure and the performance of maternal functions place her at a disadvantage," the Court found that "the physical well-being of woman becomes an object of public interest and care." Louis Brandeis, the state's attorney, amassed statistical, sociological, and economic data, rather than traditional legal arguments, to support his arguments. The "Brandeis Brief" became a common strategy for lawyers defending the constitutionality of progressive legislation.

The new field of American sociology concentrated on the rapidly changing nature of community. German social theorist Ferdinand Tönnies developed an extremely influential model for describing the recent evolution of western society from *Gemeinschaft* to *Gesellschaft*: from a static, close-knit, morally unified community to a dynamic, impersonal, morally fragmented society. If the new urban-industrial order had weakened traditional sources of morality and values—the family, the church, the small community—then where would the mass of people now learn these values?

This question provided the focus for Edward A. Ross's landmark work *Social Control* (1901), a book whose title became a key phrase in progressive thought. Ross argued that society needed an "ethical elite" of citizens "who have at heart the general welfare and know what kinds of conduct will promote this welfare." The "surplus moral energy" of this elite— ministers, educators, professionals—would have to guide the new mechanisms of social control needed in America's *Gesellschaft* communities.

SOCIAL CONTROL AND ITS LIMITS

Many middle- and upper-class Protestant progressives feared that immigrants and large cities threatened the stability of American democracy. They worried that alien cultural practices were disrupting what they viewed as traditional American morality. Viewing themselves as part of what sociologist Edward Ross called the "ethical elite," progressives often believed they had a mission to frame laws and regulations for the social control of immigrants, industrial workers, and African Americans. This was the moralistic and frequently xenophobic side of progressivism, and it provided a powerful source of support for the regulation of drinking, prostitution, leisure activities, and schooling. Organizations devoted to social control constituted other versions of reform communities. But these attempts at moral reform met with mixed success amid the extraordinary cultural and ethnic diversity of America's cities.

The more extreme proponents of these views also embraced the new pseudo-science of eugenics, based on the biological theories of the English scientist Francis Galton. Eugenicists stressed the primacy of inherited traits over environmental conditions for understanding human abilities and deficiencies. They argued that human society could be bettered only by breeding from the best stock and limiting the offspring of the worst. By the 1920s, these theories had gained enough influence to contribute to the drastic curtailing of immigration to America (see Chapter 23).

The Prohibition Movement

During the last two decades of the nineteenth century, the Woman's Christian Temperance Union had grown into a powerful mass organization. The WCTU appealed especially to women angered by men who used alcohol and then abused their wives and children. It directed most of its work toward ending the production, sale, and consumption of alcohol. But local WCTU chapters put their energy into nontemperance activities as well, including homeless shelters, Sunday schools, prison reform, child nurseries, and woman suffrage. The WCTU thus provided women with a political forum in which they could fuse their traditional moral posture as guardians of the home with broader public concerns. By 1911 the WCTU, with a quarter million members, was the largest women's organization in American history.

Other temperance groups had a narrower focus. The Anti-Saloon League, founded in 1893, began by organizing local-option campaigns in which rural counties and small towns banned liquor within their geographical limits. It drew much of its financial support from local businessmen, who saw a link between closing a community's saloons and increasing the productivity of workers. The league was a one-issue pressure group that played effectively on anti-urban and anti-immigrant prejudice. League lobbyists targeted state legislatures, where big cities were usually underrepresented. They hammered away at the close connections among saloon culture, liquor dealers, brewers, and big-city political machines.

The prohibition movement found its core strength among Protestant, native-born, small-town, and rural Americans. But prohibition found support as well in the cities, where the battle to ban alcohol revealed deep ethnic and cultural divides within America's urban communities. Opponents of alcohol were generally "pietists" who viewed the world from a position of moral absolutism. These included native-born, middle-class Protestants associated with evangelical churches along with some old-stock Protestant immigrant denominations. Opponents of prohibition were generally "ritualists" with less arbitrary notions of personal morality. These were largely new-stock, working-class Catholic and Jewish immigrants, along with some Protestants, such as German Lutherans.

The Social Evil

Many of the same reformers who battled the saloon and drinking also engaged in efforts to eradicate prostitution. Crusades against "the social evil" had appeared at intervals throughout the nineteenth century. But they reached a new level of intensity between 1895 and 1920. In part, this new sense of urgency stemmed from the sheer growth of cities and the greater visibility of prostitution in red-light districts and neighborhoods. Antiprostitution campaigns epitomized the diverse makeup and mixed motives of so much progressive reform. Male business and civic leaders joined forces with feminists, social workers, and clergy to eradicate "commercialized vice."

Between 1908 and 1914 exposés of the "white slave traffic" became a national sensation. Dozens of books, articles, and motion pictures alleged an international conspiracy to seduce and sell girls into prostitution. Most of these materials exaggerated the practices they attacked. They also made foreigners, especially Jews and southern Europeans, scapegoats for the sexual anxieties of native-born whites. In 1910 Congress passed legislation that permitted the deportation of foreign-born prostitutes or any foreigner convicted of procuring or employing them. That same year, the Mann Act made it a federal offense to transport women across state lines for "immoral purposes."

But most antiprostitution activity took place at the local level. Between 1910 and 1915, thirty-five cities and states conducted thorough investigations of prostitution. The progressive bent for defining social problems through statistics was nowhere more evident than in these reports. Vice commission investigators combed red-light districts, tenement houses, hotels, and dance halls, drawing up detailed lists of places where prostitution took place. They interviewed prostitutes, pimps, and customers. These reports agreed that commercialized sex was a business run by and for the profit and pleasure of men. They also documented the dangers of venereal disease to the larger community. The highly publicized vice reports were effective in forcing police crackdowns in urban red-light districts.

Reformers had trouble believing that any woman would freely choose to be a prostitute; such a choice was antithetical to conventional notions of female purity and sexuality. But for wage-earning women, prostitution was a rational choice in a world of limited opportunities. Maimie Pinzer, a prostitute, summed up her feelings in a letter to a wealthy female reformer: "I don't propose to get up at 6:30 to be at work at 8 and work in a close, stuffy room with people I despise, until dark, for $6 or $7 a week! When I could, just by phoning, spend an afternoon with some congenial person and in the end have more than a week's work could pay me." The antivice crusades succeeded in closing down many urban red-light districts and larger brothels, but these were replaced by the streetwalker and call girl, who were more vulnerable to harassment and control by policemen and pimps. Rather than eliminating prostitution, reform efforts transformed the organization of the sex trade.

The Redemption of Leisure

Progressives faced a thorny issue in the growing popularity of commercial entertainment. For large numbers of working-class adults and children, leisure meant time and money spent at vaudeville and burlesque theaters, amusement parks, dance halls, and motion picture houses. These competed with municipal parks, libraries, museums, YMCAs, and school recreation centers. For many cultural traditionalists, the flood of new urban commercial amusements posed a grave threat. As with prostitution, urban progressives sponsored a host of recreation and amusement surveys detailing the situation in their individual cities. "Commercialized leisure," warned Frederic C. Howe in 1914, "must be controlled by the community, if it is to become an agency of civilization rather than the reverse."

By 1908 movies had become the most popular form of cheap entertainment in America. One survey estimated that 11,500 movie theaters attracted 5 million patrons each day. For five or ten cents "nickelodeon" theaters offered programs that might include a slapstick comedy, a Western, a travelogue, and a melodrama. Early movies were most popular in the tenement and immigrant districts of big cities, and with children. As the films themselves became more sophisticated and as "movie palaces" began to replace cheap storefront theaters, the new medium attracted a large middle-class clientele as well.

Progressive reformers seized the chance to help regulate the new medium as a way of improving the commercial recreation of the urban poor. Movies held out the promise of an alternative to the older entertainment traditions, such as concert saloons and burlesque theater, that had been closely allied with machine politics and the vice economy. In 1909, New York City movie producers and exhibitors joined with the reform-minded People's Institute to establish the voluntary National Board of Censorship (NBC). Movie entrepreneurs, most of whom were themselves immigrants, sought to shed the stigma of the slums, attract more middle-class patronage, and increase profits. A revolving group of civic activists reviewed new movies, passing them, suggesting changes, or condemning

John Sloan, *Movies*, 1913 oil painting. The Toledo Museum of Art.

Movies, by John Sloan, 1913, the most talented artist among the so-called Ashcan realist school of painting. Active in socialist and bohemian circles, Sloan served as art editor for The Masses *magazine for several years. His work celebrated the vitality and diversity of urban working-class life and leisure, including the new commercial culture represented by the motion picture.*

them. Local censoring committees all over the nation subscribed to the board's weekly bulletin. They aimed at achieving what John Collier of the NBC called "the redemption of leisure." By 1914 the NBC was reviewing 95 percent of the nation's film output.

Standardizing Education

Along with reading, writing, and mathematics, schools inculcated patriotism, piety, and respect for authority. Progressive educators looked to the public school primarily as an agent of "Americanization." Elwood Cubberley, a leading educational reformer, expressed the view that schools could be the vehicle by which immigrant children could break free of the parochial

ethnic neighborhood. "Our task," he argued in *Changing Conceptions of Education* (1909), "is to break up these groups or settlements, to assimilate and amalgamate these people as a part of our American race, and to implant in their children, so far as can be done, the Anglo-Saxon conception of righteousness, law and order, and popular government."

The most important educational trends in these years were the expansion and bureaucratization of the nation's public school systems. In most cities centralization served to consolidate the power of older urban elites who felt threatened by the large influx of immigrants. Children began school earlier and stayed there longer. Kindergartens spread rapidly in large cities.

They presented, as one writer put it in 1903, "the earliest opportunity to catch the little Russian, the little Italian, the little German, Pole, Syrian, and the rest and begin to make good American citizens of them." By 1918 every state had some form of compulsory school attendance. High schools also multiplied, extending the school's influence beyond the traditional grammar school curriculum. In 1890 only 4 percent of the nation's youth between fourteen and seventeen were enrolled in school; by 1930 the figure was 47 percent.

High schools reflected a growing belief that schools be comprehensive, multifunctional institutions. In 1918 the National Education Association offered a report defining Cardinal Principles of Secondary Education. These included instruction in health, family life, citizenship, and ethical character. Academic programs prepared a small number of students for college. Vocational programs trained boys and girls for a niche in the new industrial order. Boys took shop courses in metal trades, carpentry, and machine tools. Girls learned typing, bookkeeping, sewing, cooking, and home economics. The Smith-Hughes Act of 1917 provided federal grants to support these programs and set up a Federal Board for Vocational Education.

Educational reformers also established national testing organizations such as the College Entrance Examination Board (founded in 1900) and helped standardize agencies for curriculum development and teacher training. In 1903 E. L. Thorndike published *Educational Psychology*, which laid the groundwork for education research based on experimental and statistical investigations. Progressives led in the development of specialized fields such as educational psychology, guidance counseling, and educational administration.

WORKING-CLASS COMMUNITIES AND PROTEST

The industrial revolution, which had begun transforming American life and labor in the nineteenth century, reached maturity in the early twentieth. In 1900, out of a total labor force of 28.5 million, 16 million people worked at industrial occupations and 11 million on farms. By 1920, in a labor force of nearly 42 million, almost 29 million were in industry, but farm labor had declined to 10.4 million. The world of the industrial worker included large manufacturing towns in New England; barren mining settlements in the West; primitive lumber and turpentine camps in the South; steelmaking and coal-mining cities in Pennsylvania and Ohio; and densely packed immigrant ghettos from New York to San Francisco, where workers toiled in garment trade sweatshops.

All these industrial workers shared the need to sell their labor for wages in order to survive. At the same time, differences in skill, ethnicity, and race proved powerful barriers to efforts at organizing trade unions that could bargain for improved wages and working conditions. So, too, did the economic and political power of the large corporations that dominated much of American industry. Yet there were also small, closely knit groups of skilled workers, such as printers and brewers, who exercised real control over their lives and labors. And these years saw many labor struggles that created effective trade unions or laid the groundwork for others. Industrial workers also became a force in local and national politics, adding a chorus of insistent voices to the calls for social justice.

The New Immigrants

On the eve of World War I, close to 60 percent of the industrial labor force was foreign-born. Most of these workers were among the roughly 9 million new immigrants from southern and eastern Europe who arrived in the United States between 1900 and 1914. In the nineteenth century, much of the overseas migration had come from the industrial districts of northern and western Europe. English, Welsh, and German artisans had brought with them skills critical for emerging industries such as steelmaking and coal mining. Unlike their predecessors, the new Italian, Polish, Hungarian, Jewish, and Greek immigrants nearly all lacked indus-

IMMIGRATION TO THE UNITED STATES (1901–1920)

Total: 14,532,000		% of Total
Italy	3,157,000	22%
Austria-Hungary	3,047,000	21
Russia and Poland	2,524,000	17
Canada	922,000	6
Great Britain	867,000	6
Scandinavia	709,000	5
Ireland	487,000	3
Germany	486,000	3
France and Low Countries (Belgium, Netherlands, Switz.)	361,000	2
Mexico	268,000	2
West Indies	231,000	2
Japan	213,000	2
China	41,000	*
Australia and New Zealand	23,000	*

*Less than 1% of total

Source: U.S. Bureau of the Census, *Historical Statistics of the United States from Colonial Times to 1970*, Washington, D.C., 1975.

trial skills. They thus entered the bottom ranks of factories, mines, mills, and sweatshops.

These new immigrants had been driven from their European farms and towns by several forces, including the undermining of subsistence farming by commercial agriculture; a falling death rate that brought a shortage of land; and religious and political persecution. American corporations also sent agents to recruit cheap labor. Except for Jewish immigrants, a majority of whom fled virulent anti-Semitism in Russia and Russian Poland, most newcomers planned on earning a stake and then returning home. Hard times in America forced many back to Europe. In the depression year of 1908, for example, more Austro-Hungarians and Italians left than entered the United States.

The decision to migrate usually occurred through social networks—people linked by kinship, personal acquaintance, and work experience. These "chains," extending from places of origin to specific destinations in the United States, helped migrants cope with the considerable risks entailed by the long and difficult journey. A study conducted by the U.S. Immigration Commission in 1909 found that about 60 percent of the new immigrants had their passage arranged by immigrants already in America. An Italian who joined his grandfather and cousins in Buffalo in 1906 recalled, "In western New York most of the first immigrants from Sicily went to Buffalo, so that from 1900 on, the thousands who followed them to this part of the state also landed in Buffalo."

Immigrant communities used ethnicity as a collective resource for gaining employment in factories, mills, and mines. One Polish steelworker recalled how the process operated in the Pittsburgh mills: "Now if a Russian got his job in a shear department, he's looking for a buddy, a Russian buddy. He's not going to look for a Croatian buddy. And if he sees the boss looking for a man he says, 'Look, I have a good man,' and he's picking out his friends. A Ukrainian department, a Russian department, a Polish department. And it was a beautiful thing in a way." Such specialization of work by ethnic origin was quite common throughout America's industrial communities.

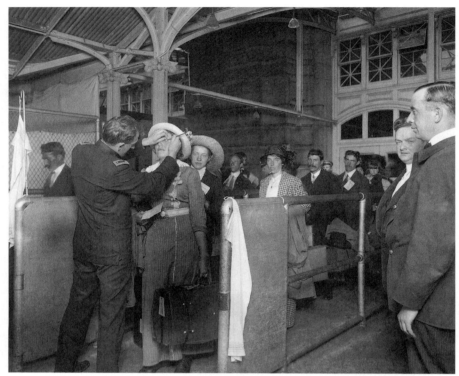

In 1892 the federal government opened the immigration station on Ellis Island, located in New York City's harbor, where about 80 percent of the immigrants to the United States landed. As many as 5,000 passengers per day reported to federal immigration officers for questions about their background and for physical examinations, such as this eye exam. Only about 1 percent were quarantined or turned away for health problems.

The low-paid, backbreaking work in basic industry became nearly the exclusive preserve of the new immigrants. In 1907, of the 14,359 common laborers employed at Pittsburgh's U.S. Steel mills, 11,694 were eastern Europeans. For twelve-hour days and seven-day weeks, two-thirds of these workers made less than $12.50 a week, one-third less than $10.00. This was far less than the $15.00 that the Pittsburgh Associated Charities had estimated as the minimum for providing necessities for a family of five. Small wonder that the new immigration was disproportionately male. One-third of the immigrant steelworkers were single, and among married men who had been in the country less than five years, about two-thirds reported that their wives were still in Europe. Workers with families generally supplemented their incomes by taking in single men as boarders.

Not all the new immigrants came from Europe. Between 1898 and 1907 more than 80,000 Japanese entered the United States. The vast majority were young men working as contract laborers in the West, mainly in California. American law prevented Japanese immigrants (the Issei) from obtaining American citizenship, because they were not white. This legal discrimination, along with informal exclusion from many occupations, forced the Japanese to create niches for themselves within local economies. Most Japanese settled near Los Angeles, where they established small communities centered around fishing, truck farming, and the flower and nursery business. In 1920 Japanese farmers produced 10 percent of the dollar volume of California agriculture on 1 percent of the farm acreage. By 1930 over 35,000 Issei and their children (the Nisei) lived in Los Angeles.

Mexican immigration also grew in these years, providing a critical source of labor for the West's farms, railroads, and mines. Between 1900 and 1914, the number of people of Mexican descent living and working in the United States tripled, from roughly 100,000 to 300,000. Economic and political crises spurred tens of thousands of Mexico's rural and urban poor to emigrate north. Large numbers of seasonal agricultural workers regularly came up from Mexico to work in the expanding sugar beet industry and then returned. But a number of substantial resident Mexican communities also emerged in the early twentieth century.

Throughout Texas, California, New Mexico, Arizona, and Colorado, western cities developed barrios, distinct communities of Mexicans. Mexican immigrants attracted by jobs in the smelting industry made El Paso the most thoroughly Mexican city in the United States. In San Antonio, Mexicans worked at shelling pecans, becoming perhaps the most underpaid and exploited group of workers in the country. By 1910, San Antonio contained the largest number of Mexican immigrants of any city. In southern California, labor agents for railroads recruited Mexicans to work on building new interurban lines around Los Angeles. Overcrowding, poor sanitation, and deficient public services made many of these enclaves unhealthy places to live. Mexican barrios suffered much higher rates of disease and infant mortality than surrounding Anglo communities.

Urban Ghettos

In large cities, new immigrant communities took the form of densely packed ghettos. By 1920, immigrants and their children constituted almost 60 percent of the population of cities over 100,000. They were an even larger percentage in major industrial centers such as Chicago, Pittsburgh, Philadelphia, and New York. The sheer size and dynamism of these cities made the immigrant experience more complex than in smaller cities and more isolated communities. Workers in the urban garment trades toiled for low wages and suffered layoffs, unemployment, and poor health. But conditions in the small, labor-intensive shops of the clothing industry differed significantly from those in the large-scale, capital-intensive industries like steel.

New York City had become the center of both Jewish immigration and America's huge ready-to-wear clothing industry. The city's Jewish population was 1.4 million in 1915, almost 30 percent of its inhabitants. New York produced 70 percent of all women's clothing and 40 percent of all men's clothing made in the country. In small factories, lofts, and tenement apartments some 200,000 people, most of them Jews, some of them Italians, worked in the clothing trades. Most of the industry operated on the grueling piece-rate, or task, system, in which manufacturers and subcontractors paid individuals or teams of workers to complete a certain quota of labor within a specific time.

The garment industry was highly seasonal. A typical work week was sixty hours, with seventy common during busy season. But there were long stretches of unemployment in slack times. Even skilled cutters, all men, earned an average of only $16 per week. Unskilled workers, nearly all of them young single women, made only $6 or $7 a week. Perhaps a quarter of the work force, classified as "learners," earned only $3 to $6 a week. Often forced to work in cramped, dirty, and badly lit rooms, garment workers strained under a system in which time equaled money. Morris Rosenfeld, a presser of men's clothing who wrote Yiddish poetry, captured the feeling:

> *The tick of the clock is the boss in his anger*
> *The face of the clock has the eye of a foe*
> *The clock—I shudder—Dost hear how it draws me?*
> *It calls me "Machine" and it cries to me "Sew!"*

In November 1909 two New York garment manufacturers responded to strikes by unskilled women workers by hiring thugs and prostitutes to beat up pickets. The strikers won the support of the Women's Trade Union League, a group of sympathetic female reformers that included Lillian Wald, Mary Dreier, and prominent society figures. At a dramatic mass meeting in Cooper Union Hall, Clara Lemlich, a teenage working girl speaking in Yiddish, made an emotional plea for a general strike. She called for everyone in the crowd to take an old Jewish oath: "If I turn traitor to the cause I now pledge, may this hand wither from the arm I now raise." The Uprising of the 20,000, as it became known, swept through the city's garment district.

The strikers demanded union recognition, better wages, and safer and more sanitary conditions. They drew support from thousands of suffragists, trade unionists, and sympathetic middle-class women as well. Hundreds of strikers were arrested, and many were beaten by police. After three cold months on the picket line, the strikers returned to work without union recognition. But the International Ladies Garment Workers Union (ILGWU), founded in 1900, did gain strength and negotiated contracts with some of the city's shirt-

New York City Police set up this makeshift morgue to help identify victims of the disastrous Triangle Shirtwaist Company fire, March 25, 1911. Unable to open the locked doors of the sweatshop and desperate to escape from smoke and flames, many of the 146 who died had leaped eight stories to their death.

waist makers. The strike was an important breakthrough in the drive to organize unskilled workers into industrial unions. It opened the doors to women's involvement in the labor movement and created new leaders, such as Lemlich, Pauline Newman, and Rose Schneiderman.

On March 25, 1911, the issues raised by the strike took on new urgency when a fire raced through three floors of the Triangle Shirtwaist Company. As the flames spread, workers found themselves trapped by exit doors locked from the outside. Fire escapes were nonexistent. Within half an hour, 146 people, mostly young Jewish women, had been killed by smoke or had leaped to their death. In the bitter aftermath, women progressives led by Florence Kelley and Frances Perkins of the National Consumers' League joined with Tammany Hall leaders Al Smith, Robert Wagner, and Big Tim Sullivan to create a New York State Factory Investigation Commission. Under Perkins's vigorous leadership, the commission conducted an unprecedented round of public hearings and on-site inspections, leading to a series of state laws that dramatically improved safety conditions and limited the hours for working women and children.

Company Towns

Immigrant industrial workers and their families often established their communities in a company town, where a single large corporation was dominant. Cities such as Lawrence, Massachusetts; Gary, Indiana; and Butte, Montana, revolved around the industrial enter-

prises of Pacific Woolen, U.S. Steel, and Anaconda Copper. Workers had little or no influence over the economic and political institutions of these cities. In the more isolated company towns, residents often had no alternative but to buy their food, clothing, and supplies at company stores, usually for exorbitantly high prices. But they did maintain some community control in other ways. Family and kin networks, ethnic lodges, saloons, benefit societies, churches and synagogues, and musical groups affirmed traditional forms of community in a setting governed by individualism and private capital.

On the job, modern machinery and industrial discipline meant high rates of injury and death. In Gary, immigrant steelworkers suffered twice the accident rate of English-speaking employees, who could better understand safety instructions and warnings. A 1910 study of work accidents revealed that nearly a fourth of all new steelworkers were killed or injured each year. As one Polish worker described the immigrant's lot to his wife: "If he comes home sick then it is trouble, because everybody is looking only for money to get some of it, and during the sickness most will be spent." Mutual aid associations, organized around ethnic groups, offered some protection through cheap insurance and death benefits.

In steel and coal towns, women not only maintained the household and raised the children, they also boosted the family income by taking in boarders, sewing, and laundry. Many women also tended gardens and raised chickens, rabbits, and goats. Their produce and income helped reduce dependence on the company store. Working-class women felt the burdens of housework more heavily than their middle-class sisters. Pump water, indoor plumbing, and sewage disposal were often available only on a pay-as-you-go basis. The daily drudgery endured by working-class women far outlasted the "man-killing" shift worked by the husband. Many women struggled with the effects of their husbands' excessive drinking and faced early widowhood.

The adjustment for immigrant workers was not so much a process of assimilation as adaptation and resistance. Efficiency experts, such as Frederick Taylor (see Chapter 19), carefully observed and analyzed the time and energy needed for each job, then set standard methods for each worker. In theory, these standards would increase efficiency and give managers more control over their workers. But work habits and Old World cultural traditions did not always mesh with factory discipline or Taylor's "scientific management." A Polish wedding celebration might last three or four days. A drinking bout following a Sunday funeral might cause workers to celebrate "St. Monday" and not show up for work. Employers made much of the few Slavs allowed to work their way up into the ranks of skilled workers and foremen. But most immigrants were far more concerned with job security than with upward mobility. The newcomers learned from more skilled and experienced British and American workers that "slowing down" or "soldiering" spread out the work. As new immigrants became less transient and more permanently settled in company towns, they increased their involvement in local politics and union activity.

The power of large corporations in the life of company towns was most evident among the mining communities of the West, as was violent labor conflict. The Colorado Fuel and Iron Company (CFI) employed roughly half of the 8,000 coal miners who labored in that state's mines. In mining towns such as Ludlow and Trinidad, the CFI thoroughly dominated the lives of miners and their families. "The miner," one union official observed, "is in this land owned by the corporation that owns the homes, that owns the boarding houses, that owns every single thing there is there . . . not only the mines, but all the grounds, all the buildings, all the places of recreation, as well as the school and church buildings." By the early twentieth century, new immigrants, such as Italians, Greeks, Slavs, and Mexicans, composed a majority of the population in these western mining communities. About one-fifth of CFI miners spoke no English.

In September 1913, the United Mine Workers led a strike in the Colorado coalfields, calling for improved safety, higher wages, and recognition of the union. Thousands of miners' families moved out of company housing and into makeshift tent colonies provided by the union. In October, Governor Elias Ammons ordered the Colorado National Guard into the tense strike region to keep order. The troops, supposedly neutral, proceeded to ally themselves with the mine operators. By spring the strike had bankrupted the state, forcing the governor to remove most of the troops. The coal companies then brought in large numbers of private mine guards who were extremely hostile toward the strikers. On April 20, 1914, a combination of guardsmen and private guards surrounded the largest of the tent colonies at Ludlow, where more than a thousand mine families lived. A shot rang out (each side accused the other of firing), and a pitched battle ensued that lasted until the poorly armed miners ran out of ammunition. At dusk, the troops burned the tent village to the ground, routing the families and killing fourteen, eleven of them children. Enraged strikers attacked mines throughout southern Colorado in an armed rebellion that lasted ten days, until President Woodrow Wilson ordered the U.S. Army into the region. News of the Ludlow Massacre shocked millions and aroused widespread protests and demonstrations against the policies of Colorado Fuel and Iron and its owner, John D. Rockefeller Jr.

The AFL: "Unions, Pure and Simple"

Following the depression of the 1890s, the American Federation of Labor emerged as the strongest and most stable organization of workers. Samuel Gompers's strategy of recruiting skilled labor into unions organized by craft had paid off. Union membership climbed from under 500,000 in 1897 to 1.7 million by 1904. Most of this growth took place in AFL affiliates in coal mining, the building trades, transportation, and machine shops. The national unions—the United Mine Workers of America, the Brotherhood of Carpenters and Joiners, the International Association of Machinists—represented workers of specific occupations in collective bargaining. Trade autonomy and exclusive jurisdiction were the ruling principles within the AFL.

But the strength of craft organization also gave rise to weakness. In 1905 Gompers told a union gathering in Minneapolis that "caucasians" would not "let their standard of living be destroyed by negroes, Chinamen, Japs, or any others." Those "others" included the new immigrants from eastern and southern Europe, men and women, who labored in the steel mills and garment trades. Each trade looked mainly to the welfare of its own. Many explicitly barred women and African Americans from membership. There were some important exceptions. The United Mine Workers of America followed a more inclusive policy, recruiting both skilled underground pitmen and the unskilled aboveground workers. The UMWA even tried to recruit strikebreakers brought in by coal operators. With 260,000 members in 1904, the UMWA became the largest AFL affiliate.

AFL unions had a difficult time holding on to their gains. Economic slumps, technological changes, and aggressive counterattacks by employer organizations could be devastating. Trade associations using management-controlled efficiency drives fought union efforts to regulate output and shop practices. The National Association of Manufacturers, a group of smaller industrialists founded in 1903, launched an "open shop" campaign to eradicate unions altogether. "Open shop" was simply a new name for a workplace where unions were not allowed. The NAM supplied strikebreakers, private guards, and labor spies to employers. It also formed antiboycott associations to prevent unions in one trade from supporting walkouts in another.

Unfriendly judicial decisions also hurt organizing efforts. In 1906 a federal judge issued a permanent injunction against an iron molders strike at the Allis Chalmers Company of Milwaukee. In the so-called Danbury Hatters' Case (*Loewe v. Lawler*, 1908), a federal court ruled that secondary boycotts, aimed by strikers at other companies doing business with their employer, such as suppliers of materials, were illegal under the Sherman Antitrust Act. Long an effective labor tactic, secondary boycotts were now declared a conspiracy in restraint of trade. Not until the 1930s would unions be able to count on legal support for collective bargaining and the right to strike.

The IWW: "One Big Union"

Some workers developed more radical visions of labor organizing. In the harsh and isolated company towns of Idaho, Montana, and Colorado, miners suffered from low wages, poor food, and primitive sanitation, as well as injuries and death from frequent cave-ins and explosions. The Western Federation of Miners (WFM) had gained strength in the metal mining regions of the West by leading several strikes marred by violence. In 1899, during a strike in the silver mining district of Coeur d'Alene, Idaho, the Bunker Hill and Sullivan Mining Company had enraged the miners by hiring armed detectives and firing all union members. Desperate miners retaliated by destroying a company mill with dynamite. Idaho's governor declared martial law and obtained federal troops to enforce it. In a pattern that would become familiar in western labor relations, the soldiers served as strikebreakers, rounding up hundreds of miners and imprisoning them for months in makeshift bullpens.

In response to the brutal realities of labor organizing in the West, most WFM leaders embraced socialism and industrial unionism. In 1905, leaders of the WFM, the Socialist Party, and various radical groups gathered in Chicago to found the Industrial Workers of the World (IWW). The IWW charter proclaimed bluntly, "The working class and the employing class have nothing in common. . . . Between these two classes a struggle must go on until the workers of the world unite as a class, take possession of the earth and the machinery of production, and abolish the wage system."

William D. "Big Bill" Haywood, an imposing, one-eyed, hard-rock miner, emerged as the most influential and flamboyant spokesman for the IWW, or Wobblies, as they were called. Haywood, a charismatic speaker and effective organizer, regularly denounced the AFL for its conservative emphasis on organizing skilled workers by trade. He insisted that the IWW would exclude no one from its ranks. The Wobblies concentrated their efforts on miners, lumberjacks, sailors, "harvest stiffs," and other casual laborers. They glorified transient and unskilled workers in speeches and songs, aiming to counter their hopelessness and degradation. Openly contemptuous of bourgeois respectability, the IWW stressed the power of collective direct action on the job—strikes and, occasionally, sabotage.

The IWW briefly became a force among eastern industrial workers, tapping the rage and growing militance of the immigrants and unskilled. In 1909, an IWW-led steel strike at McKees Rocks, Pennsylvania, challenged the power of U.S. Steel. In the 1912 "Bread and Roses" strike in Lawrence, Massachusetts, IWW organizers turned a spontaneous walkout of textile workers into a successful struggle for union recognition. Wobbly leaders such as Haywood, Elizabeth Gurley Flynn, and Joseph Ettor used class-conscious rhetoric and multilingual appeals to forge unity among the ethnically diverse Lawrence work force of 25,000.

These battles gained the IWW a great deal of sympathy from radical intellectuals, along with public scorn from the AFL and employers' groups. The IWW failed to establish permanent organizations in the eastern cities, but it remained a force in the lumber camps, mines, and wheat fields of the West. In spite of its militant rhetoric, the IWW concerned itself with practical gains. "The final aim is revolution," said one Wobbly organizer, "but for the present let's see if we can get a bed to sleep in, water enough to take a bath in and decent food to eat."

The occasional use of violence by union organizers sometimes backfired against the labor movement. On October 1, 1910, two explosions destroyed the printing plant of the *Los Angeles Times*, killing twenty-one workmen. When John and James McNamara, two brothers active in the ironworkers' union, were charged with the bombing and indicted for murder, unionists of all political persuasions rallied to their defense. Leaders of the AFL, IWW, and Socialist Party joined in a massive campaign that stressed the labor-versus-capital aspects of the case. The *Los Angeles Times* and its influential owner Harrison Gray Otis, they noted, were strongly antiunion and had helped keep Los Angeles a largely nonunion city. Some even suggested that Otis himself, looking to give labor a black eye, was responsible for the bombs. On Labor Day 1911, as the trial approached, huge crowds in America's largest cities gathered to proclaim the McNamara brothers innocent. But they were guilty. In the middle of the trial, the McNamaras confessed to the dynamiting, shocking their many supporters. A Socialist candidate for mayor of Los Angeles, favored to win the election, was decisively defeated, and the city remained a nonunion stronghold.

Rebels in Bohemia

During the 1910s, a small but influential community of painters, journalists, poets, social workers, lawyers, and political activists coalesced in the New York City neighborhood of Greenwich Village. These cultural radicals, nearly all of middle-class background and hailing from provincial American towns, shared a deep sympathy toward the struggles of labor, a passion for modern art, and an openness to socialism and anarchism. "Village bohemians," especially the women among them, challenged the double standard of Victorian sexual morality, rejected traditional marriage and sex roles, advocated birth control, and experimented with homosexual relations. They became a powerful national symbol for rebellion and the merger of political and cultural radicalism.

The term "bohemian" referred to anyone who had artistic or intellectual aspirations and who lived with disregard for conventional rules of behavior. Other American cities, notably Chicago at the turn of the century, had supported bohemian communities. But the Village scene was unique, if fleeting. The neighborhood offered cheap rents, studio space, and good ethnic restaurants, and it was close to the exciting political and labor activism of Manhattan's Lower East Side. The world view of the Village's bohemian community found expression in *The Masses*, a monthly magazine founded in 1911 by socialist critic Max Eastman, who was also its editor. "The broad purpose of *The Masses*," wrote John Reed, one of its leading writers, "is a social one—to everlastingly attack old systems, old morals, old prejudices—the whole weight of outworn thought that dead men have saddled upon us." Regular contributors included radical labor journalist Mary Heaton Vorse, artists John Sloan and George Bellows, and writers Floyd Dell and Sherwood Anderson.

At private parties and public events, the Village brought together a wide variety of men and women looking to combine politics, art, and support for the labor movement. Birth control activist Margaret Sanger found a sympathetic audience, as did IWW leader Big Bill Haywood. Journalist Walter Lippmann lectured on the new psychological theory of Sigmund Freud. Anarchist and feminist Emma Goldman wooed financial supporters for her magazine *Mother Earth*. Photographer Alfred Stieglitz welcomed artists to his gallery-studio "291."

For some, Greenwich Village offered a chance to experiment with sexual relationships or work arrangements. For others, it was an escape from small-town conformity or a haven for like-minded artists and activists. Yet the Village bohemians were united in their search for a new sense of community. Mary Heaton Vorse expressed their deeply pessimistic conviction that modern American society could no longer satisfy the elemental needs of community. "This is our weakness," she wrote. "Our strength does not multiply in our daily lives. There is a creative force in people doing things together." Intellectuals and artists, as well as workers, feeling alienated from the rest of society, sought shelter in the collective life and close-knit social relations of the Village community.

The Paterson, New Jersey, silk workers' strike of 1913 provided the most memorable fusion of bohemian sensibility and radical activism. After hearing Haywood speak about the strike at Mabel Dodge's apartment, John Reed offered to organize a pageant on the strikers' behalf at Madison Square Garden. The idea was to publicize the strike to the world and also raise money. The Villagers helped write a script, designed sets and scenery, and took care of publicity. A huge crowd watched more than a thousand workers reenact the silk workers' strike, complete with picket line songs, a funeral, and speeches by IWW organizers.

The spectacular production was an artistic triumph. One critic described the pageant as "a new art form, a form in which the workers would present their own story without artifice or theatricality, and therefore with a new kind of dramatic power." But the pageant was also a financial disaster. The Village bohemia lasted only a few years, a flame snuffed out by the chill political winds accompanying America's entry into World War I. Yet for decades Greenwich Village remained a mecca for young men and women searching for alternatives to conventional ways of living.

Publicity poster for the 1913 pageant, organized by John Reed and other Greenwich Village radicals, supporting the cause of striking silk workers in Paterson, New Jersey. This poster drew on aesthetic styles associated with the Industrial Workers of the World, typically including a heroic, larger than life image of a factory laborer.

WOMEN'S MOVEMENTS AND BLACK AWAKENING

Progressive era women were at the forefront of several reform campaigns, such as the settlement house movement, prohibition, suffrage, and birth control. Millions of others took an active role in new women's associations that combined self-help and social mission. These organizations gave women a place in public life, increased their influence in civic affairs, and nurtured a new generation of female leaders.

In fighting racial discrimination, African Americans had a more difficult task. As racism gained ground in the political and cultural spheres, black progressives fought defensively to prevent the rights they had secured during Reconstruction from being further undermined. Still, they managed to produce leaders, ideas, and organizations that would have a long-range impact on American race relations.

The New Woman

The settlement house movement discussed in the opening of this chapter was just one of the new avenues of opportunity that opened to progressive era women. A steady proliferation of women's organizations attracted growing numbers of educated, middle-class women in the early twentieth century. With more men working in offices, more children attending school, and family size declining, the middle-class home was emptier. At the same time, more middle-class women were graduating from high school and college. In 1900, only 7 percent of Americans went to high school, but 60 percent of those who graduated were women. Moreover, in 1870, only 1 percent of college-age Americans had attended college, about 20 percent of them women; by 1910 about 5 percent of college-age Americans attended college, but the proportion of women among them had doubled to 40 percent.

Single-sex clubs brought middle-class women into the public sphere by celebrating the distinctive strengths associated with women's culture: cooperation, uplift, service. The formation of the General Federation of Women's Clubs in 1890 brought together 200 local clubs representing 20,000 women. By 1900 the federation boasted 150,000 members, and by World War I it claimed to represent over a million women. The women's club movement combined an earlier focus on self-improvement and intellectual pursuits with newer benevolent efforts on behalf of working women and children. The Buffalo Union, for example, sponsored art lectures for housewives and classes in typing, stenography, and bookkeeping for young working women. It also maintained a library, set up a "noon rest" downtown where women could eat lunch, and ran a school for training domestics. In Chicago the Women's

Club became a powerful ally for reformers, and club member Louise Bowen, a Hull House trustee, gave the settlement three-quarters of a million dollars.

For many middle-class women the club movement provided a new kind of female-centered community. As one member put it: "What college life is to the young woman, club life is to the woman of riper years, who amidst the responsibilities and cares of home life still wishes to keep abreast of the time, still longs for the companionship of those who, like herself, do not wish to cease to be students because they have left school." Club activity often led members to participate in other civic ventures, particularly "child-saving" reforms, such as child labor laws and mothers' pensions. Some took up the cause of working-class women, fighting for protective legislation and offering aid to trade unions. As wives and daughters of influential and well-off men in their communities, clubwomen had access to funds and could generate support for projects they undertook.

Other women's associations made even more explicit efforts to bridge class lines between middle-class homemakers and working-class women. The National Consumers' League (NCL), started in 1898 by Maud Nathan and Josephine Lowell, sponsored a "white label" campaign in which manufacturers who met safety and sanitary standards could put NCL labels on their food and clothing. Under the dynamic leadership of Florence Kelley, the NCL took an even more aggressive stance by publicizing labor abuses in department stores and lobbying for maximum-hour and minimum-wage laws in state legislatures. In its efforts to protect home and housewife, worker and consumer, the NCL embodied the ideal of "social housekeeping." "The home does not stop at the street door," said Marion Talbot, dean of women at the University of Chicago in 1911. "It is as wide as the world into which the individual steps forth."

Birth Control

The phrase "birth control," coined by Margaret Sanger around 1913, described her campaign to provide contraceptive information and devices for women. Sanger had seen her own mother die at age forty-nine after bearing eleven children. In 1910, Sanger was a thirty-year-old nurse and housewife living with her husband and three children in a New York City suburb. Excited by a socialist lecture she had attended, she convinced her husband to move to the city, where she threw herself into the bohemian milieu. She became an organizer for the IWW, and in 1912 she wrote a series of articles on female sexuality for a socialist newspaper.

When postal officials confiscated the paper for violating obscenity laws, Sanger left for Europe to learn more about contraception. She returned to New York determined to challenge the obscenity statutes with her own magazine, the *Woman Rebel*. Sanger's journal

Margaret Sanger (second from left) is shown outside the first birth control clinic, which she founded in Brooklyn, New York, in 1916. Sanger campaigned tirelessly to educate working-class women about contraception: she wrote and distributed pamphlets, lectured around the country, and invited arrest by publicly breaking obscenity laws. "Women cannot be on an equal footing with men," she wrote, "until they have full and complete control over their reproductive function."

celebrated female autonomy, including the right to sexual expression and control over one's body. When she distributed her pamphlet *Family Limitation*, postal inspectors confiscated copies and she found herself facing forty-five years in prison. In October 1914 she fled to Europe again. In her absence, anarchist agitator Emma Goldman and many women in the Socialist Party took up the cause.

An older generation of feminists had advocated "voluntary motherhood," or the right to say no to a husband's sexual demands. The new birth control advocates embraced contraception as a way of advancing sexual freedom for middle-class women as well as responding to the misery of those working-class women who bore numerous children while living in poverty. Sanger returned to the United States in October 1915. After the government dropped the obscenity charges, she embarked on a national speaking tour. In 1916 she again defied the law by opening a birth control clinic in a working-class neighborhood in Brooklyn and offering birth control information without a physician present. Arrested and jailed, she gained more publicity for her crusade. Within a few years, birth control leagues and clinics could be found in every major city and most large towns in the country.

Racism and Accommodation

At the turn of the century, four-fifths of the nation's 10 million African Americans still lived in the South, where most eked out a living working in agriculture. In the cities, most blacks were relegated to menial jobs, but a small African American middle class of entrepreneurs and professionals gained a foothold by selling services and products to the black community. They all confronted a racism that was growing in both intensity and influence in American politics and culture. White racism came in many variants and had evolved significantly since slavery days. The more virulent strains, influenced by Darwin's evolutionary theory, held that blacks were a "degenerate" race, genetically predisposed to vice, crime, and disease and destined to lose the struggle for existence with whites. By portraying blacks as incapable of improvement, racial Darwinism justified a policy of repression and neglect toward African Americans.

Southern progressives articulated a more moderate racial philosophy. They also assumed the innate inferiority of blacks, but they believed that black progress was necessary to achieve the economic and political progress associated with a vision of the New South. Their solution to the "race problem" stressed paternalist uplift. Edgar Gardner Murphy, an Episcopal clergyman and leading Alabama progressive, held that African Americans need not be terrorized. The black man, Murphy asserted, "will accept in the white man's country the place assigned him by the white man, will do his work, not by stress of rivalry, but by genial cooperation with the white man's interests."

African Americans also endured a deeply racist popular culture that made hateful stereotypes of black people a normal feature of political debate and everyday life. Benjamin Tillman, a U.S. senator from South Carolina, denounced the African American as "a fiend, a wild beast, seeking whom he may devour." Thomas Dixon's popular novel *The Clansman* (1905) described the typical African American as "half child, half animal, the sport of impulse, whim, and conceit . . . a being who, left to his will, roams at night and sleeps in the day, whose speech knows no word of love, whose passions, once aroused, are as the fury of a tiger." In northern cities "coon songs," based on gross caricatures of black life, were extremely popular in theaters and as sheet music. As in the antebellum minstrel shows, these songs reduced African Americans to creatures of pure appetite—for food, sex, alcohol, and violence. The minstrel tradition of white entertainers "blacking up"—using burnt cork makeup to pretend they were black—was still a widely accepted convention in American show business.

Amid this political and cultural climate, Booker T. Washington won recognition as the most influential black leader of the day. Born a slave in 1856, Washington was educated at Hampton Institute in Virginia, one of the first freedmen's schools devoted to industrial education. In 1881 he founded Tuskegee Institute, a black school in Alabama devoted to industrial and moral education. He became the leading spokesman for racial accommodation, urging blacks to focus on economic improvement and self-reliance, as opposed to political and civil rights. In an 1895 speech delivered at the Cotton States Exposition in Atlanta, Washington outlined the key themes of accommodationist philosophy. "Cast down your buckets where you are," Washington told black people, meaning they should focus on improving their vocational skills as industrial workers and farmers. "In all things that are purely social," he told attentive whites, "we can be as separate as the fingers, yet one as the hand in all things essential to mutual progress."

Washington's message won him the financial backing of leading white philanthropists and the respect of progressive whites. His widely read autobiography, *Up from Slavery* (1901), stands as a classic narrative of an American self-made man. Written with a shrewd eye toward cementing his support among white Americans, it stressed the importance of learning values such as frugality, cleanliness, and personal morality. But Washington also gained a large following among African Americans, especially those who aspired to business success. With the help of Andrew Carnegie he founded the National Negro Business League to preach the virtue of black business development in black communities.

Presidents Theodore Roosevelt and William Howard Taft consulted Washington on the few political patronage appointments given to African Americans. Washington also had a decisive influence on the flow of private funds to black schools in the South. Publicly he insisted that "agitation of questions of social equality is the extremest folly." But privately Washington also spent money and worked behind the scenes trying to halt disfranchisement and segregation. He offered secret financial support, for example, for court cases that challenged Louisiana's grandfather clause, the exclusion of blacks from Alabama juries, and railroad segregation in Tennessee and Georgia.

Racial Justice and the NAACP

Washington's focus on economic self-help remained deeply influential in African American communities long after his death in 1915. But alternative black voices challenged his racial philosophy while he lived. In the

In July 1905, a group of African American leaders met in Niagara Falls, Ontario, to protest legal segregation and the denial of civil rights to the nation's black population. This portrait was taken against a studio backdrop of the falls. In 1909, the leader of the Niagara movement, W.E.B. Du Bois (*second from right, middle row*) founded and edited the *Crisis*, the influential monthly journal of the National Association for the Advancement of Colored People.

early 1900s, scholar and activist W. E. B. Du Bois created a significant alternative to Washington's leadership. A product of the black middle class, Du Bois had been educated at Fisk University and Harvard, where in 1895 he became the first African American to receive a Ph.D. His book *The Philadelphia Negro* (1899) was a pioneering work of social science that refuted racist stereotypes by, for example, discussing black contributions to that city's political life and describing the wide range of black business activity. In *The Souls of Black Folk* (1903), Du Bois declared prophetically that "the problem of the twentieth century is the problem of the color line." Through essays on black history, culture, education, and politics, Du Bois explored the concept of "double consciousness." Black people, he argued, would always feel the tension between an African heritage and their desire to assimilate as Americans.

Unlike Booker T. Washington, Du Bois did not fully accept the values of the dominant white society. He worried that "our material wants had developed much faster than our social and moral standards." *Souls* represented the first effort to embrace African American culture as a source of collective black strength and something worth preserving. Spiritual striving, rooted in black folklore, religion, music, and history, were just as important as industrial education.

Du Bois criticized Booker T. Washington's philosophy for its acceptance of "the alleged inferiority of the Negro." The black community, he argued, must fight for the right to vote, for civic equality, and for higher education for the "talented tenth" of their youth. In 1905 Du Bois and editor William Monroe Trotter brought together a group of educated black men to oppose Washington's conciliatory views. Discrimination they encountered in Buffalo, New York, prompted the men to move their meeting to Niagara Falls, Ontario. "Any discrimination based simply on race or color is barbarous," they declared. "Persistent manly agitation is the way to liberty." The Niagara movement protested legal segregation, the exclusion of blacks from labor unions, and the curtailment of voting and other civil rights.

The Niagara movement failed to generate much change. But in 1909 many of its members, led by Du Bois, attended a National Negro Conference held at the Henry Street Settlement in New York. The group included a number of white progressives sympathetic to the idea of challenging Washington's philosophy. A new, interracial organization emerged from this conference, the National Association for the Advancement of Colored People. Du Bois, the only black officer of the original NAACP, founded and edited the *Crisis*, the influential NAACP monthly journal. For the next several decades the NAACP would lead struggles to overturn legal and economic barriers to equal opportunity.

NATIONAL PROGRESSIVISM

The progressive impulse had begun at local levels and percolated up. Progressive forces in both major political parties pushed older, entrenched elements to take a more aggressive stance on the reform issues of the day. Both Republican Theodore Roosevelt and Democrat Woodrow Wilson laid claim to the progressive mantle during their presidencies—a good example of how on the national level progressivism animated many perspectives. In their pursuit of reform agendas, both significantly reshaped the office of the president. As progressivism moved to Washington, nationally organized interest groups and public opinion began to rival the influence of the old political parties in shaping the political landscape.

Theodore Roosevelt and Presidential Activism

The assassination of William McKinley in 1901 made forty-two-year-old Theodore Roosevelt the youngest man to hold the office of president before or since. Born to a wealthy New York family in 1858, Roosevelt overcame a sickly childhood through strenuous physical exercise and rugged outdoor living. After graduating from Harvard he immediately threw himself into a career in the rough and tumble of New York politics. He won election to the state assembly, ran an unsuccessful campaign for mayor of New York, served as president of the New York City Board of Police Commissioners, and went to Washington as assistant secretary of the navy. During the Spanish-American War, he won national fame as leader of the Rough Rider regiment in Cuba. Upon his return, he was elected governor of New York and then in 1900 vice president. Roosevelt viewed the presidency as a "bully pulpit"—a platform from which he could exhort Americans to reform their society—and he aimed to make the most of it.

Roosevelt was a uniquely colorful figure, a shrewd publicist, and a creative politician. His three-year stint as a rancher in the Dakota Territory; his fondness for hunting and nature study; his passion for scholarship, which resulted in ten books before he became president—all these set "T.R." apart from most of his upper-class peers. Roosevelt preached the virtues of "the strenuous life," and he believed that educated and wealthy Americans had a special responsibility to serve, guide, and inspire those less fortunate.

In style, Roosevelt made key contributions to national progressivism. He knew how to inspire and guide public opinion. He stimulated discussion and aroused curiosity like no one before him. In 1902 Roosevelt demonstrated his unique style of activism when he personally intervened in a bitter strike by anthracite coal miners. Using public calls for conciliation, a series of White House bargaining sessions, and private pressure on the mineowners, Roosevelt secured a settlement that won better pay and working conditions for the miners, but without recognition of their union. Roosevelt also pushed for efficient government as the solution to social problems. Unlike most nineteenth-century Republicans, who had largely ignored economic and social inequalities, Roosevelt frankly acknowledged them. Administrative agencies run by experts, he believed, could find rational solutions that could satisfy everyone.

Trustbusting and Regulation

One of the first issues Roosevelt faced was growing public concern with the rapid business consolidations taking place in the American economy. In 1902 he directed the Justice Department to begin a series of prosecutions under the Sherman Antitrust Act. The first target was the Northern Securities Company, a huge merger of transcontinental railroads brought about by financier J. P. Morgan. The deal would have created a giant holding company controlling nearly all the long-distance rail lines from Chicago to California. The Justice Department fought the case all the way through a hearing before the Supreme Court. In *Northern Securities v. U.S.* (1904), the Court held that the stock transactions constituted an illegal combination in restraint of interstate commerce.

This case established Roosevelt's reputation as a "trustbuster." During his two terms, the Justice Department filed forty-three cases under the Sherman Antitrust Act to restrain or dissolve business monopolies. These included actions against the so-called tobacco and beef trusts and the Standard Oil Company. Roosevelt viewed these suits as necessary to publicize the issue and assert the federal government's ultimate authority over big business. But he did not really believe in the need to break up large corporations. Unlike many progressives, who were nostalgic for smaller companies and freer competition, Roosevelt accepted centralization as a fact of modern economic life.

Roosevelt considered government regulation the best way to deal with big business. After easily defeating Democrat Alton B. Parker in the 1904 election, Roosevelt felt more secure in pushing for regulatory legislation. In 1906 Roosevelt responded to public pressure for greater government intervention and, overcoming objections from a conservative Congress, signed three important measures into law. The Hepburn Act strengthened the Interstate Commerce Commission (ICC), established in 1887 as the first independent regulatory agency, by authorizing it to set maximum railroad rates and inspect financial records.

Two other laws passed in 1906 also expanded the regulatory power of the federal government. The battles surrounding these reforms demonstrate how progressive measures often attracted supporters with competing motives. The Pure Food and Drug Act established the Food and Drug Administration (FDA), which tested and approved drugs before they went on the market. The Meat Inspection Act empowered the Department of Agriculture to inspect and label meat products. In both cases, supporters hailed the new laws as providing consumer protection against adulterated or fraudulently labeled food and drugs. Sensational exposés by muckrakers, documenting the greed, corruption, and unhealthy practices in the meatpacking and patent medicine industries, contributed to public support for the measures. Upton Sinclair's best-selling novel *The Jungle*, depicting the horrible conditions in Chicago's packinghouses, was the most sensational and influential of these.

But regulatory legislation found advocates among American big business as well. Large meat packers such as Swift and Armour strongly supported stricter federal regulation as a way to drive out smaller compa-

nies that could not meet tougher standards. The new laws also helped American packers compete more profitably in the European export market by giving their meat the official seal of federal inspectors. Large pharmaceutical manufacturers similarly supported new regulations that would eliminate competitors and patent medicine suppliers. Thus these reforms won support from large corporate interests that viewed stronger federal regulation as a strategy for consolidating their economic power. Progressive era expansion of the nation-state had its champions among—and benefits for—big business as well as American consumers.

Conservation, Preservation, and the Environment

As a naturalist and outdoorsman, Theodore Roosevelt also believed in the need for government regulation of the natural environment. He worried about the destruction of forests, prairies, streams, and the wilderness. The conservation of forest and water resources, he argued, was a national problem of vital import. In 1905 he created the U.S. Forest Service and named conservationist Gifford Pinchot to head it. Pinchot recruited a force of forest rangers to manage the reserves. By 1909 total timber and forest reserves had increased from 45 to 195 million acres, and more than 80 million acres of mineral lands had been withdrawn from public sale. Roosevelt also sponsored a National Conservation Commission, which produced the first comprehensive study of the nation's mineral, water, forest, and soil resources.

On the broad issue of managing America's natural resources, the Roosevelt administration took the middle ground between preservation and unrestricted commercial development. Pinchot established the basic pattern of federal regulation based on a philosophy of what he called the "wise use" of forest reserves. "Wilderness is waste," Pinchot was fond of saying, reflecting an essentially utilitarian vision that balanced the demands of business with wilderness conservation. But other voices championed a more radical vision of conservation, emphasizing the preservation of wilderness lands against the encroachment of commercial exploitation.

The most influential and committed of these was John Muir, an essayist and founder of the modern environmentalist movement. Muir made a passionate and spiritual defense of the inherent value of the American wilderness. Wild country, he argued, had a mystical power to inspire and refresh. "Climb the mountains and get their good tidings," he advised. "Nature's peace will flow into you as the sunshine into the trees. The winds will blow their freshness into you, and the storms their energy, while cares will drop off like autumn leaves."

Muir had been a driving force behind the Yosemite Act of 1890. Yosemite Park, located in a

William Hahn, Yosemite Valley from Glacier Point (1874). *Congress established Yosemite as a national park in 1890. Paintings like this one, along with contemporary photographs, helped convince Congress of the uniqueness of Yosemite's natural beauty.*

William Hahn (1829–1887), Yosemite Valley from Glacier Point, 1874. 27¼ x 46½ inches. California Historical Society, gift of Albert M. Bender.

valley amid California's majestic Sierra Nevada range, became the nation's first preserve consciously designed to protect wilderness. Muir served as first president of the Sierra Club, founded in 1892 to preserve and protect the mountain regions of the west coast as well as Yellowstone National Park in Wyoming, Montana, and Idaho. Muir was a tireless publicist, and his writings won wide popularity among Americans, who were increasingly drawn to explore and enjoy the outdoors. By the turn of the century, misgivings about the effects of "overcivilization" and the association of untamed lands with the nation's frontier and pioneer past had attracted many to his thinking.

A bitter, drawn-out struggle over new water sources for San Francisco revealed the deep conflicts between conservationists, represented by Pinchot, and preservationists, represented by Muir. After a devastating earthquake in 1906, San Francisco sought federal approval to dam and flood the spectacular Hetch Hetchy Valley, located 150 miles from the city in Yosemite National Park. The project promised to ease the city's chronic freshwater shortage and to generate hydroelectric power. Conservationists and their urban progressive allies argued that developing Hetch Hetchy would be a victory for the public good over greedy private developers, since the plan called for municipal control of the water supply. To John Muir

and the Sierra Club, Hetch Hetchy was a "temple" threatened with destruction by the "devotees of ravaging commercialism."

Both sides lobbied furiously in Congress and wrote scores of articles in newspapers and magazines. Congress finally approved the reservoir plan in 1913; utility and public development triumphed over the preservation of nature. Although they lost the battle for Hetch Hetchy, the preservationists gained much ground in the larger campaign of alerting the nation to the dangers of a vanishing wilderness. A disappointed John Muir took some consolation from the fact that "the conscience of the whole country has been aroused from sleep." Defenders of national parks now realized that they could not make their case simply on scenic merit alone. They began to use their own utilitarian rationales, arguing that national parks would encourage economic growth through tourism and provide Americans with a healthy escape from urban and industrial areas. In 1916 the preservationists obtained their own bureaucracy in Washington with the creation of the National Park Service.

The Newlands Reclamation Act of 1902 represented another important victory for the conservation strategy of Roosevelt and Pinchot. With the goal of turning arid land into productive family farms through irrigation, the act established the Reclamation Bureau within the Department of the Interior and provided federal funding for dam and canal projects. But in practice, the bureau did more to encourage the growth of large-scale agribusiness and western cities than small farming. The Roosevelt Dam on Arizona's Salt River, along with the forty-mile Arizona Canal, helped develop the Phoenix area. The Imperial Dam on the Colorado River diverted water to California's Imperial and Coachella Valleys. The bureau soon became a key player in western life and politics, with large federally funded water projects providing flood control and the generation of electricity, as well as water for irrigation. The Newlands Act thus established a growing federal presence in managing water resources, the critical issue in twentieth-century western development.

Republican Split

When he won reelection in 1904, Roosevelt proclaimed his support for a "Square Deal" for all people. He was still essentially a conservative who supported progressive reform as the best way to head off the potential of class war. By the end of his second term, Roosevelt had moved beyond the idea of regulation to push for the most far-reaching federal economic and social programs ever proposed. He saw the central problem as "how to exercise . . . responsible control over the business use of vast wealth." To that end, he proposed restrictions on the use of court injunctions against labor strikes, as well as an eight-hour day for federal employees, a worker compensation law, and federal income and inheritance taxes.

In 1908, Roosevelt kept his promise to retire after a second term. He chose Secretary of War William Howard Taft as his successor. Taft easily defeated Democrat William Jennings Bryan in the 1908 election. During Taft's presidency, the gulf between "insurgent" progressives and the "stand pat" wing split the Republican Party wide open. To some degree, the battles were as much over style as substance. Compared with Roosevelt, the reflective and judicious Taft brought a much more restrained concept of the presidency to the White House. He supported some progressive measures, including the constitutional amendment legalizing a graduated income tax (ratified in 1913), safety codes for mines and railroads, and the creation of a federal Children's Bureau (1912). But in a series of bitter political fights involving tariff, antitrust, and conservation policies, Taft alienated Roosevelt and many other progressives.

After returning from an African safari and a triumphant European tour in 1910, Roosevelt threw himself back into national politics. He directly challenged Taft for the Republican Party leadership. In a dozen bitter state presidential primaries (the first ever held), Taft and Roosevelt fought for the nomination.

Although Roosevelt won most of these contests, the old guard still controlled the national convention and renominated Taft in June 1912. Roosevelt's supporters stormed out, and in August the new Progressive Party nominated Roosevelt and Hiram Johnson of California as its presidential ticket. Roosevelt's "New Nationalism" presented a vision of a strong federal government, led by an activist president, regulating and protecting the various interests in American society. The platform called for woman suffrage, the eight-hour day, prohibition of child labor, minimum-wage standards for working women, and stricter regulation of large corporations.

The Election of 1912: A Four-Way Race

With the Republicans so badly divided, the Democrats sensed a chance for their first presidential victory in twenty years. They chose Governor Woodrow Wilson of New Jersey as their candidate. Although not nearly as well known nationally as Taft and Roosevelt, Wilson had

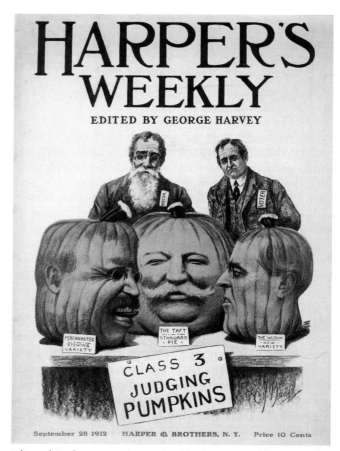

This political cartoon, drawn by Charles Jay Budd, appeared on the cover of Harper's Weekly, *September 28, 1912. It employed the imagery of autumn county fairs to depict voters as unhappy with their three choices for president. Note that the artist did not include the fourth candidate, Socialist Eugene Debs, who was often ignored by more conservative publications such as Harper's.*

built a strong reputation as a reformer. The son of a Virginia Presbyterian minister, Wilson spent most of his early career in academia. He studied law at the University of Virginia and then earned a Ph.D. in political science from Johns Hopkins. After teaching history and political science at several schools, he became president of Princeton University in 1902. In 1910, he won election as New Jersey's governor, running against the state Democratic machine. He won the Democratic nomination for president with the support of many of the party's progressives, including William Jennings Bryan.

Wilson declared himself and the Democratic Party to be the true progressives. Viewing Roosevelt rather than Taft as his main rival, Wilson contrasted his New Freedom campaign with Roosevelt's New Nationalism. Crafted largely by progressive lawyer Louis Brandeis, Wilson's platform was far more ambiguous than Roosevelt's. The New Freedom emphasized restoring conditions of free competition and equality of economic opportunity. Wilson did favor a variety of progressive reforms for workers, farmers, and consumers. But in sounding older, nineteenth-century Democratic themes of states' rights and small government, Wilson argued against allowing the federal government to become as large and paternalistic as Roosevelt advocated. "What this country needs above everything else," Wilson argued, "is a body of laws which will look after the men who are on the make rather than the men who are already made."

Socialist party nominee Eugene V. Debs offered the fourth and most radical choice to voters. The Socialists had more than doubled their membership since 1908, to more than 100,000. On election days Socialist strength was far greater than that, as the party's candidates attracted increasing numbers of voters. By 1912 more than a thousand Socialists held elective office in thirty-three states and 160 cities. Geographically, Socialist strength had shifted to the trans-Mississippi South and West.

Debs had been a national figure in American politics since the 1890s, and he had already run for president three times. An inspiring orator who drew large and sympathetic crowds wherever he spoke, Debs proved especially popular in areas with strong labor movements and populist traditions. He wrapped his socialist message in an apocalyptic vision. Socialists would "abolish this monstrous system and the misery and crime which flow from it." His movement would "tear up all privilege by the roots, and consecrate the earth and all its fullness to the joy and service of all humanity." Debs and the Socialists also took credit for pushing both Roosevelt and Wilson further toward the left. Both the Democratic and Progressive Party platforms contained proposals considered extremely radical only ten years earlier.

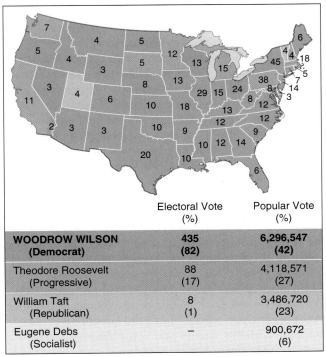

	Electoral Vote (%)	Popular Vote (%)
WOODROW WILSON (Democrat)	**435 (82)**	**6,296,547 (42)**
Theodore Roosevelt (Progressive)	88 (17)	4,118,571 (27)
William Taft (Republican)	8 (1)	3,486,720 (23)
Eugene Debs (Socialist)	–	900,672 (6)

The Election of 1912   *The split within the Republican Party allowed Woodrow Wilson to become only the second Democrat since the Civil War to be elected president. Eugene Debs's vote was the highest ever polled by a Socialist candidate.*

In the end, the divisions in the Republican Party gave the election to Wilson. He won easily, polling 6.3 million votes to Roosevelt's 4.1 million. Taft came in third with 3.5 million. Eugene Debs won 900,000 votes, 6 percent of the total, for the strongest Socialist showing in American history. Even though he won with only 42 percent of the popular vote, Wilson swept the electoral college with 435 votes to Roosevelt's 88 and Taft's 8, giving him the largest electoral majority ever to that time. In several respects, the election of 1912 was the first "modern" presidential race. It featured the first direct primaries, challenges to traditional party loyalties, an issue-oriented campaign, and a high degree of interest group activity.

Woodrow Wilson's First Term

As president, Wilson followed Roosevelt's lead in expanding the activist dimensions of the office. He became more responsive to pressure for a greater federal role in regulating business and the economy. This increase in direct lobbying—from hundreds of local and national reform groups, Washington-based organizations, and the new Progressive Party—was itself a new and defining feature of the era's political life. With the help of a Democratic-controlled Congress, Wilson pushed through a significant battery of reform proposals. By 1916 his reform program looked more like the New Nationalism that

Theodore Roosevelt had run on in 1912 than Wilson's own New Freedom platform. Four legislative achievements in Wilson's first term stand out.

The Underwood-Simmons Act of 1913 substantially reduced tariff duties on a variety of raw materials and manufactured goods, including wool, sugar, agricultural machinery, shoes, iron, and steel. Taking advantage of the newly ratified Sixteenth Amendment, which gave Congress the power to levy taxes on income, it also imposed the first graduated tax (up to 6 percent) on personal incomes. The Federal Reserve Act that same year restructured the nation's banking and currency system. It created twelve Federal Reserve Banks, regulated by a central board in Washington. Member banks were required to keep a portion of their cash reserves in the Federal Reserve Bank of their district. By raising or lowering the percentage of reserves required, "the Fed" could either discourage or encourage credit expansion by member banks. Varying the interest rate charged on loans and advances by federal reserve banks to member banks also helped regulate both the quantity and cost of money circulating in the national economy. By giving central direction to banking and monetary policy, the Federal Reserve Board diminished the power of large private banks.

Wilson also supported the Clayton Antitrust Act of 1914, which replaced the old Sherman Act of 1890 as the nation's basic antitrust law. Clayton reflected the growing political clout of the American Federation of Labor. It exempted unions from being construed as illegal combinations in restraint of trade, and it forbade federal courts to issue injunctions against strikers. But Wilson adopted the view that permanent federal regulation was necessary for checking the abuses of big business. The Federal Trade Commission (FTC), established in 1914, sought to give the federal government the same sort of regulatory control over corporations that the ICC had over railroads. Wilson believed a permanent federal body like the FTC would provide a method for corporate oversight superior to the erratic and time-consuming process of legal trustbusting. Wilson's hope that the FTC would usher in an era of harmony between government and business recalled the aims of Roosevelt and his big business backers in 1912.

On social issues, Wilson proved more cautious in his first two years. His initial failure to support federal child labor legislation and rural credits to farmers angered many progressives. A Southerner, Wilson also sanctioned the spread of racial segregation in federal offices. "I would say," he explained in 1913, "that I do approve of the segregation that is being attempted in several of the departments." As the reelection campaign of 1916 approached, Wilson worried about defections from the labor and social justice wings of his party. He proceeded to support a rural credits act providing government capital to federal farm banks, as well as federal aid to agricultural extension programs in schools. He also came out in favor of child labor reform and a worker compensation bill for federal employees. But by 1916 the dark cloud of war in Europe had already begun to cast its long shadow over progressive reform.

CONCLUSION

The American political and social landscape was significantly altered by progressivism, but these shifts reflected the tensions and ambiguities of progressivism itself. A review of changes in election laws offers a good perspective on the inconsistencies that characterized progressivism. Nearly every new election law had the effect of excluding some people from voting while including others. For African Americans, progressivism largely meant disfranchisement from voting altogether. Direct primary laws eliminated some of the most blatant abuses of big-city machines, but in cities and states dominated by one party, the majority party's primary effectively decided the general election. Stricter election laws made it more difficult for third parties to get on the ballot, another instance in which progressive reform had the effect of reducing political options available to voters. Voting itself steadily declined in these years.

Overall, party voting became a less important form of political participation. Interest group activity, congressional and statehouse lobbying, and direct appeals to public opinion gained currency as ways of influencing government. Business groups such as the National Association of Manufacturers and individual trade associations were among the most active groups pressing their demands on government. Political action often shifted from legislatures to the new administrative agencies and commissions created to deal with social and economic problems. Popular magazines and journals grew significantly in both number and circulation, becoming more influential in shaping and appealing to national public opinion.

Social progressives and their allies could point to significant improvements in the everyday lives of ordinary Americans. On the state level, real advances had been made through a range of social legislation covering working conditions, child labor, minimum wages, and worker compensation. Social progressives, too, had discovered the power of organizing into extra-party lobbying groups such as the National Consumers' League and the National American Woman Suffrage Association. Yet the tensions between fighting for social justice and the urge toward social control remained unresolved. The emphasis on efficiency, uplift, and rational administration often collided with humane impulses to aid the poor, the immigrant, the slum dweller. The large majority of African Americans, blue-collar workers, and urban poor remained untouched by federal assistance programs.

Progressives had tried to confront the new realities of urban and industrial society. What had begun as a discrete collection of local and state struggles had by 1912 come to reshape state and national politics. Politics itself had been transformed by the calls for social justice. Federal and state power would now play a more decisive role than ever in shaping work, play, and social life in local communities. That there was so much contention over the "true meaning" of progressivism is but one measure of its defining role in shaping early-twentieth-century America.

CHRONOLOGY

1889	Jane Addams founds Hull House in Chicago
1890	Jacob Riis publishes *How the Other Half Lives*
1895	Booker T. Washington addresses Cotton States Exposition in Atlanta, emphasizing an accommodationist philosophy
	Lillian Wald establishes Henry Street Settlement in New York
1898	Florence Kelley becomes general secretary of the new National Consumers' League
1900	Robert M. La Follette elected governor of Wisconsin
1901	Theodore Roosevelt succeeds the assassinated William McKinley as president
1904	Lincoln Steffens publishes *The Shame of the Cities*
1905	President Roosevelt creates U.S. Forest Service and names Gifford Pinchot head
	Industrial Workers of the World is founded in Chicago
1906	Upton Sinclair's *The Jungle* exposes conditions in the meatpacking industry
	Congress passes Pure Food and Drug Act and Meat Inspection Act and establishes Food and Drug Administration
1908	In *Muller v. Oregon* the Supreme Court upholds a state law limiting maximum hours for working women
1909	Uprising of the 20,000 in New York City's garment industries helps organize unskilled workers into unions
	National Association for the Advancement of Colored People (NAACP) is founded
1911	Triangle Shirtwaist Company fire kills 146 garment workers in New York City
	Socialist critic Max Eastman begins publishing *The Masses*
1912	Democrat Woodrow Wilson wins presidency, defeating Republican William H. Taft, Progressive Theodore Roosevelt, and Socialist Eugene V. Debs
	Bread and Roses strike involves 25,000 textile workers in Lawrence, Massachusetts
	Margaret Sanger begins writing and speaking in support of birth control for women
1913	Sixteenth Amendment, legalizing a graduated income tax, is ratified
1914	Clayton Antitrust Act exempts unions from being construed as illegal combinations in restraint of trade
	Federal Trade Commission is established
	Ludlow Massacre occurs
1916	National Park Service is established

REVIEW QUESTIONS

1. Discuss the tensions within progressivism between the ideals of social justice and the urge for social control. What concrete achievements are associated with each wing of the movement? What were the driving forces behind them?

2. Describe the different manifestations of progressivism at the local, state, and national levels. To what extent did progressives redefine the role of the state in American politics?

3. What gains were made by working-class communities in the progressive era? What barriers did they face?

4. How did the era's new immigration reshape America's cities and workplaces? What connections can you draw between the new immigrant experience and progressive era politics?

5. Analyze the progressive era from the perspective of African Americans. What political and social developments were most crucial, and what legacies did they leave?

6. Evaluate the lasting impact of progressive reform. How do the goals, methods, and language of progressives still find voice in contemporary America?

RECOMMENDED READING

John D. Buenker, *Urban Liberalism and Progressive Reform* (1973). Explores the contributions of urban ethnic voters and machine-based politicians to the progressive movement.

Robert M. Crunden, *Ministers of Reform: The Progressives' Achievement in American Civilization, 1889–1920* (1982). Emphasizes the moral and religious traditions of middle-class Protestants as the core of the progressive ethos.

Alan Dawley, *Struggles for Justice: Social Responsibility and the Liberal State* (1991). Offers an important interpretation of progressivism that focuses on how the working class and women pushed the state toward a more activist role in confronting social problems.

Susan A. Glenn, *Daughters of the Shtetl: Life and Labor in the Immigrant Generation* (1990). A sensitive analysis of the experiences of immigrant Jewish women in the garment trades.

Dewey Grantham, *Southern Progressivism: The Reconciliation of Progress and Tradition* (1982). Examines the contradictions within the southern progressive tradition.

James R. Green, *The World of the Worker: Labor in Twentieth Century America* (1980). Includes a fine overview of life and work in company towns and urban ghettos in the early twentieth century.

Morton Keller, *Regulating a New Society: Public Policy and Social Change in America, 1900–1930* (1994). A comprehensive study of public policy making on local and national levels in early twentieth-century America.

Arthur Link and Richard L. McCormick, *Progressivism* (1983). The best recent overview of progressivism and electoral politics.

Kathryn Kish Sklar, *Florence Kelley and the Nation's Work* (1995). The first installment in a two-volume biography, this book brilliantly brings Florence Kelley alive within the rich context of late-nineteenth-century women's political culture.

Robert Wiebe, *The Search for Order, 1877–1920* (1967). A pathbreaking study of how the professional middle classes responded to the upheavals of industrialism and urbanization.

ADDITIONAL BIBLIOGRAPHY

The Currents of Progressivism

Walter M. Brasch, *Forerunners of Revolution: Muckrakers and the American Social Conscience* (1990)

John D. Buenker, John C. Burnham, and Robert M. Crunden, *Progressivism* (1977)

Mina Carson, *Settlement Folk: Social Thought and the American Settlement Movement, 1885–1930* (1990)

Allen F. Davis, *Spearheads for Reform: The Social Settlements and the Progressive Movement, 1890–1914* (1967)

Leon Fink, *Progressive Intellectuals and the Dilemmas of Democratic Commitment* (1997)

Richard Hofstadter, *The Age of Reform: From Bryan to FDR* (1955)

James T. Kloppenberg, *Uncertain Victory: Social Democracy and Progressivism in European and American Thought, 1870–1920* (1986)

William A. Link, *The Paradox of Southern Progressivism, 1880–1930* (1992)

Richard McCormick, *The Party Period and Public Policy* (1986)

Nell Irvin Painter, *Standing at Armageddon: The United States, 1877–1919* (1987)

Martin J. Schiesl, *The Politics of Efficiency: Municipal Administration and Reform in America* (1977)

Social Control and Its Limits

Paul M. Boyer, *Urban Masses and Moral Order in America, 1820–1920* (1978)

Mark T. Connelly, *The Response to Prostitution in the Progressive Era* (1980)

Eldon J. Eisenach, *The Lost Promise of Progressivism* (1994)

Alan M. Kraut, *Silent Travelers: Germs, Genes, and the "Immigrant Menace"* (1994)

W. J. Rorabaugh, *The Alcoholic Republic* (1979)

Ruth Rosen, *The Lost Sisterhood: Prostitutes in America, 1900–1918* (1982)

David Tyack and Elizabeth Hansot, *Managers of Virtue: Public School Leadership in America, 1820–1980* (1982)

Working-Class Communities and Protest

John Bodnar, *The Transplanted* (1985)

Melvyn Dubofsky, *We Shall Be All: A History of the Industrial Workers of the World* (1969)

Leslie Fishbein, *Rebels in Bohemia* (1982)

Alice Kessler-Harris, *Out to Work: A History of Wage Earning Women in the United States* (1969)

J. Anthony Lukas, *Big Trouble* (1997)

David Montgomery, *The Fall of the House of Labor* (1987)

Kathy Peiss, *Cheap Amusements: Working Women and Leisure in Turn of the Century New York* (1986)

Roy Rosenzweig, *Eight Hours for What We Will* (1983)

Ronald Takaki, *Strangers from a Different Shore: A History of Asian Americans* (1989)

Women's Movements and Black Awakening

Paula Baker, *The Moral Frameworks of Public Life* (1991)

Mari Jo Buhle, *Women and American Socialism* (1983)

Ellen Fitzpatrick, *Endless Crusade: Women Social Scientists and Progressive Reform* (1990)

Linda Gordon, *Woman's Body, Woman's Right: A Social History of Birth Control* (1976)

Louis R. Harlan, *Booker T. Washington: Wizard of Tuskegee, 1901–1915* (1983)

Charles F. Kellogg, *NAACP* (1967)

J. Morgan Kousser, *The Shaping of Southern Politics* (1974)

Molly Ladd-Taylor, *Mother Work: Women, Child Welfare, and the State, 1890–1930* (1994)

David Levering Lewis, *W.E.B. Du Bois: Biography of a Race, 1868–1919* (1993)

Elaine Tyler May, *Great Expectations: Marriage and Divorce in Post Victorian America* (1980)

National Progressivism

Kendrick A. Clements, *The Presidency of Woodrow Wilson* (1992)

John M. Cooper Jr., *The Warrior and the Priest: Theodore Roosevelt and Woodrow Wilson* (1983)

Stephen R. Fox, *The American Conservation Movement: John Muir and His Legacy* (1981)

Lewis L. Gould, *The Presidency of Theodore Roosevelt* (1991)

Thomas K. McCraw, *Prophets of Regulation* (1984)

Michael McGerr, *The Decline of Popular Politics* (1986)

Roderick Nash, *Wilderness and the American Mind* (1967)

Melvin I. Urofsky, *Louis D. Brandeis and the Progressive Tradition* (1981)

Biography

Ellen Chesler, *Woman of Valor: Margaret Sanger and the Birth Control Movement in America* (1992)

Allen F. Davis, *American Heroine: The Life and Legend of Jane Addams* (1973)

Helen L. Horowitz, *The Power and Passion of M. Carey Thomas* (1994)

J. Joseph Huthmacher, *Senator Robert F. Wagner and the Rise of Urban Liberalism* (1971)

Justin Kaplan, *Lincoln Steffens* (1974)

W. Manning Marable, *W.E.B. Du Bois* (1986)

Nick Salvatore, *Eugene V. Debs: Citizen and Socialist* (1982)

David P. Thelen, *Robert M. La Follette and the Insurgent Spirit* (1976)

Bernard A. Weisberger, *The LaFollettes of Wisconsin* (1994)

Robert Westbrook, *John Dewey and American Democracy* (1991)

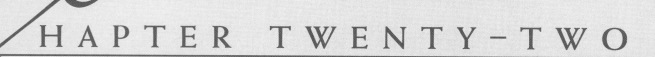
WORLD WAR I

1914–1920

McClure's Win-the-War Cover, 1918.

AMERICAN COMMUNITIES
Vigilante Justice in Bisbee, Arizona

Early in the morning of July 12, 1917, two thousand armed vigilantes swept through Bisbee, Arizona, acting on behalf of the Phelps-Dodge mining company and Bisbee's leading businessmen to break a bitter strike that had crippled Bisbee's booming copper industry. The vigilantes seized miners in their homes, on the street, and in restaurants and stores. Any miner who wasn't working or willing to work was herded into Bisbee's downtown plaza, where two machine guns commanded the scene. From the Plaza more than 2,000 were marched to the local baseball park. There, mine managers gave them a last chance to return to work. Hundreds accepted and were released. The remaining 1,400 were forced at gunpoint onto a freight train, which took them 173 miles east to Columbus, New Mexico, where they were dumped in the desert.

The Bisbee deportation occurred against a complex backdrop. America had just entered World War I, corporations were seeking higher profits, and labor militancy was on the rise. Bisbee was only one of many American communities to suffer vigilantism during the war. Any number of offenses—not displaying a flag, failing to buy war bonds, criticizing the draft, alleged spying, any apparently "disloyal" behavior—could trigger vigilante action. In western communities like Bisbee, vigilantes used the superpatriotic mood to settle scores with labor organizers and radicals.

Arizona was the leading producer of copper in the United States. With a population of 8,000, Bisbee lay in the heart of the state's richest mining district. The giant Phelps-Dodge Company dominated Bisbee's political and social life. It owned the town's hospital, department store, newspaper, library, and largest hotel. With the introduction of new technology and open pit mining after 1900, unskilled laborers—most of them Slavic, Italian, Czech, and Mexican immigrants—had increasingly replaced skilled American and English-born miners in Bisbee's workforce.

America's entry into the war pushed the price of copper to an all-time high, prompting Phelps-Dodge to increase production. Miners viewed the increased demand for labor as an opportunity to flex their own muscle and improve wages and working conditions. Two rival union locals, one affiliated with the American Federation of Labor (AFL), the other with the more radical Industrial Workers of the World (IWW), or "Wobblies," sought to organize Bisbee's workers. On June 26, 1917, Bisbee's Wobblies went on strike. They demanded better mine safety, an end to discrimination against union workers, and a substantial pay increase. The IWW, making special efforts to attract lower-paid foreign-born workers to their cause, even hired two Mexican organizers. Although the IWW had only 300 or 400 members in Bisbee, more than half the town's 4,700 miners supported the strike.

The walkout was peaceful, but Walter Douglas, district manager for Phelps-Dodge, was unmoved. "There will be no compromise," he declared, "because you cannot compromise with a rattlesnake." Douglas, Cochise County Sheriff Harry Wheeler, and Bisbee's leading businessmen met secretly to plan the July 12 deportation. The approximately 2,000 men they deputized to carry it out were members of Bisbee's Citizens' Protective League and the Workers Loyalty League. These vigilantes included company officials, small businessmen, professionals, and anti-union workers. Local telephone and telegraph offices agreed to isolate Bisbee by censoring outgoing messages. The El Paso and Southwestern Railroad, a subsidiary of Phelps-Dodge, provided the waiting boxcars.

The participants in this illegal conspiracy defended themselves by exaggerating the threat of organized labor. They also appealed to patriotism and played on racial fears. The IWW opposed American involvement in the war, making it vulnerable to charges of disloyalty. A proclamation, posted in Bisbee the day of the deportation, claimed, "There is no labor trouble—we are sure of that—but a direct attempt to embarrass and injure the government of the United States." Sheriff Wheeler told a visiting journalist he worried that Mexicans "would take advantage of the disturbed conditions of the strike and start an uprising, destroying the mines and murdering American women and children."

An army census of the deportees, who had found temporary refuge at an army camp in Columbus, New Mexico, offered quite a different picture. Of the 1,400 men, 520 owned property in Bisbee. Nearly 500 had already registered for the draft, and more than 200 had purchased Liberty Bonds. More than 400 were married with children; only 400 were members of the IWW. Eighty percent were immigrants, including nearly 400 Mexicans. A presidential mediation committee concluded that "conditions in Bisbee were in fact peaceful and free from manifestations of disorder or violence." The deported miners nonetheless found it difficult to shake the accusations that their strike was anti-American and foreign inspired.

At their camp, the miners organized their own police force and elected an executive committee to seek relief. In a letter to President Wilson, they claimed "Common American

citizens here are now convinced that they have no constitutional rights." They promised to return to digging copper if the federal government operated the nation's mines and smelters. IWW leader William D. "Big Bill" Haywood threatened a general strike of metal miners and harvest workers if the government did not return the deportees to their homes. The presidential mediation committee criticized the mine companies and declared the deportation illegal. But it also denied the federal government had any jurisdiction in the matter. Arizona's attorney general refused to offer protection for a return to Bisbee.

In September, the men began gradually to drift away from Columbus. Only a few ever returned to Bisbee. The events convinced President Wilson that the IWW was a subversive organization and a threat to national security. The Justice Department began planning an all-out legal assault that would soon cripple the Wobblies. But Wilson could not ignore protests against the Bisbee outrage from such prominent and patriotic Americans as Samuel Gompers, head of the American Federation of Labor. To demonstrate his administration's commitment to harmonious industrial relations, the president appointed a special commission to investigate and mediate wartime labor conflicts. But Arizona's mines would remain union free until the New Deal era of the 1930s.

America's entry into the war created a national sense of purpose and an unprecedented mobilization of resources. Unifying the country and winning the war now took precedence over progressive reforms. The war also aroused powerful political emotions and provided an excuse for some citizens to try to cleanse their communities of anyone who did not conform. In a 1918 speech, Arizona State Senator Fred Sutter hailed the benefits of vigilante justice. "And what are the results in Bisbee since the deportation?" he asked. "They are, sir, a practically 100 percent American camp; a foreigner to get a job there today had to give a pretty good account of himself. The mines are today producing more copper than ever before and we are a quiet, peaceful, law-abiding community and will continue so, so long as the IWWs or other enemies of the government let us alone."

Bisbee

KEY TOPICS

- America's expanding international role
- From neutrality to participation in the Great War

- Mobilizing the society and the economy for war
- Dissent and its repression
- Woodrow Wilson's failure to win the peace

BECOMING A WORLD POWER

In the first years of the new century the United States pursued a more vigorous and aggressive foreign policy than it had in the past. Presidents Theodore Roosevelt, William Howard Taft, and Woodrow Wilson all contributed to "progressive diplomacy," in which commercial expansion was backed by a growing military presence in the Caribbean, Asia, and Mexico. This policy reflected a view of world affairs that stressed moralism, order, and a special, even God-given, role for the United States. By 1917, when the United States entered the Great War, this policy had already secured the country a place as a new world power.

Roosevelt: The Big Stick

Theodore Roosevelt left a strong imprint on the nation's foreign policy. Like many of his class and background, "T.R." took for granted the superiority of Protestant Anglo-American culture and the goal of spreading its values and influence. He believed that to maintain and increase its economic and political stature, America must be militarily strong. In 1900 Roosevelt summarized his activist views, declaring, "I have always been fond of the West African proverb, 'Speak softly and carry a big stick, you will go far.'"

Roosevelt brought the "big stick" approach to several disputes in the Caribbean region. Since the 1880s, several British, French, and American companies had pursued various plans for building a canal across the Isthmus of Panama, thereby connecting the Atlantic and Pacific Oceans. The canal was a top priority for Roosevelt, and he tried to negotiate a leasing agreement with Colombia, of which Panama was a province. But when the Colombian Senate rejected a final American offer in the fall of 1903, Roosevelt invented a new strategy. A combination of native forces and foreign promoters associated with the canal project plotted a revolt against Colombia. Roosevelt kept in touch with at least one leader of the revolt, Philippe Bunau-Varilla, an engineer and agent for the New Panama Canal Company, and the president let him know that U.S. warships were steaming toward Panama.

On November 3, 1903, just as the USS Nashville arrived in Colón harbor, the province of Panama declared itself independent of Colombia. The United States immediately recognized the new Republic of Panama. Less than two weeks later, Bunau-Varilla, serving as a minister from Panama, signed a treaty granting the United States full sovereignty in perpetuity over a ten-mile-wide canal zone. America guaranteed Panama's independence and agreed to pay it $10 million initially and an additional $250,000 a year for the canal zone. Years after the canal was completed, the U. S. Senate voted another $25 million to Colombia as compensation.

The Panama Canal was a triumph of modern engineering and gave the United States a tremendous strategic and commercial advantage in the Western Hemisphere. It took eight years to build and cost hundreds of poorly paid manual workers their lives. Several earlier attempts to build a canal in the region had failed. But with better equipment and a vigorous campaign against disease, the United States succeeded. In 1914, after $720 million in construction costs, the first merchant ships sailed through the canal.

"The inevitable effect of our building the Canal," wrote Secretary of State Elihu Root in 1905, "must be to require us to police the surrounding premises." Roosevelt agreed. He was especially concerned that European powers might step in if America did not. In 1903 Great Britain, Germany, and Italy had imposed a blockade on Venezuela in a dispute over debt payments owed to private investors. To prevent armed intervention by the Europeans, Roosevelt in 1904 proclaimed what became known as the Roosevelt Corollary to the Monroe Doctrine. "Chronic wrongdoing, or an impotence which results in a general loosening of the ties of civilized society," the statement read, justified "the exercise of an international police power" anywhere in the hemisphere. Roosevelt invoked the corollary to justify U.S. intervention in the region, beginning with the Dominican Republic in 1905. To counter the protests of European creditors (and the implied threat of armed intervention), Washington assumed management of the Dominican debt and customs services. Roosevelt and later presidents cited

This 1905 *cartoon portraying President Theodore Roosevelt,* The World's Constable, *appeared in* Judge *magazine. In depicting the president as a strong but benevolent policeman bringing order in a contentious world, the artist Louis Dalrymple drew on familiar imagery from Roosevelt's earlier days as a New York City police commissioner.*

the corollary to justify armed intervention in the internal affairs of Cuba, Haiti, Nicaragua, and Mexico.

American diplomacy in Asia reflected the Open Door policy formulated by Secretary of State John Hay in 1899. Japan and the western European powers had carved key areas of China into spheres of influence, in which individual nations enjoyed economic dominance. The United States was a relative latecomer to the potentially lucrative China market, and Hay sought guarantees of equal opportunity for its commercial interests there. In a series of diplomatic notes Hay won approval for the so-called Open Door approach, giving all nations equal access to trading and development rights in China. The outbreak of war between Japan and Russia in 1905 threatened this policy. Roosevelt worried that a total victory by Russia or Japan could upset the balance of power in East Asia and threaten American business enterprises. He became especially concerned after the Japanese scored a series of military victories over Russia and began to loom as a dominant power in East Asia.

Roosevelt mediated a settlement of the Russo-Japanese War at Portsmouth, New Hampshire, in 1905 (for which he was awarded the 1906 Nobel Peace Prize). In this settlement, Japan won recognition of its dominant position in Korea and consolidated its economic control over Manchuria. Yet repeated incidents of anti-Japanese racism in California kept American-Japanese relations strained. In 1906, for example, the San Francisco school board, responding to nativist fears of a "yellow peril,"

ordered the segregation of Japanese, Chinese, and Korean students. Japan angrily protested. In 1907, in the so-called gentlemen's agreement, Japan agreed not to issue passports to Japanese male laborers looking to emigrate to the United States and Roosevelt promised to fight anti-Japanese discrimination. He then persuaded the San Francisco school board to exempt Japanese students from the segregation ordinance.

But Roosevelt did not want these conciliatory moves to be interpreted as weakness. He thus built up American naval strength in the Pacific, and in 1908 he sent battleships to visit Japan in a muscle-flexing display of sea power. In that same year, the two burgeoning Pacific powers reached a reconciliation. The Root-Takahira Agreement affirmed the "existing status quo" in Asia, mutual respect for territorial possessions in the Pacific, and the Open Door trade policy in China. From the Japanese perspective, the agreement recognized Japan's colonial dominance in Korea and southern Manchuria.

Taft: Dollar Diplomacy

Roosevelt's successor, William Howard Taft, believed he could replace the militarism of the big stick with the more subtle and effective weapon of business investment. Taft and his secretary of state, corporate lawyer Philander C. Knox, followed a strategy (called "dollar diplomacy" by critics) in which they assumed that political influence would follow increased U.S. trade and investment. As Taft explained in 1910, he advocated "active intervention to secure for our merchandise and our capitalists opportunity for profitable investment." He hoped to substitute "dollars for bullets," but he was to discover limits to this approach in both the Caribbean and Asia.

Overall American investment in Central America grew rapidly, from $41 million in 1908 to $93 million by 1914. Most of this money went into railroad construction, mining, and plantations. The United Fruit Company alone owned about 160,000 acres of land in the Caribbean by 1913. But dollar diplomacy ended up requiring military support. The Taft administration sent the navy and the marines to intervene in political disputes in Honduras and Nicaragua, propping up factions pledged to protect American business interests. A contingent of U.S. Marines remained in Nicaragua until 1933. The economic and political structures of Honduras and Nicaragua were controlled by both the dollar and the bullet.

In China, Taft and Knox pressed for a greater share of the pie for U.S. investors. They gained a place for U.S. bankers in the European consortium building the massive new Hu-kuang Railways in southern and central China. But Knox blundered by attempting to "neutralize" the existing railroads in China. He tried to secure a huge international loan for the Chinese government that would allow it to buy up all the foreign railways and develop new ones. Both Russia and Japan, which had fought wars over their railroad interests in Manchuria, resisted this plan as a threat to the arrangements hammered out at Portsmouth with the help of Theodore Roosevelt. Knox's "neutralization" scheme, combined with U.S. support for the Chinese Nationalists in their 1911 revolt against the ruling Manchu dynasty, prompted Japan to sign a new friendship treaty with Russia. The Open Door to China was now effectively closed, and American relations with Japan began a slow deterioration that ended in war thirty years later.

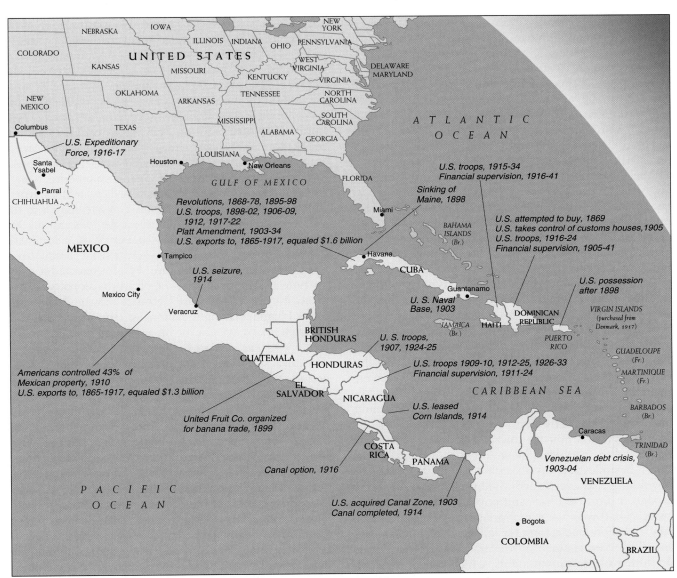

The United States in the Caribbean, 1865–1933 *An overview of U.S. economic and military involvement in the Caribbean during the late nineteenth and early twentieth centuries. Victory in the Spanish-American War, the Panama Canal project, and rapid economic investment in Mexico and Cuba all contributed to a permanent and growing U.S. military presence in the region.*

Wilson: Moralism and Realism

Right after he took office in 1913, President Woodrow Wilson observed that "it would be the irony of fate if my administration had to deal chiefly with foreign affairs." His political life up to then had centered on achieving progressive reforms in the domestic arena. As it turned out, Wilson had to face international crises from his first day in office. These were of a scope and complexity unprecedented in U.S. history. Wilson had no experience in diplomacy, but he brought to foreign affairs a set of fundamental principles that combined a moralist's faith in American democracy with a realist's understanding of the power of international commerce. He believed that American economic expansion, accompanied by democratic principles and Christianity, was a civilizing force in the world. "Our industries," he told the Democratic National Convention in 1912, "have expanded to such a point that they will burst their jackets if they cannot find a free outlet to the markets of the world. . . . Our domestic markets no longer suffice. We need foreign markets."

Wilson, like most corporate and political leaders of the day, emphasized foreign investments and industrial exports as the keys to the nation's prosperity. He believed that the United States, with its superior industrial efficiency, could achieve supremacy in world commerce if artificial barriers to free trade were removed. He championed and extended the Open Door principles of John Hay, advocating strong diplomatic and military measures "for making ourselves supreme in the world from an economic point of view." Wilson often couched his vision of a dynamic, expansive American capitalism in terms of a moral crusade. As he put it in a speech to a congress of salesmen, "[Since] you are Americans and are meant to carry liberty and justice and the principles of humanity wherever you go, go out and sell goods that will make the world more comfortable and more happy, and convert them to the principles of America." Yet he quickly found that the complex realities of power politics could interfere with moral vision.

Wilson's policies toward Mexico, which foreshadowed the problems he would encounter in World War I, best illustrate his difficulties. The 1911 Mexican Revolution had overthrown the brutally corrupt dictatorship of Porfirio Díaz, and popular leader Francisco Madero had won wide support by promising democracy and economic reform for millions of landless peasants. U.S. businessmen, however, were nervous about the future of their investments, which totaled over $1 billion, an amount greater than Mexico's own investment and more than all other foreign investment in that country combined. Wilson at first gave his blessing to the revolutionary movement, expressed regret over the Mexican-American War of 1846–48, and disavowed any interest in another war. "I have constantly to remind myself," he told a friend, "that I am not the servant of those who wish to enhance the value of their Mexican investments."

But right before he took office, Wilson was stunned by the ousting and murder of Madero by his chief lieutenant, General Victoriano Huerta. Other nations, including Great Britain and Japan, recognized the Huerta regime, but Wilson refused. He announced that the United States would support only governments that rested on the rule of law. An armed faction opposed to Huerta known as the Constitutionalists and led by Venustiano Carranza emerged in northern Mexico. Both sides rejected an effort by Wilson to broker a compromise between them. Carranza, an ardent nationalist, pressed for the right to buy U.S. arms, which he won in 1914. Wilson also isolated Huerta diplomatically by persuading the British to withdraw their support in exchange for American guarantees of English property interests in Mexico.

But Huerta stubbornly remained in power. In April 1914 Wilson used a minor insult to U.S. sailors in Tampico as an excuse to invade. American naval forces bombarded and then occupied Veracruz, the main port through which Huerta received arms shipments. Nineteen Americans and 126 Mexicans died in the battle, which brought the United States and Mexico close to war and provoked anti-American demonstrations in Mexico and throughout Latin America. Wilson accepted the offer of the ABC Powers—Argentina, Brazil, and Chile—to mediate the dispute. Huerta rejected a plan for him to step aside in favor of a provisional government. But then in August Carranza managed to overthrow Huerta. Playing to nationalist sentiment, Carranza too denounced Wilson for his intervention.

As war loomed in Europe, Mexico's revolutionary politics continued to frustrate Wilson. For a brief period Wilson threw his support behind Francisco "Pancho" Villa, Carranza's former ally who now led a rebel army of his own in the North. But Carranza's forces dealt Villa a major setback in April, 1915, and in October, its attention focused on the war in Europe, the Wilson administration recognized Carranza as Mexico's *de facto* president. Meanwhile Pancho Villa, feeling betrayed, turned on the United States and tried to provoke a crisis that might draw Washington into war with Mexico. Villa led several raids in Mexico and across the border in early 1916 that killed a few dozen Americans. The man once viewed by Wilson as a fighter for democracy was now dismissed as a dangerous bandit.

In March 1916, enraged by Villa's defiance, Wilson dispatched General John J. Pershing and an army that eventually numbered 15,000 to capture him. For a year, Pershing's troops chased Villa in vain, penetrating 300 miles into Mexico. The invasion made Villa a

Mexican revolutionary leaders and sometime allies Francisco "Pancho" Villa (center) and Emiliano Zapata (right) are shown at the National Palace in Mexico City, ca. 1916. Zapata's army operated out of a base in the southern agricultural state of Morelos, while Villa's army controlled large portions of Mexico's North. In 1914 Villa captured the imagination of American reformers, journalists, and moviemakers with his military exploits against the oppressive Huerta regime. But in 1916, after several border clashes between his forces and U.S. military units, President Wilson dispatched a punitive expedition in pursuit of Villa.

before the United States entered World War I, Wilson officially recognized the Carranza regime.

Wilson's attempt to guide the course of Mexico's revolution and protect U.S. interests left a bitter legacy of suspicion and distrust in Mexico. It also suggested the limits of a foreign policy tied to a moral vision rooted in the idea of American exceptionalism. Militarism and imperialism, Wilson had believed, were hallmarks of the old European way. American liberal values—rooted in capitalist development, democracy, and free trade—were the wave of the future. Wilson believed the United States could lead the world in establishing a new international system based on peaceful commerce and political stability. In both the 1914 invasion and the 1916 punitive expedition, Wilson declared that he had no desire to interfere with Mexican sovereignty. But in both cases that is exactly what he did. The United States, he argued, must actively use its enormous moral and material power to create the new order. That principle would soon engage America in Europe's bloodiest war and its most momentous revolution.

symbol of national resistance in Mexico, and his army grew from 500 men to 10,000 by the end of 1916. Villa's effective hit-and-run guerrilla tactics kept the U.S. forces at bay. A frustrated General Pershing complained that he felt "just a little bit like a man looking for a needle in a haystack." He urged the U.S. government to occupy the northern Mexican state of Chihuahua and later called for the occupation of the entire country.

Pershing's invasion angered the Carranza government and the Mexican public. Skirmishes between American forces and Carranza's army brought the two nations to the brink of war again in June 1916. Wilson prepared a message to Congress asking permission for American troops to occupy all of northern Mexico. But he never delivered it. There was fierce opposition to war with Mexico throughout the country. Perhaps more important, mounting tensions with Germany caused Wilson to hesitate. He told an aide that "Germany is anxious to have us at war with Mexico, so that our minds and our energies will be taken off the great war across the sea." Wilson thus accepted negotiations by a face-saving international commission. In early 1917, with America moving toward direct involvement in the European war, Wilson began withdrawing American troops. Just a month

THE GREAT WAR

World War I, or the Great War, as it was originally called, took an enormous human toll on an entire generation of Europeans. The unprecedented slaughter on the battlefields of Verdun, Ypres, Gallipoli, and scores of other places appalled the combatant nations. At the war's start in August 1914, both sides had confidently predicted a quick victory. Instead, the killing dragged on for more than four years and in the end transformed the old power relations and political map of Europe. The United States entered the war reluctantly, and American forces played a supportive rather than a central role in the military outcome. Yet the wartime experience left a sharp imprint on the nation's economy, politics, and cultural life, one that would last into the next decades.

The Guns of August

In August 1914 a relatively minor incident plunged the European continent into the most destructive war in its history until then. The last decades of the nineteenth century had seen the major European nations, especially Germany, enjoy a great rush of industrial development. During the same period, these nations acquired extensive colonial empires in Africa, Asia, and the Middle East. Only a complex and fragile system of alliances had kept the European powers at peace with each other since 1871. Two great competing camps had evolved by 1907: the Triple Alliance (also known as the Central Powers), which included Germany, Austria-Hungary, and Italy; and the Triple Entente (also known as the Allies), which included Great Britain, France, and Russia. At the heart of this division was the competition between Great Britain, long the world's dominant colonial and commercial power, and Germany, which had powerful aspirations for an empire of its own.

The alliance system managed to keep small conflicts from escalating into larger ones for most of the late nineteenth and early twentieth centuries. But its inclusiveness was also its weakness: the alliance system threatened to entangle many nations in any war that did erupt. On June 28, 1914, Archduke Franz Ferdinand, heir to the throne of the unstable Austro-Hungarian Empire, was assassinated in Sarajevo, Bosnia. The archduke's killer was a Serbian nationalist who believed the Austro-Hungarian province of Bosnia ought to be annexed to neighboring Serbia. Germany pushed Austria-Hungary to retaliate against Serbia, and the Serbians in turn asked Russia for help.

By early August both sides had exchanged declarations of war and begun mobilizing their forces. Germany invaded Belgium and prepared to move across the French border. But after the German armies were stopped at the River Marne in September, the war settled into a long, bloody stalemate. New and grimly efficient weapons, such as the machine gun and the tank, and the horrors of trench warfare meant unprecedented casualties for all involved. Centered in northern France, the fighting killed 5 million people over the next two and a half years.

American Neutrality

The outbreak of war in Europe shocked Americans. President Wilson issued a formal proclamation of neutrality and urged citizens to be "impartial in thought as well as in action." Most of the country shared the editorial view expressed that August in the New York Sun: "There is nothing reasonable in such a war, and it would be folly for the country to sacrifice itself to the frenzy of dynastic policies and the clash of ancient hatreds which is urging the Old World to destruction."

In practice, powerful cultural, political, and economic factors made the impartiality advocated by Wilson impossible. The U.S. population included many ethnic groups with close emotional ties to the Old World. Out of a total population of 92 million in 1914, about one-third were "hyphenated" Americans, either foreign-born or having one or both parents who were immigrants. Strong support for the Central Powers could be found among the 8 million German Americans, as well as the 4 million Irish Americans, who shared their ancestral homeland's historical hatred of English rule. On the other side, many Americans were at least mildly pro-Allies due to cultural and language bonds with Great Britain and the tradition of Franco-American friendship.

Both sides bombarded the United States with vigorous propaganda campaigns. The British effectively exploited their bonds of language and heritage with Americans. Reports of looting, raping, and the killing of innocent civilians by German troops circulated widely in the press. Many of these atrocity stories were exaggerated, but verified German actions—the invasion of neutral Belgium, submarine attacks on merchant ships, and the razing of towns—lent them credibility. German propagandists blamed the war on Russian expansionism and France's desire to avenge its defeat by Germany in 1870–71. It is difficult to measure the impact of war propaganda on American public opinion. As a whole, though, it highlighted the terrible human costs of the war and thus strengthened the conviction that America should stay out of it.

Economic ties between the United States and the Allies were perhaps the greatest barrier to true neutrality. Early in the war Britain imposed a blockade on all shipping to Germany. The United States, as a neutral country, might have insisted on the right of nonbelligerents to trade with both sides, as required by international law. But in practice, although Wilson protested the blockade, he wanted to avoid antagonizing Britain and disrupting trade between the United States and the Allies. Trade with Germany all but ended while trade with the Allies increased dramatically. As war orders poured in from Britain and France, the value of American trade with the Allies shot up from $824 million in 1914 to $3.2 billion in 1916. By 1917 loans to the Allies exceeded $2.5 billion compared to loans to the Central Powers of only $27 million. Increased trade with the Allies helped produce a great economic boom at home—transforming the economy in places like Bisbee, Arizona—and the United States became neutral in name only.

Preparedness and Peace

In February 1915, Germany declared the waters around the British Isles to be a war zone, a policy that it would enforce with unrestricted submarine warfare. All enemy shipping, despite the requirements of international law to the contrary, would be subject to surprise submarine attack. Neutral powers were warned that the problems of identification at sea put their ships at risk. The United States issued a sharp protest to this policy, calling it "an indefensible violation of neutral rights," and threatened to hold Germany accountable.

On May 7, 1915, a German U-boat sank the British liner Lusitania off the coast of Ireland. Among the 1,198 people who died were 128 American citizens. The Lusitania was in fact secretly carrying war materials, and passengers had been warned about a possible attack. Wilson nevertheless denounced the sinking as illegal and inhuman, and the American press loudly condemned the act as barbaric. An angry exchange of diplomatic notes led Secretary of State William Jennings Bryan to resign in protest against a policy he thought too warlike.

Tensions heated up again in March 1916 when a German U-boat torpedoed the Sussex, an unarmed French passenger ship, injuring four Americans. President Wilson threatened to break off diplomatic relations with Germany unless it abandoned its methods of submarine warfare. He won a temporary diplomatic victory when Germany promised that all vessels would be visited prior to attack. But the crisis also prompted Wilson to begin preparing for war. The National Security League, active in large eastern cities and bankrolled by conservative banking and commercial interests, helped push for a bigger army and navy and, most important, a system of universal military training. In June 1916 Congress passed the National Defense Act, which more than doubled the size of the regular army to 220,000 and integrated the state National Guards under federal control. In August, Congress passed a bill that dramatically increased spending for new battleships, cruisers, and destroyers.

Not all Americans supported these preparations for battle, and opposition to military buildup found expression in scores of American communities. As early as August 29, 1914, 1,500 women clad in black had marched down New York's Fifth Avenue in the Woman's Peace Parade. Out of this gathering evolved the American Union against Militarism, which lobbied against the preparedness campaign and against intervention in Mexico. Antiwar feeling was especially strong in the South and Midwest. Except for its vitally important cotton exports, the South generally had weaker economic ties to the Allies than other parts of the nation, as well as a historical suspicion of military power concentrated in Washington. The Midwest included communities with large German and socialist influences, both of which opposed U.S. aid to the Allies.

A group of thirty to fifty House Democrats, led by majority leader Claude Kitchin of North Carolina, stubbornly opposed Wilson's buildup. Jane Addams, Lillian D. Wald, and many other prominent progressive reformers spoke out for peace. A large

Jane Addams (right), *shown here in the late 1920s, remained active in the women's world peace movement until her death in 1935. In 1915 she had cofounded the Women's Peace Party, whose pacifist platform representing the views of the "mother half of humanity" attracted 25,000 members. But the American entry into World War I led to the Party's rapid demise.*

reservoir of popular antiwar sentiment flowed through the culture in various ways. Movie director Thomas Ince won a huge audience for his 1916 film *Civilization,* which depicted Christ returning to reveal the horrors of war to world leaders. Two of the most popular songs of 1915 were "Don't Take My Darling Boy Away" and "I Didn't Raise My Boy to Be a Soldier."

To win reelection in 1916, Wilson had to acknowledge the active opposition to involvement in the war. In the presidential campaign, Democrats adopted the winning slogan "He Kept Us Out of War." Wilson made a strong showing in the West, where antiwar sentiment was vigorous, and he managed to draw hundreds of thousands of votes away from the antiwar Socialist Party as well. Wilson made a point of appealing to progressives of all kinds, stressing his support for the eight-hour day and his administration's efforts on behalf of farmers. The war-induced prosperity no doubt helped him to defeat conservative Republican Charles Evans Hughes in a very close election. But Wilson knew that the peace was as fragile as his victory.

Safe for Democracy

By the end of January 1917, Germany's leaders had decided against a negotiated peace settlement, placing their hopes instead in a final decisive offensive against the Allies. On February 1, 1917, Germany resumed its policy of unrestricted submarine warfare, with no warnings, against all neutral and belligerent shipping. (These attacks had been temporarily restrained in 1916, following U.S. protests.) This decision was made with full knowledge that it might bring America into the conflict. In effect, German leaders were gambling that they could destroy the ability of the Allies to fight before the United States would be able to effectively mobilize manpower and resources.

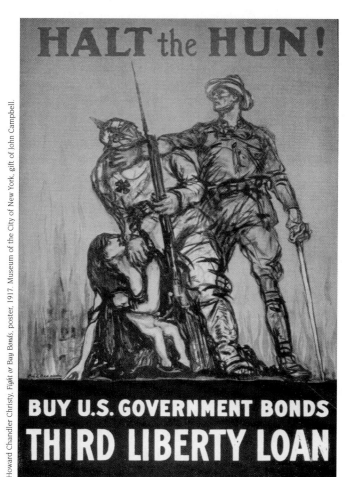

Howard Chandler Christy, *Fight or Buy Bonds,* poster, 1917. Museum of the City of New York, gift of John Campbell.

Halt the Hun. *This 1918* Liberty Loan *poster used anti-German sentiment to encourage the purchase of war bonds. Its depiction of an American soldier as the protector of an innocent mother and child implied that the Germans were guilty of unspeakable war crimes.*

Wilson was indignant and disappointed. He still hoped for peace, but Germany had made it impossible for him to preserve his twin goals of U.S. neutrality and freedom of the seas. Reluctantly, Wilson broke off diplomatic relations with Germany and called on Congress to approve the arming of U.S. merchant ships. On March 1, the White House shocked the country when it made public a recently intercepted coded message, sent by German foreign secretary Arthur Zimmermann to the German ambassador in Mexico. The Zimmermann note proposed that an alliance be made between Germany and Mexico if the United States entered the war. Zimmermann suggested that Mexico take up arms against the United States and receive in return the "lost territory in New Mexico, Texas, and Arizona." The note caused a sensation and became a very effective propaganda tool for those who favored U.S. entry into the war. "As soon as I saw it," wrote Republican senator Henry Cabot Lodge of Massachusetts, an interventionist, "I knew it would arouse the country more than any other event." The specter of a German-Mexican alliance helped turn the tide of public opinion in the Southwest, where opposition to U.S. involvement in the war had been strong.

Revelation of the Zimmermann note stiffened Wilson's resolve. He issued an executive order in mid-March authorizing the arming of all merchant ships and allowing them to shoot at submarines. In that month, German U-boats sank seven U.S. merchant ships, leaving a heavy death toll. Anti-German feeling increased, and thousands took part in prowar demonstrations in New York, Boston, Philadelphia, and other cities. Wilson finally called a special session of Congress to ask for a declaration of war.

On April 2, on a rainy night before a packed and very quiet assembly, Wilson made his case. He reviewed the escalation of submarine warfare, which he called "warfare against mankind," and said that neutrality was no longer feasible or desirable. But the conflict was not merely about U.S. shipping rights, Wilson argued:

> The world must be made safe for democracy. Its peace must be planted upon the tested foundations of political liberty. We have no selfish ends to serve. . . . We shall fight for the things which we have always carried nearest our hearts,—for democracy, for the right of those who submit to authority to have a voice in their own Governments, for the rights and liberties of small nations.

This was a bold bid to give the United States a new role in international affairs. It asserted not just the right to protect U.S. interests but called also for change in basic international structures. Wilson's eloquent speech won over the Congress, most of the press, and even his bitterest political critics, such as

Theodore Roosevelt. The Senate adopted the war resolution 82 to 6, the House 373 to 50. On April 6, President Wilson signed the declaration of war. All that remained was to win over the American public.

AMERICAN MOBILIZATION

The overall public response to Wilson's war message was enthusiastic. Most newspapers, religious leaders, state legislatures, and prominent public figures endorsed the call to arms. But the Wilson administration was less certain about the feelings of ordinary Americans and their willingness to fight in Europe. It therefore took immediate steps to win over public support for the war effort, place a legal muzzle on antiwar dissenters, and establish a universal military draft. War mobilization was above all a campaign to unify the country.

Selling the War

Just a week after signing the war declaration, Wilson created the Committee on Public Information (CPI) to organize public opinion. It was dominated by its civilian chairman, the journalist and reformer George Creel. He had become a personal friend of Wilson's while handling publicity for the 1916 Democratic campaign. Creel quickly transformed the CPI from its original function as coordinator of government news into a sophisticated and aggressive agency for promoting the war. Creel remarked that his aim was to mold Americans into "one white-hot mass . . . with fraternity, devotion, courage, and deathless determination."

To sell the war, Creel raised the art of public relations to new heights. He enlisted more than 150,000 people to work on a score of CPI committees. They produced more than 100 million pieces of literature—pamphlets, articles, books—that explained the causes and meaning of the war. The CPI also created posters, slides, newspaper advertising, and films to promote the war. It called upon movie stars such as Charlie Chaplin, Mary Pickford, and Douglas Fairbanks to help sell war bonds at huge rallies. Famous journalists like the muckraker Ida Tarbell and well-known artists like Charles Dana Gibson were recruited. Across the nation, a volunteer army of 75,000 "Four Minute Men" gave brief patriotic speeches before stage and movie shows.

Three major themes dominated the materials disseminated by the CPI: America as a unified moral community; the war as an idealistic crusade for peace and freedom; and the image of a despicable enemy. The last of these featured an aggressively negative campaign against all things German. Posters and advertisements depicted the Germans as Huns, bestial monsters outside the civilized world. The CPI supported films such as *The Kaiser: The Beast of Berlin* and *The Prussian Cur.* German music and literature, indeed

Founded by Clara Barton after the Civil War, the American Red Cross grew in both size and importance during World War I. Female volunteers, responding to humanitarian and patriotic appeals combined in posters like this one, provided most of the health and sanitary services to military and civilian casualties of the war.

the German language itself, were suspect, and were banished from the concert halls, schools, and libraries of many communities. The CPI also urged ethnic Americans to abandon their Old World ties, to become "unhyphenated Americans." The CPI's push for conformity would soon encourage thousands of local, sometimes violent, campaigns of harassment against German Americans, radicals, and peace activists.

Fading Opposition to War

By defining the call to war as a great moral crusade, President Wilson was able to win over many Americans who had been reluctant to go to war. In particular, many liberals and progressives were attracted to the possibilities of war as a positive force for social change. Many progressives identified with President Wilson's definition of the war as an idealistic crusade to defend democracy, spread liberal principles, and redeem European decadence and militarism. John Dewey, the influential philosopher, believed the war offered great "social possibilities" for developing the public good through science and greater efficiency.

Social welfare advocates, suffragists, tax reformers, even many socialists, now viewed war as a unique opportunity. War would require greater direct and coordinated involvement by the government in nearly every phase of American life. A group of prominent progressives quickly issued a statement of support for Wilson's war policy. They argued that "out of the sacrifice of war we may achieve broader democracy in Government, more equitable distribution of wealth, and greater national efficiency in raising the level of the general welfare."

The writer and cultural critic Randolph Bourne was an important, if lonely, voice of dissent among intellectuals. A former student of Dewey's at Columbia University, Bourne wrote a series of antiwar essays warning of the disastrous consequences for reform movements of all kinds. He was particularly critical of "war intellectuals" such as Dewey who were so eager to shift their energies to serving the war effort. "War is essentially the health of the State," Bourne wrote, and he accurately predicted sharp infringements on political and intellectual freedoms.

The Woman's Peace Party, founded in 1915 by feminists opposed to the preparedness campaign, dissolved. Most of its leading lights—Florence Kelley, Lillian D. Wald, and Carrie Chapman Catt—threw themselves into volunteer war work. Catt, leader of the huge National American Woman Suffrage Association (NAWSA), believed that supporting the war might help women win the right to vote. She joined the Women's Committee of the Council of National Defense and encouraged suffragists to mobilize women for war service of various kinds. A few lonely feminist voices, such as Jane Addams, continued steadfastly to oppose the war effort. But war work proved very popular among activist middle-class women. It gave them a leading role in their communities—selling bonds, coordinating food conservation drives, and working for hospitals and the Red Cross.

"You're in the Army Now"

The central military issue facing the administration was how to raise and deploy U.S. armed forces. When war was declared, there were only about 200,000 men in the army. Traditionally, the United States had relied on volunteer forces organized at the state level. But volunteer rates after April 6 were less than they had been for the Civil War or the Spanish-American War, reflecting the softness of prowar sentiment. The administration thus introduced the Selective Service Act, which provided for the registration and classification for military service of all men between ages twenty-one and thirty-five. Secretary of War Newton D. Baker was anxious to prevent the widespread, even violent, opposition to the draft that had occurred during the Civil War. Much of the anger over the Civil War draft stemmed from the unpopular provision that allowed draftees to buy their way out by paying $300 for a substitute. The new draft made no such allowances. Baker stressed the democratic procedures for registration and the active role of local draft boards in administering the process.

On June 5, 1917, nearly 10 million men registered for the draft. There was scattered organized resistance, but overall, registration records offered evidence of national support. A supplemental registration in August 1918 extended the age limits to eighteen and forty-five. By the end of the war some 24 million men had registered. Of the 2.8 million men eventually called up for service, about 340,000, or 12 percent, failed to show up. Another 2 million Americans volunteered for the various armed services.

U.S. soldiers leaving training camp, on their way to the European front, 1918. In just over a year national mobilization expanded the armed forces twentyfold, to nearly 5 million men and women. By November 1918, when the fighting ended, more than 2 million American troops were in Europe.

The vast, polyglot army posed unprecedented challenges of organization and control. But progressive elements within the administration also saw opportunities for pressing reform measures involving education, alcohol, and sex. Army psychologists gave the new Stanford-Binet intelligence test to all recruits and were shocked to find illiteracy rates as high as 25 percent. The low test scores among recent immigrants and rural African Americans undoubtedly reflected the cultural biases embedded in the tests and, for many test takers, their lack of proficiency in English. Most psychologists at the time, however, interpreted low scores in terms of racial theories of innate differences in intelligence. After the war, intelligence testing became a standard feature of America's educational system.

Ideally, the army provided a field for social reform and education, especially for the one-fifth of U.S. soldiers born in another country. "The military tent where they all sleep side by side," Theodore Roosevelt predicted, "will rank next to the public schools among the great agents of democratization." The recruits themselves took a more lighthearted view, while singing the army's praises:

Oh, the army, the army, the democratic army,
They clothe you and feed you because the army needs you
Hash for breakfast, beans for dinner, stew for suppertime,
Thirty dollars every month, deducting twenty-nine.
Oh, the army, the army, the democratic army,
The Jews, the Wops, and the Dutch and Irish Cops,
They're all in the army now!

Racism in the Military

But African Americans who served found severe limitations in the U.S. military. They were organized into totally segregated units, barred entirely from the marines and the Coast Guard, and largely relegated to working as cooks, laundrymen, stevedores, and the like in the army and navy. Thousands of black soldiers endured humiliating, sometimes violent treatment, particularly from southern white officers. African American servicemen faced hostility from white civilians as well, North and South, often being denied service in restaurants and admission to theaters near training camps. The ugliest incident occurred in Houston, Texas, in August 1917. Black infantrymen, incensed over continual insults and harassment by local whites, seized weapons from an armory and killed seventeen civilians. The army executed thirty black soldiers and imprisoned forty-one others for life, denying any of them a chance for appeal.

More than 200,000 African Americans eventually served in France, but only about one in five saw combat, as opposed to two out of three white soldiers. Black combat units served with distinction in various

The military reinforced old patterns of racism in American life by segregating African American troops and assigning most of them to menial and support tasks. Yet African Americans generally supported the war effort. The leading black newspaper of the day, the Chicago Defender, *predicted optimistically: "The colored soldier who fights side by side with the white American will hardly be begrudged a fair chance when the victorious armies return."*

divisions of the French army. The all-black 369th U.S. Infantry, for example, saw the first and longest service of any American regiment deployed in a foreign army, serving in the trenches for 191 days. The French government awarded the *Croix de Guerre* to the entire regiment, and 171 officers and enlisted men were cited individually for exceptional bravery in action. African American soldiers by and large enjoyed a friendly reception from French civilians as well. The contrast with their treatment at home would remain a sore point with these troops upon their return to the United States.

Americans in Battle

Naively, many Americans had assumed that the nation's participation in the war could be limited to supplying economic aid and military hardware. At first, the main contribution came on the sea. German U-boats were sinking Allied ships at a rate of 900,000 tons each month; one of four British ships never returned to port. The United States began sending warships and destroyers to protect large convoys of merchant ships and to aid the British navy in assaulting U-boats. Within a year, shipping tonnage lost each month to submarine warfare had been reduced to 200,000; the flow of weapons, supplies, and troops continued. No American soldiers were lost on the way to Europe.

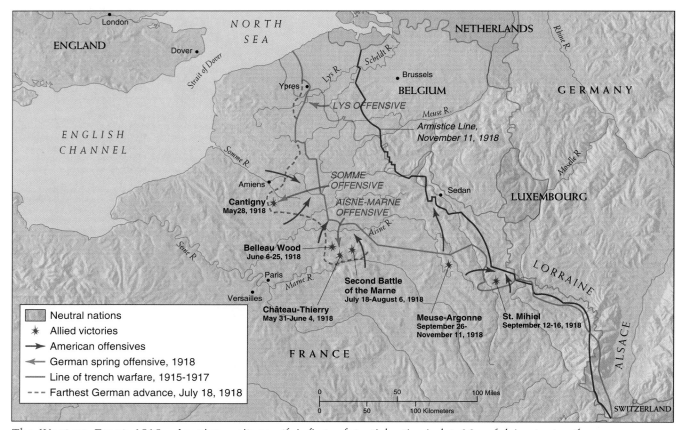

The Western Front, 1918 *American units saw their first substantial action in late May, helping to stop the German offensive at the battle of Cantigny. By September, more than 1 million American troops were fighting in a counteroffensive campaign at St. Mihiel, the largest single American engagement of the war.*

President Wilson appointed General John J. Pershing, recently returned from pursuing Pancho Villa in Mexico, as commander of the American Expeditionary Force (AEF). Pershing insisted that the AEF maintain its own identity, distinct from that of the French and British armies. He was also reluctant to send American troops into battle before they had received at least six months' training. The AEF's combat role would be brief but intense: not until early 1918 did AEF units reach the front in large numbers; eight months later the war was over.

Like Ulysses S. Grant, Pershing believed the object of war to be total destruction of the enemy's military power. He expressed contempt for the essentially defensive tactics of trench warfare pursued by both sides. But the brutal power of modern military technology had made trench warfare inevitable from 1914 to 1917. The awesome firepower of the machine gun and long-range artillery made the massed frontal confrontations of the Civil War era obsolete. The grim reality of life in the trenches—cold, wet, lice-ridden, with long periods of boredom and sleeplessness—also made a mockery of older notions about the glory of combat.

In the early spring of 1918 the Germans launched a major offensive that brought them within fifty miles of Paris. In early June about 70,000 AEF soldiers helped the French stop the Germans in the battles of Château-Thierry and Belleau Wood. In July, Allied forces led by Marshal Ferdinand Foch of France, began a counteroffensive designed to defeat Germany once and for all. American reinforcements began flooding the ports of Liverpool in England and Brest and Saint-Nazaire in France. The "doughboys" (a nickname for soldiers dating back to Civil War-era recruits who joined the army for the money) streamed in at a rate of over 250,000 a month. By September, General Pershing had more than a million Americans in his army.

In late September 1918, the AEF took over the southern part of a 200-mile front in the Meuse-Argonne offensive. In seven weeks of fighting, most through terrible mud and rain, U.S. soldiers used more ammunition than the entire Union army had in the four years of the Civil War. The Germans, exhausted and badly outnumbered, began to fall back and look for a cease-fire. On November 11, 1918, the war ended with the signing of an armistice.

The massive influx of American troops and supplies no doubt hastened the end of the war. About two-thirds of the U.S. soldiers saw at least some fighting, but even they managed to avoid the horrors of the sustained trench warfare that had marked the earlier years of the war. For most Americans at the front, the war experience was a mixture of fear, exhaustion, and fatigue. Their time in France would remain a decisive moment in their lives. In all, more than 52,000 Americans died in battle. Another 60,000 died from influenza and pneumonia, half of these while still in training camp. More than 200,000 Americans were wounded in the war. These figures, awful as they were, paled against the estimated casualties (killed and wounded) suffered by the European nations: 9 million for Russia, more than 6 million for Germany, nearly 5 million for France, and over 2 million each for Great Britain and Italy.

OVER HERE

In one sense, World War I can be understood as the ultimate progressive crusade, a reform movement of its own. Nearly all the reform energy of the previous two decades was turned toward the central goal of winning the war. The federal government would play a larger role than ever in managing and regulating the wartime economy. Planning, efficiency, scientific analysis, and cooperation were key principles for government agencies and large volunteer organizations. Although much of the regulatory spirit was temporary, the war experience started some important and lasting organizational trends in American life.

Organizing the Economy

In the summer of 1917 President Wilson established the War Industries Board (WIB) as a clearinghouse for industrial mobilization to support the war effort. Led by the successful Wall Street speculator Bernard M. Baruch, the WIB proved a major innovation in expanding the regulatory power of the federal government. It was given broad authority over the conversion of industrial plants to wartime needs, the manufacture of war materials, and the purchase of supplies for the United States and the Allies. The WIB had to balance price controls against war profits. Only by ensuring a fair rate of return on investment could it encourage stepped-up production.

The WIB eventually handled 3,000 contracts worth $14.5 billion with various businesses. Standardization of goods brought large savings and streamlined production. Baruch continually negotiated with business leaders, describing the system as "voluntary cooperation with the big stick in the cupboard." At first Elbert Gary of U.S. Steel refused to accept the government's price for steel and Henry Ford balked at limiting private car production. But when Baruch warned that he would instruct the military to take over their plants, both industrialists backed down.

In August 1917, Congress passed the Food and Fuel Act, authorizing the president to regulate the production and distribution of the food and fuel necessary for the war effort. To lead the Food Administration (FA), Wilson appointed Herbert Hoover, a millionaire engineer who had already won fame for directing a program of war relief for Belgium. He became one of the best-known figures of the war administration. Hoover imposed price controls on certain agricultural commodities, such as sugar, pork, and wheat. These were purchased by the government and then sold to the public through licensed dealers. The FA also raised the purchase price of grain so that farmers would increase production. But Hoover stopped short of imposing mandatory food rationing, preferring to rely on persuasion, high prices, and voluntary controls.

Hoover's success, like George Creel's at the CPI, depended on motivating hundreds of thousands of volunteers in thousands of American communities. The FA coordinated the work of local committees that distributed posters and leaflets urging people to save food, recycle scraps, and substitute for scarce produce. The FA directed patriotic appeals for "Wheatless Mondays, Meatless Tuesdays, and Porkless Thursdays." Hoover exhorted Americans to "go back to simple food, simple clothes, simple pleasures." He urged them to grow their own vegetables. These efforts resulted in a sharp cutback in the consumption of sugar and wheat as well as a boost in the supply of livestock. The resultant increase in food exports helped sustain the Allied war effort.

The enormous cost of fighting the war, about $33 billion, required unprecedentedly large expenditures for the federal government. The tax structure shifted dramatically as a result. Taxes on incomes and profits replaced excise and customs levies as the major source of revenue. The minimum income subject to the graduated federal income tax, in effect only since 1913, was lowered to $1,000 from $3,000, increasing the number of Americans who paid income tax from 437,000 in 1916 to 4,425,000 in 1918. Tax rates were as steep as 70 percent in the highest brackets.

The bulk of war financing came from government borrowing, especially in the form of the popular Liberty Bonds sold to the American public. Bond drives became highly organized patriotic campaigns that ultimately raised a total of $23 billion for the war effort. The administration also used the new Federal Reserve Banks to expand the money supply, making borrowing easier. The federal debt jumped from $1 billion in 1915 to $20 billion in 1920.

The Business of War

Overall, the war meant expansion and high profits for American business. Between 1916 and 1918, Ford Motor Company increased its workforce from 32,000 to 48,000, General Motors from 10,000 to 50,000. Total capital expenditure in U.S. manufacturing jumped from $600 million in 1915 to $2.5 billion in 1918. Corporate profits as a whole nearly tripled between 1914 and 1919, and many large businesses did much better than that. Annual prewar profits for United States Steel had averaged $76 million; in 1917 they were $478 million. The Bethlehem Shipbuilding Company increased its annual profits from $6 million in peacetime to $49 million in wartime. Du Pont quadrupled its assets. The demand for foodstuffs led to a boom in agriculture as well. The total value of farm produce rose from $9.8 billion in 1914 to $21.3 billion by 1918. Expanded farm acreage and increased investment in farm machinery led to a jump of 20–30 percent in overall farm production.

The most important and long-lasting economic legacy of the war was the organizational shift toward corporatism in American business. The wartime need for efficient management, manufacturing, and distribution could be met only by a greater reliance on the productive and marketing power of large corporations. Never before had business and the federal government cooperated so closely. Under war administrators like Baruch and Hoover, entire industries (such as radio manufacturing) and economic sectors (such as agriculture and energy) were organized, regulated, and subsidized. War agencies used both public and private power—legal authority and voluntarism—to hammer out and enforce agreements. Here was the genesis of the modern bureaucratic state.

Some Americans worried about the wartime trend toward a greater federal presence in their lives. As the *Saturday Evening Post* noted, "All this government activity will be called to account and re-examined in due time." Although many aspects of the government–business partnership proved temporary, some institutions and practices grew stronger in the postwar years. Among these were the Federal Reserve Board, the income tax system, the Chamber of Commerce, the Farm Bureau, and the growing horde of lobbying groups that pressed Washington for special interest legislation.

One key example of the long-range impact of the government–business partnership was the infant radio industry. Wireless communication technology found many uses among naval and ground forces in wartime. As in most industries, the Justice Department guaranteed radio manufacturers protection against patent infringement and antitrust suits. These guarantees helped stimulate research and the mass production of radios for airplanes, ships, and infantry. In 1919 the government helped create the Radio Corporation of America (RCA), which bought out a British company that had dominated America's wireless system. As part of the deal, the U.S. military was allowed a permanent representative on the RCA board of directors. The creation of RCA, jointly owned by General Electric, American Telephone and Telegraph, and Westinghouse, assured the United States a powerful position in the new age of global communications. It also set the stage for the new radio broadcasting industry of the 1920s.

Labor and the War

Organized labor's power and prestige, though by no means equal to those of business or government, clearly grew during the war. The expansion of the economy, combined with army mobilization and a decline in immigration from Europe, caused a growing wartime labor shortage. As the demand for workers intensified, the federal government was forced to recognize that labor, like any other resource or commodity, would have to be more carefully tended to than in peacetime. For the war's duration, working people generally enjoyed higher wages and a better standard of living. Trade unions, especially those affiliated with the American Federation of Labor (AFL), experienced a sharp rise in membership. In effect, the government took in labor as a junior partner in the mobilization of the economy.

Samuel Gompers, president of the AFL, emerged as the leading spokesman for the nation's trade union movement. An English immigrant and cigar maker by trade, Gompers had rejected the socialism of his youth for a philosophy of "business unionism." By stressing the concrete gains that workers could win through collective bargaining with employers, the AFL had reached a total membership of about 2 million in 1914. Virtually all its members were skilled white males, organized in highly selective crafts in the building trades, railroads, and coal mines.

Gompers pledged the AFL's patriotic support for the war effort, and in April 1918 President Wilson appointed him to the National War Labor Board (NWLB). During 1917 the nation had seen thousands of strikes involving more than a million workers. Wages were usually at issue, reflecting workers' concerns with spiraling inflation and higher prices. The NWLB, co-chaired by labor attorney Frank Walsh and former president William H. Taft, acted as a kind of supreme court for labor, arbitrating disputes and working to prevent disruptions in production. The great majority of these interventions resulted in improved wages and reduced hours of work.

Most important, the NWLB supported the right of workers to organize unions and furthered the acceptance of the eight-hour day for war workers—central aims of the labor movement. It also backed time-and-a-half pay for overtime, as well as the principle of equal pay for women workers. AFL unions gained more than a million new members during the war, and overall union membership rose from 2.7 million in 1914 to more than 5 million by 1920. The NWLB established important precedents for government intervention on behalf of labor.

Wartime conditions often meant severe disruptions and discomfort for America's workers. Overcrowding, rapid workforce turnover, and high inflation rates were typical in war-boom communities. In Bridgeport, Connecticut, a center for small-arms manufacturing, the population grew by 50,000 in less than a year. In 1917 the number of families grew by 12,000, but available housing stock increased by only 6,000 units. Chronic congestion became common in many cities; Philadelphia reported the worst housing shortage in its history.

In the Southwest, the demand for wartime labor temporarily eased restrictions against the movement of Mexicans into the United States. The Immigration Act of 1917, requiring a literacy test and an $8 head tax, had cut Mexican immigration nearly in half, down to about 25,000 per year. But employers complained of severe shortages of workers. Farmers in Arizona's Salt River Valley and southern California needed hands to harvest grain, alfalfa, cotton, and fruit. El Paso's mining and smelting industries, Texas's border ranches, and southern Arizona's railroads and copper mines insisted they depended on unskilled Mexican labor as well.

Responding to these protests, in June 1917 the Department of Labor suspended the immigration law for the duration of the war and negotiated an agreement with the Mexican government permitting some 35,000 Mexican contract laborers to enter the United States. Mexicans let in through this program had to demonstrate they had a job waiting before they could cross the border. They received identification cards and transportation to their place of work from American labor contractors. Pressure from southwestern employers kept the exemptions in force until 1921, well after the end of the war, demonstrating the growing importance of cheap Mexican labor to the region's economy.

If the war boosted the fortunes of the AFL, it also spelled the end for more radical elements of the U.S. labor movement. The Industrial Workers of the World (IWW) had followed a different path from the "pure and simple" trade unionism of Gompers. Unlike the AFL, the IWW concentrated on organizing unskilled workers into all-inclusive industrial unions. The Wobblies denounced capitalism as an unreformable system based on exploitation and they opposed U.S. entry into the war. IWW leaders advised their members to refuse induction for "the capitalists' war."

With vigorous organizing, especially in the West, the IWW had grown in 1916 and 1917. It gained strength among workers in several areas crucial to the

For Every Fighter a Woman Worker, 1917, by Ernest Hamlin Baker. This poster, part of the United War Work Campaign of the Young Women's Christian Association, depicted America's women as a civilian army, ready and able to take the place of male workers gone off to fight.

war effort: copper mining, lumbering, and wheat harvesting. In September 1917, just after the vigilante attack in Bisbee and the IWW's efforts to expose it, the Wilson administration responded to appeals from western business leaders for a crackdown on the Wobblies. Justice Department agents, acting under the broad authority of the recently passed Espionage Act, swooped down on IWW offices in more than sixty towns and cities, arresting more than 300 people and confiscating files. The mass trials and convictions that followed broke the back of America's radical labor movement and marked the beginning of a powerful wave of political repression.

Women at Work

For many of the 8 million women already in the labor force, the war meant a chance to switch from low-paying jobs, such as domestic service, to higher-paying industrial fields. About a million women workers joined the labor force for the first time. Of the estimated 9.4 million workers directly engaged in war work, some 2.25 million were women. Of these, 1.25 million worked in manufacturing. Female munitions plant workers, train engineers, drill press operators, streetcar conductors, and mail carriers became a common sight around the country.

In response to the widened range of female employment, the Labor Department created the Women in Industry Service (WIS). Directed by Mary Van Kleeck, the service advised employers on using female labor and formulated general standards for the treatment of women workers. The WIS represented the first attempt by the federal government to take a practical stand on improving working conditions for women. Its standards included the eight-hour day, equal pay for equal work, a minimum wage, the prohibition of night work, and the provision of rest periods, meal breaks, and restroom facilities. These standards had no legal force, however, and WIS inspectors found that employers often flouted them. They were accepted nonetheless as goals by nearly every group concerned with improving the conditions of working women.

Many women resented the restrictiveness of the WIS guidelines. Myrtle Altenburg, a Wisconsin widow, complained of being prevented from working on a local railroad. "It is my belief," she wrote the state railway commission, "that a woman can do everything that a man can do that is within her strength. Hundreds and hundreds of women might work and release men for war or war work, could they, the women, be employed on the railroads." Even when hired, women suffered discrimination over pay. Government surveys found that women's average earnings were roughly half of men's in the same industries.

At war's end, women lost nearly all their defense-related jobs. Wartime women railroad workers, for example, were replaced by returning servicemen through the application of laws meant to protect women from hazardous conditions. But the war accelerated female employment in fields already dominated by women. By 1920, more women who worked outside the home did so in white-collar occupations—as telephone operators, secretaries, and clerks, for example—than in manufacturing or domestic service. The new awareness of women's work led Congress to create the Women's Bureau in the Labor Department, which continued the WIS wartime program of education and investigation through the postwar years.

Woman Suffrage

The presence of so many new women wageworkers, combined with the highly visible volunteer work of millions of middle-class women, helped finally to secure the vote for women. Volunteer war work—selling bonds, saving food, organizing benefits—was very popular among housewives and clubwomen. These women played a key role in the success of the Food Administration, and the Women's Committee of the Council of National Defense included a variety of women's organizations.

Until World War I, the fight for woman suffrage had been waged largely within individual states. Western states and territories had led the way. Various forms of woman suffrage had become law in Wyoming in 1869, followed by Utah (1870), Colorado (1893), Idaho (1896), Washington (1910), California (1911), Arizona and Oregon (1912), and Montana and Nevada (1914). The reasons for this regional pattern had less to do with dramatically different notions of gender roles in the West than with the distinctiveness of western politics and society. Rocky Mountain and Pacific coast states did not have the sharp ethnocultural divisions between Catholics and Protestants that hindered suffrage efforts in the East. The close identification in the East between the suffrage and prohibition movements led many Catholic immigrants and German Lutherans to oppose the vote for women because they feared it would lead to prohibition. Mormons in Utah supported woman suffrage as a way to preserve polygamy and defend their distinctive social order from attack.

The U.S. entry into the war provided a unique opportunity for suffrage groups to shift their strategy to a national campaign for a constitutional amendment granting the vote to women. The most important of these groups was the National American Woman Suffrage Association. Before 1917, most American suffragists had opposed the war. Under the leadership of Carrie Chapman Catt, NAWSA threw its support behind the war effort and doubled its membership to 2 million. Catt gambled that a strong show of patriotism would help clinch the century-old fight to win the vote for women. NAWSA pursued a moderate policy of lobbying Congress for a constitutional amendment and calling for state referendums on woman suffrage.

At the same time, more militant suffragists led by a young Quaker activist, Alice Paul, injected new energy and more radical tactics into the movement. Paul had spent several years in England working with militant suffragists there, and in 1913 she returned to the United States to form the Congressional Union within the NAWSA to lobby for a federal amendment. Dissatisfied with the NAWSA's conservative strategy of quiet lobbying and orderly demonstrations, Paul left the organization in 1916. She joined forces with western women voters to form the National Woman's Party. Borrowing from English suffragists, this party pursued a more aggressive and dramatic strategy of agitation. Paul and her supporters picketed the White House, publicly burned President Wilson's speeches, and condemned the president and the Democrats for failing to produce an amendment. In one demonstration they chained themselves to the White House fence and after their

Members of the National Woman's Party picketed President Wilson at the White House in 1917. Their militant action in the midst of the war crisis aroused both anger and sympathy. The NWP campaign helped push the president and the Congress to accept woman suffrage as a "war measure."

arrest went on a hunger strike in jail. The militants generated a great deal of publicity and sympathy.

Although some in the NAWSA objected to these tactics, Paul's radical approach helped make the NAWSA position more acceptable to Wilson. Carrie Chapman Catt used the president's war rhetoric as an argument for granting the vote to women. The fight for democracy, she argued, must begin at home, and she urged passage of the woman suffrage amendment as a "war measure." She won Wilson's support, and in 1917 the president urged Congress to pass a woman suffrage amendment as "vital to the winning of the war." The House did so in January 1918 and a more reluctant Senate approved it in June 1919. Another year of hard work was spent convincing the state legislatures. In August 1920, Tennessee gave the final vote needed to ratify the Nineteenth Amendment to the Constitution, finally making woman's vote legal nationwide.

Prohibition

Significantly, another reform effort closely associated with women's groups triumphed at the same time. The movement to eliminate alcohol from American life had attracted many Americans, especially women, since before the Civil War. Temperance advocates saw drinking as the source of many of the worst problems faced by the working class, including family violence, unemployment, and poverty. By the early twentieth century

the Woman's Christian Temperance Union, with a quarter-million members, had become the single largest women's organization in American history.

The moral fervor that accompanied America's entry into the war provided a crucial boost to the cause. With so many breweries bearing German names, the movement benefited as well from the strong anti-German feeling of the war years. Outlawing beer and whiskey would also help to conserve precious grain, prohibitionists argued.

In 1917, a coalition of progressives and rural fundamentalists in Congress pushed through a constitutional amendment providing for a national ban on alcoholic drinks. The Eighteenth Amendment was ratified by the states in January 1919 and became the law of the land one year later. Although Prohibition would create a host of problems in the postwar years, especially as a stimulus for the growth of organized crime, many Americans, particularly native Protestants, considered it a worthy moral reform.

Public Health

Wartime mobilization brought deeper government involvement with public health issues, especially in the realm of sex hygiene, child welfare, and disease prevention. The rate of venereal disease among draftees was as high as 6 percent in some states, presenting a potential manpower problem for the army. In April 1917 the War Department mounted a vigorous campaign against venereal disease, which attracted the energies of progressive era sex reformers—social hygienists and antivice crusaders. Under the direction of Raymond Fosdick and the Commission on Training Camp Activities, the military educated troops on the dangers of contracting syphilis and gonorrhea and distributed condoms to soldiers. "A Soldier who gets a dose," warned a typical poster, "is a Traitor." More than a hundred red-light districts near military bases were closed down, and the army established five-mile "pure zones" to keep prostitutes away from the camps. Yet the sexual double standard still operated. Female activists angrily protested when military authorities, while refusing to arrest soldiers for patronizing prostitutes, arrested women en masse and held them in detention centers.

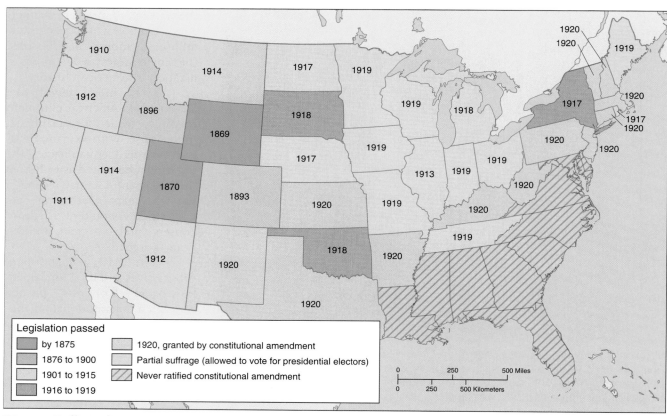

Woman Suffrage by State, 1869–1919 *Dates for the enactment of woman suffrage in the individual states. Years before ratification of the Nineteenth Amendment in 1920, a number of western states had legislated full or partial voting rights for women. In 1917 Montana suffragist Jeannette Rankin became the first woman elected to Congress.*

Source: Barbara G. Shortridge, *Atlas of American Women* (New York: Macmillan, 1987).

The scientific discussions of sex to which recruits were subjected in lectures, pamphlets, and films were surely a first for the vast majority of them. Venereal disease rates for soldiers declined by more than 300 percent during the war. The Division of Venereal Diseases, created in the summer of 1918 as a branch of the U.S. Public Health Service, established clinics offering free medical treatment to infected persons. It also coordinated an aggressive educational campaign through state departments of health.

The wartime boost to government health work continued into the postwar years. The Children's Bureau, created in 1912 as a part of the Labor Department, undertook a series of reports on special problems growing out of the war: the increase in employment of married women, finding day care for children of working mothers, and the growth of both child labor and delinquency. In 1918 Julia C. Lathrop, chief of the bureau, organized a "Children's Year" campaign designed to promote public protection of expectant mothers and infants and to enforce child labor laws. Millions of health education pamphlets were distrib-

uted nationwide, and mothers were encouraged to have their infants and children weighed and measured. Thousands of community-based committees enrolled some 11 million women in the drive.

In 1917, Lathrop, who had come to the Children's Bureau from the settlement house movement, proposed a plan to institutionalize federal aid to the states for protection of mothers and children. Congress finally passed the Maternity and Infancy Act in 1921, appropriating over $1 million a year to be administered to the states by the Children's Bureau. In the postwar years, clinics for prenatal and obstetrical care grew out of these efforts and greatly reduced the rate of infant and maternal mortality and disease.

The disastrous influenza epidemic of 1918–19 offered the most serious challenge to national public health during the war years. Part of a worldwide pandemic that claimed as many as 20 million lives, few Americans paid attention to the disease until it swept through military camps and eastern cities in September 1918. A lethal combination of the "flu" and respiratory complications (mainly pneumonia) killed roughly

550,000 Americans in ten months. Most victims were young adults between ages twenty and forty. Professional groups such as the American Medical Association called for massive government appropriations to search for a cure. Congress did appropriate a million dollars to the Public Health Service to combat and suppress the epidemic, but it offered no money for research.

The Public Health Service found itself overwhelmed by calls for doctors, nurses, and treatment facilities. Much of the care for the sick and dying came from Red Cross nurses and volunteers working in local communities across the nation. With a war on, and the nation focused on reports from the battlefront, even a public health crisis of this magnitude went relatively unnoticed. Although funding for the Public Health Service continued to grow in the 1920s, public and private expenditures on medical research were barely one-fiftieth of what they would become after World War II.

REPRESSION AND REACTION

World War I exposed and intensified many of the deepest social tensions in American life. On the local level, as exemplified by the Bisbee deportations, vigilantes increasingly took the law into their own hands to punish those suspected of disloyalty. The push for national unity led the federal government to crack down on a wide spectrum of dissenters from its war policies. The war inflamed racial hatred, and the worst race riots in the nation's history exploded in several cities. At war's end, a newly militant labor movement briefly asserted itself in mass strikes around the nation. Over all these developments loomed the 1917 Bolshevik Revolution in Russia. Radicals around the world had drawn inspiration from what looked like the first successful revolution against a capitalist state. Many conservatives worried that similar revolutions were imminent. From 1918 through 1920 the federal government directed a repressive antiradical campaign that had crucial implications for the nation's future.

Muzzling Dissent: The Espionage and Sedition Acts

The Espionage Act of June 1917 became the government's key tool for the suppression of antiwar sentiment. It set severe penalties (up to twenty years' imprisonment and a $10,000 fine) for anyone found guilty of aiding the enemy, obstructing recruitment, or causing insubordination in the armed forces. The act also empowered the postmaster general to exclude from the mails any newspapers or magazines he thought treasonous. Within a year the mailing rights of forty-five newspapers had been revoked. These included several anti-British and pro-Irish publications, as well as such

leading journals of American socialism as the Kansas-based *Appeal to Reason*, which had enjoyed a prewar circulation of half a million, and *The Masses*.

To enforce the Espionage Act, the government had to increase its overall police and surveillance machinery. Civilian intelligence was coordinated by the newly created Bureau of Investigation in the Justice Department. This agency was reorganized after the war as the Federal Bureau of Investigation (FBI). In May 1918 the Sedition Act, an amendment to the Espionage Act, outlawed "any disloyal, profane, scurrilous, or abusive language intended to cause contempt, scorn, contumely, or disrepute" to the government, Constitution, or flag.

In all, more than 2,100 cases were brought to trial under these acts. They became a convenient vehicle for striking out at socialists, pacifists, radical labor activists, and others who resisted the patriotic tide. The most celebrated prosecution came in June 1918 when federal agents arrested Eugene Debs in Canton, Ohio, after he gave a speech defending antiwar protesters. Sentenced to ten years in prison, Debs defiantly told the court: "I have been accused of having obstructed the war. I admit it. Gentlemen, I abhor war. I would oppose the war if I stood alone." Debs served thirty-two months in federal prison before being pardoned by President Warren G. Harding on Christmas Day 1921.

The Supreme Court upheld the constitutionality of the acts in several 1919 decisions. In *Schenck v. United States* the Court unanimously agreed with Justice Oliver Wendell Holmes's claim that Congress could restrict speech if the words "are used in such circumstances and are of such a nature as to create a clear and present danger." The decision upheld the conviction of Charles Schenck for having mailed pamphlets urging potential army inductees to resist conscription. In *Debs v. United States*, the Court affirmed the guilt of Eugene Debs for his antiwar speech in Canton, even though he had not explicitly urged violation of the draft laws. Finally, in *Abrams v. United States*, the Court upheld Sedition Act convictions of four Russian immigrants who had printed pamphlets denouncing American military intervention in the Russian Revolution. The nation's highest court thus endorsed the severe wartime restrictions on free speech.

The deportation of striking miners in Bisbee offered an extreme case of vigilante activity. Thousands of other instances took place as government repression and local vigilantes reinforced each other. The American Protective League, founded with the blessing of the Justice Department, mobilized 250,000 self-appointed "operatives" in more than 600 towns and cities. Members of the league, mostly businessmen, bankers, and former policemen, spied on their neighbors and staged a series of well-publicized "slacker" raids on antiwar protesters and draft evaders. Many communities, inspired by Committee on Public Information campaigns, sought to

VERVIEW

THE GREAT MIGRATION: BLACK POPULATION GROWTH IN SELECTED NORTHERN CITIES, 1910–1920

City	1910		1920		
	No.	Percent	No.	Percent	Percent Increase
New York	91,709	1.9%	152,467	2.7%	66.3%
Chicago	44,103	2.0	109,458	4.1	148.2
Philadelphia	84,459	5.5	134,229	7.4	58.9
Detroit	5,741	1.2	40,838	4.1	611.3
St. Louis	43,960	6.4	69,854	9.0	58.9
Cleveland	8,448	1.5	34,451	4.3	307.8
Pittsburgh	25,623	4.8	37,725	6.4	47.2
Cincinnati	19,739	5.4	30,079	7.5	53.2
Indianapolis	21,816	9.3	34,678	11.0	59.0
Newark	9,475	2.7	16,977	4.1	79.2
Kansas City	23,566	9.5	30,719	9.5	30.4
Columbus	12,739	7.0	22,181	9.4	74.1
Gary	383	2.3	5,299	9.6	1,283.6
Youngstown	1,936	2.4	6,662	5.0	244.1
Buffalo	1,773	0.4	4,511	0.9	154.4
Toledo	1,877	1.1	5,691	2.3	203.2
Akron	657	1.0	5,580	2.7	749.3

Source: U.S. Department of Commerce.

ban the teaching of the German language in their schools or the performance of German music in concert halls.

The Great Migration and Racial Tensions

Economic opportunity brought on by war prosperity triggered a massive migration of rural black Southerners to northern cities. From 1914 to 1920, somewhere between 300,000 and 500,000 African Americans left the rural South for the North. Chicago's black population increased by 65,000, or 150 percent; Detroit's by 35,000, or 600 percent. Acute labor shortages led northern factory managers to recruit black migrants to the expanding industrial centers. The Pennsylvania Railroad alone drew 10,000 black workers from Florida and south Georgia. Black workers eagerly left low-paying jobs as field hands and domestic servants for the chance at relatively high-paying work in meat-packing plants, shipyards, and steel mills.

Kinship and community networks were crucial in shaping what came to be called the Great Migration. They spread news about job openings, urban residential districts, and boardinghouses in northern cities. Black clubs, churches, and fraternal lodges in southern communities frequently sponsored the migration of their members, as well as return trips to the South. Single African American women often made the trip first because they could more easily obtain steady work as maids, cooks, and laundresses. One recalled that "if [white employers] liked the way the women would work in their homes or did ironing, they might throw some work to your husband or son." Relatively few African American men actually secured high-paying skilled jobs in industry or manufacturing. Most had to settle for work as construction laborers, teamsters, janitors, porters, or other low-paid jobs.

The persistence of lynching and other racial violence in the South no doubt contributed to the Great Migration. But racial violence was not limited to the South. Two of the worst race riots in American history occurred as a result of tensions brought on by wartime migration. On July 2, 1917, in East St. Louis, Illinois, a ferocious mob of whites attacked African Americans, killing at least 200. Before this riot, some of the city's manufacturers had been steadily recruiting black labor as a way to keep local union demands down. Unions had refused to allow black workers as members, and politicians had cynically exploited white racism in appealing for votes. In Chicago, on July 27,

1919, antiblack rioting broke out on a Lake Michigan beach. For two weeks white gangs hunted African Americans in the streets and burned hundreds out of their homes. Twenty-three African Americans and 15 whites died, and more than 500 were injured.

In both East St. Louis and Chicago, local authorities held African Americans responsible for the violence. President Wilson refused requests for federal intervention or investigation. A young black veteran who had been chased by a mob in the Chicago riot asked: "Had the ten months I spent in France been all in vain? Were all those white crosses over dead bodies of those dark skinned boys lying in Flanders field for naught? Was democracy a hollow sentiment?"

In terms of service in the armed forces, compliance with the draft, and involvement in volunteer work, African Americans had supported the war effort as faithfully as any group. In 1917, despite a segregated army and discrimination in defense industries, most African Americans thought the war might improve their lot. "If we again demonstrate our loyalty and devotion to our country," advised the *Chicago Defender*, "those injustices will disappear and the grounds for complaint will no longer exist." By the fall of 1919, writing in the *Crisis*, the journal of the National Association for the Advancement of Colored People (NAACP), black author James Weldon Johnson gloomily concluded that "an increased hatred of race was an integral part of wartime intolerance."

This southern African American family is shown arriving in Chicago around 1915. Black migrants to northern cities often faced overcrowding, inferior housing, and a high death rate from disease. But the chance to earn daily wages of $6 to $8 (the equivalent of a week's wages in much of the South), as well as the desire to escape persistent racial violence, kept the migrants coming.

Black disillusionment about the war grew quickly. So did a newly militant spirit. A heightened sense of race consciousness and activism was evident among black veterans and the growing black communities of northern cities. Taking the lead in the fight against bigotry and injustice, the NAACP held a national conference in 1919 on lynching. It pledged to defend persecuted African Americans, publicize the horrors of lynch law, and seek federal legislation against "Judge Lynch." By 1919 membership in the NAACP had reached 60,000 and the circulation of its journal exceeded half a million.

Labor Strife

The relative labor peace of 1917 and 1918 dissolved after the armistice. More than 4 million American workers were involved in some 3,600 strikes in 1919 alone. This unprecedented strike wave had several causes. Most of the modest wartime wage gains were wiped out by spiraling inflation and high prices for food, fuel, and housing. With the end of government controls on industry, many employers withdrew their recognition of unions. Difficult working conditions, such as the twelve-hour day in steel mills, were still routine in some industries. The quick return of demobilized servicemen to the labor force meant layoffs and new concerns about job security.

Several of the postwar strikes received widespread national attention. They seemed to be more than simple economic conflicts, and they provoked deep fears about the larger social order. In February 1919 a strike in the shipyards of Seattle, Washington, over wages escalated into a general citywide strike involving 60,000 workers. A strike committee coordinated the city's essential services for a week in a disciplined, nonviolent fashion. But the local press and Mayor Ole Hanson denounced the strikers as revolutionaries. Hanson effectively ended the strike by requesting federal troops to occupy the city.

In September, Boston policemen went out on strike when the police commissioner rejected a citizens' commission study that recommended a pay raise. Massachusetts governor Calvin Coolidge called in the National Guard to restore order and won a national reputation by crushing the strike. The entire police force was fired. Coolidge declared, "There is no right to strike against the public safety by anybody, anywhere, any time."

The biggest strike took place in the steel industry, involving some 350,000 steelworkers. Centered in several midwestern cities, this epic struggle lasted from September 1919 to January 1920. The AFL had hoped to build on wartime gains in an industry that had successfully resisted unionization before the war. The major demands were union recognition, the eight-hour day, and wage increases. The steel companies used black strike-

The General Strike Committee of Seattle distributed groceries to union families in February 1919. The Seattle general strike had been triggered when shipyard workers walked off the job after failing to gain wage hikes to offset spiraling postwar inflation. The conservative Los Angeles Times *saw the strike as evidence that Bolshevism was a right here and now American menace.*

breakers and armed guards to keep the mills running. Elbert Gary, president of U.S. Steel, directed a sophisticated propaganda campaign that branded the strikers as revolutionaries. Public opinion turned against the strike and condoned the use of state and federal troops to break it. A riot in Gary, Indiana, left eighteen strikers dead. The failed steel strike proved to be the era's most bitter and devastating defeat for organized labor.

AN UNEASY PEACE

The armistice of November 1918 ended the fighting on the battlefield, but the war continued at the peace conference. In the old royal palace of Versailles near Paris, delegates from twenty-seven countries spent five months hammering out a settlement. Yet neither Germany nor Russia was represented. The proceedings were dominated by leaders of the "Big Four": David Lloyd George (Great Britain), Georges Clemenceau (France), Vittorio Orlando (Italy), and Woodrow Wilson (United States). President Wilson saw the peace conference as a historic opportunity to project his domestic liberalism onto the world stage. But the stubborn realities of power politics would frustrate Wilson at Versailles and lead to his most crushing defeat at home.

The Fourteen Points

Wilson arrived in Paris with the United States delegation in January 1919. He brought with him a plan for peace that he had outlined a year earlier in a speech to Congress on U.S. war aims. The Fourteen Points, as they were called, had originally served wartime purposes: to appeal to war opponents in Austria-Hungary and Germany, to convince Russia to stay in the war, and to help sustain Allied morale. As a blueprint for peace, they contained three main elements. First, Wilson offered a series of specific proposals for setting postwar boundaries in Europe and creating new countries out of the collapsed Austro-Hungarian and Ottoman empires. The key idea here was the right of all peoples to "national self-determination." Second, Wilson listed general principles for governing international conduct, including freedom of the seas, free trade, open covenants instead of secret treaties, reduced armaments, and mediation for competing colonial claims. Third, and most important, Wilson called for a League of Nations to help implement these principles and resolve future disputes.

The Fourteen Points offered a plan for world order deeply rooted in the liberal progressivism long associated with Wilson. The plan reflected a faith in efficient government and the rule of law as means for solving international problems. It looked to free trade and commercial development as the key to spreading prosperity. It advocated a dynamic democratic capitalism as a middle ground between Old World autocracy and revolutionary socialism. Wilson's vision was a profoundly moral one, and he was certain it was the only road to a lasting and humane peace.

The most controversial element, both at home and abroad, would prove to be the league. The heart of the league covenant, Article X, called for collective security as the ultimate method of keeping the peace: "The members of the League undertake to respect and preserve as against external aggression the territorial integrity and existing political independence of all Members." In the United States, Wilson's critics would focus on this provision as an unacceptable surrender of the nation's sovereignty and independence in foreign affairs. They also raised constitutional objections, arguing that the American system vested the power to declare war with the Congress. Would membership in the league violate this basic principle of the Constitution?

Wilson in Paris

The president was pleased when the conference at first accepted his plan as the basis for discussions. He also enjoyed wildly enthusiastic receptions from the public in Paris and several other European capitals he visited. France's Clemenceau was less enamored. He sarcastically observed, "God gave us the Ten Commandments, and we broke them. Wilson gave us the Fourteen Points. We shall see." Wilson's plan could not survive the hostile atmosphere at Versailles.

Much of the negotiating at Versailles was in fact done in secret among the Big Four. The ideal of self-determination found limited expression. The independent states of Austria, Hungary, Poland, Yugoslavia, and Czechoslovakia were carved out of the homelands of the beaten Central Powers. But the Allies resisted Wilson's call for independence for the colonies of the defeated nations. A compromise mandate system of protectorates gave the French and British control of parts of the old German and Turkish empires in Africa and West Asia. Japan won control of former German colonies in China. Among those trying, but failing, to influence the treaty negotiations were the sixty-odd delegates to the first Pan African Congress, held in Paris at the same time as the peace talks. The group included Americans W.E.B. Du Bois and William Monroe Trotter as well as representatives from Africa and the West Indies. All were disappointed with the failure of the peace conference to grant self-determination to thousands of Africans living in former German colonies.

Another disappointment for Wilson came with the issue of war guilt. He had strongly opposed the extraction of harsh economic reparations from the Central Powers. But the French and British, with their awful war losses fresh in mind, insisted on making Germany pay. The final treaty contained a clause attributing the war to "the aggression of Germany," and a commission later set German war reparations at $33 billion. Bitter resentment in Germany over the punitive treaty helped sow the seeds for the Nazi rise to power in the 1930s.

The final treaty was signed on June 28, 1919, in the Hall of Mirrors at the Versailles palace. The Germans had no choice but to accept its harsh terms. President Wilson had been disappointed by the secret deals and the endless compromising of his ideals, no doubt underestimating the stubborn reality of power politics in the wake of Europe's most devastating war. He had nonetheless won a commitment to the League of Nations, the centerpiece of his plan, and he was confident that the American people would accept the treaty. The tougher fight would be with the Senate, where a two-thirds vote was needed for ratification.

The Treaty Fight

Preoccupied with peace conference politics in Paris, Wilson had neglected politics at home. His troubles had actually started earlier. Republicans had captured both the House and the Senate in the 1918 elections.

Woodrow Wilson, Georges Clemenceau, and David Lloyd George are among the central figures depicted in John Christen Johansen's Signing of the Treaty of Versailles. But all the gathered statesmen appear dwarfed by their surroundings.

Wilson had then made a tactical error by including no prominent Republicans in the U.S. peace delegation. He therefore faced a variety of tough opponents to the treaty he brought home.

Wilson's most extreme enemies in the Senate were a group of about sixteen "irreconcilables," opposed to a treaty in any form. Some were isolationist progressives, such as Republicans Robert M. La Follette of Wisconsin and William Borah of Idaho, who opposed the League of Nations as steadfastly as they opposed American entry into the war. Others were racist xenophobes like Democrat James Reed of Missouri. He objected, he said, to submitting questions to a tribunal "on which a nigger from Liberia, a nigger from Honduras, a nigger from India, and an unlettered gentleman from Siam, each have votes equal to the great United States of America."

The less dogmatic but more influential opponents were led by Republican Henry Cabot Lodge of Massachusetts, powerful majority leader of the Senate. They had strong reservations about the League of Nations, especially the provisions for collective security in the event of a member nation's being attacked. Lodge argued that this provision impinged on congressional authority to declare war and placed unacceptable restraints on the nation's ability to pursue an independent foreign policy. Lodge proposed a series of amendments that would have weakened the league. But Wilson refused to compromise, motivated in part by the long-standing hatred he and Lodge felt toward each other. The president decided instead to take his case directly to the American people.

In September, Wilson set out on a speaking tour across the country to drum up support for the league and the treaty. His train traveled 8,000 miles—through the Midwest, to the Pacific, and then back East. The crowds were large and responsive, but they did not change any votes in the Senate. The strain took its toll. On September 25, after speaking in Pueblo, Colorado, the sixty-three-year-old Wilson collapsed from exhaustion. His doctor canceled the rest of the trip. A week later, back in Washington, the president suffered a stroke that left him partially paralyzed. In November, Lodge brought the treaty out of committee for a vote, having appended to it fourteen reservations—that is, recommended changes. A bedridden Wilson stubbornly refused to compromise and instructed Democrats to vote against the Lodge version of the treaty. On November 19, Democrats joined with the "irreconcilables" to defeat the amended treaty, 39 to 55.

Wilson refused to budge. In January, he urged Democrats to either stand by the original treaty or vote it down. The 1920 election, he warned, would be "a great and solemn referendum" on the whole issue. In the final vote, on March 19, 1920, twenty-one Democrats broke with the president and voted for the Lodge version, giving it a majority of 49 to 35. But this was seven votes short of the two-thirds needed for ratification. As a result, the United States never signed the Versailles Treaty, nor did it join the League of Nations. The absence of the United States weakened the League and made it more difficult for the organization to realize Wilson's dream of a peaceful community of nations.

The Russian Revolution and America's Response

Since early 1917, the turmoil of the Russian Revolution had changed the climate of both foreign affairs and domestic politics. The repressive and corrupt regime of Czar Nicholas II had been overthrown in March 1917 by a coalition of forces demanding change. The new provisional government, headed by Alexander Kerensky, vowed to keep Russia in the fight against Germany. But the war had taken a terrible toll on Russian soldiers and civilians, and had become very unpopular. The radical Bolsheviks, led by V. I. Lenin, gained a large following by promising "peace, land, and bread," and they began plotting to seize power. The Bolsheviks followed the teachings of German revolutionary Karl Marx, emphasizing the inevitability of class struggle and the replacement of capitalism by communism.

In November 1917 the Bolsheviks took control of the Russian government. In March 1918, to the dismay of the Allies, the new Bolshevik government negotiated a separate peace with Germany, the Treaty of Brest-Litovsk. Russia was now lost as a military ally, and her defection made possible a massive shift of German troops to the Western Front. As civil war raged within Russia, British and French leaders wanted to help counterrevolutionary forces overthrow the new Bolshevik regime, as well as reclaim military supplies originally sent for use against the Germans.

Although sympathetic to the March revolution overthrowing the czar, President Wilson refused to recognize the authority of the Bolshevik regime. Bolshevism represented a threat to the liberal-capitalist values that Wilson believed to be the foundation of America's moral and material power and that provided the basis for the Fourteen Points. At the same time, however, Wilson at first resisted British and French pressure to intervene in Russia, citing his commitment to national self-determination and noninterference in other countries' internal affairs. "I believe in letting them work out their own salvation, even though they wallow in anarchy for a while," he wrote to one Allied diplomat.

By August 1918, as the Russian political and military situation became increasingly chaotic, Wilson agreed to British and French plans for sending troops to Siberia and northern Russia. Meanwhile, Japan poured troops into Siberia and northern Manchuria in a bid to control the commercially important Chinese Eastern and Trans-Siberian Railways. After the Wilson administration negotiated an agreement that placed these strategic railways under international control, the restoration and protection of the railways became the primary concern of American military forces in Russia. Wilson justified the intervention on trade and commercial grounds, telling Congress, "It is essential that we maintain the policy of the Open Door." But however reluctantly, the United States had in fact become an active, anti-Bolshevik participant in the Russian civil war.

Wilson's idealistic support for self-determination had succumbed to the demands of international power politics. Eventually, some 15,000 American troops served in northern and eastern Russia, with some remaining until 1920. They stayed for two reasons: to counter Japanese influence, and because Wilson did not want to risk alienating the British and French, who opposed withdrawal. The Allied armed intervention widened the gulf between Russia and the West. In March 1919, Russian Communists established the Third International, or Comintern. Their call for a worldwide revolution deepened Allied mistrust, and the Paris Peace Conference essentially ignored the new political reality posed by the Russian Revolution.

The Red Scare

In the United States, strikes, antiwar agitation, even racial disturbances were increasingly blamed on foreign radicals and alien ideologies. Pro-German sentiment, socialism, the IWW, and trade unionism in general, all were conveniently lumped together. The accusation of Bolshevism became a powerful weapon for turning public opinion against strikers and political dissenters of all kinds. In the 1919 Seattle general strike, for example, Mayor Ole Hanson claimed against all evidence that the strikers "want to take possession of our American Government and try to duplicate the anarchy of Russia." Months later the Seattle *Post-Intelligencer,* referring to the IWW, said: "We must smash every un-American and anti-American organization in the land. We must put to death the leaders of this gigantic conspiracy of murder, pillage, and revolution."

In truth, by 1919 the American radicals were already weakened and badly split. The Socialist Party had around 40,000 members. Two small Communist Parties, made up largely of immigrants, had a total of perhaps 70,000. In the spring of 1919, a few extremists mailed bombs to prominent business and political leaders. That June, simultaneous bombings in eight cities killed two people and damaged the residence of Attorney General A. Mitchell Palmer. With public alarm growing, state and federal officials began a coordinated campaign to root out subversives and their alleged Russian connections.

Palmer used the broad authority of the 1918 Alien Act, which enabled the government to deport any immigrant found to be a member of a revolutionary organization prior to or after coming to the United States. In a series of raids in late 1919, Justice Department agents in eleven cities arrested and roughed up several hundred members of the IWW and the Union of Russian Workers. Little evidence of revolutionary intent was found, but 249 people were deported, including prominent anarchists Emma Goldman and Alexander Berkman. In early 1920 some 6,000 people in thirty-three cities, including many U.S. citizens and noncommunists, were arrested and herded into prisons and bullpens. Again, no evidence of a grand plot was found, but another 600 aliens were deported. The Palmer raids had a ripple effect around the nation, encouraging other repressive measures against radicals. In New York, the state assembly refused to seat five duly elected Socialist Party members.

A report prepared by a group of distinguished lawyers questioned the legality of the attorney general's tactics. Palmer's popularity had waned by the spring of 1920, when it became clear that his predictions of revolutionary uprisings were wildly exaggerated. But the Red Scare left an ugly legacy: wholesale violations of constitutional rights, deportations of hundreds of innocent people, fuel for the fires of nativism and intolerance. Business groups, such as the National Association of Manufacturers, found "Red-baiting" to be an effective tool in postwar efforts to keep unions out of their factories. Indeed, the government-sanctioned Red Scare reemerged later in the century as a powerful political force.

The Red Scare took its toll on the women's movement as well. Before the war, many suffragists and feminists had maintained ties and shared platforms with socialist and labor groups. The suffrage movement in particular had brought together women from very different class backgrounds and political perspectives. But the calls for "100 percent Americanism" during and after the war destroyed the fragile alliances that had made a group such as the National American Woman Suffrage Association so powerful. After the war, many women's organizations that had been divided over American involvement in the war reunited under the umbrella of the National Council for Prevention of War. But when military spokesmen in the early 1920s attacked the group for advocating communism, two of its largest affiliates—the General Federation of Women's Clubs and the Parent-Teacher Association—withdrew in fear. Hostility to radicalism marked the political climate of the 1920s, and this atmosphere narrowed the political spectrum for women activists.

The Election of 1920

The presidential contest of 1920 suggested that Americans wanted to retreat from the internationalism, reform fervor, and social tensions associated with the war. Woodrow Wilson had wanted the 1920 election to be a "solemn referendum" on the League of Nations and his conduct of the war. Ill and exhausted, Wilson did not run for reelection. A badly divided Democratic Party compromised on Governor James M. Cox of Ohio as its candidate. A proven vote-getter, Cox distanced himself from Wilson's policies, which had come under withering attack from many quarters.

The Republicans nominated Senator Warren G. Harding of Ohio. A political hack, the handsome and genial Harding had virtually no qualifications to be president, except that he looked like one. Harding's campaign was vague and ambiguous about the Versailles Treaty and almost everything else. He struck a chord with the electorate in calling for a retreat from Wilsonian idealism. "America's present need," he said, "is not heroics but healing; not nostrums but normalcy; not revolution but restoration."

The notion of a "return to normalcy" proved very attractive to voters exhausted by the war, inflation, big government, and social dislocation. Harding won the greatest landslide in history to that date, carrying every state outside the South and taking the popular vote by 16 million to 9 million. Republicans retained their majorities in the House and Senate as well. Socialist Eugene

Debs, still a powerful symbol of the dream of radical social change, managed to poll 900,000 votes from jail. But the overall vote repudiated Wilson and the progressive movement. Americans seemed eager to pull back from moralism in public and international controversies. Yet many of the economic, social, and cultural changes wrought by the war would accelerate during the 1920s. In truth, there could never be a "return to normalcy."

CHRONOLOGY

1903	U.S. obtains Panama canal rights
1904	Roosevelt Corollary justifies U.S. intervention in the Americas
1905	President Theodore Roosevelt mediates peace treaty between Japan and Russia at Portsmouth Conference
1908	Root-Takahira Agreement with Japan affirms status quo in Asia and Open Door policy in China
1911	Mexican Revolution begins
1914	U.S. forces invade Mexico Panama Canal opens First World War begins in Europe President Woodrow Wilson issues proclamation of neutrality
1915	Germany declares war zone around Great Britain German U-boat sinks *Lusitania*
1916	Pancho Villa raids New Mexico, is pursued by General Pershing Wilson is reelected National Defense Act establishes preparedness program
1917	February: Germany resumes unrestricted submarine warfare March: Zimmermann note, suggesting a German-Mexican alliance, shocks Americans April: U.S. declares war on the Central Powers Committee on Public Information is established May: Selective Service Act is passed June: Espionage Act is passed July: Race riot occurs in East St. Louis

	War Industries Board is established August: Food Administration and Fuel Administration are established November: Bolshevik Revolution begins in Russia
1918	January: Wilson unveils Fourteen Points April: National War Labor Board is established May: Sedition Act is passed June: Eugene Debs is arrested for defending antiwar protesters U.S. troops begin to see action in France U.S. troops serve in Russia November: Armistice ends war
1919	January: Eighteenth Amendment (Prohibition) is ratified Wilson serves as Chief U.S. negotiator at Paris Peace Conference June: Versailles Treaty is signed in Paris July: Race riot breaks out in Chicago Steel strike begins in several midwestern cities September: Wilson suffers stroke while touring country in support of Versailles Treaty November: Henry Cabot Lodge's version of the Versailles Treaty is rejected by the Senate Palmer raids begin
1920	March: Senate finally votes down Versailles Treaty and League of Nations August: Nineteenth Amendment (woman suffrage) is ratified November: Warren G. Harding is elected president

CONCLUSION

Compared to the casualties and social upheavals endured by the European powers, the Great War's impact on American life might appear slight. Yet the war created economic, social, and political dislocations that helped reshape American life long after Armistice Day. Republican administrations invoked the wartime partnership between government and industry to justify an aggressive peacetime policy fostering cooperation between the state and business. Wartime production needs contributed to what economists later called "the second industrial revolution." Patriotic fervor and the exaggerated specter of Bolshevism were used to repress radicalism, organized labor, feminism, and the entire legacy of progressive reform.

The wartime measure of national prohibition evolved into perhaps the most contentious social issue of peacetime. Sophisticated use of sales techniques, psychology, and propaganda during the war helped define the newly powerful advertising and public relations industries of the 1920s. The growing visibility of immigrants and African Americans, especially in the nation's cities, provoked a xenophobic and racist backlash in the politics of the 1920s. More than anything else, the desire for "normalcy" reflected the deep anxieties evoked by America's wartime experience.

REVIEW QUESTIONS

1. What central issues drew the United States deeper into international politics in the early years of the century? How did American presidents justify a more expansive role? What diplomatic and military policies did they exploit for these ends?
2. Compare the arguments for and against American participation in the Great War. Which Americans were most likely to support entry? Which were more likely to oppose it?
3. How did mobilizing for war change the economy and its relationship to government? Which of these changes, if any, spilled over to the postwar years?
4. How did the war affect political life in the United States? What techniques were used to stifle dissent? What was the war's political legacy?
5. To what extent was the war an extension of progressivism?
6. Analyze the impact of the war on American workers. How did the conflict affect the lives of African Americans and women?
7. What principles guided Woodrow Wilson's Fourteen Points? How would you explain the United States' failure to ratify the Treaty of Versailles?

RECOMMENDED READING

Robert H. Ferrell, *Woodrow Wilson and World War I* (1985). A close analysis of Wilson's handling of wartime diplomacy and domestic politics.

Martin Gilbert, *The First World War: A Complete History* (1994). An ambitious overview of the Great War from a global perspective.

Maureen Greenwald, *Women, War, and Work* (1980). The best account of the impact of the war on working women.

David M. Kennedy, *Over Here* (1980). The best, most comprehensive one-volume history of the political and economic impact of the war on the domestic front.

Thomas J. Knock, *To End All Wars: Woodrow Wilson and the Quest for a New World Order* (1992). A fine analysis of Wilson's internationalism, its links to his domestic policies, and his design for the League of Nations.

Walter LaFeber, *The American Age* (1989). A fine survey of the history of U.S. foreign policy that includes an analysis of the pre–World War I era.

Paul L. Murphy, *World War I and the Origin of Civil Liberties* (1979). A good overview of the various civil liberties issues raised by the war and government efforts to suppress dissent.

Ronald Schaffer, *America in the Great War: The Rise of the War Welfare State* (1991). Excellent material on how the war transformed the relationship between business and government and spurred improved conditions for industrial workers.

Joe William Trotter Jr., ed., *The Great Migration in Historical Perspective* (1991). An excellent collection of essays examining the Great Migration, with special attention to issues of class and gender within the African American community.

Neil A. Wynn, *From Progressivism to Prosperity: World War I and American Society* (1986). An illuminating account of the social impact of the war on American life. Effectively connects the war experience with both progressive era trends and postwar developments in the 1920s.

ADDITIONAL BIBLIOGRAPHY

Becoming a World Power

Richard H. Collin, *Theodore Roosevelt's Caribbean* (1990)
John Dobson, *America's Ascent: The United States Becomes a Great Power, 1880–1914* (1978)
Akira Iriye, *Pacific Estrangement* (1972)
Friedrich Katz, *The Secret War in Mexico* (1981)
Burton I. Kaufman, *Efficiency and Expansion* (1974)
Walter LaFeber, *The Panama Canal* (1978)
Lester E. Langley, *The Banana Wars: An Inner History of American Empire, 1900–1934* (1983)
Emily S. Rosenberg, *Spreading the American Dream* (1982)

The Great War

Lloyd E. Ambrosius, *Woodrow Wilson and the American Diplomatic Tradition* (1987)
Paul Fussell, *The Great War and Modern Memory* (1973)
James Joll, *The Origins of the First World War* (1984)
C. Roland Marchand, *The American Peace Movement and Social Reform, 1898–1918* (1973)

American Mobilization

A. E. Barbeau and Florette Henri, *The Unknown Soldiers: Black American Troops in World War I* (1974)
John W. Chambers, *To Raise an Army: The Draft in Modern America* (1987)
J. Garry Clifford, *Citizen Soldiers* (1972)
Edward M. Coffman, *The War to End All Wars* (1968)
Charles Gilbert, *American Financing of World War I* (1970)
Stephen Vaughn, *Holding Fast the Inner Lines: Democracy, Nationalism, and the Committee on Public Information* (1980)
Russell Weigley, *The American Way of War* (1973)

Over Here

Daniel R. Beaver, *Newton D. Baker and the American War Effort, 1917–1919* (1966)
Allen J. Brandt, *No Magic Bullet: A Social History of Venereal Disease in the United States since 1880* (1985)
Valerie J. Conner, *The National War Labor Board* (1983)
Frank L. Grubbs Jr., *Samuel Gompers and the Great War* (1982)
Ellis W. Hawley, *The Great War and the Search for Modern Order*, 2d ed. (1992)
Jeffrey Haydu, *Making American Industries Safe for Democracy* (1997)
John F. McClymer, *War and Welfare: Social Engineering in America, 1890–1925* (1980)
David Montgomery, *The Fall of the House of Labor* (1987)
Barbara Steinson, *American Women's Activism in World War I* (1982)

Repression and Reaction

David Brody, *Labor in Crisis: The Steel Strike of 1919* (1965)
James P. Grossman, *Land of Hope: Chicago, Black Southerners, and the Great Migration* (1989)
Florette Henri, *Black Migration: Movement Northward, 1900–1920* (1975)
Frederick C. Luebke, *Bonds of Loyalty: German Americans and World War I* (1974)
Harold C. Peterson and Gilbert Fite, *Opponents of War, 1917–1918* (1968)
William Preston Jr., *Aliens and Dissenters: Federal Suppression of Radicals, 1903–1933* (1966)
William M. Tuttle Jr., *Race Riot: Chicago in the Red Summer of 1919* (1970)

An Uneasy Peace

Dana Frank, *Purchasing Power: Consumer Organizing, Gender, and the Seattle Labor Movement, 1919–1929* (1994)
Lloyd Gardner, *Safe for Democracy: The Anglo-American Response to Revolution, 1913–1923* (1984)
Robert D. Johnson, *The Peace Progressives and American Foreign Relations* (1995)
N. Gordon Levin Jr., *Woodrow Wilson and World Politics* (1968)
Robert K. Murray, *Red Scare: A Study in National Hysteria, 1919–1920* (1955)
Richard Polenberg, *Fighting Faiths: The Abrams Case, the Supreme Court, and Free Speech* (1987)
Stuart Rochester, *American Liberal Disillusionment in the Wake of World War I* (1977)
Ralph Stone, *The Irreconcilables: The Fight against the League of Nations* (1970)

Biography

Bruce Clayton, *Forgotten Prophet: The Life of Randolph Bourne* (1984)
Kendrick Clements, *Woodrow Wilson: World Statesman* (1987)
Stanley Coben, *A. Mitchell Palmer* (1963)
Arthur S. Link, *Woodrow Wilson: War, Revolution, and Peace* (1979)
Jordan Schwarz, *The Speculator: Bernard M. Baruch in Washington, 1917–1965* (1981)
Frank E. Vandiver, *Black Jack: The Life and Times of John J. Pershing* (1977)
Jacqueline van Voris, *Carrie Chapman Catt* (1987)

APPENDIX

THE DECLARATION OF INDEPENDENCE

When in the course of human events it becomes necessary for one people to dissolve the political bands which have connected them with another and to assume, among the powers of the earth, the separate and equal station to which the laws of nature and of nature's God entitle them, a decent respect to the opinions of mankind requires that they should declare the causes which impel them to the separation.

We hold these truths to be self-evident, that all men are created equal; that they are endowed by their Creator with certain unalienable rights; that among these are life, liberty, and the pursuit of happiness. That, to secure these rights, governments are instituted among men, deriving their just powers from the consent of the governed; that, whenever any form of government becomes destructive of these ends, it is the right of the people to alter or to abolish it, and to institute a new government, laying its foundation on such principles, and organizing its powers in such form, as to them shall seem most likely to effect their safety and happiness. Prudence, indeed, will dictate that governments long established should not be changed for light and transient causes; and, accordingly, all experience hath shown that mankind are more disposed to suffer, while evils are sufferable, than to right themselves by abolishing the forms to which they are accustomed. But when a long train of abuses and usurpations, pursuing invariably the same object, evinces a design to reduce them under absolute despotism, it is their right, it is their duty, to throw off such government and to provide new guards for their future security. Such has been the patient sufferance of these colonies, and such is now the necessity which constrains them to alter their former systems of government. The history of the present King of Great Britain is a history of repeated injuries and usurpations, all having, in direct object, the establishment of an absolute tyranny over these States. To prove this, let facts be submitted to a candid world:

He has refused his assent to laws the most wholesome and necessary for the public good.

He has forbidden his governors to pass laws of immediate and pressing importance, unless suspended in their operation till his assent should be obtained; and, when so suspended, he has utterly neglected to attend to them.

He has refused to pass other laws for the accommodation of large districts of people, unless those people would relinquish the right of representation in the legislature, a right inestimable to them and formidable to tyrants only.

He has called together legislative bodies at places unusual, uncomfortable, and distant from the depository of their public records, for the sole purpose of fatiguing them into compliance with his measures.

He has dissolved representative houses, repeatedly for opposing, with manly firmness, his invasions on the rights of the people.

He has refused, for a long time after such dissolutions, to cause others to be elected; whereby the legislative powers, incapable of annihilation, have returned to the people at large for their exercise; the state remaining, in the meantime, exposed to all the danger of invasion from without and convulsions within.

He has endeavored to prevent the population of these States; for that purpose, obstructing the laws for naturalization of foreigners, refusing to pass others to encourage their migration hither, and raising the conditions of new appropriations of lands.

He has obstructed the administration of justice by refusing his assent to laws for establishing judiciary powers.

He has made judges dependent on his will alone for the tenure of their offices and the amount and payment of their salaries.

He has erected a multitude of new offices and sent hither swarms of officers to harass our people and eat out their substance.

He has kept among us, in time of peace, standing armies, without the consent of our legislatures.

He has affected to render the military independent of, and superior to, the civil power.

He has combined with others to subject us to a jurisdiction foreign to our Constitution and unacknowledged by our laws, giving his assent to their acts of pretended legislation—

For quartering large bodies of armed troops among us;

For protecting them, by mock trial, from punishment for any murders which they should commit on the inhabitants of these States;

For cutting off our trade with all parts of the world;

For imposing taxes on us without our consent;

For depriving us, in many cases, of the benefit of trial by jury;

For transporting us beyond seas to be tried for pretended offences;

For abolishing the free system of English laws in a neighboring province, establishing therein an arbitrary government, and enlarging its boundaries, so as to render it at once an example and fit instrument for introducing the same absolute rule into these colonies;

For taking away our charters, abolishing our most valuable laws, and altering, fundamentally, the powers of our governments.

For suspending our own legislatures and declaring themselves invested with power to legislate for us in all cases whatsoever.

He has abdicated government here by declaring us out of his protection and waging war against us.

He has plundered our seas, ravaged our coasts, burnt our towns, and destroyed the lives of our people.

He is, at this time, transporting large armies of foreign mercenaries to complete the works of death, desolation, and tyranny already begun with circumstances of cruelty and perfidy scarcely paralleled in the most barbarous ages, and totally unworthy the head of a civilized nation.

He has constrained our fellow citizens, taken captive on the high seas, to bear arms against their country, to become the executioners of their friends and brethren, or to fall themselves by their hands.

He has excited domestic insurrections amongst us and has endeavored to bring on the inhabitants of our frontiers, the merciless Indian savages, whose known rule of warfare is an undistinguished destruction of all ages, sexes, and conditions.

In every stage of these oppressions, we have petitioned for redress in the most humble terms; our repeated petitions have been answered only by repeated injury. A prince whose character is thus marked by every act which may define a tyrant is unfit to be the ruler of a free people.

Nor have we been wanting in attention to our British brethren. We have warned them, from time to time, of attempts made by their legislature to extend an unwarrantable jurisdiction over us. We have reminded them of the circumstances of our emigration and settlement here. We have appealed to their native justice and magnanimity, and we have conjured them, by the ties of our common kindred, to disavow these usurpations, which would inevitably interrupt our connections and correspondence. They, too, have been deaf to the voice of justice and consanguinity. We must, therefore, acquiesce in the necessity which denounces our separation, and hold them, as we hold the rest of mankind, enemies in war, in peace, friends.

We, therefore, the representatives of the United States of America, in general Congress assembled, appealing to the Supreme Judge of the world for the rectitude of our intentions, do, in the name and by the authority of the good people of these colonies, solemnly publish and declare, that these united colonies are, and of right ought to be, free and independent states: that they are absolved from all allegiance to the British Crown, and that all political connection between them and the state of Great Britain is, and ought to be, totally dissolved; and that, as free and independent states, they have full power to levy war, conclude peace, contract alliances, establish commerce, and to do all other acts and things which independent states may of right do. And, for the support of this declaration, with a firm reliance on the protection of Divine Providence, we mutually pledge to each other our lives, our fortunes, and our sacred honor.

THE CONSTITUTION OF THE UNITED STATES OF AMERICA

We the people of the United States, in order to form a more perfect union, establish justice, insure domestic tranquillity, provide for the common defense, promote the general welfare, and secure the blessings of liberty to ourselves and our posterity, do ordain and establish this Constitution for the United States of America.

Article I

Section 1. All legislative powers herein granted shall be vested in a Congress of the United States, which shall consist of a Senate and House of Representatives.

Section 2. 1. The House of Representatives shall be composed of members chosen every second year by the people of the several States, and the electors in each State shall have the qualifications requisite for electors of the most numerous branch of the State legislature.

2. No person shall be a representative who shall not have attained to the age of twenty-five years, and been seven years a citizen of the United States, and who shall not, when elected, be an inhabitant of that State in which he shall be chosen.

3. Representatives and direct taxes[1] shall be apportioned among the several States which may be included within this Union, according to their respective numbers, which shall be determined by adding to the whole number of free persons, including those bound to service for a term of years, and excluding Indians not taxed, three fifths of all other persons.[2] The actual enumeration shall be made within three years after the first meeting of the Congress of the United States, and within every subsequent term of ten years, in such manner as they shall by law direct. The number of representatives shall not exceed one for every thirty thousand, but each State shall have at least one representative; and until such enumeration shall be made, the State of New Hampshire shall be entitled to choose three, Massachusetts eight, Rhode Island and Providence Plantations one, Connecticut five, New York six, New Jersey four, Pennsylvania eight, Delaware one, Maryland six, Virginia ten, North Carolina five, South Carolina five, and Georgia three.

4. When vacancies happen in the representation from any State, the executive authority thereof shall issue writs of election to fill such vacancies.

5. The House of Representatives shall choose their speaker and other officers; and shall have the sole power of impeachment.

Section 3. 1. The Senate of the United States shall be composed of two senators from each State, chosen by the legislature thereof,[3] for six years; and each senator shall have one vote.

2. Immediately after they shall be assembled in consequence of the first election, they shall be divided as equally as may be into three classes. The seats of the senators of the first class shall be vacated at the expiration of the second year, of the second class at the expiration of the fourth year, and of the third class at the expiration of the sixth year, so that one third may be chosen every second year; and if vacancies happen by resignation, or otherwise, during the recess of the legislature of any State, the executive thereof may make temporary appointments until the next meeting of the legislature, which shall then fill such vacancies.[4]

3. No person shall be a senator who shall not have attained to the age of thirty years, and been nine years a citizen of the United States, and who shall not, when elected, be an inhabitant of that State for which he shall be chosen.

4. The Vice President of the United States shall be President of the Senate, but shall have no vote, unless they be equally divided.

5. The Senate shall choose their other officers, and also a president pro tempore, in the absence of the Vice President, or when he shall exercise the office of the President of the United States.

6. The Senate shall have the sole power to try all impeachments. When sitting for that purpose, they shall be on oath or affirmation. When the President of the United States is tried, the chief justice shall preside: and no person shall be convicted without the concurrence of two thirds of the members present.

7. Judgment in cases of impeachment shall not extend further than to removal from office, and disqualification to hold and enjoy any office of honor, trust or profit under the United States: but the party convicted shall nevertheless be liable and subject to indictment, trial, judgment and punishment, according to law.

Section 4. 1. The times, places, and manner of holding elections for senators and representatives, shall be prescribed in each State by the legislature thereof; but the Congress may at any time by law make or alter such regulations, except as to the places of choosing senators.

2. The Congress shall assemble at least once in every year, and such meeting shall be on the first Monday in December, unless they shall by law appoint a different day.

Section 5. 1. Each House shall be the judge of the elections, returns and qualifications of its own members, and a majority of each shall constitute a quorum to do business; but a smaller number may adjourn from day to day, and may be authorized to compel the attendance of absent members, in such manner, and under such penalties as each House may provide.

2. Each House may determine the rules of its proceedings, punish its members for disorderly behavior, and, with the concurrence of two thirds, expel a member.

3. Each House shall keep a journal of its proceedings, and from time to time publish the same, excepting such parts as may in their judgment require secrecy; and the yeas and nays of the members of either House on any ques-

---

[1]See the Sixteenth Amendment.
[2]See the Fourteenth Amendment.
[3]See the Seventeenth Amendment.

---

[4]See the Seventeenth Amendment.

tion shall, at the desire of one fifth of those present, be entered on the journal.

4. Neither House, during the session of Congress, shall, without the consent of the other, adjourn for more than three days, nor to any other place than that in which the two Houses shall be sitting.

Section 6 1. The senators and representatives shall receive a compensation for their services, to be ascertained by law, and paid out of the Treasury of the United States. They shall in all cases, except treason, felony, and breach of the peace, be privileged from arrest during their attendance at the session of their respective Houses, and in going to and returning from the same; and for any speech or debate in either House, they shall not be questioned in any other place.

2. No senator or representative shall, during the time for which he was elected, be appointed to any civil office under the authority of the United States, which shall have been created, or the emoluments whereof shall have been increased, during such time; and no person holding any office under the United States shall be a member of either House during his continuance in office.

Section 7 1. All bills for raising revenue shall originate in the House of Representatives; but the Senate may propose or concur with amendments as on other bills.

2. Every bill which shall have passed the House of Representatives and the Senate, shall, before it become a law, be presented to the President of the United States; If he approves he shall sign it, but if not he shall return it, with his objections, to that House in which it shall have originated, who shall enter the objections at large on their journal, and proceed to reconsider it. If after such reconsideration two thirds of that House shall agree to pass the bill, it shall be sent, together with the objections, to the other House, by which it shall likewise be reconsidered, and if approved by two thirds of that House, it shall become a law. But in all such cases the votes of both Houses shall be determined by yeas and nays, and the names of the persons voting for and against the bill shall be entered on the journal of each House respectively. If any bill shall not be returned by the President within ten days (Sundays excepted) after it shall have been presented to him, the same shall be a law, in like manner as if he had signed it, unless the Congress by their adjournment prevent its return, in which case it shall not be a law.

3. Every order, resolution, or vote to which the concurrence of the Senate and the House of Representatives may be necessary (except on a question of adjournment) shall be presented to the President of the United States; and before the same shall take effect, shall be approved by him, or being disapproved by him, shall be repassed by two thirds of the Senate and House of Representatives, according to the rules and limitations prescribed in the case of a bill.

Section 8 The Congress shall have the power

1. To lay and collect taxes, duties, imposts, and excises, to pay the debts and provide for the common defense and general welfare of the United States; but all duties, imposts, and excises shall be uniform throughout the United States.

2. To borrow money on the credit of the United States;

3. To regulate commerce with foreign nations, and among the several States, and with the Indian tribes;

4. To establish a uniform rule of naturalization, and uniform laws on the subject of bankruptcies throughout the United States;

5. To coin money, regulate the value thereof, and of foreign coin, and fix the standard of weights and measures;

6. To provide for the punishment of counterfeiting the securities and current coin of the United States;

7. To establish post offices and post roads;

8. To promote the progress of science and useful arts, by securing for limited times to authors and inventors the exclusive right to their respective writings and discoveries;

9. To constitute tribunals inferior to the Supreme Court;

10. To define and punish piracies and felonies committed on the high seas, and offenses against the law of nations;

11. To declare war, grant letters of marque and reprisal, and make rules concerning captures on land and water;

12. To raise and support armies, but no appropriation of money to that use shall be for a longer term than two years;

13. To provide and maintain a navy;

14. To make rules for the government and regulation of the land and naval forces;

15. To provide for calling forth the militia to execute the laws of the Union, suppress insurrections and repel invasions;

16. To provide for organizing, arming, and disciplining the militia, and for governing such part of them as may be employed in the service of the United States, reserving to the States respectively, the appointment of the officers, and the authority of training the militia according to the discipline prescribed by Congress;

17. To exercise exclusive legislation in all cases whatsoever, over such district (not exceeding ten miles square) as may, by cession of particular States, and the acceptance of Congress, become the seat of the government of the United States, and to exercise like authority over all places purchased by the consent of the legislature of the State in which the same shall be, for the erection of forts, magazines, arsenals, dockyards, and other needful buildings; and

18. To make all laws which shall be necessary and proper for carrying into execution the foregoing powers, and all other powers vested by this Constitution in the government of the United States, or any department or officer thereof.

Section 9 1. The migration or importation of such persons as any of the States now existing shall think proper to admit, shall not be prohibited by the Congress prior to the year one thousand eight hundred and eight, but a tax or duty may be imposed on such importation, not exceeding ten dollars for each person.

2. The privilege of the writ of habeas corpus shall not be suspended, unless when in cases of rebellion or invasion the public safety may require it.

3. No bill of attainder or ex post facto law shall be passed.

4. No capitation, or other direct, tax shall be laid, unless in proportion to the census or enumeration hereinbefore directed to be taken.[5]

5. No tax or duty shall be laid on articles exported from any State.

6. No preference shall be given by any regulation of commerce or revenue to the ports of one State over those of another: nor shall vessels bound to, or from, one State be obliged to enter, clear, or pay duties in another.

7. No money shall be drawn from the treasury, but in consequence of appropriations made by law; and a regular statement and account of the receipts and expenditures of all public money shall be published from time to time.

8. No title of nobility shall be granted by the United States: and no person holding any office of profit or trust under them, shall, without the consent of the Congress, accept of any present, emolument, office, or title, of any kind whatever, from any king, price, or foreign State.

Section 10. 1. No State shall enter into any treaty, alliance, or confederation; grant letters of marque and reprisal; coin money; emit bills of credit; make any thing but gold and silver coin a tender in payment of debts; pass any bill of attainder, ex post facto law, or law impairing the obligation of contracts, or grant, any title of nobility.

2. No State shall, without the consent of the Congress, lay any imposts or duties on imports or exports, except what may be absolutely necessary for executing its inspection laws: and the net produce of all duties and imposts laid by any State on imports or exports, shall be for the use of the treasury of the United States; and all such laws shall be subject to the revision and control of the Congress.

3. No State shall, without the consent of the Congress, lay any duty of tonnage, keep troops, or ships of war in time of peace, enter into any agreement or compact with another State, or with a foreign power, or engage in war, unless actually invaded, or in such imminent danger as will not admit of delay.

Article II

Section 1. 1. The executive power shall be vested in a President of the United States of America. He shall hold his office during the term of four years, and, together with the Vice President, chosen for the same term, be elected, as follows:

2. Each State shall appoint, in such manner as the legislature thereof may direct, a number of electors, equal to the whole number of senators and representatives to which the State may be entitled in the Congress: but no senator or representative, or person holding any office of trust or profit under the United States, shall be appointed an elector.

The electors shall meet in their respective States, and vote by ballot for two persons, of whom one at least shall not be an inhabitant of the same State with themselves. And they shall make a list of all the persons voted for, and of the number of votes for each; which list they shall sign and certify, and transmit sealed to the seat of the government of the United States, directed to the president of the Senate. The president of the Senate shall, in the presence of the Senate and House of Representatives, open all the certificates, and the votes shall then be counted. The person having the greatest number of votes shall be the President, if such number be a majority of the whole number of electors appointed; and if there be more than one who have such majority, and have an equal number of votes, then the House of Representatives shall immediately choose by ballot one of them for President; and if no person have a majority, then from the five highest on the list the said House shall in like manner choose the President. But in choosing the President, the votes shall be taken by States, the representation from each State having one vote; a quorum for this purpose shall consist of a member or members from two thirds of the States, and a majority of all the States shall be necessary to a choice. In every case after the choice of the President, the person having the greatest number of votes of the electors shall be the Vice President. But if there should remain two or more who have equal votes, the Senate shall choose from them by ballot the Vice President.[6]

3. The Congress may determine the time of choosing the electors, and the day on which they shall give their votes; which day shall be the same throughout the United States.

4. No person except a natural born citizen, or a citizen of the United States, at the time of the adoption of this Constitution, shall be eligible to the office of President; neither shall any person be eligible to the office who shall not have attained to the age of thirty-five years, and been fourteen years a resident within the United States.

5. In case of the removal of the President from office, or of his death, resignation, or inability to discharge the powers and duties of the said office, the same shall devolve on the Vice President, and the congress may by law provide for the case of removal, death, resignation or inability, both of the President and Vice President, declaring what officer shall then act as President, and such officer shall act accordingly until the disability be removed, or a President shall be elected.

6. The President shall, at stated times, receive for his services a compensation which shall neither be increased nor diminished during the period for which he shall have been elected, and he shall not receive within that period any other emolument from the United States, or any of them.

7. Before he enter on the execution of his office, he shall take the following oath or affirmation:—"I do

[5]See the Sixteenth Amendment.

[6]Superseded by the Twelfth Amendment.

solemnly swear (or affirm) that I will faithfully execute the office of President of the United States, and will to the best of my ability, preserve, protect and defend the Constitution of the United States."

Section 2. 1. The President shall be commander in chief of the army and navy of the United States, and of the militia of the several States, when called into the actual service of the United States; he may require the opinion in writing, of the principal officer in each of the executive departments, upon any subject relating to the duties of their respective offices, and he shall have power to grant reprieves and pardons for offenses against the United States, except in cases of impeachment.

2. He shall have power, by and with the advice and consent of the Senate, to make treaties, provided two thirds of the senators present concur; and he shall nominate, and by and with the advice and consent of the Senate, shall appoint ambassadors, other public ministers and consuls, judges of the Supreme Court, and all other officers of the United States, whose appointments are not herein otherwise provided for, and which shall be established by law; but the Congress may by law vest the appointment of such inferior officers, as they think proper, in the President alone, in the courts of laws, or in the heads of departments.

3. The President shall have power to fill up all vacancies that may happen during the recess of the Senate, by granting commissions which shall expire at the end of their next session.

Section 3. He shall from time to time give to the Congress information of the state of the Union, and recommend to their consideration such measures as he shall judge necessary and expedient; he may, on extraordinary occasions, convene both Houses, or either of them, and in case of disagreement between them with respect to the time of adjournment, he may adjourn them to such time as he shall think proper; he shall receive ambassadors and other public ministers; he shall take care that the laws be faithfully executed, and shall commission all the officers of the United States.

Section 4. The President, Vice President, and all civil officers of the United States, shall be removed from office on impeachment for, and conviction of, treason, bribery, or other high crimes and misdemeanors.

Article III

Section 1. The judicial power of the United States shall be vested in one Supreme Court, and in such inferior courts as the Congress may from time to time ordain and establish. The judges, both of the Supreme and inferior courts, shall hold their offices during good behavior, and shall, at stated times, receive for their services, a compensation, which shall not be diminished during their continuance in office.

Section 2. 1. The judicial power shall extend to all cases, in law and equity, arising under this Constitution, the laws of the United States, and treaties made, or which shall be made, under their authority;—to all cases of admiralty and maritime jurisdiction;—to controversies to which the United States shall be a party;[7]—to controversies between two or more States;—between a State and citizens of another State;—between citizens of different States;—between citizens of the same State claiming lands under grants of different States, and between a State, or the citizens thereof, and foreign States, citizens or subjects.

2. In all cases affecting ambassadors, other public ministers and consuls, and those in which a State shall be party, the Supreme Court shall have original jurisdiction. In all the other cases before mentioned, the Supreme Court shall have appellate jurisdiction, both as to law and fact, with such exceptions, and under such regulations as the Congress shall make.

3. The trial of all crimes, except in cases of impeachment, shall be by jury; and such trial shall be held in the State where the said crimes shall have been committed; but when not committed within any State, the trial shall be such place or places as the congress may by law have directed.

Section 3. 1. Treason against the United States shall consist only in levying war against them, or in adhering to their enemies, giving them aid and comfort. No person shall be convicted of treason unless on the testimony of two witnesses to the same overt act, or on confession in open court.

2. The Congress shall have power to declare the punishment of treason, but no attainder of treason shall work corruption of blood, or forfeiture except during the life of the person attained.

Article IV

Section 1. Full faith and credit shall be given in each State to the public acts, records, and judicial proceedings of every other State. And the Congress may by general laws prescribe the manner in which such acts, records and proceedings shall be proved, and the effect thereof.

Section 2. 1. The citizens of each State shall be entitled to all privileges and immunities of citizens in the several States.[8]

2. A person charged in any State with treason, felony, or other crime, who shall flee from justice, and be found in another State, shall on demand of the executive authority of the State from which he fled, be delivered up to be removed to the State having jurisdiction of the crime.

3. No person held to service or labor in one State under the laws thereof, escaping into another, shall, in consequence of any law or regulation therein, be discharged from such service or labor, but shall be delivered up on claim of the party to whom such service or labor may be due.[9]

Section 3. 1. New States may be admitted by the Congress into this Union; but no new State shall be formed or erected within the jurisdiction of any other State, nor any State be formed by the junction of two or more States, or parts of States, without the consent of the legislatures of the States concerned as well as of the Congress.

---

[7] See the Eleventh Amendment.
[8] See the Fourteenth Amendment, Sec. 1.
[9] See the Thirteenth Amendment.

2. The Congress shall have power to dispose of and make all needful rules and regulations respecting the territory or other property belonging to the United States; and nothing in this Constitution shall be so construed as to prejudice any claims of the United States, or of any particular State.

Section 4. The United States shall guarantee to every State in this Union a republican form of government, and shall protect each of them against invasion; and on application of the legislature, or of the executive (when the legislature cannot be convened) against domestic violence.

Article V

The Congress, whenever two thirds of both Houses shall deem it necessary, shall propose amendments to this Constitution, or, on the application of the legislatures of two thirds of the several States, shall call a convention for proposing amendments, which in either case shall be valid to all intents and purposes, as part of this Constitution, when ratified by the legislatures of three fourths of the several States, or by conventions in three fourths thereof, as the one or the other mode of ratification may be proposed by the Congress; Provided that no amendment which may be made prior to the year one thousand eight hundred and eight shall in any manner affect the first and fourth clauses in the ninth section of the first article; and that no State, without its consent, shall be deprived of its equal suffrage in the Senate.

Article VI

1. All debts contracted and engagements entered into, before the adoption of this Constitution, shall be as valid against the United States under this Constitution, as under the Confederation.[10]

2. This Constitution, and the laws of the United States which shall be made in pursuance thereof; and all treaties made, or which shall be made, under the authority of the United States, shall be the supreme law of the land; and the judges in every State shall be bound thereby, any thing in the Constitution or laws of any State to the contrary notwithstanding.

3. The senators and representatives before mentioned, and the members of the several State legislatures, and all executive and judicial officers, both of the United States and of the several States, shall be bound by oath or affirmation to support this Constitution; but no religious test shall ever be required as a qualification to any office or public trust under the United States.

Article VII

The ratification of the conventions of nine States shall be sufficient for the establishment of this Constitution between the States so ratifying the same.

Done in Convention by the unanimous consent of the States present the seventeenth day of September in the year of our Lord one thousand seven hundred and eighty-

seven, and of the independence of the United States of America the twelfth. In witness whereof we have hereunto subscribed our names.

[Names omitted]

* * *

Articles in addition to, and amendment of, the Constitution of the United States of America, proposed by Congress, and ratified by the legislatures of the several States, pursuant to the fifth article of the original Constitution.

Amendment I [First ten amendments ratified December 15, 1791]

Congress shall make no law respecting an establishment of religion, or prohibiting the free exercise thereof; or abridging the freedom of speech, or of the press; or the right of the people peaceably to assemble, and to petition the government for a redress of grievances.

Amendment II

A well regulated militia, being necessary to the security of a free State, the right of the people to keep and bear arms, shall not be infringed.

Amendment III

No soldier shall, in time of peace be quartered in any house, without the consent of the owner, nor in time of war, but in a manner to be prescribed by law.

Amendment IV

The right of the people to be secure in their persons, houses, papers, and effects, against unreasonable searches and seizures, shall not be violated, and no warrants shall issue, but upon probable cause, supported by oath or affirmation, and particularly describing the place to be searched, and the persons or things to be seized.

Amendment V

No person shall be held to answer for a capital or otherwise infamous crime, unless on a presentment or indictment of a grand jury, except in cases arising in the land or naval forces, or in the militia, when in actual service in time of war or public danger; nor shall any person be subject for the same offense to be twice put in jeopardy of life or limb; nor shall be compelled in any criminal case to be a witness against himself, nor be deprived of life, liberty, or property, without due process of law; nor shall private property be taken for public use, without just compensation.

Amendment VI

In all criminal prosecutions, the accused shall enjoy the right to a speedy and public trial, by an impartial jury of the State and district wherein the crime shall have been committed, which district shall have been previously ascertained by law, and to be informed of the nature and cause of the accusation; to be confronted with the witnesses against him; to have compulsory process for obtaining witnesses in his favor, and to have the assistance of counsel for his defense.

---

[10]See the Fourteenth Amendment, Sec. 4.

Amendment VII

In suits at common law, where the value in controversy shall exceed twenty dollars, the right of trial by jury shall be preserved, and no fact tried by a jury shall be otherwise reexamined in any court of the United States, than according to the rules of the common law.

Amendment VIII

Excessive bail shall not be required, nor excessive fines imposed, nor cruel and unusual punishments inflicted.

Amendment IX

The enumeration in the Constitution of certain rights shall not be construed to deny or disparage others retained by the people.

Amendment X

The powers not delegated to the United States by the Constitution, nor prohibited by it to the States, are reserved to the States respectively, or to the people.

Amendment XI [January 8, 1798]

The judicial power of the United States shall not be construed to extend to any suit in law or equity, commended or prosecuted against one of the United States by citizens of another State, or by citizens or subjects of any foreign State.

Amendment XII [September 25, 1804]

The electors shall meet in their respective States, and vote by ballot for President and Vice President, one of whom, at least, shall not be an inhabitant of the same State with themselves; they shall name in their ballots the person voted for as President, and in distinct ballots the person voted for as Vice President, and they shall make distinct lists of all persons voted for as President and of all persons voted for as Vice President and of the number of votes for each, which lists they shall sign and certify, and transmit sealed to the seat of the government of the United States, directed to the President of the Senate;—The President of the Senate shall, in the presence of the Senate and House of Representatives, open all the certificates and the votes shall then be counted;—The person having the greatest number of votes for President, shall be the President, if such number be a majority of the whole number of electors appointed; and if no person have such majority, then from the persons having the highest numbers not exceeding three on the list of those voted for as President, the House of Representatives shall choose immediately, by ballot, the President. But in choosing the President, the votes shall be taken by States, the representation from each State having one vote; a quorum for this purpose shall consist of a member or members from two thirds of the States, and a majority of all the States shall be necessary to a choice. And if the House of Representatives shall not choose a President whenever the right of choice shall devolve upon them, before the fourth day of March next following, then the Vice President shall act as President, as in the case of the death or other constitutional disability of the President.

The person having the greatest number of votes as Vice President shall be the Vice President, if such number be a majority of the whole number of electors appointed, and if no person have a majority, then from the two highest numbers on the list, the Senate shall choose the Vice President; a quorum for the purpose shall consist of two thirds of the whole number of Senators, and a majority of the whole number shall be necessary to a choice. But no person constitutionally ineligible to the office of President shall be eligible to that of Vice President of the United States.

Amendment XIII [December 18, 1865]

Section 1. Neither slavery nor involuntary servitude, except as a punishment for crime whereof the party shall have been duly convicted, shall exist within the United States, or any place subject to their jurisdiction.

Section 2. Congress shall have power to enforce this article by appropriate legislation.

Amendment XIV [July 28, 1868]

Section 1. All persons born or naturalized in the United States, and subject to the jurisdiction thereof, are citizens of the United States and of the State wherein they reside. No State shall make or enforce any law which shall abridge the privileges or immunities of citizens of the United States; nor shall any State deprive any person of life, liberty, or property, without due process of law; nor deny to any person within its jurisdiction the equal protection of the laws.

Section 2. Representatives shall be apportioned among the several States according to their respective numbers, counting the whole number of persons in each State, excluding Indians not taxed. But when the right to vote at any election for the choice of electors for President and Vice President of the United States, representatives in Congress, the executive and judicial officers of a State, or the members of the legislature thereof, is denied to any of the male inhabitants of such State, being twenty-one years of age, and citizens of the United States, or in any way abridged, except for participating in rebellion, or other crime, the basis of representation there shall be reduced in the proportion which the number of such male citizens shall bear to the whole number of male citizens twenty-one years of age in such State.

Section 3. No person shall be a senator or representative in Congress, or elector of President and Vice President, or hold any office, civil or military, under the United States, or under any State, who having previously taken an oath, as a member of Congress, or as an officer of the United States, or as a member of any State legislature, or as an executive or judicial officer of any State, to support the Constitution of the United States, shall have engaged in insurrection or rebellion against the same, or given aid or comfort to the enemies thereof. But Congress may by a vote of two thirds of each House, remove such disability.

Section 4. The validity of the public debt of the United States, authorized by law, including debts incurred for payment of pensions and bounties for services in suppressing insurrection or rebellion; shall not be questioned.

But neither the United States nor any State shall assume or pay any debt or obligation incurred in aid of insurrection or rebellion against the United States, or any claim for the loss or emancipation of any slave; but all such debts, obligations, and claims shall be held illegal and void.

Section 5. The Congress shall have the power to enforce, by appropriate legislation, the provisions of this article.

Amendment XV [March 30, 1870]

Section 1. The right of citizens of the United States to vote shall not be denied or abridged by the United States or by any State on account of race, color, or previous condition of servitude.

Section 2. The Congress shall have power to enforce this article by appropriate legislation.

Amendment XVI [February 25, 1913]

The Congress shall have power to lay and collect taxes on incomes, from whatever source derived, without apportionment among the several States, and without regard to any census or enumeration.

Amendment XVII [May 31, 1913]

The Senate of the United States shall be composed of two senators from each State, elected by the people thereof, for six years; and each senator shall have one vote. The electors in each State shall have the qualifications requisite for electors of the most numerous branch of the State legislature.

When vacancies happen in the representation of any State in the Senate, the executive authority of such State shall issue writs of election to fill such vacancies: *Provided,* That the legislature of any State may empower the executive thereof to make temporary appointments until the people fill the vacancies by election as the legislature may direct.

This amendment shall not be so construed as to affect the election or term of any senator chosen before it becomes valid as part of the Constitution.

Amendment XVIII[1] [January 29, 1919]

After one year from the ratification of this article, the manufacture, sale, or transportation of intoxicating liquors within, the importation thereof into, or the exportation thereof from the United States and all territory subject to the jurisdiction thereof for beverage purposes is thereby prohibited.

The Congress and the several States shall have concurrent power to enforce this article by appropriate legislation.

This article shall be inoperative unless it shall have been ratified as an amendment to the Constitution by the legislatures of the several States, as provided in the constitution, within seven years from the date of the submission hereof to the States by Congress.

---

[1]Repealed by the Twenty-first Amendment.

Amendment XIX [August 26, 1920]

The right of citizens of the United States to vote shall not be denied or abridged by the United States or by any State on account of sex.

Congress shall have the power to enforce this article by appropriate legislation.

Amendment XX [January 23, 1933]

Section 1. The terms of the President and Vice President shall end at noon on the 20th day of January and the terms of Senators and Representatives at noon on the 3d day of January, of the years in which such terms would have ended if this article had not been ratified; and the terms of their successors shall then begin.

Section 2. The Congress shall assemble at least once in every year, and such meeting shall begin at noon on the 3d day of January, unless they shall by law appoint a different day.

Section 3. If, at the time fixed for the beginning of the term of President, the President-elect shall have died, the Vice President-elect shall become President. If a President shall not have been chosen before the time fixed for the beginning of his term, or if the President-elect shall have failed to qualify, then the Vice President-elect shall act as President until a President shall have qualified; and the Congress may by law provide for the case wherein neither a President-elect nor a Vice President-elect shall have qualified, declaring who shall then act as President, or the manner in which one who is to act shall be selected, and such person shall act accordingly until a President or Vice President shall have qualified.

Section 4. The Congress may by law provide for the case of the death of any of the persons from whom, the House of Representatives may choose a President whenever the right of choice shall have devolved upon them, and for the case of the death of any of the persons from whom the Senate may choose a Vice President whenever the right of choice shall have devolved upon them.

Section 5. Sections 1 and 2 shall take effect on the 15th day of October following the ratification of this article.

Section 6. This article shall be inoperative unless it shall have been ratified as an amendment to the Constitution by the legislatures of three-fourths of the several States within seven years from the date of its submission.

Amendment XXI [December 5, 1933]

Section 1. The Eighteenth Article of amendment to the Constitution of the United States is hereby repealed.

Section 2. The transportation or importation into any State, Territory, or possession of the United States for delivery or use therein of intoxicating liquors in violation of the laws thereof, is hereby prohibited.

Section 3. This article shall be inoperative unless it shall have been ratified as an amendment to the Constitution by conventions in the several States, as provided in the Constitution, within seven years from the date of the submission thereof to the States by the Congress.

Amendment XXII [*March* 1, *1951*]

No person shall be elected to the office of the President more than twice, and no person who has held the office of President, or acted as President, for more than two years of a term to which some other person was elected President shall be elected to the office of the President more than once.

But this article shall not apply to any person holding the office of President when this article was proposed by the Congress, and shall not prevent any person who may be holding the office of President, or acting as President, during the term within which this article becomes operative from holding the office of President or acting as President during the remainder of such term.

This article shall be inoperative unless it shall have been ratified as an amendment to the Constitution by the legislatures of three-fourths of the several States within seven years from the date of its submission to the States by the Congress.

Amendment XXIII [*March* 29, *1961*]

Section 1. The District constituting the seat of Government of the United States shall appoint in such manner as the Congress may direct.

A number of electors of President and Vice President equal to the whole number of Senators and Representatives in Congress to which the District would be entitled if it were a State, but in no event more than the least populous State; they shall be in addition to those appointed by the States, but they shall be considered, for the purposes of the election of President and Vice President, to be electors appointed by a State; and they shall meet in the District and perform such duties as provided by the twelfth article of amendment.

Section 2. The Congress shall have power to enforce this article by appropriate legislation.

Amendment XXIV [*January* 23, *1964*]

Section 1. The right of citizens of the United States to vote in any primary or other election for President or Vice President, for electors for President or Vice President, or for Senator or Representative in Congress, shall not be denied or abridged by the United States or any State by reason of failure to pay any poll tax or other tax.

Section 2. The Congress shall have power to enforce this article by appropriate legislation.

Amendment XXV [*February* 10, *1967*]

Section 1. In case of the removal of the President from office or of his death or resignation, the Vice President shall become President.

Section 2. Whenever there is a vacancy in the office of the Vice President, the President shall nominate a Vice President who shall take office upon confirmation by a majority of both Houses of Congress.

Section 3. Whenever the President transmits to the President pro tempore of the Senate and the Speaker of the House of Representatives his written declaration that he is unable to discharge the powers and duties of his office, and until he transmits to them a written declaration to the contrary, such powers and duties shall be discharged by the Vice President as Acting President.

Section 4. Whenever the Vice president and a majority of either the principal officers of the executive departments or of such other body as Congress may by law provide, transmit to the President pro tempore of the Senate and the Speaker of the House of Representatives their written declaration that the President is unable to discharge the powers and duties of his office, the Vice President shall immediately assume the powers and duties of the office as Acting President.

Thereafter, when the President transmits to the President pro tempore of the Senate and the Speaker of the House of Representatives his written declaration that no inability exists, he shall resume the powers and duties of his office unless the Vice President and a majority of either the principal officers of the executive departments or of such other body as Congress may by law provide, transmit within four days to the President pro tempore of the Senate and the Speaker of the House of Representatives their written declaration that the President is unable to discharge the powers and duties of his office. Thereupon Congress shall decide the issue, assembling within forty-eight hours for that purpose if not in session. If the Congress, within twenty-one days after receipt of the latter written declaration, or, if Congress is not in session, within twenty-one days after Congress is required to assemble, determines by two-thirds vote of both Houses that the President is unable to discharge the powers and duties of his office, the Vice President shall continue to discharge the same as Acting President; otherwise, the President shall resume the powers and duties of his office.

Amendment XXVI [*June* 30, *1971*]

Section 1. The right of citizens of the United States who are eighteen years of age or older to vote shall not be denied or abridged by the United States or by any State on account of age.

Section 2. The Congress shall have power to enforce this article by appropriate legislation.

Amendment XXVII[12] [*May* 7, *1992*]

No law, varying the compensation for services of the Senators and Representatives, shall take effect until an election of Representatives shall have intervened.

---

[12]James Madison proposed this amendment in 1789 together with the ten amendments that were adopted as the Bill of Rights, but it failed to win ratification at the time. Congress, however, had set no deadline for its ratification, and over the years—particularly in the 1980s and 1990s—many states voted to add it to the Constitution. With the ratification of Michigan in 1992 it passed the threshold of 3/4ths of the states required for adoption, but because the process took more than 200 years, its validity remains in doubt.

PRESIDENTS AND VICE PRESIDENTS

1. George Washington (1789)
   John Adams (1789)

2. John Adams (1797)
   Thomas Jefferson (1797)

3. Thomas Jefferson (1801)
   Aaron Burr (1801)
   George Clinton (1805)

4. James Madison (1809)
   George Clinton (1809)
   Elbridge Gerry (1813)

5. James Monroe (1817)
   Daniel D. Thompkins (1817)

6. John Quincy Adams (1825)
   John C. Calhoun (1825)

7. Andrew Jackson (1829)
   John C. Calhoun (1829)
   Martin Van Buren (1833)

8. Martin Van Buren (1837)
   Richard M. Johnson (1837)

9. William H. Harrison (1841)
   John Tyler (1841)

10. John Tyler (1841)

11. James K. Polk (1845)
    George M. Dallas (1845)

12. Zachary Taylor (1849)
    Millard Fillmore (1849)

13. Millard Fillmore (1850)

14. Franklin Pierce (1853)
    William R. King (1853)

15. James Buchanan (1857)
    John C. Breckinridge (1857)

16. Abraham Lincoln (1861)
    Hannibal Hamlin (1861)
    Andrew Johnson (1865)

17. Andrew Johnson (1865)

18. Ulysses S. Grant (1869)
    Schuyler Colfax (1869)
    Henry Wilson (1873)

19. Rutherford B. Hayes (1877)
    William A. Wheeler (1877)

20. James A. Garfield (1881)
    Chester A. Arthur (1881)

21. Chester A. Arthur (1881)

22. Grover Cleveland (1885)
    T. A. Hendricks (1885)

23. Benjamin Harrison (1889)
    Levi P. Morgan (1889)

24. Grover Cleveland (1893)
    Adlai E. Stevenson (1893)

25. William McKinley (1897)
    Garret A. Hobart (1897)
    Theodore Roosevelt (1901)

26. Theodore Roosevelt (1901)
    Charles Fairbanks (1905)

27. William H. Taft (1909)
    James S. Sherman (1909)

28. Woodrow Wilson (1913)
    Thomas R. Marshall (1913)

29. Warren G. Harding (1921)
    Calvin Coolidge (1921)

30. Calvin Coolidge (1923)
    Charles G. Dawes (1925)

31. Herbert C. Hoover (1929)
    Charles Curtis (1929)

32. Franklin D. Roosevelt (1933)
    John Nance Garner (1933)
    Henry A. Wallace (1941)
    Harry S. Truman (1945)

33. Harry S. Truman (1945)
    Alben W. Barkley (1949)

34. Dwight D. Eisenhower (1953)
    Richard M. Nixon (1953)

35. John F. Kennedy (1961)
    Lyndon B. Johnson (1961)

36. Lyndon B. Johnson (1963)
    Hubert H. Humphrey (1965)

37. Richard M. Nixon (1969)
    Spiro T. Agnew (1969)
    Gerald R. Ford (1973)

38. Gerald R. Ford (1974)
    Nelson A. Rockefeller (1974)

39. James E. Carter Jr. (1977)
    Walter F. Mondale (1977)

40. Ronald W. Reagan (1981)
    George H. Bush (1981)

41. George H. Bush (1989)
    James D. Quayle III (1989)

42. William J. Clinton (1993)
    Albert Gore (1993)

PRESIDENTIAL ELECTIONS

Year	Number of States	Candidates	Party	Popular Vote*	Electoral Vote[†]	Percentage of Popular Vote
1789	11	GEORGE WASHINGTON	No party designations		69	
		John Adams			34	
		Other Candidates			35	
1792	15	GEORGE WASHINGTON	No party designations		132	
		John Adams			77	
		George Clinton			50	
		Other Candidates			5	
1796	16	JOHN ADAMS	Federalist		71	
		Thomas Jefferson	Democratic-Republican		68	
		Thomas Pinckney	Federalist		59	
		Aaron Burr	Democratic-Republican		30	
		Other Candidates			48	
1800	16	THOMAS JEFFERSON	Democratic-Republican		73	
		Aaron Burr	Democratic-Republican		73	
		John Adams	Federalist		65	
		Charles C. Pinckney	Federalist		64	
		John Jay	Federalist		1	
1804	17	THOMAS JEFFERSON	Democratic-Republican		162	
		Charles C. Pinckney	Federalist		14	
1808	17	JAMES MADISON	Democratic-Republican		122	
		Charles C. Pinckney	Federalist		47	
		George Clinton	Democratic-Republican		6	
1812	18	JAMES MADISON	Democratic-Republican		128	
		DeWitt Clinton	Federalist		89	
1816	19	JAMES MONROE	Democratic-Republican		183	
		Rufus King	Federalist		34	
1820	24	JAMES MONROE	Democratic-Republican		231	
		John Quincy Adams	Democratic-Republican		1	
1824	24	JOHN QUINCY ADAMS	Democratic-Republican	108,740	84	30.5
		Andrew Jackson	Democratic-Republican	153,544	99	43.1
		William H. Crawford	Democratic-Republican	46,618	41	13.1
		Henry Clay	Democratic-Republican	47,136	37	13.2
1828	24	ANDREW JACKSON	Democrat	647,286	178	56.0
		John Quincy Adams	National-Republican	508,064	83	44.0
1832	24	ANDREW JACKSON	Democrat	687,502	219	55.0
		Henry Clay	National-Republican	530,189	49	42.4
		William Wirt	Anti-Masonic	} 33,108	7	} 2.6
		John Floyd	National-Republican		11	

*Percentage of popular vote given for any election year may not total 100 percent because candidates receiving less than 1 percent of the popular vote have been omitted.

[†]Prior to the passage of the Twelfth Amendment in 1904, the electoral college voted for two presidential candidates; the runner-up became Vice-President. Data from *Historical Statistics of the United States, Colonial Times to 1957* (1961), pp. 682–683, and *The World Almanac*.

PRESIDENTIAL ELECTIONS
(continued)

Year	Number of States	Candidates	Party	Popular Vote	Electoral Vote	Percentage of Popular Vote
1836	26	MARTIN VAN BUREN	Democrat	765,483	170	50.9
		William H. Harrison	Whig		73	
		Hugh L. White	Whig		26	
		Daniel Webster	Whig	739,795	14	49.1
		W. P. Mangum	Whig		11	
1840	26	WILLIAM H. HARRISON	Whig	1,274,624	234	53.1
		Martin Van Buren	Democrat	1,127,781	60	46.9
1844	26	JAMES K. POLK	Democrat	1,338,464	170	49.6
		Henry Clay	Whig	1,300,097	105	48.1
		James G. Birney	Liberty	62,300		2.3
1848	30	ZACHARY TAYLOR	Whig	1,360,967	163	47.4
		Lewis Cass	Democrat	1,222,342	127	42.5
		Martin Van Buren	Free-Soil	291,263		10.1
1852	31	FRANKLIN PIERCE	Democrat	1,601,117	254	50.9
		Winfield Scott	Whig	1,385,453	42	44.1
		John P. Hale	Free-Soil	155,825		5.0
1856	31	JAMES BUCHANAN	Democrat	1,832,955	174	45.3
		John C. Frémont	Republican	1,339,932	114	33.1
		Millard Fillmore	American ("Know Nothing")	871,731	8	21.6
1860	33	ABRAHAM LINCOLN	Republican	1,865,593	180	39.8
		Stephen A. Douglas	Democrat	1,382,713	12	29.5
		John C. Breckinridge	Democrat	848,356	72	18.1
		John Bell	Constitutional Union	592,906	39	12.6
1864	36	ABRAHAM LINCOLN	Republican	2,206,938	212	55.0
		George B. McClellan	Democrat	1,803,787	21	45.0
1868	37	ULYSSES S. GRANT	Republican	3,013,421	214	52.7
		Horatio Seymour	Democrat	2,706,829	80	47.3
1872	37	ULYSSES S. GRANT	Republican	3,596,745	286	55.6
		Horace Greeley	Democrat	2,843,446	*	43.9
1876	38	RUTHERFORD B. HAYES	Republican	4,036,572	185	48.0
		Samuel J. Tilden	Democrat	4,284,020	184	51.0
1880	38	JAMES A. GARFIELD	Republican	4,453,295	214	48.5
		Winfield S. Hancock	Democrat	4,414,082	155	48.1
		James B. Weaver	Greenback-Labor	308,578		3.4
1884	38	GROVER CLEVELAND	Democrat	4,879,507	219	48.5
		James G. Blaine	Republican	4,850,293	182	48.2
		Benjamin F. Butler	Greenback-Labor	175,370		1.8
		John P. St. John	Prohibition	150,369		1.5
1888	38	BENJAMIN HARRISON	Republican	5,447,129	233	47.9
		Grover Cleveland	Democrat	5,537,857	168	48.6
		Clinton B. Fisk	Prohibition	249,506		2.2
		Anson J. Streeter	Union Labor	146,935		1.3

*Because of the death of Greeley, Democratic electors scattered their votes.

PRESIDENTIAL ELECTIONS
(continued)

Year	Number of States	Candidates	Party	Popular Vote	Electoral Vote	Percentage of Popular Vote
1892	44	GROVER CLEVELAND	Democrat	5,555,426	277	46.1
		Benjamin Harrison	Republican	5,182,690	145	43.0
		James B. Weaver	People's	1,029,846	22	8.5
		John Bidwell	Prohibition	264,133		2.2
1896	45	WILLIAM MCKINLEY	Republican	7,102,246	271	51.1
		William J. Bryan	Democrat	6,492,559	176	47.7
1900	45	WILLIAM MCKINLEY	Republican	7,218,491	292	51.7
		William J. Bryan	Democrat; Populist	6,356,734	155	45.5
		John C. Woolley	Prohibition	208,914		1.5
1904	45	THEODORE ROOSEVELT	Republican	7,628,461	336	57.4
		Alton B. Parker	Democrat	5,084,223	140	37.6
		Eugene V. Debs	Socialist	402,283		3.0
		Silas C. Swallow	Prohibition	258,536		1.9
1908	46	WILLIAM H. TAFT	Republican	7,675,320	321	51.6
		William J. Bryan	Democrat	6,412,294	162	43.1
		Eugene V. Debs	Socialist	420,793		2.8
		Eugene W. Chafin	Prohibition	253,840		1.7
1912	48	WOODROW WILSON	Democrat	6,296,547	435	41.9
		Theodore Roosevelt	Progressive	4,118,571	88	27.4
		William H. Taft	Republican	3,486,720	8	23.2
		Eugene V. Debs	Socialist	900,672		6.0
		Eugene W. Chafin	Prohibition	206,275		1.4
1916	48	WOODROW WILSON	Democrat	9,127,695	277	49.4
		Charles E. Hughes	Republican	8,533,507	254	46.2
		A. L. Benson	Socialist	585,113		3.2
		J. Frank Hanly	Prohibition	220,506		1.2
1920	48	WARREN G. HARDING	Republican	16,143,407	404	60.4
		James M. Cox	Democrat	9,130,328	127	34.2
		Eugene V. Debs	Socialist	919,799		3.4
		P. P. Christensen	Farmer-Labor	265,411		1.0
1924	48	CALVIN COOLIDGE	Republican	15,718,211	382	54.0
		John W. Davis	Democrat	8,385,283	136	28.8
		Robert M. La Follette	Progressive	4,831,289	13	16.6
1928	48	HERBERT C. HOOVER	Republican	21,391,993	444	58.2
		Alfred E. Smith	Democrat	15,016,169	87	40.9
1932	48	FRANKLIN D. ROOSEVELT	Democrat	22,809,638	472	57.4
		Herbert C. Hoover	Republican	15,758,901	59	39.7
		Norman Thomas	Socialist	881,951		2.2
1936	48	FRANKLIN D. ROOSEVELT	Democrat	27,752,869	523	60.8
		Alfred M. Landon	Republican	16,674,665	8	36.5
		William Lemke	Union	882,479		1.9
1940	48	FRANKLIN D. ROOSEVELT	Democrat	27,307,819	449	54.8
		Wendell L. Willkie	Republican	22,321,018	82	44.8
1944	48	FRANKLIN D. ROOSEVELT	Democrat	25,606,585	432	53.5
		Thomas E. Dewey	Republican	22,014,745	99	46.0

PRESIDENTIAL ELECTIONS
(continued)

Year	Number of States	Candidates	Party	Popular Vote	Electoral Vote	Percentage of Popular Vote
1948	48	HARRY S. TRUMAN	Democrat	24,105,812	303	49.5
		Thomas E. Dewey	Republican	21,970,065	189	45.1
		J. Strom Thurmond	States' Rights	1,169,063	39	2.4
		Henry A. Wallace	Progressive	1,157,172		2.4
1952	48	DWIGHT D. EISENHOWER	Republican	33,936,234	442	55.1
		Adlai E. Stevenson	Democrat	27,314,992	89	44.4
1956	48	DWIGHT D. EISENHOWER	Republican	35,590,472	457[*]	57.6
		Adlai E. Stevenson	Democrat	26,022,752	73	42.1
1960	50	JOHN F. KENNEDY	Democrat	34,227,096	303[†]	49.9
		Richard M. Nixon	Republican	34,108,546	219	49.6
1964	50	LYNDON B. JOHNSON	Democrat	42,676,220	486	61.3
		Barry M. Goldwater	Republican	26,860,314	52	38.5
1968	50	RICHARD M. NIXON	Republican	31,785,480	301	43.4
		Hubert H. Humphrey	Democrat	31,275,165	191	42.7
		George C. Wallace	American Independent	9,906,473	46	13.5
1972	50	RICHARD M. NIXON[‡]	Republican	47,165,234	520	60.6
		George S. McGovern	Democrat	29,168,110	17	37.5
1976	50	JIMMY CARTER	Democrat	40,828,929	297	50.1
		Gerald R. Ford	Republican	39,148,940	240	47.9
		Eugene McCarthy	Independent	739,256		
1980	50	RONALD REAGAN	Republican	43,201,220	489	50.9
		Jimmy Carter	Democrat	34,913,332	49	41.2
		John B. Anderson	Independent	5,581,379		
1984	50	RONALD REAGAN	Republican	53,428,357	525	59.0
		Walter F. Mondale	Democrat	36,930,923	13	41.0
1988	50	GEORGE BUSH	Republican	48,901,046	426	53.4
		Michael Dukakis	Democrat	41,809,030	111	45.6
1992	50	BILL CLINTON	Democrat	43,728,275	370	43.2
		George Bush	Republican	38,167,416	168	37.7
		H. Ross Perot	United We Stand, America	19,237,247		19.0
1996	50	BILL CLINTON	Democrat	45,590,703	379	49.0
		Robert Dole	Republican	37,816,307	159	41.0
		H. Ross Perot	Reform	7,874,283		8.0

[*]Walter B. Jones received 1 electoral vote.

[†]Harry F. Byrd received 15 electoral votes.

[‡]Resigned August 9, 1974: Vice President Gerald R. Ford became President.

ADMISSION OF STATES INTO THE UNION

State	Date of Admission	State	Date of Admission
1. Delaware	December 7, 1787	26. Michigan	January 26, 1837
2. Pennsylvania	December 12, 1787	27. Florida	March 3, 1845
3. New Jersey	December 18, 1787	28. Texas	December 29, 1845
4. Georgia	January 2, 1788	29. Iowa	December 28, 1846
5. Connecticut	January 9, 1788	30. Wisconsin	May 29, 1848
6. Massachusetts	February 6, 1788	31. California	September 9, 1850
7. Maryland	April 28, 1788	32. Minnesota	May 11, 1858
8. South Carolina	May 23, 1788	33. Oregon	February 14, 1859
9. New Hampshire	June 21, 1788	34. Kansas	January 29, 1861
10. Virginia	June 25, 1788	35. West Virginia	June 20, 1863
11. New York	July 26, 1788	36. Nevada	October 31, 1864
12. North Carolina	November 21, 1789	37. Nebraska	March 1, 1867
13. Rhode Island	May 29, 1790	38. Colorado	August 1, 1876
14. Vermont	March 4, 1791	39. North Dakota	November 2, 1889
15. Kentucky	June 1, 1792	40. South Dakota	November 2, 1889
16. Tennessee	June 1, 1796	41. Montana	November 8, 1889
17. Ohio	March 1, 1803	42. Washington	November 11, 1889
18. Louisiana	April 30, 1812	43. Idaho	July 3, 1890
19. Indiana	December 11, 1816	44. Wyoming	July 10, 1890
20. Mississippi	December 10, 1817	45. Utah	January 4, 1896
21. Illinois	December 3, 1818	46. Oklahoma	November 16, 1907
22. Alabama	December 14, 1819	47. New Mexico	January 6, 1912
23. Maine	March 15, 1820	48. Arizona	February 14, 1912
24. Missouri	August 10, 1821	49. Alaska	January 3, 1959
25. Arkansas	June 15, 1836	50. Hawaii	August 21, 1959

DEMOGRAPHICS OF THE UNITED STATES

POPULATION GROWTH

Year	Population	Percent Increase
1630	4,600	
1640	26,600	478.3
1650	50,400	90.8
1660	75,100	49.0
1670	111,900	49.0
1680	151,500	35.4
1690	210,400	38.9
1700	250,900	19.2
1710	331,700	32.2
1720	466,200	40.5
1730	629,400	35.0
1740	905,600	43.9
1750	1,170,800	29.3
1760	1,593,600	36.1
1770	2,148,100	34.8
1780	2,780,400	29.4
1790	3,929,214	41.3
1800	5,308,483	35.1
1810	7,239,881	36.4
1820	9,638,453	33.1
1830	12,866,020	33.5
1840	17,069,453	32.7
1850	23,191,876	35.9
1860	31,443,321	35.6
1870	39,818,449	26.6
1880	50,155,783	26.0
1890	62,947,714	25.5
1900	75,994,575	20.7
1910	91,972,266	21.0
1920	105,710,620	14.9
1930	122,775,046	16.1
1940	131,669,275	7.2
1950	150,697,361	14.5
1960	179,323,175	19.0
1970	203,235,298	13.3
1980	226,545,805	11.5
1990	248,709,873	9.8
1996	265,557,000	6.8

Source: *Historical Statistics of the United States* (1975); *Statistical Abstract by the United States* (1991, 1997).
Note: Figures for 1630–1780 include British colonies within limits of present United States only; Native American population included only in 1930 and thereafter.

WORKFORCE

Year	Total Number Workers (1000s)	Farmers as % of Total	Women as % of Total	% Workers in Unions
1810	2,330	84	(NA)	(NA)
1840	5,660	75	(NA)	(NA)
1860	11,110	53	(NA)	(NA)
1870	12,506	53	15	(NA)
1880	17,392	52	15	(NA)
1890	23,318	43	17	(NA)
1900	29,073	40	18	3
1910	38,167	31	21	6
1920	41,614	26	21	12
1930	48,830	22	22	7
1940	53,011	17	24	27
1950	59,643	12	28	25
1960	69,877	8	32	26
1970	82,049	4	37	25
1980	108,544	3	42	23
1990	117,914	3	45	16
1995	124,900	3	46	15

Source: *Historical Statistics of the United States* (1975); *Statistical Abstract of the United States* (1991, 1996).

VITAL STATISTICS
(per thousands)

Year	Births	Deaths	Marriages	Divorces
1800	55	(NA)	(NA)	(NA)
1810	54.3	(NA)	(NA)	(NA)
1820	55.2	(NA)	(NA)	(NA)
1830	51.4	(NA)	(NA)	(NA)
1840	51.8	(NA)	(NA)	(NA)
1850	43.3	(NA)	(NA)	(NA)
1860	44.3	(NA)	(NA)	(NA)
1870	38.3	(NA)	9.6 (1867)	0.3 (1867)
1880	39.8	(NA)	9.1 (1875)	0.3 (1875)
1890	31.5	(NA)	9.0	0.5
1900	32.3	17.2	9.3	0.7
1910	30.1	14.7	10.3	0.9
1920	27.7	13.0	12.0	1.6
1930	21.3	11.3	9.2	1.6
1940	19.4	10.8	12.1	2.0
1950	24.1	9.6	11.1	2.6
1960	23.7	9.5	8.5	2.2
1970	18.4	9.5	10.6	3.5
1980	15.9	8.8	10.6	5.2
1990	16.7	8.6	9.8	4.7
1994	15.0	8.8	9.1	4.6

Source: *Historical Statistics of the United States* (1975); *Statistical Abstract of the United States* (1991, 1997).

RACIAL COMPOSITION OF THE POPULATION
(in thousands)

Year	White	Black	Indian	Hispanic	Asian
1790	3,172	757	(NA)	(NA)	(NA)
1800	4,306	1,002	(NA)	(NA)	(NA)
1820	7,867	1,772	(NA)	(NA)	(NA)
1840	14,196	2,874	(NA)	(NA)	(NA)
1860	26,923	4,442	(NA)	(NA)	(NA)
1880	43,403	6,581	(NA)	(NA)	(NA)
1900	66,809	8,834	(NA)	(NA)	(NA)
1910	81,732	9,828	(NA)	(NA)	(NA)
1920	94,821	10,463	(NA)	(NA)	(NA)
1930	110,287	11,891	(NA)	(NA)	(NA)
1940	118,215	12,866	(NA)	(NA)	(NA)
1950	134,942	15,042	(NA)	(NA)	(NA)
1960	158,832	18,872	(NA)	(NA)	(NA)
1970	178,098	22,581	(NA)	(NA)	(NA)
1980	194,713	26,683	1,420	14,609	3,729
1990	205,710	30,486	2,065	22,354	7,458
1996	219,749	30,503	2,288	28,269	9,743

Source: U.S. Bureau of the Census, *U.S. Census of Population: 1940*, vol. II, part 1, and vol. IV, part 1; *1950*, vol. II, part 1; *1960*, vol. I, part 1; *1970*, vol. I, part B; and *Current Population Reports*, P25-1095 and P25-1104; *Statistical Abstract of the United States* (1997), and unpublished data.

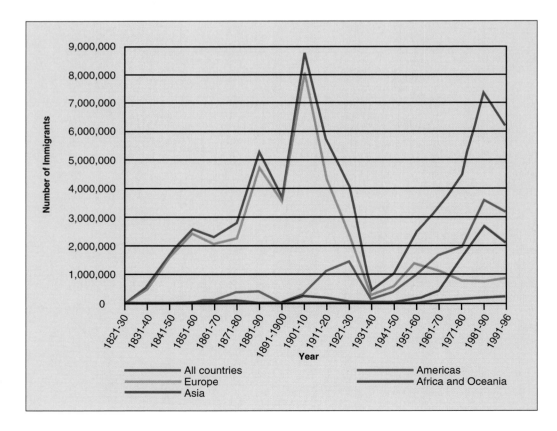

Immigration to the United States since 1820

Source: *Statistical Yearbook of the Immigration and Naturalization Service*, 1996.

PHOTO AND TEXT CREDITS

Chapter 1: Photos: Cahokia Mounds State Historic Site, xxxii (vols. I, II, A, B, C)/xlviii (combined edition); Jerry Jacka/Arizona State Museum, University of Arizona, 6; Denver Museum of Natural History, 7; American Museum of Natural History, 11; National Museum of the American Indian/Smithsonian Institution, 13; Helga Teiwes, Arizona State Museum, 13; David Hiser/David Muench Photography, Inc., 14; George Gerster/Comstock, 15; Rota/American Museum of Natural History, 20 Text: "Emergence Song" (excerpt) from William Brandon, *The Magic World: American Indian Songs and Poems.* Copyright © 1971 by William Brandon. Reprinted with the permission of William Morrow and Company, Inc., 5; Winnebago song, "This Newly Created World," from the Winnebago Medicine Rite as recorded in Raul Radin, *The Road to Life and Death: A Ritual Drama of the American Indians* (Bollinger Series V), p. 254. Copyright 1945 and © renewed 1972 by Princeton University Press. Reprinted with the permission of the publishers., 10

Chapter 2: Photos: The Granger Collection, 25; Art Resource, Musee Conde, Chantilly/Giraudon, Art Resource, NY, 29; From THE SHIP, AN ILLUSTRATED HISTORY by Bjorn Landstrom, Copyright © 1961 by Bokforlaget Forum AB. Used by permission of Doubleday, a division of Bantam Doubleday Dell Publishing Group, Inc., 31; The Granger Collection, 32; The British Library, 34; Library of Congress, 35; The British Library, 36; Jacques Le Moyne, "Rene de Loudonniere and Chief Athore," 1564, watercolor, The New York Public Library, NY, 41; Capitaine de la Nation, *Codex Canadienses,* artist Louis Nicolas, from the collection of Gilcrease Museum, Tulsa, OK, 42; The Bridgeman Art Library, 43; The Granger Collection, 44 Text: "The African, Indian and European Population of the Americas" from Colin McEvedy and Richard Jones, *Atlas of World Population History.* Copyright © 1978 by Colin McEvedy and Richard Jones. Reprinted with the permission of Penguin Putnam, Inc., 39

Chapter 3: Photos: Jerry Jacka Photography, 49; New York Public Library, 53; (left) "Princeton University Library," Manuscripts Division. Department of Rare Books and Special Collections. Princeton University Library, 55; Library of Congress, 55; Library of Congress, 56; Library of Congress, 60; The John Carter Brown Library, at Brown University, 61; The Fine Arts Museum of San Francisco, 62; The New York Historical Society, 65; The Historical Society of Pennsylvania, 66; Courtesy, American Antiquarian Society, 68

Chapter 4: Photos: The British Library, 73; Library of Congress, 77; The Bridgeman Art Library, 79; Library of Congress, 81; The Granger Collection, New York, 82; American Antiquarian Society, 83; The Maryland Historical Society, 85; Carolina Art Association/Gibbes Museum of Art, 86; Colonial Williamsburg Foundation, 90; The Philbrook Museum of Art, 91; Michael Holford/The Victoria and Albert Museum, 93; The Saint Louis Art Museum, 96; Virginia Museum of Fine Arts, 99 Text: "Estimated Number of Africans Imported to British North America," from R.C. Simmons, *The American Colonies: From Settlement to Independence* (London:Longman, 1976). Copyright © 1976 by R.C. Simmons. Reprinted with the permission of The Peters Fraser and Dunlop Group Limited, 80

Chapter 5: Photos: Colonial Williamsburg Foundation, 103; The Historical Society of Pennsylvania, 106; Jack W. Dykinga & Associates, 110; United States Geological Survey, 112; William Johnson/Stock, Boston, 113; Henry Glassie, Pattern in the Material Folk Culture of the Eastern United States, 114; (left) Courtesy, American Antiquarian Society, 118; Library of Congress, 118; Schalkwijk/Art Resource, NY, 121; American Antiquarian Society, 124; John Carter Brown Library, Brown University, 127 Text: "Distribution of Assessed Taxable Wealth in Eighteenth-Century Chester County, Pennsylvania," Copyright © 1968 by Peter N. Stearns. Reprinted with the permission of the publishers. 122; "Wealth Held by Richest 10 Percent of the Population: Northern and Southern Colonies Compared, 1770," Copyright © by Princeton University Press, renewed 1993 by Jackson Turner Main. Reprinted with the permission of Princeton University Press, 122

Chapter 6: Photos: The Granger Collection, 132; National Gallery of Canada, 138; Treaty, dated 13 July 1765, between Sir William Johnson and representatives of the Delaware, Shawnee, and Mingo nations. On parchment, 16" x 24.5". Photo by Carmelo Guadagno. Photograph courtesy of National Museum of the American Indian/Smithsonian Institution. Neg. 39369, 140; Massachusetts Historical Society, 142; Museum of Fine Arts, Boston, 144; Library of Congress, 145; The Granger Collection, 146; Library of Congress, 147; Library of Congress, 149; Christie's Images, 150; Connecticut Historical Society, 154; The Granger Collection, 156; The Granger Collection, 158

Chapter 7: Photos: Sam Holland, South Carolina State House, 162; Anne S. K. Brown Military Collection, Brown University Library, 166; Museum of Fine Arts, Boston, 167; The Granger Collection, 168; (top) Gilbert Stuart. "The Mohawk Chief Joseph Brant," 1786. Oil on canvas, 30" x 25". New York State Historical Association, Cooperstown, NY, 172; The Bostonian Society/Old State House, 172; Library of Congress, 176; Data available from U.S. Geological Survey, EROS Data Center, Sioux Falls, SD, 181; Corbis-Bettmann, 185; Library of Congress, 186; Art Resource, NY, 189

Chapter 8: Photos: The Granger Collection, 193; Print and Picture Collection, The Free Library of Philadelphia, 197; Collection of The New York Historical Society, 200; "The Republican Court," 1861, by Daniel P. Huntington. Oil on canvas. Gift of the Crescent Boys' Club. Brooklyn Museum of Art, 201; Indiana Historical Society Library (negative no. C2584), 205; "General George Washington Reviewing the Western Army...," by Francis Kemmelmeyer, after 1794. Oil on paper backed with linen. Dimensions 18 1/8" x 23 1/8". Courtesy of Winterthur Museum, 206; Collection of The New York Historical Society, 210; The Granger Collection, 212; Pennsylvania Academy of the Fine Arts, 213; Library of Congress, 214; Courtesy of American Antiquarian Society, 216; Library Company of Philadelphia, 217 Text: "Housing Values," Copyright © 1985 by Social Science History Association. Reprinted with the permission of Duke University Press, 215

Immigration & Community, to 1800: Photos: The Granger Collection, 225; The Granger Collection, 226 Text: "The Ancestry of the British Colonial Population" from Thomas L. Purvis, "The European Ancestry of the United States Population" in *William and Mary Quarterly,* 61 (1984): 85–101. Copyright © 1984 by the Institute of Early American History and Culture. Reprinted with the permission of the publishers., 223

Chapter 9: Photos: Henry Ford Museum & Greenfield Village, 228; Friedrich H. von Kittlitz, A View of the Russian Capital, 1827, from F.P. Litke. Alaska and Polar Regions, Department, Elmer E. Rasmusen Library Rare books, University of Alaska, Fairbanks, 232; Launching of ship "Fame" from Becket's Shipyard, Essex, Massachusetts, 1802, oil on canvas, by George Ropes. Mark Sexton, Peabody Essex Museum, 236; top, Library of Congress, 237; Library of Congress, 237; Museum of Early Southern Decorative Arts, 238; Thomas Gilcrease Institute of American History and Art, 243; Field Musuem of Natural History, 245; Library of Congress, 245; Library of Congress, 249; Library of Congress, 250; The New York Historical Society, 253

Chapter 10: Photos: NationsBank, 261; Walters Art Gallery, 268; Library of Congress, 270; The Maryland Historical Society, 273; Munson-Williams-Proctor Institute, 275; Chicago Historical Society, 277; Museum of the City of New York, 282; Library of Congress, 285; "Collection of the

Boston Athenaeum," 289; New York Public Library, 290 Text: "The Impact of the Erie Canal on Household Textile Manufacture" from Arthur Harrison Cole, The American Wool Manufacture. Copyright 1926 by the President and Fellows of Harvard College. Reprinted with the permission of Harvard University Press, 274

Chapter 11: Photos: Chicago Historical Society, 294; Library of Congress, 298; Wilson S. Armistead, University of Michigan Press, 299; Library of Congress, 307; The Historic New Orleans Collection, 308; Sophia Smith Collection, Smith College, 309; Library of Congress, 310; American Numismatic Society of New York, (left and right), 311; Daughters of the Republic of Texas, Yanaguana Society Collection, 312; The Historic New Orleans Collection, 315; National Archives, 317; Library of Congress, 319

Chapter 12: Photos: American Textile History Museum, 324; Abby Aldrich Rockefeller Folk Art Center, Williamsburg, VA, 328; Museum of Fine Arts, Boston, 329; Library of Congress, 332; Rhode Island Historical Society, 333; James L. Amos, National Geographic Society, (top & bottom) 336; High-Pressure Steamboat Mayflower, 1855, color lithograph by N. Currier. The Bettmann Archive. Corbis-Bettmann, 338; Baker Library, Graduate School of Business Administration, Harvard University, 340; Musuem of Fine Arts, Boston, 343; Mathew Brady/Brown Brothers, 344; The New York Historical Society, 346; Library of Congress, 347

Chapter 13: Photos: The New York Historical Society, 351; The Granger Collection, 358; Library of Congress, 360; Zelsa P. Mackay Collection, Courtesy George Eastman House, 362; "Seabury Champlin's June 3, 1791 Certificate of Membership in NY Mechanic Society," Abraham Godwin, print. Courtesy Winterthur Museum, 363; Frank and Marie-Therese Wood Print Collections, The Picture Bank, 364; The Schlesinger Library, Radcliffe College, 367; Library of Congress, 369; Hannah Harrison, Hancock Shaker Village, 371; Library of Congress (left & right), 373; Sophia Smith Collection, Smith College, 374; Lynn Historical Society, 376

Immigration & Community, 1800–1860: Photos: Dover Publications, Inc., 383; Museum of the City of New York, 384

Chapter 14: Photos: San Jacinto Museum of History Association, 386; Walters Art Gallery, 390; Henry E. Huntington Library and Art Gallery, 395; American Antiquarian Society, 397; The Walters Art Gallery, Baltimore, 398; Art Resource, NY, 399; Brown University Library, 404; National Gallery of Art, 406; The New York Historical Society, 408; California State Library, 409; Bigelow Collection, Museum of Fine Arts, Boston, 410; Steven Laschever/Museum of American Political Life/University of Hartford, 413 Text: "Overland Emigration to Oregon, California, and Utah, 1840-1860" from John Unruh, Jr., The Plains Across: The Overland Emigrants and the Trans-Mississippi West, 1840-60. Copyright © 1979 by the Board of Trustees of the University of Illinois. Reprinted with the permission of the University of Illinois Press., 396; "California in the Gold Rush," from Warren A. Beck and Ynez D. Haase, Historical Atlas of California. Copyright © 1974 by the University of Oklahoma Press. Reprinted with the permission of the publishers., 407

Chapter 15: Photos: The Granger Collection, 417; Harriet Beecher Stowe Center, Hartford, CT, Stowe-Day Foundation, 422; Courtesy American Antiquarian Society, 423; Library of Congress, 424; The Granger Collection, 431; Corbis-Bettmann, 432; New York Public Library, 434; Library of Congress, 435; Museum of the City of New York, 436; The Granger Collection, 437; Library of Congress, 440; United States Senate, 443

Chapter 16: Photos: Armen Shamalian Photographers, Art Resource, NY, 447; Courtesy Museum of Fine Arts, Boston, 451; The Picture Bank, 455; Alexander Gardner, National Archives, 456; Library of Congress, 458; Valentine Museum Library, (left) 459; Library of Congress, 459; Reproduced from Pauli Murray, Proud Shoes: The Story of an American Family,

HarperCollins Publishers, Inc., 1987, 466; Center of Military History, U.S. Army, 468; The Metropolitan Museum of Art, 469; Culvery Pictures, Inc., 471; Thomas C. Roche, Library of Congress, 475; Army Military History Institute, 476; Library of Congress, 477

Chapter 17: Photos: The Metropolitan Museum of Art, 481; National Archives, 485; Chicago Historical Society, 486; The Granger Collection, 488; The Susan B. Anthony House, Rochester, NY, 492; The Picture Bank/Harper's Weekly, 495; Library of Congress, 498; Library of Congress, 499; The University of North Carolina, (left) 501; Rutherford B. Hayes Presidential Center, 501; The Granger Collection, New York, 505; The Picture Bank, Frank and Marie-Therese Wood Print Collection, 507

Chapter 18: Photos: Christie's Images, 513; National Anthropological Archives, 518; Marion Koogler McNay Art Museum, 519; Timothy O'Sullivan, Amon Carter Museum, 522; Witte Museum, 525; Harper's Weekly, 527; Nebraska State Historical Society, Solomon D. Butcher Collection, 531; Library of Congress, 532; The Metropolitan Museum of Art, 537; Library of Congress, 538; Photo courtesy of State Historical Society of Iowa, Iowa City, 541; Edward Truman/The Denver Public Library, Western History Collection, 542 Text: "Oklahoma Territory" from John W. Morrois, Charles R. Goins, and Edwin C. McReynolds, Historical Atlas of Oklahoma, Third Edition. Copyright © 1965, 1976, 1986 by the University of Oklahoma Press. Reprinted with the permission of the publishers., 515; History and the Land feature and "Ethnic Composition of North Dakota, 1900," from John R. Shortridge, "The Great Plains" in Mary Kupiec Cayton, Elliott J. Gorn, and Peter W. Williams, Encyclopedia of American Social History II. Copyright © 1993 by Charles Scribner's Sons. Reprinted with the permission of Scribner's, an imprint of Simon & Schuster Macmillan. 528–529

Chapter 19: Photos: The Granger Collection, 547; U.S. Department of the Interior, National Park Service, Edison National Historic Site, 551 Chicago Historical Society, 553; Color engraving by J. Keppler from Puck, February 23, 1881, Collection of The New York Historical Society, New York City, 554; The Denver Public Library, Western History Collection, 556; Museum of the City of New York, 563; National Archives, 565; Terra Museum of American Art, 568; The Granger Collection, 570; Rhode Island School of Design, 573 Text: "U.S. Economy, 1873-1900" from Bernard Bailyn et al., The Great Republic, Third Edition. Copyright © 1985 by D.D. Heath and Company. Reprinted with the permission of Houghton Mifflin Company., 557

Chapter 20: Photos: Vermont State House, 578; Sally Anderson-Bruce/Museum of American Political Life, 583; Library of Congress, 585; Library of Congress, 588; Library of Congress, 590; The Granger Collection, New York, 594; National Archives, 596; Library of Congress, 601; Library of Congress, 603; Library of Congress, 604

Chapter 21: Photos: San Diego Museum of Art, 609; Lewis W. Hine/George Eastman House, 614; Henry Street Settlement, 615; Museum of the City of New York, 618;The Toledo Museum of Art, 622; Brown Brothers, 624; UPI/Corbis-Bettmann, 626; Collection of The American Labor Museum, Botto House National Landmark, 629; Planned Parenthood ® Federation of America, Inc. At, 810 Seventh Avenue, New York, NY, 10019., 631; Schomburg Center for Research in Black Culture, 632; California Historical Society, 635; Theodore Roosevelt Collection, Harvard College Library/The Houghton Library, Harvard University, 636

Chapter 22: Photos: Corbis-Bettmann, 642; The Granger Collection, 646; Culver Pictures, Inc., 649; Wallace Kirkland Papers, Jane Addams Memorial Collection, Special Collections, The University Library, University of Illinois at Chicago, 651; The Granger Collection; 652; Library of Congress, 653; National Archives, 654; National Archives, 655; Virginia War Museum/War Memorial Museum of Virginia, 659; Library of Congress, 661; Stock Montage Inc./ Historical Pictures Collection, 665;

INDEX